BENJAMIN BLYTH

BETTINA A. NORTON

Benjamin Blyth

SALEM'S 18TH-CENTURY LIMNER
IN A TIME OF RADICAL UPHEAVAL

TIDEPOOL PRESS

CAMBRIDGE, MASSACHUSETTS

2025

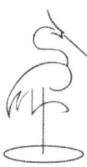

TIDEPOOL PRESS, LLC
6 Maple Avenue, Cambridge, Massachusetts 02139
www.tidepoolpress.com

LIBRARY OF CONGRESS CATALOGING-IN-PUBLICATION DATA
Bettina A. Norton, 1936-
Benjamin Blyth: Salem's 18th-Century Limner in a Time of Radical Upheaval
1. Blyth, Benjamin--catalog of works   2. Pastels, American 18th-c.
3. Portraits, American 18th-c.   4. Salem, Massachusetts, history
I. Title

LIBRARY OF CONGRES CATALOGUE NUMBER: 2025931245
ISBN 978-8-9901334-1-9

PRINTED IN THE UNITED STATES

To my husband
JOHN MERRILL NORTON
(1934–2023)
and to our son
JAMES ANTHONY NORTON
(1957–2016)

... taking a leaf from the dedication of
Faces of a Family by the late Andrew Oliver
to his son Peter:
"sapientissimo carissimo ...
memoriaeque sanctissimae sacrum ..."

CONTENTS

FOREWORD

THE Massachusetts Historical Society's iconic portraits of America's second president, John Adams, and his wife Abigail, were created soon after their marriage in 1764. They are a fine complement to the invaluable collection of the Adams Papers at the MHS. The only known portrait from life of Dr. Ezekiel Hersey, whose bequest to Harvard College in 1770 of £1000 led to the founding of Harvard Medical School, now hangs in the office of the Hersey Professor of the Theory and Practice of Physick (Medicine). Here at the MHS, our serialized publication, *Sibley's Harvard Graduates*, contains, in addition to Hersey and Adams, at least another nine portraits that are the only images of their subjects.

The artist of these singular images was Benjamin Blyth, who lived and worked in Salem from the mid–1760s until the early 1780s when he moved to Virginia. Because he signed almost no works, and almost no written documentation exists, Blyth has been unsung. This book by Bettina A. Norton aims to correct this oversight. She has added attributions and removed a few erroneous Blyth attributions, greatly increasing the number of pastels and oil paintings, and with the inclusion of miniatures, drawings and the sources for four prints has created a catalogue of 153 portraits. Four are in the collections of the MHS.

Blyth's primary medium was pastel. For many years, some of these were believed to have been the work of New England's premier portraitist of the time, John Singleton Copley. Beginning in the 1930s with the fine work of Barbara Neville Parker and Anne Wheeler for the Museum of Fine Arts, Boston, some of these attributions were questioned. They knew, as do we, that Blyth was not Copley. Art historian Henry Wilder Foote, in an article for *The Proceedings of the Massachusetts Historical Society* in 1957, identified a number of previously unacknowledged works by Blyth. However, even when Blyth was held in less regard than he is now, he was credited with depicting the character of his sitters. Other scholars have noted this as well. Frank W. Bayley, a century ago, noted that he did so faithfully. And Andrew Oliver, lawyer and gentleman scholar who in the early 1980s wrote of the portrait collections at both the MHS and the then-Essex Institute, dubbed Blyth's pastels, perhaps a bit hyperbolically, "superb."

Bettina—Toni to her friends—describes each of Blyth's techniques. The catalogue lists each portrait, illustrating those for which an image exists, plus missing ones. She visited or corresponded with over 150 institutions and individuals throughout the United States and has also done extensive research to correct misattributions and establish fuller and more accurate biographies of the sitters. Toni explains why the chronology of his work seems to confound the idea of stylistic development and delves into the complex problem of whether Blyth's brother, Samuel, executed any portraits. Venturing into previously uncharted territory for the chapter on miniatures, she puts forth a well-researched, thorough argument for the fact that he was the artist and offers plausible examples.

At the MHS, Toni looked at a number of our portraits and aided in the identification of two, not previously researched, to other contemporaries of Blyth. She found much information in our Bayley collection, which she called "essential" to the sad story of fraudulent attributions to Blackburn in the late 1920s. Toni puts Blyth in the context of his time, both within the political and commercial life of Salem in the 1760s and 1770s, as well as relating his work to the other contemporary artists in Salem and Boston. Perhaps most significantly, her discoveries have brought life to an important period in American history.

Dennis A. Fiori
President Emeritus, Massachusetts Historical Society

INTRODUCTION

❦

OVER THE COURSE of two centuries, the Peabody Essex Museum (PEM) and its predecessor institutions the Essex Institute and the East India Marine Society (later the Peabody Academy of Science and then the Peabody Museum of Salem) have collected works of art, objects, and natural history specimens from Salem, Essex County and around the world. With a collection dating back more than 200 years, PEM has many works whose original creators lie shrouded in obscurity. Eighteenth-century portraitist Benjamin Blyth, working primarily in pastels, has until now fallen into this category. While not an artist with the technical skill of his near contemporary John Singleton Copley, Blyth still managed to create lively portraits that successfully convey the character of their sitters. They are also frequently the only known representations of prominent citizens of Salem and Boston. For this reason, Blyth portraits have often been used to illustrate these citizens in publications such as *Sibley's Harvard Graduates*. But Blyth himself and the body of his work have been studied only sporadically, and no systematic project to catalog his output or understand his work has been undertaken until now.

Bettina (Toni) Norton first developed an interest in the work of Benjamin Blyth when she served as registrar at the Essex Institute and authored the book *Prints at the Essex Institute* (1978). Through a careful examination of style and technique, and a thorough investigation of documentary evidence, Toni Norton has added significantly to the body of work that can be attributed to Blyth. She has been gathering the material for this catalogue since 2015, and much of that work has involved the collections, library, and archives at PEM, which I oversee. In the seven years I have worked at PEM, I have grown to know Toni for her relentless pursuit of information, tracking down leads and sources, and her tenacious insistence on double and triple-checking her facts and conclusions, to be sure that her arguments are as persuasive as possible.

Before Toni began her work on this book, PEM had seventeen works attributed to Benjamin Blyth. Over the course of many visits and email exchanges, close examinations and deep dives into documentary records, Toni has convincingly added twelve pastels, oils and miniatures to this list. These twenty-nine portraits at PEM constitute by far the largest collection of works by Blyth at any one institution. PEM is proud to be the repository of such an important representation of the creative expression of the people of Essex County and Eastern Massachusetts at the end of the eighteenth century.

But in the catalog on the following pages, Toni has done so much more than simply identify and illustrate a series of works attributed to Benjamin Blyth. She uses Blyth's portraits, documentary evidence, and often written accounts by contemporaries, to illustrate the lives and achievements … and often frustrations … of the subjects of Blyth's portraits. In so doing, she has used Blyth's portraits to take us into the world of late eighteenth-century Salem and Boston, to paint a broader picture of that time and place, and to provide glimpses into the character of its inhabitants.

John D. Childs
James B. and Mary Lou Hawkes Director of Collections, Peabody Essex Museum

BENJAMIN BLYTH
PORTRAYER OF PEOPLE

"A good portrait, even an indifferent one if none better can be found,
is as a lighted candle with which to read biography."

—Thomas Carlyle, quoted in Oliver, *Windows on the Past*

Inescapably, every portrait is the product of a three-way negotiation
between what the subject imagines they look like,
the artist's unstoppable urge to complicate that self-image,
and the expectations of whoever ends up living with the result.
. . . Portraits have always been made with an eye to posterity.

—Simon Schama
The Face of Britain; A History of the Nation Through Its Portraits

PORTRAIT PAINTING is not generally an easy path, but its pursuit during wartime is even more difficult. Such was the experience of Benjamin Blyth (1746–1811), an artist who worked primarily in Salem, Massachusetts, from the mid-1760s until the early 1780s, including during the American Revolution. Blyth left a legacy of more than 150 portraits. He was there, recording military officers, ship captains, merchants, artisans, political leaders, clergy, privateers during the war, their wives, and sometimes their children.

Portraiture historically had been the province of the elite. However, the people whom Blyth drew or painted represented a broader view of Salem at the time: in addition to its prominent citizenry, he depicted many from its prosperous middle class. Few, if any other, colonial towns were as well documented.

Blyth's insightful portrayals, primarily pastels but also including oils and miniatures and the original drawings for a few prints, bring the community to life. Some of the portraits are the only known images of these sitters. Many are compelling for their visual appeal and their portrayal of personality. They show us *people*—introspective, proud, melancholy, nervous, self-important, shy. Portraits, after all, were, and are, of living people. They show the viewer who they were, as their family, neighbors and friends probably knew them.

Yet Blyth is not well known. This can be attributed to several factors. Almost none of his portraits were signed, and very few records from or about him have survived, so many of his portraits were designated "anonymous." Museum resources are rarely spared to research holdings of unattributed art. Also, Blyth was competing at the same time and for some of the same clientele as Copley, the premier portraitist of that generation. Nonetheless, Blyth drew more than eighty pastels during this period, of which at least a dozen had been erroneously attributed to Copley.

There well may have been more. Perhaps most significantly, the American Revolution disrupted Blyth's livelihood at the height of his success.

From the early days of his career, Benjamin's older brother Samuel made the frames for the portraits. Soon after the Revolution began, Samuel's new brother-in-law, Joseph Hiller, moved to Salem and began producing mezzotints of major figures of the war that were in the Boston-Salem area. Both Benjamin and Samuel contributed to this venture. Benjamin provided the original art for at least four of the prints. Samuel colored many of them, then began to produce mezzotints of some of the war's generals by himself. He also began drawing portraits in pastels. As there is not one bit of correspondence or other writings by Benjamin or any immediate family members, there is no way of knowing if Samuel was trying to help his brother or actively competing against him. Whether this was a contributing factor or not, before the war was over, Benjamin Blyth had left Salem forever.

This book, which almost triples those works attributed to Blyth, demonstrates that he deserves greater recognition in the story of American art and social history as an important portraitist of the latter eighteenth century. Research began with known portraits, comparing them to anonymous works, seeking out other possibilities in museums and private collections, and tracing provenance as well as possible sitters' biographies. More than two dozen portraits at the Peabody Essex Museum in Salem now can be credited to Benjamin Blyth—not only pastels, but also oils and miniatures. This is by far the greatest number of portraits by him in any collection, and several of them are among the museum's most interesting and earliest accessions. Blyth's portraits also can be found in many other museums such as the Harvard Portrait Collection, the Massachusetts Historical Society, the Museum of Fine Arts Boston, the American Antiquarian Society, the Smithsonian Institution, the Metropolitan Museum of Art, the Yale University Art Gallery, the Princeton Art Museum, the Bayou Bend Collection at the Museum of Fine Arts, Houston, and many historical societies as well as private collections.

As a welcome addition to the record of Salem, Benjamin Blyth's perspective on each sitter's personality complements much of the commentary at the time by the verbose and opinionated Salem minister, the Reverend William Bentley.

SETTING THE SCENE:
THE MASSACHUSETTS BAY COLONY TOWN OF SALEM

WHEN BENJAMIN BLYTH was born in 1746, Salem was a major eastern seaport, second in importance only to Boston in the large Province of Massachusetts Bay, with an active trade, coastal as well as transatlantic. Maritime and commercial aspects of the town were evident, with ship captains and mariners, farmers, tradesmen, and—a given of every New England town—tavern owners and clergymen. Great fortunes were being made by those who were successful at fishing and maritime trading. At the time, Salem was a compact town with mansions, churches, small shops, and wharves and docks in proximity.

The young lawyer John Adams, staying at the house of his brother-in-law in Salem while trying several cases at the court, recorded in his diary on August 13, 1766, "[T]he houses are the most

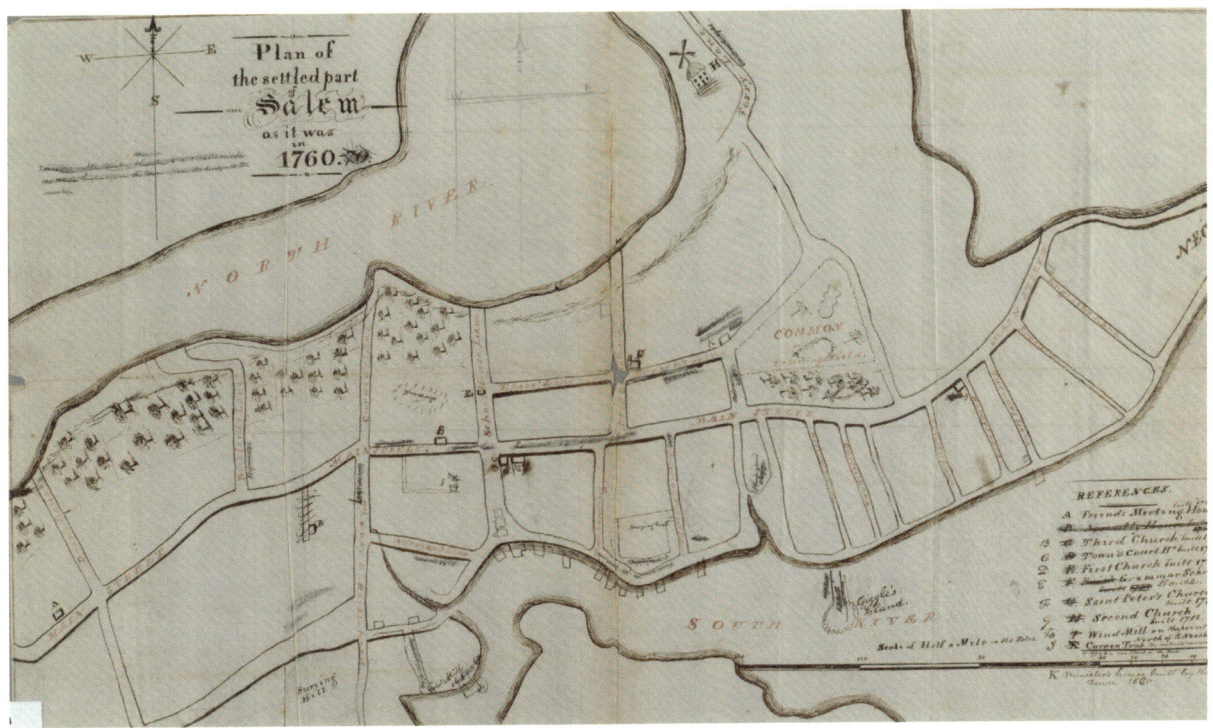

Plan of the settled part of Salem as it was in 1760.
Pen and ink drawing, anonymous, ca. 1920
Courtesy of the Phillips Library, Peabody Essex Museum, Rowley, MA. G3764. S2/P536

elegant and grand that I have seen in any of the maritime towns."[1] Adams would have seen the mansion, gardens, and surrounding buildings built about fifteen years earlier by Col. Benjamin Pickman (1740–1819).[2] The Pickman family was among Salem's elite by the mid-eighteenth century, and Benjamin wanted a house that reflected his wealth and stature, so he built a mansion in the new Georgian style. Finished around 1748, it was a "very elegant house . . . equal to any in Salem for convenience and beauty." Pickman "glorified" the codfish, by which he and other merchants of the time made their fortune, by "placing its image, carved in wood, on every step of his spacious stairway." His daughter, Love Rawlins Pickman, like young ladies of the time, made needlework pictures, of which four framed examples are now in the textile collection at the Museum of Fine Arts, Boston. One depicts what well could be a composite scene of the Pickman

1. Charles Francis Adams, *Works of John Adams*, 10 vols. (Boston: Charles C. Little and James Brown, 1850), 2:198.

2. In 1759 and 1769, Benjamin Pickman Sr. was the second wealthiest man in estimated value. By 1769 his son, Col. Benjamin Pickman, was fifth, but the first among the "new elites." The additional thirty-two names in the sixty-five wealthiest residents were sons of the same wealthiest sixty-five of a decade earlier, according to Richard J. Morris, "Redefining the Economic Elite in Salem, Massachusetts, 1759–1799," *The New England Quarterly* 73, no. 4 (Dec. 2000). "The stability of the elite is even more apparent when one examines the reasons for dropping out of the group. Twenty-one of the thirty-two men . . . had died." Proud of his own house and an amateur historian, Col. Pickman in 1793 compiled voluminous notes on the description, owners, and location of Salem houses at the time. "Some Account of Houses and Other Buildings in Salem. From a Manuscript of the Late Col. Benj. Pickman," *Historical Collections of the Essex Institute,* 6 (1864):93–99.

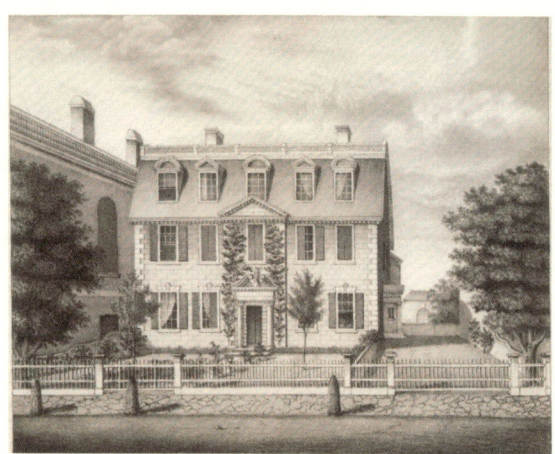

Benjamin Pickman house,
formerly at 165 Essex Street, Salem
Lithograph by James F. Colman (attr.), ca. 1830
Pendleton's Lithography, 21.8 x 27.1 cm.
Courtesy of the Boston Athenaeum A B64Sa Re. p. (no. 1)

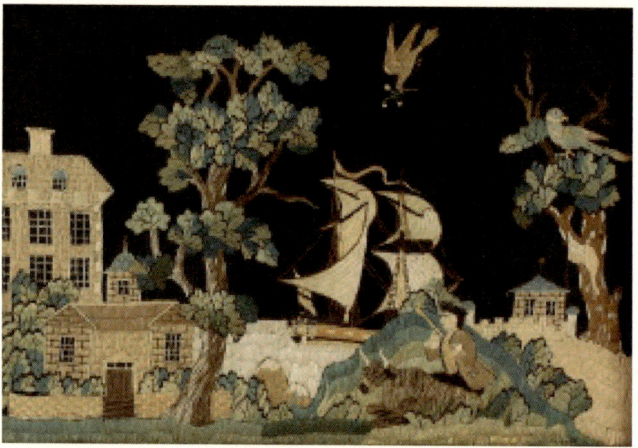

Needlework by Love Rawlins Pickman
Silk on silk, ca. 1750, 12 x 17⅝ in.
Courtesy of the M. and M. Karolik Collection, Department of
Textile and Fashion Arts, Museum of Fine Arts, Boston. 39. 241

estate: a Georgian mansion with gambrel roof, dormers and quoins; a shepherd tending a cow in the large, enclosed garden with a garden house; and a two-masted brig—the class of ships used by her father in his seafaring trade, in the distance. The house, shown in a mid-nineteenth-century lithograph, stood on land that is now the west wing of the Peabody Essex Museum. But by 1940, the once-elegant mansion was in ruins and was subsequently torn down.

Blyth must have been as aware as Adams of the importance of the Pickmans in Salem. A portrait of Love's mother, Abigail Love Rawlins Pickman (Cat. 105), was one of the earliest pastels drawn by him, although it exists only in a book illustration, with no attribution to its artist.

By the second quarter of the eighteenth century, a good number of residents of Salem were wealthy enough to sit for portraits by all the major artists in New England—John Smibert, Joseph Badger, Robert Feke, John Greenwood, William Johnston, Joseph Blackburn, and Copley. In fact, the town "proved a fertile field for portrait painters well into the nineteenth century," wrote William H. Gerdts.[3] Benjamin Blyth had ample chance to see and learn from the portraits of these eminent townsmen's families and their wives hanging in his neighbors' houses, as is evidenced by his making copies of earlier oil portraits for such a Salem notable as Mary Vial Holyoke.

Once Benjamin became interested in becoming a portraitist himself, he was well prepared to embark on a well-established tradition.

*

THE BLYTH FAMILY (also Bly, Blith, or Blythe) had been in Salem since shortly after it was founded in 1626. John Bly, Benjamin's great-grandfather the original immigrant, was in Salem by 1653, at the age of fourteen. Salem's historian Sidney Perley noted a number of incidents that

---

3. William H. Gerdts, *Art Across America: Two Centuries of Regional Painting in America, 1720–1920.* New York: Abbeville Press, 1990, 3 vols., 1:61.

Blyths had been involved in, according to early town records.[4] In 1673, "John Blith" was one of those "negligent in complying with the law" on educating their children, which "the town took measures to correct." In 1683, Jno. Bly's tax bill was one of the smallest, one shilling and eight pence, when the average was two shillings. In February 1693/4, "John Bly was approved to sell cider at his *new* [italics added] dwelling house." In 1701 "John Bligh and his family, who belonged in Boston" were among those warned to leave Salem, most likely because the town did not wish to end up supporting them. John's son Jonathan Bly, a shipwright and tallow chandler, also could not keep out of trouble; in December 1712, he and six other men rowed out to the sloop *Betty*, while the owner was in church, and "riotously and illegally boarded" it.

The Blyths then seem to have settled into the established life of the community. Jonathan married Sarah Gustin in 1719. The prominent merchant Timothy Orne noted in his diary the death of "Granny Blyth," on December 10, 1747, and of her husband, "old Jon^a Blyth," the following September.[5] One wonders what Orne's connection with the elder Blyths might have been, but the family must have been on familiar terms with one of the wealthiest men in Salem at the time. Their eighth child, Samuel, a sailmaker, married Abigail Massey, of another family of early settlers, and they had seven sons. When he died in 1774, his estate was valued at £333 6s 8d.

Three of his sons, however, eschewed a maritime trade and took up painting—Samuel, the eldest, born in 1744, became a house and ship painter. William, the youngest, also a house painter, decamped to Beverly and worked from time to time with his brother.[6] And Benjamin, born in 1746, became the portrait painter. He was baptized in Salem's First Parish, but by the time he was four, the Blyths had become members of Salem's newly established Anglican Church, St. Peter's. Benjamin's mother's family, the Masseys, had been among fifty-two petitioners for an Anglican church ten years earlier.

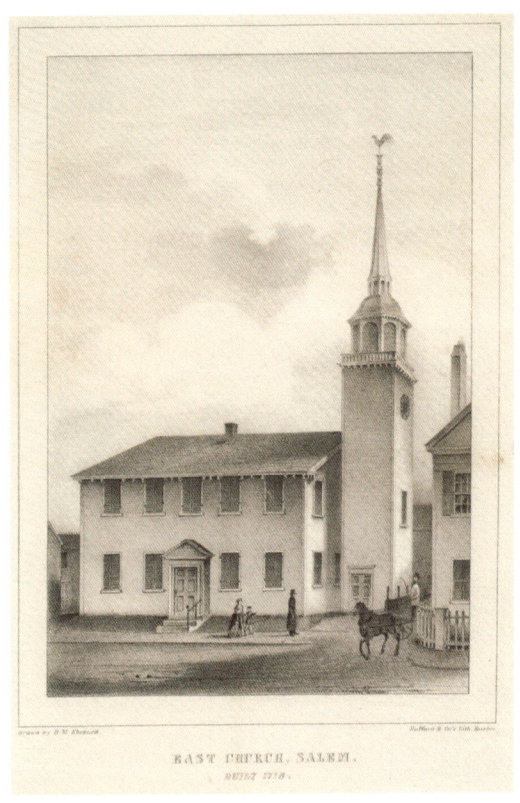

St. Peter's Church, Salem
Watercolor of the original wooden building by George Augustus Perkins, 1833. Courtesy of the Peabody Essex Museum 119581, gift of Miss Mary B. Perkins, 1928. Photography by Don McPhee

---

4. Sidney Perley, *The History of Salem, Massachusetts*, 3 vols. (Salem: S. Perley, 1924–28), 2:45, 280, 3:64, 85, 108–9, 420, 304, 349-50. see also Joseph B. Felt, *Annals of Salem*, 2d ed., 2 vols. (Salem, Massachusetts: W. & S. B. Ives; Boston: J. Munroe, 1845, 1849), 2:156.

5. Timothy Orne, *Almanac*, 1747 and 1748, Orne Family Papers, MSS 41, Box 16, Folder 3. Courtesy of Phillips Library, Peabody Essex Museum, Rowley, MA.

6. William, a soldier of the Revolution, lived in Salem in 1777 and then Beverly, according to Perley. Benjamin's wife and three children were listed, but Perley neglected to mention his profession. Perley, *History of Salem*, 3:369.

At the time, there were relatively few Anglican churches in the colonies, especially in the Puritan- and Pilgrim-founded colonies of Massachusetts Bay. Anglicans worshiped in decorated churches with organ music included in the services.

The Blyth family developed extensive ties to St. Peter's Church, and through it, links to Anglican churches in Boston. A Boston artist, John Gibbs, Sr., had decorated the interior of Boston's Christ Church ("Old North") and Trinity Church with the Ten Commandments and the Lord's Prayer in gold script in the chancel and winged cherubs' heads on the spandrels of the nave or on the ceiling of the apse. His son, John Gibbs, Jr. (ca. 1704–after 1770), followed the same scheme when he decorated the interior of St. Peter's.[7] Samuel Blyth, whose house was on the same short street as St. Peter's, was its organist by 1766 and served until 1773. He also helped with various development and restoration campaigns and served as vestryman and warden.[8] Although he was not involved in its interior decoration, he might have learned another skill from Gibbs—painting coats of arms to decorate coffins or for customers to hang in their front halls.[9]

Samuel Blyth's multi-faceted career mirrored that of another Bostonian and fellow Anglican, Thomas Johnston (ca. 1708–1767), a prominent printmaker and artisan, japanner, engraver, house painter and decorator, painter of coats of arms, church singer, pioneer builder of organs in New England, and frame maker.[10] Johnston and his workmen had many intersections with Salem that undoubtedly brought him into contact often with the Blyths and influenced their careers. Both Johnston's shop in Boston and Samuel's in Salem sold "colors" and numerous other tools and supplies for all kinds of painting. Johnston also made the new organ for St. Peter's, which was installed when Samuel Blyth was organist. Another instance provides clues to other Boston artisans: the memorandum from Salem merchant Benjamin Gerrish, in which he explained that his father, who had died the year before, had negotiated with Gawen Brown of Boston for the clock

7. Bettina A. Norton, "Anglican Embellishments; The Contributions of John Gibbs, Junior, and William Price to the Church of England in Eighteenth-century Boston," *Annual Proceedings / the Dublin Seminar for New England Folklife, 1979* (Boston: Boston University Press, [1980]), 84.

8. *Historical Collections of the Essex Institute*, 101:215; Felt, *Annals of Salem*, 2:185, 195; Harriet Sylvester Tapley, *St. Peter's Church in Salem, Massachusetts, before the Revolution* (Salem: The Essex Institute, 1944), 30, 62-3, 81; Henry Wyckoff Belknap, *Artists and Craftsmen of Essex County, Massachusetts* (Salem: The Essex Institute, 1927), 29.

9. Samuel Blyth's professional work included painting houses and decorating the exteriors and interiors of ships, chaises, and coffin boxes. On June 2, 1767, he billed Joseph Cabot for painting the brig *Tartar*. L. Vernon Briggs, "The Cabot's Ships Papers," *History and Genealogy of the Cabot Family, 1475–1927*. 3 vols. (Boston: Charles E. Goodspeed & Co., 1927), 1:xx, 121. Samuel Blyth is now credited with the arms of at least the Erwin, Holyoke, Putnam, Rawlins, and Pickman families.

10. In February 1747/8, Johnston billed the estate of the Hon[ble] Anthony Stoddard, Esq[r], for making hatchments for his wife's funeral, "inSide and OutSide frames," the iron dogs for putting them up, and 10 silk escutcheons with two yards of "Taffety" for a total cost of £7 4s. A month later, Johnston provided Sundries, including one dozen silk escutcheons and a "Brest Plate of the Coffin" for Stoddard's own funeral. This entry page also recorded credit of £5 to the estate for an "Old Hatchment frame." Massachusetts Historical Society, Stoddard Papers. The accounts of Samuel P. Savage note a payment to Johnston on Sept. 8, 1764. "To making a handsome Half length Picture Frame/ inside edge Car[vd] & Gilt" for £2 13s. 4, and "To 1 Handsome frame y[r] Picture" also £2 13s. 4d.; one can assume that the entry for April 23, 1763, was for the portrait of his wife. Samuel P. Savage Account Book, Massachusetts Historical Society.

for St. Peter's Church, and that "[t]he Case was given B. Gerrish by John Greenwood Painter & James Buck Frame maker."[11] Brown, it developed, kept shop "at Mr. Johnson's Japanner, in Brattle Street, Boston, near Mr. Copper's [sic] Meeting House.[12]

BLYTH'S MENTORS

IF BENJAMIN BLYTH as a lad assisted in his older brother's shop, he would have been aware of—if not trying out—the various painting supplies for sale there. He may even have helped paint houses or ships. By the time that Benjamin would have decided on a career as an artist, all but one of those active in his youth were gone. The prolific John Smibert, who worked throughout the colony and painted at least two people from Salem, the noted colonial magistrate Benjamin Lynde, and Margaret Mitchell Sewall, had died in 1751. Robert Feke, another prominent portraitist of the era, although he does not seem to have painted any Salem resident, died in 1752. Joseph Badger painted many portraits of Bostonians in the 1740s and 1750s, as well as John Gerry of Marblehead and members of the Timothy Orne family of Salem. But Badger died in 1765. Another portrait artist, William Johnston, Thomas Johnston's eldest son, did paint a few Boston and Essex County-area folk, but he was primarily active in Connecticut. John Greenwood, the most prolific portraitist of Salem sitters in the mid-eighteenth century, painted at least nineteen members of prominent families—Pickman, Clarke, and Gerrish—between 1751 and 1752.[13] However, Greenwood decamped for Surinam in 1752. Joseph Blackburn painted Salem residents Timothy Fitch and his wife Eunice Brown Fitch, Abigail Curwen, and several members of the Orne family. However, Blackburn does not seem to have painted any more portraits after the early 1760s, and as a Loyalist, he too left the area before the outbreak of the American Revolution.

The one artist still painting portraits in the region when Benjamin began his career was John Singleton Copley (1738–1815). Although he painted primarily full-figure oil portraits, he also was the first artist in New England to undertake pastels. They quickly became "a standard part of his repertoire" and "a medium in which he came to excel," as Theodore E. Stebbins has observed.[14] Blyth must have seen some of these pastel portraits. How else would he have learned of the

---

11. Tapley, *St. Peter's Church*, 35. The Greenwood portraits of Benjamin Gerrish Jr., Abigail Gerrish and her grandmother, and Margaret (Cabot) Gerrish are in the Peabody Essex Museum.

12. Mr. Cooper is the Rev. Samuel Cooper, minister of the Brattle Square Church from 1747 to 1783. "Gawen Brown of Boston, Massachusetts. A pre-revolutionary tall case clock," www. delaneyantiqueclocks. com. Brown had only recently arrived from London when he set up in Johnston's shop. About three years later, he was on his own and soon had a thriving career. See also David Hansen, "Gawen Brown, Soldier and Clockmaker," *Old-Time New England*, 30 no. 1 (July 1939): 1-9, brought to the attention of the author through the courtesy of Paul Foley. Nina Fletcher Little, in "Carved Figures," pointed out that Mabel Swan wrote that Salem and Boston craftsmen in the late eighteenth century were "closely connected in many joint enterprises," Essex Institute Historical Collections, 93:187. This was the case by the 1740s and maybe even earlier.

13. Greenwood's portrait of "Madam" Gibbs (Old York Museum is possibly of the wife or mother of the artist John Gibbs who decorated the interior of St. Peter's Church. Greenwood took up engraving many years later, when he moved to London.

14. Theodore E. Stebbins, et al, *American Paintings at Harvard: Paintings, Watercolors, and Pastels by Artists Born before 1826*, 2 vols. (Cambridge: Harvard Art Museum, New Haven: Yale University Press, 2014), 1:131.

medium? He must have realized its advantages: the easily portable supplies, enabling travel to potential clients who did not have to come to him, and a very appealing medium for its emphasis on character and a sense of intimacy as well as its tactile and visual charms. The sitter in pastels of the period most often dominates the picture, to the exclusion of renderings of landscape, telescopes, draperies, books, columns, &c., seen often in oil portraits; and the format can eliminate the depiction of hands, which are notoriously difficult to draw. He also must have realized that a pastel portrait would be less expensive for potential clients than a more ambitious portrait in oils.

Copley, who produced his first dated pastel in 1758, had already made more than a dozen before Blyth made any. Could Blyth have learned how to do so from Copley, eight years his senior?[15]

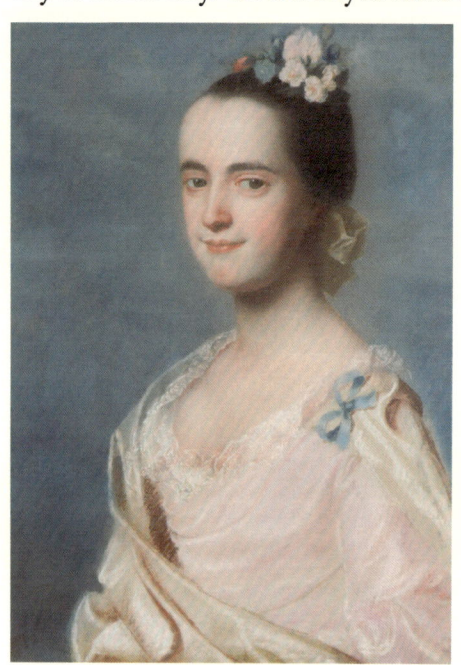

Mary (Mrs. Joseph) Greene
Pastel by John Singleton Copley, 1767
Private collection

Several art historians have noted that Copley really left no "school" behind him; he was not known to have instructed any other emerging artists beyond his younger half-brother, Henry Pelham. This did not preclude Blyth encountering Copley and perhaps asking him for technical advice or where to buy pastel crayons, but it does not intimate any direct role of advisor. Nor can it be assumed that, because the artists knew or knew of each other, Copley would have extended a helping hand. Copley once wrote that "there has not been one portrait brought that is worthy to be called a picture."[16] Indeed, he was probably referring to Blyth, in his letter to Benjamin West, January 17, 1768, when he wrote that he "had never seen 'more than three heads done in Crayons' and none 'that could possibly be esteem'd.'"[17]

Would he have been referring to Blyth's portraits of John and Abigail Adams (Cats. 3,2), Joseph and Elizabeth Warren (Cats. 129, 128), Elizabeth Cabot and her son George (Cats. 23, 25), or Abigail Pickman (Cat. 106)? Even if Copley thought his comments an honest assessment, were they

15. The reverse is suggested in Marjorie Shelley, "American Drawings and Watercolors in the Metropolitan Museum of Art," in *A Catalogue of Works by Artists Born before 1835*, Kevin E. Avery, ed. (New York: Metropolitan Museum of Art, 2002),1:86. The entry for the pastel of Ebenezer Storer by Copley states that he "may have been inspired by the pastel portraits of other artists working in and near Boston, such as Joseph Blackburn (ca. 1703–1787), Benjamin Blyth (ca.1740–ca. 1787), and Thomas Johnston (ca. 1708–1767)." However, it is not possible that Copley was influenced by Blyth: he was born in 1746 (Salem Vital Records), not 1740, as appears incorrectly in such early sources as Mantle Fielding, *American Engravers upon Copper and Steel:* Biographical sketches and check lists of engravings. a supplement to David McNeely Stauffer's *American Engravers* (Philadelphia, 1917). Also American Portrait Inventory, 1663–1860 (Newark NJ: The Historical Records Society [WPA], 1940. Blyth's correct birth date is in George Cuthbert Groce and David H. Wallace, *The New-York Historical Society's Dictionary of Artists in America* (New Haven: Yale University Press, 1957), 57. Also, Blackburn is not believed to have drawn any pastels.
16. Flexner, *First Flowers of Our Wilderness*, 213.
17. Marjorie Shelley, "Painting in Crayon: The Pastels of John Singleton Copley," *John Singleton Copley in America* (New York: The Metropolitan Museum of Art, 1995), 127-41.

also an attempt to cast aspersion on a possible rival? He undoubtedly realized the potential of Salem, the colony's second most important town, as a rich source of clients. Might Blyth's emergence have spurred the ambitious Copley to resume work in this genre after that break of two or three years and deliberately target wealthy residents of the North Shore, to stake out his claim to superior pastel portraiture over a potential rival? Indeed, at the time, he painted some of Salem's leading citizens.[18] Nonetheless, Blyth clearly had established himself with his patrons. In 1769, according to his newspaper advertisement, he occupied a room in a house owned by his father "in the great Street leading towards Marblehead." It was either the Ruck house or very near it, according to Boston art dealer Frank W. Bayley. The house was occupied for a time by Abigail Adams's sister and husband, Richard Cranch, whom John and Abigail often visited in 1766–67.[19]

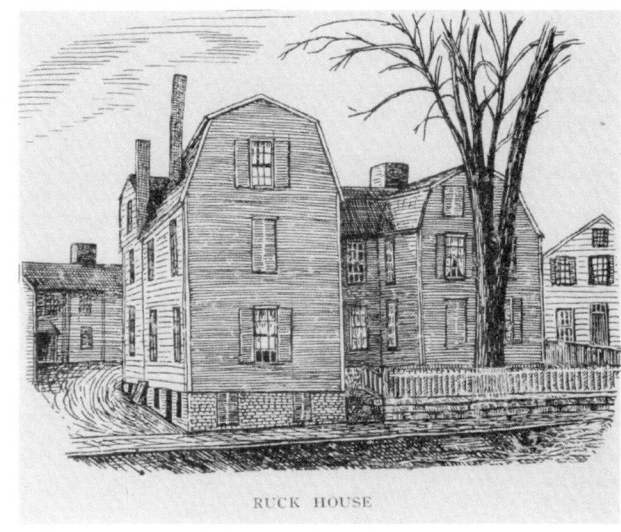

Ruck House, Salem
Illustration from
Sidney Perley, *History of Salem, Massachusetts* (1924) 2:317
Courtesy of the Boston Athenaeum

Within a few years, even Copley was gone. As a Loyalist fearful of the impending threat of violence in Boston and having been courted for years to move to London by expatriate American artist Benjamin West, he departed for England in 1774. That left the field open to Blyth.

He learned by copying, even after his career was underway. He drew a copy of Copley's pastel of Gov. Jonathan Belcher (Cat. 14), probably in the early 1770s. The Unknown Man (Cat. 145) may well be another. Indeed, Blyth learned well: Frank W. Bayley, owner of Copley Gallery in Boston's Back Bay who wrote extensively on New England portraiture, listed the Belcher and five other pastels as being by Copley. They have since been credited to Blyth. The similarities between the two artists hampered proper identification by early art historians who wrote on Copley, but they also served Bayley as a potential commercial benefit as well as a vehicle for prestige in the academic community. Both dealers and owners knew a Copley would be more highly valued than the work of a less well-known artist and it may have influenced attribution, whether unintentionally or intentionally.

Thomas Johnston also seemed a likely precursor for Blyth learning how to draw pastels. However, the one portrait currently attributed to Johnston, a pastel of Newburyport distiller Dudley

---

18. Parker, Barbara and Anne Wheeler, *John Singleton Copley: American Portraits in Oil, Pastel, and Miniature* (Boston: Museum of Fine Arts, 1938), 6. A legend widely circulated for years is that, ostensibly to encourage portrait commissions, Copley had rented the Ruck house in Salem. The first known source is Sidney Perley's *History of Salem, Massachusetts* (1924) 2:317, who gave the time as "just before the Revolution," although the main year given is 1767. To date, it has been impossible to confirm the Copley occupancy. There is no reference in the Perley Papers at the Peabody Essex Museum's Phillips Library, nor in the Cranch Papers at the Massachusetts Historical Society. The mitigating factor is that Perley is considered a careful annotator.

19. Bayley pamphlet, *Little Known Early American Portrait Painters* (Boston: Copley Gallery), 1917, unpaginated.

Atkins (1731–1767), is probably neither by Thomas Johnston nor of this Atkins.[20]

Another possible artist from whom Blyth might have learned the technique of pastel is Joseph Blackburn (ca. 1703–1787)[21], one of colonial New England's most prominent portraitists who arrived in Boston around 1754—except that Blackburn never made any pastels, or at least, not these four. The first one so attributed, of Thomas Dering, was given to the Metropolitan Museum in New York in 1917 with several family portraits done by Blackburn. The donor noted that the artist of the pastel, however, was unknown. Nonetheless, in the report of the gift in the museum's annual report for the year, the Dering pastel was erroneously also credited to Blackburn.

In the late 1920s, Frank W. Bayley, undoubtedly aware of the attribution in the Met's annual report, subsequently sold three other "Blackburn" pastels, ostensibly signed and dated 1760. They were identified as "Lt. Gov. Thomas Oliver," "Mrs. Oliver," and "Lt. Gov. Thomas Hutchinson," attributions soon determined to be false. Bayley also sold other portraits with fictitious documentation. The Boston Athenaeum, the Museum of Fine Arts, Boston, and the Massachusetts Art Commission accepted the attributions and provenance of portraits they bought from Bayley, because of his known scholarship. His writings included several important early monographs on Smibert,

---

20. The portrait is at the Massachusetts Historical Society. The coat worn by the sitter is of a style dating to about thirty years after Johnston's death in 1767, the same year as the death of the supposed subject. Fine Arts dealer James Kochan suggests that this is a portrait of Atkins's grandson, David Atkins Tyng. Francis Higginson Atkins, *History of the Atkins Family*, Dudley Atkins, Book & Job Printers, 1891, noted that the surname was added "at the instance of Mrs. Sarah Tyng Winslow (1719–1791); she had no children and was known as "the protectress of her maiden name Tyng." Sometime after her death family members dropped the "Tyng"; also, the name of the publishing company for the family history, a century after her death, does not use "Tyng." The author believes the portrait may have been done by Thomas Johnston's son, John. In addition, the surmise of Frederick W. Coburn in 1932 that Thomas Johnston painted the two oil portraits of "Mr. Gee" and "Dr. Mayhew" recorded in the inventory of his estate does not hold up. The "Mayhew" probably was not the Copley pastel, now lost, but more likely, the oil of the Reverend Jonathan Mayhew done ca. 1750 by Johnston's former apprentice, John Greenwood. The "Gee" must be the Reverend Joshua Gee, copied from Gee's portrait by Smibert, now at Harvard. The copy is now at the Massachusetts Historical Society, with Smibert's portrait of Mrs. Gee. The inscription giving Gee's age, "Ætat:33", seems to have been done by the same hand as "—moriar Mercerus" in the portrait of Andrew Le Mercier by John Greenwood, in the Peabody Essex Museum. This, plus the overall handling of the portrait of Gee, suggests that it also can now be attributed to this artist, and that it likely was the "Gee" in Johnston's shop at his death. Would these portraits of Mayhew and Gee have been in the shop for frames, or were they the personal possession of Thomas Johnston? Is it relevant that both the sitters were clergymen; could it be that neither they nor their congregations chose to buy them? Does their being in Johnston's possession mean that Greenwood, when he left for Surinam, intended to return, as some writers have suggested? Or did he relinquish them to his former employer? Intriguing questions all, but these portraits cannot be attributed to Thomas Johnston.

21. The date of Joseph Blackburn's death, which had been unknown to art historians for years, was provided by Neil Jeffares, pastel expert, in an email to the author, Nov. 20, 2015. The British register of St. Nicholas, 1787 (reference 852 Worcester St. Nicholas BA3790/1b) noted that Blackburn was buried at St. Nicholas Church, now the Slug and Lettuce, on July 11, 1787. Unlike the portraitists who preceded him in New England, it is widely assumed that Blackburn had received professional guidance in England, most likely from the eighteenth-century portraitist, Thomas Hudson. Although more than 250 oil portraits are credited to Hudson (with his workshop), no pastel is known. C. H. Collins Baker, "Notes on Joseph Blackburn and Nathaniel Dance," *The Huntington Library Quarterly* 9, no 1 (Nov. 1945):33-48, disputed that Blackburn's level of professional skill indicated that he had been a student of Hudson in England and that the theory of Blackburn's training in New England put forth by H. W. French, might be "redeemed from contempt," 40.

Feke, Blackburn, and John Johnston. Bayley devoted an entire pamphlet in his series *Little Known Early American Portrait Painters* (1917), to Johnston, calling him "[a]mong the best of the little-known American portrait painters." In an ironic twist, in one of these booklets Bayley promoted Benjamin Blyth's pastels, giving him two pages instead of the usual one for each artist. In 1915, Bayley published a book on John Singleton Copley. These writings were well regarded at the time.[22] Furthermore, among Bayley's friends were John Hill Morgan and Lawrence Park, like-minded art historians of American art whom he sometimes joined on scholarly pursuits. Therefore, the myth that Blackburn was a pastel artist seemed credible. Presumably, if Bayley had thought the pastels could pass as Copleys, he would have so marketed them. Soon after the fraud was exposed in 1932, Bayley committed suicide. One unfortunate outcome is that neither the sitters nor the artists of these pastels are definitively known, although it is likely that Benjamin Blyth drew two of them.

There is too little documentation on Blackburn to say how he himself might have helped Blyth. But it seems clear that Blackburn's work exerted a good deal of influence on the young artist. Blyth made a pastel copy of Blackburn's oil portrait of Mary Holyoke's grandfather, Deacon Jonathan Simpson, in 1771 (Cat. 117). It is a very accomplished, accurate rendering of the original and provided Blyth with ample opportunity to study the older artist's techniques. Blyth undoubtedly saw another Blackburn portrait, Samuel Curwen's wife, Abigail, since he was doing pastels of the family.[23] In fact, Bayley, who

22. Bayley "deserves the highest praise for the manner in which he has traced the works of America's first 'old master' and for his appreciative and intelligent compilation", *American Art News*, 13, no. 19 (Feb. 13, 1915):7. In 1929, Bayley published *Five Colonial Artists*, with numerous full-page illustrations, in which he also credited Morgan with having found Blackburn's correct first name, corroborating what he himself had found in *The New Hampshire Gazette* of October 30, 1761. And Bayley supplied the texts for the MFA's *Loan Exhibition of One Hundred Colonial Portraits*, organized for the Massachusetts Tercentenary. The printed catalogue contained a number of errors by the MFA, which Bayley noted with annoyance in an undated letter to Charles K. Bolton at the Boston Athenaeum. Its copy of the catalogue, in the Boston Athenaeum Rare Book Room, has the letter pasted in, to which corrections were made in pen. The discovery of Blackburn's first name is in Frank W. Bayley, *Five Colonial Artists of New England: Joseph Badger, Joseph Blackburn, John Singleton Copley, Robert Feke, John Smibert* (Boston: Privately printed, 1929), 51-52.

23. Might Blyth have been the artist who made the copy of her portrait in oil? Once in the collection of James Cooley, Washington, DC, in the 1980s, the original was sold by Northeast Auctions in 2010; its current whereabouts is unknown. Lawrence Park listed the portrait in 1923 in the estate of Henry R. Dalton, Boston, MA. In the description, Park mentions that the original is reproduced in Alice Morse Earle, *Two Centuries of Costume in America, MDCXX —MDCCXX*, (New York: The Macmillan Company, 1903), "where it states that the portrait is in the Essex Institute, but the reproduction differs slightly and may refer to a different picture." Lawrence Park, "Joseph Blackburn," Repr. from *The Proceedings of the American Antiquarian Society for Oct. 1922*, (Worcester: Published by the Society, 1923), 29-30.

Samuel Curwen had complained to a Mary Russell that it was time his pictures were finished, and she answered in a letter from Boston dated February 1757 that she agreed, and that she would speak to the artist. Park, "Joseph Blackburn," 5-6; a note penciled in the margin of the Boston Athenaeum copy states that Ogden Codman said this letter writer was wrongly attributed, and it was not from Mrs. Richard Russell, but from Mrs. Chambers Russell. The paint strokes are much smoother than Blyth is known to have used, and the copy might have been done before he became active in the medium. The copyist might be William Johnston. A telling comparison is Abigail Curwen's face with that in William Johnston's portrait of Mrs. Jacob Hurd (and baby) at the Metropolitan Museum, NY. There is also a copy. PEM not only has the original Blackburn of Mrs. Fitch, but an early copy. It, too, might have been made by William Johnston or John Greenwood; more examination is warranted. Other Blackburn portraits Blyth probably saw are of the Rev. Peter Bours, rector of St. Michael's Church in Marblehead, and Salem residents Mrs. Samuel Gardner, Timothy Fitch, and his wife, Eunice Brown Fitch.

was a good judge of art, may have realized this affinity when he sold the three pastels as Blackburns.

Blyth adopted many of Blackburn's attributes, such as the same noticeable brown lip line and almond eyes and rich flesh tones—two of the clear indications of Blackburn influence. Blyth also took note of the white dot always present in the eyes of Blackburn's subjects, a technique that effectively brings eyes to life. The Blackburn portrait of the Reverend Daniel Greenleaf is a very persuasive example of the affinity of this artist to the younger Blyth. Lawrence Park noted that Blackburn was "particularly fond of introducing pearls" and "betrays an almost effeminate affection for laces and satins, and at his best these are drawn with a startling veri-similitude [*sic*]."[24] Blyth most likely learned how to paint lace by copying portraits by Blackburn, although lacking his virtuosity. Some of Blyth's most effective renderings of pearls, with dabs of white for "capturing light," are, not surprisingly, on pastel portraits for which he devoted much care—strands of pearls worn by Lydia Phippen Fisk (Cat. 53) and Rachel(?) Baty (Cat. 13), the visible earring of Mrs. J. Gardner (Cat. 58), and even the strand in Elizabeth Rogers' hair (Cat. 110).

The two artists also shared such traits as work that was uneven and lacking any evidence of artistic development or progression of skill. And both artists had a common problem: they were being outshone by the ambitious Copley. Indeed, Park, while noting that Copley early on was influenced by Blackburn, added that the Copley's increasing excellence may have caused Black-

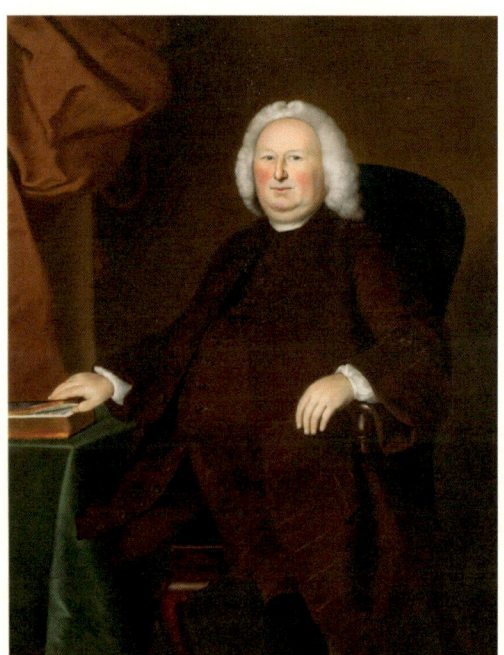

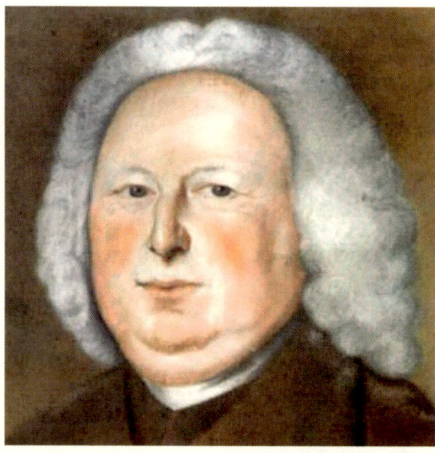

Jonathan Simpson
Detail of pastel by
Benjamin Blyth, probably 1771

Portrait of Deacon Jonathan Simpson
Oil on canvas by Joseph Blackburn, 1757
Courtesy of the Michele and Donald D'Amour Museum of Fine Arts,
Springfield Massachusetts, gift of Mrs. Lewis Tifft, 57. 29
Photography by John Polak

---

24. Lawrence Park, "Joseph Blackburn," 10. Lace is especially prominent in the Blackburn portraits of Margaret Temple (Mrs. Nathaniel Dowse, MHS) as well as in Sarah Wentworth McPheadris and Mrs. Jonathan Warner (both at the Warner House Assoc., NH). The Warner portraits were some of the many portraits that generations of descendants claimed (believed?) were by Copley and were so recorded in the town history: C. S. Gurney, *Portsmouth: Historic and Picturesque,* (Portsmouth, NH: C. S. Gurney, 1902).

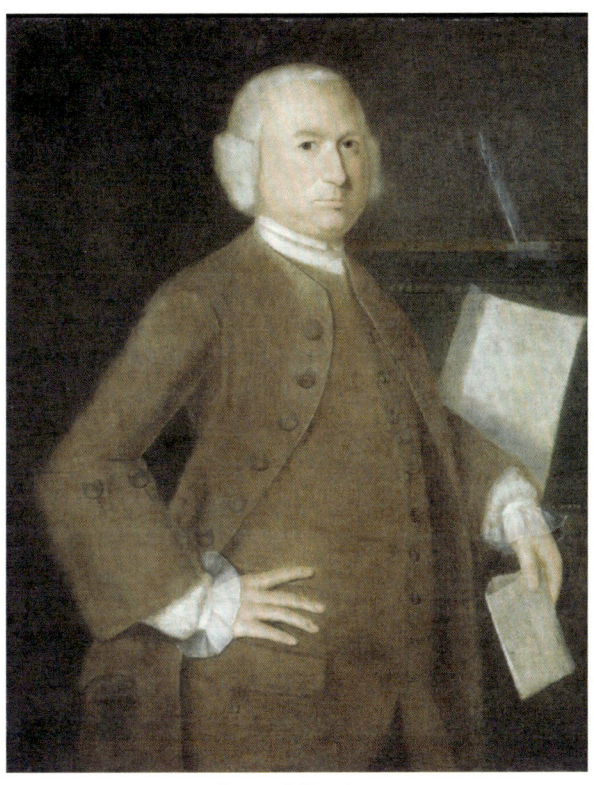

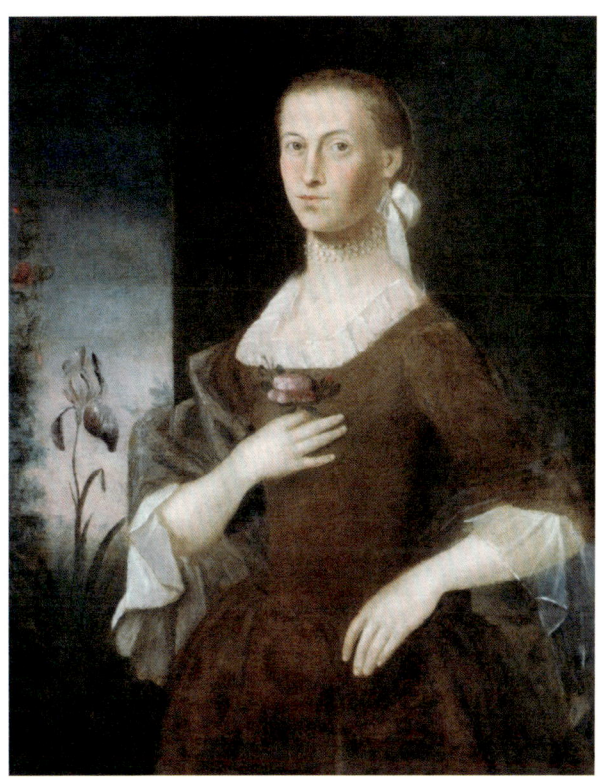

Samuel Gardiner
Oil portrait by William Johnston, 1763
Courtesy of the Metropolitan Museum 283.2,
gift of Edgar William and Bernice Chrysler Garbisch, 1970

Mrs. Samuel Gardiner
Oil portrait by William Johnston, 1763
Courtesy of the Metropolitan Museum 283.3,
gift of Edgar William and Bernice Chrysler Garbisch, 1970

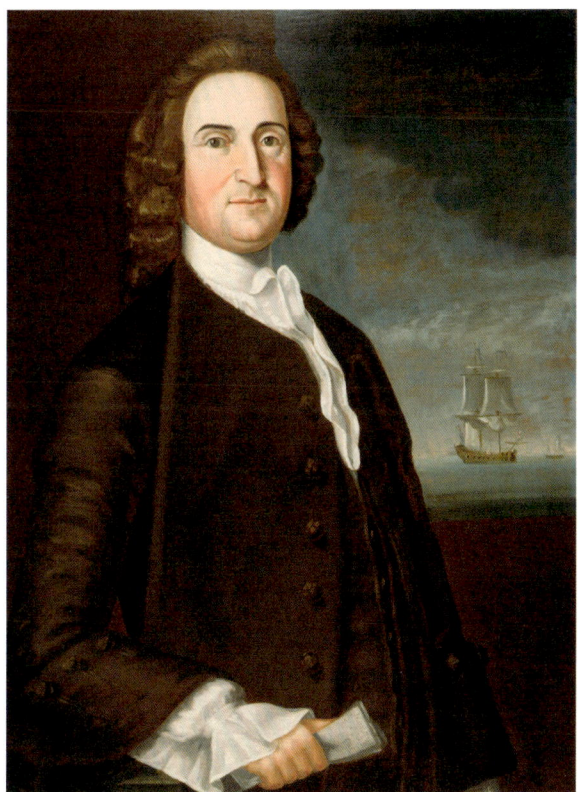

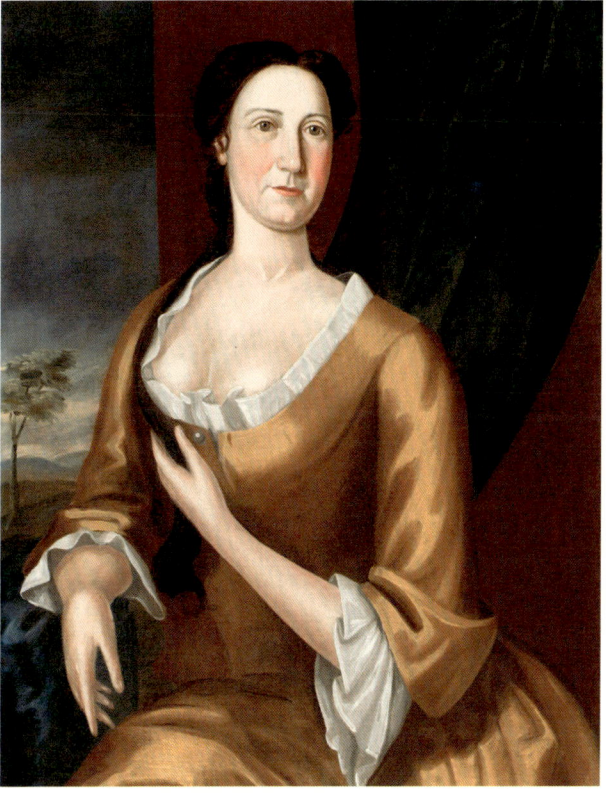

Benjamin Pickman
Oil portrait by John Greenwood, ca. 1750
Courtesy of the Peabody Essex Museum 100135,
gift of Dr. Hersey Derby Pickman, 1903

Abigail Rawlins Pickman
Oil portrait by John Greenwood, ca. 1750
Courtesy of the Peabody Essex Museum 112438,
gift of Miss Martha C. Codman, 1921

burn's departure.[25] It certainly didn't seem to cut into Blyth's career, as has been noted; many of his pastels were drawn while Copley was still in New England.

Portrayal of character, however, was not Blackburn's strong suit. Bolton and Binsse noted that "perhaps Blackburn's chief artistic demerits are the lack of characterization in his face and the general monotony of his work." Art historian James Flexner wrote that Blackburn was not interested in this aspect of portraiture.[26] Unlike Blackburn, Blyth captured his subjects' individuality in his portraits.

Two other artists active in the region whose work Blyth might well have seen were William Johnston (1732–1772) and John Greenwood (1727–1792). Johnston's hard-edged style, like that of Blackburn, is also stylistically a precursor of Benjamin Blyth's oil portraits, and his portrait of Jacob Hurd exhibits the same lip line and white dot in the eye used by Blackburn and adopted later by Blyth. Although Greenwood left for Surinam in 1752, when Blyth was six years old, Blyth also could have learned much from studying his portraits, starting with the scheme of assembling facial details. Blyth's hands, when he did them, were curving arcs without knuckles, not unlike the right hand of Abigail Love Rawlins Pickman, by Greenwood, in the Peabody Essex Museum (Acc. 112438).[27] Also, the apparition-like landscapes that serve as backgrounds of such Greenwood portraits as that of Mrs. Samuel Gardner at the Massachusetts Historical Society and Benjamin Gerrish and Mrs. Gerrish at the Peabody Essex Museum (Acc. 105414 and 105415)—the dark and cloudy skies, the hills in Tuscan-School-like blues and greens—reappear in Blyth's pastel of the Sarah Moses child with pet bird (Cat. 95) and in his oil of young William Luscomb (Cat. 88), both of which, however, may have also been worked on by Samuel Blyth.

In sum, although Blyth may have learned about working in pastels from seeing some early ones by Copley, he probably learned as much if not more on technique and composition in general from studying the oil portraits by Joseph Blackburn, William Johnston, and John Greenwood. Blyth, like many other early to mid-eighteenth-century artists in Boston, also may have learned about both pastels and painting in oils by visiting the well-patronized shop started by John Smibert in Boston, or he simply may have learned about the technique of pastel drawing from some books from England that were available in Boston at the time.[28]

---

25. Lawrence Park, "Joseph Blackburn," 11.

26. Flexner, *First Flowers*, 204, 210. Also, Theodore Bolton and Harry Lorin Binsse, "An American Artist of Formula: Joseph Blackburn, *Antiquarian* 15 (Nov. 1930): 50-53, 88-92.

27. It is possible that Greenwood's later portrait of his extended family at the Museum of Fine Arts, Boston, (MFA 1983. 34), concentrates so obviously on hands, to show, perhaps, that he had learned how to do them.

28. Smibert is discussed in Walter K. Watkins, "The New England Museum and the Home of Art in Boston," *Bostonian Society Publications*, 2 (1917):112–14. Among the "effects" at Smibert's death, along with thirty-five portraits, "history pieces" and "landskips, were a 'Library' and "Prints and Books of prints, drawings, etc." Marjorie Shelley cites in the *Bulletin, Metropolitan Museum of Art*, Spring 2011, *The Principles of Painting* by Roger de Piles, published in 1743, as a possible source. She also cites Janice G. Schimmelman's article, "Books on Drawing and Painting Techniques Available in Eighteenth-Century American Libraries and Bookstores," *Winterthur Portfolio*, 19:2-3, 193-205. An email from Neil Jeffares (website pastellists.com) to the author in 2015 noted that there were other crayon suppliers in Boston from Smibert on; his nephew John Moffat, who was alive until 1777; John Gore, who advertised "crayons . . . sold cheap for cash" in the *Boston Gazette* of Sept. 3, 1761, and five years later, "crayons in sets."

SALEM'S NINETEENTH-CENTURY historian Joseph B. Felt made note of Benjamin Blyth's January 1769 advertisement in *The Essex Gazette* that he "draws crayons at his father's house in the great street leading to Marblehead." It has long been assumed that this announced the start of Blyth's career. However, the newspaper had been established only a few months earlier; this notice was simply Blyth's first opportunity to advertise in it.[29]

His earliest pastel portraits, from the mid- to late 1760s, are primarily those of wealthy, elderly matrons who would have been sympathetic to the young aspiring artist: as well as Abigail Love Rawlins Pickman (Cat. 106), previously

Advertisement posted by Benjamin Blyth
The Essex Gazette, Jan. 17, 1769
Courtesy of the Boston Athenaeum

noted, he drew Margaret Gibbs Appleton (Cat. 5), and the recently widowed Elizabeth Cabot (Cat. 23). The portrait of Cabot's son George (Cat. 25), presumably done at about the same time, is the only one known to have been signed by Blyth. And at that, twice.

He soon seized the opportunity to do portraits of John Adams, an up-and-coming lawyer, and his young wife, Abigail. The newly married couple was staying with the Cranch family while John Adams tended to his legal duties in the Essex County courts.[30] Blyth also drew Dr. Joseph Warren and his wife. Warren, a friend of Adams, was already making himself known for his opposition to English rule.

On September 18, 1769, Benjamin Blyth married Mehitabel Cook, daughter of a mariner and shoreman from another old Salem family; they had two sons, Benjamin, baptized on February 10,

---

29. *Essex Gazette*, 1, no. 25, Jan. 17, 1769. Various published citations give the date of commencement of publication as 1769. However, it was in August 1768. And the date of the issue in which the advertisement appeared was also given as May 10–17. The Boston Athenaeum's bound copy does not have the initial issues, but a page of penciled notes on the front free endpaper provides the information. Neither the Peabody Essex Museum nor the American Antiquarian Society has this issue.

30. Foote made the cogent argument that Blyth did the portraits between late 1764 and 1766, and that the pastels were proficient enough to suggest they were not Blyth's first—two plausible hypotheses now upheld by some new attributions. The Cranch family moved to Boston in 1767. Perley, *History of Salem,* 2:317. Adams, in his diary, recorded arriving at the "brother Cranch's" on August 16, 1766, staying at least the next day. There are no entries for Friday through Sunday, nor from August 21 until Nov. 3, when the Adamses again went to Salem and brother Cranch's through Thursday, Nov. 6, cited in Charles Francis Adams, ed., *Works of John Adams,* (Boston: Charles C. Little and James Brown, 1850), 2:199. "By summer [1766] Abigail had to juggle schedules to find a week for the two of them to visit her favorite sister in Salem. It is likely during this vacation that the Adamses sat for the portraits by Benjamin Blyth," cited in James Grant, *John Adams, Party of One,* (New York: Farrar, Straus and Giroux, 2005),70. See also Janet Whitney, *Abigail Adams,* (Boston: Little, Brown & Co., 1947), 43. The Ruck house, at the northern end of Mill St. between Norman and Creek Streets, had been built ca. 1645 and was added on to before 1742. Copley rented the newer part from Samuel Bacon, who had bought it from Joseph McIntire, joiner, in 1754—three years before the birth of his famous son, architect Samuel McIntire; but the family may never have lived there. However, there is no mention of either Copley or Cranch in Felt, *Annals of Salem,* and only one irrelevant one of John Adams. Yet Felt's wife was a niece of "Mrs. John Adams" (Abigail), according to Earle, in the caption for illustration "Fans and Pieces of Brocade Gown" in Earle, *Two Centuries of Costume,* 2:xi.

1771, and Frank, baptized on January 3, 1773. The family was living either in the Ruck house—the Cranch family had moved to Boston in November 1767—or nearby. Among Blyth's early patrons were Holyoke, Curwen, then Derby families. He also was busy drawing pastels of many clergy and other prominent people from Salem and other Essex County towns. In fact, the early 1770s were the most productive in his career as a portraitist, despite the presence of Copley.

Benjamin and Samuel's father died in 1774. Samuel was one of the administrators of the estate, along with his brother, Verrin, his brother-in-law Joseph Hiller, listed as "Watchmaker," and Samuel Flagg (Cat. 55) — but not Benjamin. In the distribution of assets, each of the four brothers received £66 13s 4d. The probate record for their father's estate, valued at £333 6s, also listed "7 Portrait Prints @ [0]/4, 6 Lanskip Dito @ [0]/1/9 ½, 5 Small Pictures @ [0]/1, 1 Coat of Arms @ [0]/8." Could the coat of arms have been made by Samuel Jr. for his father, or had it been made by the Boston printmaker and coat of arms painter, Thomas Johnston? The first, and significant, item in this list is "1 Family Portrait Picture @ 0/14/0." Who was depicted, what medium was it, and who made it? The family circumstances of earlier generations would seem to preclude an oil portrait, and the value belies this. Could it have been a Blyth pastel? Samuel shortly advertised a proposed boarding school "for females," with instruction consisting of the usual, "with French and dancing,"[31] an addition to his livelihood that may have come about with the help of his inheritance. Whether it actually was established is not known.

On May 13, 1774, Gen. Thomas Gage, Commander-in-Chief, and military governor of the British forces in North America, arrived in Boston. About four weeks later, probably coinciding with, if not the motive for, Lt. Gov. Thomas Hutchinson's state visit to Salem, Gage moved the General Court there. For a while, he was wined and dined by sympathetic Salemites.[32] However, within a few months, after the British mandated the embargo of the port of Boston, 125 Salem residents signed a document objecting to its closing. Some prominent townspeople were ambivalent, suffering from their allegiance with close friends on both sides of the impending conflict. Other Salem luminaries signed a friendly letter to Hutchinson, who was popular with many of the town's elite, although several signers, including both ministers Thomas Barnard, senior and junior, were compelled later to retract it.[33] Tensions between colonists and the British government were beginning to rise. The political discontent building up in Salem was about to affect Benjamin Blyth's burgeoning career as an artist.

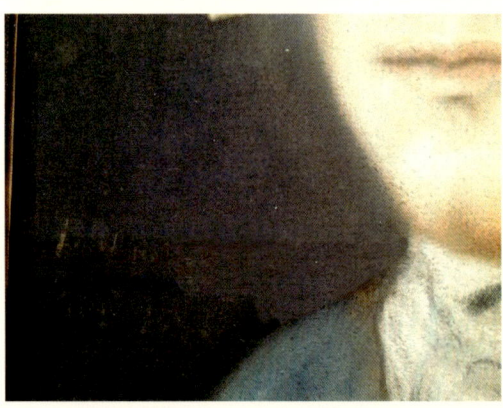

Signature B Blyth on portrait of George Cabot
Detail of pastel (now illegible), probably 1767

31. Felt, *Annals of Salem*, 1:452; also, Phillips, *Salem in The Eighteenth Century*, 323.

32. Charles S. Osgood and H. M. Batchelder, *Historical Sketch of Salem:1626–1879* (Salem: Essex Institute, 1879).

33. Hutchinson was popular among prominent citizens of Boston as well; the Rev Jonathan Mayhew, an instigator of the Stamp Act Rebellion, owned a portrait of Hutchinson, now in the collections of the Massachusetts Historical Society.

Gen. Gage soon attempted to stop political meetings, such as the one publicized with printed handbills by the Committee of Correspondence to be held in Salem on August 24, 1774, to elect delegates to an upcoming county convention in Ipswich. It met anyway and established its own independent organization on October 7, 1774, an event considered of "peculiar significance, and it can be justly claimed as the first official act of the Province by which she put herself in open, actual opposition to the home government."[34] John Hancock, a wealthy Boston merchant already known for his objection to British rule, was elected president, becoming one of the first major local heroes of the emerging American Revolution. After the account of the incident reached England, a British satirical print *A Political Lesson*, published later that year, shows Gage, personifying the British government, toppling from his horse onto the dirt road. Rarely noted in descriptions of this print, but most telling, is that the signpost points "*to Salem.*"[35] "Shortly after these stirring events," wrote Gilbert L. Streeter, "the hated Governor Gage, with his soldiers and his myrmidons, returned to Boston. His attempts to control the contumacious town of Salem had signally failed. The people would neither be silenced by alluring bribes of increased trade and commerce nor be cowed by the display of military power."[36]

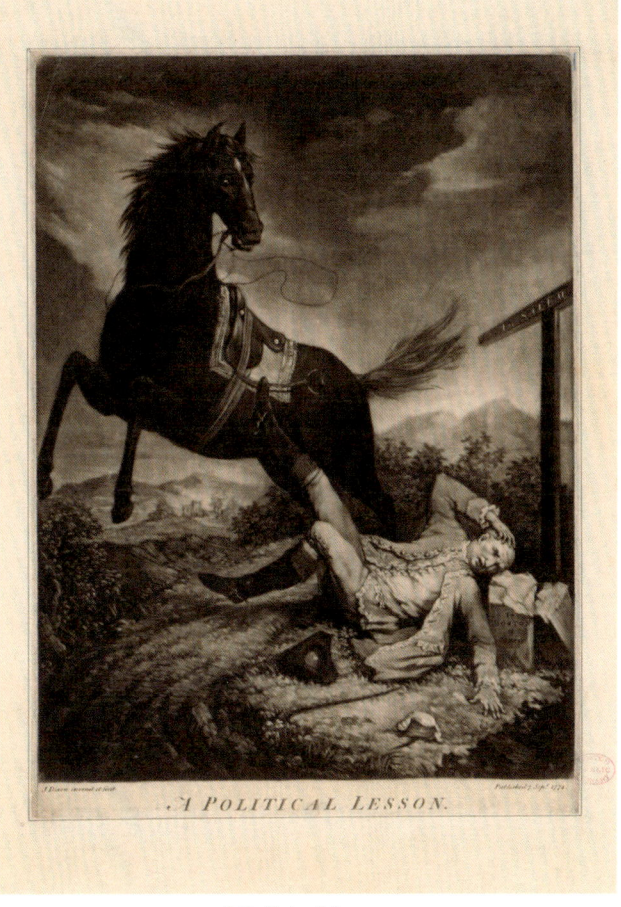

A Political Lesson.
Mezzotint. J. Dixon invenit et fecit. Published 7 Sepr 1774. Printed for John Bowles at No. 13, in Cornhill [London] [corner torn] —
1s 6 d.
Courtesy of the Boston Public Library,
Americana Collection

The next *contretemps* in Salem was the potentially bloody confrontation on February 26, 1775, between the locals and the British troops under the command of Colonel Alexander Leslie, who had been sent to find hidden ammunition. The crisis was eventually defused by the intervention of the Rev. Thomas Barnard, Jr. It was possibly around this time that Benjamin Blyth drew his pastel

34. Osgood, *Historical Sketch of Salem*, 47. See also Phillips, *Salem in the Eighteenth Century*, 333.
35. The print is described in E. McSherry Fowble, *Two Centuries of Prints in America: 1680–1880/ A Selective Catalogue of the Winterthur Museum Collection*, (Charlottesville: Published for the Henry Francis du Pont Winterthur Museum by the University Press of Virginia, 1987), 149. Impressions of the British satirical print are also in the collections of Colonial Williamsburg, Harvard, Metropolitan Museum of Art, and Winterthur.
36. Gilbert Streeter, "Salem Before the Revolution," EIHS 32:83.

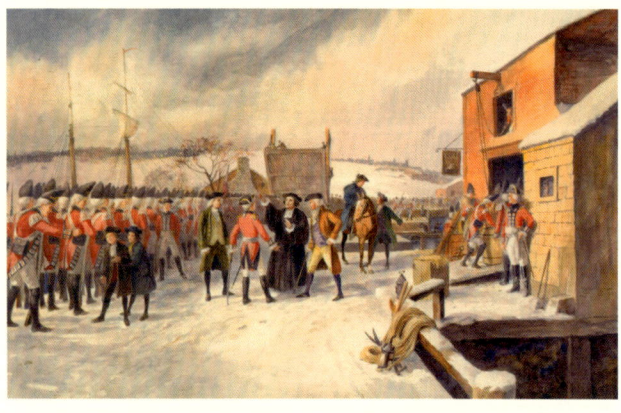

The Repulse of Leslie at the North Bridge, Sunday February 26, 1775 Watercolor by Lewis Jesse Bridgman, 1901, 22¾ x 32¾ in. Courtesy of the Peabody Essex Museum 106721, purchase 1918

Joseph Hiller ad, *The Essex Gazette*, May 8–15, 1770
Courtesy of the American Antiquarian Society

portrait of the minister (Cat. 8).

It can be argued that the American Revolution came close to beginning in Salem, although the inevitable conflict finally sprouted into actual fighting two months later, over another British search for stashed ammunitions in Lexington and Concord. Salem men then participated in overwhelming numbers to the costly battle of Bunker Hill on June 17, 1775, at which Joseph Warren was killed.

Disaffection with British rule had already begun to spread after the publication in Boston five years earlier of a print of the "Bloody Massacre" by Paul Revere. His prints were becoming an increasingly important propaganda tool for the emerging Patriot cause. So, a wave of print publishing began in Salem. It was started by Joseph Hiller, a clockmaker, watchmaker, and silversmith who had moved from Boston to Salem and in 1775 married Samuel Blyth's sister-in-law. Both Samuel and Benjamin soon became a vital part of the printmaking project.

Hiller's first contributions in 1775–76 were mezzotints of John Hancock and Joseph Warren. For the print of Hancock, the notation "Jos. Hiller feci" suggests that he did the original drawing and mezzotinting, based on the oil portrait by John Singleton Copley, painted between 1770 and 1772.[37]

---

37. The painting is now at the Massachusetts Historical Society. Of the known impressions of the print, the one at the Peabody Essex Museum has very little coloring, while the impression in the Smithsonian Institution's National Portrait Gallery shows the extensive use of color, complete with strong opaque white accents attributable to Samuel Blyth.

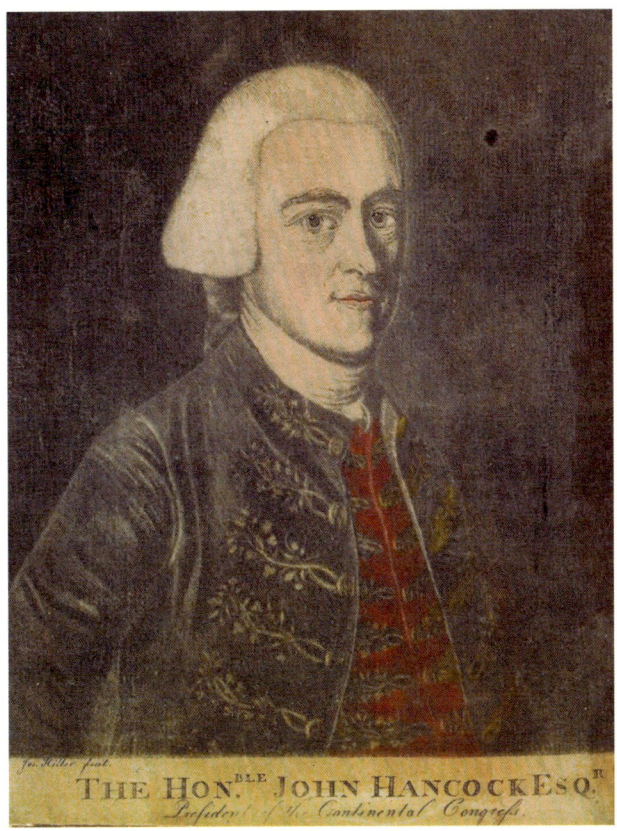

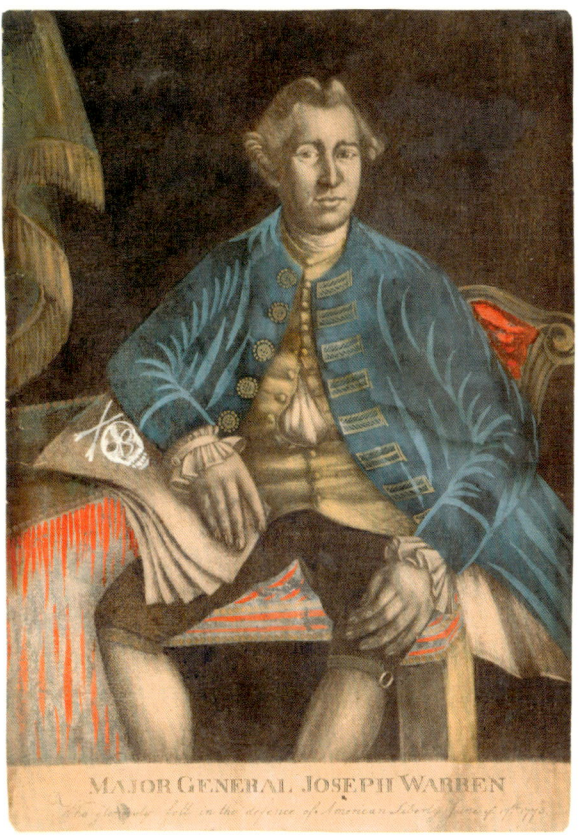

THE HON^{BLE} JOHN HANCOCK, ESQ^R
Preſident of the Continental Congreſs
Jos. Hiller fecit
Mezzotint with hand coloring, ca. 1775, 25.1 x 20 cm.
Courtesy of the Peabody Essex Museum 106937,
Museum purchase, 1918

MAJOR GENERAL JOSEPH WARREN
Who glorioufly fell in the defence of American Liberty
June ye 17th 1775
Joseph Hiller (attr.)
Mezzotint with hand coloring, ca. 1775, 32.8 x 23.2 cm. (sheet)
Courtesy of the Yale University Art Gallery, Mabel Grady
Garvin Collection, 1946.3.960.

The print of Warren, based on the Copley portrait now at the Museum of Fine Arts, Boston, also is attributed to Hiller; the elegantly scripted subtitle for both it and the Hancock engravings are characteristic of the work of one would expect from a silversmith—florid, flowing, from swell to fine point.[38] Samuel Blyth probably did the coloring of this impression. The added imagery of skull and crossbones on the anatomical drawings under his right (left, in the painting) arm, a ref-

In another impression at the Smithsonian National Museum of American History, neither Hiller's name nor the second line of the text, "Preſident of the Continental Congress," appear. Hancock's coat was covered with a wash of light gray, then numerous slashes of intense red, obliterating any detail. But on examination, the text area shows no evidence of burnishing, so it is seen to be a proof, suggesting that Samuel was involved in the early stages of the original printing. 38. The Peabody Essex Museum owns a silver porringer made by Hiller for the marriage of his niece, engraved J. H. to S. F. The letters "J" and "H" are identical to the inscription on Hiller's print of John Hancock, although it can be argued that the style is common. Hiller had access to the oil portrait of Warren painted by Copley ca. 1765, now at the Museum of Fine Arts, Boston. Because the image, somewhat simplified, was drawn on the plate as it appeared, it printed in reverse. The maker of the mezzotint was listed as "Anonymous" in the 1904 exhibition catalogue of the Museum (No. 37). Other collections: Metropolitan Museum, bequest of Charles Munn, 1924; Elkins Collection, Free Library of Philadelphia.

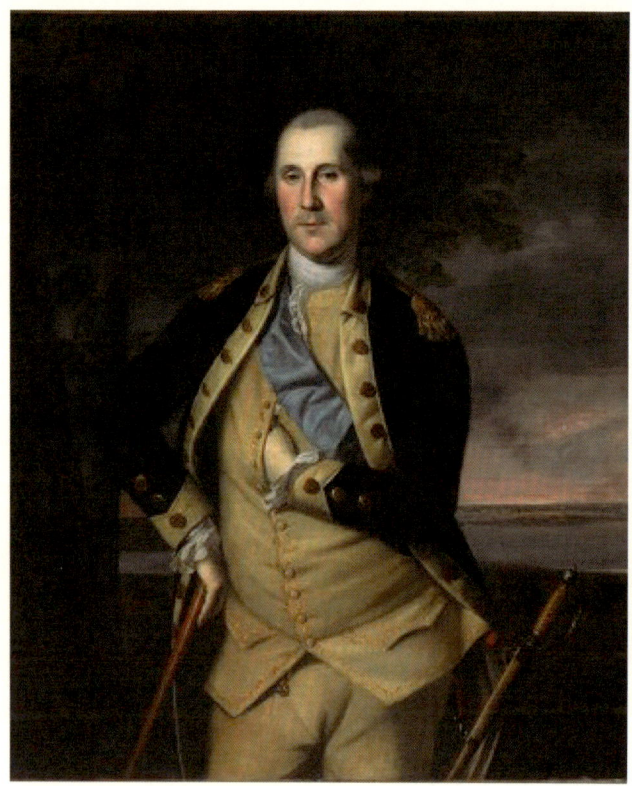

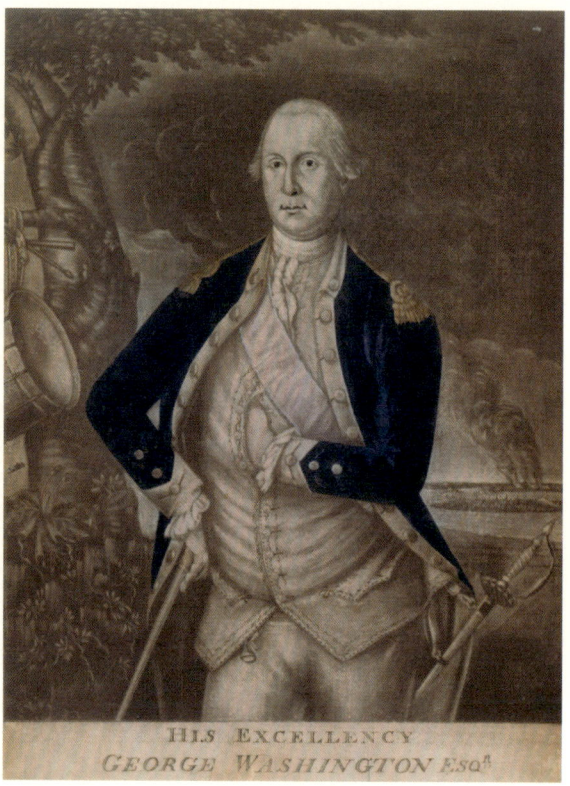

George Washington
Charles Willson Peale, 1775–6. Oil on canvas, 44 x 38 5/16 in.
Courtesy of the Brooklyn Museum, Dick S. Ramsay Fund,
34.1178

His Excellency George Washington Esqʳ
Joseph Hiller (attr.)
Mezzotint with hand coloring, probably 1776, 26.4 x 17.2 cm.
Courtesy of the Metropolitan Museum Department of
Drawings and Prints 24.90.212, bequest of Charles Allen
Munn, 1924

erence to Warren being a doctor, were painted in the highly visible opaque white that was typical of Samuel Blyth, who used allusions, either graphic or literary, in several of his prints.

On June 19, 1775, two days after the Battle of Bunker Hill, George Washington was made commander-in-chief of the colonial forces on Cambridge Common. Hiller, recognizing the importance of the occasion, soon produced a pair of mezzotints, *His Excellency George Washington, Esqʳ* and the companion portrait of *Lady Washington.*

Hiller's mezzotint of Washington was based on the oil portrait of him commissioned by John Hancock from Charles Willson Peale (1741–1827). The Philadelphia-based artist was staying in Cambridge at the time. The sought-after print became the first of the nearly 900 entries in Charles Henry Hart's monumental 1904 *Catalogue of the Engraved Portraits of Washington.* Four years later, Charles Allen Munn wrote that it was "the engraving which is considered by collectors in many respects the most prized of all portraits of the general. It is the first engraved portrait of Washington published in this country."[39]

---

39. Charles Allen Munn, *Three Types of Washington Portraits* (New York: Privately printed [The Gilliss Press], 1908), 27. Other collections that own the prints include the Museum of Fine Arts, Boston, the Massachusetts Historical Society, the New-York Historical Society, the Peabody Essex Museum, and the Yale University Art Gallery, John Hill Morgan Collection.

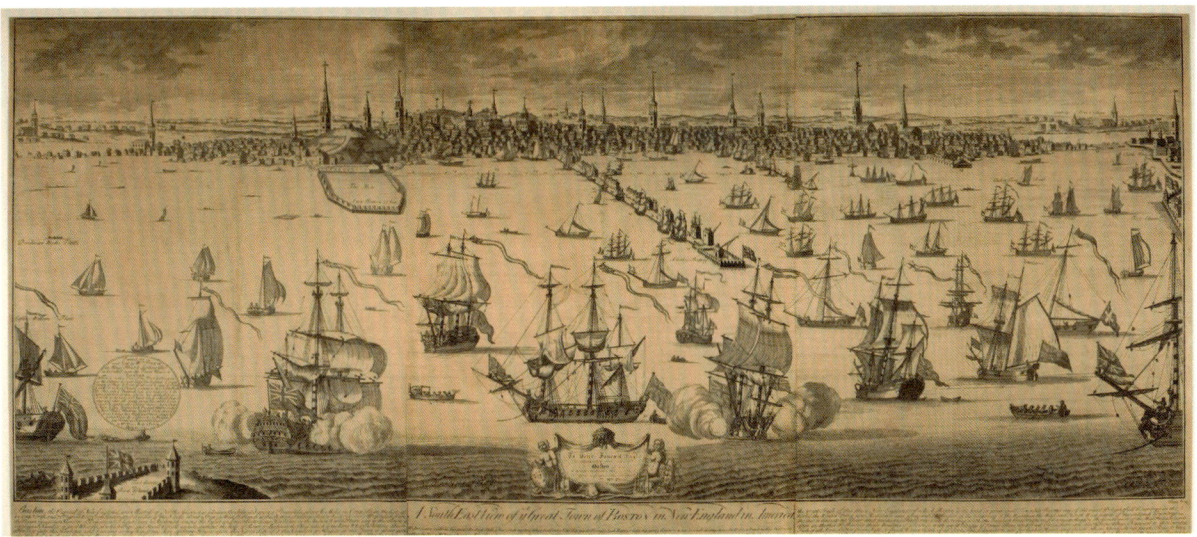

A South East View of yᵉ Great Town of Boston in New England in America.
W. Burgis Delin./I.Harris Sculp.
Printed and Sold by Wᵐ. Price Print & Mapseller . . . 1743
Courtesy of the American Antiquarian Society

For many years, the identity of the engraver had been the subject of speculation, until Wendy Shadwell, then curator of prints at the New-York Historical Society, made a convincing case for Hiller. Another opinion, from collector of Washingtoniana J. Robert Maguire, concluded that the pair of mezzotint portraits were the work of Samuel Blyth because of the way they were hand-colored.[40] The coloring is indeed attributable to him. However, the more finely drawn, detailed draftsmanship of the figure of the general, along with the well-executed landscape, particularly the foliage and the drum hanging from a tree branch in the left foreground, are more skillfully handled than is found in any mezzotint attributable to Samuel Blyth. (The awkward depiction of the general's right arm is a faithful reproduction of how it appears in the Peale painting!) Nonetheless, this print of Washington seems to have been the first of the printmaking efforts indicating that Hiller intended more collaboration if not outright partnership with the Blyth brothers.

An intriguing detail in the print is the identity of the distant landscape that appears surrounded by water. The vignette, which is in the oil portrait by Peale, proves to be a view of Boston, a peninsula at the time. Peale probably used as his source the well-disseminated view issued by William Price in 1743, which incorporated many new church spires and other buildings to the earlier version of *South East View of yᵉ Great Town of Boston in New England in America*, drawn by William Burgis and engraved by J. Harris in 1725. The Peale painting simplified the image by eliminating Long Wharf and many vessels in the harbor. (The well-known print of Boston by Paul Revere, *The town of Boston*

40. Wendy J. Shadwell, "An Attribution for His Excellency and Lady Washington," *The Magazine Antiques* 95 no. 2 (Feb. 1969): 240-41. J. Robert Maguire, "His Excellency and Lady Washington: A Pair of Mezzotint Portraits by Joseph Hiller, Sr., or Samuel Blyth?" *Imprint* 30 no. 2 (Autumn 2005), 22-33. They also were illustrated in Nina Fletcher Little, "The Blyths of Salem: Benjamin, Limner in Crayons and Oil, and Samuel, Painter and Cabinetmaker," *EIHC* 108 (1972), 49-57, illus. betw. 56-57.

in New-England and Brittish [sic] ships of war landing their troops, published in 1768, is not the source; it only pictured the north half of the town, as its focus was on Long Wharf.) That the background landscape in the painting has escaped mention is especially surprising, as Peale is known for his care in providing relevant identifiable background details.

However, Hiller took the image one step further in his mezzotint. He added the plumes of smoke, presumably to indicate Charlestown on fire. It had been destroyed in the Battle of Bunker Hill on June 17, 1775. Hiller took a bit of artistic license, as Charlestown is depicted with a few buildings at the right edge of this view, with "Cambridge Town & Colleges" behind it. Therefore, Washington could be imagined to be on Dorchester Heights, from which his troops liberated Boston in March 1776. Both events would have made this print particularly popular.

Art historian Mantle Fielding, in *American Engravers upon Copper and Steel*, considered the companion print of *Lady Washington* "the first graphic representation" of her. Its origin is unknown, although her head was probably based on her miniature by Peale in 1772. The mezzotint is attributed to Hiller, who probably created the rest of the composition. The scene from the window may represent the landscape from the Vassall House in Cambridge, which the Washington family then occupied, when the vista was open to the Charles River. The source of the sobriquet "Lady Washington" is said to have been given by the troops encamped at Valley Forge from late 1777 to 1778, where she endeared herself to the soldiers by visiting them, providing food and clothing, prevailing on local women to do so, and nursing those who were ill or dying. However, this print shows that the sobriquet was in use a year or two earlier.

Benjamin Blyth contributed the original artwork for Hiller's next mezzotint, of Gen. Israel Putnam (Cat. 108). Whether the original of Putnam by Blyth was a drawing, pastel, or oil painting has long been a mystery. A drawing seems likely, as was probably the case with the second of the full-length mezzotint portraits of General Washington now attributed to Hiller in the Elkins Collection. This mezzotint of Washington resembles the above-mentioned image of the general signed "B. Blyth Pinx^t," which may have been the model. Washington's face was not colored, revealing its similarity to that of Montgomery, below, the engraving of which is attributed to Hiller.

In addition to the two Washington prints, two other mezzotints in the Elkins Collection, of

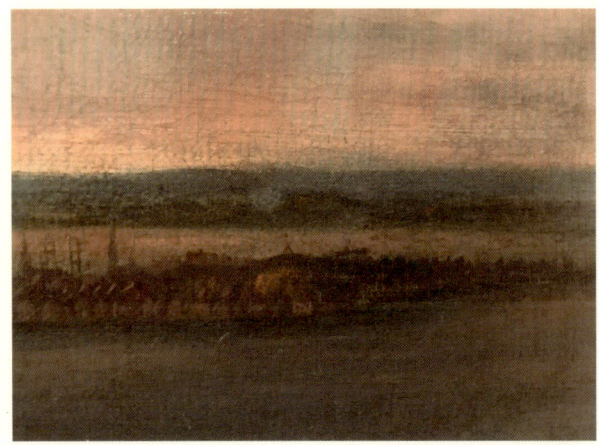

Detail of oil portrait of Washington by Charles Willson Peale

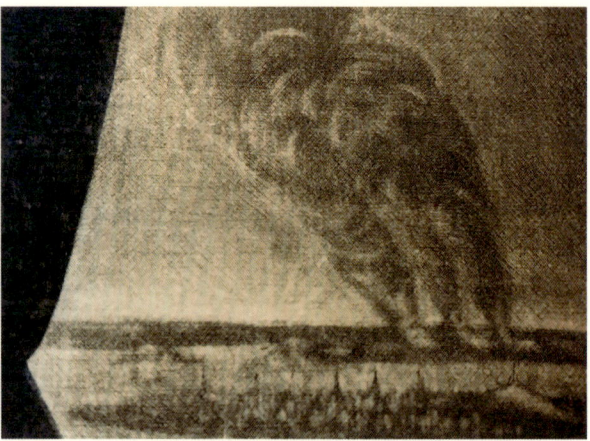

Detail of mezzotint of Washington by Joseph Hiller

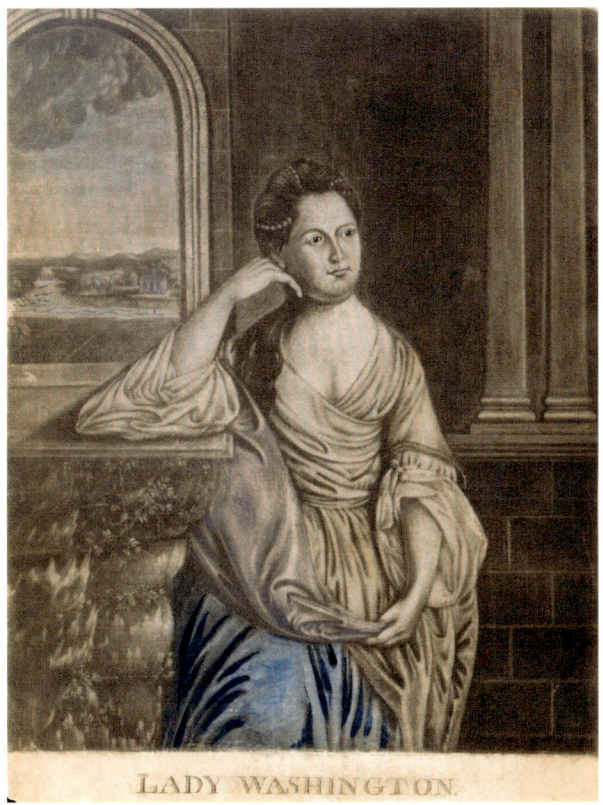

LADY WASHINGTON
Joseph Hiller (attr.)
Mezzotint, ca. 1776, 32 x 24.1 cm. (with text)
Courtesy of the Metropolitan Museum
Department of Drawings and Prints 24.90.213,
bequest of Charles Allen Munn, 1924

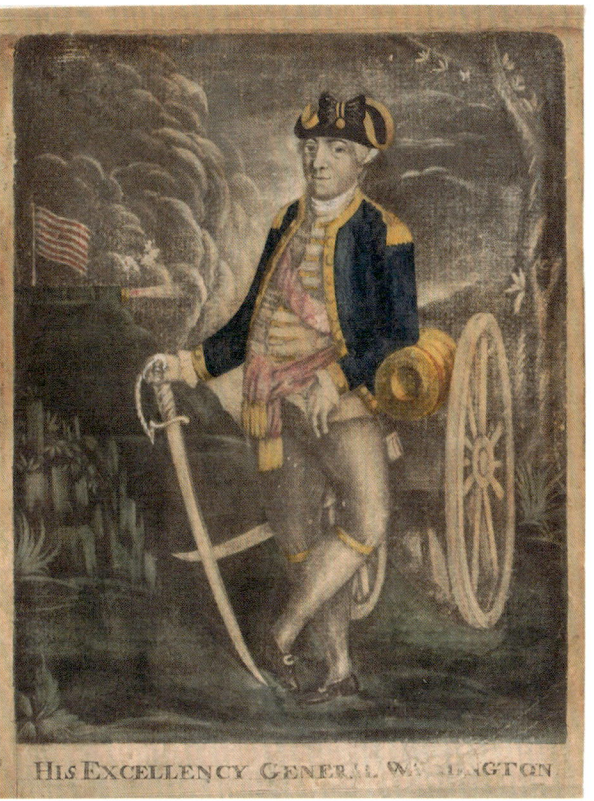

HIS EXCELLENCY GENERAL WASHINGTON
Joseph Hiller (attr.)
Mezzotint with hand coloring, ca. 1776–77, 21.7 x 17.5 cm.;
sheet (sight), (23 x 18 cm.)
Courtesy of the William M. Elkins Collection of
Americana, Rare Book Department, Free Library of
Philadelphia ELK0040001

generals Richard Montgomery (1738–1775) and Charles Lee (1731–1782), both seemingly unique impressions, are also attributed here primarily to Hiller. Both portraits are fictitious, as there are no known other portraits of either general.[41] Blyth's composition for Putnam was presumably used by Hiller for his mezzotint of Gen. Montgomery, as seen in such features as his uniform and the background, especially the distant hillock with an encampment and the clouds. However, his coat is red and lower legs were added to the three-quarter figure of Putnam. Samuel Blyth again was probably responsible for the coloring, with his characteristic features—extensive coverage and distinctive, noticeable slashes of opaque white.

Although Hiller's prints of Hancock, George Washington, and Martha Washington were copied from original oil portraits owned at the time by John Hancock, this was not the case with the Lee. Hiller based his portrait on a fictitious print of the General published in London in October 1775 by C. Shepherd & Tomlinson. In the eighteenth century, pirating prints by other artists was

41. The only known oil portrait of Montgomery is posthumous, by Charles Willson Peale, in the late 1780s. The most likely source for Peale's portrait is the engraving by J. Norman, 1781.

commonplace. So for colonial printmakers at the onset of the American Revolution and years before the U. S. Copyright Act of 1790, copying imagery from British prints was akin, in a way, to privateering—what they considered legitimate, appropriating the cargoes of British ships—especially when the prints that their English counterparts were issuing were of the Colony's own local heroes.[42] Because the image was copied directly, save for changing the position of the sword and eliminating a brick wall, it, like that of Warren, was printed in reverse.

This impression from the William M. Elkins Collection of Americana, Free Library of Philadelphia, is the only one known of the complete image; the other three known impressions were all cut down. It is likely that Hiller intended these mezzotints to be part of a series, as the British were issuing at the time. Several examples lack credits and are now the "only known impression." Does their rarity suggest that there was no market for their prints in Salem? Did Hiller abandon the idea of issuing them? Or were there troubles with the partnership? This begs the additional question of whether these unique prints in the Elkins Collection once were from Hiller's estate.[43]

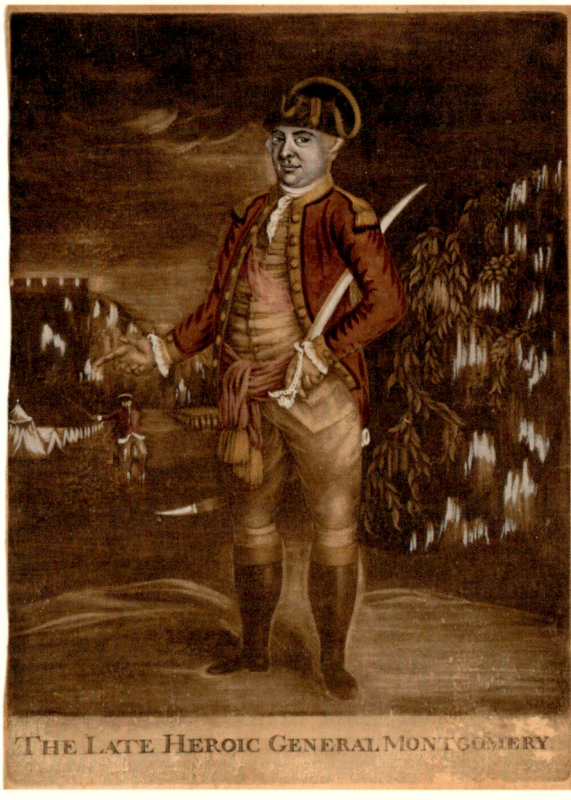

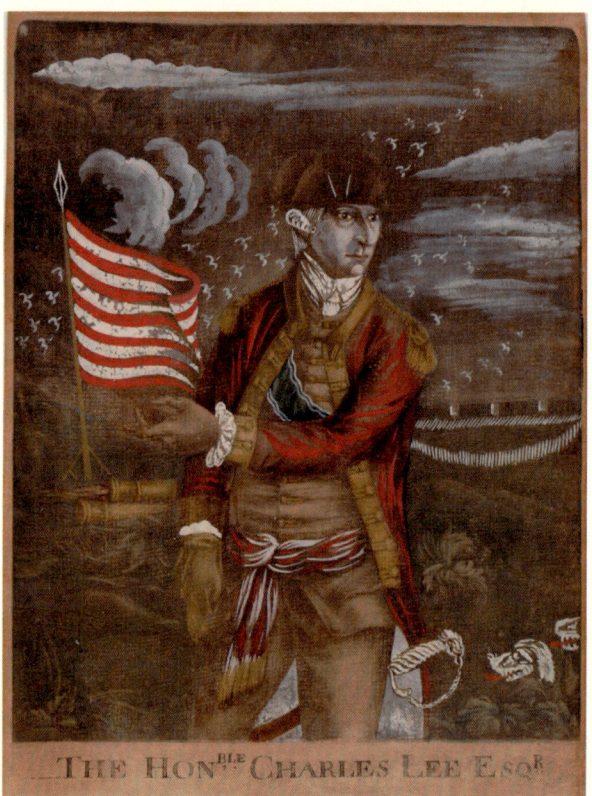

THE LATE HEROIC GENERAL MONTGOMERY
Joseph Hiller (attr.)
Mezzotint, ca. 1776, 33 x 24.5 cm. (sight)
Courtesy of the William M. Elkins Collection of Americana,
Rare Book Department, Free Library of Philadelphia
ELK0010001

THE HON.BLE CHARLES LEE ESQR.
Joseph Hiller (attr.)
Mezzotint with hand coloring, ca. 1778, 30.25 x 24 cm., image
Courtesy of the William M. Elkins Collection of Americana,
Rare Book Department, Free Library of Philadelphia
ELK0050001

42. The first British Copyright Law was passed in 1710.
43. While Elkins was at Harvard in the early 1900s, he frequented Goodspeed's Book Shop in Boston, but the shop has no relevant purchase records. It is a question for future historians.

The war began to take its toll, disrupting maritime activity and dividing Salem families. Jonathan Gardner, who is likely the Gardner portrayed by Benjamin Blyth (Cat. 57), had recorded in his Memorandum Book for April 23, 1775, "No meeting on account of the grate surprise the people were in, and fearing that Ships of War should come in to Salem and Distroy the town. It was allso expected a seasure of Provisions so that there was from three to four hundred teams in for Provisions & Goods, which made grate Confusion."[44] Families such as the Fryes, the Curwens, and the Olivers, were divided in their allegiances; some members fled to other parts of the county or abroad, and others stayed. There also were several incidents of vandalism to the homes of those suspected of Tory sympathies or who traded in English goods. The houses of both Peter Frye (Cat. 56) and John Appleton were burned, and arson was suspected.[45] The family life of Samuel Curwen (Cat. 33), who also was a signatory of the letter of support for Gov. Hutchinson, became a casualty of the war. Blyth drew pastels of many of these people, probably before hostilities erupted.

Although Benjamin Blyth's production of pastel portraits seems to have slowed down when the American Revolution was underway, he did manage to draw over two dozen between 1775 and 1780, including twelve extended members of Salem's noted family, the Derbys. And Blyth began paintings in oils well as miniatures. But he also became involved in privateering.

With Salem's traditional trade in jeopardy, privateering was seen as not only patriotic, but lucrative. Robbery on the high seas had been a common threat to trade, so merchant ships were already armed. Once war broke out, authenticity to engage in privateering was easily established. The provisional government issued commissions, also referred to as letters of marque, allowing the holders to attack foreign vessels and take them as prizes, dividing the booty among the privateer's sponsors, shipowners, captains and crew. As the ports of Boston and New York were being ruined by the enemy, "the main reliance was on the shipping of Salem," wrote Samuel Eliot Morison, adding that 626 letters of marque were issued to Massachusetts vessels, and some thousand more by the General Court. "[S]uccess in this legalized piracy was probably the greatest contribution of seaboard Massachusetts to the common cause. . . . In the earlier years of the war, large profits were made from privateering by everyone connected with it. A favorite speculation for merchants was to buy, in advance of his cruise, half a privateer's share of his forthcoming prizes."[46] Economic historian Richard J. Morris explained the demographics of privateering: "Of the thirty-nine new elites, additions to the names of Salem's wealthiest residents in 1777, only four were uninvolved." On the other hand, ninety percent of the new elites "owned or captained privateers. . . . The en-

---

44. *EIHC* 13:236. The memorandum book, primarily with notes on preachers and their texts, contains occasional comments on public affairs such as this one.

45. *EIHC* 13:28-29; 43:116. John Langdon Sibley, *Biographical Sketches of Graduates of Harvard University in Cambridge, Massachusetts*, (Cambridge: C. W. Sever, 1873–1973), 14:128.

46. Morison, *The Maritime History of Massachusetts, 1783–1860*, (Boston: Houghton Mifflin, 1961), 30, 28. Although large profits were made in the early years of the war, noted Morison, the Derby firm was said to have been the only one "to retain a favorable balance, when peace was concluded." It was followed by "the worst economic depression Massachusetts has ever known," although "the war closed with little change in the social system of provincial days, . . . maritime interests were still supreme." Nonetheless, the citizens were suffering from trying to practice their livelihoods; lives were disrupted, and money was spent on other needs. In explanation of "worst": Morison's book was published in 1921.

terprise also provided the middle class with opportunities not available in the absence of war."[47]

Benjamin Blyth became one of them. He no doubt noted the vast number of Salemites who took up privateering, including one of his major patrons, Elias Hasket Derby. To finance such a venture, Blyth and another artist, John Coles, became agents for the six-gun brig *Brandywine*.[48] Blyth appears to have played only a minor role in privateering, as neither his name nor that of this vessel have been discovered in published accounts. There is no evidence that he, in addition to being an agent, actually went to sea. However, he was served a number of legal suits in 1774, for which he was listed as "late of Salem" and "out of the Province" for several months.[49] For unknown reasons, including his obvious lack of background in maritime activities, he does not seem to have realized any great profits from the privateering venture. He might also have been too late. By the last years of the war, the British had tightened their blockades and "captured a large number of our fleet, and drove the rest into port."[50] Blyth's misfortune also included incurring a huge debt for repairs of the *Brandywine*, for which he was prime agent. It had lost its mast in the Caribbean in May 1779, and was repaired in St. Pierre, Martinique, by a Mr. Hutchinson, who billed Blyth for £37,901. (Hutchinson did lade the ship to the gunwales with salable cargo to help offset the debt.) Hutchinson in turn owed money to several debtors, including Elias Hasket Derby. So Derby, believing that he would be unlikely to collect from Hutchinson and his co-investors in 1782, sued Blyth and thirty others, including John Coles, Samuel Blyth, and other merchants, mariners, apothecary, shipwright, yeoman and tanner to recover the sums they owed Hutchinson.[51] The magnitude of the debt may have been among the reasons that led Benjamin Blyth to abandon Salem by 1783. And he may have felt betrayed by one of his most important supporters.

Salem's entire population suffered. By 1777, the third year of fighting, there were only 1,193 males over age sixteen in Salem; and at the end of the war in 1783, almost half of its 6,665 residents were under that age or were widows (almost 16 percent). Many townspeople had disappeared, some were Loyalists, many had died; others were newly impoverished.[52] It was hardly the environment for portraiture. Nonetheless, Benjamin Blyth was still doing a few pastels, such as one of Capt. Samuel Flagg (Cat. 55), the leader of the Rhode Island Expedition in August 1778. At least eight of the eighty-one men on that expedition, as well as several of their wives, were drawn at some

---

47. Morris, "Redefining the Economic Elite in Salem, Massachusetts, 1759–1799," 614.

48. Coles would undertake one print venture later, with Benjamin. Felt, *Annals of Salem*, mentions the *Brandywine* in a "List of other Salem Privateers," 2:276.

49. Successful suits were brought against Benjamin Blyth by William Browne, Abner Chase, Benjamin Daland, and Benjamin Coats of Salem. Even Samuel Blyth, as administrator of their father's estate, brought two suits against his brother. *Essex County Court Records*, 6:225-27.

50. Morison, *Maritime History of Massachusetts*, 30.

51. Ipswich Court of Common Pleas, May 23, 1783, 7:358-9. Derby sought £126 0s. 9d and costs of £4 15s. 4d., and John Brown & Christopher Ellery of Providence, Merchants, sought £357 12s. 4d. and costs of £7 5s. 6d. Bettina A. Norton, "The Brothers Blyth: Salem in its Heyday," *New England Meeting House and Church, 1630–1850*, ed. Peter Benes, associate editor, Jane Montague Benes, (Boston, Mass.: Boston University, [1980]), 55-56.

52. William Bentley, D. D., *The Diary of William Bentley, D. D., Pastor of the East Church, Salem, Massachusetts.* 4 vols., (Salem: The Essex Institute, 1905-14), 1:7; Phillips, *Salem in the Eighteenth Century*, 348-49.

time by Blyth.[53] Both his brother Samuel and their fellow printmaker Joseph Hiller were listed among those who had served in the war, but Benjamin's name does not appear. It is believed, however, that he did accompany the Expedition, a handy explanation for his doing the pastel portraits of William Goddard (Cat. 63), and Aaron Lopez (Cat. 86).[54]

There is no further indication of how Benjamin Blyth spent his time in the Revolution, what he thought, or whether he was a member of the militia, as were many men his age in Salem, including his two younger brothers William and Verrin. Traveling with the troops also might explain the gap of seven years before the birth of his third child, Samuel, baptized on July 2, 1780.[55] In the process of establishing some sort of chronology for his portraits—dating is problematic—there seems to be a dearth of portraits of those not involved in either militia service or privateering from the mid-1770s until about 1778, when he returned to painting in oils.

*

EARLY IN HIS CAREER, Blyth had painted two oil portraits, one an original and one a copy of a print. The first, of Dr. Ezekiel Hersey (Cat. 66), was done in the late 1760s to 1770. At about the same time, Blyth made a copy in oils of the English eighteenth-century New Lights preacher, the Reverend George Whitefield (Cat. 139), who died in Newburyport in 1770. Blyth's portrait was based on an English print by John Greenwood—who had left the Boston area ten years earlier.

Historically, copying paintings has been done for one or more reasons: aspiring artists wishing to learn technique of former masters to hone their own skills; duplicates sought to provide an image for another family member, institution, or collectors, as Salem's eighteenth-century diarist Bentley did for his own collection of portraits; or replacements made for damaged originals. The Peabody Essex Museum owns several portraits copied by Salem artist George Southward (1803–1876): Timothy Pickering, after Gilbert Stuart; George Washington, after Joseph Wright; and Richard Derby, Sr. after, it is now believed, a missing pastel by Benjamin Blyth. Southward also painted the copy of Blyth's lost oil portrait of Gen. Stephen Abbot (Cat. 1).

Blyth himself copied at least four portraits, all as duplicates for family members or admirers. The only oil, of the Reverend Whitefield, was for the Reverend John Chipman of Beverly. The others are pastel copies of oil portraits: Gov. John Endecott (Cat. 51), for a descendant; Gov. Jonathan Belcher (Cat. 14), for an unknown person; and Jonathan Simpson (Cat. 117), for Simpson's granddaughter Mary Vial Holyoke.

Blyth's own pastels have been copied as well. Known examples are Benjamin Crowninshield (Cat. 31), Richard Derby, Sr. (Cat. 47), and Peter Frye (Cat. 56), in the collections of the Peabody Essex Museum; Reverend John Chipman (Cat. 28), at the Second Church of Beverly; Hugh Hill (Cat. 68),

---

53. Presumably listed in order of rank, they were Benjamin Ropes, Jr; Jona. Gardner, Jr; George Dodge, Jr; Francis Cabot, Jr; Abijah Northey; George Abbot; David Ropes; Benjamin Moses; and possibly Joseph Hiller. *EIHC* I:112–13.
54. If Blyth had gone as crew, he would not have been listed on manifests; much information is available on ships and their captains, but little on their crews. One of the main sources of information on service during the Revolution were requests for compensation at the end of the war, but because Blyth had moved south by then, he may never have put in a claim, if he indeed were entitled.
55. The baptism was at the Third Church because St. Peter's, an Anglican church, was closed from 1775 until 1782, during the Revolution. Tapley, *St. Peter's Church*, 55, 83.

at Historic Beverly; Sarah Hersey Derby, at Derby Academy (Cat. 66); and John Lowell (Cat. 87) in a private collection. The only pastel by Blyth that was copied but for which the original still exists is of Frye, and it, along with one copy by L. P. Cutts, is in the Peabody Essex Museum.

In the late 1770s, Blyth began paintings portraits in oil, several of which were companion pieces of husband and wife with child. With almost no existing documentation such as bills or diary entries by sitters that Blyth was an artist in *any* medium, it is not surprising that it has taken so long to identify him as the artist of other, previously unattributed, oil portraits. The astute Nina Fletcher Little recognized the value of the two Moses portraits. They were not identified as by Blyth in the 1936 catalogue of portraits in the Essex Institute. Although they are signed and dated, 1781, this is almost illegible, so for years their identity had escaped notice. Nina Little borrowed them for an exhibition at the Museum of Fine Arts, Boston, in 1984, thereby spurring interest in knowing more about Blyth and what he might have done. The total number of portraits in oil now stands at fifteen.

Blyth also took up painting miniatures. They appealed to families in Salem and other seacoast towns in Essex County, often separated by months if not years by the seafaring trade. The Revolution, when even more men were off to war, appears to have fueled demand. To date, fourteen miniatures are attributed to him.

At the same time, Benjamin began drawing pastels of young children. Why would Benjamin Blyth have begun producing children's portraits at all? Perhaps Blyth's portraits of Anstiss Derby (Cat. 40) and her younger brother, Ezekiel Derby (Cat. 45), may have inspired other Salem families to have their children drawn as well. Blyth had already begun painting oil portraits of a man with a companion portrait of his wife and a young child, which also may have spurred interest.

From the outset of Benjamin's career in the mid-1760s, he had been helped by Samuel, who had connections in Salem and with many other visiting workmen from Boston. Samuel also possibly sent clients his brother's way. Most significant, he began supplying the black ebonized wood Hogarth-type frame, with carved and gilded inner lining, for many of his brother's pastels. The progenitor for the Hogarth frame, in common use for prints and small paintings at the time, was an anglicized version of the Dutch frame, influenced by Calvinist thought that eschewed ornately carved and gilded ones. The frame became popular in England for smaller works of art, and thence in the colonies. Occasionally the maker of a frame impressed his signature motif on one side of the frame. The Dutch also were responsible for building the trade in ebony from Africa, which became the predominant wood used.

Little has been written about frames for American colonial portraits, and rarely are frames shown when images of portraits are reproduced.[56] Yet frames can prove a vital part of the artifact for dating and providing object information. They enhance the portrait and testify to the links among the practicing artists, especially for ones in Boston and Salem. Few references to any frames exist in eighteenth-century diaries or other documents, but one is mentioned in Samuel Curwen's will. He left to his grandnephew's wife Jane "a profile of myself set in a black ebony

---

56. See Morrison M. Hecksher, "Copley's Picture Frames," *John Singleton Copley in America* (New York: The Metropolitan Museum of Art, 1995), 143-69; and Henry Heydenryk, *The Art and History of Frames: An Inquiry into the Enhancement of Paintings,* (New York: James H. Heineman, Inc., 1963), for in-depth discussions.

frame." The portrait (Cat. 33) was drawn by Benjamin Blyth and the frame was made by Samuel Blyth. Curwen valued it sufficiently to arrange for its disposition.

For years, the frames have been a factor for attribution to Benjamin. Elias Hasket Derby's account book in the Peabody Essex Museum Library lists a payment of £18 to Samuel Blyth for six frames in 1775; possibly it was for some of the Derby family portraits believed to have been drawn that year by his brother. Samuel Blyth frames are on the pastels of Anstiss, Elizabeth, and Ezekiel; the others now have later frames.

Of the 122 pastels attributed to Benjamin, forty-eight are known to have frames made by Samuel, and an additional six were probably originally also by him, as the sitters were spouses. He may also have made many, if not most, of the thirty-seven for which there is no information, or which were later reframed. That makes a potential ninety-one frames by Samuel for his brother's pastels, almost eighty percent. The bill from Benjamin Blyth to the widow of General John Thomas, in the Thomas Papers at the Massachusetts Historical Society, itemizes "one frame and glaſs . . . 1=16=." Unfortunately, this portrait no longer has its original frame.

This bill, dated "Salem, Febrᵃʳʸ 14th 1777," is invaluable for providing the only currently known information on the price Blyth received for a pastel, 4-40-[0?] as well as one of the rare examples of his handwriting. Two other informative notations in this document record other rarely found information: that "Widow Thomas" was charged 0-3 for a "Box," used to transport the pastel, and "Mr. Very will Deliver [it to] you." At the bottom of this document is yet another notation recording the conclusion of the transaction: "Salem, June 28, 1777, by the hand of Geo Williams the above [indecipherable, presumably recording the payment], Benja Blyth."

Salem's nineteenth-century historian Joseph B. Felt recorded "an individual, supposed to be a Very, who in 1774 advertised a post chaise between Salem and Boston, to go on a Wednesday and return on a Thursday . . . for passengers, letters, and bundles."[57]

Almost all of Benjamin Blyth's pastels, drawn on paper and backed with rough linen or canvas, were attached with nails to a wood frame, called a strainer. In the very few cases in which a Blyth pastel has a stretcher—a frame with thin wedges, also called keys, in the corners to allow for contraction or expansion—it had probably been conserved and reframed. This assembly was then fitted to the outer frame. The common method of hanging the picture was to install two metal screw eyes on the top of the frame, from which one or two wires were hung, to be attached either to a peg in the wall or to metal clips that would fit over molding running along the top of the wall.[58]

Samuel Blyth had probably learned to make frames from Thomas Johnston. Although a little-known aspect of Johnston's career, it is confirmed in a letter his son William wrote to him in 1762 from New London, Connecticut: "The frames I wrote for I Hope are Ship'd on Board of [Ayres?]. I Shall soon have Occation for more, two in the ½ Lengths, I have Considerable Buſineſs Engag'd at New Haven."[59] John Greenwood worked in Thomas Johnston's shop, and most of his paintings have frames that presumably were made there.

57. Felt, *Annals of Salem* I, 317

58. . Adair, *The Frame in America, 1700–1900*, 26.

59. William wrote to him in 1762 from New London, Connecticut: Samuel P. Savage Papers II and accounts with

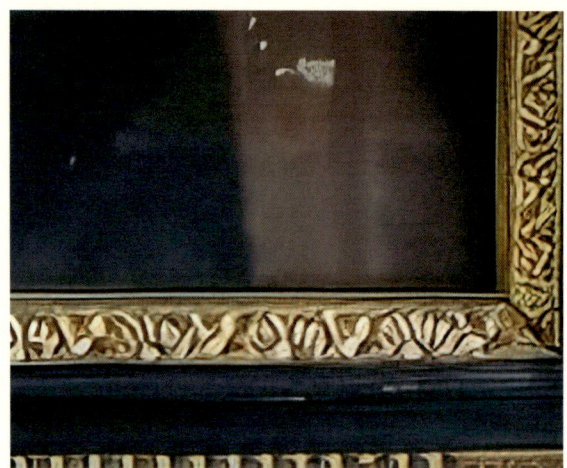

Detail of frame by Samuel Blyth
for pastel of Thomas Barnard

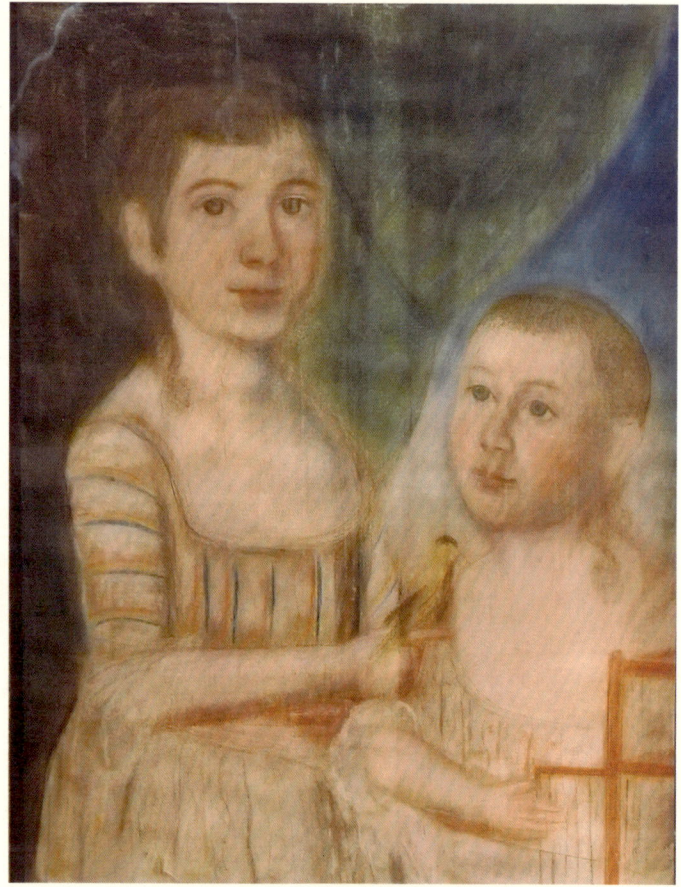

Advertisement posted by Samuel Blyth
The Essex Gazette, May 28, and June 4, 1771
Courtesy of the American Antiquarian Society

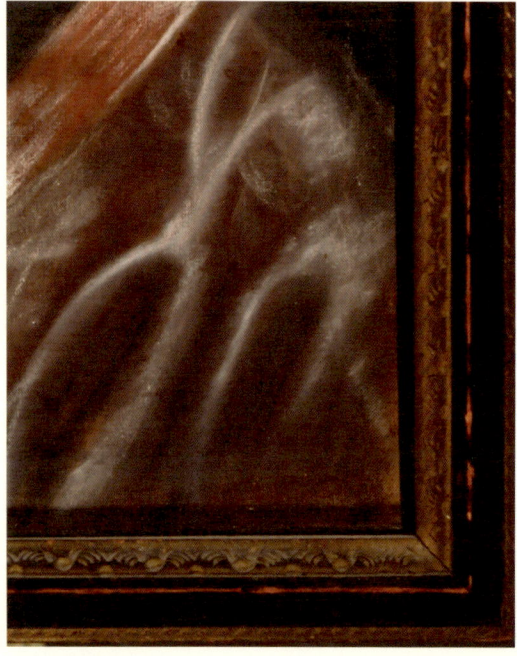

Detail of frame by Samuel Blyth for pastel of
Thomas Cary

RIGHT: *Babson sisters*, Samuel Blyth (attr.)
Pastel on paper, 1784–86,
22½ x 17 1/8 in. (57.15 x 43.50 cm.), Samuel Blyth frame
Courtesy of the Mount Desert Island Historical
Society, Mount Desert, ME

The young girls are the daughters of John (Jr.) and Susanna (Rogers) Babson, originally from Gloucester, Massachusetts. Rachel, born there in 1776, married Abraham Somes II, son of the founder of the Somes Settlement in Somesville, Maine, and Susan, born in 1780 in Amesbury, married a Trask, also from Somesville.

Blyth's most common motif for the gilt inner molding of his frames was a course of three or four convex arcing lines radiating around a central half circle, flat side against the edge, with a raised motif between each set. It is very closely related to the frame configuration on Johnston's portrait at the Nichols House Museum. The more elaborate version of this motif with a sand-encrusted gilt band between inner molding and frame was used by Johnston for his son William Johnston's paintings.[60] Some of the Blyth frames have gilded outer edges, with a thin strip of small rectangular shapes. Samuel also used several variations, but the gouging tool he seemed to employ in most of them was that which produced the curving arcs, sometimes at right angles with the picture edge, sometimes flipped.[61] However, it is a very common style of molding, described by William B. Adair as "a very standard 18th c. imbricated edge ornament."[62] Another variation was to make the motifs concave rather than convex.

A few of Samuel Blyth's frames, like that of the Reverends Thomas Barnard (Cat. 8) and Thomas Cary (Cat. 27), still have their original two hooks for hanging from wall moldings. One of the most elaborate frames by Blyth, with a wide inner strip of sand-encrusted gilding, it was used for the coat of arms for the Holyoke family as well as pastels now attributed to him.

On May 28, and June 4, 1771, Samuel placed an advertisement in *The Essex Gazette*, more than two years after Benjamin had published his. The advertisement seems to encompass the entire produc-

---

Samuel P. Savage 1762–1764, 8 September 1764, Lemuel Shaw Papers, Massachusetts Historical Society. The portraits by William Johnston (1732–72), with Hogarth frames, now at the Connecticut Historical Society include Col. Eliphalet Dyer (1721–1807), Eleazer Lord (1699–1768) and Mrs. Lord (1708–80), the Hon. Jabez Hamlin (1709–91), Capt. Ashbel Riley (1733/4–94), Mrs. Thomas Seymour (ca. 1735–1807), and the Rev. Elnathan Whitman. Johnson's portraits at the Metropolitan Museum, New York, are of Mr. and Mrs. Gardiner, Samuel and Jacob Hurd, and Mrs. Hurd with child. Others are portraits of Mehitabel Deane at the Kent-DeLord House Museum in Plattsburg, NY, and Sarah Deshon at the Lyman Allyn Museum. Johnston also is a probable artist for the copy of the Blackburn portrait of Abigail Curwen in the Peabody Essex Museum. A comparison of her face to that of Mrs. Jacob Hurd by Johnston makes a strong case, as do many other elements in the two paintings. The child is holding the rattle seen in Badger and Blyth portraits of children.

It is likely that Thomas Johnston himself made the frame for his own portrait in the dining room of the Nichols House Museum on Beacon Hill. There were other frame-makers in Boston during the eighteenth century, but evidence abounds that he provided frames to a number of these local artists. The production of frames is another key to understanding his broad influence over the art world in the area at the time. Another Johnston son, John, also a portrait painter, later made frames under the firm Rea and Johnston. The firm's Account Book at the Baker Library, Harvard Business School, record not only painting and gilding frames for others, but occasionally making the actual frame.

60. It was also used on the portraits of Eleazer and Abigail Cheseborough Mumford Lord at the Connecticut Historical Society. Other portraits at the Society by William Johnston that have that additional gilt inner strip include Jabez Hamlin, Eliphalet Dyer, Col. Ashbel Riley, Mrs. Thomas Seymour and the Seymour coat of arms (although the gilt is almost entirely gone), and Elnathan Whitman.

61. Although the gilt is eroded on some, this is the motif for the frames (known so far) on Benjamin Blyth's pastels of the Rev. Thomas Barnard, George Cabot, the Rev. Thomas Cary and Mrs. Cary, Samuel Curwen, Sarah Curwen, Anstiss Derby, Lydia Phippen Fisk, John Gibaut, William Goddard, Rebecca Hooper, Molly Hoyt, Edward Lang, Joseph Lemmon, Eunice Diman Mason, Thomas Mason, William Messervy, Sarah "Sally" Moses, Abijah Northey, Elizabeth Rogers, David Ropes, Priscilla Ropes, Capt. John Somes, Gen. Thomas, Patty Webb, Elizabeth Stone White, Joseph White, an anonymous woman of the Hedge family, and the Unknown Boy "from Salem."

62. Email from William B. Adair to the author, Apr. 30, 2014. Adair, owner of Gold Leaf Studio in Washington, D.C., is author of *The Frame in America, 1700–1900: A Survey of Fabrication Techniques and Styles*. The American Institute of Architects Foundation:1983, revised in 2013. It is still used as a reference for American frame history.

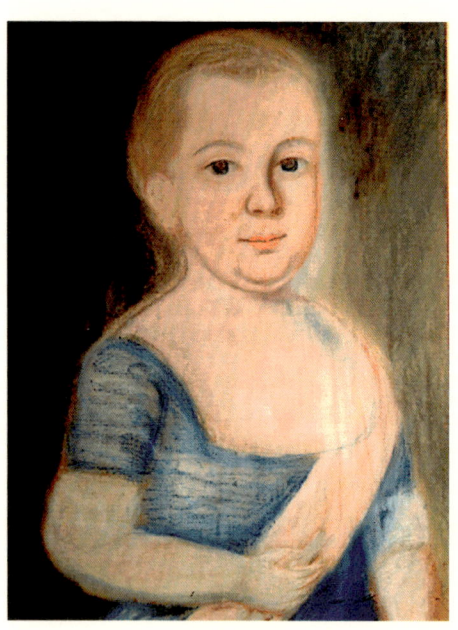

*Jones child
(Eunice, b. 1777?)*
Samuel Blyth (attr.)
Pastel on paper, ca.
1783–84, 14 x 10½ in.
(35.56 x 26.67 cm.),
Hogarth-type frame,
possibly later addition
Courtesy of the Golden
Ball Tavern, Weston,
MA

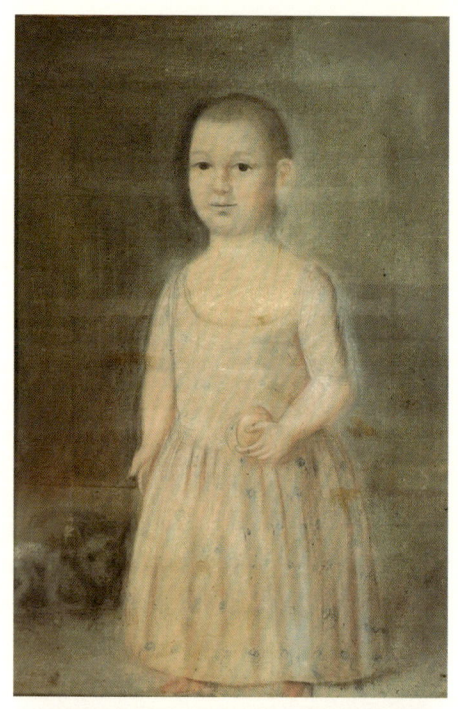

Putnam child
Samuel Blyth (attr.)
Pastel on paper, ca.
1783–85, 22¾ x 17 in.
(57. 8 x 43.2 cm.),
Samuel Blyth frame
Courtesy of the Pea-
body Essex Museum
132417, gift of Harry
Sutton, Jr. in memory of
Elinor Putnam Gardner
Sutton, 1970 (donor also
given as Mrs. Robert
Saltonstall)

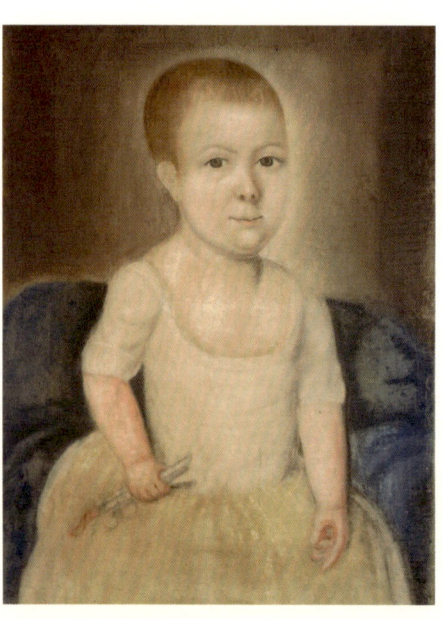

*Elizabeth Safford
(1781–1812)*
Samuel Blyth (attr.)
Pastel on paper mount-
ed on fabric, 1783–84,
22 x 16 in. (55.88 x 40.64
cm.), plain black frame
Courtesy of the Pea-
body Essex Museum
124689, gift of Miss
Maude O[sgood]
Webber, 1941

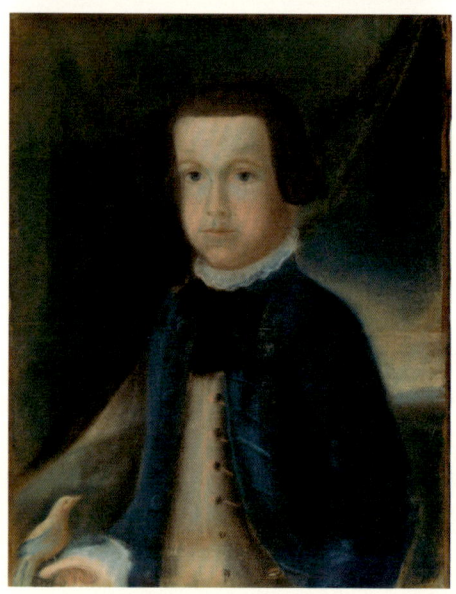

*John Warden, Jr. (?)
(ca. 1778–after 1850)*
Samuel Blyth (attr.)
Pastel on two pieces
of paper on canvas,
ca. 1783–85, 22¼ x 16¾
in. (56.52 x 42.54 cm.),
framed
Courtesy of the
Shelburne Museum
1958–147.4, gift of Mrs.
Katherine Pren-
tis Murphy
Photography by Andy
Duback

Elizabeth Safford was the daughter of William and Thankful Safford.
Henry Wilder Foote, in "Benjamin Blyth of Salem:. . . ," *Proceedings
of the Massachusetts Historical Society*, Third Series, 71:79, 101), credited the pastel, as "Stafford," to Benjamin but wrote that it "was not
well drawn."

A label identifies the subject as Francis Warden, "taken prisoner by
the British in Revolutionary War, and died on the Prison Ship 'New
York' at about eighteen years of age." He was too old to have been
the subject. More likely, it was his nephew, John Warden, whose
daughter, Anne Ross Warden once owned the pastel.

tion from his shop. Yet characteristics of the problematic pastel child portraits suggest that Samuel
did produce some of them, although close to a decade later. The pastels now attributed to Samuel
are not as well drawn as those attributed to his brother. They seem almost factory-produced to a

stock unvarying metric, showing less skill (or attention), with neither his grace nor subtlety, and too awkward. Henry Wilder Foote expressed reservations as early as his article on the Blyth brothers for the Massachusetts Historical Society in 1957.[63] Samuel was, after all, primarily a copyist, so he would have had ample opportunity to study Benjamin's portraits, as he framed so many of them in his shop. Could he have used his brother's pastel of the Messervy boy (Cat. 92), for example, as a template? He was probably also familiar with Benjamin's oil portrait of Sarah Moses and her daughter Betsy (Cat. 94)—although comparisons must be tempered with the fact that the portrait underwent restoration many years ago that altered the painting from that of the original.

Another clue to Samuel's work is that he included objects in his pastels. The children all hold an animal or a toy. Such props were typical of child portraits of the time—presumably to make them more appealing; the animals are a human touch, as is the rattle, which is also a symbol of the family's prosperity.[64] As for the birds present in several of these portraits, birds appear in Samuel's coats of arms, like that for the Pickman family. The treatment of the heads of several of these less successful child portraits resembles the Moses portrait by Benjamin: the telltale curved, untampered prominent dark line for the lip divide, the ear that should be receding but is parallel to the picture plane, the close-cropped hair. However, the noses on these other child portraits, especially the nostrils, are drawn with less skill, out of proper perspective, and too dominant.

The most important pastel portrait now attributed to Samuel Blyth is one of two known at this time by him that depict adults. It is of Samuel McIntire (1757–1811), the leading architect of the Federal style in Salem. He and Samuel Blyth were friends and had many intersections over the years, whereas McIntire was just coming into prominence when Benjamin Blyth was leaving Salem. The two Samuels worked together on the details of some of the architect's buildings, and both were musicians who arranged concerts and probably performed together; Samuel Blyth played the organ and presumably, the harpsichord. McIntire also taught singing, composed, played the bass viol and the organ, and built cases for them. He had "an ear of exquisite nicety," Bentley wrote, calling him "among our best Judges and most able performers." McIntire's estate inventory included a "large Hand Organ with 10 barrels," a violin and double bass, music, Handel's *Messiah* and two lots of music books, "Large" and "Small," and an Organ Chest. McIntire substantially remodeled the Assembly House (now the Cotting-Smith Assembly House), part of the Peabody Essex Museum, for a consortium of Salem notables that included Samuel Blyth.

The draftsmanship of the McIntire pastel is like that in the mezzotint of Capt. Mugford, now attributed to Samuel Blyth. The mouths are both visibly outlined, with a prominent curved upper

63. Foote, "Benjamin Blyth, of Salem: Eighteenth-Century Artist," *Proceedings of the Massachusetts Historical Society, Third Series,* 71 (Oct. 1953–May 1957): 79. Two other oil portraits, copies of earlier ones of Massachusetts Bay Colony governors Simon Bradstreet and John Endecott, have been historically attributed to Samuel. Nonetheless, here the oil of Bradstreet has been eliminated and the pastel of Endecott is assigned to Benjamin.

64. Blyth may have seen the oil portrait painted by Joseph Badger in 1745 of three-year-old John Gerry, from the famous Marblehead family, with a bird perched on his hand. Oil paintings by Joseph Badger of children in Salem homes at the time, like Lois and Rebecca Orne, had props. Another portrait of two children (not identified) shows one with a squirrel and the other with a silver and coral rattle. William Johnston's portrait of Mrs. Jacob Hurd and child, now at the Brooklyn Museum, has the identical rattle, very well detailed.

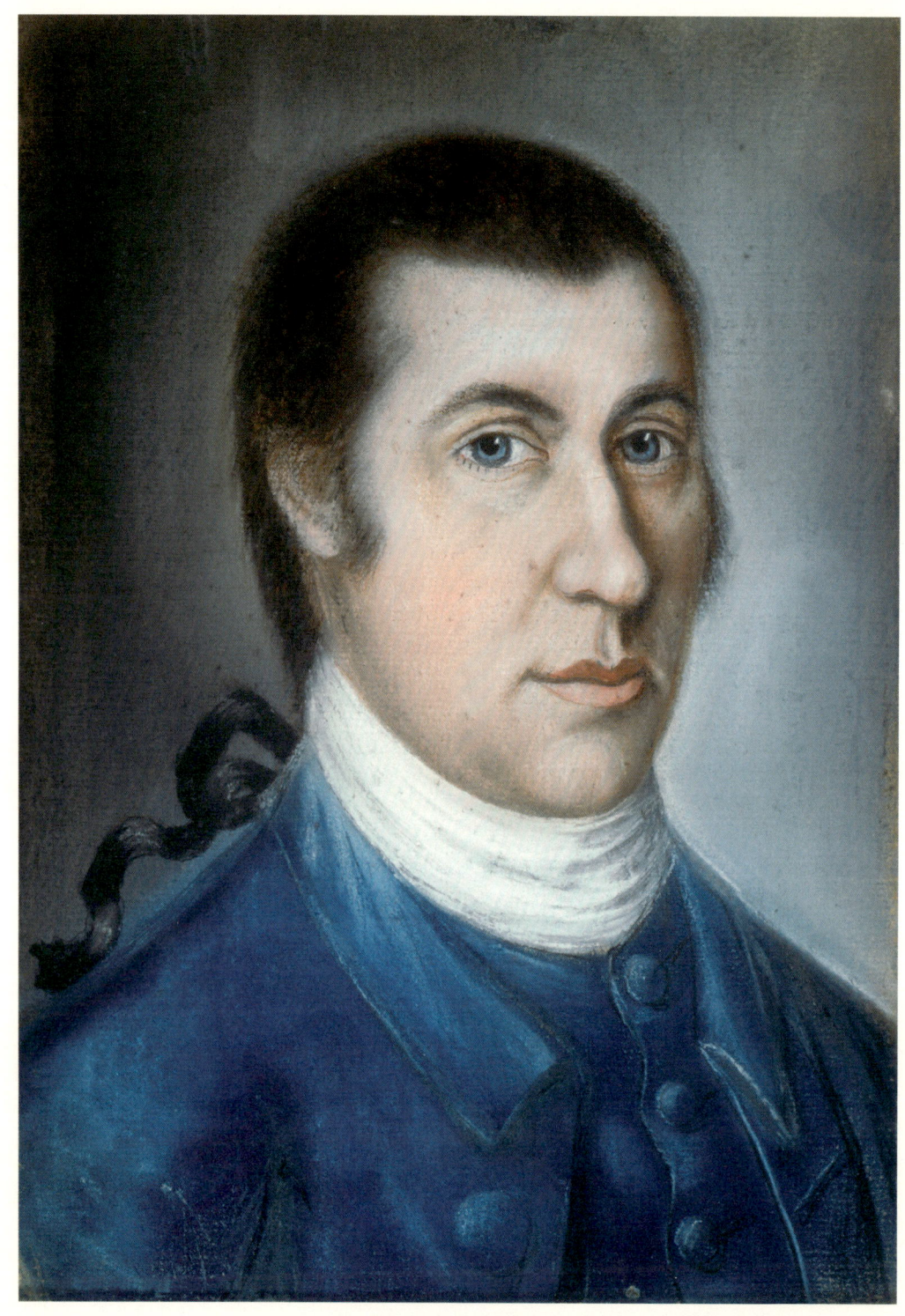

Samuel McIntire (1757–1811)
Samuel Blyth (attr.)
Pastel on paper on canvas, probably after 1783, 14 x 9 3/4 in. (35.6 x 24.8 cm.)
Courtesy of the Peabody Essex Museum 123420, gift of the estate of George W. Low, 1938

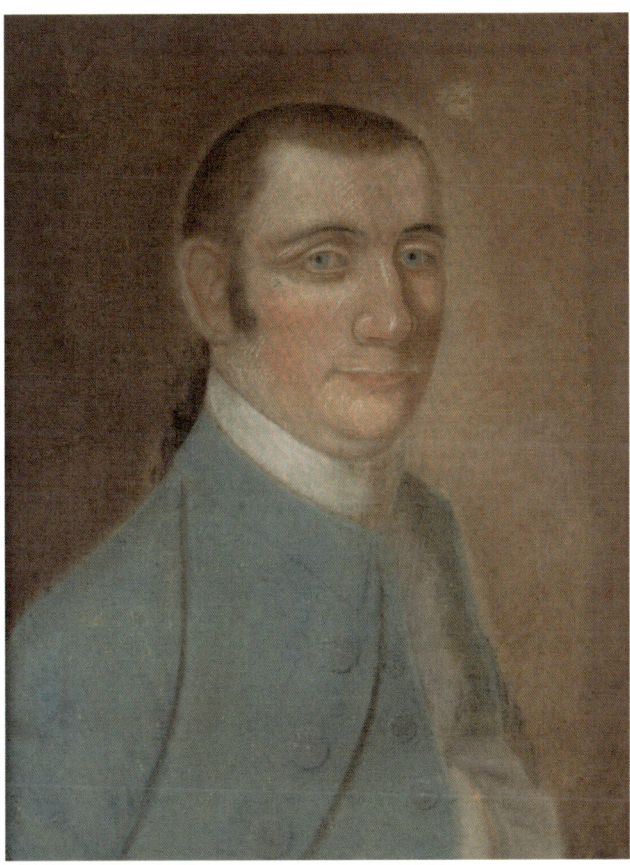

Unknown Man with Queue, in Blue Coat
Samuel Blyth (attr.)
Pastel on paper, ca. 1782–85, 18 x 14 in, (45.7 x 35.56 cm.),
Samuel Blyth frame
Courtesy of the Peabody Essex Museum 108312, source unknown,
acquisition prior to 1919

Another portrait of a young man with dark brown hair in a pony-tail, long sideburns, and 'Egyptian-like' eyes was either hastily done or abandoned. The proportions of features of the face are out-of-scale and awkward. It is listed in The American Portraits in Mass 2564, under Unidentified: Man in Light Blue Coat, among three works attributed to Samuel Blyth. Foote also thought it too poor to have been drawn by Benjamin and assigned it to Samuel.

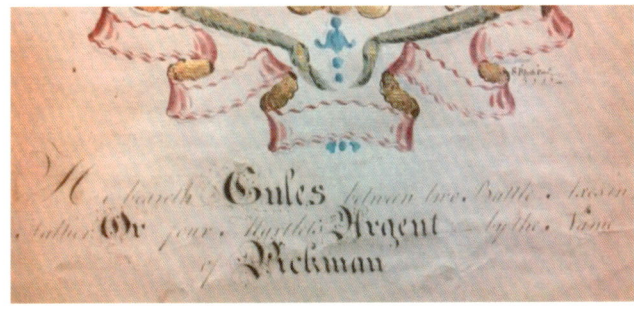

Pickman coat of arms, detail of ribbon

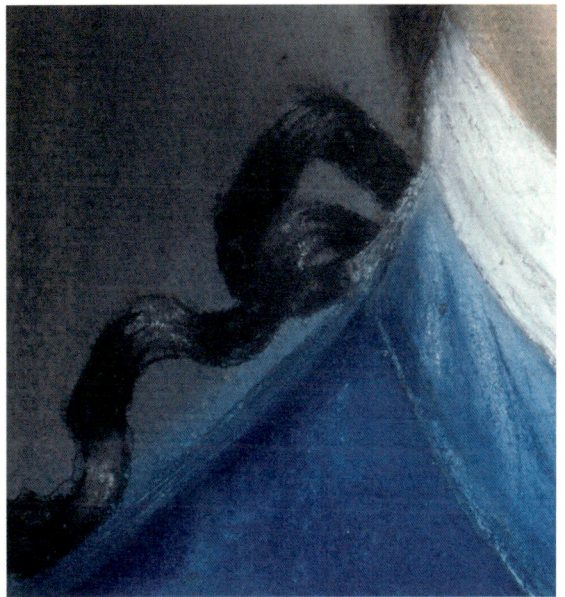

Samuel McIntire pastel, detail of ribbon

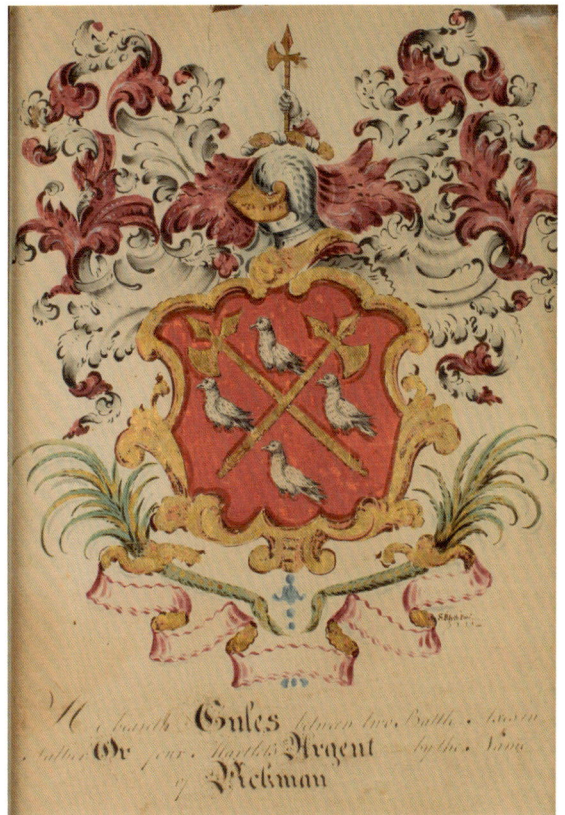

Pickman coat of arms
S. Blyth Pinxt
Watercolor, 13¾ x 9½ in. Courtesy of the Peabody Essex
Museum, 105350. gift of Miss Martha C. Codman, 1916

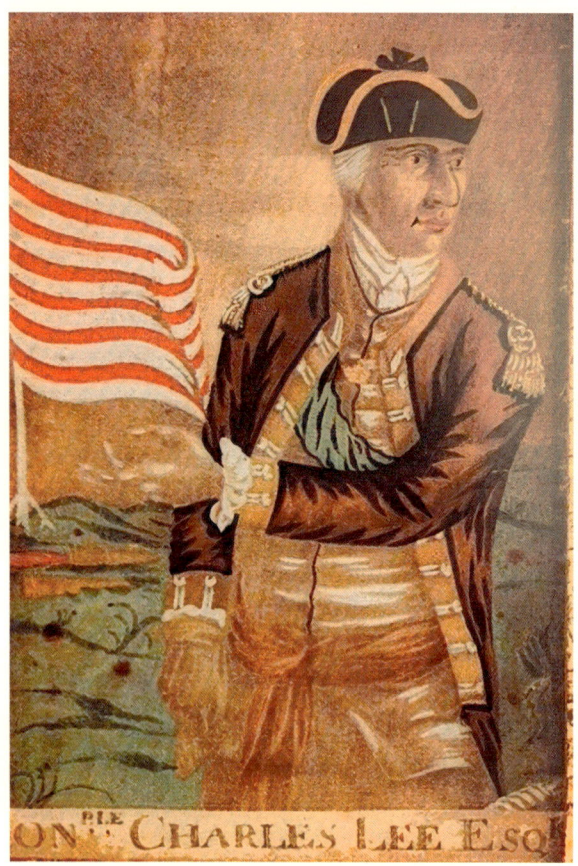

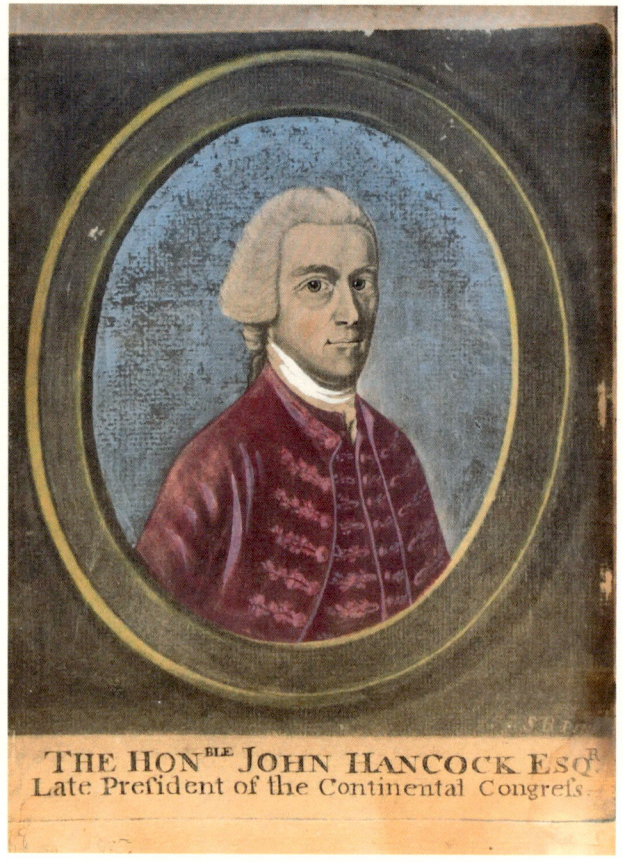

HON^{BLE} CHARLES LEE, ESQ^R
Samuel Blyth
Mezzotint restrike/second state with hand coloring,
1778–80, 24.1 x 17 cm., (sight), cropped
Courtesy of the Dr. Gary M. Milan Collection

This better-known print of Lee was struck from the original plate now attributed to Joseph Hiller; but both known
impressions of this version were cropped on all sides, with
the title simply cut out and pasted over the lower part of the
print. The reissue probably reflected continued local sympathy for Lee. As in the Hiller print, almost all engraved areas
are obscured by extensive use of watercolor, an attribute of
Samuel Blyth that hinders determining if this plate was simply a restrike or reworked, as a second state. The impression
at the New York Public Library Prints and Photographs
department shows more of the original.

THE HON^{BLE} JOHN HANCOCK, ESQ^R.
Late Preſident of the Continental Congreſs
SB [within image]
Mezzotint with hand coloring, ca. 1780, 22.5 x19 cm.
From the Hall Park McCullough Collection, now in a private
collection

The image of Hancock appears at first to have been made from
the same plate as the print issued earlier by Samuel Blyth's
brother-in-law, Joseph Hiller. However, the bust of Hancock is
smaller by about a third and is enclosed in on oval frame. Blyth's
source might have been the English print of Hancock done in
1776. Blyth signed it by burnishing his initials at the bottom right,
within the image, further denoting this as his own image.

lip. The ribbon tying back McIntire's hair is depicted in flourishes typical of Blyth's work for his coats of arms, like the streamers on those for Erwin, Pickman, and Rawlins.[65]

At some point, around 1778–80, Samuel began making mezzotints. Three were essentially reissues, and one is on a classical theme, depicting a well-known event of ancient history. As with most of his output, it was a copy.[66] Two seem to be original compositions.

The assumption by American print historians has been that Samuel copied his brother Benjamin's image of Gen. Putnam for his later mezzotint portrait. However, Samuel actually reused this original copperplate as he did for that of Charles Lee. The reissue may have been prompted by Putnam's death in 1779. Blyth lengthened the image area by eliminating the elaborate text below to add more to Putnam's legs and the tip of the sword blade. For the figure of Putnam, Samuel left the face alone but added the officers' hat, rifle barrel, and fringed cloth around Putnam's waist—although he confused it with the honorary riband. He also completely reworked the background by adding a line of soldiers, his signature gnarled tree and decorative flora in the foreground, and dark clouds edged with sunlight. Samuel covered almost all his mezzotints with pigments—the print medium to him was simply the base for what he evidently considered a more fulsome portrayal, bright with color—so correlation of the work on the impressions was not easy to come by. Nonetheless, in comparing the Benjamin Blyth print to the Samuel Blyth impression of Putnam in the blue coat, with less added coloring than on the other two impressions, enough of the original mezzotint still shows through the attempted disguising to suggest the correlation.

Capt. James Mugford (1749–1776) of Marblehead was credited with a major contribution to the victory of the colonists in the American Revolution. He was already a successful captain in the early 1770s, making many trips across the Atlantic. Soon after the start of the war, he requested permission to be authorized as a privateer. In May 1776, his schooner, the *Franklin*,

---

65. McIntire's great-grandson George W. Low, owner of the pastel in the early 1900s, may have taken it to the Copley Gallery for conservation and restoration; the treatment of the eyelashes is similar to those that appear on other Blyth pastels restored at the gallery. Dean Lahikainen, in *Samuel McIntire, Carving in an American Style* (2007), cited the date of this portrait as 1786, explaining that the text originally read "before 1786," referring to the last known date for Benjamin Blyth at the time, but that "before" had been edited out. It may actually be closer to correct, as this portrait appears to be the work of Samuel, not Benjamin, Blyth.

McIntire himself also may have tried engraving. The 1904 exhibition of engravings at the Museum of Fine Arts, Boston included a bookplate, Cat. 478, for "Cpt John Lee," signed below right, "S. McIntire." Charles Dexter Allen called it "A crude name-label, with a border suggestive of nothing." He thought so little of this engraving that it was not cited in the index, either under sitter, engraver, or "Massachusetts book-plates." There was another S. McIntire, a mariner from Danvers (as was Capt. Lee), who may have made the engraving, although its stylistic elements, "framed in scroll-work, with cornucopias in a small oval above," suggest the architect rather than the mariner. The mezzotint, listed under "Anonymous," was exhibited at the Museum of Fine Arts, Boston, in 1904 and subsequently published in the catalogue (No. 31).

66. The print depicting Cleopatra committing suicide, signed S. Blyth below the image on the right, is the only known example of an ancient historical subject by him. The source was a print with the same name and text engraved by Charles Spooner (d. 1767), a native of County Wexford, Ireland, although Blyth's version has misspellings, and the image was printed in reverse. A few of Spooner's engravings were after his own drawings, but the bulk of his output, like that of Samuel Blyth, consisted of copying popular prints of his contemporaries. An impression of Samuel Blyth's *Cleopatra* is in the New York Public Library, Thomas Addis Emmet Collection.

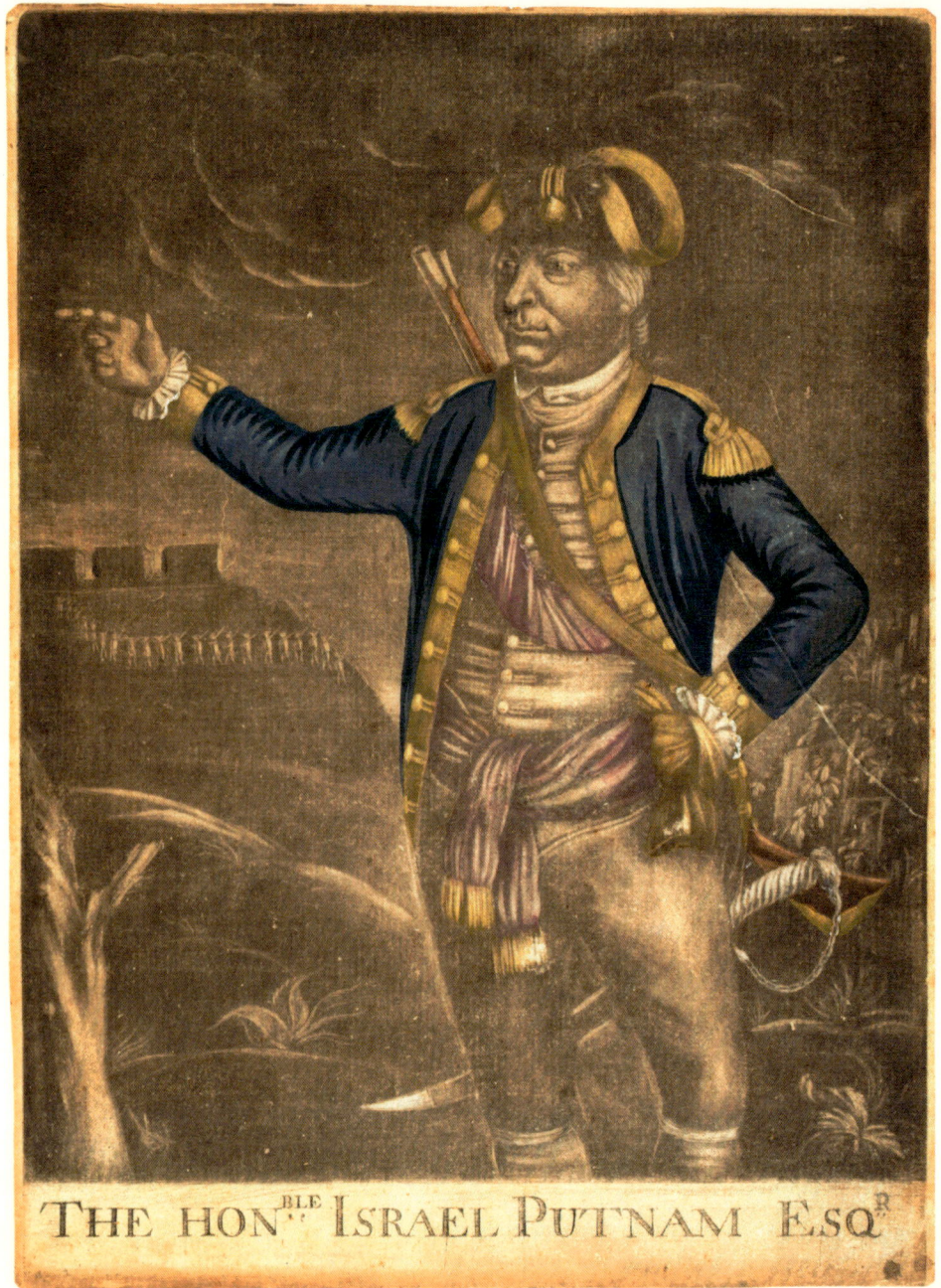

THE HON^{BLE} ISRAEL PUTNAM ESQ^R

THE HON^{BLE}
**ISRAEL PUTNAM,
ESQ**^R**,**
Samuel Blyth
Mezzotint, second state with
hand coloring, 1779–82, 30.5 x
24 cm., (sight)
Courtesy of the William
M. Elkins Collection of
Americana, Rare Book
Department, Free Library of
Philadelphia. ELK0177541

forced the British ship *Hope*, heading toward Boston Harbor, into a tidal inlet where she was grounded in low tide. Local patriots unloaded all the precious gunpowder, other tools and weapons and turned them over to the Continental Navy. It was a great prize, and a great boost to the patriotic cause. However, during the night of May 19, the *Franklin* was attacked by the British and Mugford was killed.

The mezzotint is unusual for a Samuel Blyth image, as his prints were usually almost entirely colored. This one has only sparse use of blue, white, and black pigment, so enough of the mezzotint image is visible to make attribution fairly certain. Outlines show up for the lower part of Mugford's face and the outer edge of his coat, left side. The most cogent stylistic comparison is to Samuel

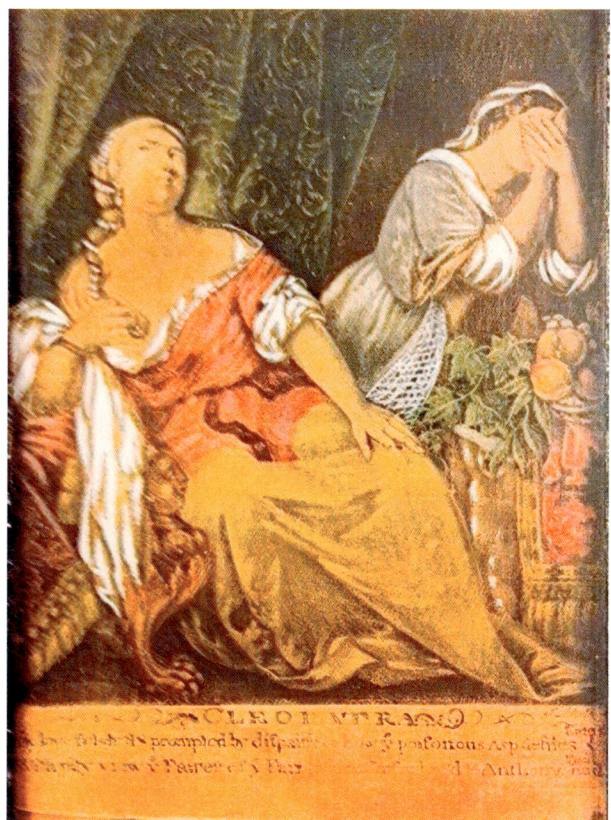

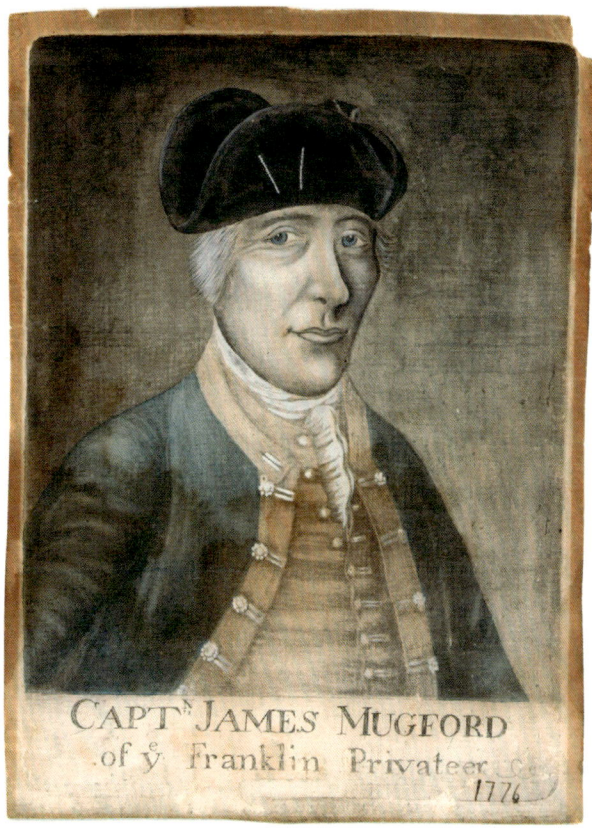

CLEOPATRA, S. Blyth [l.r., below image]
Mezzotint with hand coloring, ca. 1780, 32 x 24 cm.
Courtesy of the Dr. Gary M. Milan Collection
Text below image:
By love fubdu'd & prompted by difpair
With pity view ye Fairest of ye Fair
See how ye poifonous Asp defiles ye Breaft
Which Cæfar lov'd & Anthony had Prest

CAPT^N JAMES MUGFORD/
of ye Franklin Privateer
Samuel Blyth (attr.)
Mezzotint with hand coloring, ca. 1778–80, 21.59 x 15.24 cm.
Courtesy of the Marblehead Museum and
Historical Society 1979.6

Blyth's mezzotint of Gen. Charles Lee. The treatment of facial details and hair are almost identical, as are the strokes of paint used in such details as the buttonholes. The distinct lettering, also, is like the Lee, as well as other Samuel Blyth prints. This seems to be the only impression.[67]

The story of the capture of Major John André must have fascinated Salem. André was a British Revolutionary war officer captured on September 23, 1780, outside Tarrytown, New York and put on trial as a spy because he was out of uniform, against the rules of war at the time. Among the sixteen senior military officers convened to hear the case against him were Brig. Gen. John Glover of Marblehead. André was found guilty and was hanged on October 2, 1780, after General

---

67. Blyth's image of Mugford, from an unknown if not fictional source, became the center vignette of a large, tinted lithograph, *Capt. James Mugford, of the Schr. Franklin*, one of two commemorative prints printed in 1854 by L. H. Bradford & Company of Boston and published by Glover Broughton, Town Clerk of Marblehead. Below the image is a long paragraph describing the engagement, basically claiming that, were it not for Mugford, the war might have had a different outcome. The text concludes: "Who can estimate the real value of that capture?" The Peabody Essex Museum has an impression of the lithograph, as do the Prints and Photographs Department of the Museum of Fine Arts, Boston, and the Mariners Museum, Newport News, VA.

Washington had refused his request for a more honorable (and less painful) death by firing squad. Reverend Enos Hitchcock, on leave as minister of the Second Parish in Beverly to serve as a chaplain to the Continental Army, witnessed André's execution: "He appeared a most Genteel young fellow—handsomely drest in his regimentals. When he came to the Galows, he said he knew well his fate but was disappointed in the mode, He ascended the wagon cheerfully, fixed the halter round his own neck and bound his Eyes—said, smiling, a few moments would settle the whole—was asked if he had anything to offer, lifting up the handkerchief that covered his Eyes, said Gentlemen, you will all bear witness that I meet my fate like a brave man. Gen. Marquis de Lafayette, who was also present, broke down in tears."[68]

The first-known depiction of the incident, this print was probably made shortly after André was hanged. Samuel Blyth may have gotten his inspiration for the poem beneath the print, which he evidently composed, from such precedents as the Henry Pelham print on the Boston Massacre, "Fruits of Arbitrary Power," published in 1770, or from earlier colonial prints as "The Patriotic American Farmer," published in Philadelphia in 1768.

Belying the gravity of the event, the mezzotint is charming, even to the cheerful, benign faces of everyone involved. The colonial captors look like overgrown putti in uniform, all with cherubic wide-eyed expressions bordering on inanely cheerful. (E. McSherry Fowble called them "look-alike mannequins with simplistic smiles."[69]) André is shown offering what looks like a cookie to the men who apprehended him. But it was intended to depict a bribe, a dubious claim. Also inaccurately—and a factor that would have exonerated André, if true—the hand-coloring shows him the red coat of a British officer. Nonetheless, the verse beneath the print conveys much less sympathy for the British officer.

At the right is the familiar Samuel Blyth imagery of a gnarled tree trunk. His landscape backgrounds are predominantly in light browns and blue-greens, with pronounced accents of white, which could be considered his trademark. Unlike his brother, elements stressed receding perspective, like the tents—again, depicted in strong white accents—that line a road in the background of the print.

By the late 1770s, the collaborative printmaking venture of Hiller with the Blyth brothers ceased, although each of them later made at least one print, both with John Coles. Hiller is believed to have made Salem's early seals after he became Collector of the Port.[70]

An allegorical mezzotint in tribute to the impending success of the war for American independence, it has to post-date March 1, 1781, when Maryland became the thirteenth state to join

68. Sibley, *Graduates of Harvard University*, 16:479

69. E. McSherry Fowble, *Two Centuries of Prints in America*, Cat. 308, 438-39. Bettina A. Norton, *Prints at the Essex Institute*, Essex Institute Museum Booklet Series. Other impressions are at the William M. Elkins Collection of Americana, Rare Book Department, Free Library of Philadelphia, and the Henry Francis du Pont Winterthur Museum.

70. Salem Maritime National Historic Site has a seal designed by Hiller. Louis S. Middlebrook, a scholar of Colonial maritime history, thought incorrectly that it was "quite possible" that it was Blyth. However, his list in "New England Engravers" in *EIHC* 62:359, does not include Joseph Hiller. Hiller's son, Joseph Jr., produced a dry-point etching in profile of George Washington in 1794 that was used as a model for a triumphal arch erected in Salem Common. Hart, *Catalogue of the Engraved Portraits of Washington*, (New York: The Grolier Club, 1904), (author-annotated copy at the Boston Athenaeum), Cat. 138; W. S. Baker, *The Engraved Portraits of Washington*, Cat. 7. Hiller Jr. died at sea shortly thereafter.

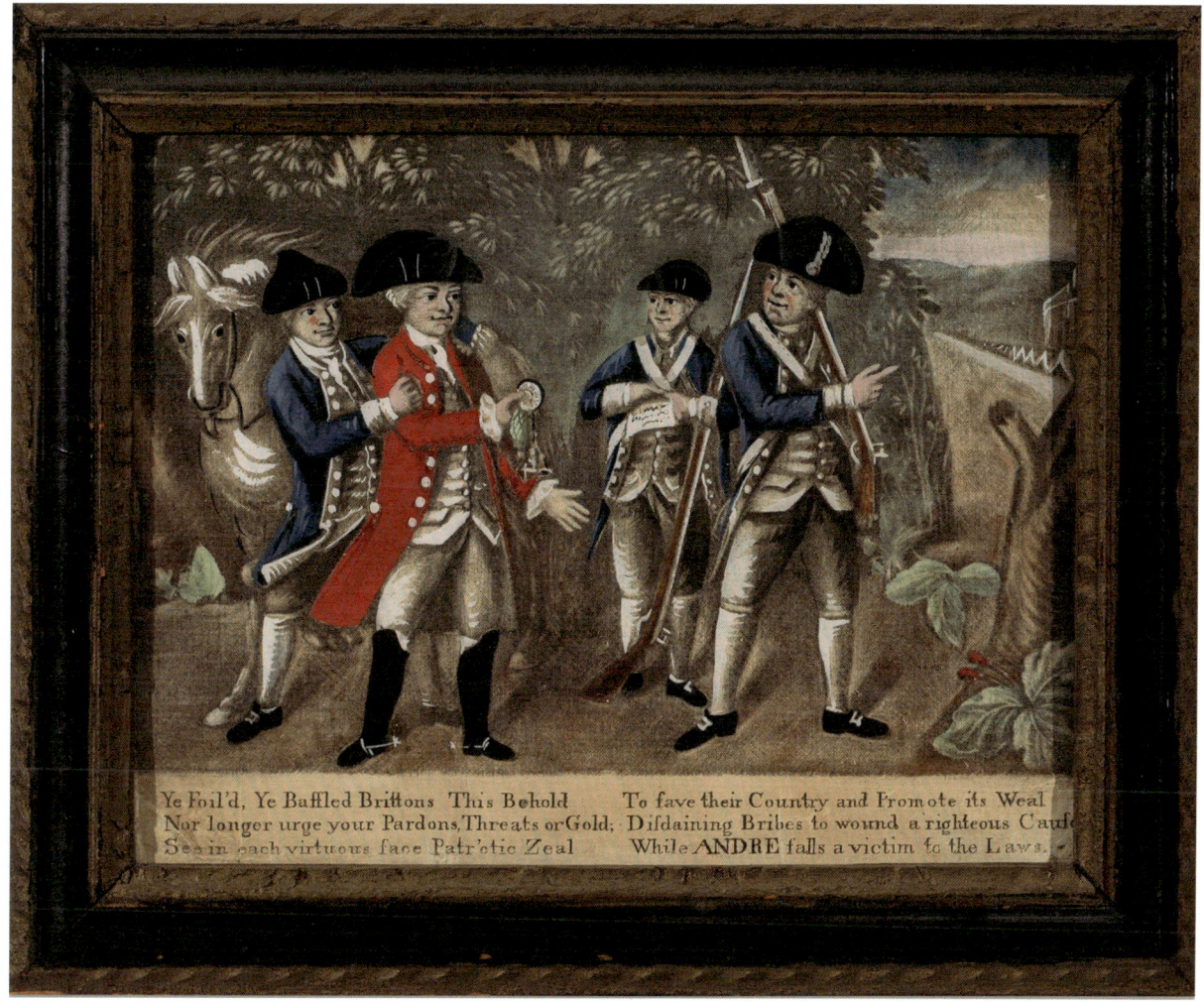

[Capture of Major André]
Samuel Blyth
Ye Foil'd, Ye Baffled Brittons This Behold/ Nor longer urge your Pardons, Threats, or Gold;
See in each virtuous face Patr'otic Zeal/ To ſave their Country and Promote its Weal.
Disdaining Bribes to wound a righteous Cauſe/ While ANDRÉ falls a victim to it Laws.
Mezzotint with hand coloring, probably 1780, 17 x 23.7 cm.
Courtesy of the Peabody Essex Museum, 103215f

the union. The Museum of Fine Arts 1904 catalogue credited the print to Benjamin Blyth. However, although he provided much original artwork, he is not known to have made any mezzotints. Such a wealth of imagery is more characteristic of decoration for coats of arms, the province of both Samuel Blyth and Coles. Blyth also probably taught Coles how to draw coats of arms. Further evidence of the connection with Samuel is his suit against Coles for an unpaid promissory note of £37 7s. 6d. dated June 1, 1782.[71] So, it can be assumed that "Blyth Fecit" refers to Samuel.

71. Suffolk County Court of Common Pleas, no. 94,894. The loan "may have been made in connection with the publication of the Washington engravings," wrote Walter Kendall Watkins in his article, "John Coles, Heraldry Painter," for *Old-Time New England* in 1931.

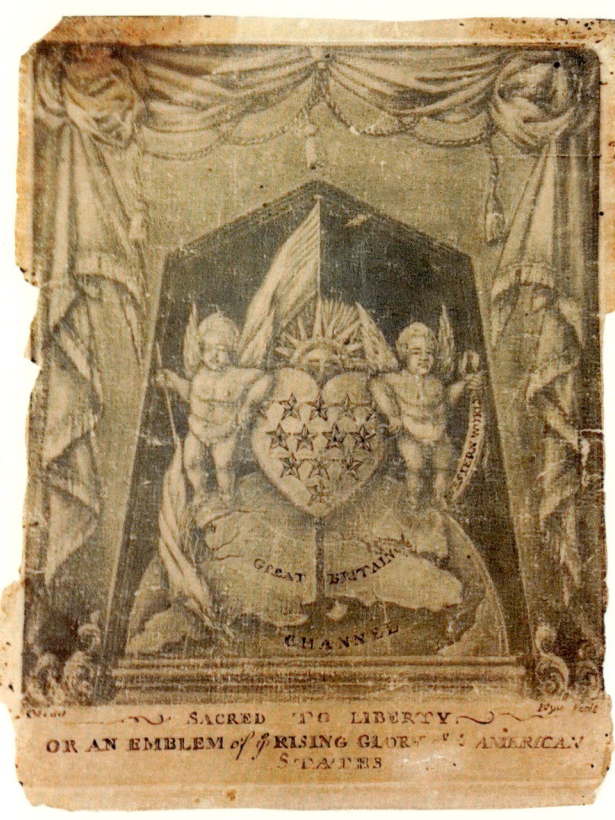

Sacred to Liberty or an Emblem of ye Rising Glory of ye
American States
Cole [sic.] del. / Blyth Fecit
Mezzotint, 1781–82, 8.11 x 7.12 cm.
Courtesy of the American Antiquarian Society, AAS 523947

In 1781, Hiller was appointed "Worshipful Master" of the Essex Lodge of Freemasons. Benjamin Blyth joined the following year, at the same meeting as Edward Lang, another silversmith, whose portrait Blyth painted in oil (Cat. 83). Hiller's son married silversmith Edward Lang's daughter in 1796. There were clearly strong connections among these men.

However, few of the members of the Lodge were prominent in Salem history, and even Bentley, a very active member, thought at one point a few years later that its membership should be turned in, "Salem not being the soil for such an institution."[72] Hiller was a good friend of Bentley, who referred to him as "Major."[73]

In 1802, Hiller moved to Lancaster, in central Massachusetts, where he died in 1814. The lengthy inventory of his estate showed his wealth, his household with numerous fine furnishings, and his intense interest in intellectual and artistic pursuits.[74] Among the inventory were collections of prints, including two of Washington. It is not a stretch to suggest that Hiller owned some of the prints that he engraved along with the brothers Blyth, and others of American generals published in London in 1775. They were valued at $5,00. If only it were known which prints they were, or their trail of ownership! The inventory also makes no mention of any printmaking materials.[75] However,

---

72. Bentley, *Diary*, Feb. 26, 1787, 1:56. Not many Lodge members were drawn or painted by Blyth; in truth, not many of the men from prestigious older families of Salem who were likely to want portraits were members of the Masons, with the exception of Benjamin Crowninshield, Jr. (Cat. 31), and he seems to have been a bit of a maverick. The Lodge later reorganized, with help from Bentley.

73. "Major Hiller spent the evening with me very agreably on my part. The state of our western territories, the west india island, & France the subjects of our conversation, & of public attention," wrote Bentley. Other evenings were spent "looking over the work of the celebrated Lavater on Physiognomy," or with his "agreable family. We had excellent music, & free conversation. Bentley, *Diary*, 1:345, 310, 418. Bentley does not mention his former friend again, even on his death in 1814.

74. Phillips, *Salem in the Eighteenth Century*, 265. Charles Henry Hart mentioned a portrait of Hiller, "painted from life, which was presented by his descendants" then (1907) at the Salem Custom House. (*EIHC* 43:4-5). Transferred to the collections of the Salem Maritime National Historic Site, it is attributed to Auguste Saint-Memin (1770–1852). The PEM contains examples of silver made by Hiller. The illustration on the title page of Belknap's *Artists and Craftsmen of Essex County* is a drawing of a nutmeg grater made by Hiller.

75. At his death, he owned thirty-one cartons of books, including the complete run from 1732 to 1785 of England's

his "cornelian seal" of Washington was valued at $25. There were also five miniatures—one of himself, valued at $1. 00; two unidentified, valued at $1.00; one at 50 cents; and one in a gold case of his son, Joseph Hiller, Jr., who had drowned at age twenty-two, almost twenty years earlier, which was valued at $5.00. One wonders if Benjamin Blyth might have done one or more of those miniatures.

Samuel Blyth never joined the Masons, however, but was continuously active in church and town affairs. His name appears on several town petitions on political issues. Relating an anecdote about the agitation over a proposal for a bridge to be erected over the North Ferry to Beverly in 1787, the mid-nineteenth-century historian of Salem Joseph B. Felt recounted that Samuel, "noted for his ingenious play on words, said, on the occasion, that he never knew a bridge built without railing on both sides."[76]

Shortly after Benjamin Blyth left Salem, around 1783, Samuel also stopped producing portraits. He continued to be quite successful and more prominent in town affairs, twice enlarging his house on Prison Lane, which in later years was called a "mansion." He died in 1789, at age fifty. The probate inventory of his estate, with numerous carpentry tools and paint supplies, indicates that his major business was, as other evidence attests, house painting and providing wood elements such as window sash.[77] However, Felt later referred to him as a "limner." And a century later, Harriet Sylvester Tapley in her book about St. Peter's Church, stated in a footnote on the Blyth family, "Some of them were pastel artists."[78] Yet the fact that there seems to be no artwork done by Samuel Blyth after his brother was gone for a year or so seems to validate that it was intimately tied to his affairs.

Without correspondence or other corroborating evidence, one can only speculate whether their relationship may have been fractured by potentially conflicting roles and the partnership turned into rivalry, or whether Samuel was trying to help Benjamin. His departure and the scattering of his family hint at some sort of crisis in his life. The circumstances remain elusive.

At the time, Bentley probably hardly knew, or even knew of, Blyth. The minister's arrival to as-

anti-Tory journal, *London Magazine*, and "numerous viols," a flute, a spinet, and music sheets. Worcester County, MA: Probate File Papers, 173101881, 29557.

76. Felt, *Annals of Salem*, 1:307.

77. His debts included £150 to his younger brother William, also a painter, who occasionally worked for him. His will provided a small sum, £10, for his son Stephen, leaving the rest of his entire estate in thirds to his wife and two daughters. Stephen Cleveland Blyth vacillated among professions, religions, and domiciles. He tried various faiths in his travels, temporarily changed his and his family's surname to Blydon, and moved to Montreal, where he authored a book in 1815, *Apology for the conversion of Stephen Cleveland Blythe, to the faith of the Catholic, Apostolic and Roman Church, respectfully addressed to Protestants of every denomination*, (Montreal: Printed by Nahum Mower, 1815). (A copy is at the American Antiquarian Society.) He also practiced medicine in Boucherville, Canada (north of Montreal). Back in Salem, he opened an academy for young ladies, applied (but was not chosen) for headmaster of a school for Blacks, then became an assistant in a newspaper, *The Essex Register*, which was lampooned in "The Fool," a half-sheet newspaper. Bentley often disparaged Stephen Cleveland Blyth[e], noting in one entry, " . . . a native of Salem, self-taught, & who has been abroad as a Dr. in the West Indies, lately returned to Salem, & opened a School for young Ladies . . . . He has repeatedly complained of ill success, which he by no means imputes to his want of talents." Bentley, *Diary*, 3:259, 277, 294, 310; and "Charles Willson Peale with Patron and Populace," Transactions of the American Philosophical Society, The American Philosophical Society, May 1969, 17:277, 21:265-6.

78. Felt, *Annals of Salem*, 1:307. Tapley, *St. Peter's Church*, fn. 35, 35.

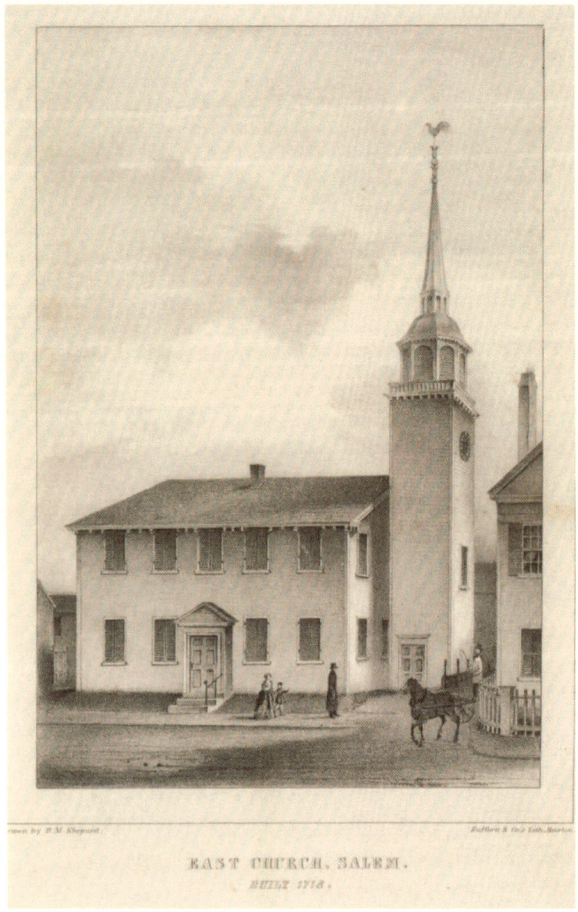

East Church, Salem. /Built 1718
Drawn by B. M. Shepard/ Bufford & Co.'s Lith., Boston
Lithograph, ca. 1855, image 22.5 x 16.1 cm.
Courtesy of the Boston Athenaeum

sist at the East Church in Salem in 1783 came at the waning of the artist's career, although Bentley either did not see or chose not to comment on Blyth's pastels in the houses of his parishioners, especially the portrait of the young John Gibaut, one of Bentley's best friends and one of Benjamin Blyth's best pastels.

Benjamin's family seems to have moved to the northern reaches of the Massachusetts Bay Colony—Maine. Whether Benjamin originally left with his family or whether they went their separate ways when his youngest son was around three years old is still unknown. There is no evidence of him or his wife Mehitabel there. In fact, Ancestry.com has no record anywhere of a Mehitabel Blyth from 1778 through 1840. However, the three references there are to Blyths in Maine into the early years of the nineteenth century are the names of Benjamin and Mehitabel's three children: Benjamin, born in 1771; Frank, born in 1773; and Samuel, born in 1780. A Benjamin Blyth appeared in a list of "Master Mariners before 1800" in Pownalborough, with the brigantine *Franklin*. A Capt. Samuel Blyth died in 1813 in Portland. And a Francis, not Frank, Blyth is listed in Pownalborough, Maine, in the 1800 census; he was between the ages of twenty-six and forty-four, with children under age ten. According to records, he had been born in 1773 in Massachusetts—as was Benjamin's son Frank—and died at Pownalborough in 1806. John Bentley, the brother of Salem's contemporary diarist, the Reverend William Bentley, who was so critical of the work of Benjamin Blyth, married Elizabeth Blythe, daughter of Francis Blyth, on July 15, 1792.[79] Although Benjamin's son was too young to be the father of this Elizabeth and there seems to be no known connection, the name "Francis Blyth" was uncommon in colonial America. It would be ironic if the minister who so disparaged the work of Benjamin Blyth might prove to have been related to him.

No sign of Benjamin was found in the vital records in the New England states or in any state between Massachusetts and Virginia for the next two or three years. Blyth's first known residence after he left Salem was in Richmond, Virginia, in 1785. It is not known whether he knew that a

79. Bentley, *Diary*, 2:121, 4:292.

former Boston bookseller, William Pelham, Jr., Peter Pelham's grandson, was living in nearby Williamsburg at the time.[80] The first notice of Blyth's presence in Richmond was publication of his marriage to a widow, Mary Dougle, on February 12, 1785.[81]

Half a year later, in July, Blyth once again advertised his services: "Benjamin Blyth, limner, informs the public he has opened a house near the City Coffee-House for the performance on limning in oil, crayons and miniature."[82] Having been a Mason in Salem, he joined Richmond's Manchester Lodge No. 14, Richmond, Virginia, when it was founded in 1786, and provided much of its original decoration. Two figures of a winged Mercury drawn by Benjamin Blyth were made by a silversmith named Jacob Ege into badges in 1786. Worn by the Senior and Junior Deacons until 1963, they are now on long-term loan to the Allen. E. Roberts Grand Lodge of Virginia Museum in Richmond. Blyth also designed the ornament for the tops of two wands carried by Masonic leaders.[83] The square and compass with the sun at the center was used on top of the staff carried by the Senior Deacon. The Junior Deacon's staff had the square and compass with the moon in the center, and the staffs carried by the Stewards had cornucopias. These emblems, along with the figures of Mercury, are the only evidence of Blyth's work in Virginia. They are still in use.

No portraits, pastels, oils, or miniatures have been found in Virginia institutions that can be attributed to Benjamin Blyth. The only records other than his marriage are his other dealings with the Lodge. He also sold other items to the association, including "some lambskins." As a newcomer to the Richmond area, despite becoming involved in the Masons, he must not have been able to establish the family connections or the patronage that had helped him in Salem. And then he disappeared, showing up again in Ohio, then part of the newly established Northwest Territory. Several other families with Salem or Essex County roots also emigrated nearby. The Rufus Putnam family settled in the town of Marietta. William Pelham also turned up in 1810 in Zanesville, Ohio, where Blyth was living at the time, and where he died a year later, at age sixty-five.

Unlikely as it seems that Benjamin Blyth ended up in another state with a third wife, Elleanor [*sic*], the signatures in his probate record (he died intestate) are almost identical to the one he penned from Salem in 1776 on the bill to the widow of Gen. John Thomas.

---

80. William Pelham was born in Williamsburg, VA, in 1759 but was in Boston by 1796, as a bookseller. He moved to Zanesville, OH, where Blyth was then living, around 1810. Pelham died in New Harmony, IN, on February 3, 1827. Charles K. Bolton, *Circulating Libraries in Boston, 1765–1865,* (Boston, 1907), 203-4.

81. "Marriage Bonds of Norfolk County [Virginia]," *The William and Mary Quarterly*, Williamsburg, Va.: Institute of Early American History and Culture, 1944, Second Series, 8:171; Married again at age thirty-nine, Blyth and his new wife could have had children, but there are no records of births (or marriages or deaths). It was not unheard of for eighteenth- and early-nineteenth-century artists between states or new territories to shed a wife without benefit of legal separation when moving to another state or territory, like John Ramage (1748–1802) and Edwin Whitefield (1816–1892), for two. As genealogists know, the combination of massive migrations west after the Revolution and lack of churches keeping accurate documentation has made tracing families in this period difficult.

82. *The Virginia Genealogist*, 142. Blyth had sold the Lodge a Bible published in 1775, which in 1994 the Lodge claimed was "now a very rare edition."

83. Bernard L. Brock, correspondence from June 13, 1994; Manchester Lodge papers, Mss3 F8774 a FA2 and Marie Barnett, correspondence.

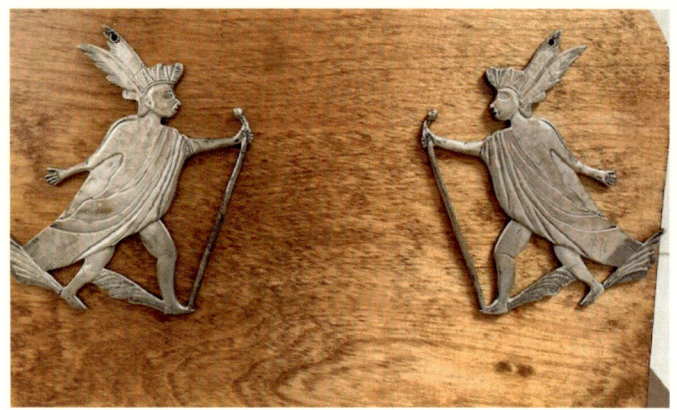

Mercury, Two Figures
From original drawings by Benjamin Blyth, 1786
Metal, 4½ x 3¾ in. Originals drawings lost
Courtesy of the Allen. E. Roberts Grand Lodge of Virginia Museum,
Richmond, VA

Among Blyth's belongings at his death, the only ones beyond the frugal furnishings of a household and farmer were four volumes of the Bible and six of Doddridge's works, plus a silver watch.[84] From what is known of Blyth's interest in depicting the clergy and in matters intellectual, Doddridge would have been someone Blyth admired: along with a New Testament commentary and other theological works, Doddridge also wrote more than 400 hymns. As for the silver watch, Blyth may have received or bought it from his friend and fellow Mason in Salem, silversmith Edward Lang. The inventory confirms that Blyth evidently became a farmer with no pretentions of continuing a career as an artist. No records survive on any of his three wives, and he ended his life selling Bibles in Ohio.

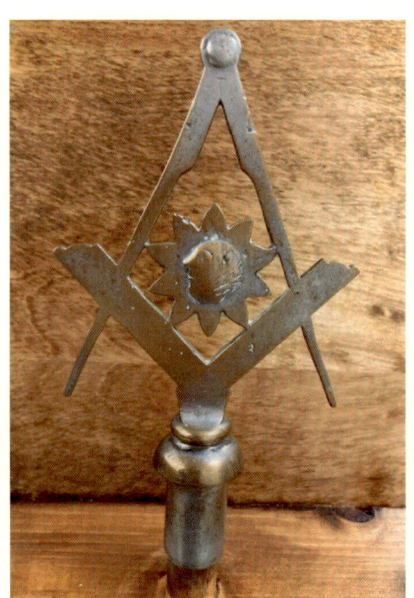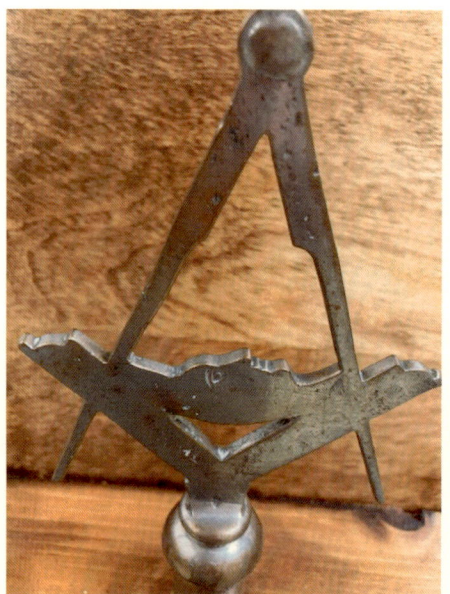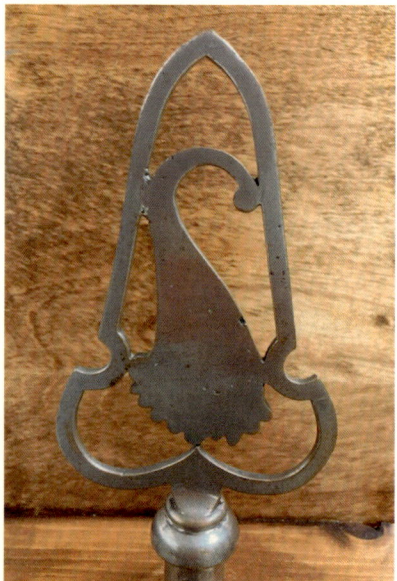

Three Masonic Emblems from drawings by Benjamin Blyth, 1786
Metal, (a) Emblem Square and Compass with Face in Sun, 6⅞ x 3¾ in. (b) Cornucopia, 7 ¾ x 3 ½ in. (c) Square and Compass Recline
Face, 6 ½ x 3¾ in.
Courtesy of the Allen E. Roberts Grand Lodge of Virginia Museum, Richmond, VA

---

84. Muskingum Will Book A, Case 39, 203.

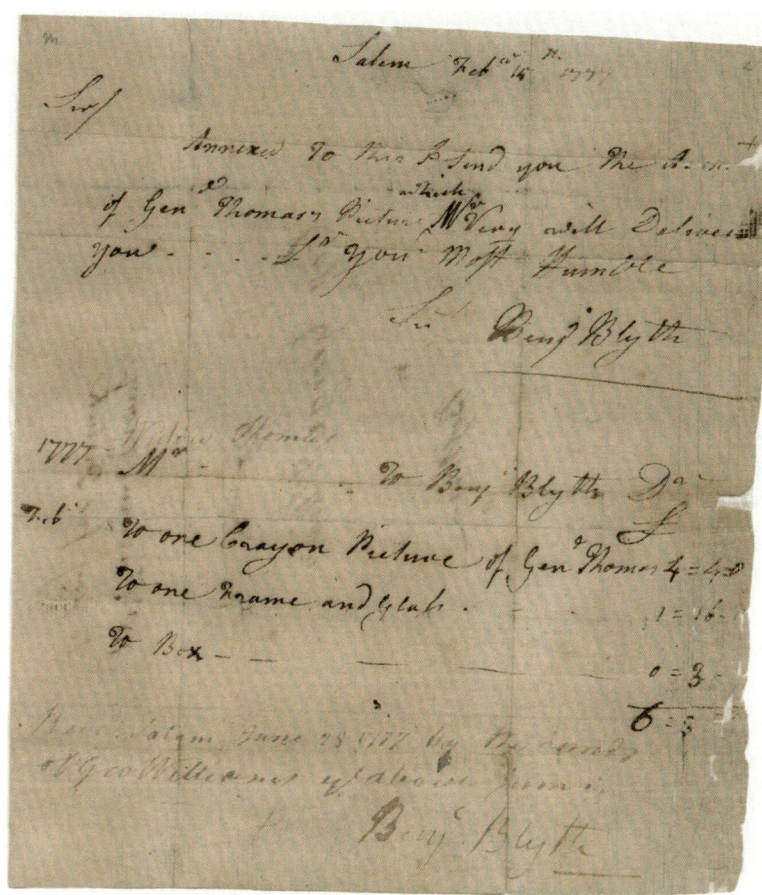

*Benjamin Blyth's signature on his bill
to the widow of John Thomas, 1776*
Courtesy of the Massachusetts Historical Society, John Thomas Papers

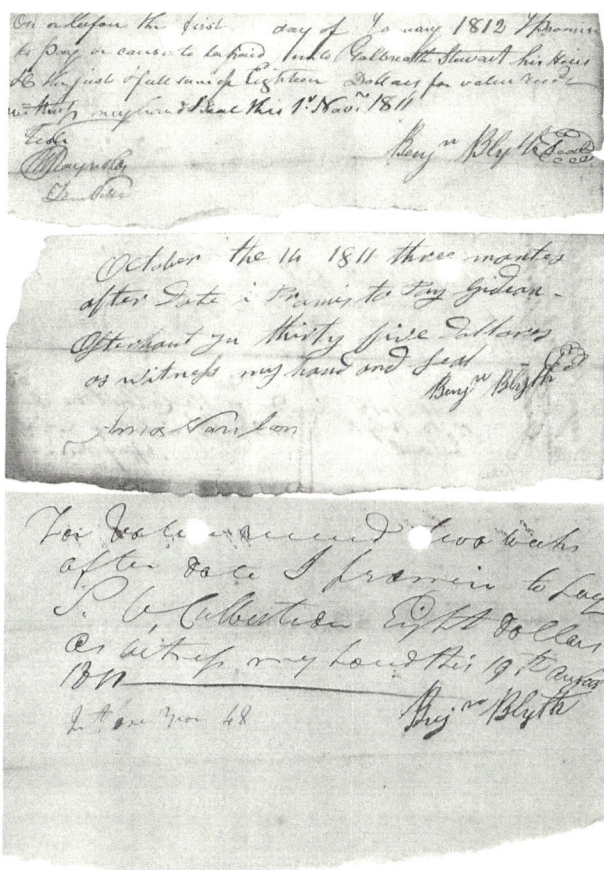

Blyth signature on a promissory note, 1811
Courtesy of the Muskingum County Probate Records, E-1811,
MU Will Book A, 203

BENJAMIN BLYTH'S ART

PASTELS: HIS SIGNATURE MEDIUM

THE AMERICAN HISTORIAN Bernard Bailyn praised the pastel portraits of John and Abigail Adams, as a newlywed couple: "[A]n even more revealing witness of the significance of the marriage—more revealing in some ways even than the famous correspondence between John and Abigail Adams . . . is the portraits of the two, drawn in pastel by an obscure but evidently discerning colonial artist, Benjamin Blyth." Bailyn noted a "marked contrast" between John's "likable but unimpressive face: round, rather soft-looking, bland, and withdrawn . . ." and Abigail's, "extraordinary, not so much for its beauty, which, in a masculine way, is clearly enough there, as for the maturity and the power of personality it expresses. . . . about as confident, controlled, and commanding a face, as a woman can have and still remain feminine."[85] This astute observation from a prominent historian captures what makes Blyth pastels so worthy—revealing the character of his sitters. As was pointed out earlier (p. 23), the early-twentieth-century Boston art dealer Frank W. Bayley thought well enough of Blyth's pastels to give him two pages instead of one in his *Little Known Early American Portrait Painters* (1917).

On the other hand, an early-twentieth-century art critic/collector, Malcolm Vaughn (1896–1962), harshly criticized Blyth's technique based on knowledge of ten "extant" pastels. His example was the pastel of Sarah Curwen (Cat. 34). "Typical of his early or pre-Revolutionary manner, . . . [I]t shows at a glance that he could not be counted on to preserve the medium through a time of stress. His talent was too small; his training too meager. Mrs. Curwen is badly spaced, awkwardly drawn and anatomically absurd. . . . Also as a colorist he is poor. Mrs. Curwen is painted against a neutral background, and the tints are a lifeless brown for the hair, eyes of a nondescript brownish hue, and the flesh the blanched tones of an invalid."[86] In fact, Blyth *was* portraying an invalid; Curwen died at age thirty-one, a year after her portrait was drawn.

What Vaughn meant by "times of stress" is unclear; Blyth produced many fine pastel portraits leading up to and during the American Revolution. When Vaughn praised John Johnston for his "doubly pleasing" work, the best of the four Johnstons known to him was the "remarkable pastel bust of Col. Samuel Flagg," which he credited with "something of the Colonial earnestness, vigor and sturdiness . . . straightforward, unsophisticated and virile." Vaughn was assessing this pastel in

---

85. Bernard Bailyn, "Butterfield's Adams: Notes for a Sketch," *The William and Mary Quarterly*, 3d Ser., 19, no. 2 (April 1962): 249-50. Bailyn's comments were cited in part in an article on the Adams portraits by Andrew Oliver et al., Portraits of John and Abigail Adams (Cambridge: The Belknap Press of Harvard University Press, 1967), 9.
86. Malcolm Vaughn, "American pastels: late eighteenth century," *International Studio* 89, April 1928:1-65. Among Vaughn's other mistaken opinions, he accepted the thesis perpetrated by Frank W. Bayley that Blackburn drew pastels, a ruse that was exposed in the early 1930s by John Hill Morgan.

terms that in fact apply to some works of Benjamin Blyth. Moreover, the Flagg has been credited to him, and not John Johnson, for over a half century.

How Blyth used pastel crayons to begin his compositions is shown in unfinished works such as Unknown Boy in Brown Suit (Cat. 141), Thomas Mason (Cat. 90), or Hannah Breck Porter (Cat. 107). Brown or black was used for the outlines. These would be crayoned over with added layers of color or would evolve to parts of shadow in finished portraits. Sometimes there is an underlayer of blue that emerges as shadow. This shows up well in the extensively abraded portrait of Gen. John Thomas (Cat. 122). The background coloring in a Blyth pastel is almost always neutral, with dark gray, brown, or black tones predominant, although he used blue on at least five. He also used blue for clothing, although Prussian blue was not a dependable pigment at the time. Also, there was no green crayon until the introduction of cobalt in the 1780s. As for wigs, Blyth depicted them as the lifeless puffs that they are, but white pastel proved very adaptable to convey their powdery makeup. Blyth's modeling of faces, generally very proficient, exhibits variations in skin color and texture that show sensitivity to form, as seen also in the soft folds of flesh for

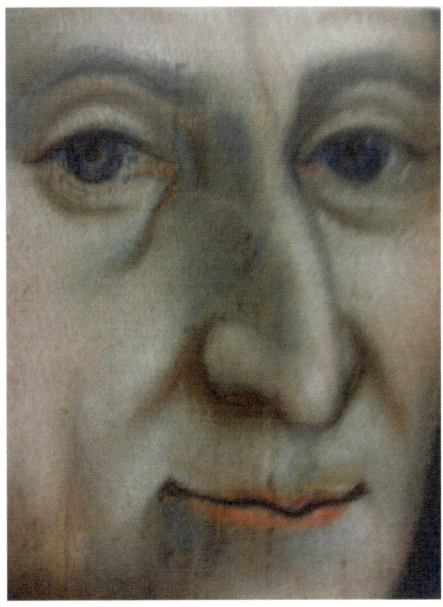

Gen. John Thomas, detail of face showing underlying blue pigment
from the pastel by Benjamin Blyth

breasts, especially in Elizabeth Dabney (Cat. 39) and Sarah Putnam(?) Gardner (Cat. 58). Blyth likely gleaned some techniques from copying Blackburn's work, if not him personally.[87]

Blyth's characteristic stylistic elements are a too-prominent dark brown lip line with little or no swell or tapering, an ear that is and parallel to the picture plane and sometimes oversized, and prominently delineated eyes that are usually the same, with no allowance for perspective for the distant one. Women's hair was treated as an ancillary element, lacking life. Blyth with a few exceptions did not draw loose, decorative curls, although the hair often is enhanced with jewels or flowers. The backgrounds, added last, sometimes constrict the hair that frames the face. In others, they do suggest some "air" around the figures. Blyth's portraits rarely included hands, a bonus for him, as he could not execute them convincingly. He used the prevalent artists' trick of portraying them tucked inside a waistcoat or jacket. When he did draw hands, the fingers are outlined, curved, and seemingly lack knuckles.

However, Blyth seemed to delight in drawing ruffles and edgings of lace. The same holds for the seam lines of the buttonholes in jackets of the 1760s and '70s and the threads or metal of the buttons; Blyth conveyed them with deft strokes. His lace cuffs often show delicate transparency. Again, this skill may have been learned by studying portraits that he might have seen in Salem, such as those of Mrs. Samuel Gardiner and Mrs. Jacob Hurd by William Johnston, now at the Metropoli-

---

87. D[avid] P[ulllins], in Stebbins et al., *American Paintings at Harvard*, 1:95. See also the subheading, "Blyth's Mentors."

tan Museum, or of Abigail Curwen by Blackburn, recently sold to a private collector. However, Blyth never learned, or bothered to learn, how to render skillfully the varying textures and sheens of fabric like satin, although he did a creditable job with Elizabeth Dabney's ivory satin dress (Cat. 39) and Elizabeth Derby's lace-trimmed jacket (Cat. 43). Last, Blyth's pastels generally eschewed extraneous details such as representative or decorative elements, although there are exceptions: a glimpse of a chair back, a quill pen, a hand holding a book.

As for the children's pastel portraits by Benjamin Blyth, the format is the same as in his other pastels— a bust portrait against a plain background, with concentration on the face of the sitter, such as the Unknown Boy "from Salem" (Cat. 140) or the Unknown Boy in Brown Suit (Cat. 141). The few times that he included animals as children's pets, they resemble hairless rats. Blyth's technique is better seen in the delicate, well-drawn touches of lace, such as found on Sarah Moses's dress (Cat. 95) or the pleats on Patty Webb's dress (Cat. 133). What defines these children's portraits from those now thought to have been done by Blyth's brother Samuel, in addition to better draftsmanship, is the emphasis on character. The more one looks at their faces, the more haunting the images become. This is especially true of Patty Webb, carefully and expertly restored by her current owners, and the prize of all, John Gibaut (Cat. 59).

Blyth appears to have signed only one pastel, that of George Cabot—twice, with different dates. This raises the possibility that neither inscription is in Blyth's hand. (See illustration of one on page 28; the other is almost illegible.) In fact, one bill and two promissory notes are the extent of his known writings.

Also, almost nothing is known of what Blyth charged or was paid (with one exception: that of Gen. John Thomas, for which the bill was £4 4s. for the portrait and £1 6s. for the frame, and one possible reference: Edward Lang's account book, which allowed £4 1s. 4d. to square the account for two unfinished pictures). Although one cannot assume much for a person about whom documentation is so scant, it seems logical that Blyth charged a higher price for the more ambitious portrayals, such as for the husband-and-wife portraits of the Gardner, Ropes, Moses, and Baty families. On the other hand, it cannot be discounted that occasionally Blyth painted a portrait simply because he wished to do so, *gratis* or not, to promote his calling, as might have been the case with the Adams portraits; it must have been seen as a coup to capture the likeness of the rising lawyer who had just saved some sailors on a Marblehead ship from imprisonment or death. Perhaps Blyth was not much of a businessman. Rather telling, it seems, is that he was passed over to help administer the estate of his father for his older and younger brothers.

Many of Blyth's portraits were done in the early 1770s. Moreover, all this activity was taking place while Copley was still in the area and focused occasionally on Salem for sitters. Although no Copley is known to have been mistaken for a Blyth, the reverse has occurred at least a dozen times. Copley's pastel of Mary (Mrs. Joseph) Greene, which so closely resembles work Blyth might have done, encapsulates the difference between the two artists. The women's eyes and brows also are quite similar, although Mrs. Greene's farther eye is appropriately smaller. The same prominent upward-curved brown line separating the lips on both women is one of Blyth's most salient characteristics, but the fleshy part in that of Mrs. Greene is more softly modeled, like the almost sexy

Details from pastels by Benjamin Blyth

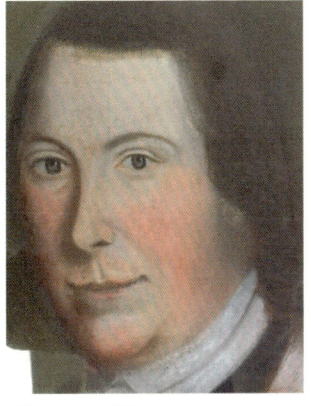 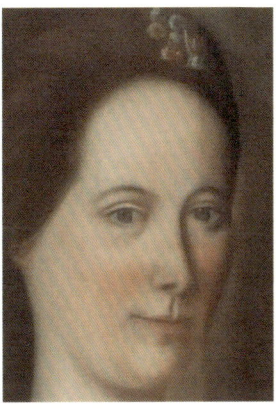 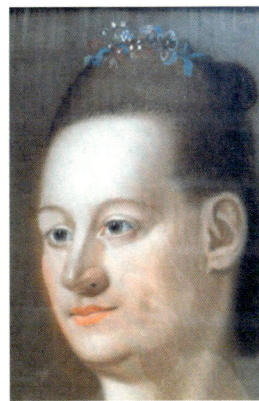 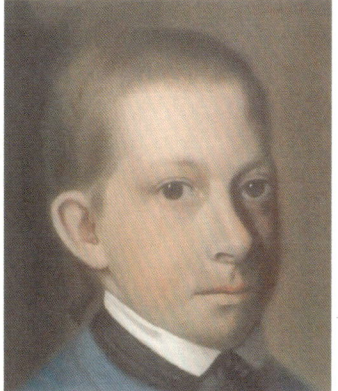

Close-up of faces noting characteristic treatment of eyes, lips, and ears: Thomas Cary (Cat. 27), Sarah Curwen (Cat. 34), Elizabeth Dabney (Cat. 39), John Gibaut (Cat. 59)

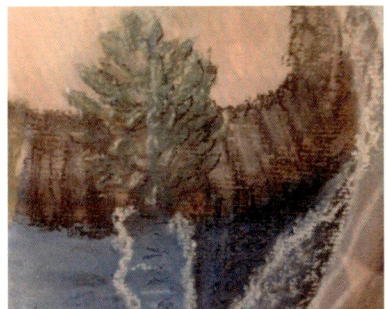 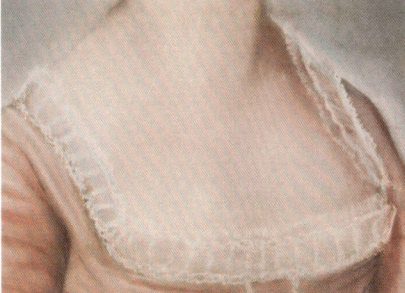 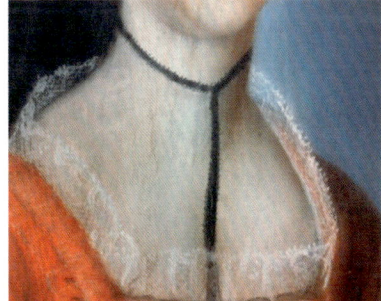

Lace details: Woman in Blue Dress with Black Lace (Cat. 151), Elizabeth Rogers (Cat. 110), Elizabeth White (Cat. 136)

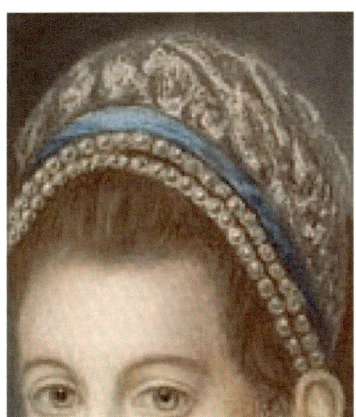 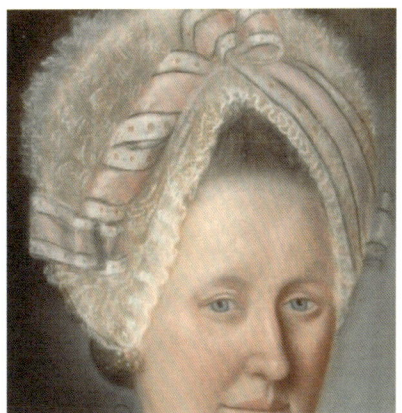 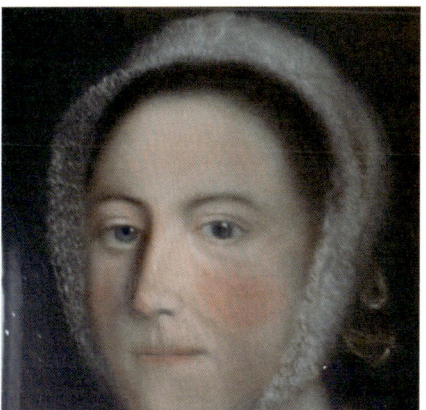

Hats: Lydia Phippen Fisk (Cat. 53), Mrs. J. Gardner (Cat. 58), Hepzibah Sharp (Cat. 116)

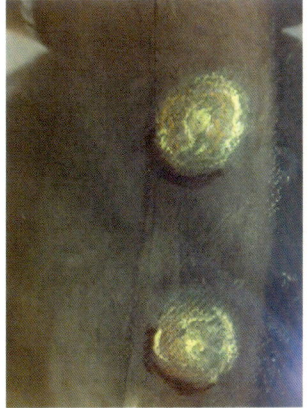 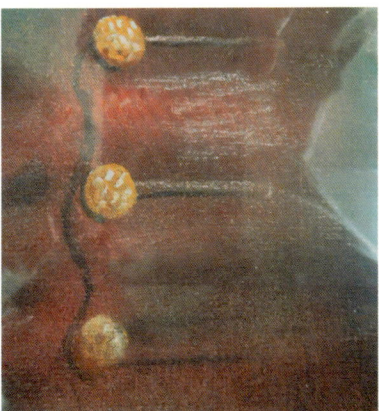 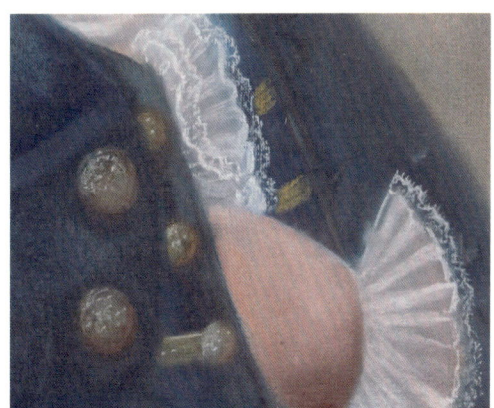

Buttons: Samuel Curwen (Cat. 33), David Ropes (Cat. 111), John Somes (Cat. 120)

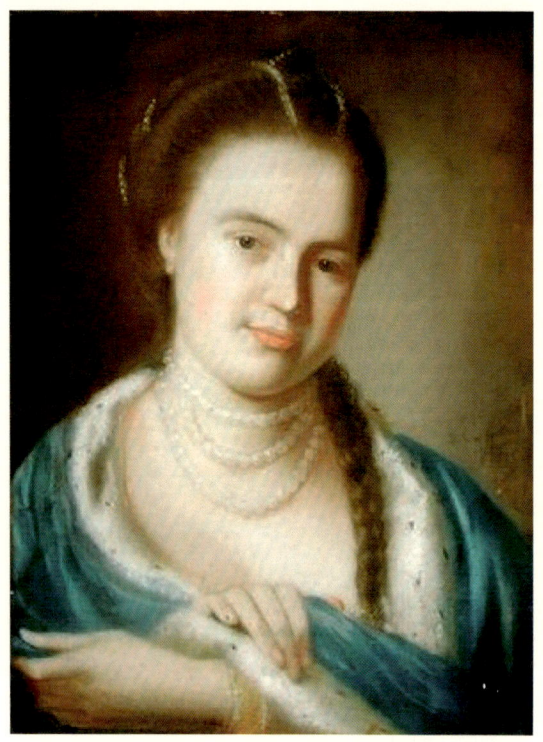

Mrs. Gawen Brown (Elizabeth Byles)
Pastel by John Singleton Copley, 1763
Courtesy of the Museum of Fine Arts, Houston, B.54.21

lips of Mrs. Gawen Brown (illustrated here), Mrs. Joseph Barrell, and Lady Temple. Copley and Blyth both portrayed the Reverend Thomas Cary (Cat. 27), about which Theodore E. Stebbins, Jr., demurred, "Cary's rather unusual, elfin face looks very similar in both pictures."[88]

It is difficult to pinpoint any stylistic development for Blyth. A number of his early pastels are very accomplished, although the portrait of the young John Gibaut (Cat. 59), ca. 1780, one of the later ones and indisputably one of his best, belies the notion that his technique did not advance. Blyth indeed rendered Gibaut's face with more plasticity and unity of features than he did, say, with the earlier portrait of John Adams (Cat. 3), whose nose seems to float detached from his right cheek. Neil Jeffares, author of the online art reference "Pastels and Pastellists" (http://www.pastellists.com), in correspondence with the author, also noted that the treatment of the folds in Gibaut's coat had advanced from the much earlier pastel of George Cabot (Cat. 25).

A major constraint on attributing pastels is the damage to the originals from loss of pigment or subsequent touching-up. Pastel is a fragile medium, and a significant number of Blyth portraits (in both institutional and private collections) have suffered from wear and/or water damage, exposure to harmful atmospheric conditions, poor storage, or other problems. The surfaces of pastels that were not under glass are frequently speckled with fly droppings that, by the nature of the medium, are difficult to remove. A worse fate befell the pastels that were pasted directly onto board; as the wood expanded and contracted with humidity, the paper bubbled and cracked, or the surface was stained with tannin, such as seen in the pastels of Thankful/Rachel Baty (Cat. 13) Gen. John Thomas (Cat. 122), and Benjamin West (Cat. 134). The glass put on the front of pastels, ostensibly for protection, also sometimes actually damaged them by inadvertent abrading of the crayon. Plexiglass creates a static field that removes crayon particles, as it did on the pastel of Peter Frye (Cat. 56).

Some of Blyth's pastels that suffered damage over the years were copied to preserve the images, and the originals were lost or destroyed. Among these are the pastels of Benjamin Crowninshield (Cat. 31) and Richard Derby, Sr. (Cat. 47), given to the former Essex Institute; Hugh Hill at the Beverly Historical Society and Museum (Cat. 67); Sarah Derby Hersey (Cat. 66) at Derby Academy; the Rev. John Chipman (Cat. 28), at the First Church in Beverly; and John Lowell (Cat. 87), in a private collection.

---

88. Stebbins et al., *American Paintings at Harvard*, 83.

Only one image of an original Blyth portrait and its copy are extant—Peter Frye (Cat. 56). There are two pastels of him in the Peabody Essex Museum, both of which, until this study, were believed to be copies by L. P. Cutts of the original Blyth portrait. However, examination of one revealed written in pencil on the mat: "Conservation note: portrait was mistakenly framed under plexiglass for many years and had considerable surface mold growth ... carefully and lightly brushed off with a fine sable brush. The portrait has been in sunlight for about two hours/ JHW." (John Hardy Wright was assistant curator of the Essex Institute at the time.) Another note, on the catalogue card, records that the pastel was later sent to the Museum of Fine Arts, Boston, for conservation for use in the EI exhibition, "Patriots and Loyalists." The notes established two important points. First, they explain why the puzzling reproduction of Frye in *Sibley's Harvard Graduates*, published in 1960, was slightly different from either of the two pastels in the collection. Some of the dashing strokes of white chalk shown on Frye's wig were unavoidably lost, as were losses softening the eyes and mouth—although the latter were subtle enough almost to have escaped notice. (Nonetheless, the needed repairs to that pastel were meticulously done.) Second, that portrait was the original by Blyth. The full force of Frye's somewhat acerbic personality that Blyth had caught so well is still evident, though slightly diminished.

Sometimes, pastels were redrawn to obscure the identity of the original artist for one that is better known. Occasionally, however, a clue appears. During an examination of the once-called

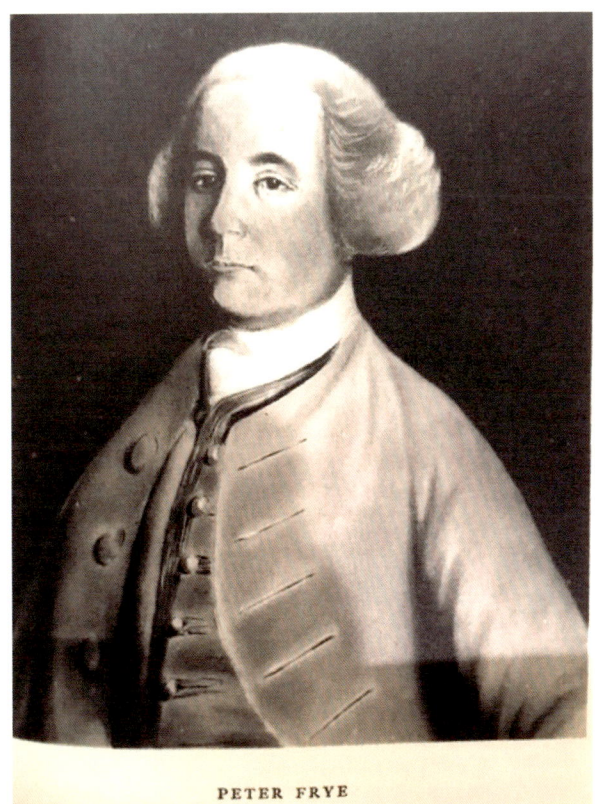

PETER FRYE

Photograph of pastel of Peter Frye
Illustration from *Sibley's Harvard Graduates*, 11 (1960), opp. 404
Courtesy of the Boston Athenaeum

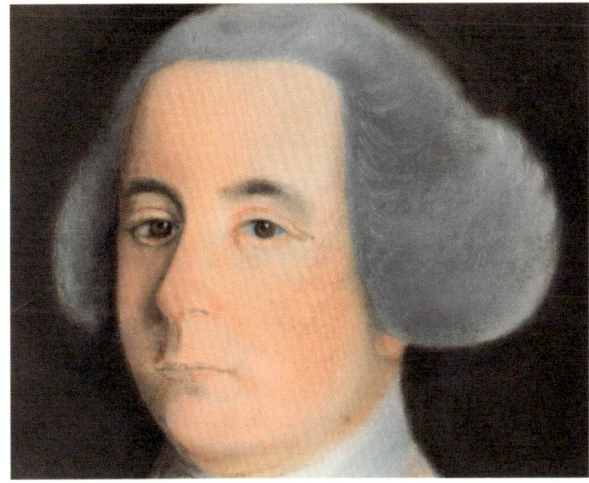

Peter Frye, detail after restoration in 1973
from the pastel by Benjamin Blyth

"Lt. Gov. Oliver" (Cat. 145), now in the Museum of Fine Arts, Boston, the technique of the draftsmanship around the eyes was found to resemble closely Blyth's pastel of Hannah Paine (Cat. 101) at the Worcester Art Museum. The inscription on the back of a photograph of her portrait, part of the Bayley Collection of about 600 glass-plate negatives at Historic New England, noted that it was "made by Baldwin Coolidge, Boston, Jan. 24, 1906." The back of the portrait itself revealed the identical inscription, except that instead of the word "made," it was "Restored." Bayley's gallery offered such services, both to institutions and to private collectors. Thus, Hannah's portrait would have been improved upon when it was still in the family; it did not enter the collection of the Museum until 1952.

The pastels purportedly of Lt. Gov. Oliver, along with that of Lt. Gov. Hutchinson (Cat. 144), did undergo the same redrawing of facial elements, with the purpose of passing them off as drawn by Joseph Blackburn. The most likely person to have done the extensive redrawing was Baldwin Coolidge. He was not only the photographer for hundreds of portraits that passed through Bayley's gallery, but he was also an artist.[89] His oil portrait of Charles Francis Adams II at the Massachusetts Historical Society shows the same telltale strokes for eyelashes as in the Gideon Baty pastel (Cat. 11), which also may have been touched up by Bayley's gallery. The characteristic addition of eyelashes to the lower eyelids is apparent, as are thin delicate strokes of the same black crayon to his wig and along the edge of the near collar of his blue coat. Baty's left eye also has radiating strokes surrounding the blue iris. If Coolidge were responsible for reworking these pastels, he most likely was unaware of the fraudulent attributions. Coolidge had left Boston for California in 1917 and died there in 1928. Bayley sought to sell the fraudulent "Blackburns" the year following Coolidge's death.[90] Bayley's attributions to Blackburn were clever: he felt that Blyth was underappreciated but also recognized the influence of the better-known artist. The so-called restoration work at Copley Gallery was expertly done.

Overall, Benjamin Blyth's pastels show a great variety of execution, sometimes very careful, sometimes seemingly rushed and done with disinterest, sometimes unfinished. There is a distinct dichotomy in his portraiture, between those that are softly, carefully modeled, and those that have prominent features, almost outlined. Yet there is no discernible "progression" from one year to the next. Without Blyth's correspondence or other personal documents, it cannot be ascertained why some portraits were superior to others; perhaps he, like artists before and after him, simply put more effort into some than others, possibly due to size of commissions or simply empathy with the subject. There is no record of Blyth's interests or his friends, but among his more accomplished pastels are people

---

89. Historic New England's library and archives has more than 2,000 glass plate negatives by Coolidge in the Bayley Collection. See Reichlin, Ellie, "Double Exposure: Baldwin Coolidge and William Sumner Appleton" *Old-Time New England* 69, nos. 3-4, (Winter-Spring 1979), Serial Nos. 255-256, 34-43.

90. John Hill Morgan had been offered the portraits by Bayley but turned them down and later wrote of his concerns to the officials of Boston's Museum of Fine Arts. The accompanying biographies of the offered paintings were peppered with human-interest tidbits ("The Olivers were very fond of Mrs. Vassall") and that a purported sitter was an "intimate friend" of other important colonial figures. Frank William Bayley Papers, folder "Blackburn, Joseph & Badger, Joseph," Massachusetts Historical Society, 60. Bayley ascribed the biographies to a Robert M. de Forest, said to be a New York art dealer, and then simply rewrote and typed them for potential clients. R. M. de Forest is listed in the 1920 City Directory for New York City, but no profession is given. His name does not appear in www. americanancestors.org. Also, no connection has been found between de Forest and the president of the Metropolitan Museum board, also a de Forest. For further discussion, see Bettina Norton, "A Foray into Forgery and the Boston Athenaeum's Role in Exposing It." https://soundcloud. com/bostonathenaeum/bettina-norton-a-foray-into-forgery-and-the-boston-athenaeums-role-in-exposing-it.

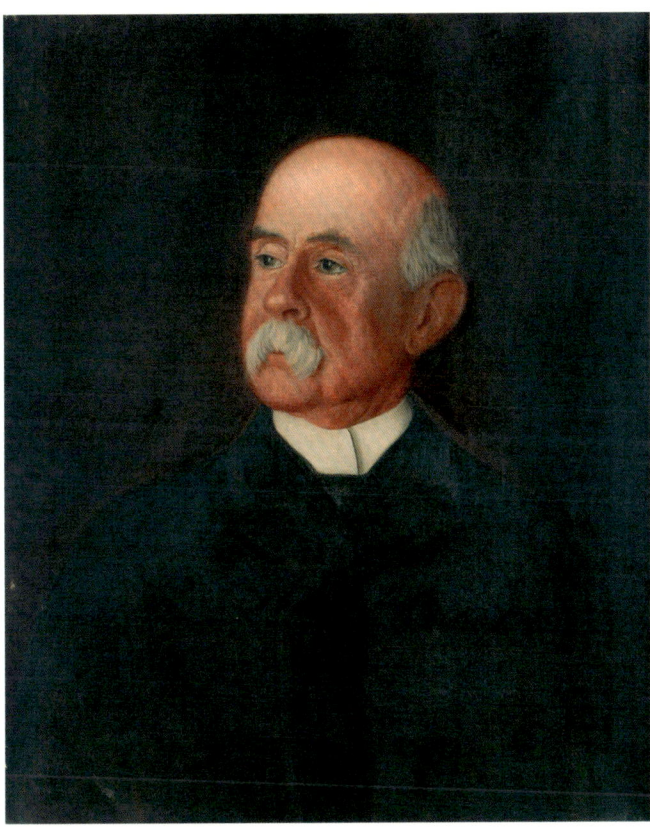

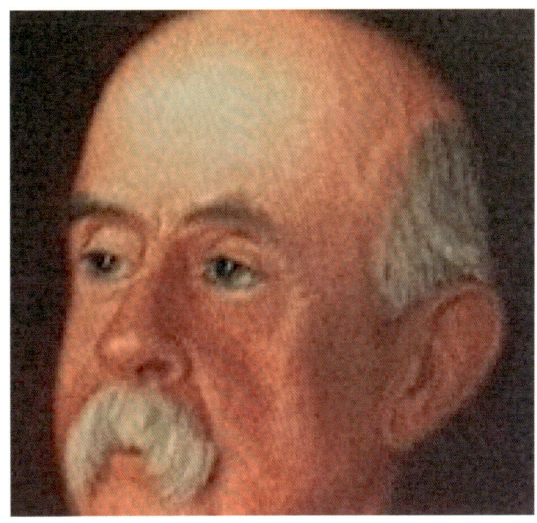

Charles Francis Adams
Oil on canvas by Baldwin Coolidge, circa 1911
Courtesy of the Massachusetts Historical Society,
Artwork 01.315. Photograph by Christopher Minty

Charles Francis Adams, detail of face, showing eyes
From the oil painting by Baldwin Coolidge
Courtesy of the Massachusetts Historical Society

with lively intellects—such as John Gibaut (Cat. 59), Thomas Barnard (Cat. 8), John Adams (Cat. 3), Edward Holyoke (Cat. 70), Joseph Lemmon (Cat. 85), and Samuel Curwen (Cat. 33)—and women with some sense of personal worth and independence—such as Abigail Adams (Cat. 2), Elizabeth Higginson Cabot (Cat. 23), Elizabeth Dabney (Cat. 39), Eunice Diman Mason (Cat. 90), Lydia Dodge (Cat. 50), and Hannah Paine (Cat. 101). Blyth's compelling portrait of Elizabeth Cabot shows her as a thoughtful, kindly, and charitable soul in her senior years. The Reverend Thomas Barnard's (Cat. 8) displays the gentle resoluteness that he used to defuse the confrontation between the British troops marching into Salem to uncover a cache of hidden arms and the colonists determined to keep them hidden that almost began the American Revolution.

The portrayal of character so evident in Blyth is not confined to facial characteristics. An assumed sense of superiority is portrayed in the poses of some figures such as the Unknown Man once known as Lt. Gov. Oliver (Cat. 145) and Peter Frye (Cat. 56), both Tories, or the Reverend Thomas Fitch Oliver (Cat. 99), disdainful of non-Anglicans, or, at the other end of the political spectrum, Thomas Melville (Cat. 92), Tea Party participant. Particularly striking is the pastel of the "wealthiest man in America" at the time, Elias Hasket Derby (Cat. 41), that shows a serene, gentle man, eager to portray his standing as an attentive businessman.

When Copley left for England in 1774, it would seem to have provided a clear market for Blyth, but soon, the American Revolution would disrupt society.

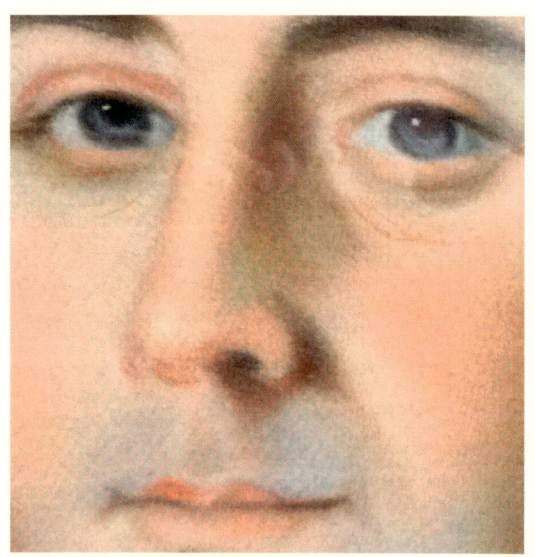

John Adams, details of eyes and nose
from the pastel by Benjamin Blyth

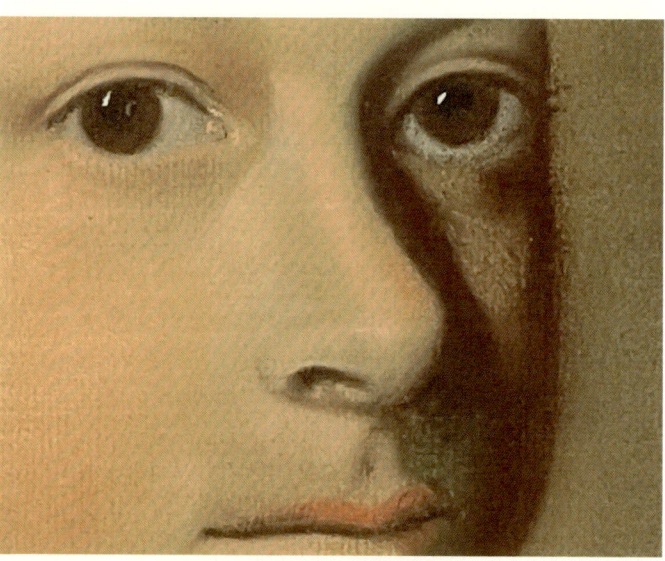

John Gibaut, detail of nose
from the pastel by Benjamin Blyth

THE interest in early American portraits is increasing rapidly, and the work of the pioneers in American art who left the only record we have of the features of our ancestors is now more appreciated than ever before. These portraits teach and encourage pride in ancestry and make the characters in our history real. Many of these portraits are more or less cracked, blistered or wrinkled. Others are dry and colorless from dirt or lack of varnish; backgrounds are lost, flesh color entirely unlike the work of the painter, perhaps the canvas torn or broken,— all owing to neglect. In nearly every case portraits may be restored without injury or in any way altering the work of the artist, by intelligent and careful attention. I am familiar with the technique and manner of nearly all the early American portrait painters, and am prepared to consult without expense with owners of old portraits as to their condition and advise with them as to what is necessary for their preservation. This work is done under my personal supervision and I have an extensive list of references.

FRANK W. BAYLEY.

Bayley pamphlet page offering restoration services, in Little Known Early American Portrait Painters, nos. 3, 4, or 5 (1915)
Courtesy of the Boston Athenaeum, Arthur and Charlotte Vershbow Rare Book Room, URQ5 .B34

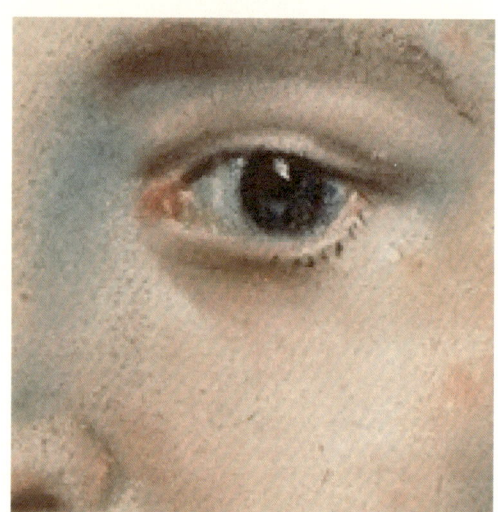

Hannah Paine, detail of eyes
from the pastel by Benjamin Blyth

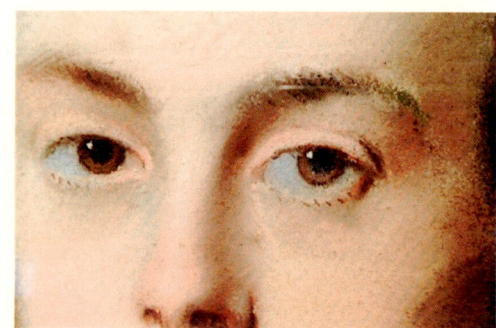

*Unknown man, formerly "Lt. Gov. Oliver,"
detail of eyes*
from the pastel attributed to Benjamin Blyth

PORTRAITS IN OILS

WHEN THE FRICK ART REFERENCE LIBRARY began cataloguing American portraits in the 1940s, only two oil portraits were attributed to Blyth—Benjamin Moses and his wife and child, Sarah and Betsy (Cats. 94, 95). When this study began, ten were attributed to Benjamin Blyth. Now there are five more. They are of two types, bust or half-figure and three-quarter-figure ending at mid-calf, which avoided the necessity of Blyth having to deal with the perspective of his subject's feet. All are also original compositions, except for the Reverend George Whitefield (Cat. 139), which was based on a print. Four are in the three-quarter-figure format and include an object or background view of biographical significance. The fifth one, although bust only now, was "cut from a larger canvas." Four of these newly attributed portraits have been in the collections of the Peabody Essex Museum for years but were never further catalogued. The other, known only in a book illustration, was destroyed in the Salem fire of 1914.

The number of surviving oil portraits that can be attributed to Blyth is small, compared to the number of pastels. Although there is only one oil portrait with a date—1781—it cannot be assumed he did not start painting in that medium until later in his career. One of his oils is of Dr. Ezekiel Hersey (Cat. 66), who died in 1770, and that of the Rev. George Whitefield was probably done from a print shortly after his death in the same year. So the mystery remains. A major determinant is the treatment of the faces. Those that have not been overpainted still show that Blyth was able to capture the personality of his sitters, as he did with his pastels. This discussion of the ten portraits already attributed to him will clarify the rationale for the addition of the five new ones. Perhaps it will also bring other possibilities to light.

*

PROBABLY THE BEST-KNOWN oil portraits by Benjamin Blyth are of Benjamin Moses and the companion portrait of his wife Sarah and child Betsy (Cats. 94, 95). That of Benjamin Moses is the one signed *and* dated—"B Blyth 1781." Despite the importance of this authentication, this portrait does not provide a good litmus test to his style, the key to making other attributions, because it suffered major paint loss and was heavily overpainted, especially on the face, and not to advantage. It also obscured the subtlety of character Blyth originally portrayed, and for which his portraits are valued.

The two oil portraits long attributed to Blyth, the small one of Dr. Hersey (Cat. 66) and the larger one of Whitefield (Cat. 139) prove more helpful for looking at Blyth's technique. Both portraits, the earliest known oils by Blyth, were painted around 1771, about a decade before the Moses portraits. Yet both show impressive facility in rendering details. Hersey's half-figure portrait also shows no damage or overpainting. His face is tight, almost schematic. The right eye is problematic with its faulty perspective, so that his head seems to float distinct from his body, and with the over-emphasis of the eye's solid black outline and iris. This problem with the distant eye is found frequently enough to be an identifying feature in many portraits by Blyth. However, Dr. Hersey's lace cuff is well rendered. The snuff box, also beautifully rendered, demonstrates that Blyth was able to handle metals like its brass end very well, beginning with his earliest oil portraits. Hersey's fingers, moreover, are rendered more anatomically convincing than those painted later for Moses.

The portrait of Whitefield has suffered overall damage of crackling paint and has been mended in several areas, though none occur on the main parts of the image. The eighteenth-century clergyman shown in the act of preaching was based on the then-popular British engraving of Whitefield by John Greenwood done in 1769 after a painting by Nathaniel Hone. Blyth did a creditable job of reproducing the print in oils, capturing the evangelist's pose and employing deft strokes, especially the elements in white paint—the cuff on his right arm, the left "preaching tab" of his clerical collar showing its folds and thickness, and the well-worn pages along with the delicate red on the edge of the cover of the Bible.

The portrait of "Nancy" Lane and child Betsy (Cat. 82) also is a better template because it had not suffered much if any damage, such as the early "restoration" of the Moses portraits or the all-over crackling in the Whitefield. Not only does the Lane portrait have the identical composition of Sarah Moses and baby Betsy, but it has every identifiable Blyth feature. The rattle held by Betsy also appears in several of Blyth's portraits of children. A similar rattle was used several times by Joseph Badger in his portraits of children, including Lois Orne, daughter of Salem's Timothy Orne, and Mrs. Jacob Hurd and child. Blyth's practice of companion portraits of a husband and wife holding a small, standing child on her lap begs the question that there may once have been a portrait of Nancy Lane's husband Nathaniel.

Blyth seems to have painted no other oils during the next few years, when he was either traveling with troops or acting as a privateer agent. Unlike the paraphernalia for pastels, those for oils usually involve a larger canvas and are therefore much more cumbersome, i.e., reasons why they are usually done in an artist's studio. He was certainly back in Salem by 1779. In the early 1780s, Blyth again painted three oil portraits that were bust or half-figure only on a neutral background, continuing the formula he used for the earlier oil of Hersey and in his pastels.

One was of Edward Lang (Cat. 83), a silversmith who joined Salem's Masonic Lodge on the same day, March 1, 1881, as Benjamin Blyth. Lang's wife's portrait (Cat. 84), currently unaccounted for, is inferred through the reference in Lang's account book at the Peabody Essex Museum and corroborated in a reference to the portraits of Edward and Rachel Lang in the checklist of a mid-twentieth-century exhibition of portraits in Iowa.

Two later portraits show improvement in Blyth's handling of the medium. The portrait of Deborah Prince Cary (Cat. 26), second wife of the Reverend Thomas Cary (Cat. 27) of Newburyport, is considered as one of Blyth's most successful. It shows more developed handling of the medium of oil, and the facial modeling is much improved. The other portrait, of Moses Brown— "Gentleman Brown" (Cat. 21)—is very similar in subdued palette, composition, and execution to Blyth's portraits of Edward Lang and Deborah Cary. Blyth has begun to solve his problem of the handling of the distant eye. The eyes are not as strongly outlined, although the distant one is still too large and not painted at an angle to indicate depth.

There are questions about the oil portrait of William Luscomb (Cat. 89) attributed tentatively to Benjamin Blyth. The figure of the young boy and the dog is credibly by Blyth, but the curving, truncated tree that frames one side of the painting is an image that his brother, Samuel, used repeatedly. And Samuel was known for his wit, as in the reference to the Pope couplet on the dog's collar. Given that Samuel was beginning to draw some pastel portraits at the time, it is conceivable that he added the background, especially the tiny cartoon-like horses in the Luscomb portrait that seem unlikely for Benjamin to have done. If so, Samuel was either helping out his brother by finishing the portrait or taking it over after his brother left town.

The five oil portraits newly attributed to Benjamin Blyth all share characteristics with these already attributed to him. The portrait of Gen. Stephen Abbot is unmistakably by Benjamin Blyth. It is the mirror image of the figure of Benjamin Moses, but Abbot is proudly attired in his militia uniform. The painting was destroyed in the Salem Fire of 1914, but fortunately it had been photographed just a few years earlier for the fourth volume of the Rev. William Bentley's published diaries.

The snuff box so beautifully rendered in the Hersey portrait aided in the identification of another husband-and-wife pair of oils of Benjamin and Sarah King and daughter Ann (Cats. 80, 81), in the collections of the Peabody Essex Museum. The silver box evinces similar skill to that shown in the telescope held by Benjamin King. The portraits also are the same compositional format as both the Lane and Moses portraits but have been subjected to some heavy-handed overpainting in red that obscures the modeling, the color, and the brush strokes, hindering the attribution to Benjamin Blyth.

Capt. Edward Allen's portrait (Cat. 4), also in the collections of the Peabody Essex Museum, was heavily worked on, but unlike the "restoration" on the Moses or the King portraits, it was done before it entered the collection, and competently. The additions of the eyelashes and the deft use of dark accents point to Baldwin Coolidge at Copley Gallery, who worked on a number of Blyth pastels. Indeed, a label pasted to the back of the portrait of Allen states, "This picture was/ RESTORED/ at the Copley Gallery/103 Newbury Street Boston/June 19–1916." The result was that Blyth was not considered as the possible artist. Again, however, there are signs of his work: the treatment of Allen's distant eye with the bulge, the lip line still visible under the restoration work, his ear, his stock, similar to that of Edward Lang, and the portrayal of his lively personality. Allen also was a likely subject; he was related through his wife to the Derbys, whose extended family accounted for twelve other portraits by Blyth.

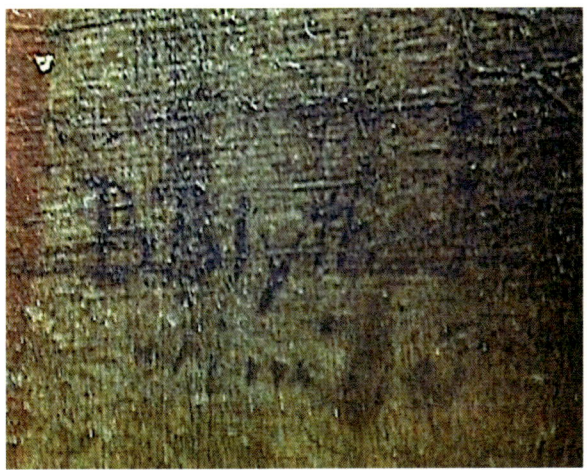

Blyth signature and date on oil portrait of Benjamin Moses by Benjamin Blyth

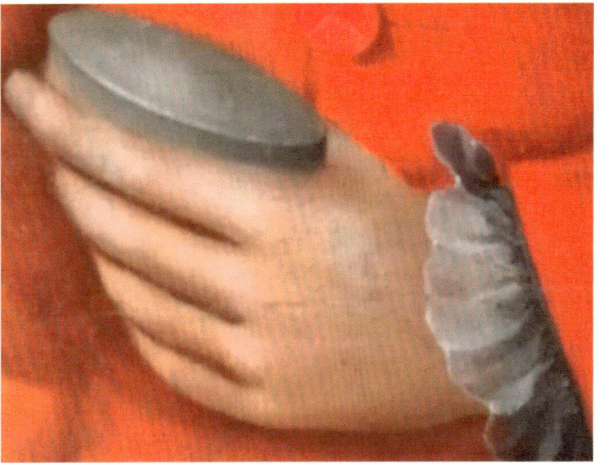

Ezekiel Hersey, detail of hand, cuff, and snuff box
from the oil portrait by Benjamin Blyth

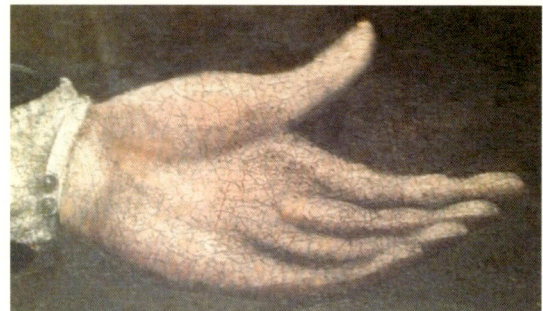

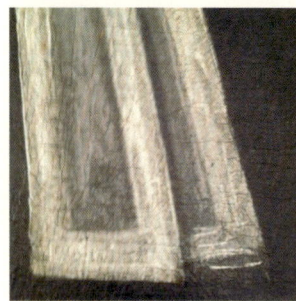

The Rev. George Whitefield, details of cuff and hand from the oil portrait by Benjamin Blyth

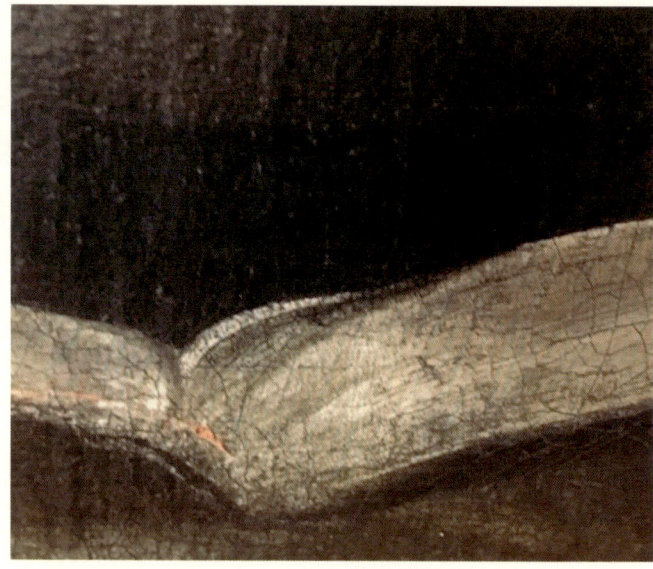

Detail of the Bible's well-worn pages from the oil portrait by Benjamin Blyth

The fourth previously unattributed portrait from the collections of the Peabody Essex Museum is of an unknown Revolutionary War officer credibly identified by arts and antiques dealer James Kochan as Gen. Henry Jackson. A further clue to the identity of Jackson as the subject is his pointing to what is now believed to be the location of the battle of Butts Hill, part of the August 1778 Rhode Island Campaign. The portrait, like that of Capt. Allen, was also extensively and competently restored throughout, which again obscured the identity of the artist. However, there are clues to Blyth: the out-of-perspective larger eye on the far side, the lip line (although altered), the cuff, and the pattern of buttons and folds of the vest, and the portrayal of character—the self-satisfied demeanor of Gen. Jackson (Cat. 79). Another clue is what looks like a fingernail (although this one is anatomically impossible). Blyth indicated fingernails, outlined in brown, in every oil portrait in which fingers appear, namely, in Dr. Hersey, Benjamin and Sarah King, Nancy Lane, Benjamin and Sarah Moses, and the Rev. George Whitefield.

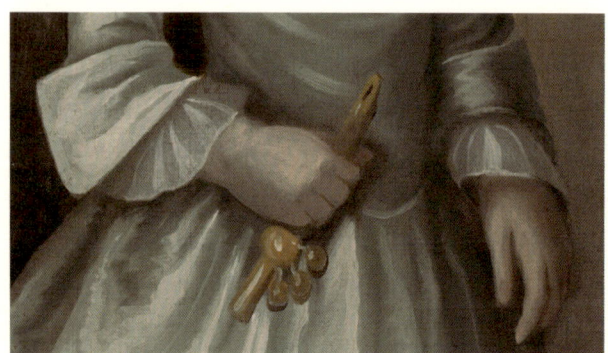

Lois Orne, detail of rattle
from the oil portrait by Joseph Badger, 1757
Courtesy of the Worcester Art Museum, Eliza S. Paine Fund in
memory of William R. and Frances T. C. Paine, 1971.102

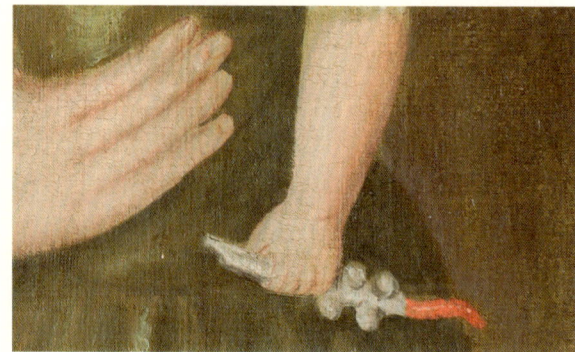

Nancy Lane and Betsy, detail of rattle
from the oil portrait by Benjamin Blyth

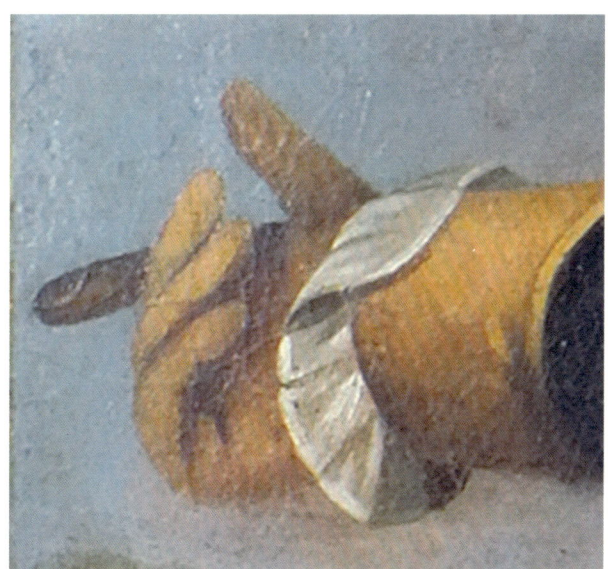

Gen. Henry Jackson, detail of hand
from the oil portrait attributed to Benjamin Blyth

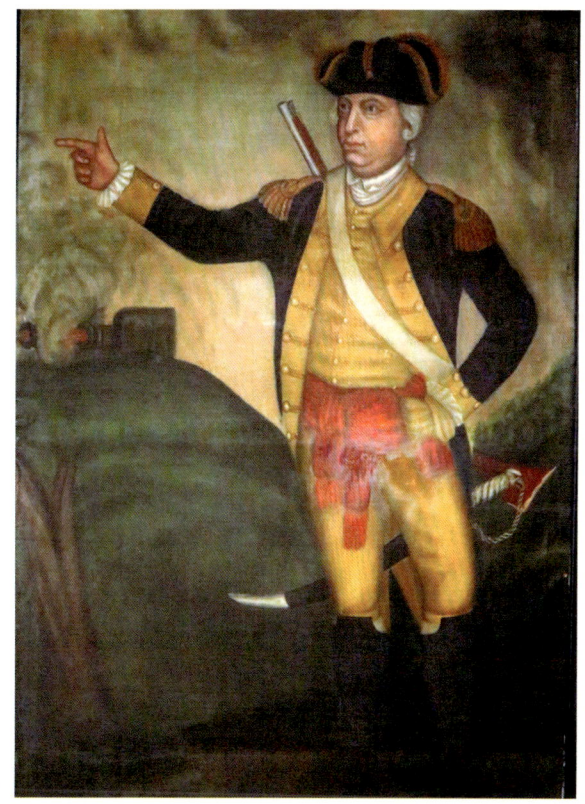

Gen. Israel Putnam, oil painting by an unknown artist
Courtesy Campus Martius,
Ohio History Connection H19180

Several portraits once thought to be possible oils by Benjamin Blyth are no longer considered so. One is the painting of Gen. Israel Putnam in the collections at Campus Martius, a satellite of the Ohio History Connection. Blyth provided the source for the rare mezzotint of Gen. Putnam, a major officer of the Revolution, but as the credit line reads "B Blyth del" and not "pinxit," it is unlikely that it was an oil and may simply have been a drawing, as was also probably the case for the less well-known print of George Washington he supplied for Hiller. In addition, the Campus Martius oil depiction of Putnam was based on the *second* state of the mezzotint, produced by Samuel Blyth, who had added a military tricorn hat with gold braid, sashes, and a rifle and altered the landscape. According to legend, the painting was taken to Ohio by the general's son, William Pitt Putnam, who had gone with his cousin Rufus Putnam to settle new lands in the Ohio country in 1795.[91] The painting, which measures 6 ft. 9 in. x 5 ft. 4 in., is said to have been cut into three pieces to make it easier to transport. This seemed implausible—it could simply have been rolled up, and in fact the upper of the supposed two "cuts" is actually a fold. The conclusion is that the original canvas depicted a three-quarter figure, and the bottom piece of canvas was sewn on to the original painting at a later time.

The main portion of the painting seems to have been done at one time and by one hand and shows no evidence of having been altered. It might have been done by Samuel at the request of

91. William Putnam was born in Pomfret, CT, in 1770 and lived in nearby Woodstock. He went twice to Ohio. The first trip began in December 3, 1787. It is more likely that he took the portrait on his second trip, with his family, in 1790.

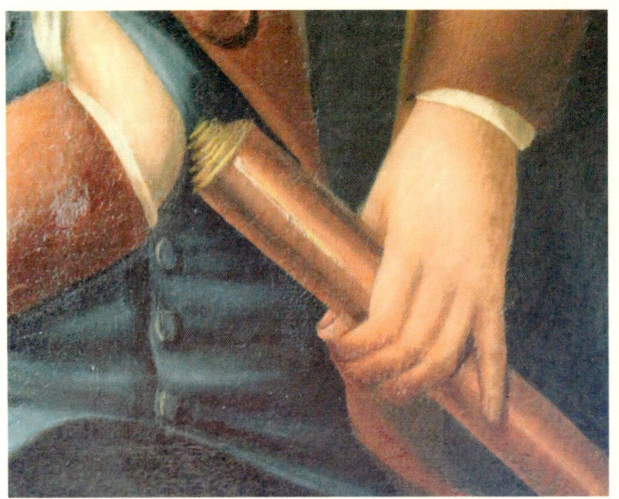

Benjamin King, detail of hands and telescope
from the oil portrait by Benjamin Blyth

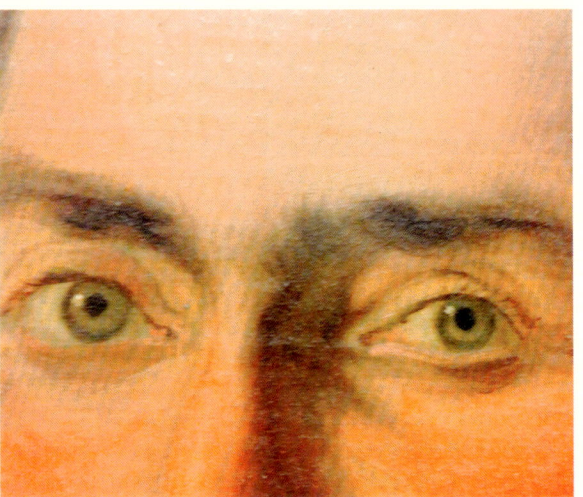

Capt. Edward Allen, detail of eyes
from the oil painting by Benjamin Blyth

the Putnam family, after he had issued his mezzotint. However, there is no known example of an oil portrait by Samuel Blyth. Neither of the two portraits in oil that for years were credited to Samuel, of the colonial Massachusetts governors John Endecott and Simon Bradstreet, is now believed to have been done by him, although it is suspected that he might have worked on two of the portraits credited to his brother. While it is a very faithful rendering of Samuel's version of the Benjamin Blyth mezzotint, the artist is still unknown.

Several portraits once thought to be by Benjamin Blyth are now considered to have been painted by other artists. In the 1980s, the three-quarter-figure portraits of Elisha Doane and Jane Cutler Doane in the collections of the National Gallery of Art were tentatively attributed to Blyth. There are indeed many similarities, especially in the face details. However, the treatment of fabrics and use of white accents is more skillful in Doane's portrait, greatly enhancing the volume of the figure, as well as details such as his hair. Also, the Doanes were from Cohasset, although that does not necessarily preclude Blyth from having painted them. Most cogently, the portraits could not have been done until after their marriage in 1783, by which time there is little evidence of Blyth still being in the area. So the attribution is dubious. A portrait believed to be of William Welstead Prout at the Historical Society of Old Newbury seems to be by the same artist who painted the Doane portraits and probably also dates from the mid–1780s. There may be others that have yet to be identified.

Any analysis of Benjamin Blyth's work in oils is hindered by the condition of so many of them, the meager documentation of any kind, and the difficulty of accounting for both the disparity in style and chronology of development of skills. His oil portraits do not measure up in technique to his work in pastels. His brush technique and skill at modeling facial features and hands improved (although the treatment of facial features remains distinctively his); but he was less skilled in this medium than in pastel. While this general conclusion is true, his portraits are unabashed character portrayals, a redeeming feature of his work, with no attempt at flattery. Despite some awkwardness of technique, Blyth's revelation of his sitters' character remains paramount.

MINIATURES

AFTER BLYTH SETTLED in Virginia, he took out an advertisement in *The Virginia Gazette* for July 19, 1786. "Benjamin Blyth, limner, informs the public he has opened a house near the City Coffee-House for the performance of limning in oil, crayons and miniature." If Blyth advertised himself as able to "perform" (as he put it) miniatures when he arrived in Virginia, he must have had some experience producing them earlier, in Salem. He did. There are two pieces of evidence for this. First, the Reverend Manasseh Cutler, minister of the Congregational Church in Ipswich, noted in his diary, "Jan. 25, 1782, Mr Bly drew the profile of Mrs. Cutler and myself in miniature."[92] However, they currently are unaccounted for, which therefore robs us of any matrix, as the George Cabot and Warren portraits provides for Blyth's pastels, or the Moses portraits presumably do for his oils. Second, an entry in the account books of the gold- and silversmith Edward Lang (Cat. 83) notes that in October 1781, he sold four lockets at three shillings apiece to Benjamin Blyth. Miniatures were encased in jewelry, either as brooches or pendants, or both. Blyth returned two of the lockets in 1783, leading one to believe that he might have used the other two for his miniature portraits of the Derbys (Cats. 42, 44).

There is ample evidence of the presence of miniatures in Salem at the time. Capt. Jacob Crowninshield paid silversmith Edward Lang for "Setting a Lockett in gold" in March 1770, and a month later, for "a stone Lockitt Edg'd with gold." Lang sold Miles Ward a small silver "broach" in August 1774. He mended a "Broach" for Maj. Joseph Sprague in 1779 and supplied his brother William in July 1783 with a locket and a double locket. Elias Hasket Derby also paid Lang "for mending a broach."[93] And John Gibaut's inventory at his death listed two "images with cases." The inventory of Joseph Hiller's estate after his death in Lancaster in 1814 mentions five miniatures, including one of him and one of his son. Hiller's time in Salem overlapped with Blyth for twelve or thirteen years, and they collaborated on several prints, so it is possible that the latter might have painted some of those miniatures (but not the one of Hiller's son, who was born in 1777).[94]

Boston portrait painter John Smibert made the first known miniature in the colonies, in 1734. It is believed to have been a copy of his three-quarter-length portrait of Samuel Browne; but Smibert is believed to have done only one or two others.[95] From the mid-1750s to the early 1770s, there were only three known artists doing miniatures in Salem or in the Boston area. Most prominent was John Singleton Copley, who painted a number of them between 1755 and 1761, although his interest seemed to have been revived in the late 1760s. His subjects included prominent Salem and Marblehead residents.[96]

---

92. *William Parker* Cutler, *The Life, Journals and Correspondence of Rev. Manasseh Cutler, L. L. D.*, 2 vols. (Cincinnati, Ohio: R. Clarke & Co., 1888), 1:89.

93. Edward Lang Account Book, MSS 1212, Phillips Library, Peabody Essex Museum.

94. The Hiller miniatures might have been done by one or another of the later miniaturists in Salem, before Hiller left in 1802. Or, less likely, they could have been done in Lancaster. A miniature of Joseph Hiller Jr. is in the PEM (Cat. #128, in *EIHC* 71:154-55).

95. Carol Aiken, "The Emergence of the Portrait Miniature in New England," *Annual Proceedings of the Dublin Seminar for New England Folklife* (Boston: Boston University Press), 1994, 41-42.

96. Harry B. Wehle, *American Miniatures, 1730–1850: One Hundred and Seventy-three Portraits Selected with a Descriptive Account*, (Garden City, NY: published for the Metropolitan Museum of Art by Doubleday, Page & Company,

However, just before the outbreak of the Revolution, Copley had permanently left the Boston area. The second miniature artist of the time was Copley's younger half-brother Henry Pelham.[97] But he produced a small number before he also left for England in 1776, and they are different—delicately drawn and not at all linear—from those attributed to Blyth. Charles Willson Peale, who also painted miniatures, visited Copley when he was in Boston in 1765.[98] Although no images of Salem sitters by Peale are known so far, his style also is distinctive and identifiable.

Miniature artist John Ramage was briefly in the Boston area in 1775–76, but as a Loyalist, he too left Boston for Halifax.[99] William Verstille (1757–1803) was painting miniatures during the Revolution. However, he did not appear in Salem until around 1790. "A Mr. Verstille has at present great fame & it is believed great success," Bentley wrote in October 1802.[100]

More miniaturists began to appear in Boston and Salem in the last decades of the eighteenth century. John Hazlitt advertised himself as a miniaturist in Salem in 1785. Bentley observed in his diary in November 1818 that his portrait had been done by "Haslitt [*sic*] . . . now celebrated in London." There must be other Salem sitters for Hazlitt, but none is known at this time. Another is "Henry W. Rogers. Flourished 1782, Salem/Miniature painter"; however, almost nothing is known of him.[101] Nathaniel Hancock also painted miniatures of Salem residents when he first arrived in Boston from England in 1792.[102] His dates, plus known images, make a clear case that Hancock is not the artist for the portraits attributed here to Benjamin Blyth. William M. S. Doyle

1927), 24. Wehle wryly noted about Copley that "most Boston miniatures, even up to 1790, [are] stoutly claimed for him . . ." as were ones in Charleston and New York, although he was not known to have done many there. This book is an excellent source for descriptions of the styles of the different miniaturists. Eight were attributed by Perkins to Copley, ten by Frank Bayley. Barbara Neville Parker and Anne Wheeler, in *John Singleton Copley: American Portraits in Oil, Pastel, and Miniature* (Boston: Museum of Fine Arts, 1938), suggested that nineteen miniatures previously listed as "attributed" to Copley were stylistically incompatible or not verifiable.

97. Wehle, *American Miniatures*, 26. The list includes Pelham miniatures seen from various sources includes Edward Holyoke, after Copley's portrait, 1760; Peter Chardon, (attr.), after a Copley pastel; Zechariah Hitchcock(?) (attr.) 1776; Mrs. Peter Oliver Jr., 1773; and Joseph Hooper, ca.1770, although Parker and Wheeler thought this one might have been done by Copley from the larger portrait. Wehle, 245.

98. Wehle, *American Miniatures*, 95, also Baker, *Engraved Portraits of Washington*, 11. Peale's brother James also was a prolific miniaturist, but he does not seem to have visited the Boston area.

99. Bolton, *Early Draughtsmen*, 57. Ramage, a goldsmith and engraver, also made his own frames.

100. Bentley, *Diary*, 2:452, 4:561. Verstille miniatures of Capt. John Carlton and John Dabney are at the Peabody Essex Museum, as are a number by Hancock. Verstille also painted the Boston and Salem publisher Thomas C. Cushing and his wife, the former Catherine Sewall Orne, Joshua Ward and his wife Susannah Holyoke Ward, Anstiss Stone, John Dabney, Jacob Crowninshield, and Mary Crowninshield Silsbee. Bentley noted that he had Verstille change the clothing on the miniature that had been done of him by Hazlitt. Indeed, miniature expert Dale T. Johnson considers that the Salem portraits by Verstille are among his best. Dale T. Johnson, *American Portrait Miniatures in the Manney Collection* (New York: Metropolitan Museum of Art, distributed by Harry N. Abrams, Inc., New York, 1990), 17. Verstille's method of drawing is unlike Blyth's. In all images seen to date, except one, the sitters face left. And at least ten are signed.

101. Theodore Bolton, *Early American Portrait Painters in Miniature*, 137, and *EIHC* 57:147-48. Miniature expert Edward Sheppard provided his full name: Henry W. Rogers. Felt lists notices in Salem newspapers for miniatures from Hancock (1805), Hazlitt (1785), Verstille, and Purinton (1802), 2:79-80.

102. Bentley, *Diary*, 4:561; Cutler, *Life, Journals*, 131; *EIHC* 57:147. Hancock's miniatures are found in the collections of the Peabody Essex Museum.

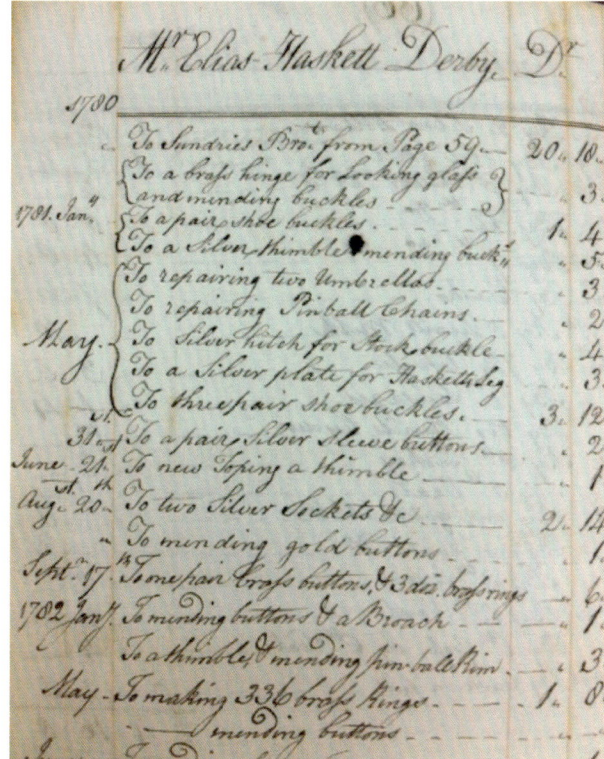

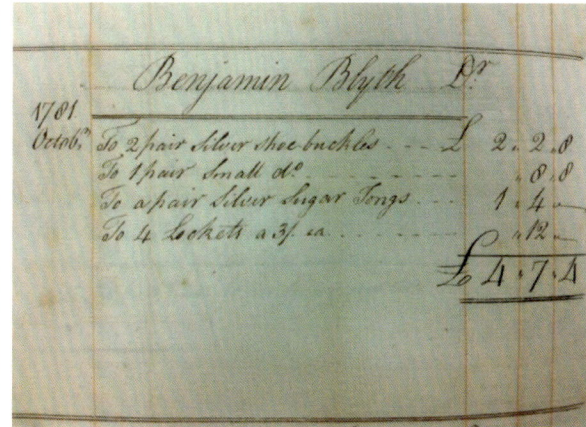

Lang Account Book, record for Benjamin Blyth,
Octob' 1781, showing purchase of four lockets
Courtesy of the Phillips Library, Peabody Essex Museum,
Rowley, MA

Lang Account Book, record for Elias Hasket Derby,
Aug. 20th 1781, for two "Silver Lockets &c"
Two lines below is the entry of Sept' 17th
that includes "3 doz. brafs rings"
Courtesy of the Phillips Library, Peabody Essex Museum,
Rowley, MA

(1769–1828) was working in Boston by 1796; all his miniatures, however, date from the first two decades of the nineteenth century.

Joseph Dunkerley (1752–1806) turned up in the Boston area in 1774. The son and grandson of London jewelers, he arrived in the colonies as a private in the British 38th Regiment of Foot but soon deserted, joining the Continental army and becoming an officer before finally resigning in 1778, in fear for his life as a previous member of the British forces.[103] His earliest known miniature, of William Gale, now at the Yale University Art Gallery, is signed and dated "ID/1776."[104] Although there is no direct evidence of Joseph Dunkerley living in Salem, he painted miniatures of Essex County residents Capt. George Smith of Salem, Elbridge Gerry and his wife, Ann (Thompson), of Marblehead, and Mrs. Joan Bartlett Titcomb of Newburyport. Dunkerley's name also was inscribed on the frame of the portrait of Mary (Mrs. George) Burroughs, probably a woman of that name from Haverhill, 1742/3–1823).[105] Most relevant to his likely presence in Salem, however, is that a "John Dunckley," presumably a son, was an apprentice to gunsmith Richard

---

103. Carrie Rebora Barratt, and Lori Zabar, *American Portrait Miniatures in the Metropolitan Museum of Art.* A miniature of James Dunkerley (1728–1802) suggests that he was the father of Joseph, but there is no recorded birth of a Joseph in England's VRs for that period. For an account of Dunkerly's life in the colonies, see Dan. N. Hagist, "He'd Rather Be Painting," *Journal of the American Revolution,* Feb. 21, 2014, on his website: allthingsliberty. com.
104. The sitter might be the William Gale who died in Cambridge on June 20, 1812, age sixty-five, would have been about thirty years old at the time of the portrait. G[rave] R[ecord] 3, (Mount Auburn Cemetery), [i. e., b. 1746–47]
105. Wehle, *American Miniatures,* 4, in an exhibition of miniatures at the Metropolitan Museum in 1927.

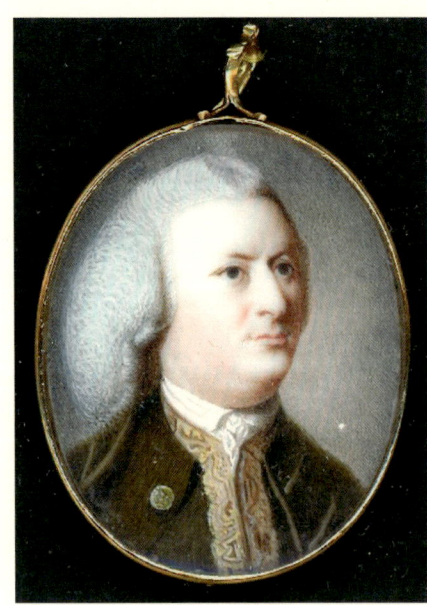

Jeremiah Lee
Miniature by John Singleton Copley,
ca. 1769
Courtesy of the Marblehead Museum,
Mrs. Mary L. Kinsman through her son,
Dr. Frederick J. Bryants, 1935.163

Manning in Salem from December 18, 1786 to January 2, 1787, according to the account book of Edward Lang, who provided schooling to the apprentice between those dates. John Dunkerley became a blacksmith and married Abigail Porter in 1794. Their son born in 1800 was named Joseph—the same name as the miniaturist. So John Dunkerley is presumed to have been his son.

Miniatures by Dunkerley have been said to have been mistaken for those of Copley,[106] but few images support that surmise. His technique was more linear and less modeled than Copley's, more akin to ones now attributed to Blyth. In fact, it seems likely that Blyth learned the technique from Dunkerley. Their miniatures have many similarities. The main stylistic difference can be summarized in the treatment of hair: for men, Dunkerley often used short, sharp, parallel strokes of gray, cascading from the crania of his sitters, and for women, he embellished them with a multitude of curls. Also, many of his men are portrayed with drooping shoulders. A critical difference between the two artists is the treatment of the sitters' character. Donald Shelton, an historian and a collector, has stated that Dunkerley "often had a sort of small, almost screwed up face, and included more of the body in the miniature."[107] Indeed, the facial expressions of almost all of his sitters seem placid to sweet—probably a not-unappealing characteristic that contributed to the artist's success, but

106. Bolton, *Early American Portrait Miniatures*, New York: Frederick Fairchild Sherman, 1921. 17. Bolton noted, however, because the *surfaces* are different—copper or ivory— the *technique* is not the same. Once washes are laid, they cannot be altered; because the surface takes so long to dry and care must be shown in placing the paint, miniaturists used both cross-hatching and stippling. The artist must be especially careful not to touch the surface (a caveat that applies as well to drawing on a lithographic stone). These difficulties could be learned; in fact, a number of the practitioners were self-taught. And because of the nature of the medium, the images might have suffered from surface damage, but they would not have been tampered with; the artist's style would be there to analyze.
107. Email from Shelton to the author, Sept. 2016. Some unattributed Salem miniatures that contain many of the similar characteristics of Blyth and Dunkerley probably now can be attributed to the latter, on the basis of their later dates of execution, after Blyth had left town. These include Joseph Cabot and Capt. Robert Hale Ives, at the Peabody Essex Museum (though the subjects' biographies also raise questions on both their identities and possible dates of execution), and Capt. William Gray, at the Massachusetts Historical Society. The miniature of Dr. Thomas Kast, once thought to be a Copley, could be by either Blyth or Dunkerley. (The name appears in several variations of spelling.) Some miniatures that are signed with JD (for Dunkerley) might in fact be "altered" Blyths. Dealers know that a work of art credited to a specific artist is more valuable than one by an anonymous painter. Email from Shelton to the author, Oct. 2016: "[T]he collector and dealer, Edward Grosvenor Paine . . . had a reputation, among dedicated miniature experts (a very limited field!), for having added signatures to early American, and other miniatures. See the discussion of Paine (1911–1989) on Shelton's website, where he notes, "Modern opinion does not always agree with his attributions, hence signed American miniature need to be approached with caution."

but not one associated with Blyth's depictions of his sitters' more discernible personalities. A comparison of the Dunkerley miniatures of Mr. and Mrs. Ebenezer Pemberton at the Yale University Art Gallery show more benign personalities than suggested in the Copley pastels of them at the Harvard Art Museums, on which they were based. By 1787, Dunkerley had moved to Jamaica, established his miniature business, and died there in 1806.[108]

The technique for painting miniatures is different from that used for oil or pastels. Meticulous work is done with brushes holding a small number of bristles that come to a sharp point, to paint very thin lines. It is a painstaking process. Miniaturists also were often skilled in making mezzotints.[109] This is an intriguing additional factor in considering whether Blyth was involved in that aspect of the process, although nothing has been discovered to suggest or corroborate this.

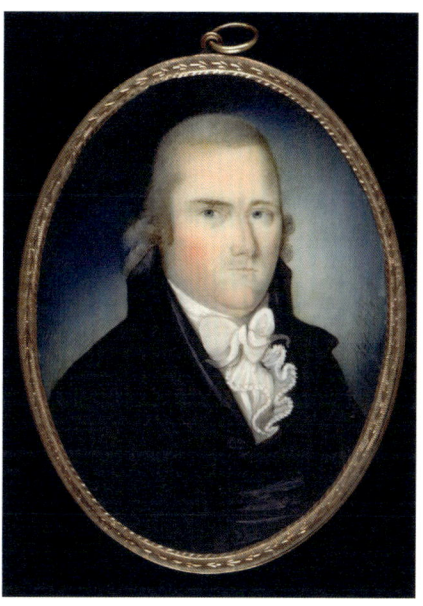

Capt. Robert Lillibridge
Miniature by William Verstille, signed, ca. 1795
Courtesy of the Smithsonian Institution
National Museum of American Art,
1975. 59. 1

The characteristics of miniatures that might prove attributable to Blyth are similar to those seen in his pastels. Frederic Fairchild Sherman observed in 1920 that "most of the artists were painters of portraits in oil as well—and a painter's mannerisms are so much a part of himself that they remain essentially the same on the smallest ivory as on the largest canvas."[110] For Blyth, these are: brown lip line of unvarying thickness, prominent ear askew from proper perspective, eyes that are the same size despite one being further away, lack of interest in depicting hair, delicate strokes and dots that indicate edges of lace, tinting of the background that is lighter on the face side of the figures. He also was able to convey his interest in personality.

Several criteria for attributing some miniatures to Blyth are relevant. One is the subjects' biographical information and therefore probable dates of execution. Another is size. Blyth began producing miniatures in the late 1770s to early 1780s, when the ivories or copper bases were on average no more than an inch-and-a-half or so, either dimension. Cases would be another clue, although a number of the miniatures either were given later cases (like those for the Derbys, in later, ill-fitting wooden frames) or now lack them. A fourth factor is consistency or orientation;

108. Notebook of Edward Lang, Phillips Library, Peabody Essex Museum. The only other Dunkerley (Dunklee) family in Massachusetts was in Danvers. That some of the Dunkerley family might have remained in the Salem area is suggested by the reference to a John "Duncklee" apprenticed to a gunsmith, Richard Manning, in Salem in 1786–87 and 1789, when he was a teenager and attended Edward Lang's night school. A John "Dunkley," presumably the same one, married Abigail Porter on July 15, 1794, in Salem, and his child who died there at the age of one month, in 1800, was named Joseph *Dunkerley* (John's father's name). In addition, a Sarah "Dunkelly" was married in Salem in 1784, and Elizabeth Deliverance Dunkly in 1788. The Dunkerley surname, even with its variant spellings, was extremely rare in the colonies at the time.

109. Dale T. Johnson, *American Portrait Miniatures in the Manney Collection,* (New York: Metropolitan Museum of Art, distributed by Harry N. Abrams, Inc., New York, 1990), 15.

110. Frederic Fairchild Sherman, *Early American Portraiture,* (New York: Privately printed, 1930), 20.

miniaturists generally painted their subjects from the same angle. The Cutler miniatures being in profile does not preclude that all other miniatures attributed to Blyth so far are three-quarter-facing portraits. Although this was the format for most of his pastels, he did draw Dr. Holyoke and his wife as well as Samuel Curwen in profile. The miniature of Francis Cabot, although now known only in a poor book illustration, is still useful for showing identifiable Blyth elements. Its case also provides a key to the type that Blyth probably used: a simple metal case, with plain loop at the top, perpendicular to the wearer's chest so that the case would lie flat. Miniature expert Elle Shushan, in emails to the author in November 2021, agreed that the miniatures of Francis Cabot and John Glover could be by Blyth, although she attributes the cases for them to Dunkerley. This is credible if the two artists worked together, as is posited here. She also felt that the miniature of the Rev. Samuel Parker has Blyth attributes.

So far, fourteen miniatures can be attributed to Benjamin Blyth, some tentatively. There could be more, including one of Elizabeth (Safford) White in the collections of the Peabody Essex Museum that is currently not located. Another missing miniature, of Abijah Northey, exhibited at the Museum of Fine Arts and cited by Parker and Wheeler as a questionable Copley, might also prove to be by Blyth. Northey was a friend of the Blyth family and Benjamin did draw a pastel of him (Cat. 97). Other unattributed miniatures may also turn out to have been painted by Blyth.[111]

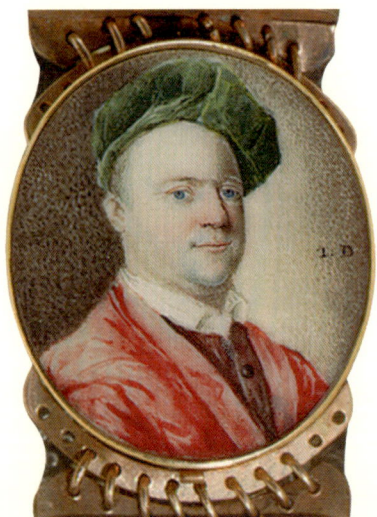 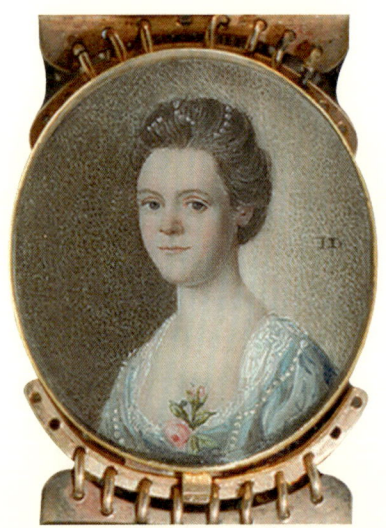

Ebenezer Storer
Miniature by Joseph Dunkerley, signed, 1785
Courtesy of the Yale University Art Gallery, 1949.96

Elizabeth Green (Mrs. Ebenezer) Storer
Miniature by Joseph Dunkerley, signed, 1785
Courtesy of the Yale University Art Gallery, 1949. 97

The recovery of the missing miniatures of the Reverend Manasseh Cutler and his wife would assist in substantiating all the attributions to date and further differentiate Blyth's work from Dunkerley's. They might help clarify attributions to other artists, including Verstille and Hancock.[112] However, the "science" of attribution remains an imperfect one.

---

111. Two from the list in Parker and Wheeler, *Copley,* 260, that are "Attributed": Christopher Bartlett and Daniel Dunbar, are suggested as possible Dunkerleys.

112. The portraits of Capt. Nathaniel West and Elizabeth (Crowninshield Derby) West, once thought to have been

CONCLUSION

BENJAMIN BLYTH created an extensive visual record of the residents of Essex County in the late eighteenth century, leading up to and into the early years of the American Revolution. He was the only artist of the time to depict so many people from a single region in the American colonies. He made portraits not only of the predictable ship owners and maritime traders of Salem, but also mariners, artisans, tavern owners, widows, clergy, Masons, Quakers, teachers, and the area's lively intelligentsia. There also are portraits of infants and young children.

The biographies in the catalogue are drawn from public and family records as well as many references sources such as the diaries of the Reverend William Bentley. They provide an overview of each sitter's life as part of an evolving community: their interconnections and mutual acquaintances, their inter-family marriages, their roles in the American Revolution and the family rifts caused by it, the organizations they belonged to and supported, the tragedies or successes of their lives—stories that lend much flavor to understanding these individuals and a tumultuous period in which they lived.

Blyth garnered support from several leading families of Essex County. Elias Hasket Derby's extended family accounted for thirteen; five were done for the Cabot and Curwen families; and descendants of the Reverend John Rogers (1666–1745), of the First Church of Ipswich—the Rogers, Homans, Babson, and Somes families—account for six. In addition, Blyth received commissions to copy several ancestral portraits.

The research for this book has yielded many more portraits as part of Benjamin Blyth's oeuvre. When work began, fifty-nine were attributed to him, some tentatively. A few of those have been eliminated, but two-and-a-half times that number are now added. However, there probably are more, yet to be discovered. Some portraits were likely destroyed in fires or floods or through neglect, while other portraits, unsigned, traveled with their families to other parts of the country and may have lost their identity along the way. Others may be still unattributed because Blyth neither signed his name nor used a monogram, as did John Singleton Copley. Yet Blyth drew or painted many portraits while Copley was still in the area.

Copley's portraits are admired as much for his handling of fabrics and flesh as they are for the names of the sitters. He was successful at "emulating the elegance and charm of London portrait painters."[113] However, as has been observed by American historian Simon Schama, "Inescapably, every portrait is the product of a three-way negotiation between what the subject imagines they look like, the artist's unstoppable urge to complicate that self-image, and the expectations of whoever ends up living with the result."[114] Copley seems to have understood this, in that he would "complicate" the images by surrounding the women in his portraits with complimentary sky-blue backgrounds, emphasizing their luxurious dress, and de-emphasizing their physical imperfections, in the effort to please his patrons.

---

painted by Malbone, are listed in the Smithsonian Institution Research Information System as possibly by William Lovett. An unidentified sitter, once attributed to Hancock, now has been attributed to Dunkerley.

113. E.P. Richardson, *Copley's New York Portraits*, Winterthur Portfolio Vol. 2 (1965), The University of Chicago Press, 1–13.

114. Simon Schama, *The Face of Britain; A History of the Nation Through Its Portraits*, "Pre-face," xx.

In contrast, Blyth's portraits do not convey elegance and charm. He did devote attention to such elements as colorful costumes and lace, but his vital contribution is that he conveyed the sitter's character as he read it. John Gibaut (Cat. 59) is seen as a serious young scholar. The Reverend Thomas Barnard (Cat. 8) wears his heart on his sleeve. Elizabeth Cabot (Cat. 23) is suffering from the loss of her husband. John Somes (Cat. 120) looks as if he had a hidden agenda. Hannah Paine (Cat. 101) is coquettish. Samuel Curwen (Cat. 33) is curmudgeonly, strait-laced and opinionated. Elias Hasket Derby, despite his wealth, seems more concerned with recording his accountability—on financial as well as moral grounds. Joseph White (Cat. 138), whom the Reverend Bentley disdained for his lack of concern about trading in slaves, is seen as unpleasant, if not nasty.

Blyth's output declined as the Revolution progressed. As soon as it was over, Salem quickly recovered and began to trade once again, establishing a reputation in faraway China that it was a country unto itself. Bentley's diary continued to be peppered with requests for prayers for men at sea or lost on voyages. In this fruitful period, Salem residents amassed large fortunes in the China trade and started the East India Marine Society, now the Peabody Essex Museum, to exhibit the exotic items they brought back from voyages. The townspeople built Federal mansions, many designed and embellished by local architect Samuel McIntire. Salem was enjoying great wealth, but by then Benjamin Blyth had already left.

Blyth's own story remains a mystery. We know nothing of his own concerns, interests, or attitudes, beyond a few tentative assumptions. He does not seem to have drawn his own portrait, nor any of his family. He left no letters or other writing. He is rarely mentioned in the accounts and diaries of the time. Perhaps more information about Blyth himself will come to light. Blyth's reputation also has suffered over the years because he was not as good a painter as Copley. Nonetheless, Blyth was a skilled observer. The nineteenth-century Scottish historian and essayist Thomas Carlyle noted, "A good portrait, even an indifferent one if none better can be found, is as a lighted candle with which to read biography."[115] Blyth provided "a lighted candle" not only to inform us of what the sitters looked like or their standing in society but to provide glimpses into their personalities. His portraits are his legacy.

---

115. quoted in Oliver, *Windows on the Past*. Carlyle was a major contributor to the establishment of the National Portrait Gallery in London and in Edinburgh.

THE CATALOGUE

THE MAIN CATALOGUE of people listed as definitively portrayed by or attributed to Benjamin Blyth includes 153 portraits—pastels, oils, miniatures, and prints, dating from around 1765 to 1783. Every effort has been made to present the subjects as individuals, not simply art objects. Careful checking revealed that some data on the sitters provided by donors, institutions, and dealers was incomplete or erroneous—for instance, when artists and/or sitters were incorrectly identified or descendants mixed up generations or branches of a family in their attributions, so additional research was called for. Town Vital Records were the main source for much biographical information. Nonetheless, the identity of some portrait subjects could not be ascertained. Also, the current locations of forty-two of them of them are still not known. Five are known through copies of the lost originals, and some are documented through photographs, but for seven of them, there is no image at all. They are known through references or other related documentation. In a few cases, it was not possible to view the objects or obtain additional information. It must be noted that, when appropriate or possible, institutions or private owners were consulted about suggested changes.

Dates of portraits have been estimated by biographical information on the sitter and their costumes, other written records, and provenance. For example, dating by costume can be later, but not earlier, than a new look. However, for various reasons a sitter might stick with his or her wardrobe and not adopt the fashion trends. For women in the mid-to-late 1760s, bodices were v-necked, and gossamer shawls called "handkerchiefs" covered shoulders and chest. Scoop-necked dresses edged with fine lace, often with a small bow centered at the front, were introduced around 1770. In some portraits of the 1770s, women are still wearing handkerchiefs, but by then they are simply draped over shoulders. Hair fashions such as a very high head dress, often stuffed with wire underpinning and ornamented with strands of pearls and fabric flowers, indicate that the portrait could not have been done before the very late 1760s, and more commonly, the early 1770s. For men, clothing from 1765 to the early 1770s consisted of a waistcoat and a coat with no collar. Buttons were commonly plated or woven; shirts had ruffles at bosom and cuffs. Collars and lapels are seen by the mid-1770s, with the high coat collar coming into fashion in the late 1770s. Wigs generally went out of favor after 1770, although traditionalists continued to wear them, and gradually, men adopted the fashion of tying their hair in a queue or tying it behind their back with a ribbon (usually black). The uniforms for officers in the American Revolution can also be dated.

At least twelve husband-and-wife companion portraits were drawn or painted by Blyth. Most were done in the conventional manner, to be hung as "pendants" slightly facing each other. However, he occasionally veered from the accepted format. The portraits of Elias Hasket and Elizabeth Derby, Dr. Edward Augustus and Mary Holyoke, or possibly Samuel and Abigail Curwen, among the most illustrious couples of Salem at the time, do not complement each other.

The main catalogue is followed by three additional lists: Possible Attributions, including recorded but unseen pastels; Possible Sitters, primarily spouses of known sitters for whom there is no identified portrait; and Dubious Attributions, portraits previously attributed to Blyth but considered too uncertain to assign to either Benjamin or Samuel. Historian Henry Wilder Foote wrote in his article on Blyth for the Massachusetts Historical Society in 1957 that "he may easily have drawn two or three times as many" as he had found. Foote also wrote that his attributions were arrived at "with varying degrees of assurance." His first assumption is fulfilled here, and his reservation also holds with this publication, along with the hope that it engenders future discoveries.

A note on provenance: The order followed is given from current owner backwards, i.e., in reverse chronological order. In the citations of sources, when authors have more than one work in the bibliography, key words from the relevant title are used. For works not listed in the Bibliography, full citations are given. Commonly used references, abbreviated or simplified, include:

Bentley: *The Diary of William Bentley, D. D.*
EIHC: Essex Institute Historical Collections
EIMS: *Portraits of Members of the East India Marine Society Salem, Massachusetts*
FARL: Frick Art Reference Library Photoarchives
HNE: Historic New England
Jeffares: Jeffares, pastellists.com/Articles/Blyth.pdf
MFA: Museum of Fine Arts, Boston
MHS: Massachusetts Historical Society
NEHGS: New England Historic Genealogical Society
PEM: Peabody Essex Museum
Sibley: *Biographical Sketches of Graduates of Harvard University . . .*
SIRIS: Smithsonian Institution Reference Information System
VR: Vital Records, by individual towns
WPA: American portraits, 1620–1825 found in Massachusetts, National Portrait Survey

[1]

Stephen Abbot (1749–1813)

Benjamin Blyth, 1779–80
Oil painting, probably 47½ x 35½ in.
Destroyed; owned in 1914 by Charlotte A. Chase, Salem, MA

The portrait of Gen. Stephen Abbot was lost in the Great Salem Fire of 1914 that destroyed more than 1,300 buildings. Fortuitously, the portrait had already been photographed for the first edition of the Reverend William Bentley's diaries that was published later that year.

Abbot was born in Andover, Massachusetts, in 1749 to Stephen Abbott [*sic*], yeoman, and Mary (Abbot). His father, at his death in 1768, left to his "Well Beloved Son" Stephen a large part of his land including his house. On September 24, 1769, Abbot married Sarah Crow, who had been born in England. They had seven children but lost the three youngest ones to "throat distemper" in November 1787. Their only surviving son Josiah Fisk, who suffered from epilepsy, died on March 30, 1899, at the age of thirteen. Two of their daughters married Quakers. Abbot's wife Sarah died on April 14, 1805, at age fifty-five, and in November, he married Mary Badger of Dunstable, New Hampshire.

Before the American Revolution, Abbot was a hatter in Salem, and after the war, he kept "a little shop in Church Street, which soon became a Grocery & from which he acquired a very handsome estate" north of St. Peter's Church, of which he was a member. As a captain in the 11th Massachusetts Regiment during the Revolution, he participated in the battles of Ticonderoga, Bennington, Stillwater, and West Point. Bentley credited him with beginning "the military reputation of the town." After the war he became head of the Second Corps of Cadets and rose to major general in 1797. The militia company served as George Washington's bodyguard during his visit to Salem in October 1789, and Abbot entertained him at his home, for tea.

At the time, Abbot lived in the former Assembly House on Federal Street, now owned by the Peabody Essex Museum. Abbot also founded The Voluntary Guard to protect residents from "suspicious persons" in the east part of town. A devoted military man, he loved ceremony and frequently hosted dinners for fellow Masons and members of the Fire Club in his "Hall."

Abbot served as warden of St. Peter's Church from 1785–87 and 1890–92, although he was not on the vestry at the same time as Samuel Blyth. Abbot also served as a pallbearer for the funerals of John Fisk (Cat. 52) and John Gibaut (Cat. 59). At Abbot's death on August 9, 1813, he was buried with Masonic honors in St. Peter's burial yard. His considerable estate included his mansion house and several other buildings, including his Potash Estate and stables. Bentley wrote of him, "He was very corpulent & very severely affected by the gout, which in the end put an end to his life, aet. 64. He was of an easy temper, firm but not very active. He held many town offices with great integrity, but was much loved in his office of Overseer of the Poor (22 years)."

He and his wife lost three sons to early deaths, but three daughters survived to adulthood. Betsy

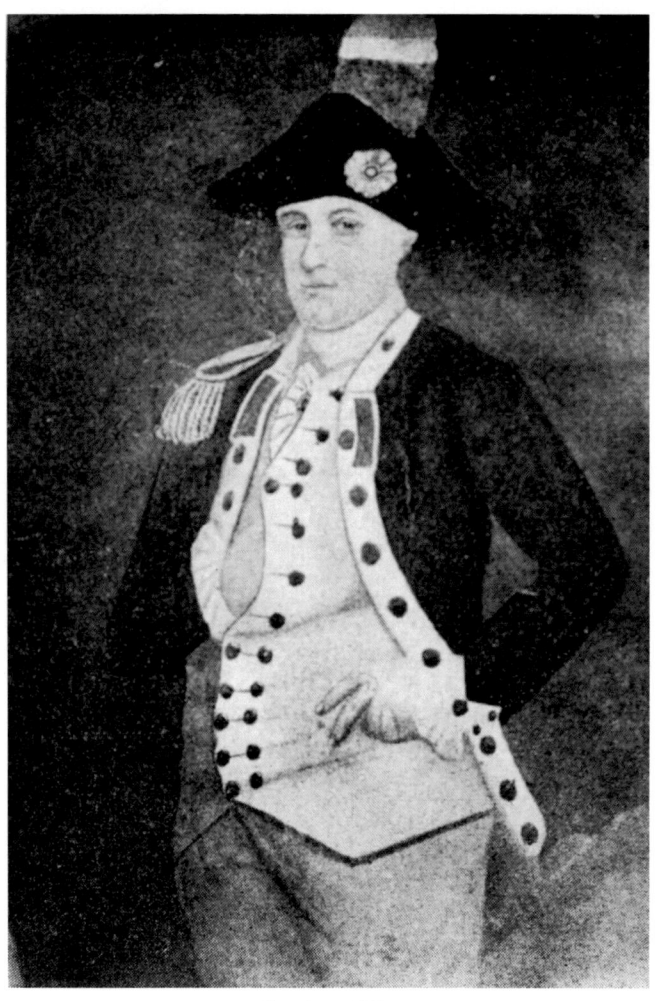

Stephen Abbot
Photograph of destroyed oil painting attributed to Benjamin Blyth,
1779–80
Illustration from *Diary of William Bentley*, 4:65
Courtesy of the Boston Athenaeum

(Betsey) married Henry Chase in 1801, and their son, George, born in 1803, was the father of Charlotte A. Chase, donor of the portrait of her great-grandfather.

This portrait, known for many years as "American School," is the mirror image of Blyth's 1881 portrait of Benjamin Moses. Because Abbot is portrayed in the dress uniform adopted by Congress in 1779, the portrait probably was painted shortly thereafter; the uniform became associated with the Cadets. Barely discernible from the early photograph, the background of the portrait seems to indicate a strip of horizontal landscape. A copy of the portrait was made in the nineteenth century by George Southward. However, the face is inferior to Blyth's depiction and the epaulet was changed. Once owned by the Armory of the Salem Cadets, the Southward copy was reproduced in Harriet Tapley's book, *St. Peter's Church before the Revolution* (1944). Now missing, it is recorded in the FARL photo archives.

Abbot Family Genealogy
Bentley 1:130,131,195, 215, 237; 2:88, 97, 217, 333, 358, 359; 3:151; 4:64–65, 186–7, illus. opp. 65
EIHC 6:162, 73:172, cat. 3; 75:54
FARL, American School, Massachusetts (1751–1800) 121–11b
Jeffares
SMS Plate 1
Tapley, *St. Peter's Church,* illus. opp. 64
WPA 2

[2]
Abigail Adams (1744–1818)

Benjamin Blyth, probably 1766
Pastel on paper, 22½ x 17½ in. (57 x 44.3 cm.), Samuel Blyth frame
Massachusetts Historical Society Artwork 01. 026, gift of John Adams, 1957; the Adams family

Abigail was born on November 22, 1744, to the Reverend William Smith (Cat. 119) pastor of the North Parish Congregational Church in Weymouth, Massachusetts, and Elizabeth (Quincy) Smith. In 1759, Abigail met John Adams when he accompanied his friend Richard Cranch on a visit to the Smith household. Cranch was courting Abigail's older sister Mary, whom he later married. Adams married Abigail on October 25, 1764, when she was a month short of twenty. They first lived in the Adams farm in Braintree, but by 1768 moved to a rented house in Boston as Adams developed his law practice. Over the next ten years, six children were born: Abigail, in 1765; John Quincy, 1767; Susanna, 1768; Charles, 1770; Thomas Boylston, 1772; and Elizabeth, (stillborn), 1777. Abigail managed the household and the family farm when John was away, especially when the British Siege of Boston was worsening and when he was in Philadelphia during the Second Continental Congress. They corresponded regularly, and these oft-quoted letters are part of the voluminous Adams Family Papers at the MHS.

Abigail and her sister Mary Cranch visited each other often, and the portraits of Abigail and John were probably done in late August or early November 1766, when he attended the Essex Court and Abigail traveled with him to Salem to stay with the Cranches, who were living there at the time. However, their son John Quincy Adams in a letter of August 7, 1839, wrote "Mrs. Greenleaf has two Portraits in Crayons, of my father and mother, which belong to me. They "were taken in the year 1765, just after the birth of my sister Abigail." Henry Wilder Foote wrote, "her face . . . is full of intelligence and vitality," as did the late Bernard Bailyn, Professor of Early American History at Harvard, quoted at the beginning of the essay on pastels.

The Reverend William Bentley's diary provides two contrasting opinions of Abigail. On March 10, 1787, he wrote, " . . . from the indecent behavior of Mrs. Adams at the Court, & the known character of Adams, I thought it best to abandon all connections with them About thirty years later, however, he wrote a rich, fulsome obituary of Abigail, who died on October 28, 1818, a month short of her seventy-fourth birthday:

> We have had notice of the death of Abigail, wife of the late President John Adams, who is still living at his home in Quincy . . . The first time I ever saw Madam was at her own house shelling her beans for a family dinner to which without any ceremony or apology she invited me but from engagements I did not accept. I saw her repeatedly at her own house to which without any impression unfavourable to her person or manners. I found a freedom in conversation which took its familiar topics. When at my own house in Salem she left the kind opinion of a respect for herself adapted to make her courtesy & conversation more valuable

& agreeable. She was in appearance of middle size, in the dress of the matrons who were in New England in my youth. . . . Everything the best but nothing different from our wealthy & modest citizens. She was possessed of the history of our country & of the great occurrences in it. She had a distinct view of our public men & measures & had her own opinions which she was free to disclose but not eager to defend in public circles. She had the vigour of a firm constitution & seemed designed for great old age. Her children are of disproportioned genius. . . . Mr. Adams always appeared in full confidence, but that of an equal & friend who had lived himself into one with the wife of his bosom Her grandson recalled that, in retirement years, "her cheerful nature 'enlivened the small social circle around her."

Early labels pasted to the back of the portraits of Abigail and John Adams credit them to "Blythe, 1763 (English Artist)." Exhibited at the Metropolitan Museum, New York, and the Fogg Art Museum in 1935–36 as by Benjamin Blyth, they remained in the Adams family until given to the MHS in 1957. The United States Bicentennial Society's 1974 "Patriot Series," issued the Blyth likeness of Abigail Adams in color on a porcelain plate with gold edges.

Both Adams portraits were treated on versos with light misting of non-aqueous basic solution to buffer slightly and reframed using archival materials to replace disintegrating wood backing, probably in the 1980s.

Adams, Charles Francis, *Works of John Adams*, 2:198–201

Adams Papers, MHS, letter from JQA, 7 Aug 1839

Bayley, *Little Known . . . Portrait Painters*, unpaginated

Bentley, 1:57; 4:556–57

Bolton, *Portrait Draughtsmen*, 7

Century Magazine (April 1889), xxxvii, 853

Cole, "Limned by Blyth," 331

Dictionary of American Biography 1 (1928): 35

FARL, Blyth, Benjamin 158-3i

Foote, "Blyth," 63–65, 67, 69–70, 82 ("Mrs. John Adams")

Grant, *John Adams, Party of One*, 70

Jeffares, http://www.pastellists.com/Articles/Blyth.pdf

Norton, "Brothers Blyth," 61

Old-Time New England, 26 (Jan. 1936): 93

Oliver, *Portraits of John and Abigail Adams*, 9, illus. 7

Sibley 7:590-91

Whitney, Janet, *Abigail Adams*, 43

WPA 5

Also reproduced in Butterfield et al., *The book of Abigail and John . . .* 1975, frontispiece; Dunlap, edition by Bayley & Goodspeed, 1918; Earle, Alice Morse, *Two Centuries of Costume . . .* 1903, 2:xi; McCullough, *John Adams*, 2001, opp. 336; Whitney, Jane, *Abigail Adams*, 1947, frontispiece, 43. The Library of Congress, Prints and Photographs Division, has a glass-plate negative made by Harris & Ewing, Photographers, Washington, D. C.

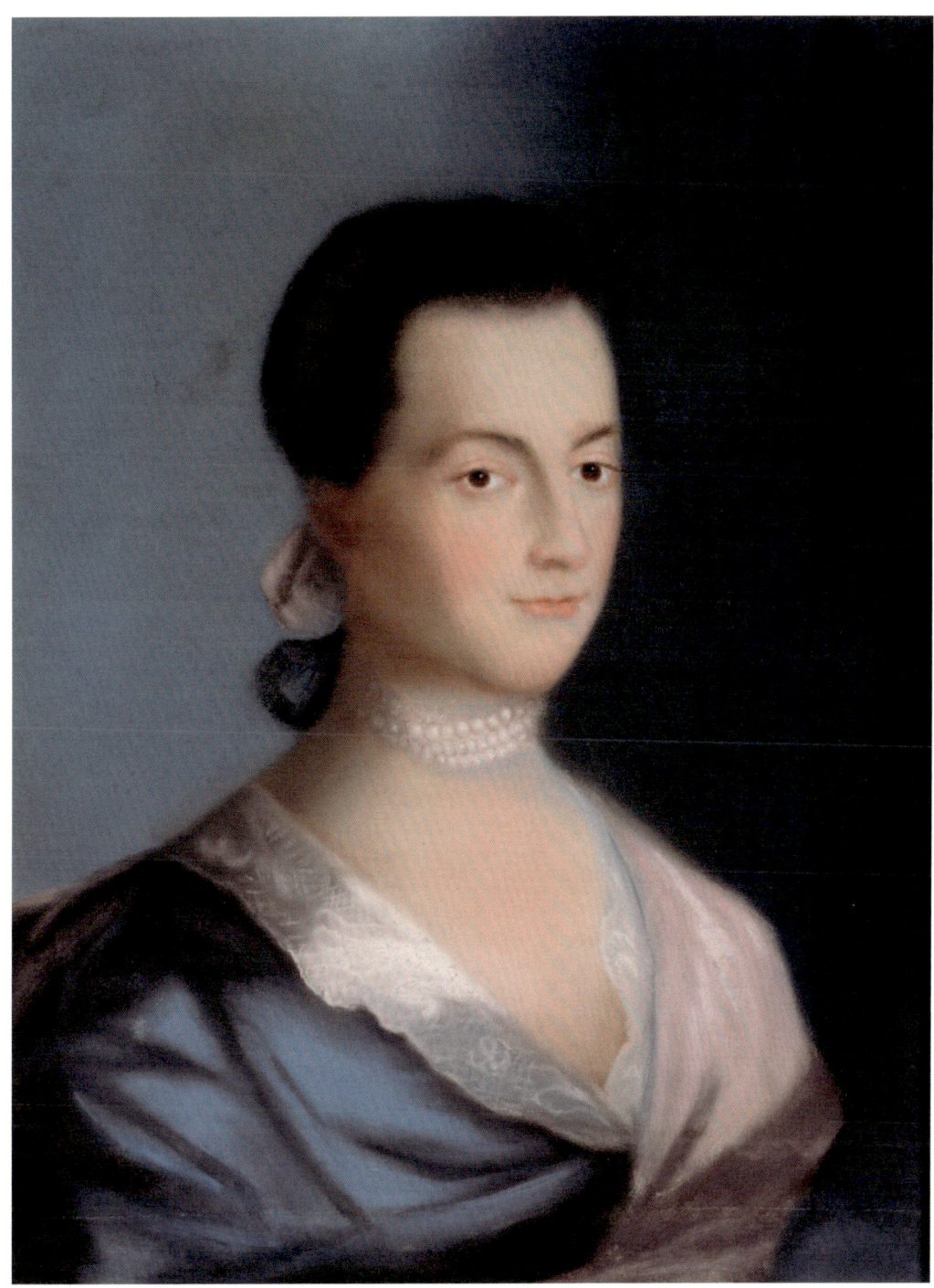

Abigail Adams
Pastel by Benjamin Blyth, probably 1766
Courtesy of the Massachusetts Historical Society Artwork 01.026, gift of John Adams, 1957

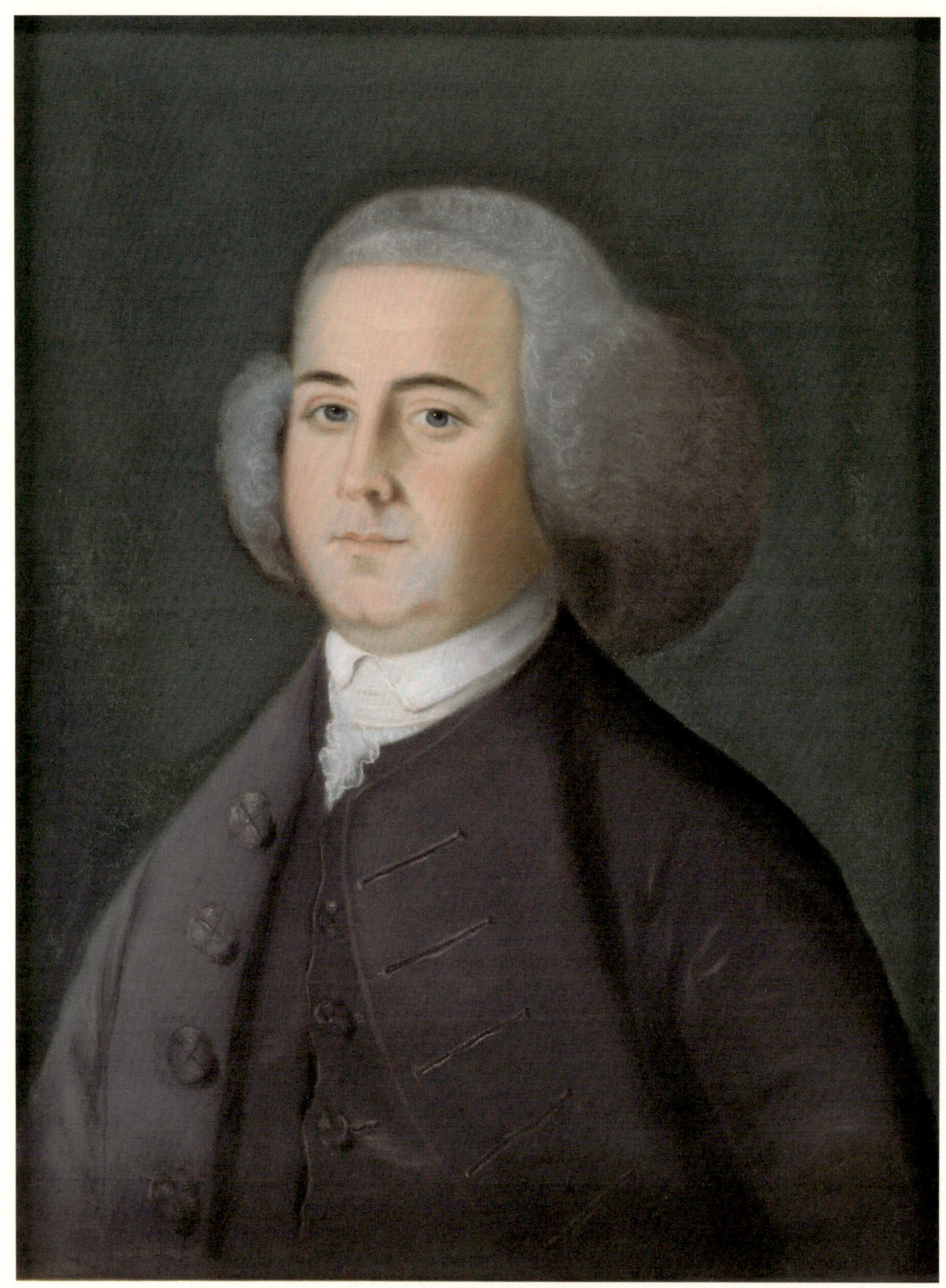

John Adams
Pastel by Benjamin Blyth, probably 1766
Courtesy of the Massachusetts Historical Society Artwork 01.027, gift of John Adams, 1957
Photograph by Christopher Minty

[*3*]

John Adams (1735–1826)

Benjamin Blyth, probably 1766
Pastel on paper, 22½ x 17⅔ in. (57.15 x 44.7), Samuel Blyth frame
Massachusetts Historical Society Artwork 01.027, gift of John Adams, 1957; the Adams family

John Adams was born to John Adams and Susanna (Boylston) Adams in Braintree (the north precinct of which later became Quincy), Massachusetts, on October 30, 1735. He and Abigail Smith were married on October 25, 1764 by her father, the Reverend William Smith. Disliking lawyers and much preferring Richard Cranch—"tall, grave, and dignified"—for a son-in-law, Smith preached on the text, "John came neither eating nor drinking, & they say he hath a devil." Smith misjudged: Adams went on to become a major figure in the history of the United States: Massachusetts delegate to the Continental Congress, Founding Father, the first vice-president and second president of the United States, and a diplomat.

Adams, as a traveling lawyer, argued cases in the Essex courts in the 1760s and took the occasion to travel to Salem with his wife; on November 3, 1766, his diary relates, "Set off with my Wife for Salem; . . . arrived at my dear Brother Cranch's about eight, and drank tea. . . ." They stayed there until November 6, and it is believed that their portraits were painted during this visit or the equally long one at the end of the previous August.

In 1769, Adams co-defended four sailors who were being tried for manslaughter for the death of an English sailor who boarded their ship. Robert Hooper of Marblehead was the ship's owner, and two of the sailors were then in jail there. Adams' argument (*Rex v. Corbet*) that the sailors feared impressment was corroborated by the testimony of Robert Traill (Cat. 124), a member of the Special Court of Admiralty, and the defendants were found not guilty, a verdict hailed throughout Essex County. Years later, Adams told Jedidiah Morse, a founder of the Massachusetts Historical Society, that he considered the Corbet case more important than the Boston Massacre trials for the American Revolution, presumably because he viewed impressment as a more valid cause.

Adams is the subject of dozens of diary entries by the Reverend William Bentley. The entry for March 29, 1791, recounted that "M^r. Adams returned from Newbury & lost his horse at Ipswich. I provided the Stage to carry him to Boston, for which he is to refund me in books." Celebrations were held annually for the anniversary of Adams's birth, with balls and decoration of ships. On September 19, 1791, Bentley wrote, "In Salem & Marblehead, several toasts have been given in honor of the Vice President, John Adams, as the protector of the Fishery. As his aristocratical principles have made parties for & against him, his friends have triumphed in these public Testimonies of affection." Bentley also noted, on May 18, 1800, the political fallout in Salem: "The affair of the sudden dismission of Mr. T. Pickering from the office of Secretary of State of U. S. by President Adams arrests the public attention. It is an event wrapt in darkness. . . . All are surprised and many glad."

John Adams' portrait shows a serious, introspective young man. David McCullough notes in the caption for the portrait in his book, *John Adams* (2001), that Abigail's "decided nature is clearly evident, while he might be almost any untested, well-fed young man of the time." A pastel copy made in 1904 by May Hallowell Loud, owned by the Quincy Historical Society, hangs in the John Quincy Adams Birthplace.

Adams, Charles Francis, *Works of John Adams* 2:199

Bayley, *Little Known . . . Portrait Painters* No. 2, unpaginated, illus.

Bentley 1:57, 240, 306; 2:337

Bolton, *Portrait Draughtsmen*, 7

Cole, "Limned by Blyth," illus. 331

FARL, Blyth, Benjamin 157-3a

Foote, "Blyth," 63–65, 81

Jeffares, http://www.pastellists.com/Articles/Blyth.pdf

MHS, Legal Papers of John Adams 2:276–78, 289, 296–97

Norton, "Benjamin Blyth," 61

Oliver, *Portraits of John and Abigail Adams*, illus. 6

WPA 10

Also reproduced in Bancroft, *History of the United States: from the discovery of the American continent . . .* Boston: Little, Brown and Company, vol. 4, 1852: frontispiece; Dunlap, William, *A History of the Rise and Progress of the Arts of Design*, A New Edition, Illustrated, Frank W. Bayley and Charles E. Goodspeed, 1918, 3: betw. 283-84; Earle, *Two Centuries of Costume in America*, "John Adams in Youth," 1903, 1:3, for his wig; Charles F. Adams, *Works of John Adams*, . . . 1914, vol. 2: frontispiece, with the caption, "John Adams in Youth"; Dunlap, edition by Bayley & Goodspeed, 1918; *OTNE* 26, 1936, illus. and caption, betw. 91–92; O'Toole, *"In the Hearts and Minds"* 1974, 64; Butterfield, *The book of Abigail and John*, 1975, frontispiece; McCullough, *John Adams*, 2001, opp. 336 (attributed to "Blythe ").

[4]

Edward Allen (1735–1803)

Benjamin Blyth (attr.), ca. 1780
Oil on canvas, 16½ x 13 in. (42 x 33 cm.), estimate of original: 26 x 17 in.; later frame
Peabody Essex Museum M371, bequest of the Misses Marion C. and Elizabeth C. Allen, 1891

"A man of many excellent qualities," Bentley wrote of his good friend, Capt. Edward Allen, a successful merchant and shipmaster. Born in 1735 in Berwick-on-Tweed, England, Allen came to America in 1757 and "by his good conduct gained esteem & employment in this Town Within two years of his arrival in Salem he married widow Ruth (Hodges) Gardner, Richard Derby, Sr.'s sister-in-law. Born fifteen years after her sister, she was seven years older than her husband. As a young man, Allen captained the *Antelope* and other ships for Richard Derby to the Leghorn, Cadiz, Gibraltar, and the Leeward Islands. By 1780, he had become owner of the *Baltick* and part owner of other vessels. A letter illustrating well his careful oversight and yet boldness instructs the captain of the *Oliver Cromwell*: "When your ship is ready & the wind invites, proceed directly for Guadaloup & on your arrival, dispose of your Cargo, & lay out the proceeds, together with the amount of your Bills (if honored) in Molasses & Cotton & return home taking particular care not to load deep . . . but don't forbid your chasing any Vessel that falls in your way, provided your ship sails fast & appearances encourage the pursuit, but even in that case you can't be too cautious."

Allen's wife died in 1774, and four years later, he married Margaret Lockhart, from North Carolina. His mansion on Derby Street was one of Salem's most sumptuous, according to Bentley, who added that Allen even took a lease on a lot "on the west side of Hardy Street only to avoid the evil of such buildings near his mansion house." Allen spent considerable time improving his farm on the Salem Neck, which he bought for summer use from E. H. Derby, "the first time the Neck has been the residence of any family but for the purposes of industry," Bentley wrote. He followed the day-by-day developments in his diary, claiming that Allen's planned artificial fishpond also was the first he knew of in the area. Bentley sometimes took one of the Allen children on trips with him. Of the nine surviving children, one son, Jordan Lockhart, had been lost overboard off the Cape of Good Hope in 1798, according to Bentley, noting that Allen "is plagued with a living one, from whom he expected great consolation." Allen joined the Salem Marine Society in 1766, the year it was founded, and became Deputy Master from 1802 until he died on July 27, 1803, at age 68. His eldest son, Edward Jr., who married a daughter of Gen. John and Lydia Phippen Fisk (Cats. 52, 53), inherited the farm and added an artificial pond, wharves, and a summer house.

Right after Allen's death, Bentley asked for his portrait, which was sent over to him; but "In the evening it was reclaimed by the daughters. . . . I had cut it down to separate the injured parts but must return it." A carefully scripted note quoting the brief biography of Allen from Bentley's diary entry, probably added during the portrait's restoration, recorded that Bentley had cut it down from "a full length picture to its present size." But the inscription is inaccurate; Bentley's diary

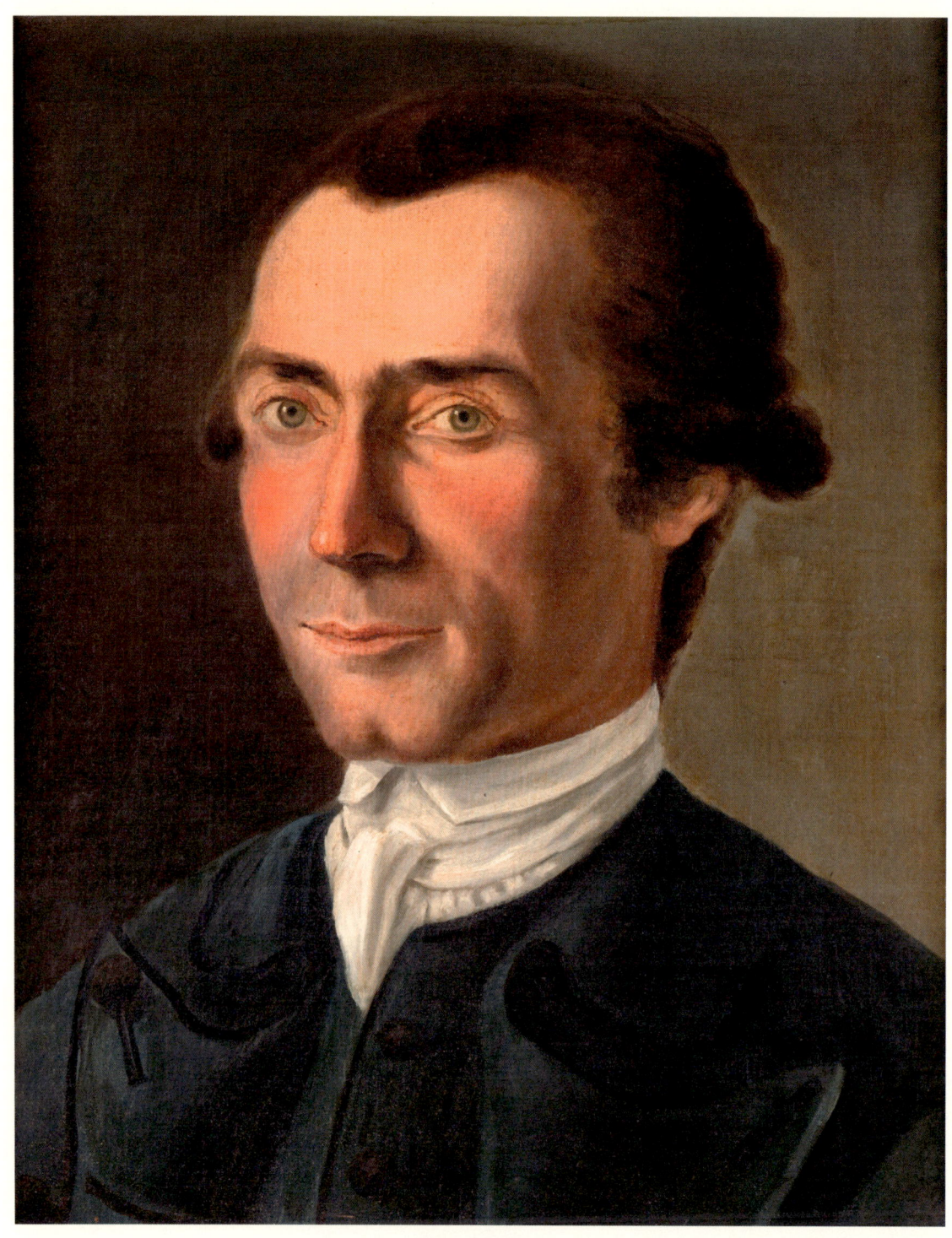

Edward Allen
Oil painting attributed to Benjamin Blyth, ca. 1780
Courtesy of the Peabody Essex Museum M371, Bequest of the Misses Marion C. and Elizabeth C. Allen, 1891

entry did not mention "full-length." Also, the uniform color of the background suggests that it was a bust portrait and is compatible in scale to Blyth's oil portrait of Moses Brown.

Examination by black light shows extensive overpainting on Allen's eyes, eyebrows, and right cheek, with other touch-ups on the stock and coat. Curls were added to the hair, and the edges of the lapel also were prominently outlined. Indeed, pasted on the reverse is the label: "This picture was/ RESTORED/ at the Copley Gallery/103 Newbury Street Boston/June 19-1916." Nonetheless, salient characteristics of Blyth's technique remain, namely the eyes, lip line, and concentration on character—Allen's genial personality and penetrating intellect. Elizabeth C. Allen, in donating the portrait to the "Peabody Academy," wrote that "our ancestor does not rejoice in manly beauty but old Dr. Bentley gives him credit for beauty of character." One can see why he was a favored friend of Bentley, although old enough to be his father.

Allen was a likely subject for Blyth: he was related to the Derbys through his wife. Also, Allen's son Edward married a daughter of Lydia Phippen Fisk and Thomas Fisk (Cats. 52 and 53), both of whom were earlier Blyth subjects. The oil of Allen and the pastel of Lydia Phippen Fisk descended in the Allen family, who bequeathed them to the Essex Institute, along with another oil of an unidentified sea captain (*EIHC* "Catalogue . . ." 373), possibly Capt. Fisk. The Allen portrait had been in the collections of the former Essex Institute, accession number 2956, but was transferred to the former Peabody Museum in 1911.

Bentley 1: xx, xxxiii, 28; 2:141, 257; 3:7, 19, 21, 32, 34; 4: 383, among many entries

EIHC, 73:172, Cat. 2 (Peabody Museum), neg. 2253

Phillips, *Salem . . . 18th C.*, 244, 420

SMS Plate 1, no. 26

Visitor's Guide to Salem (1895), 196

Whitehill, *Portraits . . . Peabody Museum*, 2

WPA 41

[5]

Margaret Gibbs Appleton (1699–1771)

Benjamin Blyth, mid-1760s
Pastel, measurements unknown
Current location not known; owned in 1969 by "Mrs. Cutter"

Blyth can be credited with the portrait of Margaret Gibbs Appleton illustrated in Elizabeth Mc-Clellan's *History of American Costume, 1607–1870*. McClellan used Mrs. Appleton's portrait because it showed "a peculiar cap in 1784." But she died in 1771, and the cap actually dates from the 1760s, as probably does the portrait. The illustration credit states, "from a photo lent by Mrs. Cutter," presumed to be the owner at the time.

Margaret Gibbs was born on July 3, 1699, to the Reverend Henry Gibbs, minister of the East Parish in Watertown, and Mercy Greenough Gibbs. Her father officiated at her marriage on June 25, 1719, to the Reverend Nathaniel Appleton, minister of the First Parish in Cambridge. He served for sixty-seven years, from 1717 until his death at age ninety in 1784, the longest tenure in the church's history.

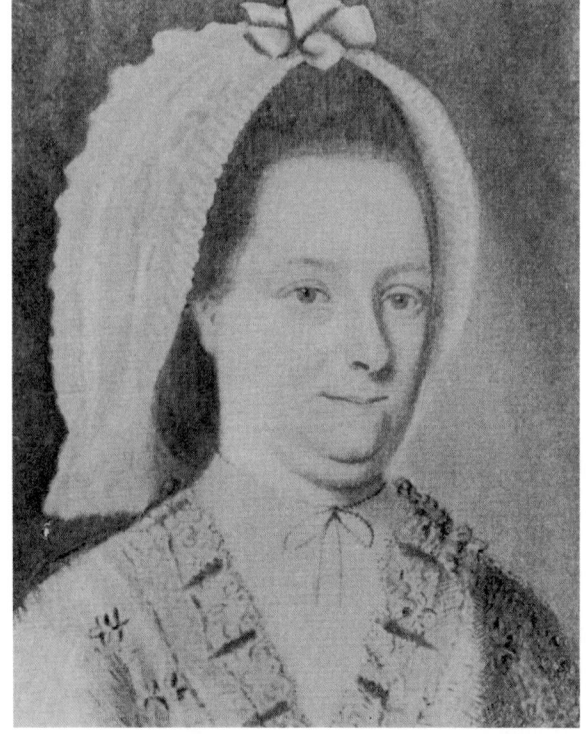

Margaret Gibbs Appleton
Photograph of unlocated pastel by Benjamin Blyth,
mid-1760s
Illustration from Elizabeth McClellan,
History of American Costume, 1607–1870, betw. 158-59

Blyth's portrait of her presumably was done on a visit to her son, Henry Gibbs, who had moved to Salem in 1734 to assume a career as a merchant. Her portrait by Copley, signed and dated 1763, is in the Harvard Portrait Collection (on loan since 1855). Both portraits show her rotund face and heavy-lidded eyes, although her double chin is more prominent in the Blyth, when she was perhaps three or four years older. She was described in *Sibley's* as "a meek and quiet Spirit; . . . agreeable and pleasant . . . prudent, inoffensive, and exemplary." Her portrait by Blyth conveys this, even outshining her more somber demeanor in the Copley portrait.

McClellan, illus. no. 202, betw.158-59
Sibley, 5:603–4
Stebbins, *American Paintings at Harvard*, 2:130–31

[6]

Gibbs Atkins (1740–1806)

Benjamin Blyth (attr.), ca. 1772
Pastel, known only in photograph and a glass plate negative at the Haverhill Public Library, Haverhill, MA
Current location not known; owned in the 1940s by Maria Gilbert, Haverhill, MA

Gibbs Atkins was born in Cambridge in 1740, but his parents' names are unknown. At the beginning of the Revolution, he was a cabinetmaker living in Boston. A Loyalist, he fled and was classified an "absentee," so his estate on Prince Street, between Salem and Hanover Streets in the North End, was sold in 1781 by the special committee headed by Richard Cranch, John Adams' brother-in-law. Gibbs did return to Boston after the war and married Hannah Sanderson in 1788. He died in 1806, and Hannah in 1838, at age eighty-eight. They are buried in Mount Auburn Cemetery.

Following publication in 1994 of this author's article "The Brothers Blyth: Salem in Its Heyday" for the Dublin Seminar for New England Folklife, the late Sing Laing of the Haverhill Public Library wrote that it had both a photograph and the glass plate negative of a pastel portrait which he thought might be another Blyth. It was of Atkins. "He or his son lived at 12 Richmond St., near Salem St. in the North End, which was owned by his descendants for several generations," Laing wrote, enclosing a photograph of the plate, "This pastel hung in the house in Roxbury & later here in Haverhill until WWI or so." Laing had no further information on it and added that

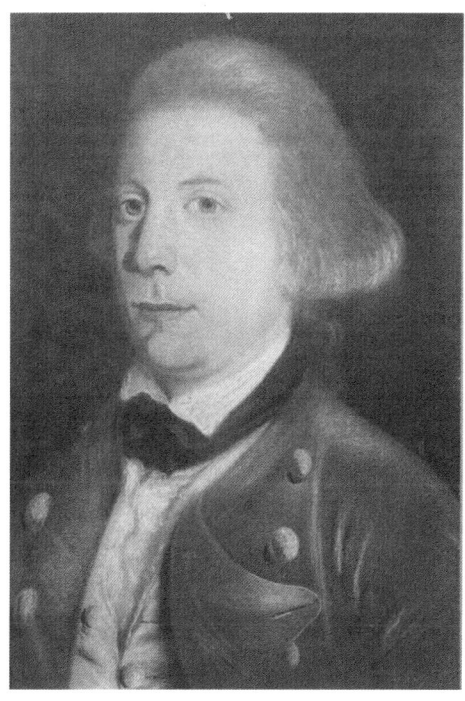

Gibbs Atkins
Photocopy by the late Sing Laing of unlocated
pastel attributed to Benjamin Blyth, ca. 1772
Haverhill Public Library, Haverhill, MA

it was not on the WPA list of portraits in Massachusetts. The portrait is comparable stylistically to that of Abijah Northey (Cat. 97).

The glass plate negative most likely was made by Baldwin Coolidge, who photographed many portraits in the early twentieth century for the Museum of Fine Arts, Boston, and Frank W. Bayley's Copley Gallery. Coolidge later donated more than 2,000 glass plate negatives to Historic New England. From the copy of the Atkins photograph sent by Laing, it looks as if the pastel was touched up; this is consistent with the assumed relationship between Coolidge and Bayley. As of 2022, neither the photograph nor the glass plate negative could be found by the Haverhill Public Library.

Haverhill Public Library, correspondence from the late Sing Laing, Nov. 1995
Inhabitants and Estates of the Town of Boston (Thwing Collection)

[7]

Josiah Barker (1728–1803)

Benjamin Blyth, probably 1778
Pastel on paper mounted on linen, 22 x 17¹³⁄₁₆ in. (55.9 x 35 cm.), frame 19th-century bronzed wood
New Bedford Whaling Museum 1946. 25.5, gift of Estate of Capt. Francis Rotch, 1946

Born in Nantucket on July 17, 1728, to Samuel and Bethiah (Folger) Barker, Josiah served with Massachusetts soldiers in the French and Indian War from 1744 and at the Crown Point Expedition under Capt. Samuel Dakin in September 1755. He married Elizabeth Mitchell in 1754. She died in 1761, and two years later he married Elisabeth Hussey Coffin, daughter of George Hussey and Elisabeth (Starbuck) and widow of Peleg Coffin. On November 17 of that year, the couple was "called" to become members of the Nantucket Quakers; the Island had a large contingent of the Society of Friends. In 1779, Barker was three-quarters owner of the brigantine *Pembroke,* "now lying at Long Island with a quantity of oil," suggesting that he was a privateer during the Revolution. He died "suddenly" in 1803, at age seventy-five.

The simplicity of Barker's clothing resembles that of a Salem Quaker, Abijah Northey (Cat. 97), and Barker's unusual light blue eyes are comparable to those of the Rev. Thomas Barnard (Cat. 8). Barker's portrait, along with fourteen related artifacts, was the gift to the New Bedford Whaling Museum from the estate of Capt. Francis Rotch, who died in Medina, Washington in 1944. Rotch, a descendant of Barker's daughter Elizabeth and Benjamin Rotch, was also a great-grandson of the New Bedford nineteenth-century artist and lithographer, Benjamin Rotch (1817–1882).

Barker's portrait is an unabashedly honest portrait of a serious-minded older man.

Edes, *Memorial of Josiah Barker,* 19

Leach, Robert J., and Peter Gow, *Quaker Nantucket: The Religious Community Behind the Whaling Empire,* (Nantucket, MA: Mill Hill Press, 1996), 312–13.

Nantucket Historical Association, Barney Genealogical Record, William C. Folger Genealogical Record ("not free from errors")

NEHGS, "Mass. soldiers in the French-Indian Wars, 1744–1755."

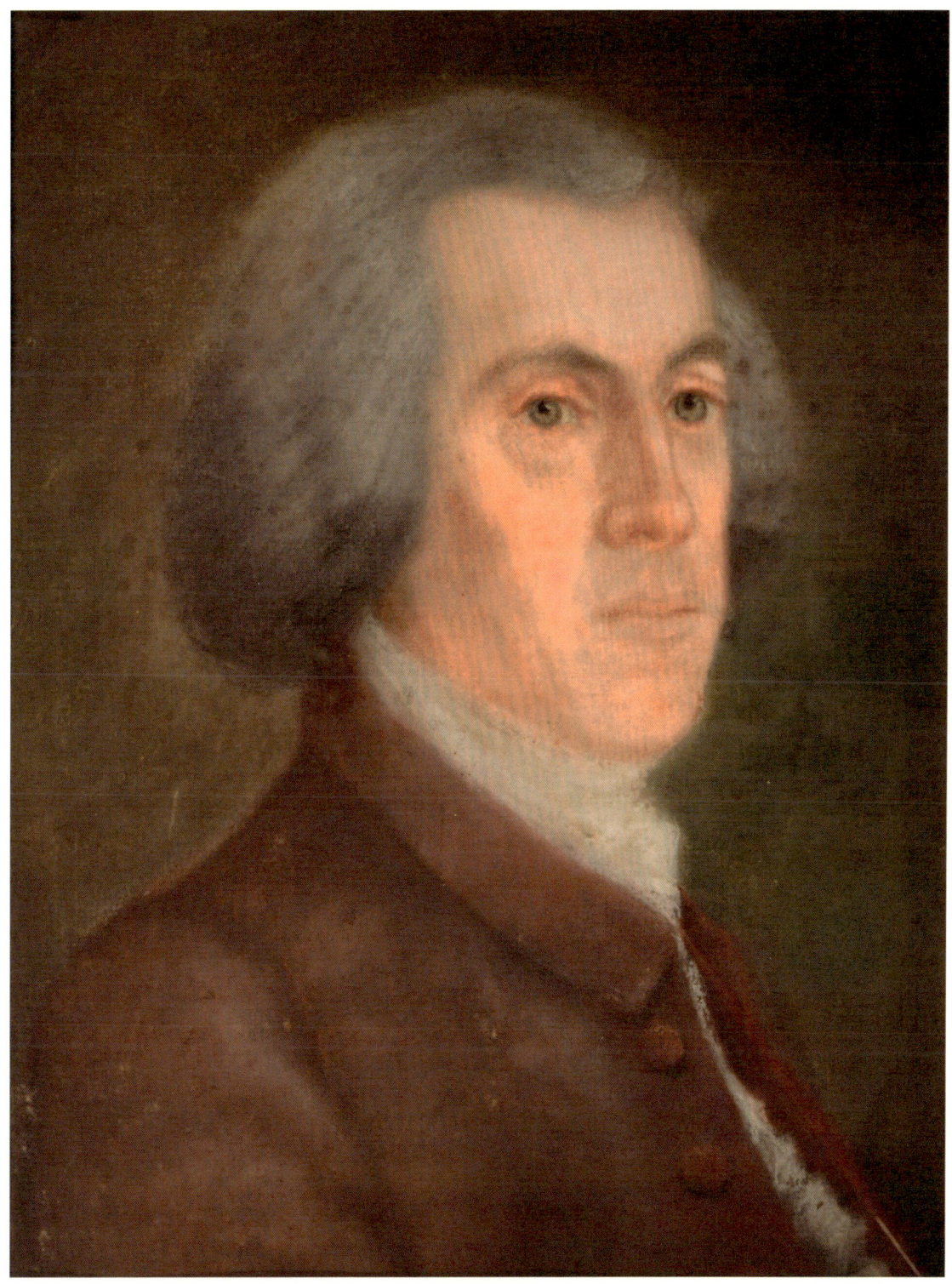

Josiah Barker
Pastel by Benjamin Blyth, probably 1778
Courtesy of the New Bedford Whaling Museum 1946. 25.5, gift of Estate of Capt. Francis Rotch, 1946

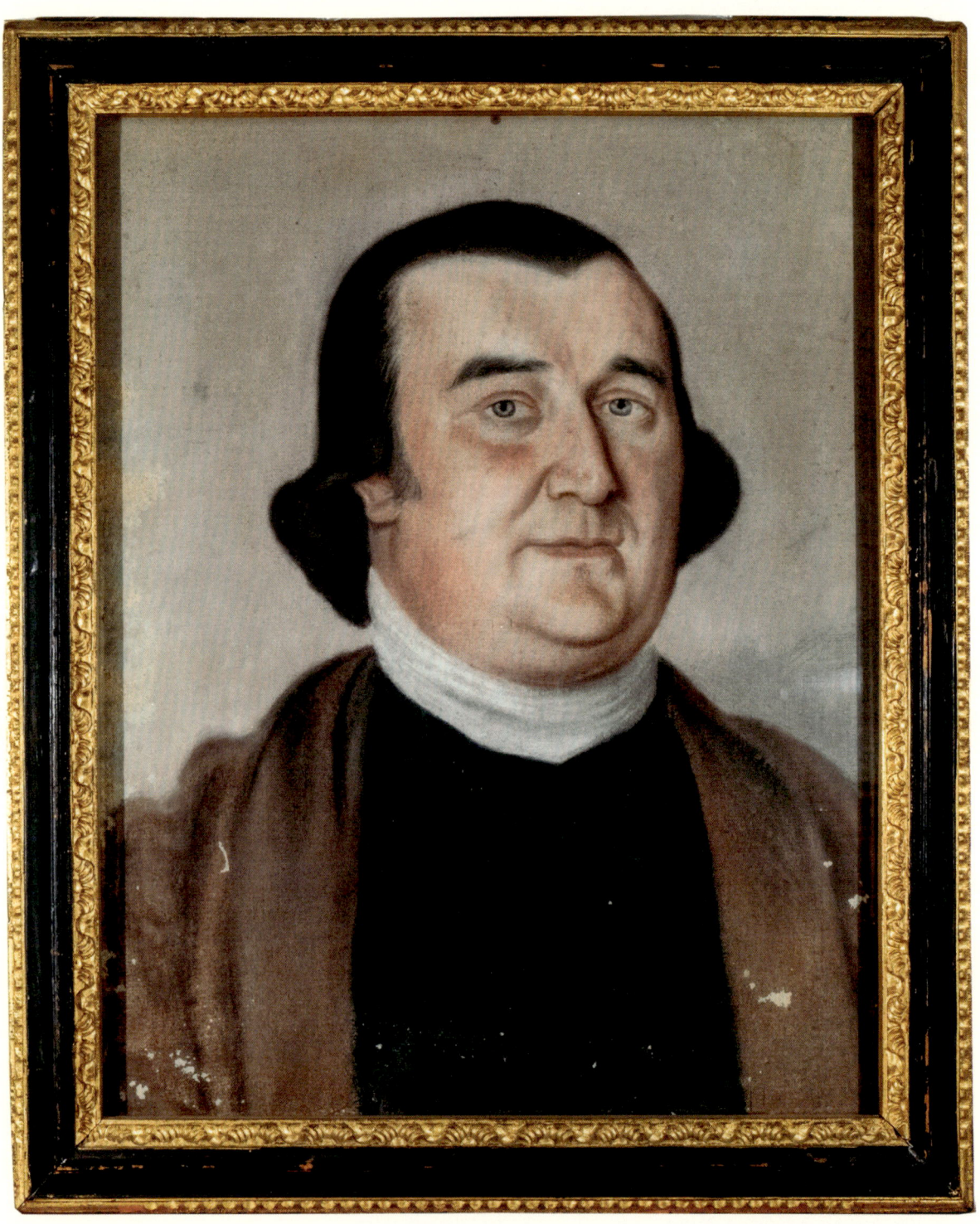

Thomas Barnard
Pastel by Benjamin Blyth, ca. 1775
Courtesy of the First Church in Salem
Photograph by Michael C. King

[8]

Thomas Barnard (1748–1814)

Benjamin Blyth, ca. 1775
Pastel on paper mounted on linen, 19½ x 15 in. (49.5 x 38 cm.),
Samuel Blyth frame with original hooks for hanging
First Church in Salem, Unitarian, gift of the Bridges family to the North Church Society

The second surviving son of the Reverend Thomas and Mary (Woodbridge) Barnard, Thomas Jr. was born in Newbury, Massachusetts, on January 30, 1748, and became the fourth generation of his family to join the ministry. The family moved to Salem in 1755, when his father became minister of the First Church. Thomas Jr. graduated from Harvard College in 1766, and four years later, when his father no longer was able to preach, was asked to assume the pulpit temporarily. However, after the Reverend Asa Dunbar was chosen in 1772 to fill the post, dissenters left to form the North Church with the younger Barnard as its first pastor. Among the early signatories for the new church were Francis Cabot, Sarah Curwen, her aunt and uncle Samuel and Abigail Curwen, Dr. E. A. Holyoke, and Priscilla Ropes, all drawn by Blyth (Cats. 24, 34, 33, 32, 69, 111).

On May 31, 1773, Barnard married Lois Gardner, "a Lady possessed of a Fortune upwards of Two Thousand Pounds Lawful Money, and second daughter of Samuel Gardner, Esq.; late an eminent Merchant of this Place, deceased" according to the Pickering genealogy. Like his father, Barnard was an active member of the rich intellectual and social life of Salem. He maintained a fine garden, from which he "dealt out his flowers with a liberal hand to the girls and boys, especially on holidays, for he was very fond of children." There were two Barnard children, a daughter, and a son, who, "ruined by Intemperance," died on March 30, 1800, less than a month before his twenty-sixth birthday.

Barnard's prominent place in Salem history was assured by defusing a potential bloody confrontation on February 26, 1775, between the locals and the British officer, Col. Alexander Leslie, who had been sent from Boston to find a stash of ammunition. Barnard crafted a compromise that allowed both sides to avoid humiliation and thus became the hero of "Leslie's Retreat" (See illus., p. 30). So the inevitable outbreak of the fighting in the American Revolution began elsewhere, when British troops went looking for more ammunition stores in Concord. Because of Barnard's reputation as a conciliator, he was the only member of a committee chosen by both sides in 1788 to help resolve a dispute involving a Topsfield clergyman.

A theological liberal who reputedly avoided mentioning the Trinity, Barnard served the church for nearly forty-two years. In 1794, he received a Doctor of Divinity degree from Rhode Island College (later to become Brown University). Soon after his death at age sixty-one, in 1814, the North Church officially became Unitarian, and in 1923 it rejoined its parent, the First Church, so Barnard's portrait is once again in the congregation that he and his father served. His family's Georgian house, built in 1740, still stands on the opposite side of Essex Street from the church.

The First Church in Salem, Unitarian, recently had the portrait and its frame restored at the Northeast Document Conservation Center and has placed it back in the newly designated Barnard Room of the Parish House.

Barnard's portrait is displayed in its elaborate Samuel Blyth frame, both inner and outer moldings gilt, with its original two hanging hooks. It conveys "a short, plump, good-natured man, greatly beloved by all his people for kindliness of heart and an earnest desire to help all," as James Duncan Phillips wrote in *Salem and the Indies*. The Pickering Genealogy noted that he was "a respected scholar, [with a] genial, sympathetic, and comprehensive manliness." The portrait captures it all.

There may have been a portrait of Barnard's wife, especially if the two Gardner portraits (Cats. 57, 58) are of her sister and brother-in-law, as is surmised here.

Barnard Diary DIA, Phillips Library, Peabody Essex Museum

Bentley 1:x, 89; 2:176, illus. opp. 359

Felt 2:518-19s

The first Centenary of the North Church 13–20, 25-27

Norton, "Benjamin Blyth," 61

Oliver, *Windows on the Past*, 33

Phillips, *Salem . . . 18th C.*, portrait (printed in reverse) and church illus. betw. 344–45

Phillips, *Salem . . . Indies*, 198-99, quoting J. B. Derby, *Reminiscences of Salem*, 1847

Pickering Genealogy, 1:11, portrait illus. 181, house illus. betw. 182-83

Sibley 16:316–322; illus. in Illus. Section

SIRIS, "unknown" painter

WPA 134, "artist unknown"

[9]

William Bartlett (1741–1794)

Benjamin Blyth (attr.), ca. 1780
Miniature on ivory, 1⁵⁄₁₆ x ⅞ in. (3.45 x 2.23 cm.)
Location of original unknown

Capt. William Bartlett was born in Beverly on June 27, 1741, to Capt. William and Anna Bartlett. In 1761, he married Joanna Herrick, daughter of Henry and Anne Herrick, members of an old and large Beverly family. Known as a "shoreman," Bartlett became a prominent citizen, very involved in the political, mercantile, religious, and intellectual life of Beverly and Salem. His papers show that he had an extensive business in sugar, flour and rice.

During the American Revolution, Gen. Washington appointed Bartlett and Jonathan Glover of Marblehead to "expedite the fitting out of armed vessels"—i. e., to take on privateering; they did so until January 1, 1776. Bartlett was named port agent for Beverly, to condemn and sell British prize vessels captured by American privateers. His schooner *Benjamin,* sailing "under the colours of Massachusetts Bay," was seized by the British off the coast of Haiti on October 21, 1776, and "condemned as American property." Its cargo included boards, hoops, staves, shingles, spermaceti, wax and tallow candles, all from Beverly.

Bartlett sold his house and land in 1782 and by 1785 he and his wife were in Westmoreland County, Pennsylvania, where he died on December 30, 1794. There is no record of children, although descendants reportedly were living in Marietta, Ohio, by the end of the century. His wife Joanna applied from Ohio for membership in the General Society of Mayflower descendants.

The original miniature of Bartlett is lost. A small reproduction exhibited at the Beverly Historical Society and Museum notes "From an original at the Peabody Essex Museum." The reproduction is from the 1886 catalogue of portraits of members of the Salem Marine Society in the collections of the Peabody Essex Museum's Phillips Library. The illustration includes a penciled notation at the bottom of the image: "Born June 27, 1744 [*sic*] Died Dec.ʳ 30, 1794." There were personal associations with the Blyths. Bartlett was an active member of St. Peter's Church in Salem and he also hired Samuel Blyth and his brother William to paint the fence at his residence, John Bond House in Beverly.

The miniature has the earmarks of Benjamin Blyth, and, typical of the artist, is a good character study. The portly William Bartlett's gaze is penetrating, yet genial.

William Bartlett
Photograph of unlocated miniature
attributed to Benjamin Blyth, ca. 1780
Illustration from *Portraits of Members. . . ,*
Salem, MA: Salem Marine Society
Courtesy of the Phillips Library, Peabody
Essex Museum, Rowley, MA

Beverly Museum, Capt. William Bartlett Papers
Cutler, Manasseh Cutler, 89, 254, 405–6
EIHC 45:7; 55:293, 303; 76:46; 81:302
SMS Plate 1, no. 12
Smith, Philip Chadwick Foster, *Portraits Marine Society*, Plate 1
Tapley, *St. Peter's,* 35

[10]

Edward Bass (1726–1803)

Benjamin Blyth, ca. 1772
Pastel on paper mounted on linen, 22¾ x 17¾ in. (57.8 x 45 cm.), Samuel Blyth frame
The Episcopal Diocese of Massachusetts, gift of the Misses Whitney, after 1960

Born in Dorchester on November 23, 1726, to Joseph and Elizabeth Bass, the Reverend Edward Bass spent almost his entire adult life in Newburyport, Massachusetts. As of 1960, even his portrait was still there, in private hands. A graduate of Harvard College in 1744, he moved in 1751 to the recently established town of Newburyport to become assistant minister of St. Paul's, a new Anglican mission under St. Anne's, Newbury. In 1754, Bass married Sarah, daughter of Deacon Joshua and Abigail Beck of Newbury. Sarah died in May 1789, and later that year, Bass married Mercy Phillips. There are no recorded children. At the death of the minister of St. Anne's, Bass became in charge of both, but the popularity of St. Paul's soon outshone the "mother" church.

Because Bass signed the address congratulating Hutchinson on his appointment as governor in 1774, as war with England was imminent, Bass and his wife were "pursued along the street by near two hundred persons, who pelted him with dust and stones, and treated him with the most indelicate language," wrote historian William S. Bartlett. Nonetheless, Bass was popular. He also contributed generously, considering his salary, to the purchase of the Brattle organ for St. Paul's. He held his parish together during the Revolution and subsequently played an important role in the early history of the Anglican Church in New England. In 1790, he chaired the committee adopting a new constitution for the newly formed Episcopal Church in the United States of America. In 1796, he was unanimously elected the first Bishop of Massachusetts and second Bishop of Rhode Island, also serving as rector of his church until his death in 1803. (At the time, there was no central office for the bishop; each administered Diocesan duties from his home parish.)

His fondness for card playing and "like social diversions" sometimes brought him reproofs. Nonetheless, the Reverend William Bentley had tea with him one day in 1791 and reported, "I found him full of useful information, ready with wit on all subjects, stored with merry tales, & very agreeable." *Sibley's Harvard Graduates* noted: "The portrait here reproduced demonstrates that the young minister could not rely on his appearance to charm his parish, ... [however] 'his pleasant, cheerful countenance' which, although it does not appear in his portrait, charmed almost everyone with whom he came into contact." Perhaps Blyth was trying to portray the sociable clergyman's wit with an amused grimace.

When photographed for *Sibley's* for volume 11, published in 1960, it was owned by "the Misses Whitney of Newburyport, but it will soon go to the Diocesan House in Boston." The pastel is in the original frame—by Samuel Blyth. It has undergone some faulty restoration, and the visible flecks are fly droppings on the glass. A stipple engraving based on the ca. 1772 original, by an anonymous early-nineteenth-century artist, is in the Prints and Photographs Department, Museum of Fine Arts, Boston.

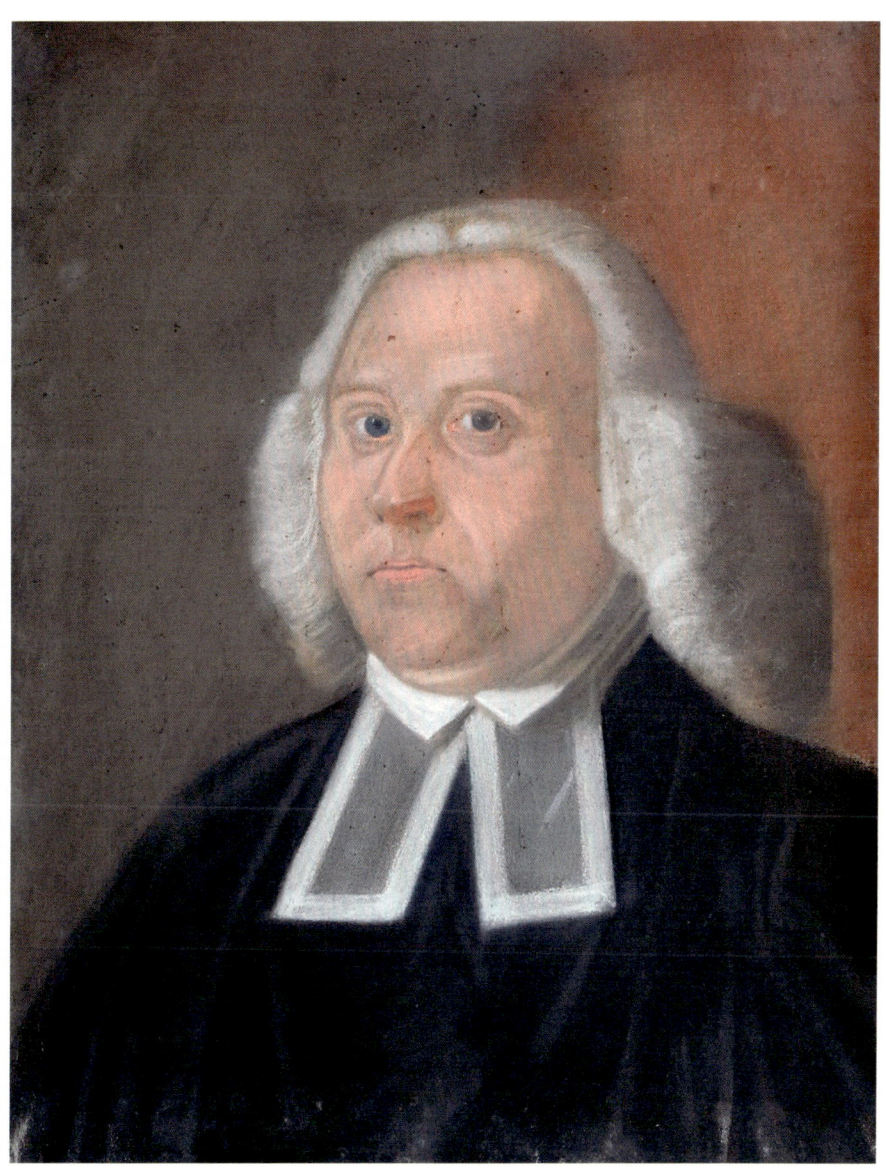

Edward Bass
Pastel by Benjamin Blyth, ca. 1772
Courtesy of the Diocesan Library and Archives, Episcopal Diocese of Massachusetts
Photograph by F. Lee Eiseman

Bartlett, *Frontier Missionary*, 312–15, illus. opp. 312

Bentley 1:87, 209, 259

The Cathedral Church of St. Paul, Boston, Library and Archives

Jeffares, http://www.pastellists.com/Articles/Blyth.pdf

Norton, "Brothers Blyth," 61

Sibley 11:342–43, 358; illus. opp. 340

[11]

Gideon Baty (1738–1787)

Benjamin Blyth, early 1770s
Pastel on paper pasted on board, 14 x 10 in. (35.6 x 25.4 cm.)
Courtesy of the collection of James and Janet Laverdiere; private collection, Cowan Auctions,
Freeman family

Gideon "Betee" was born on March 7, 1738, in Eastham, on Cape Cod. In 1766, Gideon, whose surname by then was "Baty," married Rachal Knowles [Knowls]. She was born in 1744, also in Eastham. Their first child, a daughter Sally, born on August 29, 1768, died at age eleven months. Their son Gideon was born on December 4, 1770, and a daughter Rachel, on September 21, 1773. Baty's wife died in 1777, and later that year, he married Thankful Freeman, widow of Watson Freeman, from nearby Harwich on the Cape.

By the late 1780s, Baty was a prominent merchant in Boston, although he kept his connections with the Barnstable area. Goods that he sold included clothing, fabric ("Callimanco" and "Cambleteens"), and hardware. His assets at his death in July 1787 included "Mansion house, out houses barn &c," valued at £900, three stores close to the Town Dock, valued at £850, and part ownership of a mill in Harwich. His will also reveals a wealthy, religious man, grateful to God for his good fortune. Interested in furthering the education of his children, he directed that his daughter Rachel be taught reading and arithmetic and his son Gideon, French. His wife and children shared his estate, but he also left money to his stepson Watson. The explicit instructions in Baty's will for his children, along with the facts that he and his wives were from the Sandwich area and there is no record of the deaths of either Rachel or Thankful, suggest that the family may have had been Quaker.

The portraits of Baty and his wife appeared in a 2017 sale of Americana by Cowan's Auctions. The last digit in the date, 177-, scratched on the back of the frame, is illegible. But on it hinges the identity of whether the woman portrayed in the companion portrait was his first or second wife. Born in 1738, Baty appears to be in his early to-mid-thirties, and the wig and jacket also strongly suggest the early 1770s, especially as a merchant who dealt in cloth and clothing and would be presumed to dress in fashion. However, whether he was in the vicinity of Salem at any time in the early 1770s to be a subject for Blyth, cannot be ascertained, nor whether the companion portrait was of his first or second wife.

The pastels hung for many years along with other family portraits in the Freeman Farm in Sandwich, Massachusetts. A label on the back confirms that the portraits were framed at the Copley Gallery in Boston sometime before 1933. The touch of the restorer at the gallery owned by Frank W. Bayley is seen in delicate, deft strokes of black crayon used throughout, but more detectable on his wig, on his eyebrows and right eye, and along the edge of the near collar of his blue coat. Flesh-colored strokes line his eyes and soften his lips. Baty's left eye also has radiating

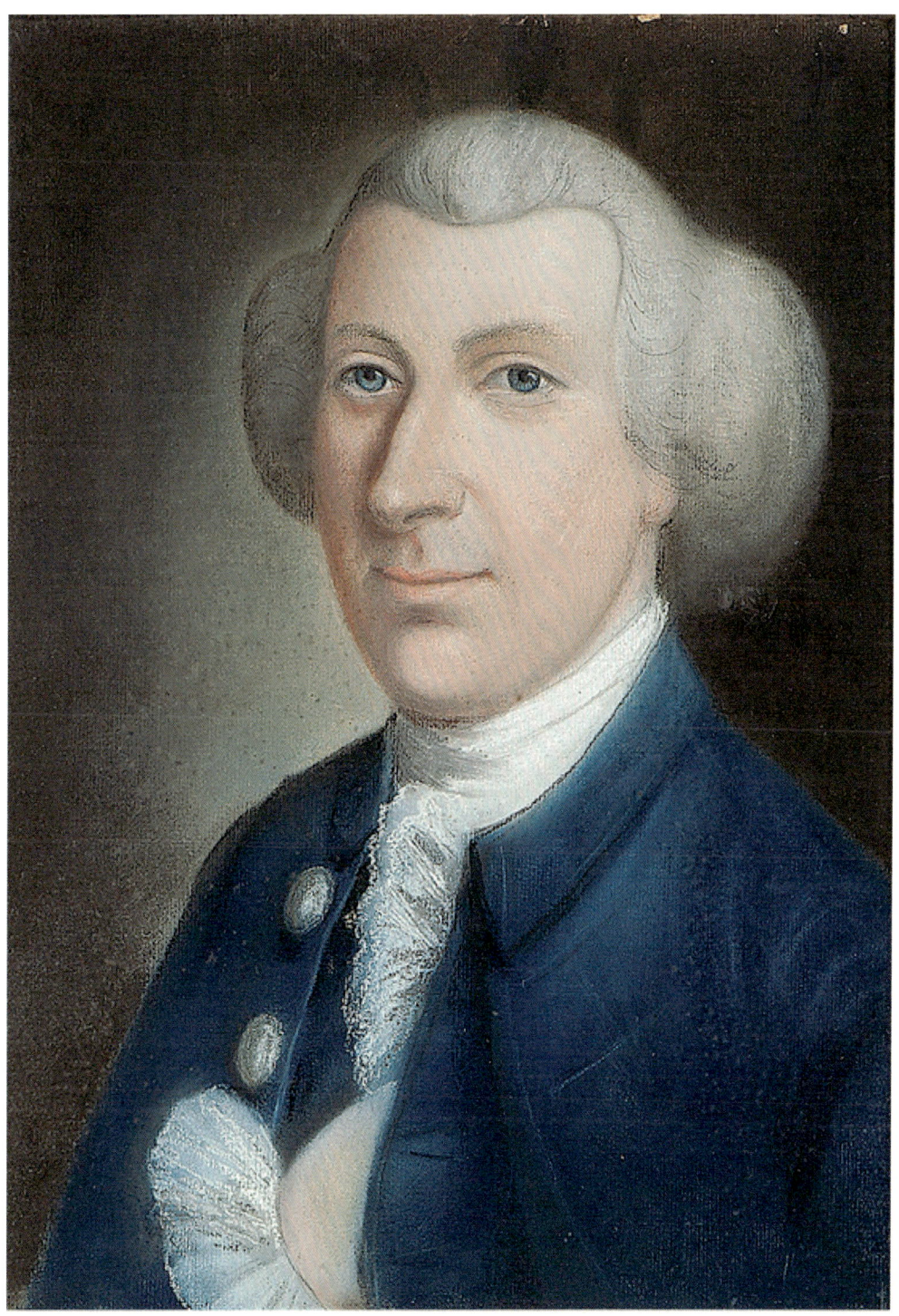

Gideon Baty
Pastel by Benjamin Blyth, early 1770s
Courtesy of the collection of James and Janet Laverdiere
Photograph by F. Lee Eiseman

strokes surrounding the blue iris. Other Blyth portraits that went through Bayley's gallery include the pastels of John and Mary Collins (Cats. 29, 30), Lydia Phippen Fisk (Cat. 53), Hannah Paine (Cat. 101), and Portrait of a Woman in Blue Dress with Black Lace (Cat. 151), along with the oil of Edward Allen (Cat. 4).

Blyth portrayed Gideon and his wife as kind and gentle.

Boston Tax Records, 1800

Cowan Auctions, 10/21/2017 - Fine & Decorative Art Featuring Americana: Day 2

Dexter Memorandum

Freeman family, correspondence with a descendant

Suffolk County Probate Records, 18931, 86:390

Gideon Baty (1738–1787)

Benjamin Blyth (attr.), probably 1778–80
Miniature, 2 x 1½ in. (5.08 x 3.81 cm.)
Private collection; Cowan Auctions, Freeman family

The miniature portrait of Baty, as in the pastel, shows characteristics attributable to Blyth. The larger collar of Baty's coat bespeaks a date of the late 1770s to very early 1780s. The miniature also shows stylistic affinity to that of the Rev. Samuel Parker, drawn probably in 1780 and here attributed to Blyth. Both are also wearing an old-fashioned "buckled" wig. One possible reason that the miniature of Baty may have been drawn later than his pastel and that of his assumed first wife is that there is, or was intended, an accompanying one of Baty's second wife. His is the only miniature attributed to Blyth that faces left rather than right.

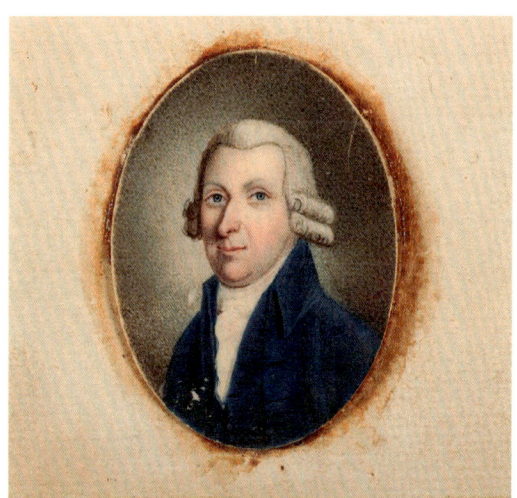

Gideon Baty
Miniature attributed to Benjamin Blyth, probably
1778–80
Private Collection

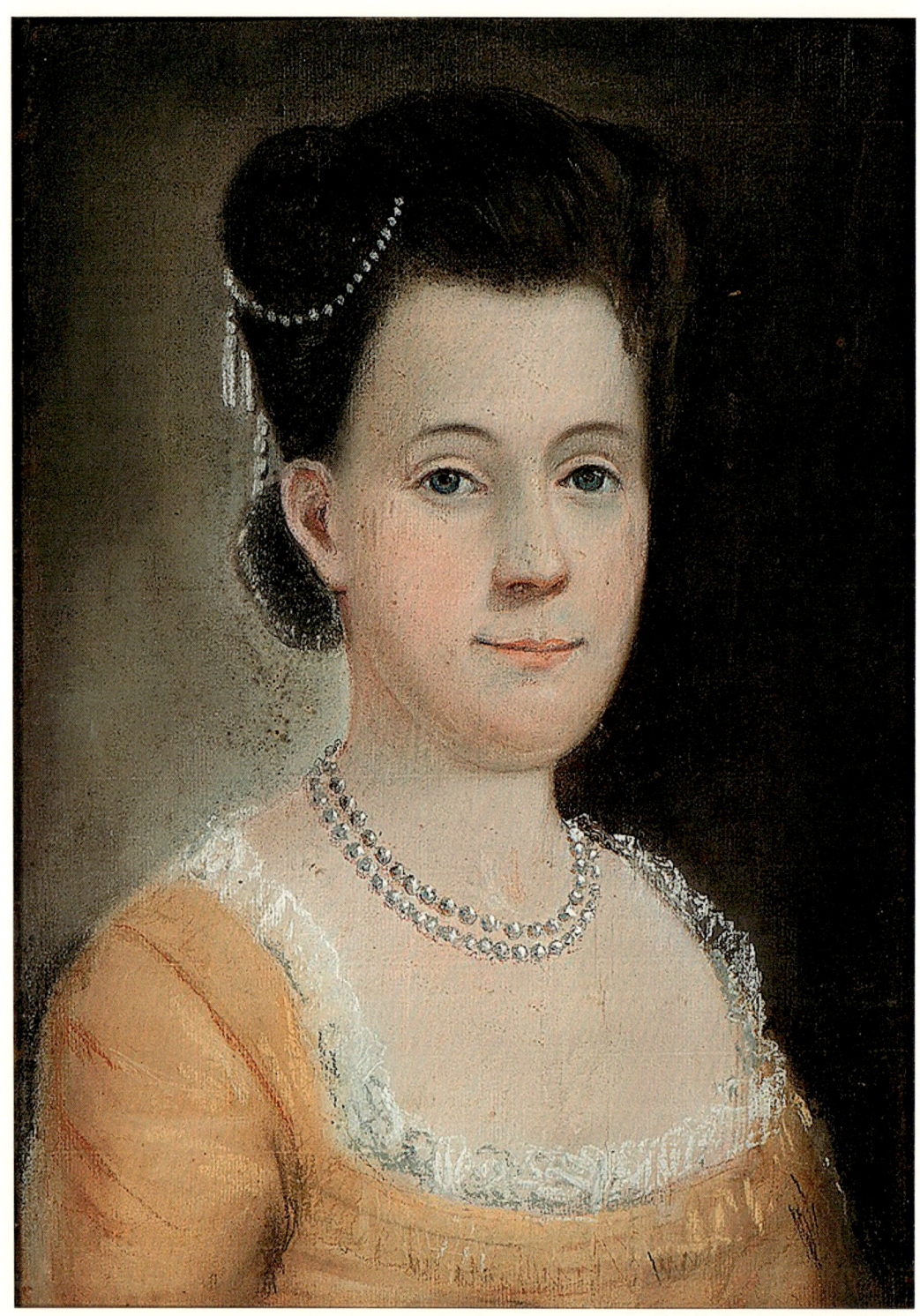

Rachel (or Thankful) Baty
Pastel by Benjamin Blyth, early 1770s(?)
Private Collection
Photograph by F. Lee Eiseman

[13]

Rachel (1743–1777) *(or Thankful)* (1741–1809) *Baty*

Benjamin Blyth, early 1770s(?)
Pastel on paper pasted on board, 14 x 10 in. (35.6 x 25.4 cm.)
Private collection; Cowan Auctions; Freeman family

Family history records this portrait as of Thankful, Gideon Baty's second wife. However, several factors suggest that it might be of his first wife, Rachel. The sitter appears to be a woman in her late twenties to early thirties, but Thankful was thirty-seven when she and Baty were married in 1777. Also, the apparel of both Gideon and his wife, plus his wig and her upswept and bejeweled hair style, suggest a date in the early 1770s.

Rachel, daughter of Amos Knowls [Knowles], was born in Eastham on January 15, 1744, and married Gideon Baty at age twenty-two on September 18, 1766. They had three children, Sally, who died before her first birthday, and Gideon and Rachel. Baty's wife Rachel died in 1777. The following year, he married Thankful, a widow whom he undoubtedly knew from Barnstable and Harwich. She was born to Benjamin Freeman Jr. and Sarah of Harwich on September 30, 1741. Her first marriage on March 18, 1762, to Watson Freeman, produced one son, Watson. No children seem to have been born from her marriage to Baty, and she died in 1809.

By 1800, Watson and his stepbrother Gideon Jr. went into business together in Boston. Their shop at Staniford and Cambridge Streets sold English goods. The neighborhood then was residential; nearby were the first mansion house of Harrison Gray Otis, built about five years earlier (now home to Historic New England), and the West Church. The families clearly were close-knit, but there is no indication through which of them the portraits descended.

Less later touching-up was done on this portrait than that of Gideon; there are a few areas on her hair with additional short black strokes, a few touches on the lace trim of her dress, strokes of yellow on her dress, and tiny dots on a few of the pearls, but none on her face. She, like her husband, looks to have been a very gentle person. The lack of information on the families in Vital Records, and the area of Cape Cod from which both came, which had an active community of Friends, suggest that they may have been Quakers.

Cowan Auctions, 10/21/2017 - *Fine & Decorative Art Featuring Americana: Day 2*
Freeman family, correspondence with a descendant, Sr. Christine Pratt, OSU
Suffolk County Probate Records 18913, 86:390

Jonathan Belcher (1682–1757)

Benjamin Blyth, copy ca. 1770 of a pastel attributed to John Singleton Copley, ca. 1756
Pastel on paper on linen, on board, 24¾ x 19 in. (62.86 x 48.26 cm.), 19th-c. frame
Massachusetts State House Art Collection 1923.2; Copley Gallery; Belcher family

In 1923 Frank W. Bayley, owner of Copley Gallery in Boston, sold this portrait, identified on the back as "J. Belcher," to the Massachusetts State Art Commission for $3,500. Bayley attributed the pastel to John Singleton Copley, done in his early "crude manner." This opinion was corroborated at the request of the Commission by art historian Lawrence Park, although he had attributed it the previous year to Joseph Blackburn. (Later, this attribution was refuted indirectly by John Hill Morgan and Henry Wilder Foote. See pp. 22–23). Evidently, neither Park nor Bayley suspected that this pastel was actually a *copy* of a Copley portrait.

Jonathan Belcher was born into a wealthy merchant family from Cambridge, Massachusetts on January 8, 1682, and graduated from Harvard College in 1699. He traveled to Europe and then joined the family business. In 1718, he was elected to the Governor's Council and was re-elected seven times during the next ten years. After the death of Gov. William Burnet in 1729, Belcher served simultaneously for more than a decade as colonial governor of the colonies of Massachusetts and New Hampshire. His tenure was controversial, and he made many powerful enemies. After a brief trip to England, he was appointed governor of New Jersey in 1747, where he attempted to mediate the conflicts between New Jersey's Quakers and large landowners. He also promoted the establishment of the College of New Jersey (later, Princeton University), along with the Reverend Ebenezer Pemberton. Through most of Belcher's tenure as royal governor, he suffered from a progressive nervous disorder and died in office in 1757.

The original pastel of Belcher was transported to England during the American Revolution and was owned by descendant Edward B. Belcher when it was seen in 1950 by John Marshall Phillips, director of the Yale University Art Gallery. He alerted Princeton, which engineered its acquisition by Carl Otto von Kienbusch '06, who then gave it to the university in 1953. A pastel portrait of Reverend Pemberton by Blyth (Cat. 104), also is owned by the university.

Belcher looks to be in his sixties, which would date the Copley oil to the mid-1750s. Blyth most likely made the copy in the early 1770s. It is an accomplished rendering, although Blyth's depiction of Belcher's personality is more subdued than the assured one portrayed by Copley. The handling also seems softer than the usual Blyth. These observations can be explained by the recent discovery of a note on the back: "Retouched with fresh crayons Nov, 1847 for/ St Andrew's Day by Mifs Jennison's friend EM Judkins." Eliza Maria Judkins [1807–1887], an artist born in Cambridge, exhibited at the Boston Athenaeum in the 1850s. Another note reads "Mifs Belcher/Clarence Lodge/ Rochampton/11thJune 1823," indicating that this pastel also was abroad at some time.

Massachusetts State House Art Collection files

Morgan, John Hill and Henry Wilder Foote, "An Extension of Lawrence Park's Descriptive List of the Work of Joseph Blackburn," *Proceedings of the American Antiquarian Society*, 46 (1936):63–64, 73.

Princeton Herald, July 22, 1953, courtesy of Princeton University Library, Special Collections

Princeton University object record PP251

SIRIS, control number 80979128, attributed to Joseph Blackburn

Wikimedia Foundation, last edited 8 November 2022, https://en.wikipedia.org/wiki/Jonathan_Belcher

WPA 174, attributed to Copley

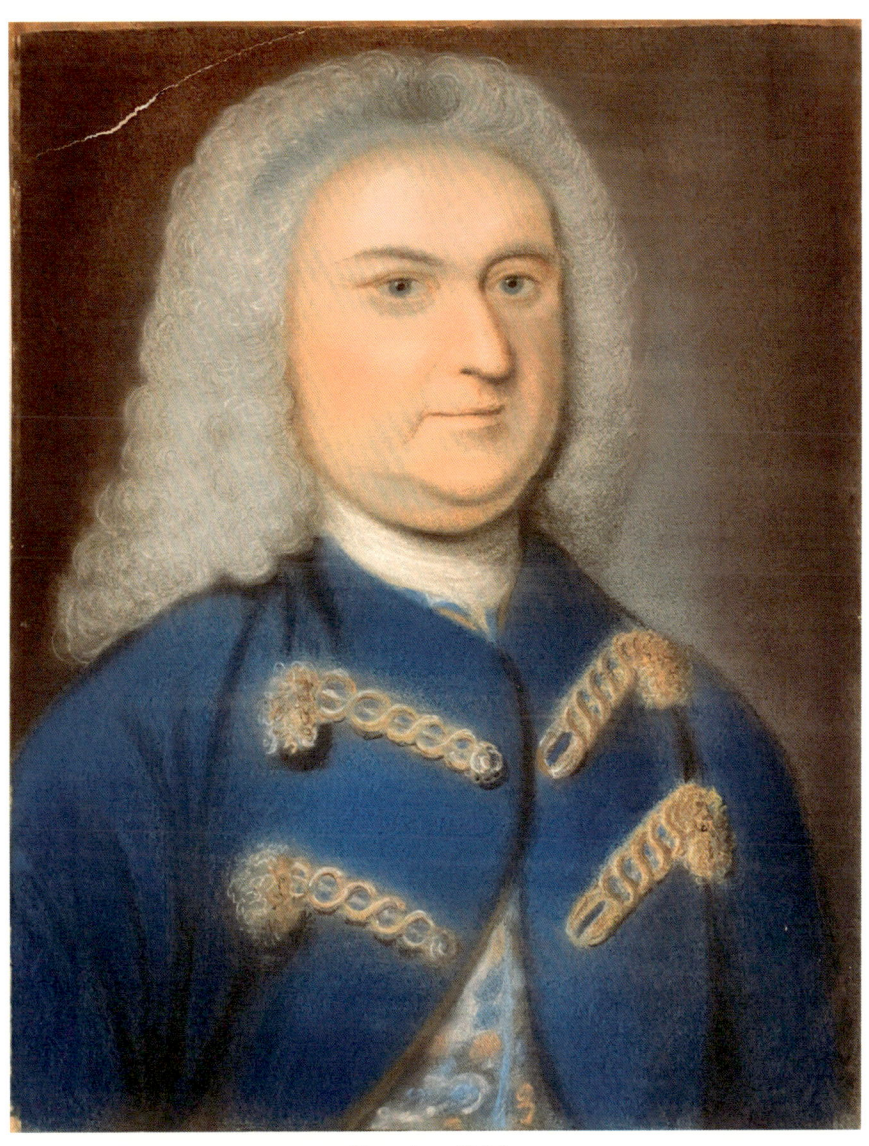

Jonathan Belcher
Pastel copy by Benjamin Blyth ca. 1770 of a pastel attributed to Copley, ca. 1756
Courtesy of Massachusetts State House Art Collection 1923. 2

[15]

Phebe Bliss (1713–1797)

Benjamin Blyth, ca. 1775
Pastel on paper mounted on linen, 21⅝ x 17¾ in. (sight), (55 x 45 cm.), Samuel Blyth frame
Ralph Waldo Emerson Memorial Association, Concord, MA; Emerson family

Phebe (Phoebe) was born in 1713 in Dighton, Massachusetts to Nathan and Abigail Walker. On July 22, 1738, she married the Reverend Daniel Bliss, who became minister of the First Parish of Concord the following year. They had three daughters and six sons. Their daughter Phebe married the Reverend William Emerson, who had assumed the pulpit. Their son William became the father of Transcendentalist Ralph Waldo Emerson, so Phebe was his great-grandmother.

When Blyth might have done the portrait of Phoebe Bliss is not clear. It is possible, though only conjecture at this point, that Benjamin Blyth participated in the engagements in Lexington and Concord, at which time he might also have done the portrait of Eleazer Brooks (Cat. 20.) She looks determined, if not set in her ways. Blyth characteristics are her facial features, with similarities to Elizabeth Cabot (Cat. 23) drawn at about the same time. Phoebe's hand is very typical of Blyth's "knuckle-less" manner, and her ermine stole is similarly drawn to that of Elizabeth Dabney (Cat. 39). It is a rare example of a Blyth portrait that shows such added elements as holding a book. Significantly, Phoebe Bliss's portrait is in a Samuel Blyth frame, a more elaborate one like that found is on the Reverend Thomas Barnard (Cat. 8).

The portrait remained in the family and is still on view in the house on Cambridge Turnpike in Concord, Massachusetts, that Emerson bought in 1835 and where he lived with his family until his death in 1882. Family members continued to live in the house until 1948. Now owned by the Ralph Waldo Emerson Memorial Association, it is open to the public on a seasonal basis.

Dighton Vital Records
Emerson House object file
Richardson, Robert D. Jr., *The Mind on Fire,* (Berkeley and Los Angeles: University of California Press, 1995)
WPA 219

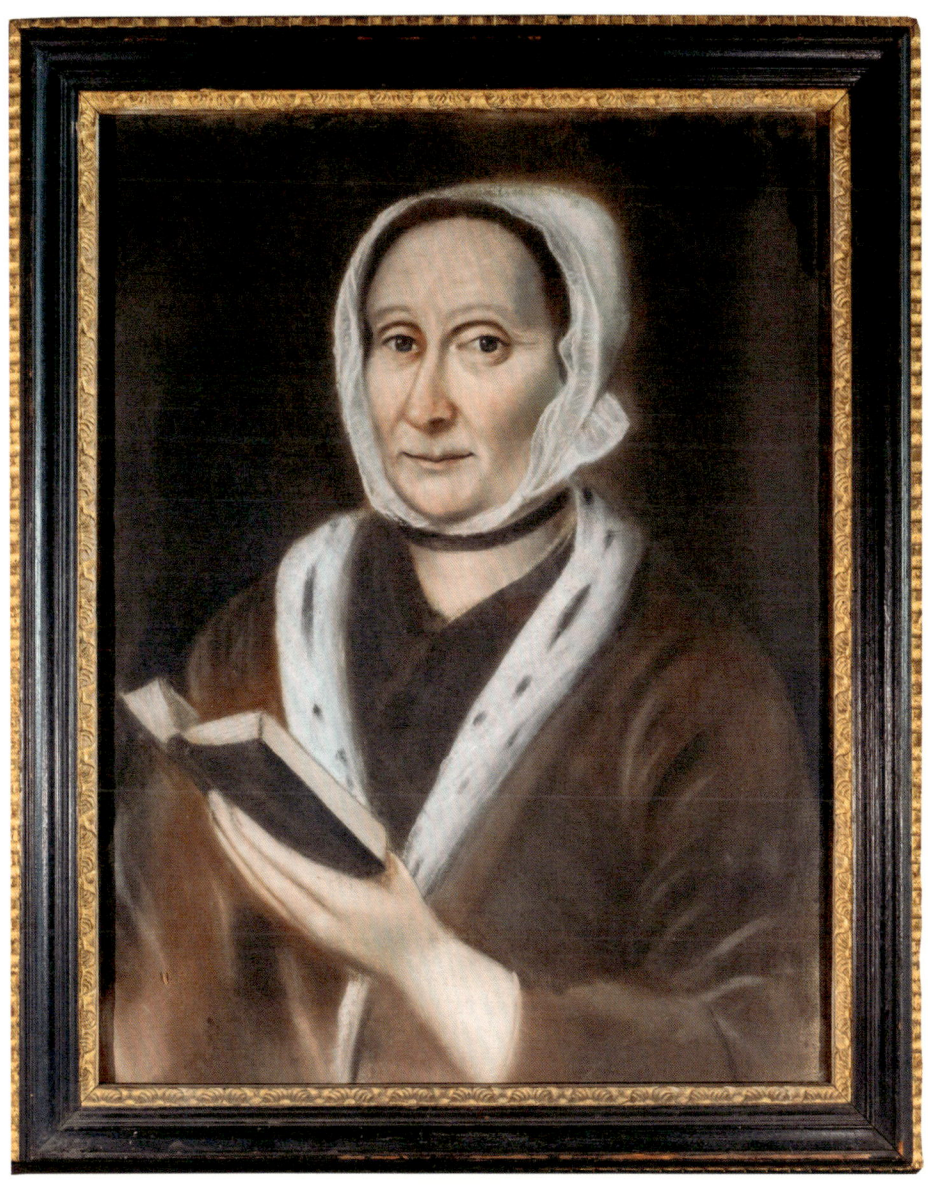

Phebe Bliss
Pastel by Benjamin Blyth, ca. 1775
Courtesy of Ralph Waldo Emerson Memorial Association, Concord, Massachusetts
Photograph by Michael C. King

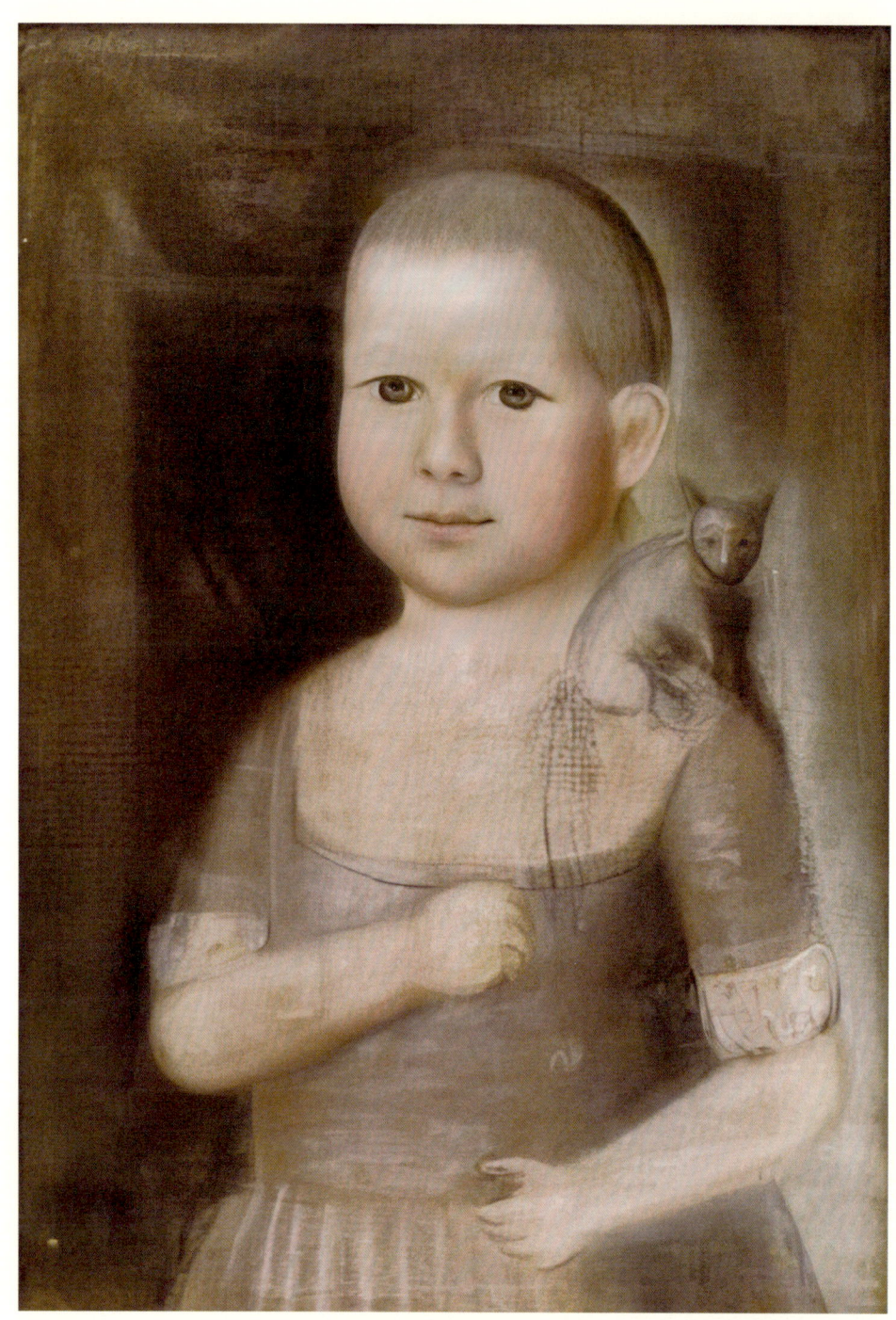

Mary Boardman
Pastel by Benjamin Blyth, ca. 1782
Private Collection

Mary Boardman (1778–1840)

Benjamin Blyth, ca. 1782
Pastel on paper mounted on linen, 21 x 16 in. (53.3 x 40.6 cm.)
Private collection; John H. Wright; CRN Auctions (Carl Nordblum), April 2005

Mary (Polly) is presumed to be the daughter of Capt. Francis and Mary Boardman of Ipswich, based on Boardman's probate inventory. In 1792, when she was about fourteen, her father, master of the schooner *Rambler*, died on a voyage from a fever he contracted in Port-au-Prince, Hispaniola. His estate, in addition to the schooner, included a mansion house and warehouse, outbuildings, "151 casks of Molasses, . . . 5 barrels of sugar, . . . silver, linens, chafing dish, and gold buttons, and & "brooch." Mary and her siblings also were beneficiaries of the substantial estate of her mother, who died in 1828.

Mary married Benjamin Crowninshield "Jr.," a son of Benjamin and Mary Crowninshield, on New Year's Day, 1804. In 1810, they commissioned a house designed by Salem's premier architect Samuel McIntire. They had nine children, including twins born in 1812. The family were said to have moved to Boston when Benjamin was elected to the Massachusetts Legislature, but a daughter, Anstiss, was born in Salem in 1815. Mary died in Cambridge in 1840 at age sixty-two and is buried at Mount Auburn Cemetery. A nineteenth-century pastel portrait of her father-in-law, Benjamin Crowninshield, in the collections of the Peabody Essex Museum, is recorded as having been based on an original miniature of him, here credited to Blyth (Cat. 31).

A news clipping on the back of the pastel identifies it as an American school portrait of Mary Boardman Crowninshield (1778?–1840) attributed to "B. Blythe." It was sold by CRN Auctions, Cambridge, MA, in 2005 for $6,325, almost half again above its top estimated price, as reported in *Maine Antique Digest*. The pastel's attribution to Benjamin Blyth has long been accepted by art historians, although it is strikingly similar to four pastels attributed in this study to Samuel Blyth (page 44). The pastel of Mary Boardman is thought to have been the prototype for Samuel Blyth, or he may have done it.

CRN Auctions, Cambridge, MA, catalogue, 2005
Geni. com/people/Mary-Crowninshield
Maine Antiques Digest, April 2005, clipping courtesy of Lois Avigad, New York City

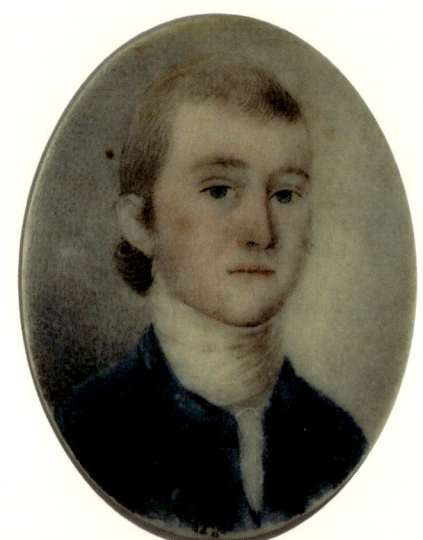

Joseph Bowditch
Miniature by Benjamin Blyth, ca. 1780
Courtesy of the Peabody Essex Museum
1980, gift of Elizabeth B. Gardner, 1878

[17]

Joseph Bowditch (1757–1800)

Benjamin Blyth, ca. 1780
Miniature on ivory, 1⅛ x ⅞ in. (2.86 x 2.22 cm.), no case
Peabody Essex Museum 1980, gift of Elizabeth B. Gardner, 1878

The Essex Institute Historical Collection's catalogue notes that this miniature portrays "a young man with fair hair," so the Joseph given as the subject, born in 1719/20, would have had to have been drawn in the 1740s. However, miniatures were not painted in the Salem area until the mid-to-late 1770s. Therefore, the subject is most likely Joseph's grandson, also a Joseph, born to Capt. Joseph Bowditch, Jr. and his second wife, Mrs. Sarah Gardner, and baptized at Salem's First Church on November 20, 1757.

The Bowditch family owned land on Essex Street, next to that of the Gardners. Although Bowditch had apprenticed to be a merchant under the tutelage of Richard Derby, he was "deposed of the estate of an Uncle by the intrigues of a Female" and was unsuccessful in business, observed the Rev. William Bentley. "He could make himself very agreeable," Bentley added, "but his anecdotes did not always gain him friendship." Becoming a "zealous Episcopalian," Bowditch joined St. Peter's Church and served on the vestry from 1785 through 1793.

He never married, and after the death of his mother in 1797, he moved to Middleton. At age forty-two, he died of "decay"—which at the time referred to "abnormal bodily weakness or feebleness." Bentley ended his account of Bowditch, "He expected death & was reconciled to it." Three weeks before his death, he made out his will, giving his estate to family of his mother, Sarah: his uncle John Gardner of Danvers and his aunts Elizabeth Gardner, Mary Andrews, and Margaret Barton, all of Salem. Bowditch was buried on May 2, 1800, in St. Peter's Church graveyard. His grandfather outlived him, dying the following October at age eighty. His grandfather's death in the same year may have occasioned the confusion of which Joseph was the subject of the miniature.

Blyth depicted a handsome young man looking quite tenuous, pale, and possibly sickly, as Bowditch was.

Bentley 2:335,
EIHC 6:97, 162; 70:182-3, cat. 22, "unknown artist"
FARL, American School, Massachusetts (1701–1750) 175-12a
Gardner, *Planter*, 378
Phillips, *Salem . . . 18th C.*, 263

Two Young Women of the Bradish Family

Benjamin Blyth, early 1770s

Pastels on paper pasted on board, each 14¾ x 10½ in. (37.5 x 26.7 cm.), 19th-c. gilt wood frames

Private Collection, Alexandria, Virginia; Skinner Inc., auction 2255, in 2004; Robinson family

These portraits went to auction accompanied by handwritten notes that identified one as Elizabeth Bradish, daughter of Col. John Bradish who "married Edward Capeu on October 9, 1803," and the other as "Sister of Elizabeth Bradish Capeu Harris."

However, the Elizabeth who married Edward Capen ("Capeu" is an incorrect transcription) was born in 1783 in Portland, Maine, to David and Abiah (Merrill) Bradish. She and her sister would have been too young, if even born, to have been subjects for Blyth. The sitters look to be at least in their late twenties or early thirties, suggesting that the sisters belong to the previous generation. The only Massachusetts birth recorded in Massachusetts of a David Bradish, wrongly identified as their father, was on October 25, 1745, in Medford to Jonathan and Abigail (Johnson) Bradish. Most likely, the sitters were his sisters and therefore aunts of the Elizabeth who was thought to have been depicted. The possibilities are Abigail ("Nabby"), born in 1744—whose second husband was the son of Peter Frye, drawn by Blyth (Cat. 56); Susanna, born in 1752; or Catherine, born in 1755, who never married. The family was then living in Charlestown.

Correspondence with the owners

Curley, Juanita Bradish, *A Genealogy & History of Robert Bradish in America*, (Northville, Mich: The Unicorn Press, 2000), 40

FARL, American School, Massachusetts (1751–1800) 158-3a drawing

Jeffares, http://www.pastellists.com/Articles/Blyth. pdf

Middlesex Probate File Papers 2453, 1788

Skinner, Inc. auction 2255, lot 215,

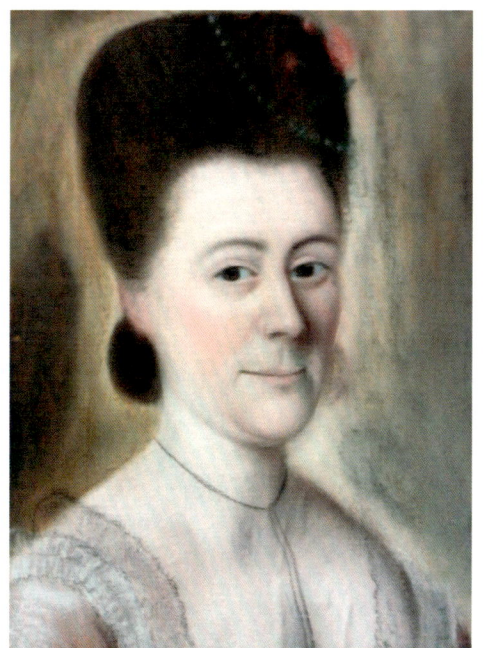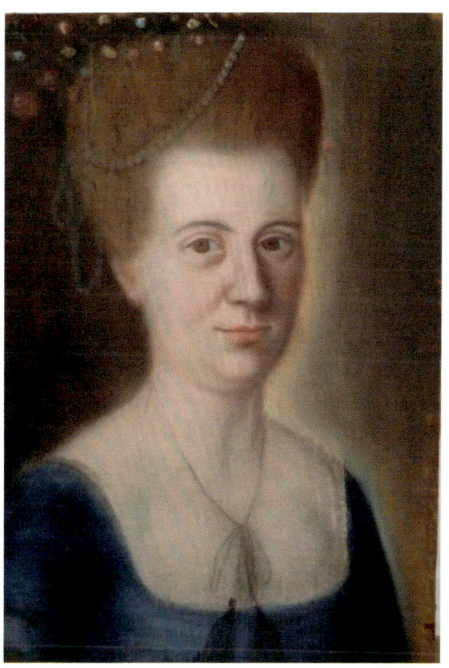

Two Young Women of the Bradish Family
Pastels by Benjamin Blyth, early 1770s
Private Collection

☞ Hannah Porter Breck (1757–1838); see Hannah Porter (Cat. 108)

[20]

Eleazer Brooks (1727–1806)

Benjamin Blyth, ca. 1775
Pastel on paper mounted on linen, 20 x 17 in. (50.8 x 43.2 cm.)
Concord Museum 2005.1, Anonymous gift with George and Lisa Foote and Candace Brooks Carr;
Sotheby's; Avis and Rockwell Gardiner, Stamford, CT; provenance unknown

Eleazer Brooks, farmer and prominent citizen and public official in Lincoln, Massachusetts, was born on September 10, 1727, to Job and Elizabeth Brooks in the section of Concord that was set off to become Lincoln in 1754. He married Mary Taylor of Concord in 1763, and the next year, they became members of the Lincoln church, for which he eventually became deacon. His wife died in 1769, and in 1777, he married Elizabeth Greenough of Boston. They had two children, Eleazer Jr. and Elizabeth.

Brooks held several town offices in Lincoln before the Revolution: surveyor of highways, treasurer (three terms), and selectman (two terms). As early advocate of separation from Britain, he was elected to Lincoln's Committee of Correspondence in 1773 and in 1774 drafted the letter in opposition to the tea tax and penned "Thoughts on Civil Government." Joining the Militia as a lieutenant, he was promoted to colonel of the 3rd Middlesex Co. Regt. On February 8, 1776, and marched his troops to reinforce the Continental Army at Dorchester Heights, then to New York. On October 15, 1778, he was promoted Brigadier-General of Militia of Middlesex County. Brooks represented Lincoln at Massachusetts's ratification of the Articles of Confederation in that year and was elected the town's first representative two years later. He died in Lincoln on November 9, 1806.

Brooks' active participation in the Revolution made him a likely subject to be drawn by Benjamin Blyth. This portrait, like that of Phebe Bliss (Cat. 15), raises the possibility that Blyth was present at the engagements in Lexington and Concord.

Brooks's expression, notably in the curve of the eyebrows and pursed mouth, bespeaks a critical outlook.

Concord (MA) Public Library Archives, Eleazar Brooks Papers
Sotheby's catalogue "American School 18th Century," No8053 lot 916, 2005

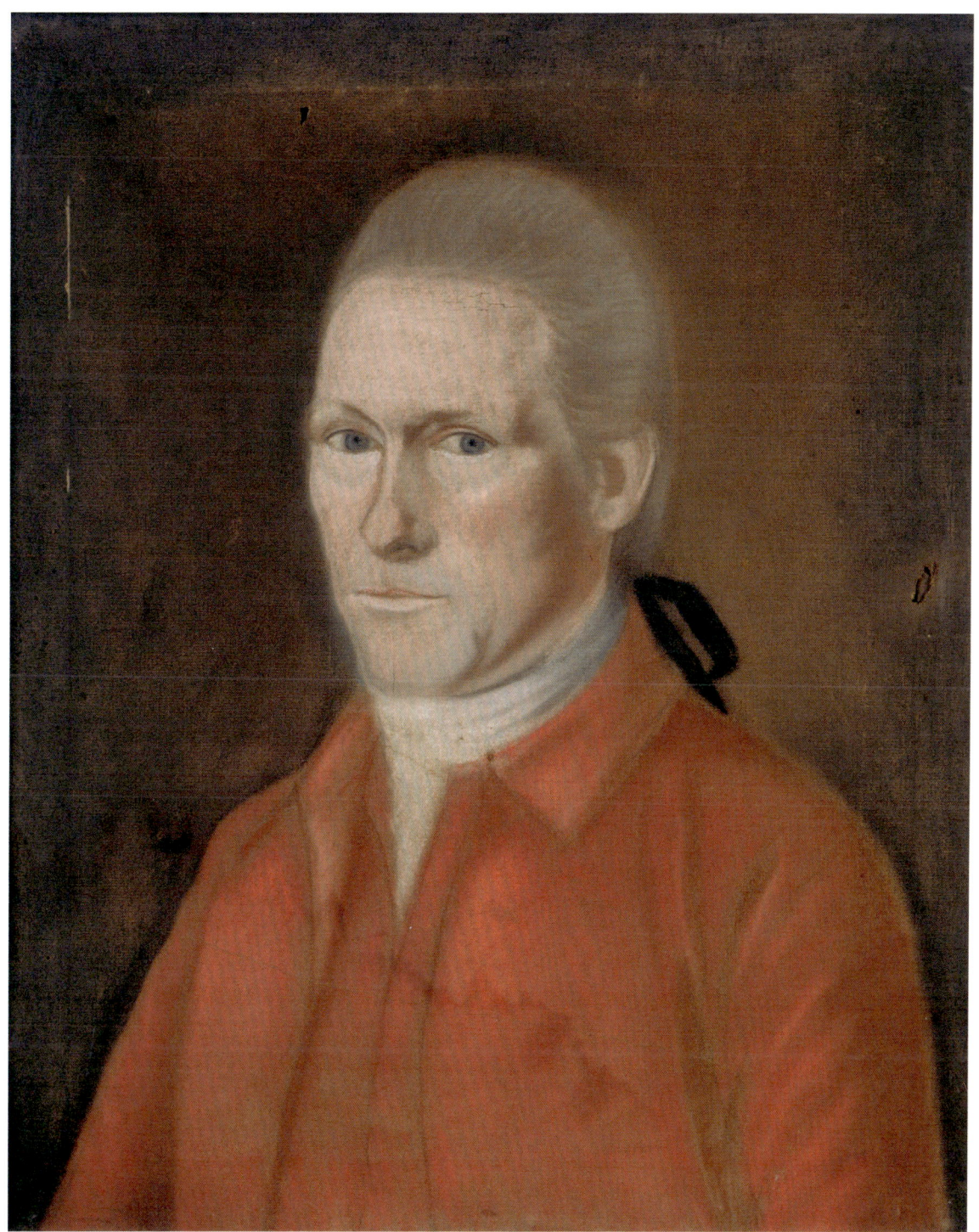

Eleazer Brooks
Pastel by Benjamin Blyth, ca. 1775
Courtesy of the Concord Museum 2005. 1, Anonymous gift with
George and Lisa Foote Candace Brooks Carr
Photograph by David Wood

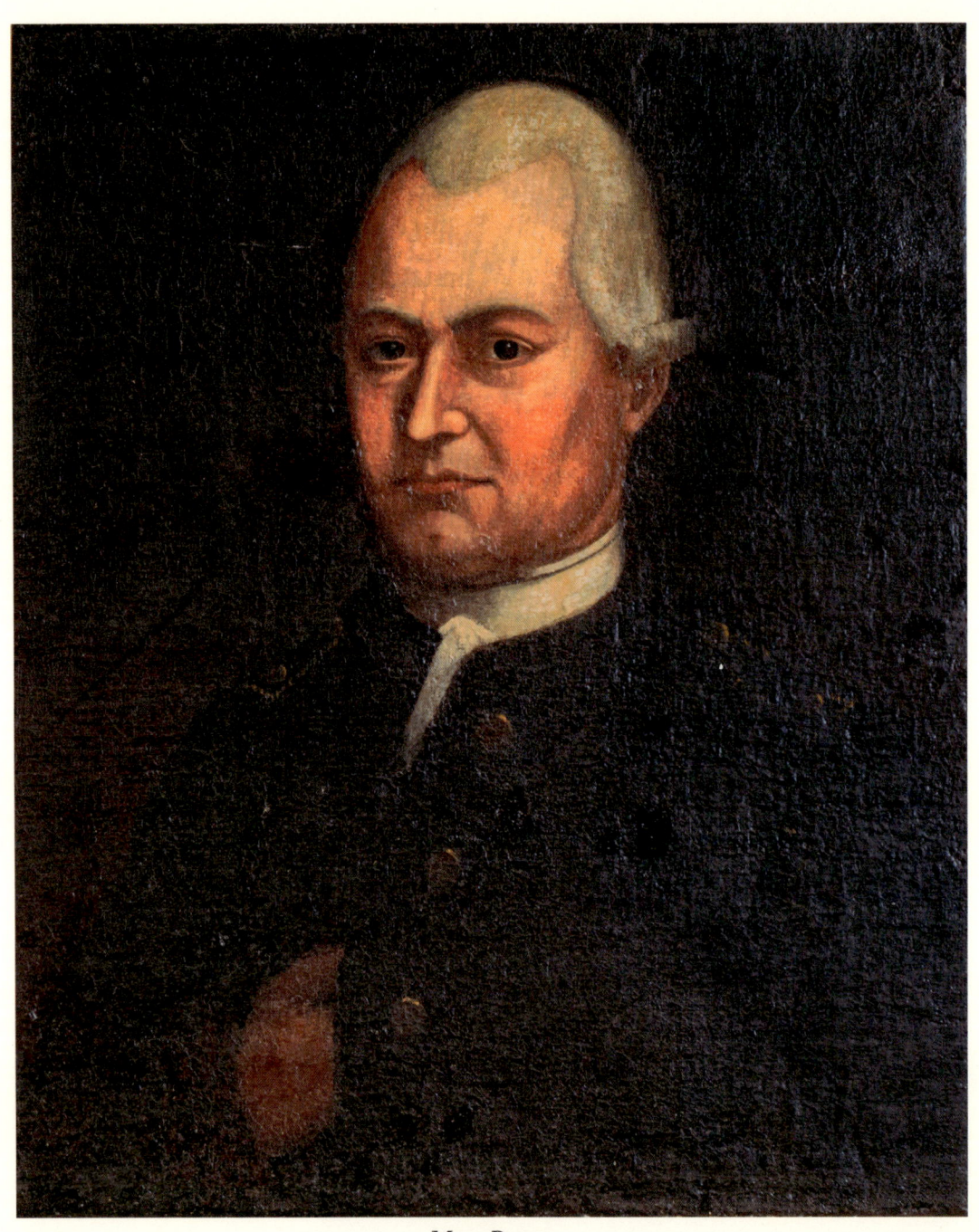

Moses Brown
Oil painting by Benjamin Blyth, 1778–1782
Courtesy of the Historical Society of Old Newbury 1975.10.1

[21]

Moses Brown (1742–1804)

Benjamin Blyth, 1778-82
Oil on canvas, 24 x 19½ in. (60.7 x 49.5 cm.)
Custom House Maritime Museum, 1975. 10. 1

Moses Brown of Newburyport, known both as "Gentleman Brown" and "Seafaring Brown," was a successful investor in the sugar, molasses, and rum trade and became the second wealthiest man in the town. He spent most of his life in naval engagements "interspersed with merchant voyages." He fought against both France and Britain, and he was taken a prisoner of war three times. Born on Ring's Island, Salisbury, to Edward and Dorothy Brown on January 23, 1742, Moses Brown was apprenticed at sea at age fifteen to Capt. William Coffin and in 1763 married Coffin's younger sister, Sarah. They had nine children born between 1765 and 1781, one of whom died as a toddler, and two who became sea captains like their father.

Like many Essex County men, Brown joined the march to Concord in April 1775 and returned with the troops to Cambridge, where company receipts show he was in May, June, October, and November. Jonathan Glover (Cat. 62) was a drummer in Brown's company in 1776. A fellow townsman in Newburyport, Samuel Newhall, petitioned with others that Brown be commissioned commander of the *General Arnold* as a privateer in 1778; it was one of six ships he commanded. In 1798, he was commissioned a captain in the U.S Navy to command the sloop of war *Merrimack*. After the Revolution, Brown became a merchant trader amassing a fortune in the pepper trade. He also he helped promote the "Salem Turnpike and Chelsea Bridge Corporation" between Salem and Boston, along with Francis and George Cabot and George Dodge, all drawn by Blyth (Cats. 24, 25, 49). Brown died from apoplexy on January 2, 1804, in Long Island Sound on a return voyage from Guadaloupe and is buried in Newburyport.

Brown's portrait is very similar in coloration, composition, and execution to Blyth's later portraits of Edward Lang (Cat. 83) and Deborah Prince Cary (Cat. 26). The military insignia on Brown's uniform indicates that he was an officer in the Continental Navy, so the portrait most likely was painted soon after he received his commission in 1778. He is wearing a wig, which, by that time, was becoming out of fashion. Although no corroborating reference to Brown's personality has surfaced so far, the portrait depicts him as quite somber, determined, even possibly ruthless.

Benes, *Old-Town and the Waterside*, 117
EIHC 5:59; 25:11; 38:242–3; 80:56–7, 88:129; 92:110; 102:305
FARL, American School, Massachusetts (1801–1850) 121-7c2
Jackson, Russell Leigh, "The Story of the Seafaring Brown," *EIHC* 80:56–57
Massachusetts Soldiers and Sailors in the American Revolution 2:666

[22]

Anna "Nancy" Cabot (1759/60–1788)

Benjamin Blyth (attr.), probably 1780
Miniature, measurements unknown
Image location unknown; John Higginson Cabot, Esq., Brookline, MA

Anna "Nancy" Clarke, daughter of Capt. John and Sarah (Pickering) Clarke, married Francis Cabot on January 28, 1780. They had three children, two boys and one girl. The first son, Francis, died at age six; another, John Higginson, died unmarried in Marseilles. Anna Cabot died on September 9, 1788, at age twenty-eight at "childbed." Her miniature was described in *Pickering Genealogy* as "a small and unsatisfactory miniature of Mrs. Cabot in the possession of her grandson, John H[igginson] Cabot, of Brookline." As her only recorded son died purportedly unmarried, the relationship is probably incorrect. The miniature of her husband, Francis Cabot, Jr. (Cat. 24), has been attributed to Blyth, who also had drawn two pastels of other Cabot family members, so the assumption that Anna was one is plausible. The miniatures were probably done at the time of the marriage of Anna and Francis.

Ellery and Bowditch, *Pickering Genealogy* 1:233

[23]

Elizabeth Higginson Cabot (1722–1781)

Benjamin Blyth, probably 1767
Pastel on paper mounted on linen, 20 x 15 in. (50.8 x 38.1 cm.), Samuel Blyth frame
with original glass and hooks
Jonathan Lee; Joseph Lee, provenance through the Lee family

Elizabeth Higginson, born in Salem in 1722 to John and Ruth (Bordman) Higginson, married Joseph Cabot in 1744. Four years later, Cabot built "the finest house then in Salem" at 365 Essex Street, and he and his wife actively engaged in the town's social life as a mercantile family. They were considered "perhaps . . . next in importance to the Pickmans," according to James Duncan Phillips. The Cabots had ten sons and one daughter. Soon after Mrs. Cabot was widowed in 1767, she moved to Beverly, "thinking to find a little better draft of water, with less costly wharfage." From Beverly, she skillfully managed her husband's company and the affairs of numerous real estate holdings. In 1773, she built the house at 115 Cabot Street, since moved around the corner onto Central Street. Artifacts from the house are now owned by the Beverly Museum and Historical Society.

In the mid-1960s, Elizabeth Cabot's portrait was hanging in the Beacon Hill house of long-time Boston School Committee member Joseph Lee, a direct descendant. At the time, the portraait was believed to be a Copley, cited as such in both the American Portrait Inventory (1941) and *History and Genealogy of the Cabot Family 1475–1927* (1927), where it is reproduced opposite page 59—with incorrect dates. His grandson, Jonathan Lee, the current owner, had it conserved, replacing the original glass but keeping the original, and has carefully archived all documents on the portrait that have accrued over the last 100 years. Elizabeth Cabot's son George (Cat. 25) also painted by Blyth is now owned by another descendant. Both portraits are still in their original Samuel Blyth frames.

Elizabeth Cabot's portrait, one of Blyth's most poignant portrayals, shows a woman alert and thoughtful, though in sorrow. It was probably done around the time of the death of her husband. A miniature said to be of him, in the collections of the Peabody Essex Museum, shows a man in 1790s costume, so it is probably not of Joseph and more likely depicts their son, Joseph Jr. Two other sons, John and Andrew, married sisters Hannah and Lydia, daughters of George and Lydia (Herrick) Dodge, who also were drawn by Blyth (Cats. 49, 50), as was a miniature of Elizabeth Higginson Cabot's son Francis (Cat. 24) and his wife, Anna (Cat. 22).

Joseph Lee (1901–1991), long-time member of the School Committee of the City of Boston, was extremely proud of his ancestor and her portrait, although he did believe that it was drawn by John Singleton Copley. For years, it hung over the fireplace of his Federal-era house on South Russell Street in Boston. His grandson is the current custodian of this most haunting pastel, now attributed to Blyth.

Briggs, . . . *Cabot Family*, 1:53, illus. opp. 59 (with the wrong dates for Elizabeth Cabot)

EIHC 55:107-8, 63:279

Foote, "Blyth," 83 ("Mrs. Joseph Cabot")

Jeffares, http://www.pastellists.com/Articles/Blyth.pdf

Lee, Jonathan, documents

Norton, "Benjamin Blyth," 62

Phillips, *Salem, 18th C.*, 245

SIRI IAP 80950004, attr. to Blyth

WPA 350, "either Blyth or Copley"

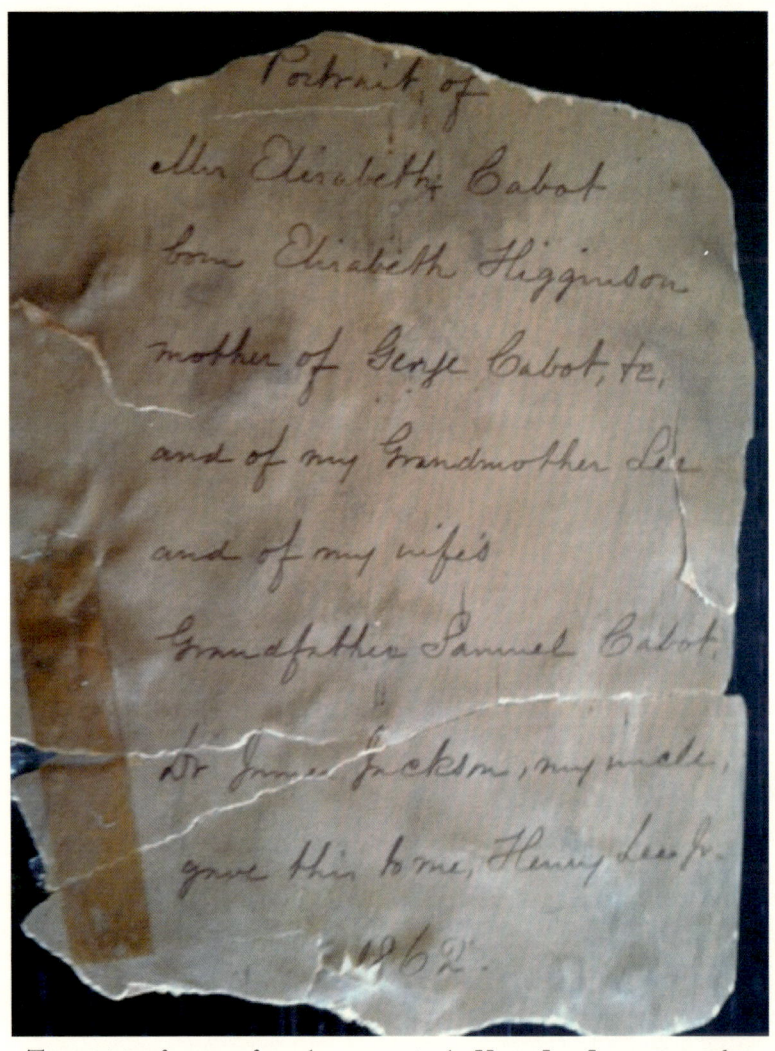

The surviving fragment from the manuscript by Henry Lee, Jr., once pasted to
the back of the portrait, giving the family genealogy up to 1862.
Courtesy of Jonathan Lee.

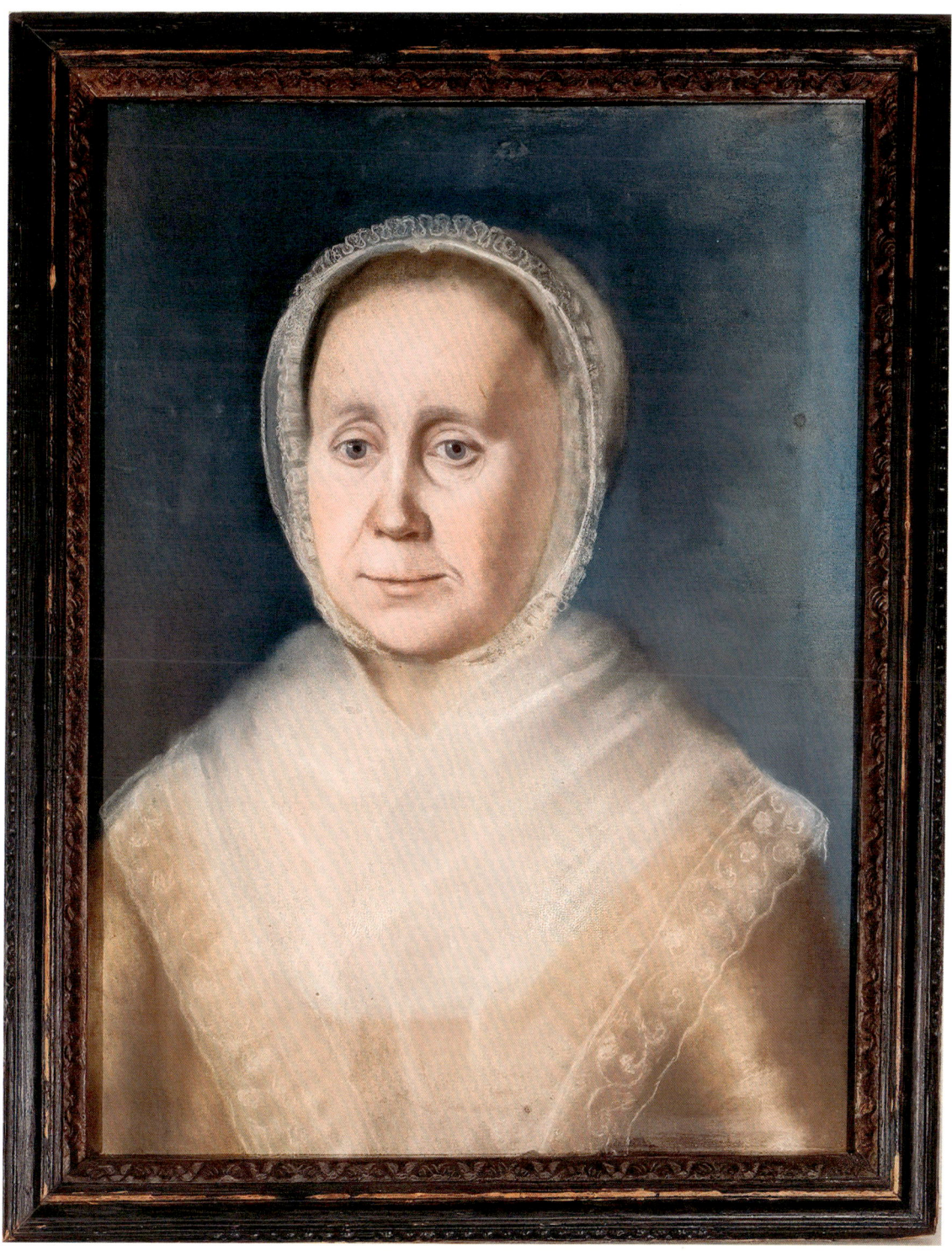

Elizabeth Higginson Cabot
Pastel by Benjamin Blyth, probably 1767
Courtesy of the collection of Jonathan Lee
Photograph by Michael C. King

[24]

Francis Cabot, Jr. (1757–1832)

Benjamin Blyth (attr.), probably 1780
Miniature, measurements unknown
Current location not known; John Higginson Cabot, Esq., Brookline, MA

Francis Cabot was actively involved in events relating to the founding of the United States, as was his older brother George Cabot (Cat. 25), an eminent merchant and Federalist. Francis was born in Salem on June 14, 1757, to Joseph and Elizabeth Higginson Cabot (Cat. 23). When he was ten years old, his father died, and his mother moved the family to Beverly. Francis—called Francis "Jr." to distinguish him from his uncle—became a merchant and moved back to Salem. He owned or partially owned several ships, including the privateers *Pilgrim* and *Spanish Packet*, with ten guns. On January 28, 1780, he married Anna "Nancy" Clark, daughter of Capt. John and Sarah (Pickering) Clarke. They had three children. After the Revolution, Francis was a major in Gen. Lincoln's brigade that suppressed Shay's Rebellion in 1787.

In 1788, his gardens were being repeatedly vandalized, according to an ad offering a reward he placed in the *Salem Mercury*. His wife Nancy died on September 9, 1788, at age twenty-eight, at "childbed," as the unusual record reads. Leaving his children to be raised by their maternal grandparents, Capt. John and Sarah (Pickering) Clarke, Francis moved to Philadelphia, then to Natchez, Mississippi, where he died in 1832. The Pickering Genealogy states that he was "said to have been a very agreeable man and to have made many friends."

The miniature is known only in illustrations in the Cabot and Pickering genealogies. Although it is credited there to Ramage, its attributes not only are more in keeping with Blyth—the eyes, lip line, and ear, and Cabot had left Salem before Ramage arrived there. Blyth also made portraits of other members of the Cabot family. This one of Francis Cabot and one of his wife, now lost, which is also attributed here to Blyth, were owned in 1897 by John Higginson Cabot of Brookline.

Bentley, 1:36, 84, 104; 2:414

Briggs, . . . *Cabot Family*, 1:194–95

Burroughs, *Limners and Likenesses*, 69–70

Ellery and Bowditch, *Pickering Genealogy* 1:233, illus. betw. 234–35

Essex County Probate Records, 1786, case 4435

EIHC 1:113, 6:108,15:44, 38:303, 55:107-8, 63:279, 73:348, 353

FARL, American School, Massachusetts (1751–1800) 175-10b

Historic Beverly, Cabot Family Papers: Cabot, Francis, Jr.

Salem Mercury, May 19, 1788

Salem Register, Aug. 9, 1832

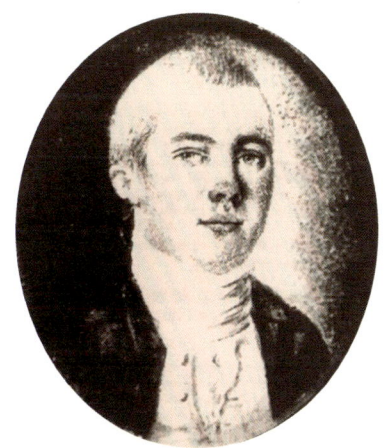

Francis Cabot
Photograph of unlocated miniature attributed to
Benjamin Blyth, probably 1780
Illustration from L. Vernon Briggs, *History and
Genealogy of the Cabot Family*
Courtesy of the Boston Athenaeum

George Cabot (1752–1823)

Benjamin Blyth, signed "1771," probably 1767
Pastel on paper mounted on linen, 16 x 12½ in. (40.6 x 31.7 cm.), Samuel Blyth frame
Collection of Henry S. Richardson; Hon. Eliot L. Richardson, Henry Lee Shattuck,
Mrs. Frederick C. Shattuck, Colonel Henry Lee

George Cabot was born to Joseph and Elizabeth Higginson Cabot (Cat. 23) on January 16, 1752. His father, who died in December 1767, provided in his will for his son's education at Harvard College until he earned one degree, and as long as he was "[c]ontinuing to belong to said Colledge and not being expelled." Nonetheless, Cabot left before graduating to go to sea for his brother-in-law, Capt. Joseph Lee, "who gave his young kinsman the full benefit of severe ship's discipline." These two records hint at some youthful problems, but the rest of his career was successful and noteworthy. Rising quickly, he was made a captain at age twenty, but after several long voyages and his marriage on February 22, 1774, to Elizabeth Higginson, a double first cousin, he gave up life at sea for mercantile pursuits at home. The Cabots had nine children, four of whom died in infancy and their firstborn at age thirteen.

During the American Revolution, Cabot and his brothers John and Andrew engaged in extensive privateering. Two of their large and heavily armed vessels were the brigantines *Hampden* and the *Oliver Cromwell*. Cabot also was a successful merchant, "thought by his contemporaries second only to Hamilton in his knowledge of finance," noted the Reverend William Bentley. At the conclusion of the Revolution, he formed a successful partnership, Lee & Cabot, with Capt. Lee but retired from active participation in 1792, when he became a U. S. Senator for Massachusetts. In 1787, Cabot was a major force behind erecting a controversial bridge at the North Ferry in Salem, to connect with Beverly. He was also involved in the move to establish the first cotton mill in the colonies in 1788.

During much of Cabot's adult life, he was involved in politics. In 1775, he was a member of the Provincial Congress, then a member of both the state Constitutional Convention and the one which ratified the U. S. Constitution. A confirmed Federalist, Cabot served as U. S. Senator from 1792 to 1796 but resigned a year before his term expired because of the vitriolic political climate. He was appointed first president of the Boston branch of the newly established United States Bank in 1791 and served until 1793. By then, the Cabot family was living in Brookline, but in 1803, upon his second appointment to the bank, they moved to Boston. He became president of the Federalist's Hartford Convention at the end of the War of 1812, to oppose the policies of presidents Jefferson and Madison. Ultimately unsuccessful, that role effectively ended Cabot's political career.

The pastel of George Cabot, dominated by the same clear blue eyes, shows the affinity Cabot must have had with his mother—a calm, thoughtful personality. This trait of portraying personal-

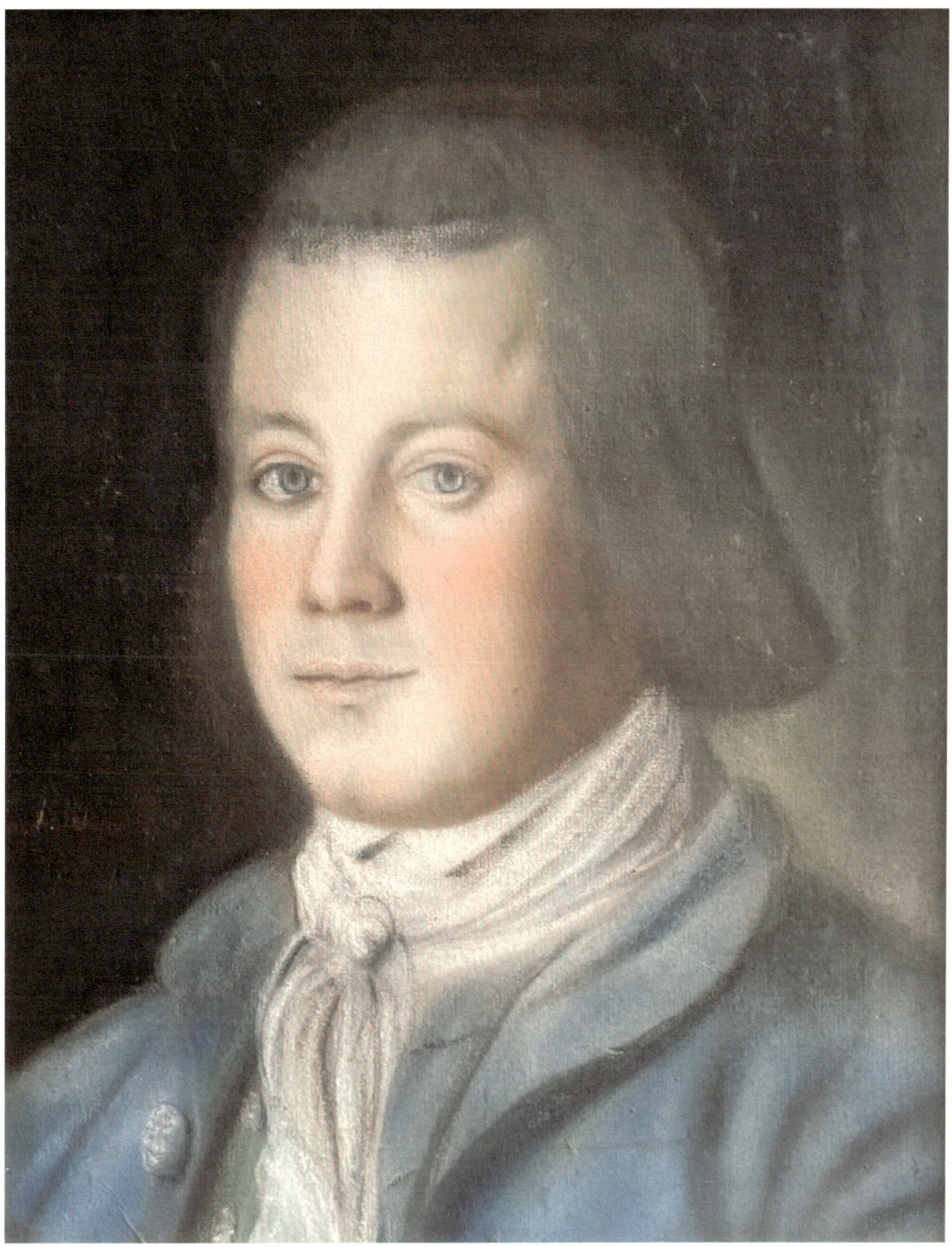

George Cabot
Pastel by Benjamin Blyth, probably 1767, signed
Courtesy of Henry S. Richardson

ity was present from the beginning of Blyth's career. The portrait, which remains in the family, is the only pastel known to have been signed, allegedly by Blyth. This, however, did not preclude it from being considered for years as a work by Copley, until the catalogue of his work was prepared in 1938 by Barbara Neville Parker and Anne Wheeler for an exhibition at Boston's Museum of Fine Arts. They noted it was "signed at lower left," but in the copy of their book at the Boston Athenaeum, someone penciled in "signed lower right." Both signatures are barely visible or credible: Henry Wilder Foote in *The Proceedings of the Massachusetts Historical Society* in 1957 noted that "B Blyth Pinx^t 1767" was at the left, but "B Blyth Pinx^t 1771" also appears on the right. According to Cabot's father's will drawn in November 1767, George was already at Harvard, though on shaky ground. The portrait most likely dates from that time.

Bayley, *Copley*, 72–73

Bentley 1:70, 79–81, 100, 102, 310 fn.; 2:343; 3:411

Bolton, *Portrait Draughtsmen*, 18

Briggs, *Cabot Genealogy*, 1:53, 185–93

Burroughs, *Limners and Likenesses*, 69

Dresser, Louisa, "Attribution and Authenticity in American Painting," *Art in America* 33 (October 1945), illus. opp. 199

EIHC 69:25-32, 102; 33:11, 13–17

FARL, Blyth, Benjamin 157-3e

Felt 1:307–8

Foote, "Blyth," 71:82–83

Jeffares, http://www.pastellists.com/Articles/Blyth.pdf

Norton, "Brothers Blyth" 48 (illus.), 62

Parker and Wheeler, *Copley*, 258

Phillips, *Salem . . . 18th C.*, 405, 409–10

Sibley 17:344–358

SMS: Plate 1, no. 54

Winsor, *Memorial History of Boston*, illus. 3:214

WPA 353

[26]

Deborah Prince Cary (1745?–1821)

Benjamin Blyth, probably late 1783
Oil on canvas, 22⅜ x 17⅛ in. (56.8 x 43.5 cm.), original Samuel Blyth frame with hooks
First Religious Society Unitarian Universalist, Newburyport, MA

Although there has been some reservation about whether this portrait is of the Rev. Thomas Cary's first or second wife, it seems most likely to be his second, the former Deborah Prince, whom he married on September 1, 1783. Cary's first wife, Esther (Carter), died in childbirth in May 1779 at age thirty. Her newborn son Jonathan died six months later, and her older son, Thomas was then two years old. The woman in the portrait looks as if she were in her late thirties to early forties, which would have been the case if the portrait was of Deborah and done around the time of their marriage. Also, both the palette and the handling support the attribution to Benjamin Blyth's work of that period.

Deborah Prince was living in Exeter, N. H., when she married the Rev. Cary, but little else is known of her. She is possibly the child born in Boston in 1745 to Moses and Jane Prince, but when Moses died in 1788, he left his estate to only one child, Abigail. Rev. Thomas and Deborah Cary had six children. A son George may have been named for George Prince, ostensibly Deborah Cary's older brother. Four children died in infancy, one as a young teenager, and another son drowned at sea in 1804. Only one child, Samuel, seems to have survived to adulthood, although no record has been found. Deborah Cary died on November 10, 1821, at age seventy-seven.

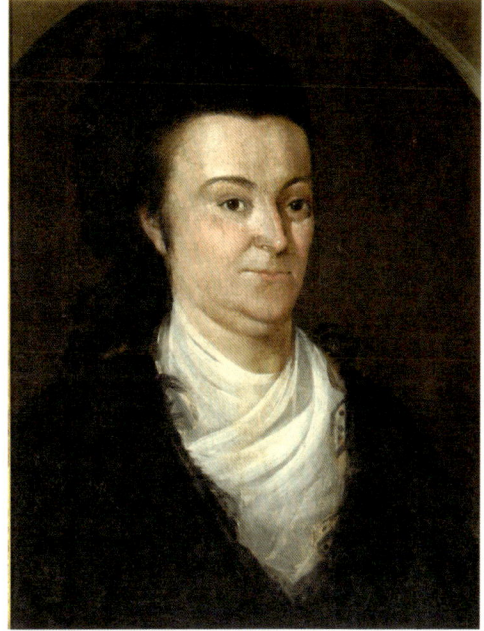

Her portrait may have been done to complement that of her husband, a pastel drawn by Blyth about ten years earlier. However, her portrait not only is an oil but is in a half-rondel, a conservative touch rarely used by Blyth but perhaps asked for by Cary or his wife. Both portraits are in Samuel Blyth frames, closely matched, with the original ring hangers to attach with chains to ceiling trim. One of Blyth's last portraits, that of Deborah Cary shows greater skill in handling the medium of oil in the modeling of her face. Severely dressed with a white throat scarf covering her chest, she appears serious-minded in her role as surrogate mother.

First Religious Society Unitarian Universalist, Newburyport, MA

Foote, "Blyth," 84-85 ("Mrs. Thomas Cary")

Deborah Prince Cary
Oil painting by Benjamin Blyth, probably late 1783
Courtesy of First Religious Society Unitarian
Universalist, Newburyport, MA

[27]

Thomas Cary (1745–1808)

Benjamin Blyth, early 1770s
Pastel on paper mounted on linen, 22 x 17¼ in. (55.9 x 43.8 cm.),
Samuel Blyth frame, original glass, and hooks
First Religious Society Unitarian Universalist, Newburyport, MA

The Reverend Thomas Cary served his parish, then the First Church in Newburyport, in a long and successful career from 1769 until his death in 1808. Born in Charlestown, Massachusetts, on October 7, 1745, to Samuel and Margaret (Graves) Cary, he graduated from Harvard College in 1761. He married Esther Beck Carter, a daughter of one of Newburyport's wealthiest residents, in 1775, whose uncle, the Reverend Edward Bass (Cat. 10) later became the first Episcopal bishop of Massachusetts. She died in 1779 after the birth of their second son, Jonathan, who also died six months later. Cary remained a widower with their older son, Thomas, for three-and-a-half years until his marriage to Deborah Prince of Exeter, New Hampshire, on September 1, 1783.

Cary's diary reflects frequent visits with friends and exchanges of pulpits with clergy in other towns. The diary of the Reverend William Bentley contains many entries of his "most worthy Friend Cary," who, he noted, was "a friend of my youth, a man whom I most highly esteemed" "a man of wealth, & of kind manners." Both men were a collegial group; in an entry about religious revivalists in Newburyport, Bentley wrote that Bishop Bass "observes his usual prudence, & Messrs. Cary and Andres of the first Church are obliged to a painful silence . . ."

The inscription on the back of Reverend Cary's portrait, dated four years after he arrived, notes: "Oct^r —^th1773/A Gift/of the/ Revd. /Thomas/Cary of/ Newburypt/ [in different ink and not the same hand] D. Balch." Henry Wilder Foote suggested in 1957 that the portrait was by Blyth, and calling it "a very pleasing one." Two important catalogues of American art, that of the Harvard collections and of the Metropolitan Museum of New York (1995), quoted here, have pointed out how well Blyth conveyed Cary's personality: "The portraits in most cases are the only known representations, so difficult to corroborate if they are accurate. However, Benjamin Blyth drew the Reverend Thomas Cary in pastel (fig. 205) at about the time that Copley painted him, and Cary's rather unusual, elfin face looks very similar in both pictures," noted Theodore L. Stebbins (see p. 64). He is the only clergyman drawn or painted by Blyth who not only was not wearing the clerical collar but wore a banyan, India-inspired leisure wear indicative of a stylish upper-class man of the time. Blyth's portrait not only is a very sympathetic portrayal of the characteristics Bentley found in his friend, but of his serenity, impressive, given the tragedies in his life.

Bentley, 1:61, 250; 2:113, 364; 3:42, 368, 391, 398
EIHC 85:159, fn.
Foote, "Blyth," 83-84

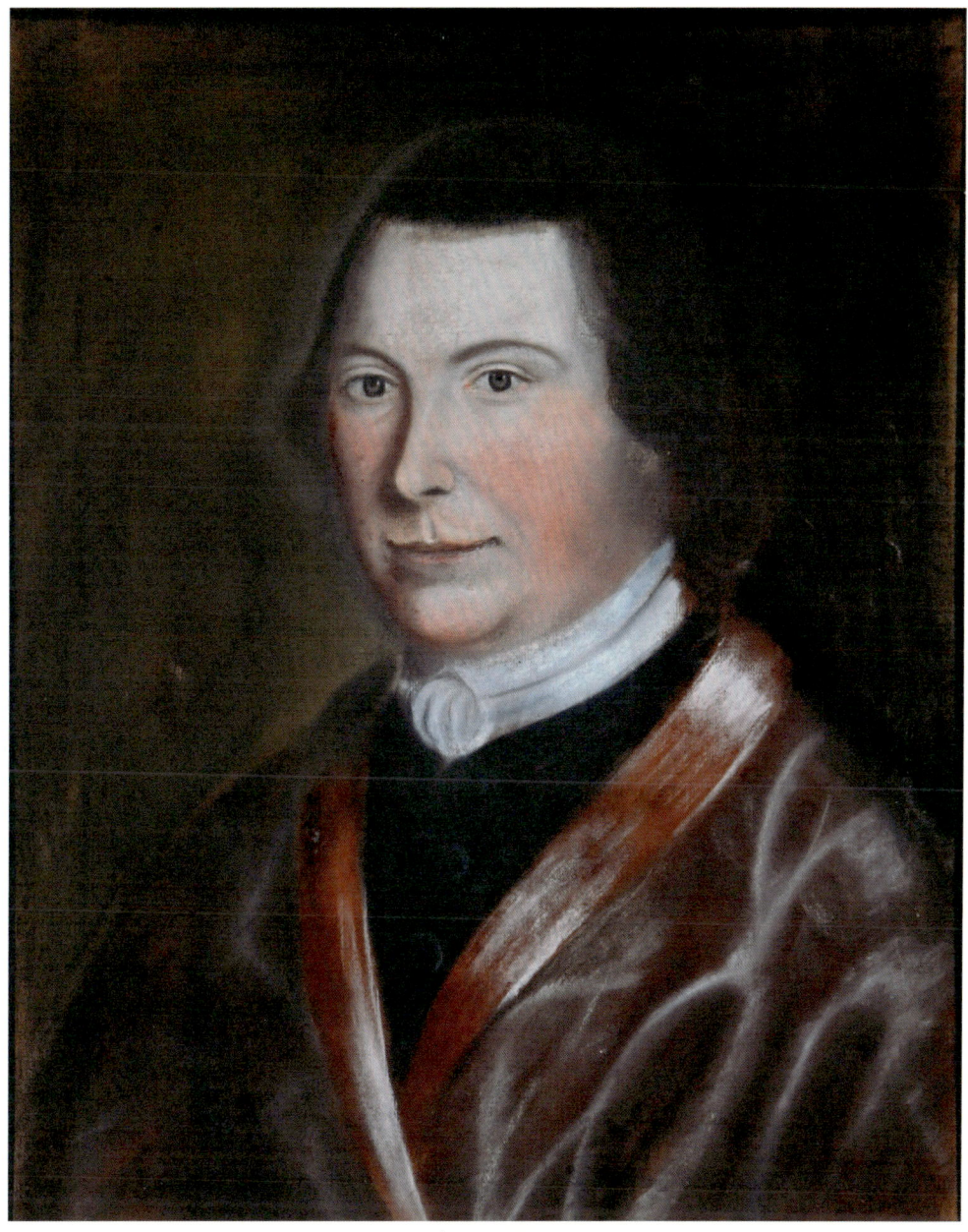

Thomas Cary
Pastel by Benjamin Blyth, early 1770s
Courtesy of the First Religious Society Unitarian Universalist, Newburyport, Massachusetts

Jeffares, http://www.pastellists.com/Articles/Blyth.pdf

New England Historic Genealogical Society, Rev. Thomas Cary Diaries

Norton, "Benjamin Blyth," 62

Prown, *Copley*, 1:104, 212

Rebora et al, *Copley in America*, 83, 286, fig. 205

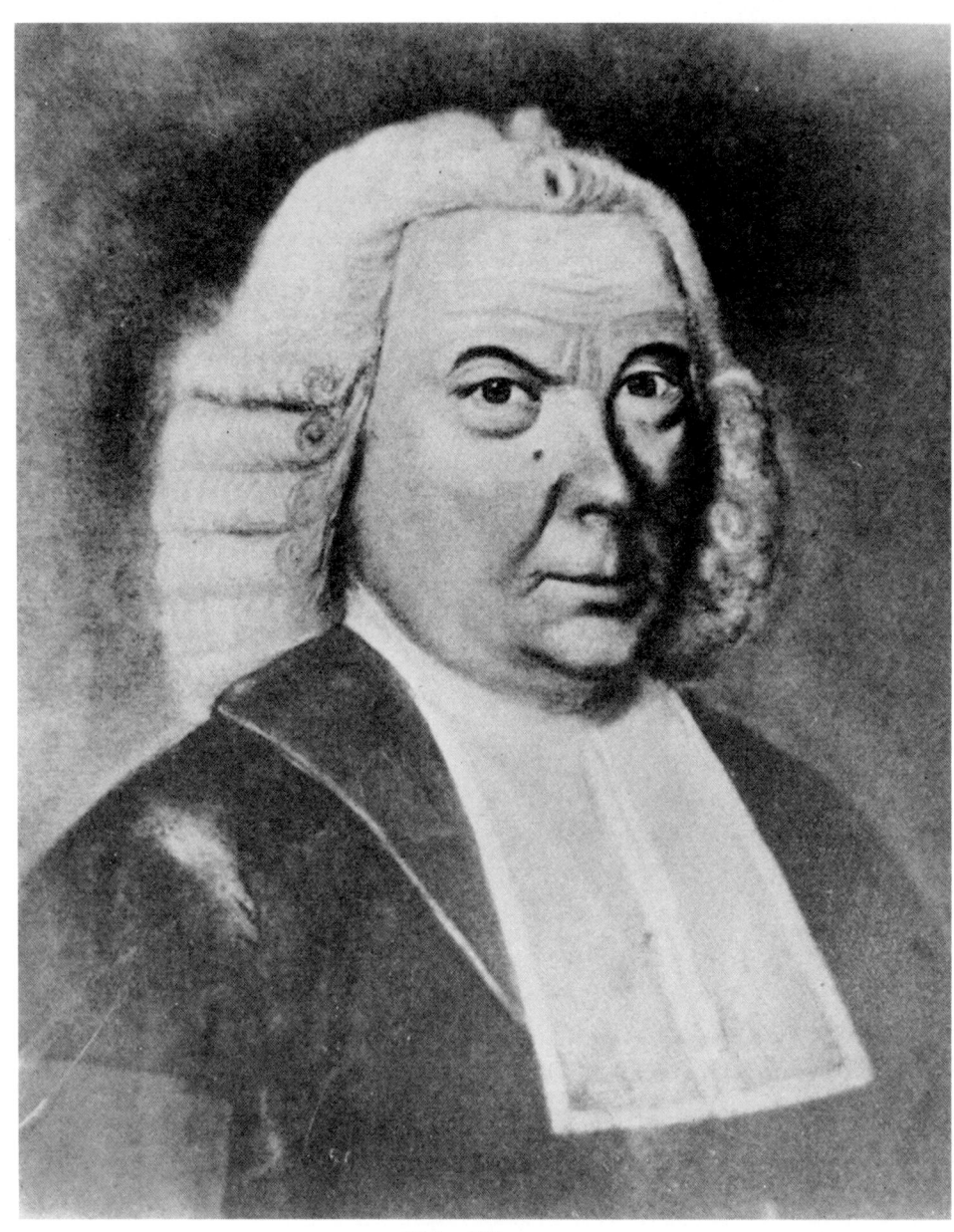

John Chipman
Photograph of pastel by Benjamin Blyth, early 1770s
Illustration from *Sibley's Harvard Graduates,* 5: opp. 563
Courtesy of the Boston Athenaeum

[28]

John Chipman (1691–1775)

Benjamin Blyth, early 1770s
Pastel, measurements unknown
Current location not known; Roland Gray, Cambridge; Mrs. John C. Gray, Boston

At one time, two Blyth portraits hung in the manse of the Reverend John Chipman—the pastel of the minister himself and an oil of the Reverend George Whitefield (Cat. 139), probably commissioned by Chipman. The British New Lights preacher's final visit to America was in 1769–70. Perhaps both portraits were done by Blyth at about the same time. The original portrait of Chipman is lost, but the church has a photographic copy on display.

John Chipman, the third of nine children, was born in Barnstable on February 16, 1691, to Samuel and Sarah (Cob) and was given the name of his grandfather, Elder John Chipman. He graduated from Harvard College in 1711 and was ordained as the first pastor of the Second Church in Beverly on December 28, 1715. His wife Rebecca (Rebekah) Hale, whom he married in 1718, was the daughter of Robert and Elizabeth (Clark) Hale, a prominent Beverly family, and the granddaughter of the Reverend John Hale, who in the 1690s called for eliminating those deemed responsible for witchcraft in Salem (until his wife was accused). The Chipman's house at 634 Cabot Street in Beverly, also known as the Exercise Conant House after the original seventeenth-century owner, was enlarged after 1715 for Chipman. He died at age eighty-four on March 23, 1775.

The portrait, dating from the early 1770s, when the minister was eighty, depicts one of the oldest of Blyth's sitters, still vigorous and a man of critical intelligence. He was also a controversial figure, embracing the "Old Lights" Calvinist stance against those of Arminians like the Reverend Balch. The Reverend William Bentley wrote that Chipman "had all the authority of a Bishop tho' his controversy with Revd. Balch of Bradford will not exhibit his powers to advantage." Chipman's portrait is now known only through several book illustrations. *Sibley's Harvard Graduates* credited its illustration of Chipman to "an oil at Historic Beverly after the Johnston pastel owned by Mr. Roland Gray of Cambridge." Foote disagreed on the attribution, as does this author. The Second Church commissioned a copy in oils in the 1940s—showing the preacher, however, in three-quarter pose with an open Bible. His face shows less critical vitality than that in the Blyth pastel.

Bentley 3:420–21, illus. 4:452
EIHC 98:139–144; 99:88–96
Foote, "Blyth," 71–72
MHS, Frank William Bayley Papers
Perley, *History of Salem*, illus 3:400
Sibley 5:xii, 563–568, illus. opp. 563
WPA 413, attributed to John Johnston

[29]

John Collins (1752–1824)

Benjamin Blyth, probably 1777
Pastel on paper mounted on coarse linen, 23 x 17 in. (58.4 x 43.2 cm.), Samuel Blyth frame
Collection of Brian L. Grimsley, Esq.; Cowan Auctions; Israel Sack, Inc., NYC; Kindig Galleries;
provenance unknown

Capt. John Collins, one of many ship captains and master mariners drawn by Blyth, was born in Salem to Joseph and Abigail (Crowel) on March 21, 1752. At age twenty-four, he married Mary Stuart (Steward). They had seven children, three of whom died young—one as an infant, two in their early twenties. Collins joined Salem's Essex Lodge of Freemasons on March 30, 1780. Like many other Salem seamen, he benefited from the explosion of wealth from trade after the war. The Collins home was on Turner's Lane, at the Old Marblehead ferry ways on the Salem side. The Reverend William Bentley noted that Collins laid the foundation of his new sea wall to square off his garden at the bottom of Turner's Lane, rebuilding it again July 1792.

The Collins portraits were probably drawn shortly after their marriage on December 15, 1776. Although once believed to be drawn by John Johnston, an idea probably perpetuated by Frank Bayley, by the time the Kindig Galleries had the portraits, they were credited to Blyth with a lengthy inscription added on the back: "Capt. John Collins/ . . . by Benjamin Blythe [*sic*]/ Salem [born] 1746." The overall handling and composition support the attribution, especially in the delicate lace-edged cuff, which he drew so well. The handling of Collins's face, especially the nostrils and mouth, and the delicate lash lines of the lower eye, lead to a suspicion that this portrait, like those of Samuel McIntire and Hannah Paine, may have undergone enhancement at Bayley's Copley Gallery in the early twentieth century. Corroborating evidence is the inscription on the back of the portrait of his wife. However, Collins' "pug nose" is as good an illustration as any that the artist does not simply apply a formulaic depiction to at least one crucial part of the face.

Salem's nineteenth-century historian Joseph B. Felt noted that Collins was known as a kind man who in June 1795 "provided for the sick and disabled at his own house" for the storm-distressed crew from the *Polly*, "out of Weathersfield" (presumably the Connecticut town on the Connecticut River). And the Essex Lodge records note that he received "a vote of thanks for his kindness to Brother Juan Mattas Charles, whom he took as a passenger hence to the West Indies." Collins's face indeed is a beneficent one.

Bentley, 1:1,127,365; 2:275; 3:101-2
EIMS, 56
FARL, Blyth, Benjamin 157-30
Felt 2:303
Foote, "Blyth," 84-85

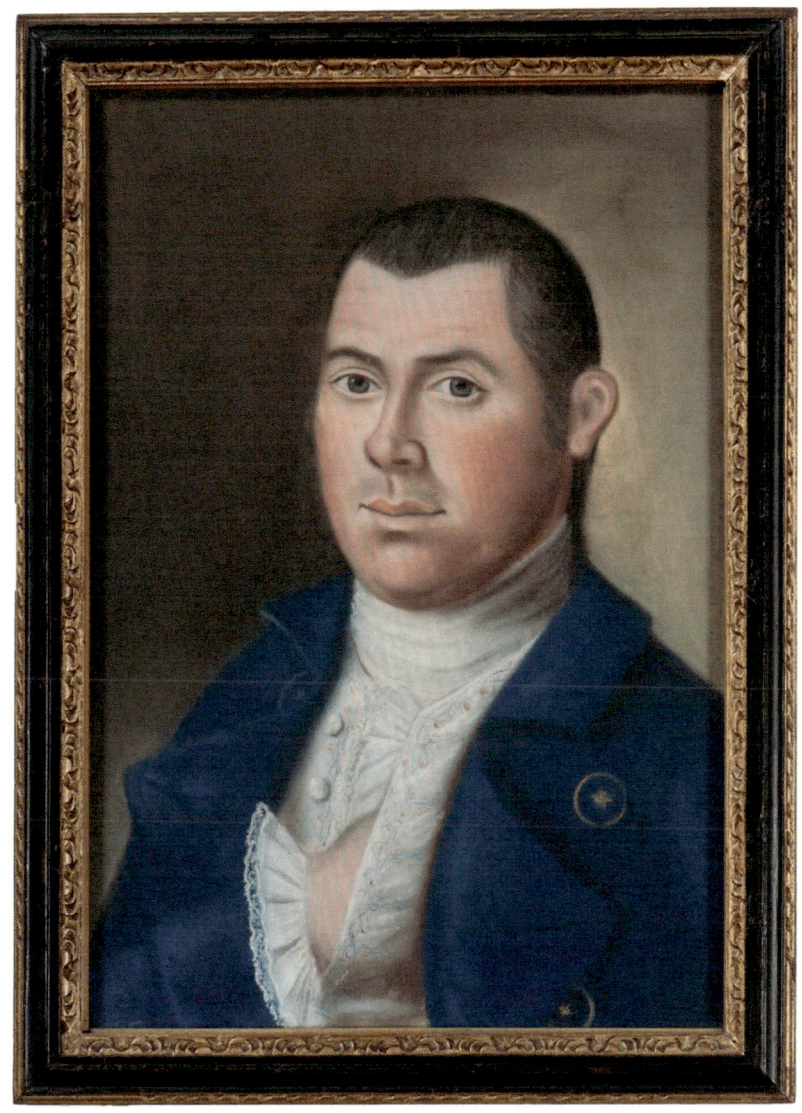

John Collins
Pastel by Benjamin Blyth, probably 1777
Courtesy of Brian L. Grimsley, Esq.

Jeffares, http://www.pastellists.com/Articles/Blyth.pdf

Norton, "Brothers Blyth," 53 (illus), 62

Phillips Library, PEM, Collins family Bible; Essex Lodge records, 125

SMS: Plate 2, no. 70

Suffolk County (MA) Probate Record 27328, Collins will, 1:224

[30]

Mary Stuart Collins (1756–1816)

Benjamin Blyth, probably 1777
Pastel on paper mounted on coarse linen, 23 x 17 in. (58.4 x 43.2 cm.), Samuel Blyth frame
Collection of Brian L. Grimsley, Esq.; Cowan Auctions; Israel Sack, Inc., NYC; Kindig Galleries;
provenance unknown

Mary Stuart was born on December 17, 1756, but there is no record of her parents. She married Capt. John Collins on December 15, 1776. Their first child, John, was lost at the age of twenty on the Grand Banks on the family's passage from Hamburg, in November 1779. The Reverend William Bentley's popular East Church, where the Collinses became members in 1779, noted the death, adding "They have three sons and two daughters left." Mary Collins and four of her children were inoculated against smallpox by Dr. William Paine (Cat. 102) during a major outbreak in Salem. One daughter, Mary, died in 1810, and another son, Henry, died the next year, at age twenty-eight, on his passage from Havana.

Mary died in October 1816 from 'hectic," a fever associated with tuberculosis, at the age of fifty-nine. The back of her portrait is inscribed on the side of the stretcher: "Mary (Stuart) Collins/Born Dec. 17—[illegible]/ Died Oct. 16, 181—[illegible]." Below, in cursive script added later: "1753 John Johnston 1818/ Boston." The handwriting looks like that of Frank W. Bayley, an early promoter of the work of Johnston, as is evident in comparing his writing to a letter the dealer sent to Charles K. Bolton of the Boston Athenaeum. But the portrait decidedly is by Benjamin Blyth. The photo of the back shows the checkered pattern of the cloth on which the paper was mounted, which was probably attached when the portrait was reframed (*viz.* the twentieth-century nails).

The transparent "handkerchief" (shawl) on her shoulders and across her chest, lovingly drawn by Blyth, and her hat, similar to the one worn by Mrs. J[onathan?] Gardner, suggest that the Collins portraits were done soon after their marriage. Mary Collins gets very little notice in Salem diaries and journals, but from her face, one detects a rather whimsical, if detached, personality.

Bayley, letter to Charles K. Bolton, Boston Athenaeum
Bentley 1:179, 409
Phillips Library, PEM, Collins Family Bible, P. R. 280,
FARL, Blyth, Benjamin 158-3j
Foote, "Blyth," 85–86 ("Mrs. John Collins")
Jeffares, http://www.pastellists.com/Articles/Blyth.pdf
Norton, "Brothers Blyth," 52 (illus.), 62

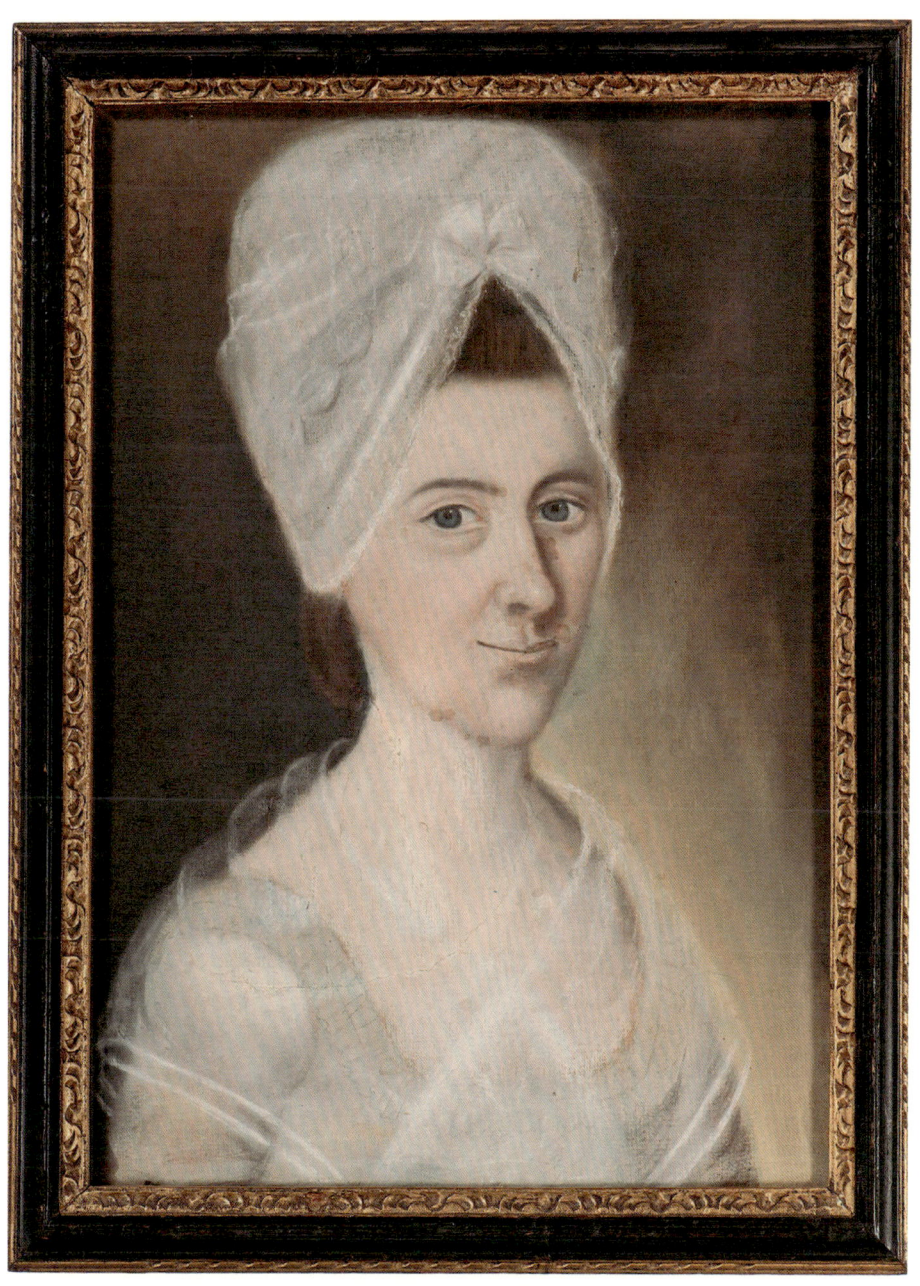

Mary Stuart Collins
Pastel by Benjamin Blyth, probably 1777
Courtesy of Brian L. Grimsley, Esq.

Benjamin Crowninshield (1758–1836)

Benjamin Blyth (attr.), ca. 1782
Miniature, measurements unknown
Current location not known; possibly destroyed

A pastel of Benjamin Crowninshield drawn by Mary Gulliver (1860–1939) "after an old miniature" was given to the Peabody Museum in 1889 by John Caspar Crowninshield. The artist of the miniature was not given, but it is now attributed to Benjamin Blyth. Crowninshield would have been in his early twenties when it was drawn, just at the time that Blyth was producing them. The details of the face in the pastel, assuming they were an accurate depiction of the original miniature, have all the earmarks of Blyth's style. Gulliver added the top hat—anachronistic, but probably to give some dash to the figure, along with the ship in the background.

Benjamin Crowninshield was born to Jacob and Hannah (Carlton) Crowninshield on February 16, 1758, in the house built around 1727 by his grandfather, Capt. John Crowninshield. After the death of Benjamin's father in 1774, his mother Hannah and sister, also Hannah, lived in the east side, where the Reverend William Bentley later boarded. In 1780, Benjamin Crowninshield married Mary Lambert. They had five children, including Benjamin Jr., born in 1782, who married Mary Boardman (Cat. 16). Bentley's diary is replete with references to the family. Three of Crowninshield's sons took Bentley for a sail in an "open boat," he noted, "the first time that I ever was 15 miles from land." He tutored Benjamin Jr. for admission to Harvard, and when he was rejected, Bentley was so upset, he wrote, "My connections with Cambridge cease." The house, moved to its current location in 1959, is now known as the Crowninshield-Bentley house in tribute to its illustrious tenants and is now part of the complex of the Peabody Essex Museum.

A master mariner known as "Sailor Ben," Crowninshield spent his life at sea. At the outbreak of the Revolution, he was serving as a midshipman on a British man-of-war. With the captain's permission, he left the ship and joined the American militia, and was wounded at Bunker Hill. He then served on the privateer *Black Prince*, that successfully disrupted British sea trade, and commanded several Crowninshield family vessels including the ships *America, Belisarius, Brutus,* and *Prudent*. He took the *America* to India in 1805, and during the War of 1812 commanded the private armed ship *John*, mounting sixteen guns and manned by 105 men, and the *Alexander*, with eighteen guns and 140 men. After the war he commanded *Cleopatra's Barge*, a yacht belonging to his cousin George Crowninshield, on the historic first "pleasure trip" to the Mediterranean by an American vessel. (Its well-appointed stateroom is now a high point in the collections of the Peabody Essex Museum.) Crowninshield later served as Collector of Customs for the Marblehead/Lynn, Massachusetts district from 1821–1830 and in the Massachusetts House of Representatives.

He was admitted to the Essex Lodge of Masons on May 16, 1782, a year after Blyth had become a member. He also was a member of the Salem Marine Society and joined the East India Marine

Society in 1799—later to become the Peabody Essex Museum—the year it was founded. He and his family moved before 1812 to Danversport, to a "Mansion House" with forty acres, known as the Crowninshield Farm, where he is reported to have given "pleasant festive gatherings." Still going to sea in 1812, Bentley wrote, "Capt. B. Crowninshield had no engagement with any armed vessels. This gives new spirits." Later, the family moved to Charlestown, where he died in 1836. His fortunes were much diminished at the time of his death and some of his property had to be sold to meet his debts.

Crowninshield's portrait shows a jaunty, well-heeled young gentleman. A later portrait, illustrated in the book of members of the Salem Marine Society (no. 152) and now in the collections of the PEM, depicts him as completely dissipated. David L. Ferguson noted that Crowninshield was known as a "'good-natured, rattling, unprincipled man,' but he was more than that, . . . a surprisingly gentle man [with] a fundamental decency."

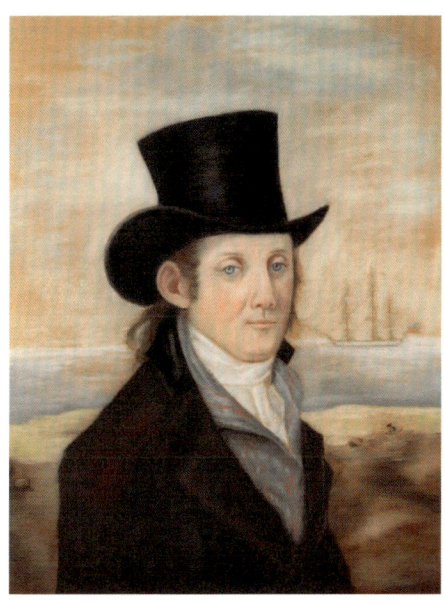

Benjamin Crowninshield
Pastel by Mary Gulliver ca. 1880, 20 x 27 in.,
after a missing miniature attributed to Benjamin Blyth, ca. 1782
Courtesy of the Peabody Essex Museum M348;
gift of John Caspar Crowninshield, 1889

Bentley, many references, including 1:43, 371; 2:274; 3:37, 40, 164; 4:106, 110, 125
EIHC 3:130; 4:264–5; 37:18; 73:279, cat. 39
EIMS, 54
FARL, Gulliver, Mary 157–3a
Ferguson, *Cleopatra's Barge*, 96
Grand Lodge of Masons Membership Cards, 1739–1990, Coo-Czu, 589
History of the Essex Lodge (illus.) 10
Phillips Library, PEM Crowninshield Papers
SMS Cat. 152
Visitor's Guide to Salem (1895), 166
Whitehill, *Portraits Peabody Museum*, Cat. 39, 33–4, illus. opp. 35
WPA 525

[32]

Abigail Curwen (1725–1793)

Benjamin Blyth, probably 1772
Pastel, assumed
Current location not known; possibly destroyed

The existence of this portrait is based on a statement that appears in the biography of Samuel Curwen in *Sibley's Harvard Graduates*: "[i]t is one of the inconsistencies of his character that he kept a silhouette of her by him during his second exile" in England. This suggests that there may have been a companion to Curwen's own portrait in silhouette by Blyth.

Abigail was born to Daniel and Rebecca Russell of Charlestown in 1725 and married Curwen on May 24, 1750. *Sibley's Harvard Graduates* records that "the marriage partook of the nature of a diplomatic alliance between the aristocracies of Salem and Charlestown." Andrew Oliver wryly called it a marriage of "convenience (inconvenience, as it developed)." The Curwens had no children. After Abigail's husband fled to England at the outbreak of the American Revolution, she was left in charge of the household, "& being not too well acquainted with business & deluded by a nephew Russel Weare, there was almost an entire sacrifice of the property," Bentley noted. "The remains of a valuable Library were sold just before his return by his nephew Richard Ward, Esqr., & it was sacrificed."

The portrait's location is unknown and may still be in England, or Samuel may have destroyed it in his distress on discovering the loss of his possessions. Presumably, the portrait would have been a companion to the profile of her husband, and therefore the only known pair by Blyth that were both silhouettes. (Dr. Holyoke also was drawn in profile, but his wife is a frontal view.) A further reason to assume that Blyth drew Abigail Curwen is that he drew pastel portraits not only of her husband but of their two nieces, Sarah and Mehitabel Ward (Cats. 34, 126).

Bentley 2:423-24
Oliver, *Samuel Curwen*, 1:xiv; 2:910–11, 1017–20, 1035–41
Sibley 9:514, 527

[33]

Samuel Curwen, Esq. (1715–1802)

Benjamin Blyth, probably 1772
Pastel on paper on linen 22 x 17 in. (55.4 x 42.4 cm.), Samuel Blyth frame
Peabody Essex Museum 4134.7, bequest of George Rea Curwen, 1900

Samuel Curwen, prominent Salem merchant, was one of the most colorful and eccentric men of eighteenth-century Salem. Another is the Reverend William Bentley, whose diary entry on April 10, 1802, described his elderly friend:

"Last night departed this life Samuel Curwen, Esqr. aet. 87. He graduated at Cambridge [Harvard College], 1735. He was of the most slender form, I ever saw, & yet the most active old man to be seen in our streets. He was a merchant in Salem. His slender habit was exceedingly irritable. He was indifferent to nothing, seized violently & preserved firmly. The times of the American Revolution were no times for him, & partly by timidity, & partly from an habitual disinclination for all popular measures, he left America & went to England. When he left our Country he possessed a Convenient House in Essex Street, not far west of North Street, & he had a good assortment of goods. . . . I got an early acquaintance with Mr. Curwin upon his return [in 1794], & frequently had him at my house, & visited him in turn. He was an excellent Antiquarian, & I profited much from the few things he had saved from the destruction which befell his Library, Cabinet & private papers. He was a good Classical Latin Scholar, well read in History. Had conversed much with men. Was much of a gentleman, & had a good address. He appeared in our street, much like a Patriarch. The English tye Wig, the long Scarlet Cloak, the heavy rings, & the golden headed cane, attracted notice after the war, tho' it was the best dress before it, for persons of condition."

Bentley, of course, knew Curwen personally only in the last eight years of his long life; other sources provide accounts of his earlier years. He was born in 1715 to the Reverend George and Mehitabel (Parkman) Curwen. He and his younger brother George were orphaned at a very early age; their father had died in 1717, a month before George was born, and their mother, exactly a year later. Although their social rank placed them near the top of the list of students at Harvard, they both were recipients of Browne scholarships. Samuel prepared for the ministry but early on became a merchant. In the French and Indian War, he was one of the captains in the victory over the French at Louisburg on June 16, 1745. Said to have been devastated by the death of a woman with whom he had been in love, Curwen married Abigail Russell of Charlestown on May 24, 1750. They built a new house, which became a social center for the town. When the First Church in the early 1770s was divided over hiring the Reverend Thomas Barnard (Cat. 8) to take over for his ailing father, the Curwen family joined him in the exodus that formed the North Church. He served for many years on the Commission of Peace for Essex County, as provincial Impost Officer and Assistant Judge of the Admiralty. He also helped start the Social Library and the Philosophical

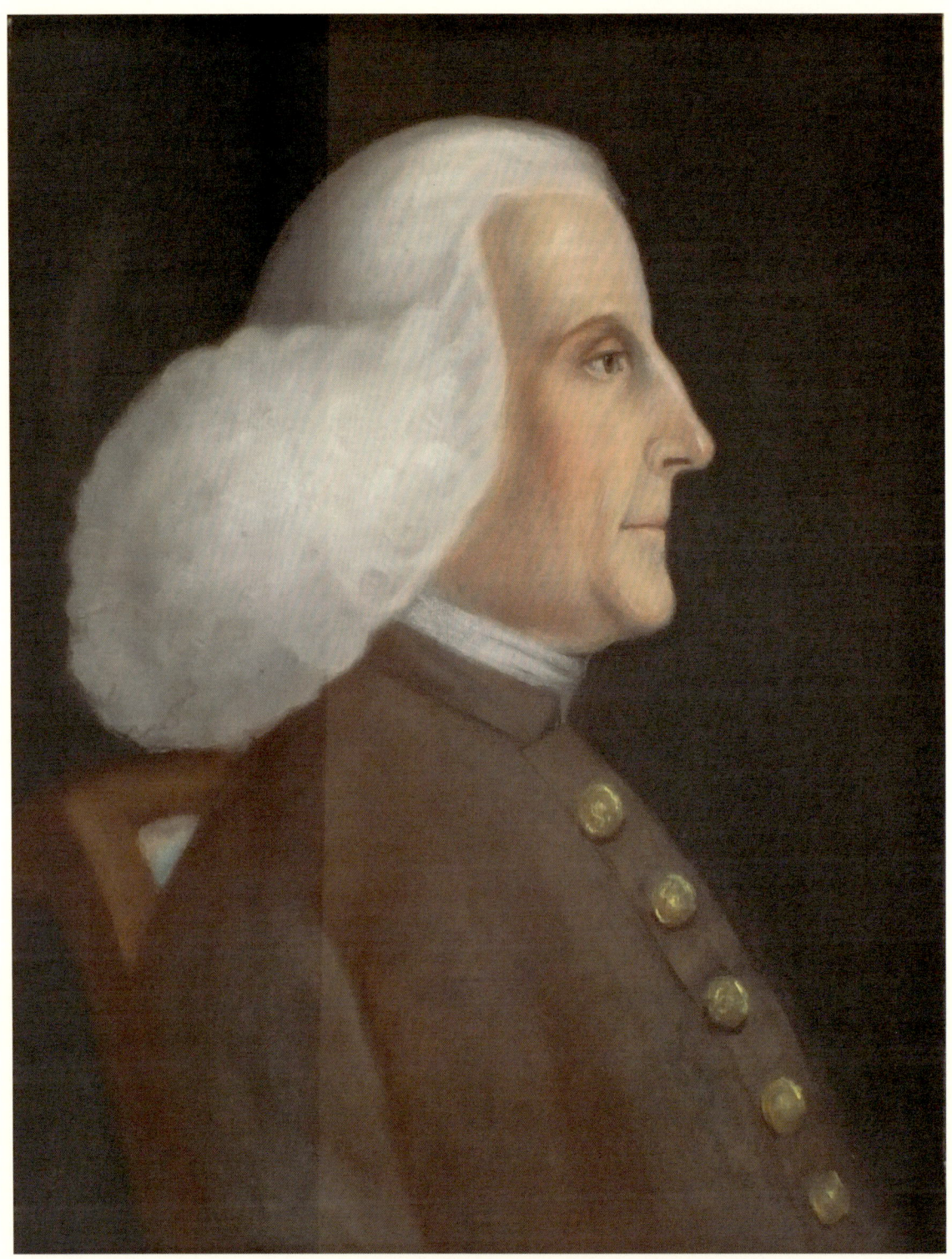

Samuel Curwen
Pastel by Benjamin Blyth, probably 1772
Courtesy of the Peabody Essex Museum, 4134.7, bequest of George Rea Curwen, 1900

Library of Salem and was a member of the Monday Night Club. He also subscribed regularly to "no less than five English magazines," according to his entry in Sibley's.

Curwen left for England on April 23, 1775, when he began this diary: "... finding the spirit of the people ... to grow more and more sour and malevolent against those whom they see fit to reproach as enemies of their Country, by the name of Tories, amongst which number I am unhappily though unjustly ranked, ... I owe myself to seek some secure asylum ...." His wife refused to leave (she had not been "left behind," as Bentley wrote). Six months later, Curwen recorded in his diary, "This being my dear wife's birthday when she enters into her 57th year, ... May it please God to continue her life as long as it shall be a blessing, and afterwards to receive her into the unutterable and inconceivable joy prepared for all the good and virtuous. Amen." Curwen also corresponded with Loyalist Peter Frye (Cat. 56), by then also in England, and with Barnard, to whom he penned a letter "expressing interest in his 'wife's return.'"

It was only later that Curwen learned of the "dreadful derangement and waste of my stock by the mismanagement of a stupid, wasteful, fuddling fellow, one Russell Wyer, nephew of my wive's." Curwen penned a lengthy diatribe, calling Wyer "[t]hat most worthless of all sottish spendthrift miscreants," among many other derisive names, and wrote to his wife to remove him from their house. Curwen returned to Salem in 1784, "much to the satisfaction of his friends, and was never molested for his political course"; however, his wife "had an hysterical fit." He was so upset at the state of his financial affairs that he returned to England, not to return until after his wife's death on March 31, 1793. Curwen wrote that he was not to be buried near her: "Should she obstinately resolve to live and die in Salem ... it is my express and peremptory order, command, and injunction on my heirs that on no consideration her dead body be entombed with my late niece or any of my family, being unwilling that her dust should be mixed with that of a family to which she bore enmity; and I should be not a little deranged in the Resurrection morning to find Abigail Curwen starting up at my side ... too mortifying a thought to indulge." He outlived her for close to nine years. And yet, as his biography in *Sibley's Harvard Graduates* pointed out, "It is one of the inconsistencies of his character that he kept a silhouette of her by him during his second exile." With the death of Dr. E.A. Holyoke in 1801, Curwen became the oldest resident of Salem. He died on April 10, 1802, at the age of eighty-seven.

His will left the portrait of his deceased unmarried niece, Sarah Curwen, to her sister, Mehitabel. To his great-grandnephew Samuel Curwen Ward, a gold watch and to Jane, "a profile of myself, set in a black ebony frame"—the portrait shown here. To his great grandnephew, the minor son of Samuel Curwen Ward, who at Curwen's request dropped the "Ward" from his name, Curwen left the rest of his estate "to the intent that he may receive if inclined an education at the University in Cambridge." Mehitabel's husband, Richard Ward, penned increasingly insistent letters to the probate court "... as my wife is heir at Law to the decd, I may have objections to what is called his will." In the third, he protested that, although Ebenezer Pope, with whom Curwen lived until his death, would testify that he was of sound mind, "I must be also Satisfied." Curwen, seemingly suspecting such a possibility, had three witnesses to his will and named a Jonathan Hodges as sole executor.

A century after Curwen's death, one of his descendants, George Rea Curwen, made a substantial bequest to the Essex Institute of one of its most famous collections that includes family portraits. Assuming that the lost portrait of Samuel Curwen's wife was a pastel, this one, her husband's, and Dr. Edward Augustus Holyoke (Cat. 70) would be the only silhouettes. Curwen's also is one of the few pastels in which Blyth included an object, the back of a very simple chair. The portrait does show a man who could be irascible, stubborn, and opinionated, but also who possessed a keen intellect and much-needed resilience.

Bayley, *Little Known . . . Portrait Painters,*

Bentley 1:132, 136; 2:360, 423–24, illus. opp. 423 (erroneously calling him "Judge"); 4:575, 631

Bolton, *Portrait Draughtsmen,* 7

Burroughs, *Limners and Likenesses,* 69–70

Cole, "Limned by Blyth," 333

Curwen Diaries (1972 ed.), 2:xiii, xiv, xxii, 1, 106–7, 910-11, 1027–30, 1035–36; illustration by Blyth opp. 260.

Curwen will, Essex County Probate Record 6951 (1802)

EIHC 70:376–77, cat. 58

FARL, Blyth, Benjamin 157–3c

Felt 2:511–12

Foote, "Blyth," 85–86

Holyoke Diaries, illus. betw. 110–11

Jeffares, http://www.pastellists.com/Articles/Blyth.pdf

Loyalists of Massachusetts, illus. Plate XV

Norton, "Brothers Blyth," 51 (illus.), 62

Oliver, *Windows on the Past,* illus. 29

Phillips, *Salem . . . 18th C.,* 391

Sibley 9:524, 525, 527; entire, 511–29

WPA 535

Sarah Curwen (1742–1773)

Benjamin Blyth, probably 1772
Pastel on paper mounted on linen, 22 x 17 in. (55.4 x 42.4 cm.), Samuel Blyth frame
Peabody Essex Museum 4134.12, Bequest of George Rea Curwen, 1900

A clipping in the object file for Joseph Lemmon at the Smithsonian Institution's National Museum of American Art is a scathing critique of Blyth's portrait of Sarah Curwen. The clipping was traced and the author has been identified as Malcolm Vaughn, a little-known art critic/collector. He wrote in 1928 of Blyth, "His portrayal of Mrs. Curwen is badly spaced, awkwardly drawn and anatomically absurd. . . . Also as a colorist he is poor. Mrs. Curwen is painted against a neutral background, and the tints are a lifeless brown for the hair, eyes of a nondescript brownish hue, and the flesh the blanched tones of an invalid. As if to attract attention to his errors, the dress is light blue with a pink bow and an edging of white lace." It is strange to criticize an outfit the sitter decided to wear. As for ". . . the blanched flesh tones of an invalid," it may be a more accurate description than the critic intended; she was sickly and died the year after her portrait was drawn.

Little is known of Sarah Curwen, except that she never married. Her portrait remained in her uncle's possession until his death, when he willed it to her sister, Mehitabel Ward. The label on the back reads "Miss Sarah Curwen, daughter of George and Sarah (Pickman) Curwen/ born in Salem Ma. Jan.[y] 1742/ died 26th Feb[y] 1773 unmarried/ Taken by Blyth in 1772" (the last two numerals in a different colored ink). George Rea Curwen gave seven Curwen portraits as part of his large legacy to the Essex Institute in 1900.

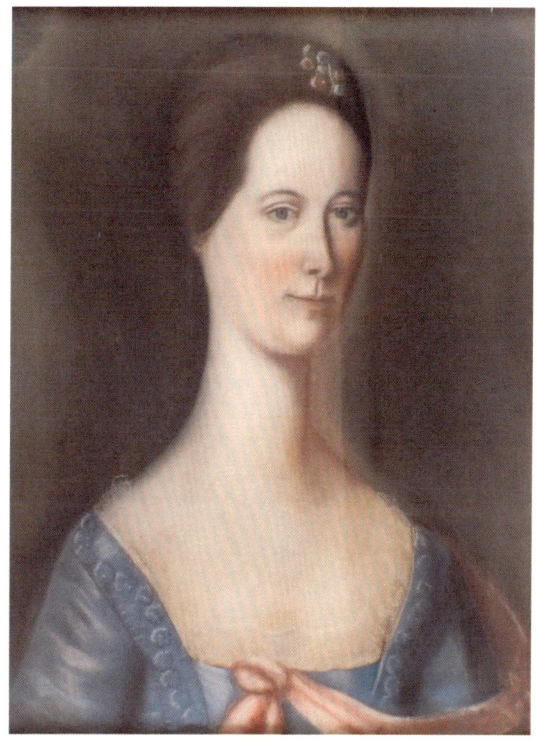

Sarah Curwen
Pastel by Benjamin Blyth, probably 1772
Courtesy of the Peabody Essex Museum 4134. 12,
Bequest of George Rea Curwen, 1900

Bolton, *Portrait Draughtsmen*, 7
Burroughs, *Limners and Likenesses*, 69-70
EIHC 70:377-8, Cat. 59
Foote, "Blyth," 86-87
Jeffares, http://www.pastellists.com/Articles/Blyth.pdf
Norton, "Benjamin Blyth," 51 (illus.), 62
Sloat, Caroline, for finding the Vaughn quote
Vaughn, "American pastels: late eighteenth century,"
International Studio vol. 5 (Apr. 1928):89
WPA 536

[35]
"Cushing" Boy
[36]
"Cushing" Girl

Benjamin Blyth, ca. 1780
Pastels on paper mounted on linen, 20¼ x 16⅜ in. (51 x 41.8 cm.),
replicas of Samuel Blyth frames with hooks
Merwin House, Stockbridge, MA, property of Historic New England, Inc.,
Bequest of Vipont de R. D. Merwin, 1966; Doane family

The identity of the children in these charming portraits is unknown. Nor is it clear how the possible connection to the Cushing family was made. Blyth obviously spent more time on these children than he did on others he painted at the time (with the exception of the Derbys), which would indicate some great sympathy for the subjects and respect for their parents, if not his fees. Blyth certainly had much reason to be cordial with the newspaper publisher and bookstore owner Thomas C. Cushing, but he was married too late to be the father of these children. Provenance, also, is not a help. The former owners of Merwin House, the Doanes and their daughter, Vipont Merwin, traveled extensively, collecting European and American furnishings and objects to decorate their home, but there are no documents showing from whom they bought the portraits.

However, there is very strong familial resemblance in the unusually deep-set, mournful large eyes of these children to Thomas Cushing III (1725–1788), shown in the Badger portrait at the Peabody Essex Museum (Acc. 106814). The children look to be between eight and twelve years old, so some possibilities are that they are either the children of Cushing's son Jonathan Cushing and his wife, Bethia, from Boston: Sarah, born in 1770, and Benjamin, born in 1772, or those of another son, Benjamin and Hannah, from Salisbury: either Hannah, born in 1768, or Mary, born in 1772, and Caleb, born in 1770.

Regardless of who the children were, unmistakable signs point to these portraits being done by Benjamin Blyth—the emphasis on the face and personality with less on the hair, the telltale ear of the young girl, the cuff lace of the boy. The girl's hand shows that Blyth finally learned how to give these appendages knuckles, and the flowers that she holds are reminiscent of the bouquet held by Ezekiel Hersey Derby (Cat. 45).

Jeffares: http://www.pastellists.com/Articles/Blyth.pdf.

Norton, "Benjamin Blyth," 62, (illus.) 61

Oliver, *Windows on the Past*, 50–51, illus. of Thomas Cushing

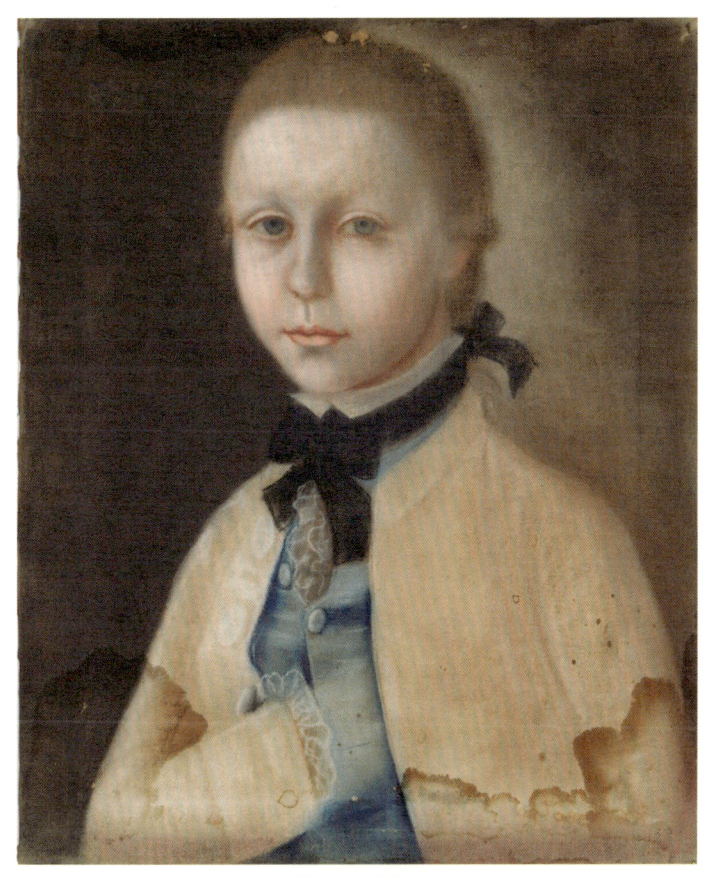

"Cushing" Boy
Pastel by Benjamin Blyth, ca. 1780
Courtesy of Historic New England, Inc., Bequest of Vipont de R. D.
Merwin, 1966, 1704

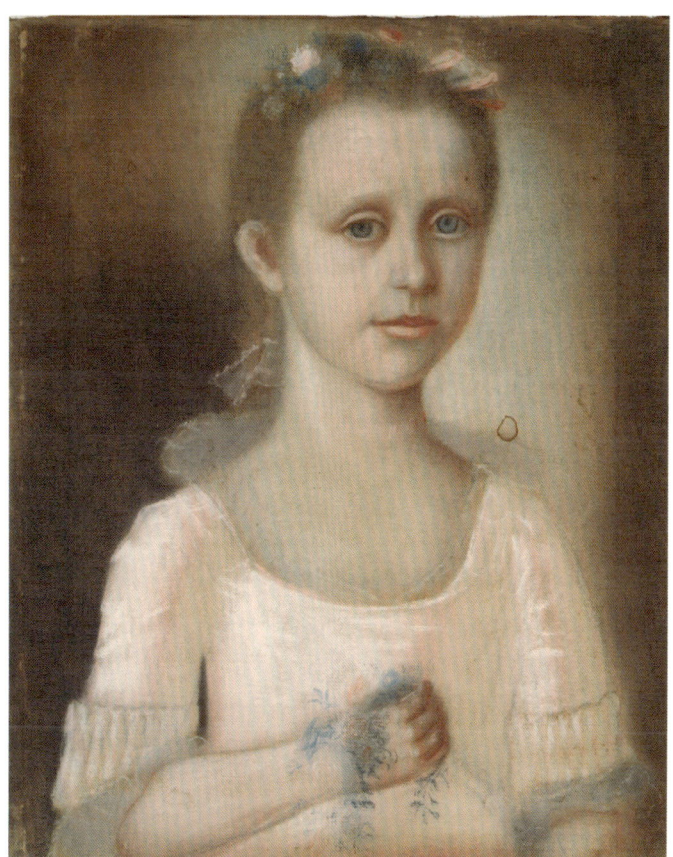

"Cushing" Girl
Pastel by Benjamin Blyth, ca. 1780
Courtesy of Historic New England, Inc., Bequest of Vipont de R. D.
Merwin, 1966, 1705

[37]

Manasseh Cutler (1742–1823)

Benjamin Blyth, 1782
Miniature, measurements
Current location not known

"Mr Bly drew the profile of Mrs. Cutler and myself in miniature," wrote the Reverend Manasseh Cutler in his diary entry for January 25, 1782, written in Hamilton, Massachusetts. This is the "smoking gun" that proved what had been suspected, that if Benjamin Blyth advertised himself in Richmond, Virginia, in 1786 as a painter of miniatures, among other skills, then he must have done some before leaving Salem.

Cutler was described as "Brilliant, versatile, distinguished," by Mrs. William Darrach and Mrs. Ernest G. Vietor in the *Essex Institute Historical Collections*. He was born in Killingly, Connecticut, on May 13, 1742, to Hezekiah and Susan (Clarke) Cutler. His college thesis at Yale College in 1765, a quote from Virgil *'Felix, qui potuit rerum cognoscere causas'* [Happy is he who can discover the causes of things] . . . seems, indeed, to have been the keynote of his character," wrote Darrach and Vietor. On September 7, 1766, Cutler married Mary Balch, daughter of the Reverend Thomas Balch of Dedham, where Cutler was teaching school. After several years as teacher, merchant, ship chandler in Martha's Vineyard, and lawyer, he decided to go into the ministry, under the tutelage of his father-in-law. In 1771, he became second pastor of the South Congregational Parish of Ipswich Hamlet (until it separated in 1793 to become the town of Hamilton), serving until his death at the parsonage on July 28, 1823.

A zealous patriot, Cutler joined the militia when the British marched through Lexington to Concord and was commissioned for a few months in 1776 as chaplain to the 11th Massachusetts Regiment. Like so many of Blyth's subjects, he went on the Rhode Island Expedition in 1778. To supplement his meager salary, he took up medicine and soon opened a boarding school that ran for twenty years, at which he tutored nine-year-old Nathaniel Silsbee and others for Harvard College. And Cutler also was involved in politics. He was a member of the Provincial Congress in 1775 and the Seventh and Eighth Congresses from 1801 until 1805, and in 1808, one of sixty-four delegates to a meeting of Federalists of Essex County in Topsfield.

In 1781, he and the Reverend John Prince of Salem gathered a group to buy the books retrieved from a captured British vessel moored in Beverly Harbor. The books, belonging to the distinguished Irish philosopher Richard Kirwan, contained the "greater part of the Philosophical Transactions of the French Academy, the Royal Society of London, and the Society of Berlin." The group then formed the Philosophical Library Company. A very learned man, Cutler wrote the first treatises on New England botany and astronomy. He was a Fellow of the American Academy of Arts and Sciences and member of the Massachusetts Historical Society, the Essex Institute Historical Association, and the American Philosophical Society. Yale awarded him an

L. L. D. in 1789. In 1812, he was supposed to be near to completing his *magnum opus* of flora of New England when a fire in his study destroyed the manuscript.

Cutler has been called the "controlling mind" behind the establishment of land grants in the Northwest Territory (Ohio), established by Congress in 1781, for which he had two objectives—providing lands for those impoverished by the Revolution and promoting the value of expansion of the colonies. "Of the nine most conspicuous names associated with the passage of the Ordinance of 1787 . . . seven . . . belong distinctively to Essex County." Among them was Rufus Putnam, of a family originally from Danvers. (A commemorative three-cent stamp was issued in 1937 for the Northwest Ordinance of 1787, with a map showing Marietta and portraits of both Cutler and Putnam.) In keeping with his life-long interests, Cutler insisted on a grant of land for a university and land for encouraging theology and schools and is considered a founder of Ohio University.

Cutler was a natural for a subject; his portrait combined three of Blyth's prominent subject interests: clergyman, patriot, and intellectual. It is unfortunate that the whereabouts of the miniature, especially of a man of the stature of Cutler and the only one for which one can analyze his style in the medium, is not known. A discovery might be made in the future by comparing an oil portrait of him done by Nathaniel Lakeman (1756–after 1830) at the Peabody Essex Museum.

Beinecke Library, Yale University, Cutler Diary, GEN MSS MISC, 89

Bentley 1:127, 371; 2:452; et al.

Cutler, Reverend Manasseh Cutler, 89

Darrach and Vietor, "Reverend Manasseh Cutler," *EIHC* 90 (1954), 111–22

EIHC 4:176, 271–2; 9. 2: 19:229; 25:165–167; 50:304; 70:379–81 cat. 63 (oil portrait); 86:164; 90: 111–22 cited at 112; 96:176–79

Sibley 16:138–54

[38]

Mary Cutler (1742–1815)

Benjamin Blyth, 1782
Miniature, measurements unknown
Current location not known

Mary Balch was born in Dedham in 1742 to the Reverend Thomas Balch, minister of the Church of Christ, and his wife Mary. The town records cite that Balch "was deservedly highly esteemed for he was a man of talents and intellectual attainments. He was orthodox and highly regarded as a preacher." In 1744, he was a chaplain in the expedition against Cape Breton during the French and Indian War.

In 1766, Mary's father officiated at her marriage to the Reverend Manasseh Cutler, who at the time was teaching school in Dedham, Massachusetts. They had eight children, some with names denoting classical references: Lavinia, Irene, Temple, and Augusta, along with Charles, Elisabeth, Hannah, Jervis, and Thomas. The Cutlers lost their first child, Temple, at the age of three months, to smallpox.

Mary died in 1815, at age seventy-three, in Hamilton. Noting that her husband was frequently away from home, Darrach and Vietor mused, "One cannot help wondering a bit about Mrs. Cutler who bore him eight children, managed to take into her house about twenty boarding students and who in her own right must have been a remarkable person."

Beinecke Library, Yale University, Cutler Diary, GEN MSS MISC, 89
Darrach and Vietor, "Reverend Manasseh Cutler," *EIHC* 90:111–22
Dedham Town Records

[39]

Elizabeth Dabney (1750–1834)

Benjamin Blyth, early 1770s

Pastel on paper mounted on linen, 23 x 18 in. (58.42 x 45.72 cm.), Samuel Blyth frame (?)

Peabody Essex Museum 118,172, gift of Mrs. John B. Hotchkiss, 1925; Fidelia Bridges

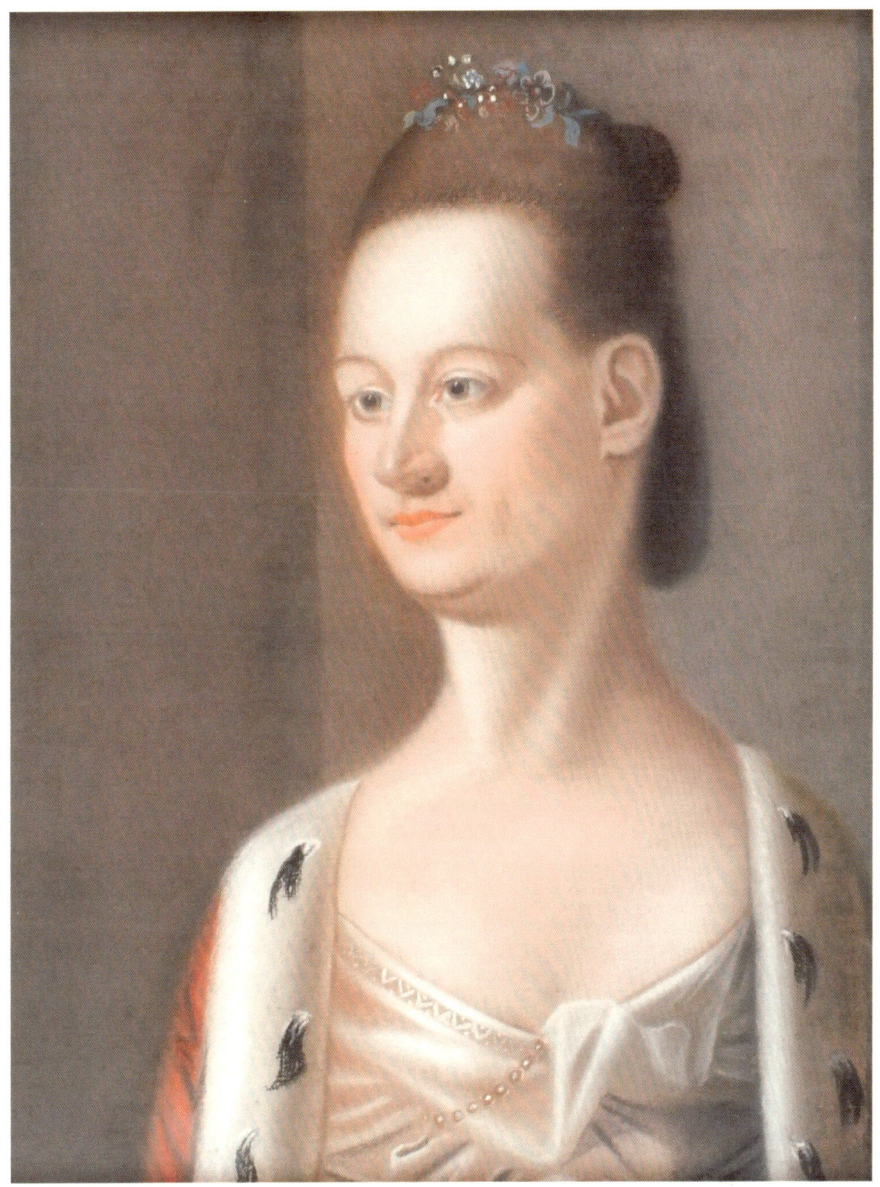

Elizabeth Dabney
Pastel by Benjamin Blyth, early 1770s
Courtesy of the Peabody Essex Museum 118,172, gift of Mrs. John B. Hotchkiss, 1925;
Fidelia Bridges

Elizabeth Dabney, widowed three times, was born in 1750 to Samuel Gardner, a prominent Salem merchant, and his first wife, Esther (Orne). Elizabeth's first marriage, date unknown, was to Nathaniel Dabney, a physician and apothecary born in Boston in 1746. His ad in the *Salem Gazette* in 1771 noted that his shop was "at the sign of Hippocrates's Head." (The shop sign is now in the collections of the Peabody Essex Museum.) A Loyalist, Nathaniel fled to Halifax and then London, where he caught up with his friend, Samuel Curwen (Cat. 33). Dabney must have returned by 1780, as a son, Nathaniel Gardner Dabney, was baptized at St. Peter's Church in 1781. Three years later, Elizabeth's husband was lost at sea. The settlement of his estate took so long that she remarried twice before it was settled. On June 21, 1787, she married James Bridges, a farmer of Andover, where they then lived. Their two children were Fidelia, born in 1788, and Henry Gardner, born in 1789. And then six months later, Bridges died, at age thirty-eight. Her third husband was Ebenezer Stevens, also a farmer, whom she married in January 1793, and her older son Nathaniel petitioned to have him named his guardian. Another child, Elizabeth Stevens, was born in February 1794. Ebenezer Stevens was the third husband to predecease his wife. He died in 1821, but Elizabeth lived to be eighty-four.

Elizabeth wore an ermine stole, an unusual luxury at the time, over her light pink dress. She was a beautiful woman, especially clear from the close-up of her face, and if one ignores the awkwardly proportioned back of her head and unfortunately overly large ear, drawn, as Blyth was wont to do, parallel to the picture plane. Still, one can sense her soulful, appealing yet dignified manner. The portrait, which descended through her daughter Fidelia Bridges, was attributed in 1925 to John Johnston by Frank W. Bayley. In the WPA Massachusetts Portraits it is attributed to Samuel Blyth, based on information provided by the Essex Institute, but Foote deemed that it had a "level of skill" comparable to Benjamin's. He also corrected the date. Elizabeth's cousin J[onathan?] Gardner and his wife also were drawn by Blyth (Cats. 57, 58). And her sister, Lois Gardner, married the Rev. Thomas Barnard, who was also drawn by Blyth, in 1773 (Cat. 8).

Bayley, *Little Known Early American Portrait Painters*

EIHC 72:251–2, Cat 304 (listed as Elizabeth Dabney-Bridges-Stevens, by unknown artist)

FARL, Johnston, John 158–3a

Felt 2:195

Foote, "Blyth," 79, 87 ("Mrs. Nathaniel Dabney")

Jeffares, http://www.pastellists.com/Articles/Blyth.pdf

Norton, "Brothers Blyth," 62

Pickering Genealogy, 185, illus. betw. 186–87 (with the wrong husband and printed in reverse)

WPA 2043, under "Stevens" and attributed to Samuel Blyth

[40]

Anstiss Derby (1769–1836)

Benjamin Blyth, 1780–82
Pastel on paper mounted on linen, 22⅕ x 16¼ in. (56.4 x 41.3 cm.), Samuel Blyth frame
Salem Maritime National Historic Site, on loan from a private collection

Anstiss was the fifth child of Elizabeth Crowninshield and Elias Hasket Derby, born on October 6, 1769. She was named for her maternal grandmother ("Anstus"). Her father, a prominent merchant with ships that went all over the world, also spent a good deal of energy on developing his land and gardens. The basket of fruit that Anstiss holds is a tribute to his efforts. On October 20, 1789, just after turning twenty, she married Benjamin Pickman, Jr., from another illustrious Salem family. They had three daughters, Anstiss, Elizabeth, and Martha, and three sons, Clark-Gayton, Francis, and Benjamin T. At her death on June 1, 1836, she was listed in the newspaper as the wife of "Hon. Benjamin."

The fruit basket in her portrait might be one of the two without handles listed in "Plated Ware" in E. H. Derby's probate inventory. If indeed drawn at the same time, as the examination suggests, it is the only example known of any still-life representation that can be attributed to Blyth. The source might have been an English print that included a still-life, as William Gerdts suggested was common at the time. Or it might have been a later addition by John Johnston, known to have been in Salem and who painted a still life in 1810, now at the St. Louis Art Museum. (A typescript by Bayley on his Copley Gallery stationery states "A still life of this period signed by Johnston is surprisingly well executed.") However, Anstiss's hand, comparable to that her brother's holding the rose, or of the Cushing girl, shows that Blyth did learn how to show articulation, and reinforces that this element can be attributed to Blyth. Exuding self-assurance and pertness, Anstiss looks to be a pre-teen.

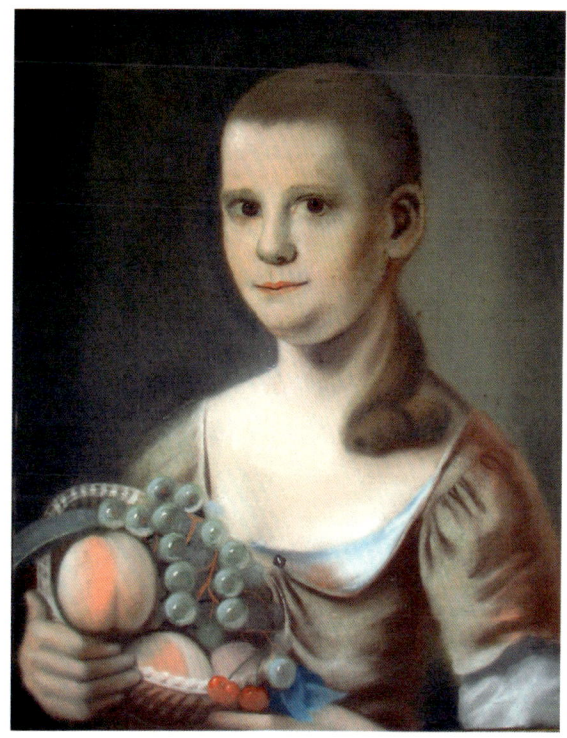

Anstiss Derby
Pastel by Benjamin Blyth, 1780–82
Courtesy of the Salem Maritime National Historic Site

Dow, *Diary and Letters of Benjamin Pickman*, illus. 28
Gerdts, *Still-Life Painting*, 21
Norton, "Brothers Blyth," 62
WPA 1695 under "Pickman"

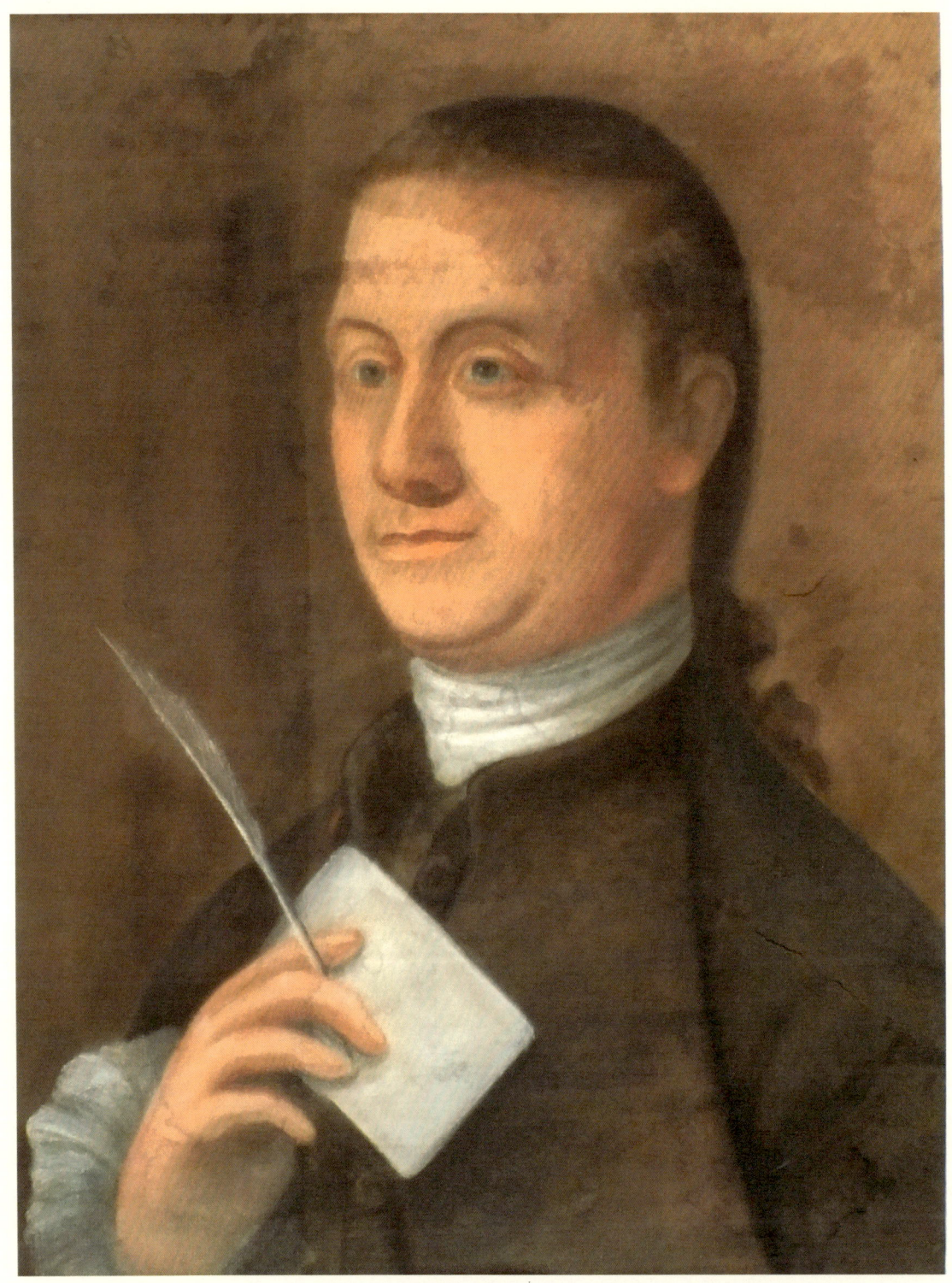

Elias Hasket Derby
Pastel by Benjamin Blyth, probably 1775
Courtesy of the Peabody Essex Museum M4315, purchase 1935

Elias Hasket Derby (1739–1799)

Benjamin Blyth, probably 1775
Pastel on paper mounted on linen; 23 x 18 in. (50.8 x 45 cm.), including later frame
Peabody Essex Museum M4315, purchase 1935, possibly from Dr. Richard Derby, Oyster Bay, NY

One of the leading citizens of Salem and a legend in its history, Elias Hasket Derby is known as New England's (alternatively, America's) first millionaire, whose name is still a byword in Salem, as Andrew Oliver noted. Born to Richard and Mary (Hodges) Derby in 1739, Elias as a young man took over the books from his father's counting house, continuing the trade with English and French ships. When the Revolution broke out, Elias Hasket Derby had seven vessels trading with the West Indies. Unlike some of his wealthy friends and neighbors, Derby refused to engage in the slave trade, although he did own at least two. As an ardent patriot, he initially made his vessels privateers, but as the war progressed and his interests began to return to commercial pursuits, the privateers were supplanted by the provisional government's sanctioned letters of marque, and Derby helped Salem send out 158 armed vessels. It was the *Astra*, as Andrew Oliver reminded readers, that brought the first shipment of tea to America "in an American bottom." The achievement for which Derby is renowned, however, is opening trade with China after the Revolution.

His business suffered greatly during the war, but he recouped quickly; in 1784, his vessels opened trade with St. Petersburg and began trade with India, and he soon took on the challenge of competing against England, France, and Holland, who had a monopoly on trade with the Far East. Many of his exploits were accomplished with his *Grand Turk*, at first Salem's most successful privateer and then providing access for him into the Indian market. From 1785 to 1799, when Derby died, he had sent out at least thirty-seven vessels on 125 voyages.

Derby married Elizabeth Crowninshield in 1761. They had eight children born between 1762 and 1777, two of whom were drawn by Blyth (Cats. 40, 45). The family lived very well; their house was furnished with ample quantities of glass, linens, silver, and pictures in almost every room, and a substantial library of books in a study and other rooms. The kitchen bespeaks an ambitious cookery, and his wine list included hundreds of bottles, from Madeira, Sicily, and Lisbon. Specific mention was made of a prize possession, a "Monteith" (a large bowl for cooling wine glasses) presented to his grandfather by the Province of Massachusetts Bay in 1749.

An avid gardener and horticulturalist, Derby continuously enlarged and improved his holdings and showed off his gardens and produce to friends such as the Reverend William Bentley. His diary includes many entries about his interactions with Derby, with whom he shared an interest in collecting books, and who showed him for the first time "the Skins of the Zebra." Bentley wrote on February 17, 1790, "Mr. Derby sent to Hardy, London, for an elegant Library of six hundred books." On one visit, when he and other clergy were invited to the Derby farm in Danvers, he wrote, "We were regaled at our arrival, after the best liquours at the house, with a feast in his Strawberry beds. . . . We saw whole nurseries of Trees . . . [and] the Swan, a stranger among us, from Virginia." Salem nineteenth-century historian Joseph B. Felt noted that Derby imported trees from India and Africa, fine horses from Copenhagen, Siberian wheat, and the largest herd of Merino sheep imported at that time.

Derby put some of his money to community use. He donated to the erection of a new courthouse designed by Samuel McIntire, who also was architect of Derby's new mansion on the waterfront. In 1792, Bentley noted that "We find mr Derby shew the same liberality to all the religious societies in Town, as a method more easy to himself, & Family than the distribution at his door." Two years later, according to Felt, Derby offered to pay for teaching 60 young seamen from Salem the art of navigation as long as the embargo lasted," adding that it "bespoke a heart, that felt its obligations to a class, too much neglected, and a mind that had clear views of commercial interests."

Bentley wrote after Derby's death on September 8, 1799, that he was "the most eminent merchant that has ever been in Salem. His industry, his manners, his economy, exactly conformed to the best character of this place. . . . His property is far beyond anything ever known in Salem." James Duncan Phillips wrote in *Salem and the Indies* that Derby had "a keen instinct for selecting good men to help him" and was "strictly honest in all his dealings and fulfilled all his engagements to the letter, and he expected the same treatment from others. He was not a man to be trifled with." His portrait seems to confirm this; it does show him to have been resolute and alert.

Although probably drawn at the same time, the portraits of Elias and Elizabeth are not companion pieces in the usual sense of the genre, i. e., three-quarter portraits somewhat facing each other. His account book lists a payment of £18 to Samuel Blyth for six frames in 1775; possibly it was for the family portraits. Walter Muir Whitehill assigned that date to Derby's portrait. It was purchased by the then-Peabody Museum in 1935, from an unrecorded source, but most likely, it was Dr. Richard Derby, of Oyster Bay, New York. The other family portraits are at the Salem Maritime National Historic Site.

Bentley, 1:147, 372, 373–74, 414; 2:73, 219, 317; many other entries

Essex County Probate Record 7571

EIHC 73:283, cat. 43, "drawn 1776," neg. 5045

EIMS, 55

FARL, Blyth, Benjamin 157-2b

Felt, *Annals of Salem*, 1:458, 2:145–48, 633

Foote, "Blyth," 75, 87–88

Jeffares, http://www.pastellists.com/Articles/Blyth.pdf

Norton, "Brothers Blyth," 62

Oliver, *Windows on the Past*, 15, illus. 29

Osgood, *Sketch of Salem*, 130–32

PEM, Phillips Library, Derby Family Papers

Phillips, *Salem . . . 18th C.*, 77, 243; other entries on privateering

Whitehill, *Portraits of Shipmasters and Merchants*, 37, illus. opp. 36

WPA 3609

Also illus. in *Portraits of Shipmasters and Merchants in The Peabody Museum of Salem*, Peabody Museum, Salem, 1939.

[42]

Elias Hasket Derby (1739–1799)

Benjamin Blyth (attr.), 1780–82
Miniature on ivory, 2¾ x 2½ in. (5.7 x 6.35 cm.), gilt wood oval frame, not original
Peabody Essex Museum 124253, purchase from Elizabeth Crowninshield Derby, 1940

Elias Hasket Derby was billed for two silver lockets by Salem silversmith Edward Lang (Cat. 83) on August 20, 1781, providing a possible date for this miniature and that of his wife, Elizabeth Crowninshield Derby. The purchase also fits within the parameters now seen to have been when Blyth was painting them. Andrew Oliver, in *Windows on the Past*, dates the Derby miniatures to ca. 1780, by an unknown artist. One might think they had been done by Verstille. However, the Derbys look to be in their early forties and are wearing clothing of an earlier style than was current when Verstille arrived in town in the 1790s. The technique is unlike Verstilles; there are no broad, bold brush strokes, nor the thin, spidery lines common to his work. The Derby miniatures are the only ones attributed to Blyth that are the larger size, although by 1780 it was being used. The frame, a later replacement, is a clumsy fit; the inner dimension is actually larger than the ivory, as can be seen along the right edge.

Dunkerley could be the artist, although his characters are unfailingly bland. Like so many Blyth portraits, this one of Derby effectively captures his character, a man who carefully supervised his affairs, was judicious, proud, and attentive. For his biography, see Elias Hasket Derby (Cat. 41).

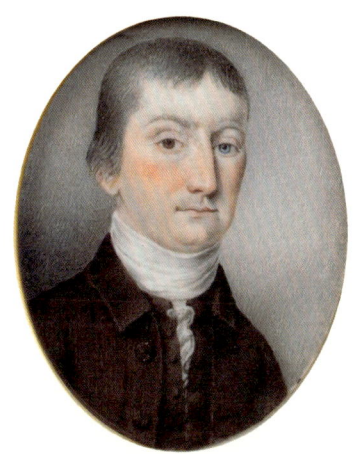

EIHC 85:324-5, cat. 29, "unknown artist"
Lahikainen, *Mcintire*, 218
Norton, "Brothers Blyth," 62
PEM, Phillips Library, Elias Hasket Derby Papers, Series II, Personal Papers
MA MH 76, B1, F 11
Oliver, *Windows on the Past*, illus. 15
Phillips, *Salem . . . 18th C.*, illus. betw. 58-59

Elias Hasket Derby
Miniature attributed to
Benjamin Blyth, 1780–82
Courtesy of the Peabody Essex
Museum 124253, purchase from
Elizabeth Crowninshield Derby,
1940

[43]

Elizabeth Crowninshield Derby (1736–1799)

Benjamin Blyth, probably 1775
Pastel on paper mounted on linen, 22½ x 16½ in. (57.2 x 41.9 cm.), Samuel Blyth frame
Salem Maritime National Historic Site; gift of Dr. Richard Derby before 1957, for the Derby Mansion

Elizabeth was born to John and Anstus (Williams) "Crowningshield" on February 23, 1736. Her marriage to Elias Hasket Derby on April 23, 1761, united two of Salem's most prestigious families. Both not only had mansion houses in Salem but tracts of land in neighboring Danvers. Elizabeth's father and grandfather were merchants in Salem, accumulating property and running successful maritime-related businesses, but future generations of the Crowninshield family achieved national prominence.

Elizabeth had grown up in the Crowninshield House, now one of the historic properties owned by the Peabody Essex Museum, but after their marriage, she and Elias Hasket raised their eight children, born between 1762 and 1777, in the Derby House, a wedding present from his father, Capt. Richard Derby, Sr. It is now part of Salem Maritime National Historic Site.

One son, Henry, was baptized on November 19, 1775, in Salisbury, where Elias Hasket sent his family to be out of harm's way at the onset of the American Revolution, but the child died before his first birthday. Salem Vital Records contain very little information on the Derbys, but Elias Hasket's will listed Elias Hasket [Jr.], John, Ezekiel Hersey, Richard, Elizabeth, Martha, and Anstiss. At Elizabeth's death on April 19, 1799, at age sixty-four, she was recorded in the newspaper with the unusual title, "Madam," indicating the social esteem in which she and her husband were held. He, of course, was "Esq." The Reverend William Bentley's diary entry noted that she "felt & enjoyed all the pride of great wealth, . . . but [was] a woman who took the greatest pride in being known as a Charitable woman, as she was indeed to the poor in general. . . . It was at her instigation the Elegant Mansion house was built . . . but she did not live long to enjoy it. All have anecdotes of her folly & vanity, but all reverence her charity & kind dispositions."

Rather clumsy "repair" work was done on the pastel, presumably many years ago: a rectangular patch runs from her right to left cheeks and across her nose. The overpainting is obvious in a round "patch" on her right cheek, halfway down her nose, at the inner corner of her left eye, and again a small round patch over the outer end of her left eyebrow. It has harmed what otherwise would have been one of Blyth's better pastels. Elizabeth is wearing a "turquerie," popular with wealthy women in the 1770s. She appears a somewhat withdrawn woman, yet, as Bentley noted, aware of her position and answering to *noblesse oblige*.

Bentley, 2:300–01
EIHC 97:84–85 Abbot Lowell Cummings, on the Crowninshield-Bentley House
Foote, "Blyth," 75, 88 ("Mrs. Elias Hasket Derby")

Jeffares, http://www.pastellists.com/Articles/Blyth.pdf

Murphy, Emily A., Ph. D., Salem Maritime National Historic Site

Norton, "Brothers Blyth," 62

Salem VR: PR 299, Bible once owned by Mrs. Alice McAlpine

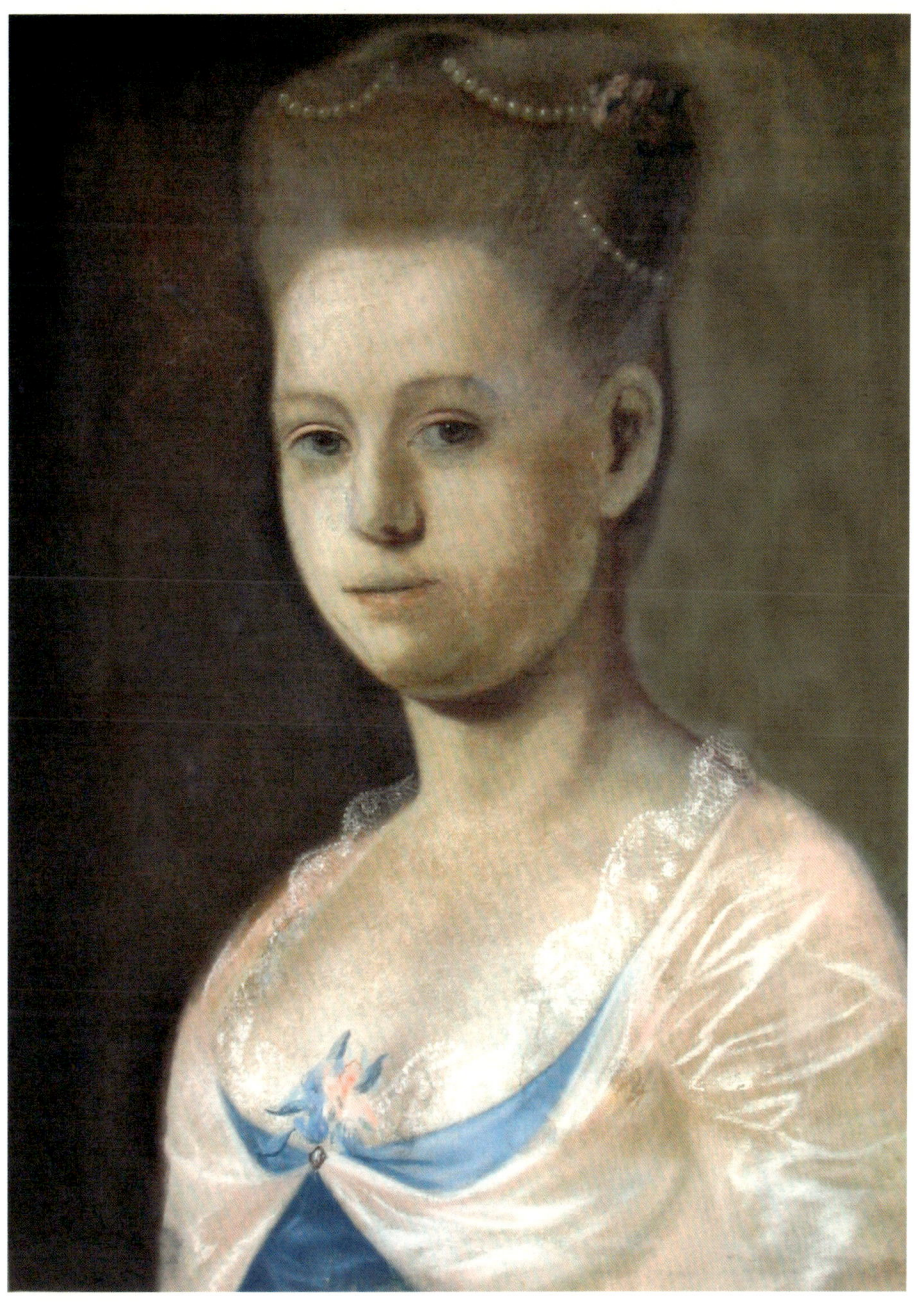

Elizabeth Derby
Pastel by Benjamin Blyth, probably 1775
Courtesy of the Salem Maritime National Historic Site

[44]

Elizabeth Crowninshield Derby (1735–1799)

Benjamin Blyth (attr.), 1780–81
Miniature on ivory, 2¾ x 2¼ in. (6.99 x 5. 7 cm.), gilt wood oval frame
Peabody Essex Museum 124,254, purchase from Elizabeth Crowninshield Derby, 1940; George Derby,
Benjamin Pickman.

This miniature of Elizabeth Derby, along with that of her husband, Elias Hasket, was probably made in 1780–81, accounting her age to be around forty-five, or about five or six years after her pastel portrait. The miniatures were removed from their original cases and given gilt wood frames. The frame is a later replacement, and it is a clumsy fit; the inner dimension is actually larger than the ivory, as can be seen along the left edge.

Long credited to an unknown artist, this miniature might be by Dunkerley, but it shows many Blyth characteristics—the ever-present lip line, the prominent eyes, and the delicate lace edging of her cap. Blyth depicted her as a serious, thoughtful woman. For her biography, see Elizabeth Crowninshield Derby (Cat. 43).

EIHC 85: 325-6, cat. 30, "unknown artist"
Lahikainen, *Mcintire*, 218
Payson, "Museum Collections," illus. 34
Phillips, *Salem . . . 18th C.*, illus. betw. 58-59

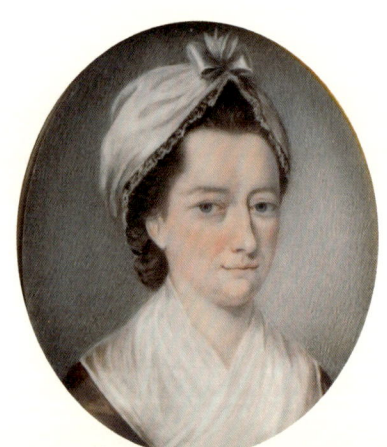

Elizabeth Derby
Miniature attributed to Benjamin Blyth,
ca. 1780–81
Courtesy of the Peabody Essex Museum
124,254, purchase from
Elizabeth Crowninshield Derby, 1940

[45]

Ezekiel Hersey Derby (1772–1852)

Benjamin Blyth, 1780–82
Pastel on paper mounted on linen, 25 x 20 in. (58.9 x 45.8 cm.), Samuel Blyth frame
Salem Maritime National Historic Site; Dr. Richard Derby before 1957, for the Derby Mansion;
gift of Salem Maritime Historical Association (Louise DuPont Crowninshield), 1959

In his portrait, the young Ezekiel is holding a rose; his devotion to flowers and agriculture occupied his entire life. Born in 1772, he was one of the sons of Elias Hasket and Elizabeth Derby. Hersey, as he was known, was born on November 1, 1772. As there were no prior Ezekiels in either family, it can be assumed that his middle name was for Dr. Ezekiel Hersey (Cat. 66). Ezekiel Derby graduated from Harvard College in 1791 and three years later, married Hannah (Browne) Fitch, daughter of Eunice Browne and Timothy Fitch, Esq. of Medford.

They had seven children, including Ezekiel Hersey, Jr. and another child, who predeceased him. Although Ezekiel Hersey had started out as a merchant following in his father's footsteps, he spent his last thirty-five years as an agriculturist, his father's major avocation, and at his death in 1852 at age eighty was listed as "Farmer." His lands in the South Fields were a "spot was long noted for its rare fruits and flowers," wrote Salem nineteenth-century historian Joseph B. Felt. The Reverend William Bentley noted that "Hearsy Derby has the Brown farm more decorated with gardens & exotics, but Colonel Pickman [married to Hersey's older sister, Anstiss, (Cat. 40)] is an example of our best agriculture & pasturage." Michel Felice Corné, in the first decade of the nineteenth century, painted a view of the farm in South Salem. Ezekiel also inherited from his father the "Brick Dwelling House on Derby Street and the Wharves and lots in front of it, also the house in Essex Street" in which Ezekiel was then living.

Although Hersey seemed to get into public brawls—"a bruising match" and "fisticuffs," Bentley recorded—Hersey was defending his sister, Elizabeth, then in an unfortunate marriage. He was devoted to his family; the opening of his will stated "… in the first place it is my will and intention that, … my wife and daughters should continue to make one family and reside together, in as nearly as possible the same manner as we have for so many years lived." He also made very specific charge for the income from the produce of "the Gardens, Green House, Fruit House, and Garden Cottage."

Foote thought the pastel of Ezekiel was probably done at the same time as those of his parents, but a case can be made that the ones of him and his sister, Anstiss, were done later. Blyth took great care in drawing this portrait; Hersey is lovingly portrayed, dressed in a sky-blue jacket and beautifully drawn linen and lace collar, a "Little Blue Boy" outfit *au courant* by the early 1780s. The pastel passed by inheritance to Dr. Richard Derby, of Oyster Bay, New York, who gave it to the Salem Maritime National Historic Site to be hung in Derby House, where it is today, along with his sister Anstiss, his mother Elizabeth, and his uncle Richard (Cats. 40, 43, 46). Peabody Essex Museum owns a later portrait of Ezekiel Hersey in oils, by Charles Osgood.

Bentley 2:353; 3:18; 4:28
EIHC 71:65, cat. 74, oil by Osgood
Felt, 2:148
Foote, "Blyth," 75, 88–89
Jeffares, http://www.pastellists.com/Articles/Blyth.pdf
NEGHS Register
Norton, "Brothers Blyth," 62
Oracle of the Day (Salem, MA), Sept. 27, 1784, 3
PEM, Phillips Library, Derby Family Papers
Salem VR, PR 79 (Holyoke Diaries)
[Illus SAMA 1675]

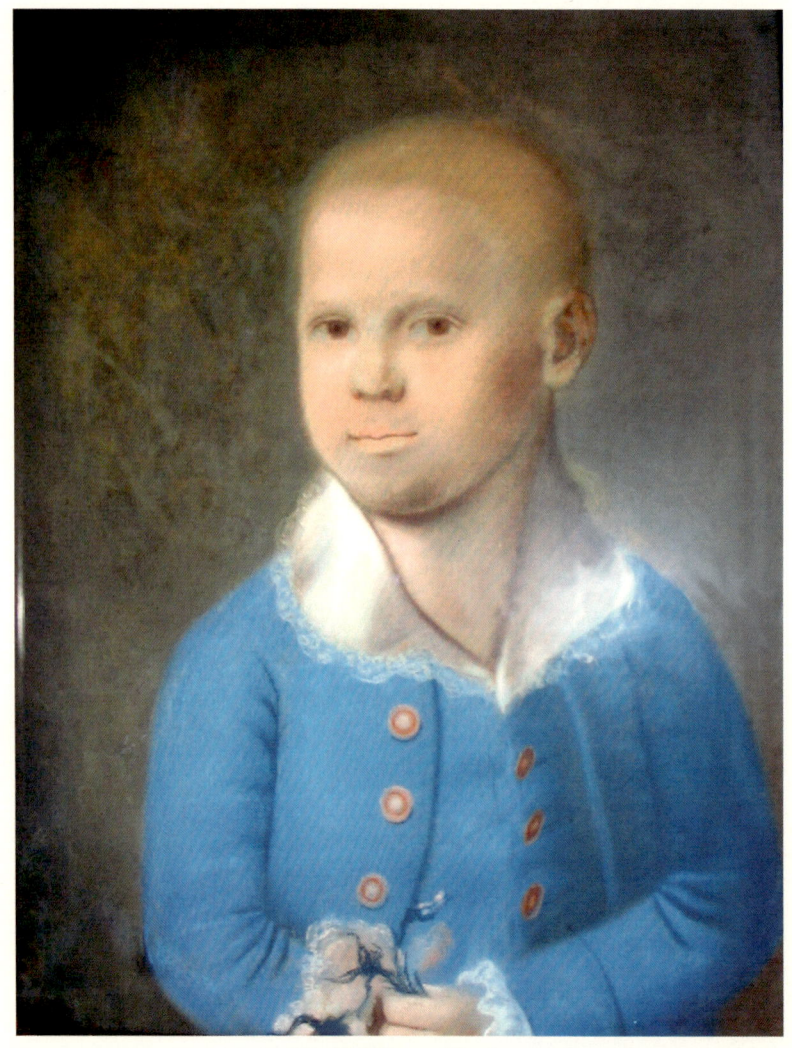

Ezekiel Hersey Derby
Pastel by Benjamin Blyth, 1780–82
Courtesy of the Salem Maritime National Historic Site

[46]

Richard Derby, Jr. (1736–1781)

Benjamin Blyth, probably 1775
Pastel on paper mounted on linen, 23¼ x 19½ in. (59. 1 x 48. 9 cm.), later frame
Salem Maritime National Historic Site, gift of Louise DuPont Crowninshield, 1955, for the Derby
House; Mrs. M. Collins, Mary Pickman Russell, Joseph Pickman, Hannah M. Derby

Richard Derby, Jr. was born on January 6, 1736, to Richard Sr. and Mary (Hodges) Derby. On September 13, 1759, Richard Jr. married Lydia Gardner, sister of Jonathan Gardner (Cat. 57)—a member of another prominent Salem family. They lived in "a Mansion House" on Herbert Street, purchased by Richard Sr. for his son on his marriage, and eventually had three daughters and five sons. Richard Jr.'s wife Lydia died in 1777. After his marriage a year later to Lucy Smith of Falmouth, Maine, he acquired the large and valuable Loyalist estate at Rial Side, Beverly, known as the "Browne Hall estate" or "Brown's Folly." In ill health for many years, he died from a fever on March 20, 1781, at a fairly young age of forty-five, predeceasing his father, Richard Derby, Sr., by two years.

Richard was twenty-one years old when his father first entrusted him with the command of a ship to foreign ports. His brother John also sailed as a crewman and later captain, while his other brother, Elias Hasket (Cat. 41), stayed ashore to help in his father's counting-house. At the end of 1768, as Salem began to lean toward patriot sympathies over Loyalist ones, Richard Derby, Jr., along with John Pickering, Jr., was elected to the House of Representatives; the following spring, they presented a detailed list of grievances written by the Salem selectmen. Derby represented Salem from 1769 to 1773 and was a counselor from 1774 to 1777. He is believed to have supported the town's enactment of a strict non-importation agreement against British goods, although records of this are scant. During his service on the council, Derby was on the committee for the building of vessels for the Massachusetts Navy. His ship *Quero*, under orders from Gen. Joseph Warren (Cat. 130), took the news of the Battle of Lexington to London. Between 1776 and 1779 Derby was one of the agents for the Massachusetts Navy, which meant he was responsible for outfitting and managing prizes captured by naval vessels, most particularly the *Tyrannicide*.

His will left the use of his extensive farm in Beverly to his wife for her lifetime, and thereafter the assets were to be divided among his children. He also left his pews in both the Beverly church and East Church in Salem and another farm in Windham, Cumberland County, then still part of Massachusetts. His personal effects were extensive, including much silver, china, Delftware, a gold and silver watch, and, an unusual entry for will inventories of the period, "10 Matzatinto pictures." He stipulated that his funeral "shall be altogether without Parade and with as little ceremony as decency will admit of."

When donated to the National Park Service, the portrait had a label on the back, "Likeness of Elias Hasket Derby, 1739-1799. Done at Salem by Benjamin Blyth. Given to Hannah M Derby, late property of Joseph Pickman, 1862." However, based on their research, the staff determined the portrait to be of Richard Derby, Jr. They also determined that the style of the uniform he is wearing is very similar to the 1760s French and Indian War uniform. George Washington wore a similar style of militia uniform for his 1772 portrait by Charles Willson Peale. Richard Jr. was captain of the First Salem Company of the First Essex Regiment of the Massachusetts Militia in 1766–1767, so it is also possible that he dusted off his old militia uniform for a portrait. Military historian James Kochan wrote, "The uniform depicted appears to be the undress uniform of a Royal Navy lieutenant under the regulations of 1748, which were continued with small changes until 1767. Richard Derby, Jr. and his brother John both commanded vessels for their father's mercantile establishment during the Seven Year's War, mostly in the West Indies."

The drawing of Derby's face is similar to that of Rev. Thomas Barnard (Cat. 8). The questionable element of the pastel is the overall execution of his coat, with the large dark, strong shadow lines, whereas the pastel in most other places shows signs of abrasions and loss of pigment, especially on the face. The coat may have been redrawn. A portly man, Derby looks kindly, if somewhat worried; he was chronically ill and would be dead within a few years. A bland copy of his portrait in oil, adding more body, was made for Phillips Academy in the mid-twentieth century.

EIHC 3:166–7; 44:201-2

Jeffares, http://www.pastellists.com/Articles/Blyth.pdf

Murphy, Emily A., Ph. D., Salem Maritime National Historic Site, correspondence

Norton, "The Brothers Blyth," 62

PEM, Phillips Library, Derby Papers, Biographical Sketches

PEM, Phillips Library, John Gardner diary

Phillips, *Richard Derby of Salem*, 26

Phillips, *Salem . . . 18th C.*, 239, 244

Phillips Academy, portrait collection

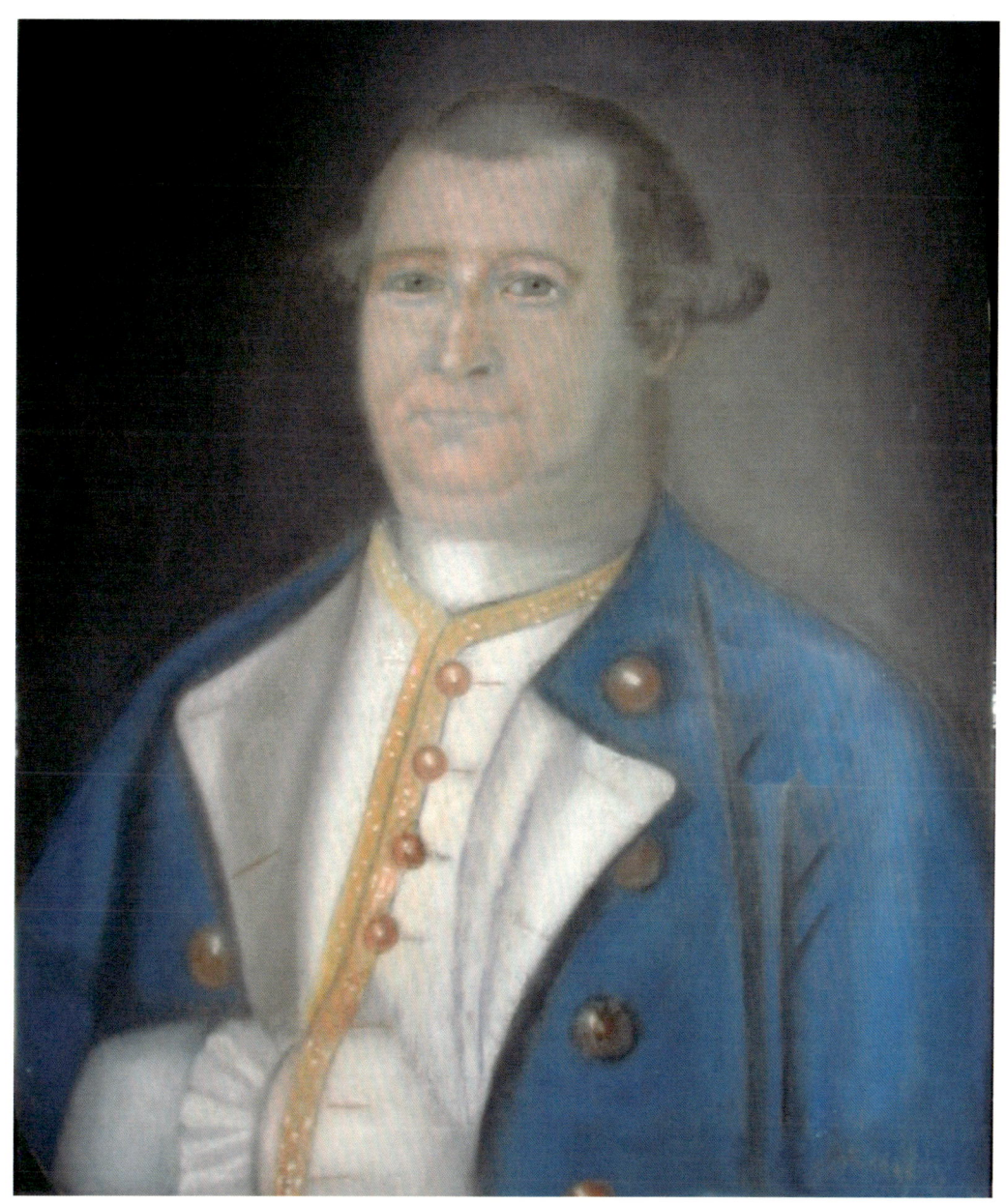

Richard Derby, Jr.
Pastel by Benjamin Blyth, probably 1775
Courtesy of the Salem Maritime National Historic Site

Richard Derby, Sr. (1712–1783)

George Southward, based on a lost pastel by Benjamin Blyth, probably 1775
Oil, 21½ x 18¾ in. ; measurements of original unknown, probably similar
Peabody Essex Museum, "Received before 1919. Unknown source"

Benjamin Blyth drew five pastels of other Derby family members in the mid-1770s, including the son of Richard Derby, Sr., so why not him as well? There are two portraits of Derby, Sr., but they are oils, not pastels, and neither is by Blyth. One is recorded in the Catalogue of Portraits of the Essex Institute, published in the 1930s, as an "unfinished copy" by George Southward (1803–76). The other is a later oil by J. Alden Weir (1852–1919), now in the collections of the Salem Maritime National Historic Site, also in Salem. Both images are recorded at the Frick Art Reference Library.

Neither portrait was painted from life. Southward copied the original portrait, whereabouts now unknown, sometime in the mid-nineteenth century. At the end of the century, Weir, evidently commissioned by family members (probably the Rogers), translated the Southward into a more imposing, full-figure oil portrait. At the time, the Rogers family was living in New Canaan, Connecticut, and Weir, by then a well-known artist, lived in the nearby towns of Wilton and Branchville. Shortly thereafter, the Southward probably entered the collections of the then-Essex Institute. Its provenance states "Received before 1919. Unknown source."

However, the Southward portrait of Derby as it appears now in the collections is not the one illustrated in the *EIHC* "Catalogue . . ." Yet the museum has no other portrait of him. The measurements, also, are basically the same. The answer was suggested by the inscription on the back of the canvas: "Restored by May E. Colbert 1952." The surmise is that she "improved" Southward's unfinished portrait, about twenty years after it had been photographed for the catalogue. This was not unusual at the Institute; several other portraits were also altered under its aegis. Examining it in storage with the author in the 1970s, then chief curator Anne Farnam commented, "Yes, that's one of the lip-sticked ones," a reference to similar conservation efforts of the mid-twentieth century. The conclusion is that the original pastel portrait of Richard Derby, Sr. by Benjamin Blyth was first copied in oils fairly accurately by Southward but was later completely painted over by Colbert. The details of the face and upper torso in the original Southward are consistent with Blyth portrayals, and Derby's age conforms to the assumed date of the mid-1770s. Also, the oil's measurements, 21¼ x 18¾, are consistent with a Blyth pastel. The original pastel probably had been damaged and destroyed, where or when is unclear.

Richard Derby established the renowned Derby seafaring trade empire in the South Atlantic and West Indian trade. Born to Richard Derby and Martha Hasket (Hescott) of Ipswich, on Sept. 12, 1712, he married Mary Hodges Feb. 3, 1734. They had six children, three girls and three boys. In the early years, Derby went to sea. In October 1761, the seizure of Salem vessels trading with the West Indies by French ships had become so prevalent that Richard Derby, Sr. and twenty-one signatories petitioned Gov. Bernard for the British ship *King George* to serve as convoy escort. It was not granted, and subsequent seizures cost Derby a substantial amount of money. "No wonder this sort of thing bred ill-feeling and disloyalty among the American merchants," wrote James Duncan Phillips. From then on, Derby stayed ashore; his sons Richard and John and Capt. Edward Allen (Cat. 4), among others, commanded his ships to Leghorn, Gibraltar, the Leeward Islands, and Cadiz. Although the Derbys had become less involved in fisheries, by 1765 they had interests in at least eight vessels, most of them involved in the European trade.

After the death of his wife Mary in 1770, Derby married Sarah Hersey (Cat. 67), widow of Dr. Ezekiel Hersey (Cat. 66), on October 2, 1771. On March 10, 1773, Derby's son Elias Hasket, perhaps in anticipation of his father's death, bought seven dozen brass rings from Edward Lang. Richard Derby died six months later. His will provided equitably for the entire family, including the children of his two children who had predeceased him. After his death, his widow re-turned to Hingham where she founded, in 1784, the school that was to become Derby Academy. She died in 1790. Coincidentally, her original pastel portrait, also used to construct a full-length portrait for Derby Academy, also is now lost, like that of her second husband.

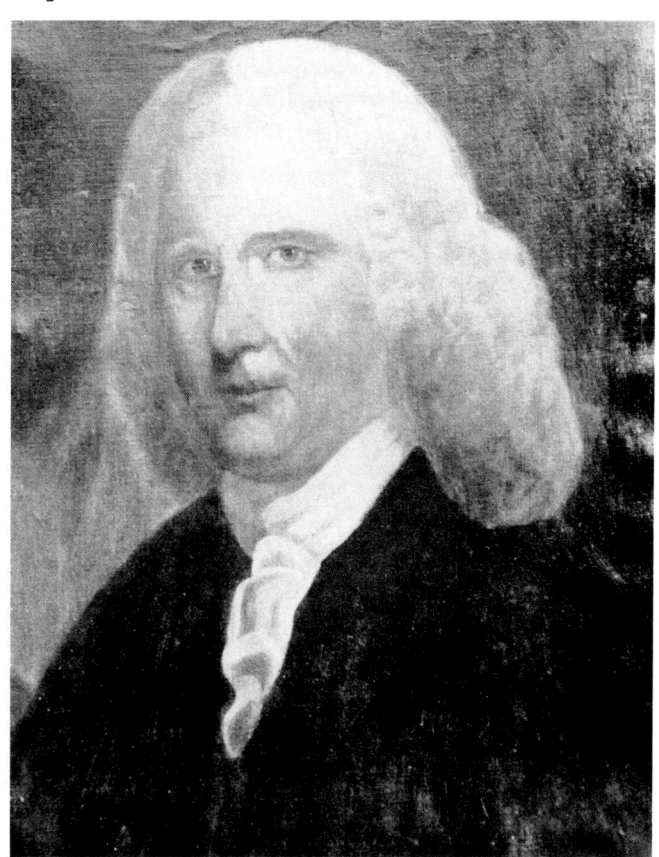

Bacon, *Reminiscences*, illus. betw. 86–87

EIHC 70: opp. 50; 71:51–52

FARL, Derby, Richard Sr: Southward, George (1803–1876); Sargent, Henry (1770–1845); Anonymous, American School, 1851–1900

Holyoke Diaries, 1709–1856, opp. 61

PEM, Phillips Library, Lang Account Book

Richard Derby, Sr.
Oil by George Southward, based on a lost pastel by Benjamin Blyth,
and before being overpainted in 1952 by May E. Colbert
Illustration from *Catalogue of Portraits in the Essex Institute* (1936),
opp. 50
Courtesy of the Boston Athenaeum

☞ Derby, Sarah Hersey, see Hersey, Sarah (Cat. 67)

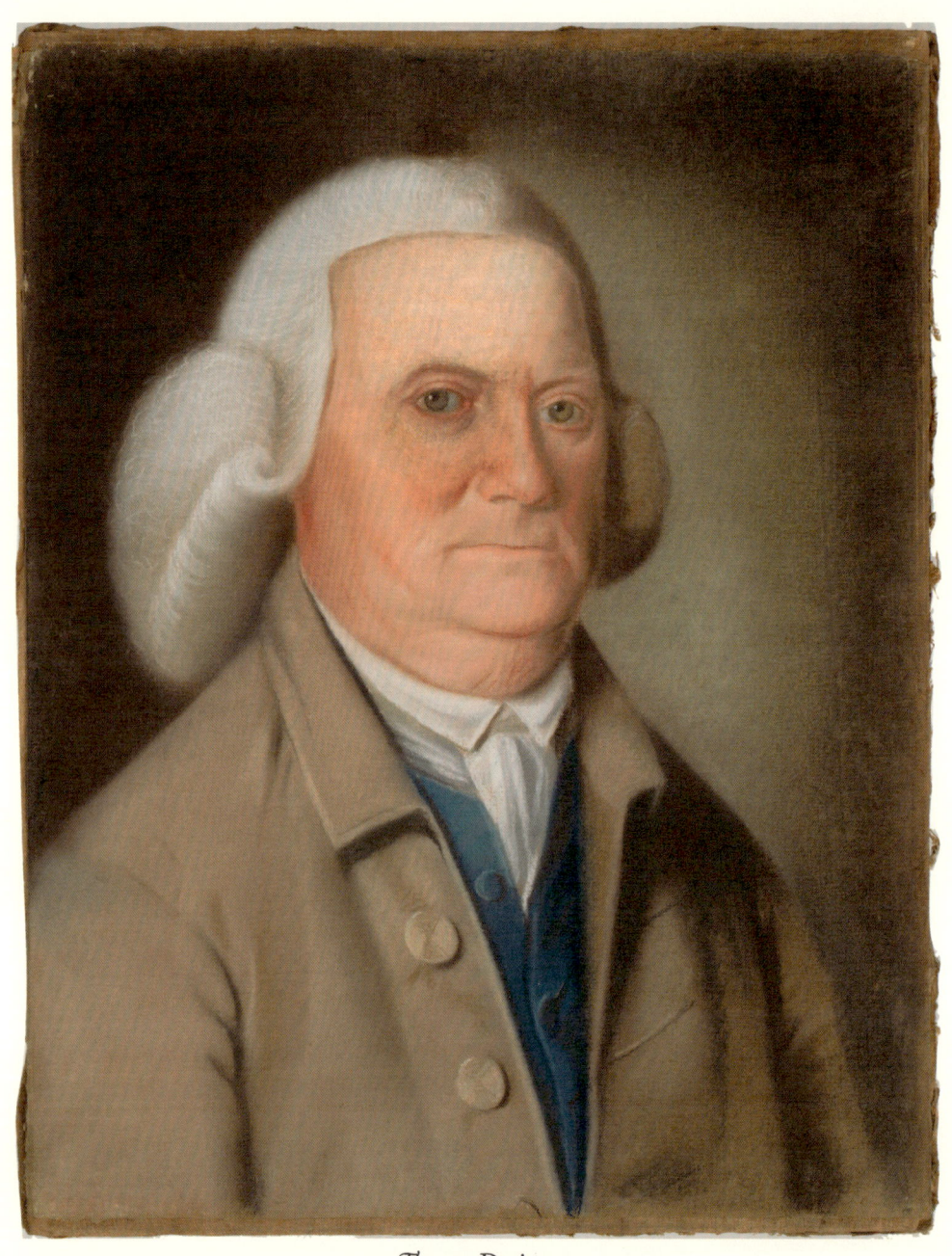

Thomas Dering
Pastel attributed to Benjamin Blyth, early 1770s
Courtesy of the Metropolitan Museum, New York 16. 68. 1, gift of Sylvester Dering, 1916

[48]

Thomas Dering (1720–1785)

Benjamin Blyth (attr.), early 1770s
Pastel on blue laid paper mounted on canvas, 22 x 16 in. (55. 9 x 40. 6 cm.), not framed
Metropolitan Museum of New York 16.68.1, gift of Sylvester Dering, 1916

Thomas Dering was primarily a New York resident and civic official, but his roots were in Massachusetts. His father emigrated to Salisbury in 1664 and subsequently moved to Boston, where Dering was born in 1720. In 1756, he married Mary Sylvester, in Newport, Rhode Island. He went into business with his father but lost everything in a devastating fire in 1761, so he took his wife and young son to the home of his father-in-law, who had built a Georgian mansion on Shelter Island, New York, which became the family home. Dering took on civic responsibilities previously held by his father-in-law, becoming town Supervisor and leader of the religious revival on the town's East End.

Although his entire family were Loyalists (his sister had married the son of then-Lt. Governor Wentworth of New Hampshire), Dering represented his community in various Provincial activities including the convention that adopted the Declaration of Independence and was elected a member of the Provincial Convention, which met in Fishkill in 1775 and 1777 to form a constitution for the State of New York. Dering moved his family to Connecticut for the duration of the Revolutionary War. He died in 1785. Sylvester Manor, a mansion on about 248 acres on Dering Harbor, is now owned by the Sylvester Manor Educational Farm Foundation.

Much confusion has been disseminated about this portrait. Inadvertently, it was mistakenly recorded when acquired by the Metropolitan Museum in its annual report to have been drawn by Joseph Blackburn. This was despite material in the object file, including the description in a letter from the donor, Sylvester Dering, in 1914: "The pictures of Mrs. Dering and her sister Mrs. Cheeseboro are oil paintings, painted in 1754 by Blackburn, . . . The picture of Thomas Dering is a Water Color painted in 1754—measures 20" x 24." I do not know the artist." The mistake was then promulgated in 1923 by Bolton in *Early American Portrait Draughtsmen in Crayon.* Then Frank W. Bayley, owner of Copley Gallery in Boston, fraudulently began to attribute other pastels to Blackburn. Both art historians John Hill Morgan and Henry Wilder Foote discounted the notion that Blackburn drew any and suggested that the Dering was by "Copley, if drawn before 1774 or Blyth if drawn thereafter." Neither historian knew at the time of the extent of Blyth's work prior to Copley's departure.

The portrait was later tentatively attributed by the Met to Blyth. The facial modeling of the Dering, especially of the lower face and neck, resembles the Blyth pastels of Reverend Thomas Barnard; the treatment of the face and wig recall that of Deacon Sharp; the woven quadrants of the buttons are like those for Jonathan Simpson. Only the eyes do not have the linearity suggestive of Blyth, but areas of the face had been damaged and repaired, and much of the pastel shows signs of having been worked on prior to its arrival at the Metropolitan Museum in 1917. The biggest hurdle to the Blyth attribution is how he may have met Dering. It possibly was in Rhode Island.

The Society for the Preservation of Long Island Antiquities owns an oil copy of the Dering portrait, of the same size.

Bolton, *Portrait Draughtsmen in Crayon*, 7, 105

Bolton and Binsse, *Antiquarian*, 90

FARL, Copley, John Singleton 157-3z

Geni website

Jeffares, http://www.pastellists.com/Articles/Blyth.pdf

MET, Archives and object file; Museum catalogue 408, by unknown artist, 1765, 16. 68. 1

MET, *Forty-seventh Annual Report*/1916. (Met, NY MCMXVII)

Morgan, letter to Edgell, 1934 MFA object file

Morgan and Foote, "An Extension . . . Joseph," 58, 70

Newport, Episcopal & Congregational Records 8:476

Shillingburg, J. E. descendant, email correspondence

Society for the Preservation of Long Island Antiquities, Dering correspondence

Sylvester Manor Educational Farm Foundation

University of Michigan, William L. Clements Library, Dering Papers

☞ Eunice Diman; see Eunice Diman Mason, Cat. 90

George Dodge (1726–1808)

Benjamin Blyth, late 1760s
Pastel on paper mounted on linen, 21¾ x 17 in. (55.2 x 43 cm.)
Current location not known; George Dodge Cabot, Weehawken, NJ, in 1957; John Cabot; Lucy Cabot; Hannah Dodge Cabot

Capt. George Dodge is the subject of one of three "case studies" of the economic elite in Salem before, during, and immediately after the American Revolution by historian Richard J. Morris. Dodge, a member of a prosperous Essex County farming family, became a successful mariner, a heavy investor in privateering, and by 1792, one of the wealthiest men in Salem.

Dodge was born on April 10, 1726, to Joshua and Hannah Rayment (Raymond,) Dodge of Beverly. In 1746, he married Lydia Herrick, daughter of Benjamin and Lidia Herrick of Wenham. They lived in Beverly, where several children were born, before moving to Salem, where he manufactured sailcloth and ran a tannery. As hostilities with Britain advanced, he became a member of the Committee of Inspection that attempted to confiscate the goods of fellow residents, including Peter Frye (Cat. 56) and Elizabeth Higginson, who were in violation of the Non-Importation Agreement. By the time of the Revolution, Dodge had become a merchant who helped finance privateers, among other ventures. After the war, he manufactured sailcloth for the burgeoning maritime trade, and he, along with the Cabots and Moses Brown (Cat. 21), was a major investor and officer in the Essex Bridge between Salem and Beverly.

For Dodge, as for so many Salem residents, the Reverend William Bentley's diary is an excellent source. Its very first entry, on April 30, 1784, records the arrival of Dodge, a member of his East Church, into Salem harbor "after sickness and a long Voiage to the W. Indies." Bentley enjoyed Dodge's company and wrote of one visit with him in 1794, "He saw an engagement of the Peguans with the Siamese in which 9,000 men were engaged & he was told the first time with fire arms.... They fought from gun Boats."

On January 20, 1808, Bentley wrote, "Last Monday morning died in this town Capt. George Dodge. He was one of the three enterprising Sea Captains who distinguished themselves in the past Generation. Thomas Mason [Cat. 91], George Williams, & G. Dodge. He outlived his contemporaries in naval enterprise & business, & often said he had doubled his estate since he was 60 years of age. He is thought to be worth between 150 & 200 thousand dollars.... He was long a Captain of a Vessel. He was a man acute in business, domestic, allowing little intercourse at his house, even to his children, who were permitted to pay short visits. Since the death of his wife a few years ago he has kept house & had the services of his g[rand]children. He was not an intemperate man but he was regularly a great drinker of wine. He had no information at all upon any subject but business & he had a very imperfect education.... Public opinion is that he was not indulgent to his children.... He had reached 82 when he died."

Dodge's estate was valued at $282,000. His carefully framed will left his two living sons the houses they then occupied and provided that his daughters receive fair shares in his estate; he also provided for the two children of his deceased son, Larkin, who inherited the "mansion house" buildings and land where Dodge had lived. His daughter Hannah was the first owner of the portraits of her parents, then her unmarried daughter, Lucy Cabot, through the family to George Dodge Cabot, ca. 1936, where the trail became lost.

The current location of the pastel is not known, but Henry Wilder Foote described it in 1957: Dodge had dark blue eyes and was wearing a dark brown coat and waistcoat, with brass buttons. The background was dark brown. The reproduction shows a sober-minded, observant man, alert to his affairs, conservatively but not ostentatiously dressed.

Bentley 1:1; 2:81–2; 3:339–40

Essex County, MA Probate File Papers, 7841 (1808)

EIHC 3:83, 30:53–105; 62:8–11

FARL, Blyth, Benjamin 157-3f

Felt 2:168

Foote, "Blyth," 89

Jeffares, http://www.pastellists.com/Articles/Blyth.pdf

Morris, 603

Norton, "Brothers Blyth," 62

Phillips, *Salem . . . 18th C.,* 249–50, 407

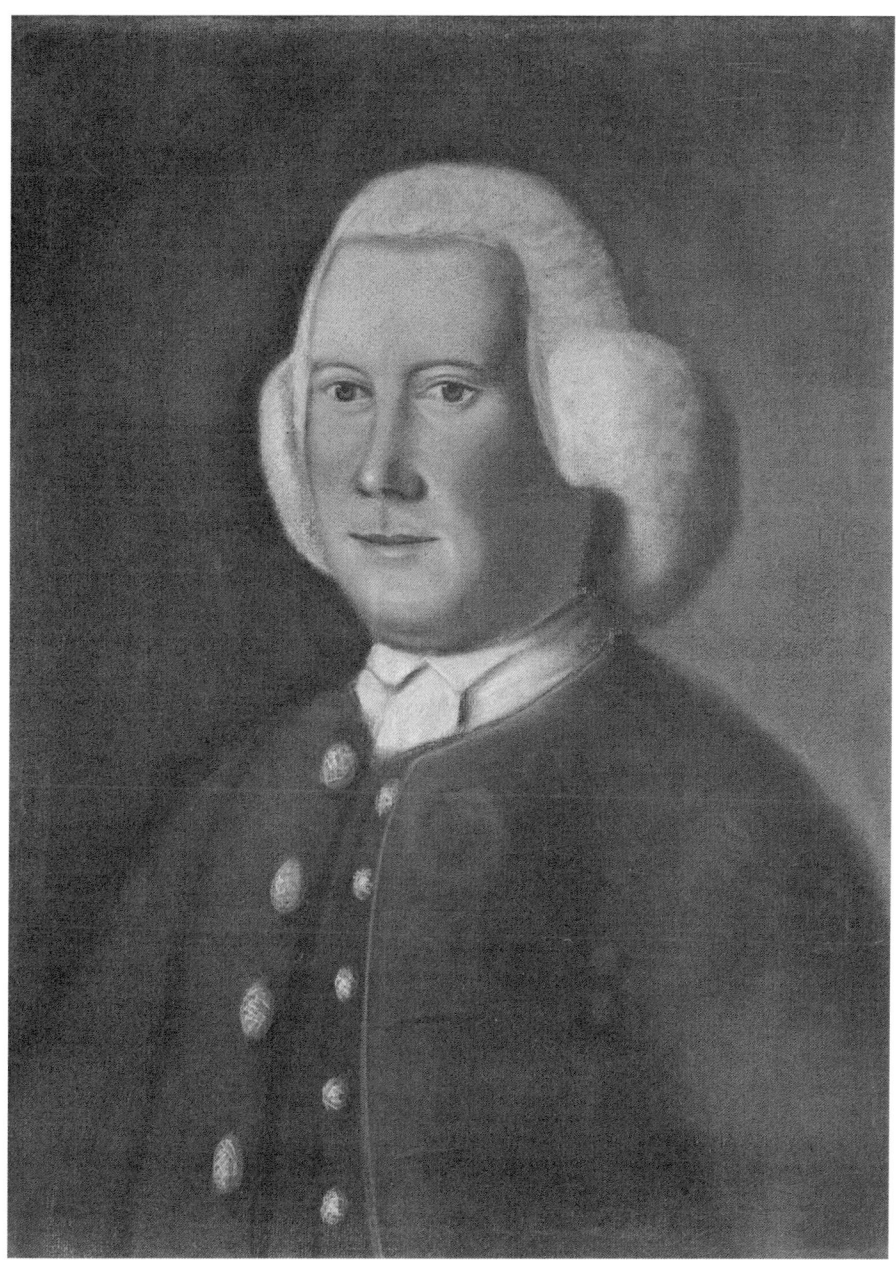

George Dodge
Photograph of unlocated pastel by Benjamin Blyth, late 1760s
Courtesy of the Frick Art Reference Library Photoarchives

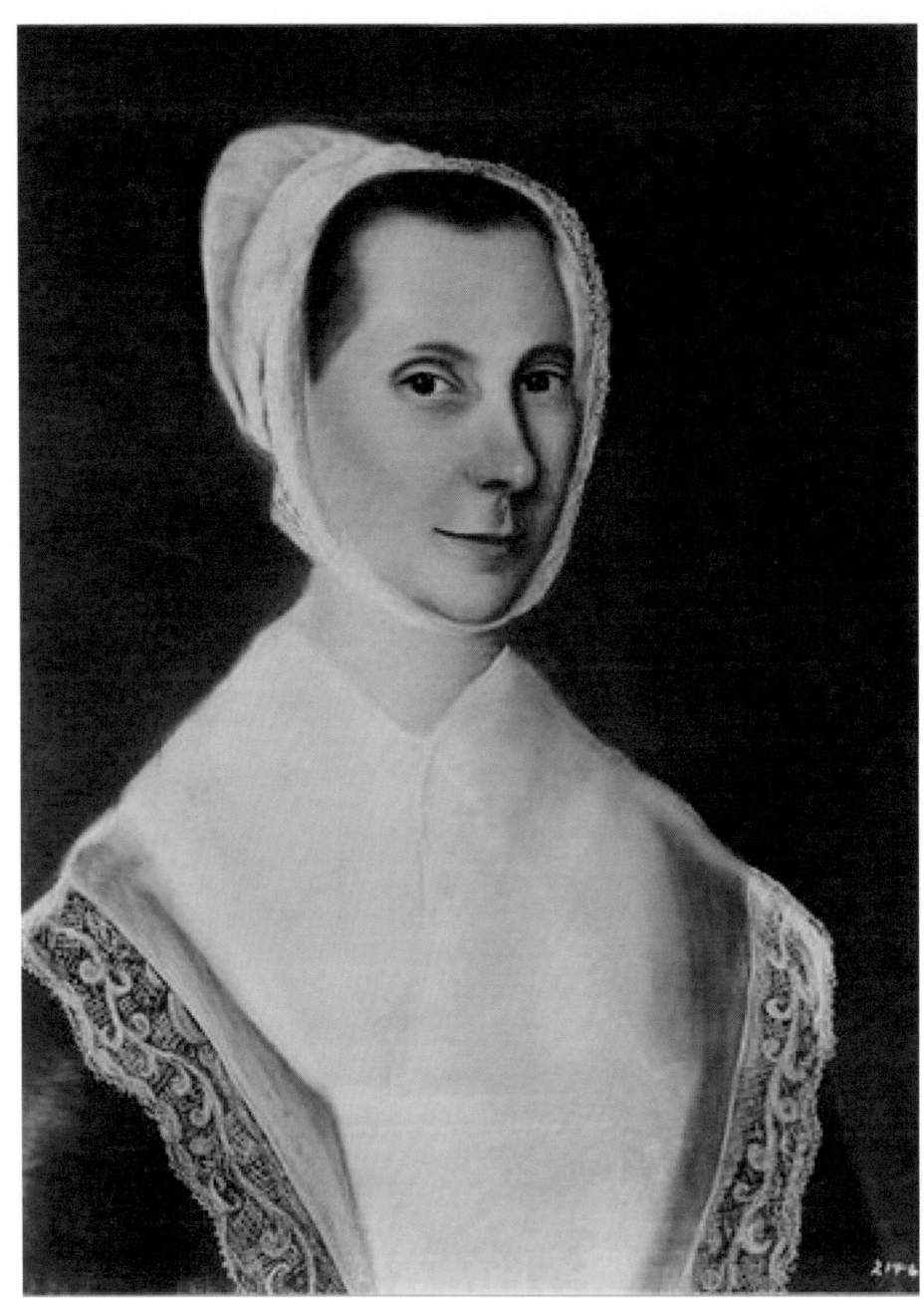

Lydia Herrick Dodge
Photograph of unlocated pastel by Benjamin Blyth, late 1760s
Courtesy of the Frick Art Reference Library Photoarchives

[50]
Lydia Herrick Dodge (1726–1798)

Benjamin Blyth, late 1760s
Pastel on paper mounted on linen, 21¾ x 17 in. (55.2 x 43 cm.)
Current location not known; Cabot family to George Dodge Cabot, Weehawken, NJ, ca. 1936

Lidia Herrick was born to Benjamin and Lidia Herrick of Wenham on May 18, 1726. She and George Dodge were married there on August 25, 1746, when both were just twenty years old. Their first son, Larkin, is reported to have been born on February 7, 1746, but this is probably an error that can be attributed to the change in the calendar, which would make it 1747—at that, less than six months after his parents' marriage. Their other children were Lydia, George, and Hannah. Larkin, who married Mehitabel Orne on January 4, 1770, had died by the time George Dodge made out his carefully drawn will, so he provided for Larkin's children, along with the rest of his and Lydia's children.

The lace trim on Lydia's hat and gossamer "handkerchief" (shawl) is masterfully drawn. Lydia Dodge's facial expression, curious and yet reserved, dominates her portrait. Henry Wilder Foote does not describe the color of her clothing but wrote that her face "suggests an outstanding personality, with a sense of humor. This is one of Benjamin Blyth's best pictures." Indeed, and among his earliest.

Beverly VR, Bible record owned by Mrs. Sophronia A. Day in 1907
FARL, Blyth, Benjamin 158–3e
Foote, "Blyth," 89–90 ("Mrs. George Dodge")
Jeffares, http://www.pastellists.com/Articles/Blyth. pdf
Norton, "Brothers Blyth," 62

John Endecott (1588/9–1665)

Benjamin Blyth, early 1770s
Pastel on paper, mounted on linen, 21¾ x 17¾ in. (sight), (55.3 x 44.2 cm.),
Samuel Blyth frame with original hooks
Massachusetts Historical Society Artwork 01.397, gift of Matthew Greif, 2016;
William Crowninshield Endicott, 1935; Henry Pickering Walcott; earlier provenance unknown

As a co-founder with Roger Conant of the town of Salem, Gov. John Endecott was a revered figure in early Massachusetts Bay Colony history as its longest-serving governor. He was also considered a rigid, somewhat over-zealous Puritan, whose theology did not allow for Anglican or other Nonconformist views. His persecutions of Quakers resulted in three being hanged. His expedition against the Indians in 1636 was part of the devastating Pequot War.

Believed to have been born in Devon, England, around 1588, he arrived from England with his first wife, Ann (Gower) in 1628 and served as first governor of the Massachusetts Bay Colony until the arrival of John Winthrop in 1630. Endecott, though sometimes controversial, did set the infant town of Salem on the road to prominence in the colony. He held major public offices, including deputy governor as well as governor for all but the year 1634 (that, a suspension from office for defacing a military ensign, which he considered an example of popish idolatry) until 1664. At his death in 1668, he had considerable holdings, including lands given him by the General Court and two Sachems of Quinebaug.

This portrait is a 2016 acquisition by the Massachusetts Historical Society, which also owns two others of Endecott. A brass plaque attached to the frame of this MHS pastel copy attributes it to Samuel Blyth, but it clearly is too proficient. The telltale right ear, parallel to the picture plane, suggests Benjamin, as do subtle folds of Endecott's voluminous collar. Benjamin Blyth is now known to have made copies of several other earlier portraits, both in pastel and in oil. This one of Endecott also comes close to the original by an anonymous artist, although elements such as the tassel were eliminated. According to a label on the back, it had once been owned by Roger Walcott, who gave it in 1935 to William Crowninshield Endicott, in honor of his friendship with Henry Pickering Walcott. The portrait then descended through the Prince family to Matthew Greif, who donated it to the MHS. Greif thinks it may have come down through his great-grandfather, Morton Prince.

This severe quality of Endecott's character, clearly demonstrated in the original, was faithfully retained in the copy by Benjamin Blyth.

Bentley 2:197-98, illus. (oil) opp. 199
Encyclopedia Britannica
Essex County, MA: Probate File Papers, 9053

EIHC 20:1–18; 71:69, 70, oil portraits, by Mitchell, Cat. 81; by Frothingham, Cat. 83

Felt, illus. vol. 1 frontispiece

Foote, "Benjamin Blyth of Salem," 71:79, attr. to Samuel Blyth

Massachusetts State House Art Collection, object file folder

Oliver, *Portraits . . . Massachusetts Historical Society*, 38, attr. to Smibert

Suffolk County Probate File Records, 385

WPA 723, attr. to Samuel Blyth, after 1783

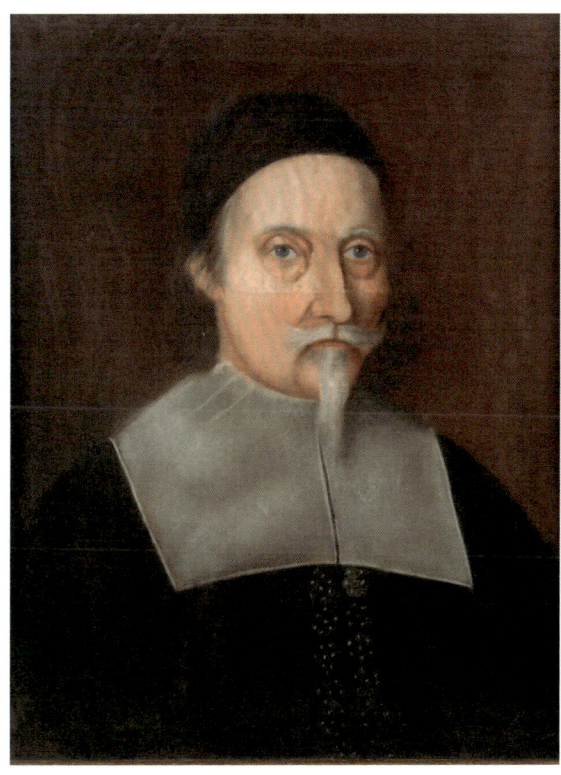 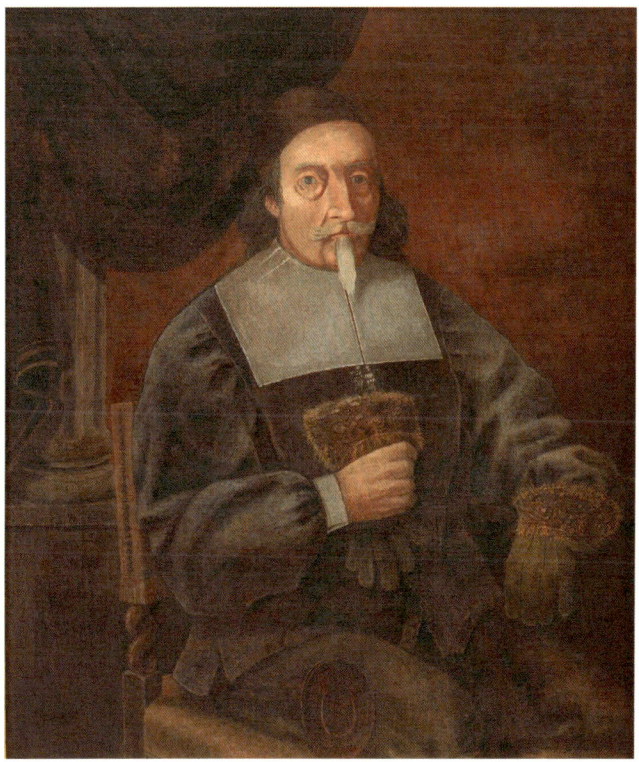

John Endecott
Pastel by Benjamin Blyth, early 1770s, copy of an original
oil by an unknown artist
Courtesy of the Massachusetts Historical Society Artwork
01. 397, gift of Matthew Greif, 2016

John Endecott
Oil by unknown artist, mid-17th century
Courtesy of the Massachusetts State House Art Commission
1941.2, Bequest of William Crowninshield Endicott 1935.
Presented 1941.

[52]

John Fisk (1744–1797)

Benjamin Blyth, early 1770s
Pastel (assumed), measurements unknown
No information on image

John Fisk was born in 1744 to one of the most contentious ministers in Salem history, the Reverend Samuel Fisk, who fought for years with some members the First Church, then formed his own parish, another "First Church" (forced to call itself the Third Church), and eventually the New Meeting House (Salem Tabernacle), from which he was turned out in 1745. His son elected to be a mariner and became one of Salem's heroes of the Revolution. Fisk commanded the privateers *Massachusetts* and *Tyrannicide*, the latter one of five vessels authorized by the Massachusetts General Court for its new Navy in February 1776. He took an active part in privateering and "probably made some money," according to James Duncan Phillips, "for after the Revolution he set up as a merchant and kept a store. . . . traded steadily in the West Indies and made better ventures there than in the Far East. He owned about a quarter of Union Wharf." Fisk had part interest in many vessels, including the *Nancy*, along with Elias Hasket Derby.

After the death of his first wife Lydia Phippen Fisk (Cat. 53) in 1782, he married Mrs. Martha Hibbert. She died two years later, and in 1786 he married the recently widowed Sarah Gerry from Marblehead. In 1792, Fisk was chosen major general of the 2nd Division of Militia and a deputy or representative to the state government. As a leading member of Salem notables, he served in various capacities at town festivities. Phillips wrote that Fisk "was a most hospitable host, entertaining distinguished strangers who came to town and some that were not so distinguished. . . . Unfortunately the rapid succession of deaths among his children and some severe financial reverses upset his mind, so that he had to be confined under the care of Dr. Kittredge in Andover for two years before his death on September 27, 1797. Reverend William Bentley recorded, "I was called from my bed at one o-clock & continued with him until 43 minutes after one next day, just after dinner, when he died." Bentley delivered Fisk's funeral sermon. "All the Vessels in the Harbour hoisted their colors half mast on the occasion," he noted. Gen. Fisk's casket was supported by friends Capt. Edward Gibaut (Cat. 59) and Gen. Abbot (Cat. 1), among others. Artillery, cadets, and the Salem Marine Society all turned out. Bentley's sermon was subsequently published by Thomas D. Cushing.

Bentley wrote of "Endeavouring from some imperfect materials to obtain a portrait of my old friend Gen. Fiske. . . . A portrait, three quarter face, was taken while he was in the Naval service, but unfinished, by Cole & Blythe. They were wretched daubers at best but they had much employment from the privateer men. None of their portraits are finished but they sometimes have taken likenesses. These were the only persons who undertook at that time. That of Fiske very bad. It is servile. His vigor, his ready soul are not easily painted." The portrait Bentley referred to is unknown, and no portrait of Fisk has been found. Bentley's account of "Cole & Blythe" is unclear. These artists made one set of engravings, of George and Martha Washington (Cats. 132, 133), but none is known of Fisk. Beyond this description, the whereabouts of this portrait of Fisk is not known. However, as noted above, Blyth drew a pastel portrait of Capt. Fisk's wife (Cat. 53).

Bentley 1:xxxvii, 24; 2:238; 3:470; many other entries

Bentley, *Parish List of Deaths 1785–1819*

Essex County, MA Probate Records, case 9503

Felt, 2:278, 373, 565

Foote, "Blyth," 76–77, 90

Jeffares, http://www.pastellists.com/Articles/Blyth.pdf

Norton, "Brothers Blyth," 62

PEM, Phillips Library, Orne Papers, Aug. 1745

Phillips, *Salem . . . Indies*, 87–8

Phillips, *Salem . . . 18th C.*, 394–5, 398

Lydia Phippen Fisk (1747–1782)

Benjamin Blyth, early 1770s
Pastel on paper mounted on canvas 20½ x 15½, in. (63.5 x 39.4 cm.), Samuel Blyth frame
Peabody Essex Museum 103698, bequest of the Misses Marion C. Allen and Elizabeth C. Allen, 1913

Born to David and Priscilla (Bickford) Phippen in Salem on January 7, 1747, Lydia Phippen was married at age nineteen to John Fisk (Cat. 52), son of the Reverend Samuel Fisk of the First Church and Anna (Gerrish). She died at age thirty-five in 1782, leaving seven children, the youngest only seventeen months old. She did not live to witness the deaths a few years later of her daughters including her namesake, seventeen, from consumption, and shortly afterwards, a son from "intemperance." One daughter, Sarah Putnam, died at age twenty-two in 1795, leaving an infant son and, as the Reverend William Bentley noted, "added to the list of bereavements, which have been multiplied in the General's family." As a friend of the family, Bentley witnessed the removal of the Fisk graves from the Charter Street Burying Ground and described in detail the decomposition of Lydia Fisk's body, as well as those of other family members.

As Blyth depicted her, Lydia Phippen Fisk was young, beautiful, and fashionable without being ostentatious. Her portrait is one of his most successful, not only for depicting her character, but for the treatment of her hat, pearls, and lace at her bodice. On the back of the portrait are several inscriptions on the newspaper used as backing that mention the engagement in which her husband participated. Several other writings have proven inscrutable: " … Ever and Ever … "; and "Mr. Eatern, Boston, July the 16th. …" The portrait was treated for mildew at the Museum of Fine Arts, Boston, in 1969, along with that of John Gibaut and David Ropes.

The donors, the Allen sisters, or possibly only Miss Marion, also gave the oil portrait of Capt. Edward Allen (Cat. 4) and an unidentified sea captain, *EIHC* Catalogue … 373. Allen's son, Edward Jr., had married Lydia and John's daughter, Ann. Presumably the unidentified sea captain was also related.

Addison Gallery of American Art, *Bulletin,* … Catalogue of the Essex County Exhibition Oct. 1935, 20-22
Appletons' Cyclopaedia of American Biography, 2:469 (1887)
Bayley, *Little Known … Portrait Painters,* "Blyth," no. 2
Bentley 1:22, 24; 2:123, 142; *Deaths,* 58
Cole, "Limned by Blyth," illus. 332
EIHC 71:74-5, cat. 88
FARL, Blyth, Benjamin 158-3c
Foote, "Blyth," 77, 90 ("Mrs. John Fisk")
Jeffares, http://www.pastellists.com/Articles/Blyth.pdf
Norton, "Brothers Blyth," 62
Salem VR P. R. 432, Bible belonging to Mrs. Nathaniel West
WPA 754

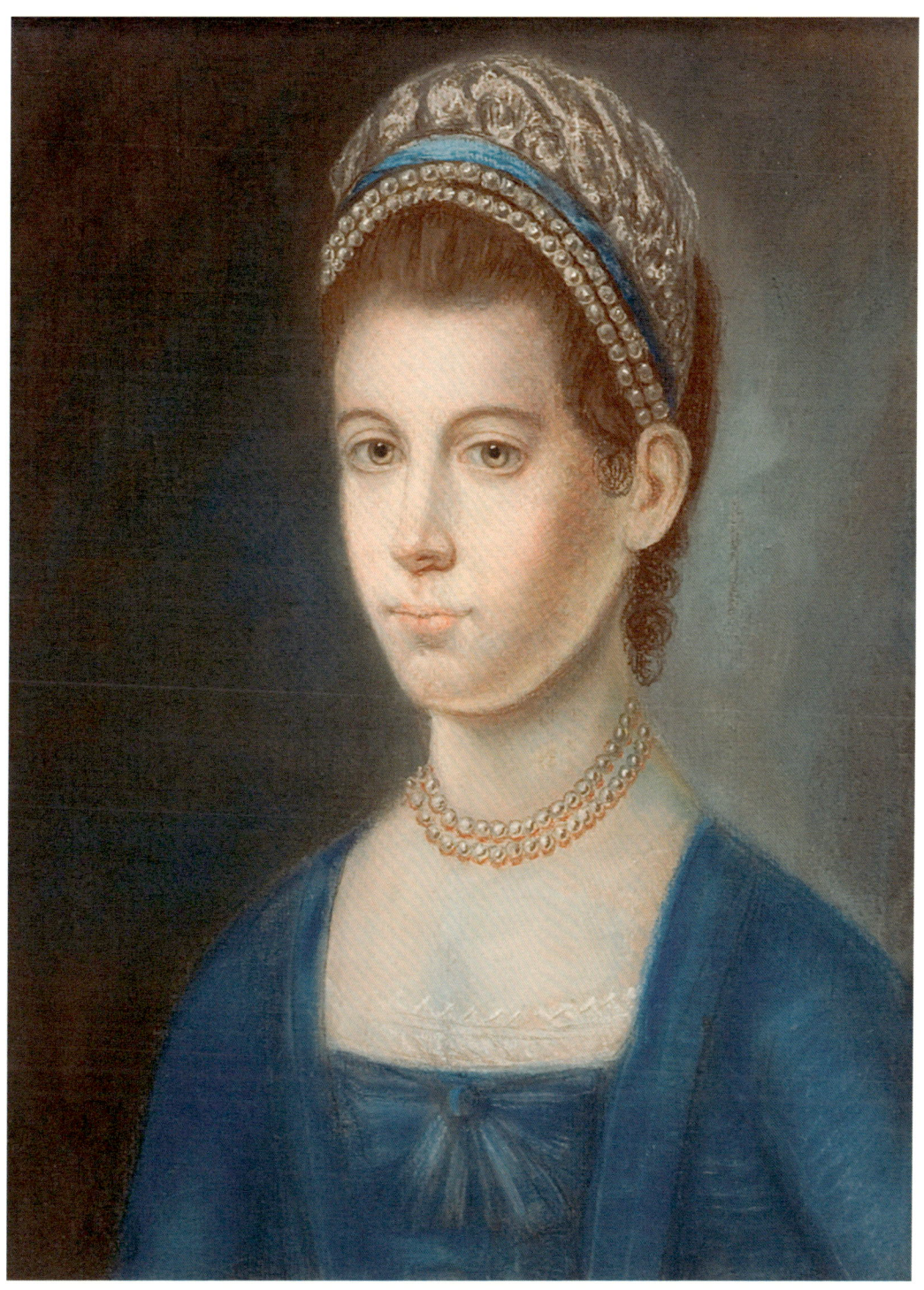

Lydia Phippen Fisk
Pastel by Benjamin Blyth, early 1770s
Courtesy of the Peabody Essex Museum 103698, bequest of the Misses Marion C. Allen
and Elizabeth C. Allen, 1913

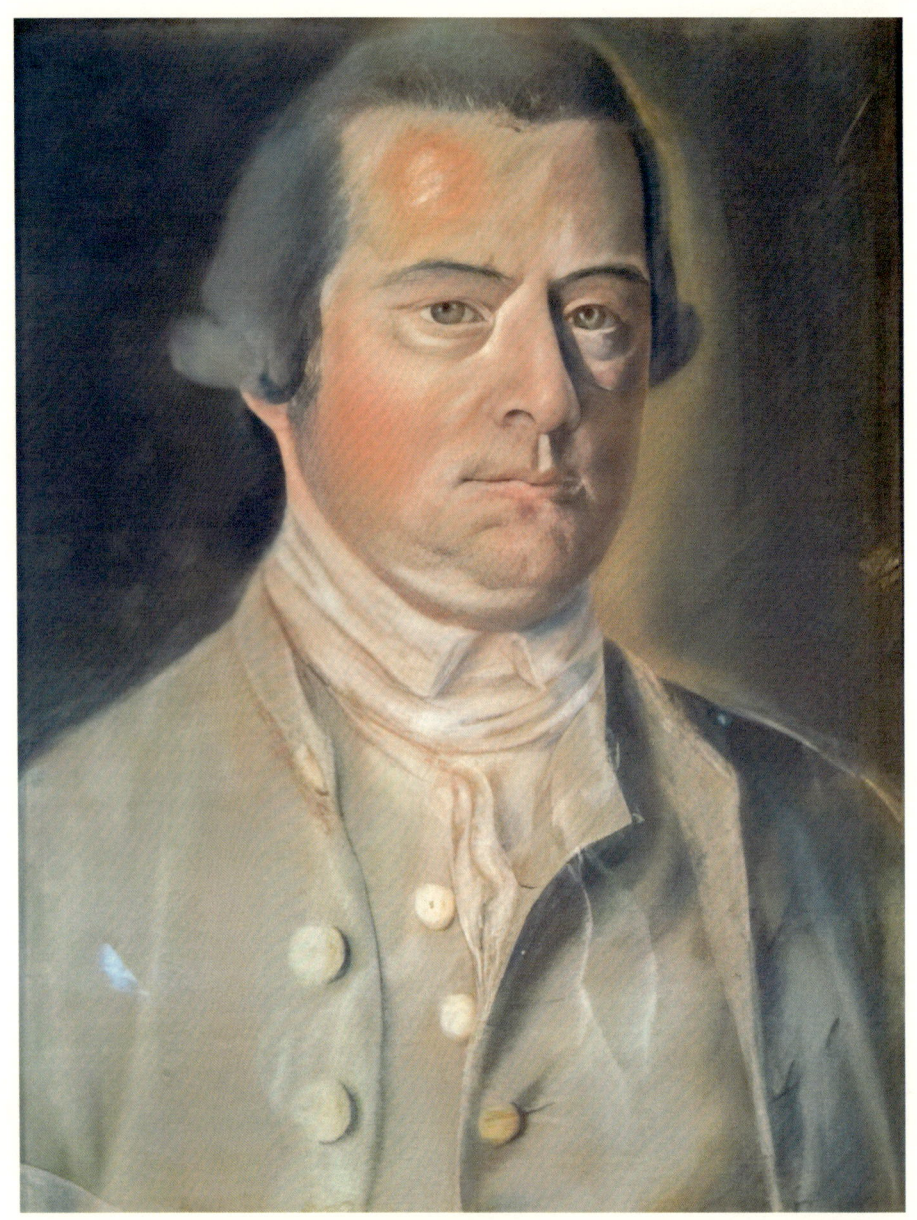

James Flagg
Pastel by Benjamin Blyth, early 1770s
Courtesy of the collection of Thomas L. Tileston

[54]

James Flagg (1739–1775)

Benjamin Blyth, early 1770s

Pastel on paper mounted on linen, 20¼ x 14¾ in. (51.4 x 37.5 cm.), Samuel Blyth frame

Thomas L. Tileston, Newport Beach, CA; Flagg and Foote families

One of the most interesting and well-documented Blyth portraits still owned by the sitter's family is of James Flagg. One of seven children of Gershom Flagg III by his second marriage to Hannah Pitson, James Flagg was born in Boston on October 28, 1739. He became a merchant and lived on the upper end of Hanover Street, eradicated in the 1960s for what is now City Hall Plaza. As a Plymouth Proprietor, Flagg also owned land in Augusta, Maine. The date when he joined the Massachusetts Grand Lodge of Masons in Boston is not known, but he was raised to Master in 1761 and is recorded as having attended the "Feast" on December 29 of that year. Flagg died in St. Eustacia, the West Indies, on June 20, 1775. He never married, so the portrait went to his sister Mary (Polly), wife of Josiah Wilder, to her daughter, Mary Wilder White, to her daughter Mary Wilder Foote (mother of historian Henry Wilder Foote), to her daughter Mary Wilder Tileston, then to her son, Thomas L. Tileston, the current owner. Flagg was also related to the family of Benjamin West (Cat. 135). Checking his family portrait may have been the impetus for Foote's heavily researched article on Blyth for the Massachusetts Historical Society in 1957.

Flagg's portrait was long credited to John Johnston until attributed to Blyth by Foote. Johnston could not be the artist because he became a portrait painter in the late 1770s, after the death of Flagg. Also, of fifty portraits credited to John Johnston in the Smithsonian Inventory of Paintings and Sculpture, only three are said to be pastels, of which none, however, is confirmed. Most significantly, the portrait is in a Samuel Blyth frame.

Bolton, *Early American Portraits in Crayon;* credited to John Johnston

FARL, American School, Massachusetts (1751–1800) 157–3f

Flagg, Norman and Lucius C. S., *The Flagg Family* [Quincy, Ill: Cadogan-Hatcher], 1907

Foote, "Blyth," 90–91

Jeffares, http://www.pastellists.com/Articles/Blyth.pdf

Massachusetts Gazette 23 May 1768

North, James W., *The History of Augusta: . . . ,* (Augusta [ME]: Clapp and North, 1870), 859

WPA 2691, in Addenda

[55]

Samuel Flagg (1740/41?–1822?)

Benjamin Blyth, mid-1770s

Pastel on paper, 19⅝ x 12½ in. (49.5 x 50 cm.)

Current location not known; Mrs. Richard Ward Greene, Worcester, MA, by 1923 to 1975

A note from an anonymous source states, "November 26, 1951. Rev. Henry Wilder Foote brought in portrait of Samuel's cousin, James Flagg, to compare with Samuel. His portrait is pastel and attr. to Blyth. No particular resemblances. Mr. Foote says he has never been able to find any biographical material on Samuel." Samuel Flagg's birth and death dates still elude researchers, but as he appears to be in his late thirties, his birth is assumed to have been in the early 1740s. By 1770, he was a dealer in pepper and dry goods in Salem. The next year, he was a captain in the 4th Salem Company, with 1st Lt. Col. Peter Frye (Cat. 56) and 2nd Lt. Col. Benjamin Pickman. On August 30, 1772, Flagg married Mrs. Dorothy Drowne, at Dunstable, New Hampshire. Because he, along with Frye and Elizabeth Higginson, refused to adhere to the Non-Importation Agreement in 1774, his goods were in danger of being confiscated. However, after war broke out, Samuel Flagg joined the Patriot cause. He served as captain of the Salem contingent of 108 volunteers for the Rhode Island Expedition in August 1778, an odyssey that, as James Duncan Phillips wrote, "seems to have appealed to all the Salem sea captains and other leading citizens" and encouraged participation from neighboring towns. Flagg later rose to the rank of colonel. He became engaged in privateering. A letter from Timothy Pickering, dated October 24, 1780, noted that "Mr. Henry Rust, Capt. Saml Flag, Joshua Ward, & Mr Whittemore of Cape Ann, are part owners of the ship Brutas which has Taken some of the valuable Quebeck Fleet." In 1778 he served as an appraiser for the estate of a Salem Quaker, David Northey, with two other men, both Quakers. Flagg was an early member of the Essex Lodge of Freemasons, organized in 1779, and was one of its first treasurers. In 1783, Flagg was the delegate or representative in the nascent Massachusetts government.

The most likely death record found for a Samuel Flagg is from Grafton, on October 17, 1822, at the age of eighty-one. The Grafton-area connection is buttressed by the fact that the portrait was owned in 1923 and again in 1975 by Mrs. Richard Ward Greene of Worcester. It also was said to have been put on deposit at the Worcester Art Museum, but the museum has no record of it.

Frank W. Bayley credited the portrait to John Johnston, as did Bolton. It was reported to be "water-stained" with "fold and scratch damage . . . face." The portrait of Samuel Flagg, like that of James Flagg (Cat. 54), stands as a Blyth. It has many of his stylistic attributes.

Bayley, *Little Known . . . Portrait Painters, John Johnston*, unpaginated

Bolton, *Portrait Draughtsmen*, 42, illus. opp. 2

Coburn, "The Johnstons of Boston," credited to John Johnston

EIHC 3:94; 29:179; 39:51; 43:16; 45:125; 54:82

Felt 2:195, 522, 565

Flagg, Norman and Lucius C. S., *The Flagg Family*, 151

Foote, "Blyth," 90–91

Jeffares, http://www.pastellists.com/Articles/Blyth.pdf

Norton, "Brothers Blyth," 62

Phillips, *Salem . . . 18th C.*, 249-50, 306–10, 376, 407

SIRIS, credited to John Johnston

WPA 768, listed "at Worcester Art Museum"

WPA 2693, under Addenda, attributed to John Johnston

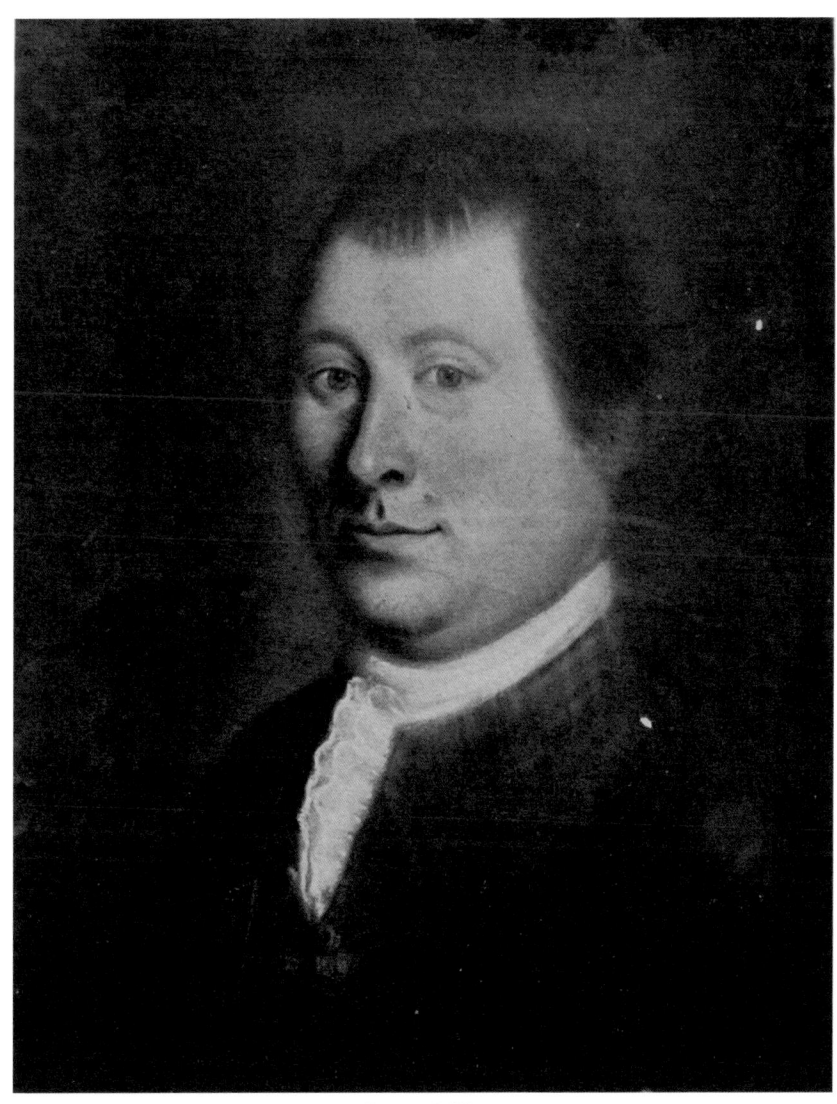

Samuel Flagg
Photograph of unlocated pastel attributed to Benjamin Blyth, mid-1770s
Illustration from Bolton, *Portrait Draughtsmen* (1923)
Courtesy of the Boston Atheneum

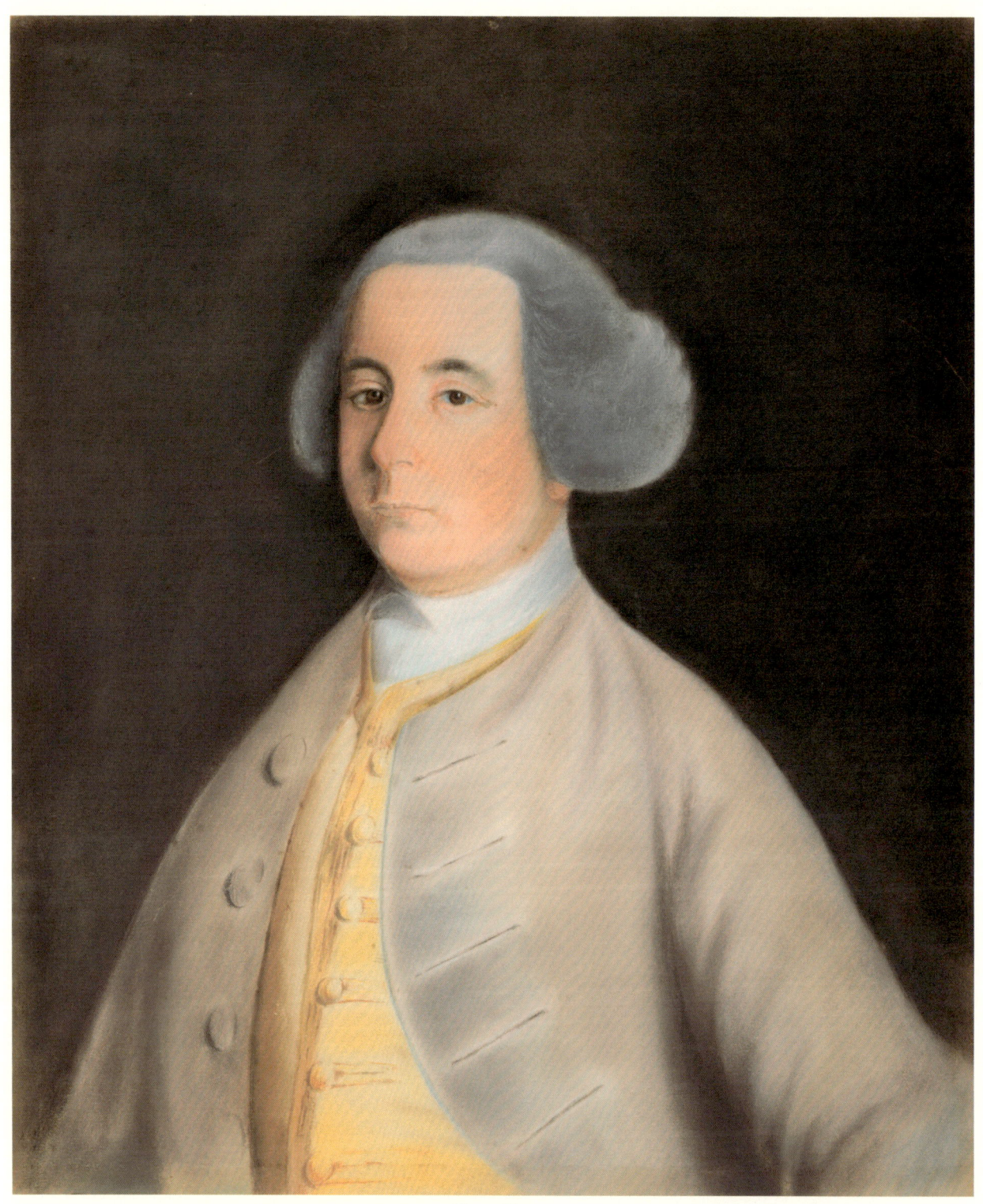

Peter Frye
Pastel by Benjamin Blyth, early 1770s
Courtesy of the Peabody Essex Museum 104296, provenance unknown

[56]
Peter Frye (1723–1820)

Benjamin Blyth, late 1760s
Pastel on paper, 25½ x 21⅝ in. (67.44 x 54.9 cm.)
Peabody Essex Museum 104296, gift to the former Peabody Museum in 1901 and transferred to the former Essex Institute on March 10, 1914; prior provenance unknown

The Frye family was among those that suffered irreparably from the Revolution. As colonial grievances flared up, Peter Frye was one of the Loyalists who, like Samuel Curwen (Cat. 33) and Nathaniel Dabney, husband of Elizabeth (Cat. 39), fled to England, leaving their wives and family behind. Born in Andover on January 3, 1723 (EIHC has February 1), to Samuel, a "respectable farmer," and Sarah (Osgood) Frye, Peter Frye graduated from Harvard College in 1744 and three years later moved to Salem to teach grammar school. In 1751, he married Love Pickman, daughter of the prominent merchant Benjamin Pickman and his wife, Abigail Love Rawlins Pickman (Cat. 106), and joined his father-in-law in business. The next year, Frye was a collector of duties on imported goods. He owned several ships with Pickman and Benjamin Lynde and was sole owner of a coastal schooner, *Swan*, becoming himself a successful importer of British goods. Frye also succeeded to his father-in-law's share in the Social Library and his place in Salem society. Although a representative for Salem in the General Court from 1767 to 1769, Frye was not re-elected because of "proclivities . . . towards the cause of the King." He also was one of seventeen men who voted against the majority that objected to the new tax imposed by Great Britain. Nonetheless, he became Colonel of Essex County Militia, Justice of the Peace, Judge of the Inferior Court of Common Pleas, and in 1773, Register of Probate.

Soon, however, Frye was one of four people from Salem who were publicly impugned for "base and infamous behavior" for circumventing the town's embargo of imported goods and for flaunting his sympathies to British troops. On October 6, 1774, his house and its outbuildings on Essex Street were destroyed by a fire "probably of incendiary origin." So in late 1775, after the start of the Revolution, he abruptly left the country, settling in England with his daughter, Love, and her husband, Dr. Peter Oliver. The fate of the family left behind, his wife and eight children, was recounted upon Love Frye's death in 1809 at age seventy-seven by her brother, Benjamin Pickman in a letter to the court. He explained why Frye did not deserve part of his wife's estate: he had deserted her and the children, she had been living in a small house on Pickman's property, and she had "no effects" but bedding and clothing. Bentley's observation was that she was "A Woman remarkable for the excentricities of her life." One son, John, had died at age thirty-seven, leaving six "destitute" children whom, it appears, she was helping to raise. Daughter Judith Stickney was widowed, and another son, Peter, who had deserted the Continental Army, was caught, and sentenced to be shot, but through the intercession of his mother was spared as "a lunatic" and spent the last twenty years of his life in the Salem Poor House, where he died of dysentery in 1815. Their father, subject of this portrait, died five years later near London at the home of Admiral Sir John Knight Camperwell, on the day he turned ninety-eight. He had one distinction at the time—he was the oldest living graduate of Harvard College.

The Peabody Essex Museum owns two pastels of Frye. The first was a gift from the Peabody Museum to the Essex Institute in 1914. The EI accession book recorded that the pastel was by S. P. Cutts. The error was repeated in the Catalogue of Portraits published serially in several volumes of *The Essex Institute Historical Collections* in the 1930s. However, on a page of "Errata" published in a subsequent volume, it was corrected to "The artist was Miss Love Pickman Cutts . . . Copy from an oil portrait. A similar pastel is in the possession of Samuel Frye Walcott, Esq." That it was copied from an oil portrait was yet another error. Moreover, on the back of the original catalogue card is a typescript containing information on Frye's death and "Executed by L. P. Cutts. March 1851." Evidently unheeded was that the typescript was a later addition to the catalogue card, and that a line below reads, "above copied from note attached to wood panel."

The second pastel of Frye in the collections, M5025, a gift to of Hon. Robert Walcott in 1941 to the Peabody Museum, also was transferred to the Essex Institute. The Peabody Museum documented it as a "Crayon portrait . . . copied from *original* [italics added] owned by Essex Institute by Miss Love Cutts," referring, it would seem, to the one it transferred to the EI a generation earlier. The other copy of the Frye pastel by Cutts, once belonging to Samuel Walcott, was recently located in a private collection in New Hampshire. Therefore it has now been ascertained, and corroborated by PEM Director of Collections John Childs, that the Frye pastel given to the former EI in 1914 is indeed the original by Blyth. It is one of Blyth's larger ones. (For the discussion of the history of its damage and restoration, see discussion under "Pastels," pp. 64–65). As Blyth drew both Frye and his mother-in-law, it is likely that he did one of his wife, Love (Pickman) Frye.

Bentley 3:419; 4:497, 558–59, illus. 558

Essex County Probate Record 10316, Love Frye

EIHC 3:152–54; 71:138, cat. 103; 73:88, "Errata"

Felt 2:548–9, 565, 593

Groce and Wallace, *New-York Historical Society Dictionary of Arts in America*, misidentifying Love Cutts as a male, 161.

Journal and Letters of the Late Samuel Curwen, 513

Osgood, *Sketch of Salem*, 44

PEM accessions book, 5025

PEM, Phillips Library, Timothy Orne Papers, May 1751

Phillips, *Salem . . . 18th C.*, 388

Reports of the First Exhibition of the Salem Charitable Mechanics Association, at the Mechanic Hall, in the city of Salem, September, 1849: 9

SMS: Plate 8, no 247

Sibley 11:xii; 399–404, illus. opp. 404

WPA 827

[57]

J(onathan?) Gardner (1728–1791)

Benjamin Blyth, early 1770s

Pastel on paper mounted on linen, 18 x 14 in. (45.7 x 35.6 cm.), in period giltwood frame

Collection of James and Janet Laverdiere; James L. Kochan, Wiscasset, Maine; Skinner, Inc.;
provenance unknown

The portraits of "Mr." and "Mrs. J." Gardner, once attributed to John Singleton Copley, are by Benjamin Blyth and are among his best, a factor that figures into their probable identities. The writing on an old cardboard backing of the man's portrait reads "*J. Gardner/ of Boston/ New England*," and the portrait is lined with a Boston newspaper. That does not necessarily mean the sitters were from Boston, nor does it necessarily date the pastel. And the cardboard backing with its possibly misleading inscription is a later addition.

As these portraits show, the Gardners were very well off and willing to pay for elaborate portraits. The sitters' clothing dates from the early 1770s. Gardner is sporting a wig, fashionable in the mid-eighteenth century but, as military historian James Kochan noted, two decades later it would signify the conservatism in dress and, possibly, outlook brought about by middle age and social position. Both sitters have double chins, so they were most likely in their forties. Of the three possible men whose names begin with "J"—John Gardner and his cousins, brothers John and Jonathan—only two can be considered; of the two brothers, John married Sarah Derby, from a family for which Blyth drew many portraits, but they are eliminated, as she was only in her mid-twenties around the time that the portraits were done and died in 1774, at age twenty-seven. His brother Jonathan and his wife Sarah (Putnam) were deemed possible, as were John Gardner and his wife Elizabeth (Pickering); they all were in their forties. However, although John and Elizabeth were still living in Salem in the early 1770s, where their children were born, he was not very active in town affairs and seemed to spend much of his time at his farm in what is now Danvers. Also, Blyth is not known to have done any portraits of the Pickering family. On the other hand, besides these two portraits, Blyth drew three other descendants of Capt. John Gardner (1661–1722): pastels of Elizabeth Gardner Dabney (Cat. 39), her brother-in-law, the Rev. Thomas Barnard (Cat. 8), and a miniature of Joseph Bowditch (Cat. 17), plus eight portraits of the Derby family and relatives.

So the most likely subject is Jonathan. A recent owner of the pastels, James Kochan, in an email of April 2022 wrote, "I think that your documentation and process of deductive reasoning is most compelling." "Commodore" Jonathan as he was often called, was a prominent merchant involved in many aspects of the town life of Salem business and society. Born on May 25, 1728, to Capt. Jonathan and Elizabeth (Gardner) Gardner, Jonathan married Sarah Putnam on January 2, 1753. His business partners included men also drawn by Blyth, such as Richard Derby, Jr. (Cat. 46), married to Jonathan Gardner's sister Lydia, and George Cabot (Cat. 25), for whom, along with

Joseph Cabot, Jonathan commanded the *Salem*. He also captained their privateer, *Two Brothers*, in the French and Indian War. During the Revolution, he was a member of the Committee of Correspondence, a Minute Man, the commander of the Essex Regiment in 1776, and a volunteer in the Rhode Island Expedition in 1778. He headed the list of the incorporators of the Salem Marine Society in 1772 and was both clerk and treasurer. He also joined the Masons as a member of Essex Lodge on April 7, 1779 (Blyth joined two years later). The Gardner family lived in a house on the north side of Essex Street, now the site of the Peabody Essex Museum's John Tucker Daland House, close to his tannery on Winter Street.

At Jonathan's death in 1791, the Reverend William Bentley wrote "A most useful Citizen, of amiable temper, inflexible integrity, and a sober friend to all useful, social & religious institutions. He was President of the Marine Society & has served the Town in every useful office. A better man is not left behind. He has left an only son & child behind." Bentley was very upset at the printed version of his funeral sermon for Gardner: "The leading idea intended, that social institutions begin with private virtue & particular exertion, is rather to be guessed at, than expressed."

Blyth took great care with these portraits, from modeling features to colors used, to such subtlety as the shadow lines where the wig meets Gardner's forehead and right cheek. The background treatment, contrasting black with the light-struck area behind Gardner, is unusually dramatic for Blyth. His ability to depict delicate lace edging is particularly marked, as on the sweeping reverse curve of Jonathan Gardner's cuff ruffle protruding from his coat sleeve. Above all, this portrait shows a man with some sense of self-importance and perhaps a touch of mischievousness.

The portraits were appropriately reframed by the owners.

Bentley 1: xxxvii, 235, 243-4, 375–76

Bentley, *Sermon . . . Jonathan Gardner*, 1791, 5

EIHC 3:121; 4:5; 6:97, 162; 13:236; 39:40–44 (John Gardner)

FARL, American School, Massachusetts (1751–1800) 158–3d

Gardner, Frank Augustine, *Gardner Memorial*, 76–77

Jeffares, http://www.pastellists.com/Articles/Blyth.pdf

Kochan, email correspondence, Apr. 20, 2022

Phillips, *Salem . . . 18th C.*, 169, 246, 251–2, 263–4, 321, 326

Skinner, Inc. Auction 2412, American Furniture and Decorative Arts, Lot 42, June 8, 2008 and sold with its companion portrait of Gardner's wife for $8,888.

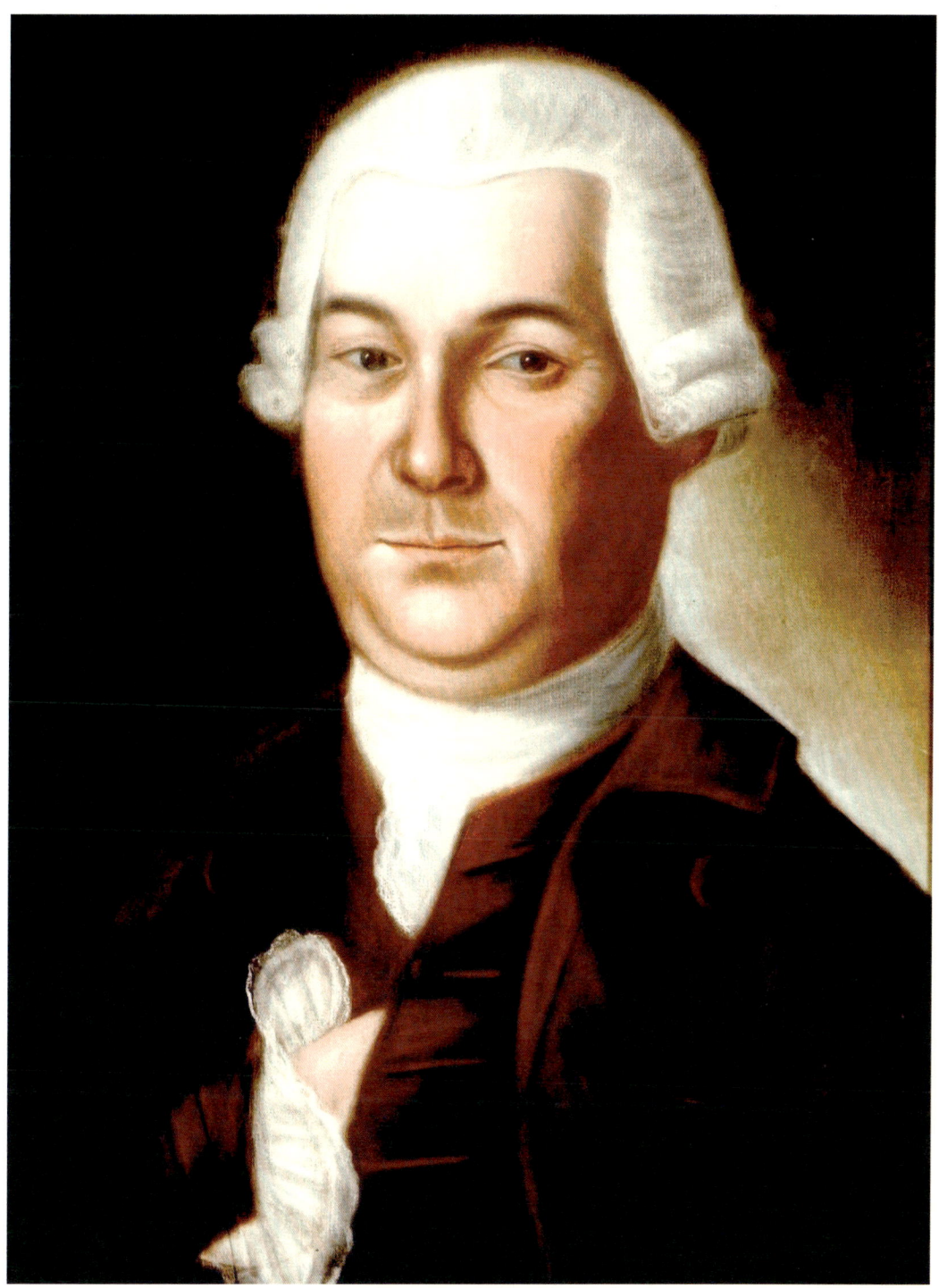

J(onathan?) Gardner
Pastel by Benjamin Blyth, early 1770s
Courtesy of the collection of James and Janet Laverdiere

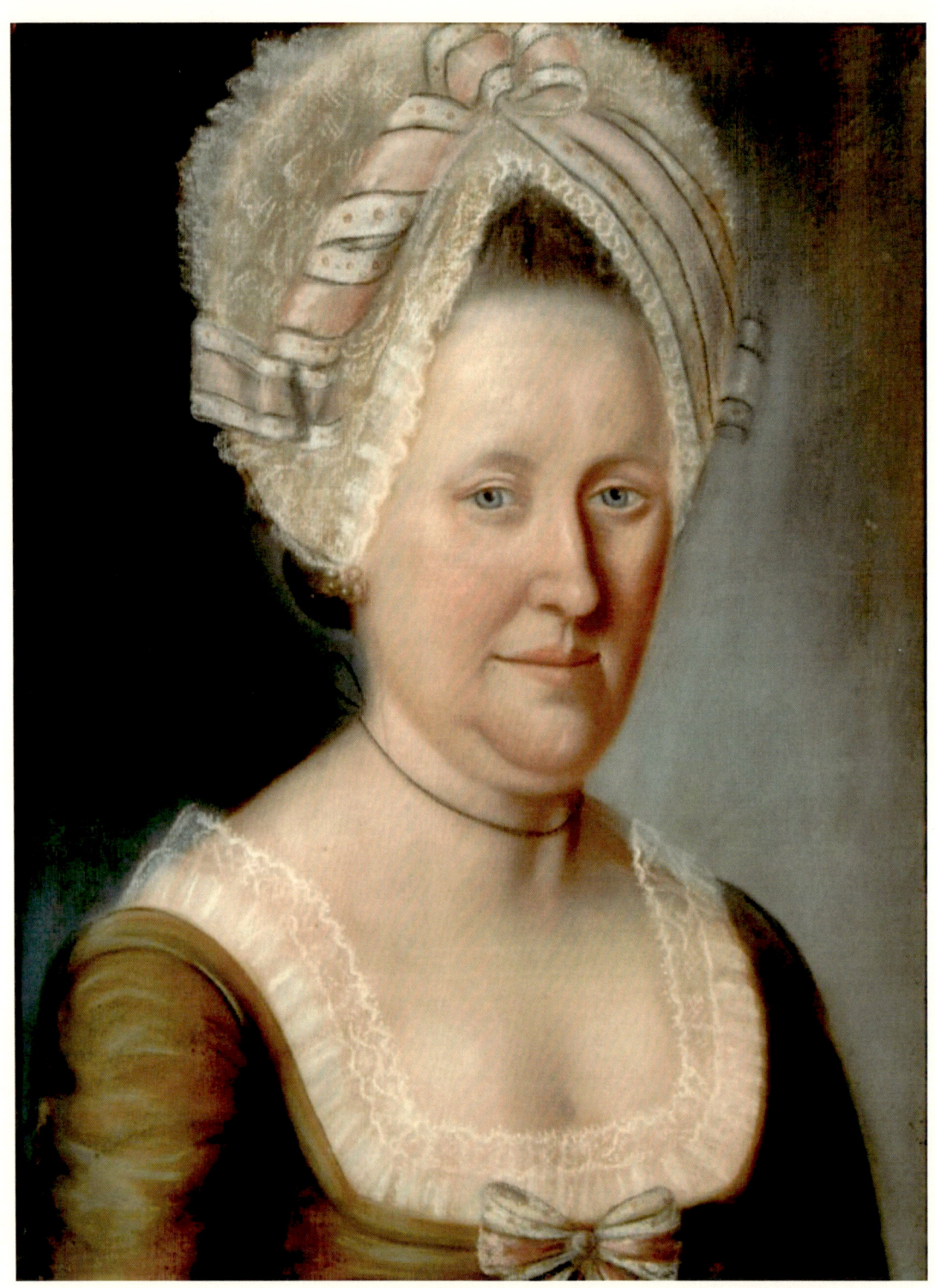

Sarah Putnam (?) Gardner
Pastel by Benjamin Blyth, early 1770s
Courtesy of the collection of James and Janet Laverdiere

Sarah Putnam (?) Gardner (1728–1791)

Benjamin Blyth, early 1770s
Pastel on paper mounted on linen, 18 x 14 in. (45.7 x 35.6 cm.), in period giltwood frame
James and Janet Laverdiere; James L. Kochan Collection, Wiscasset, Maine; Skinner, Inc. Auction,
provenance unknown

It is more probable that of the two Gardner women who could have been the sitter, this is Sarah Putnam, who married Jonathan. The Blyths had many connections with members of the Putnam family, but none with the Pickerings. Sarah, born in 1728 to William and Sarah Putnam of Salem, was five months old when her father died. Her mother married Capt. John Gardner (1706/7–1784) a year later and her namesake married her stepfather's nephew Jonathan on January 3, 1753. Existing records show that they had a small family. The only known son is Jonathan, although another boy, James, whose parents were not named, may have been theirs also. Sarah died in November 1791 from cachexia, a general physical wasting and malnutrition usually associated with chronic disease. She and her husband Jonathan, who were only a few months apart in age, also died within a few months of each other.

Mrs. Gardner's cap of fine lawn, trimmed with lace and silk ribbons, is similar to the one worn by Mary Collins (Cat. 30), and its lace and that on her dress are typical of Blyth's best work. This is also the case with Blyth's treatment of the flesh, notably in the softness of her bosom. Again, the background for Mrs. Gardner, as with that of her husband, is airier than usually associated with Blyth. Yet in comparing Sarah's portrait to her husband's, she seems to be the "sober" one.

EIHC 6:161-2

FARL, American School, Massachusetts (1751–1800) 157-3f

Jeffares, http://www.pastellists.com/Articles/Blyth.pdf

Kochan, email correspondence, Apr. 20, 2022

Skinner, Inc. Auction 2412, American Furniture and Decorative Arts, lot 42, June 8, 2008; attributed to Benjamin Blyth

[59]

John Gibaut (1766/7–1805)

Benjamin Blyth, ca. 1780
Pastel on paper mounted on fabric, 21½ x 14¾ in. (54.6 x 37.5 cm.), Samuel Blyth frame(?)
Peabody Essex Museum 2989, gift of Benjamin Barstow, Esq., 1891

The Reverend William Bentley of Salem considered John Gibaut one of his closest friends. "I became early acquainted in the family & had from it every attention. They had one son . . . by whom I entered into the intimate acquaintance I held." Both were bachelors and had many similar wide-ranging scholarly interests. Little is known of Gibaut's family, except that his father came to Salem from the island of Jersey and married Sarah Crowninshield, Elizabeth Crowninshield Derby's sister, on June 15, 1758. John Gibaut's birth is not recorded, but he was reported to be thirty-eight when he died on August 10, 1805. He had a short but colorful and distinguished career as a ship captain, closely affiliated with Salem's wealthy merchants, his uncles Elias Hasket Derby and Benjamin Crowninshield. While still at Harvard, from which he graduated after a leave of absence in 1786, he worked for Derby. In 1790, he was master and part owner of the ship *Borneo* and later commanded the *Astrea*. For twelve years, he sailed ships to and from Spain for Benjamin Pickman. In 1793, his vessel was seized while he was on a trading voyage from Madras to Pegu, and he and his second mate were held hostage, during which his mother died. Bentley called her his "unwearied benefactor" and was equally complimentary towards Gibaut's subsequent stepmother, Abigail, who died in 1818. She, "by her prudence & her affections was entitled to succeed to all the honours of a wife."

Gibaut and Bentley spent enjoyable days walking on the beach and attending parties and clubs and military parades. And they shared an interest in reading. Gibaut sent letters to Bentley from Coramandel Coast, Bengal, and the Indies; and when he arrived back in Salem from a three-year voyage to India, he gave Bentley a letter with Arabic and Persian and promised "a specimen of the Peguan language & writing." On December 29, 1790, Bentley recorded, Gibaut arrived in port with a native of Madras, who excited much curiosity. Over ten years later, on February 27, 1801, Bentley wrote of his friend, "Capt. Gibaut reached town, after his return from his East Indian Voyage. From the state of his health we have had little hopes of his return."

When Gibaut retired from seafaring, he moved with his father to Gloucester where he became Collector of Ports in 1801. Bentley visited him often, noting at one time, "He followed commercial pursuits—had the satisfaction of supporting his father in all the comforts of life." In chronically ill health, Gibaut died at age thirty-eight. He had earned the honorific "Esqʳ." The inventory of his estate included "1 Vol. Chambrs Dictionary, 8 Vols Bufour Nat. History, 4 Vols Shak plays, 2 vol. Ancien China, 3 vols. Adams's defⁿ. Constitution, 4 Vol. History England, 400 sundry books." Gibaut also had "1 Pair Imᵃges + Cases," presumably miniatures. And among the six friends to whom Gibaut left $20 to buy "some token to be held in remembrance of me" was Bentley. He visited his friend Gibaut's grave in 1819, fourteen years after his death.

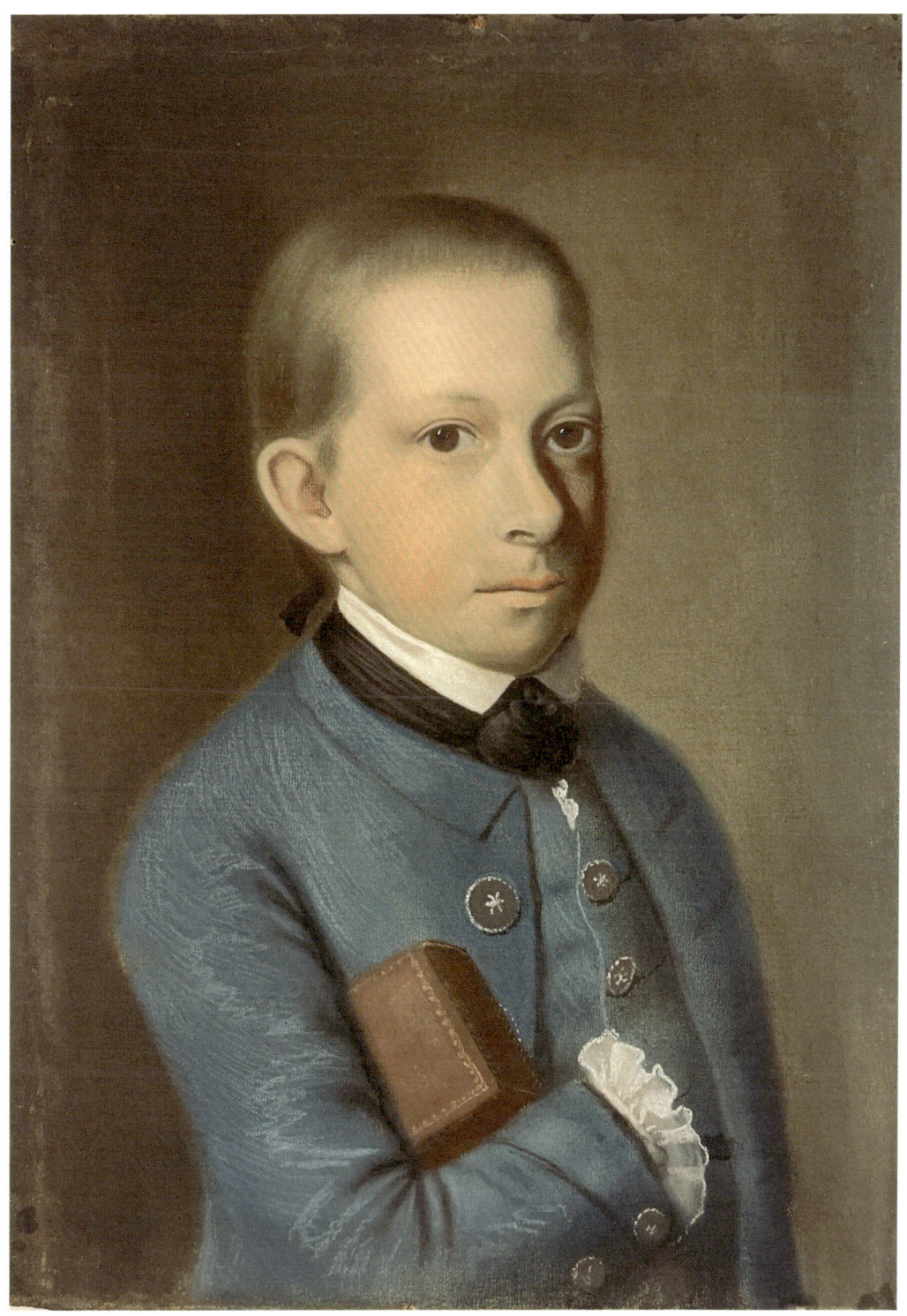

John Gibaut
Pastel by Benjamin Blyth, ca. 1780
Courtesy of the Peabody Essex Museum 2989, gift of Benjamin Barstow, Esq., 1891

It does not seem credible that Bentley, who so denigrated Blyth as an artist (albeit through lack of information), could not have known of this portrait—certainly one of the artist's finest, but he may not have known who painted it. And he might not have known Blyth at all; Bentley began preaching as a candidate for the East Church pulpit on the first Sunday in May 1783, at about the time that Blyth left Salem. An early gift to the former Essex Institute, Gibaut's portrait was not credited to Blyth for more than sixty years. It was treated for mildew by the Museum of Fine Arts, Boston, in 1969, along with the Blyth pastels of Lydia Phippen Fisk and David Ropes. Depicting a scholarly, introspective boy, it was said to have been done when he was fourteen, about to enter Harvard. One of Blyth's best and most appealing pastels, it is one of the few with any sort of personal artifact—Gibaut is clutching a book.

Bayley, *Little Known . . . Portrait Painters*, "Blyth," no. 2

Bentley, 1:228; 2:65, 88, 364; 4:515, 615; many other entries

Bolton, *Portrait Draughtsmen*, 7

Bridge St. Cemetery, Gloucester, GR 1

Essex County Probate File Papers 10804

EIHC 4:81; 71:142–3, Cat 109, by "unknown artist"

EIMS 54

Felt 2:295, 297

Foote, "Blyth," 91

Jeffares, http://www.pastellists.com/Articles/Blyth.pdf

Norton, "Brothers Blyth," 57 (illus.), 62

PEM, Phillips Library, GEN. BUS. & Pers Papers/Misc Receipts 1783–1784, B16 F9 2nd

Phillips, *Salem . . . 18th C.*, 250

Quinquennial Catalogue of Harvard University/1636–1930, 1297

Visitor's Guide to Salem, 1895, "at the age of fourteen," unknown artist, 194

WPA 859, attributed to Blyth

Abigail Glover (1726/7–1787)

Benjamin Blyth, probably 1765–67
Pastel on paper, 22 x 18 in. (55.9 x 45.7 cm., est.)
Current location not known; G. Glover Crocker in 1940s; Sarah Crocker, 1915

The Burnham family was in Ipswich by 1636, but by 1720, Job and Hannah Burnham were in Marblehead, where Abigail was baptized on June 19, 1726. She and Jonathan Glover were married there on October 10, 1748; he was seventeen, she, twenty-two. They had nine children, beginning with Mary, born on February 2, 1750. The last, Jonathan, born in 1771 when Abigail was forty-five years old, died at age five months. The first two Benjamins, named after Jonathan's guardian Benjamin Stacey, also died as infants; the third was born in 1762. Abigail died at age sixty, on April 29, 1787, and four months later her husband, then dubbed "Esq.," married Mary Greely of Boston.

Abigail Glover's portrait, along with that of her husband Jonathan, were among those once attributed to John Singleton Copley by Frank W. Bayley. Barbara Parker and Anne Wheeler first questioned this and other attributions in their book on Copley in 1937, a view echoed by Jules Prown in 1966. The portraits have since been attributed to Blyth. Abigail looks to be in her forties to early fifties, the same age and dressed similarly to Elizabeth Higginson Cabot, whose portrait was done in the late 1760s. She looks serious and thoughtful. This photograph, from an unknown source, is the only currently available image of Abigail. Photographs of the original pastel portraits of her and Jonathan were recently shown to the author, but are not available for reproduction.

Bayley, *Copley*, 120
FARL, American School, Massachusetts (1751–1800) 158-3d
Marblehead Historical Society and Museum, Glover file
Parker and Wheeler, 258
Prown, 1:239, quoting Parker
WPA 877, attributed to Copley

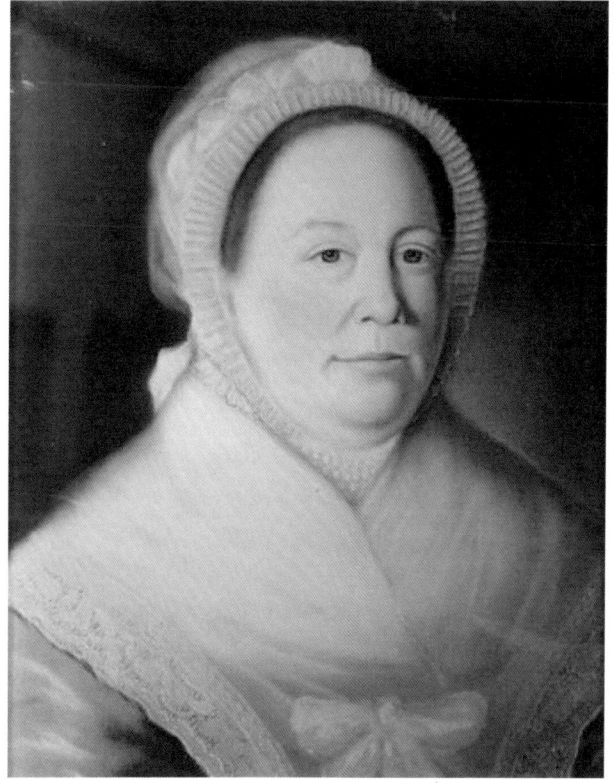

Abigail Glover
Photograph of unlocated pastel by Benjamin Blyth, probably 1765–67
Courtesy of the Frick Art Reference Library Photoarchives

[61]

John Glover (1755–1811?)

Benjamin Blyth (attr.), 1778–1780
Miniature on ivory, 1⅛ x ⅞ in. (2.85 x 22.2 cm.), gold case, with pin for a brooch
Marblehead Museum 1951.91, gift of Caroline H. Fabens, 1951

The young man in this miniature, done in the late 1770s to early 1780s, could not be the famous Marblehead American Revolutionary War Gen. John Glover (1732–1797), as had been assumed; Glover was close to fifty when the miniature would have been made, and in addition, all images of him show abundant curly hair. The source of the misattribution was possibly one of the descendants. But it probably is of his first-born son, also John, who was baptized on March 23, 1755, just short of five months after the marriage of his parents, John and Hannah (Gale). Little is known of John Jr. but what is found in vital records. It is assumed that it was his death in South Salem that was reported in the *Salem Gazette* for June 18, 1811.

His miniature descended through his sister, Mary Hooper. One possible explanation is that it was among the effects of his father, Gen. Glover, when he died in 1797. The executor was Mary's husband Robert Hooper, whom she had married in 1788. George Fabens, husband of the donor, is a direct descendent. The pin was probably added to the miniature in the nineteenth century.

Blyth also did pastels of John's uncle Jonathan and his wife, Abigail (Cats. 57, 58).

Bentley 3:180.
Salem Gazette, Phillips Library, Peabody Essex Museum

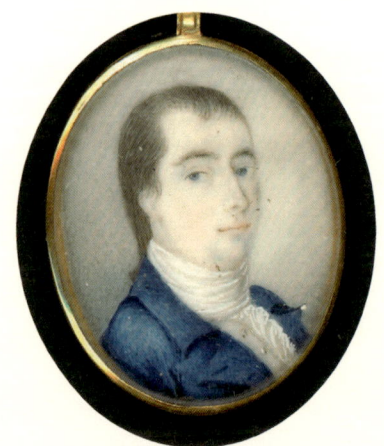

John Glover
Miniature by Benjamin Blyth (attr.), 1778-80
Courtesy of the Marblehead Museum,
Marblehead, MA, 1951.91, gift of
Caroline H. Fabens, 1951

[62]

Jonathan Glover (1731–1797)

Benjamin Blyth, probably 1765–67
Pastel on paper, 22 x 18 in. (est.)
Current location not known; G. Glover Crocker in 1940s; Sarah Crocker, 1915

Jonathan Glover, son of Jonathan Jr. and Tabitha Glover, was baptized in Salem on July 4, 1731. His father had died by 1737, and Tabitha moved to Marblehead with Jonathan and her other three sons, John, Samuel, and Daniel. Just after Jonathan turned thirteen, his mother signed him over to the guardianship of Benjamin Stacey, a feltmaker. (John, who later became a major general in the Revolution, was apprenticed to a shoemaker, Samuel to a goldsmith, and Daniel to a block-maker.) Jonathan married Abigail Burnham on October 10, 1748. He was seventeen, she was twenty-two. Their first three children were girls, followed by two Benjamins, both of whom died. The third Benjamin, born in 1762, was given the middle name of Jonathan's guardian, Benjamin Stacey. Two more girls and a boy followed. The house Jonathan built on Front Street after the Revolution was a showplace of Marblehead in its day. At the gate were two posts with gilded eagles atop, which had just become the new country's symbol. The house is extant, although it is partially hidden behind other buildings erected in its former front gardens.

Jonathan soon entered the fishing trade as a master on sailing vessels, and he and his brother John became wealthy ship owners and merchants, prominent in the political life of Marblehead. In 1773, the brothers, with Azor Orne and Elbridge Gerry, established a hospital for Smallpox on Cat Island, but it was unpopular with some Marbleheaders, and in January 1774, all the structures on the island were burned or destroyed, and the founders lost their entire investment. During the turmoil, Glover is said to have put a loaded cannon in the hall of his house and threatened rioters, who then decamped.

He was a member of the local militia for a short time in 1759 and 1762 and was a Colonel in the Fifth Essex Regiment during the Revolution but did not serve in the Continental Army or Navy "because of public responsibilities." To provide needed vessels for combat, Gen. George Washington appointed him and William Bartlett of Beverly (Cat. 9) to serve as agents until January 1, 1776. He joined the Masonic Lodge of Marblehead in June 1781, and later became treasurer. After the war, the Reverend William Bentley noted, Jonathan was asked to help with the Marblehead Lottery in protecting the lands of the Neck but seems to have "exceeded the expenses designed for it." Jonathan and John, again with Azor Orne, also were delegates to the Massachusetts Constitutional Convention in 1787.

On March 19, 1797, "Jonathan Glover . . . chartered a Vessel for N. C. & had his Son and Son in law with him," Bentley recorded. "The Vessel & Cargo were lost in the late stormy Weather in N. C. & J. G. the Master perished."

The portraits of Jonathan and his wife Abigail had not been seen since 1915, presumably when

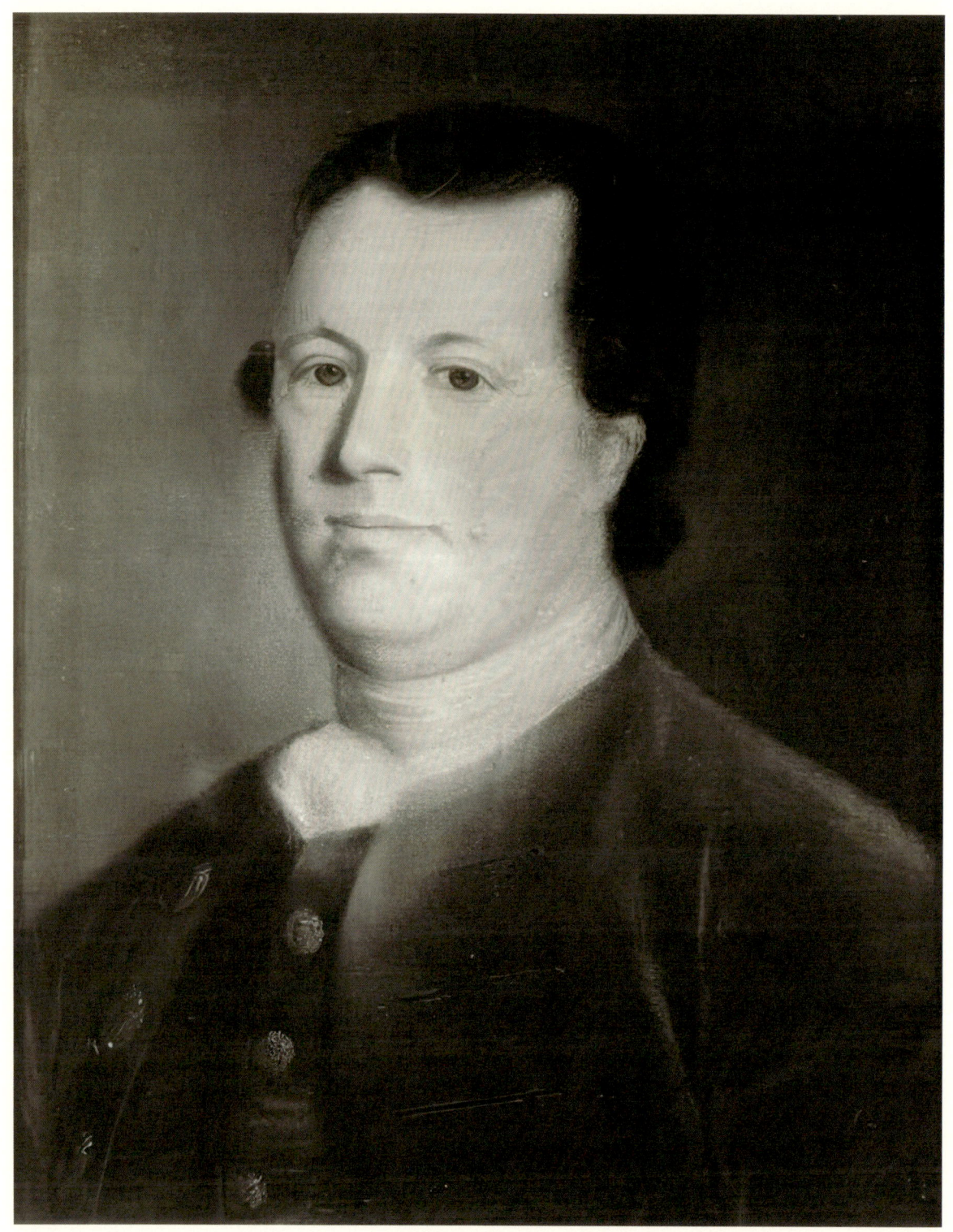

Jonathan Glover
Photograph of unlocated pastel by Benjamin Blyth, probably 1765–67
Courtesy of the Frick Art Reference Library Photoarchives

Bayley listed them as by John Singleton Copley. Parker and Wheeler, in their book on Copley in 1938, placed these portraits in the "Attributed" category and repeated their judgment again in 1943. Jules Prown simply repeated it in his "attributed" list. Both portraits show many of the characteristics attributed to Blyth. Photographs of the original pastel portraits of Jonathan and his wife Abigail were recently shown to the author, but are not available for reproduction.

Bayley, *Copley*, 120.

Bentley 1:309; 2:217, 354; 3:130; 4:544

EIHC 5:50–53

FARL, American School (1751–1800), 157-3f

Lord and Gamage, *Marblehead*, 117, 139, 265–6

Marblehead Historical Society and Museum, Glover file

Parker and Wheeler, 257–8

Prown, 1:239

WPA 879

Wright, John Hardy, source of illustration, cut from an unidentified magazine

[63]

William Goddard (1740–1817)

Benjamin Blyth, probably 1778
Pastel on paper mounted on fabric, 16¾ x 13½ in. (43.5 x. 35.5 cm.), reproduction Hogarth-type frame
Rhode Island Historical Society, John Brown House Museum; Robert Hale Ives Goddard, Jr.;
Mrs. C. Oliver Iselin; Goddard descendants

When the British colonial postmaster failed to deliver out-of-town newspapers to William Goddard because of his "over-liberal" views, he was deprived of a critical source of information, so he established independent post riders in 1773 between New England and Baltimore under the name of the 'American' or 'Constitutional Post Office.' They were "founded upon the constitutional principles of open communication, freedom from governmental interference, and the guaranteed free exchange of ideas," notes the Smithsonian's National Postal Museum website. Goddard therefore established the postal service that was adopted by the Federal Government in 1775 and is still in use today. A letter from Gen. Joseph Warren (Cat. 130) to the Rhode Island legislature written on June 15, 1775, two days before his death at the Battle of Bunker Hill, bears the only surviving example of that "Constitutional Post."

Although not a resident of Salem or Essex County, there are several reasons why Goddard was a likely subject for Blyth: he was a patriot and part of their town's community of printers, and it is quite likely (though still unproven) that Blyth accompanied the Salem men who took part during the Rhode Island Expedition in August 1778. Goddard was born in New London, Connecticut, on Oct. 20, 1740, to Dr. Giles Goddard, the Postmaster of New London, and his wife, Sarah (Updike). He moved to Providence, where, in 1762, he founded the *Providence Gazette & Country Journal*, located at Shakespeare's Head at 21 Meeting St., now the Providence Preservation Society. He later set up printing offices in New York, Philadelphia, and for twenty years, beginning in 1773, published the *Maryland Journal* and *Baltimore Advertiser* with his sister Mary Katherine Goddard. On May 25, 1786, he married Abigail Angell, daughter of Gen. James Angell of Providence, R. I. They had four children. He was elected to the American Antiquarian Society in 1813, the year after it was founded.

Mrs. C. Oliver Iselin, a direct descendant and former owner of the portrait, believed it to be the work of Benjamin Blyth, an attribution also shared by F. H. Goodyear, Jr. and Linda Eppich, former Chief Curator of the Rhode Island Historical Society. They suggested a comparison with the portrait of Samuel McIntire. Albeit Goddard's portrait is one of Benjamin Blyth's most successful and a better portrait than that of McIntire, herein attributed to Blyth's brother Samuel, the instincts of Iselin, Goodyear, and Eppich were correct. The Goddard pastel was conserved by Sarah Dove, New London, Connecticut, in 1994, when it probably received its current frame, similar to Rhode Island Historical Society's portrait of Reverend Enos Hitchcock. The condition of Goddard's portrait in the early years of the twentieth century is recorded in a photograph by Bayley's Copley Gallery. It appears to have been worked on there before it was conserved later by Dove. It contains the same use of thin black lines enhancing Goddard's face, as observed in other pastels known to have also been in Bayley's Gallery. Nonetheless, Goddard's personality was retained; he is depicted as a contemplative, gentle man.

FARL, Blyth, Benjamin 157-3L

Jeffares, http://www.pastellists.com/Articles/Blyth.pdf

Norton, "Brothers Blyth," 62

RIHS Object file

RIHS Quarterly, 9:112

Smithsonian National Postal Museum website, illus. of print from the Goddard portrait

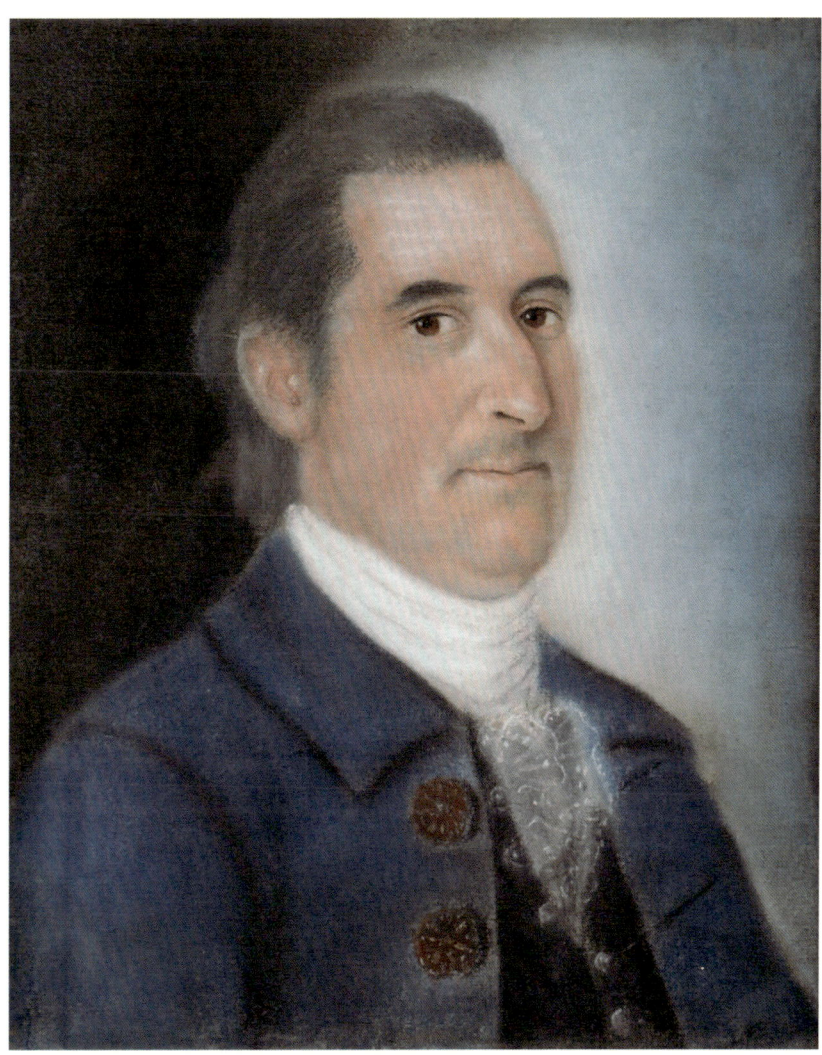

William Goddard
Pastel by Benjamin Blyth, probably 1778
Courtesy of the Rhode Island Historical Society, John Brown House Museum 1972.19.2,
gift of Robert Hale Ives Goddard, Jr.

Woman of the Hedge Family

Benjamin Blyth, early 1770s
Pastel on paper mounted on canvas, 23⅛ x 18¼ in; (58.7 x 46.4 cm.), original frame
Current location not known; Sotheby's, 1994; Nina Fletcher Little;
Roger Bacon Antiques, Exeter, NH, Hedge family

This portrait was sold at Sotheby's in 1994 from the collection of the estate of Nina Fletcher Little for $4,350. A typed jelly label pasted to the back records, "pastel of unknown lady descended in the Hedge family of Plymouth and Brookline attributed by the family to Benjamin Blythe of Salem. They believe some ancestors had Salem connections." The Holyoke diary lists the death of Susan Hedge, on August 4, 1817, and "W. K." in 1833 and the births of two unnamed Hedge children, in 1801 and 1811. These are the sole references to any Hedge family members in Salem Vital Records. Most Hedge names were from southeastern Massachusetts.

The portrait, very similar to Blyth's pastel of Mehitabel Curwen Ward (Cat. 127), done in the early 1770s, is an appealing portrait of an unostentatious but assured woman.

Little, Drs. John and Françoise, correspondence
Norton, "Brothers Blyth," 62
Sotheby's catalogue May 17, 1994, Lot O

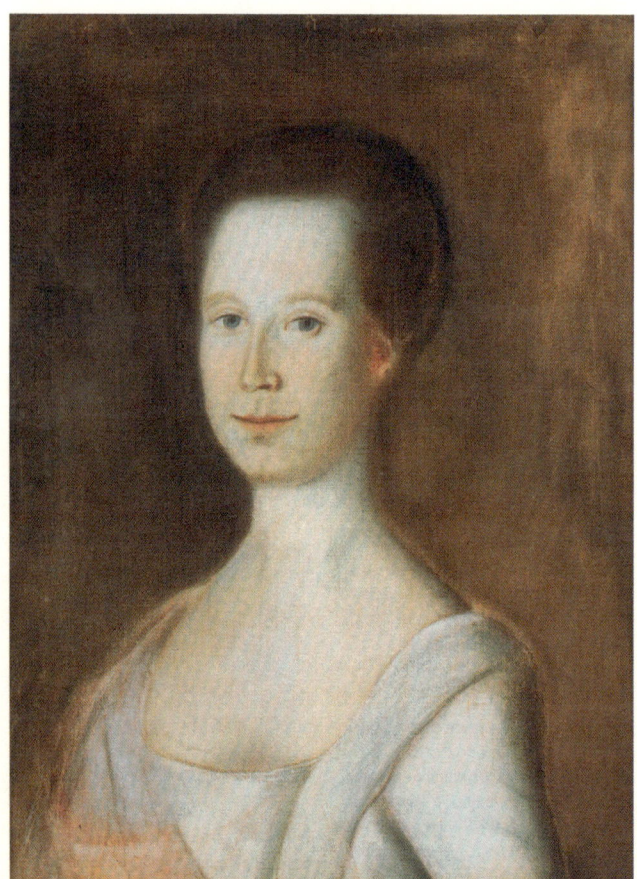

Woman of the Hedge Family
Photograph of pastel by Benjamin Blyth,
early 1770s
Photograph by F. Lee Eiseman, courtesy of
Sotheby's, 1994

[65]

Hugh Henderson (1746/7–1794)

Benjamin Blyth (attr.), late 1760s
Pastel on paper mounted on canvas, 23 x 18 in; (58.7 x 46.4 cm.), later frame
New Hampshire Historical Society; South Bay Auctions, 2025; "Collection of a former New York City museum professional, appraiser and dealer of American Art"; Sotheby's, 2005; Sotheby's, 1978; Dr. & Mrs. James W. Marvin; Lillian Blankely Cogan; Harry Arons Antiques; Gerrish family; Henderson family

This portrait of Hugh Henderson, purchased recently by the New Hampshire Historical Society, has many resemblances to work by Benjamin Blyth, especially in the facial details. The date of "Circa 1790s" given by the auction house is deemed erroneous, but a major reservation was the awkward treatment of Henderson's bright blue jacket, drawn much more prominently and vividly than typical of Blyth. However, the handling of the buttons is seen in several of Blyth's pastels, and the awkward handling of the right arm does resemble that in Blyth's pastel of Hepzibah Sharp, done probably in the late 1760s. Likewise, Hannah Paine's 1771 portrait shows her in a cloak of very vibrant blue with large creases highlighted in white. So, the conclusion is that the pastel of Hugh Henderson is an early Blyth, probably dating from the late 1760s. The portrait was given at one time to Robert Follett Gerrish, husband of Henderson's granddaughter, Sarah (1812–1901).

Henderson was born in Scotland but arrived in Boston in 1768 aboard the ship *Glasgow*. By 1770, he was in Portsmouth, New Hampshire, where he is first recorded in April in *The New-Hampshire Gazette* selling tea and "a variety of English Goods." He married Hannah Sheafe on May 11, 1772. His sympathies were Tory, so he fled to New York in 1778. In 1791, he returned to Portsmouth, where he died on August 4, 1794.

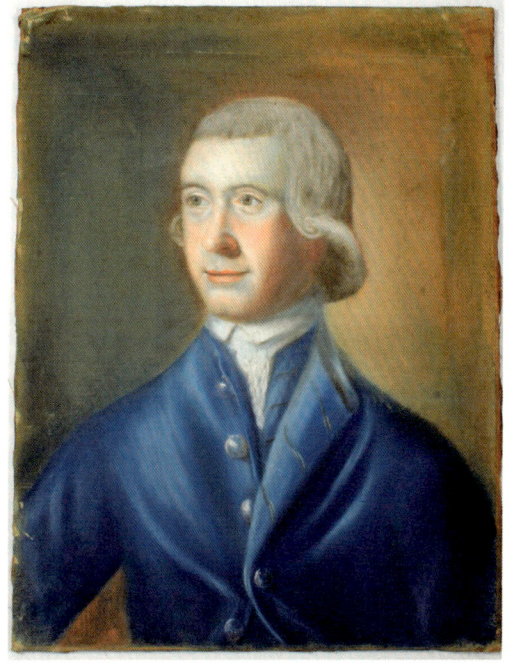

In the late 1760s, Blyth drew Gibbs Atkins, a Boston Tory. The surmise is that Blyth may have drawn these men, and probably Dr. Joseph and Elizabeth Warren, nascent Patriots, in Boston. Blyth also drew Elizabeth and George Turner from Portsmouth in the early 1770s.

"A Connecticut House in Northern New England," *Living with Antiques*, Feb. 1972, 360–366

Olly, Jonathan, Hew Hampshire Historical Society, correspondence

South Bay Auction, February 5, 2025, Lot 44

Hugh Henderson (1746/7–1794)
Pastel by Benjamin Blyth (attr.), late 1760s.
Photograph courtesy New Hampshire Historical Society

[66]

Ezekiel Hersey (1709–1770)

Benjamin Blyth, ca. 1770
Oil on canvas, 26½ x 20¾ in. (67.3 x 52.7 cm.); framed
Harvard University Portrait Collection H383, bequest of Dr. Harold C. Ernst to Harvard Medical
School, 1927; Dr. Harold C. Ernst; Mary Rivers; Mrs. Jonathan Russell; Derby Academy;
Sarah (Langlee) Hersey Derby

"Such was his fame," records *Sibley's Harvard Graduates* entry for Ezekiel Hersey (class of 1728), "that a sharp young fellow named John Adams, who was taken down to Hingham for a consultation, . . . recorded his impression of the Doctor: 'He was an everlasting talker, and ran out into history, philosophy, metaphysics, etc., and frequently put questions to me as if he wanted to sound me and see if there was anything in me besides hectic fever. . . . I gave him very modest and very diffident answers.'" As a practicing physician, Dr. Hersey was known to treat all patients equally; "Impartially he served the Acadian exiles in Hingham and the family of Chief Justice Lynde of Salem."

Hersey was born in Hingham on September 21, 1709, to James and Mary Hersey and married Sarah Langlee, also of Hingham, in 1738. Although it has been suggested that Hersey's portrait was done in Quincy, where the doctor had his office, it more likely was done in Salem, perhaps when he was tending to the Lynde family. Known for his sympathies with the Whigs, Dr. Hersey would have been a likely subject for Blyth when he was starting his career.

At his death in 1779, Hersey bequeathed £1,000 to Harvard for a Professorship of Anatomy and Physick, a sum Harvard deemed inadequate, so his widow (Cat. 67), after she married Richard Derby, Sr. of Salem (Cat. 47), added another £1,000. Supplemented with a subsequent £1,000 bequeathed from her and £500 from Dr. Hersey's brother Abner, the endowment of the first chair for what became Harvard Medical School was assured. It was established in 1782.

The college asked Sarah Hersey for a portrait in order that a copy might be made, *Sibley's* noted, adding, "However, the only portrait which Mrs. Hersey had was a small and miserable oil." Nonetheless, if it were not for Blyth's portrait of Dr. Hersey, Harvard Medical School would have no contemporary image of its founder. The portrait also succeeds well in depicting what John Quincy, in his *History of Harvard College*, called "a sense of moral rectitude . . . conscientious in the discharge of his duties, but capricious, whimsical, and exxentric [*sic*]."

A curious dichotomy exists between the well-executed snuff box and the crudely outlined eyes, which detract from the otherwise more skilled treatment of Hersey's face. Blyth's handling would improve greatly in later portraits. Two portraits of Hersey were based on the pastel. One, by an anonymous artist, shown in an early-twentieth-century photograph, is still half-figure but with the right arm. The other, attributed to Edward Savage and dated around 1785, adds an entire body to the Hersey original. He is seated in a cavernous room "in a costume and background more suitable for a great London surgeon than a Yankee country doctor," noted his biography in *Sibley's*

Harvard Graduates. It could be argued that the most honest portrait is the one by Blyth, which now hangs on the wall of the office of the Hersey Professor of the Theory and Practice of Physic (Medicine) at Harvard Medical School. A later copy in oil of Hersey's wife Sarah was also based on her original portrait by Blyth. They constitute the only known couple whose portraits by Blyth were given fictitious bodies in later, more seemingly deserving, full-figure oil portrayals.

Bentley 1:178-9

Elliott and Rossiter, eds., *Science at Harvard University* (1992), 336

Foote, "Blyth," 91-92

Loscalzo, Dr. Joseph, Harvard Medical School, correspondence

Norton, "Brothers Blyth," 62

Sibley 8:431-436, illus. opp. 432

Stebbins, *Harvard Portraits*, 92; giving the date for the Blyth portrait of Hersey "ca. 1760-62," 286; illus. 72

Quincy, *History of Harvard College*, 2:269

WPA 1022, attributed to "Blyth (?), 1770"

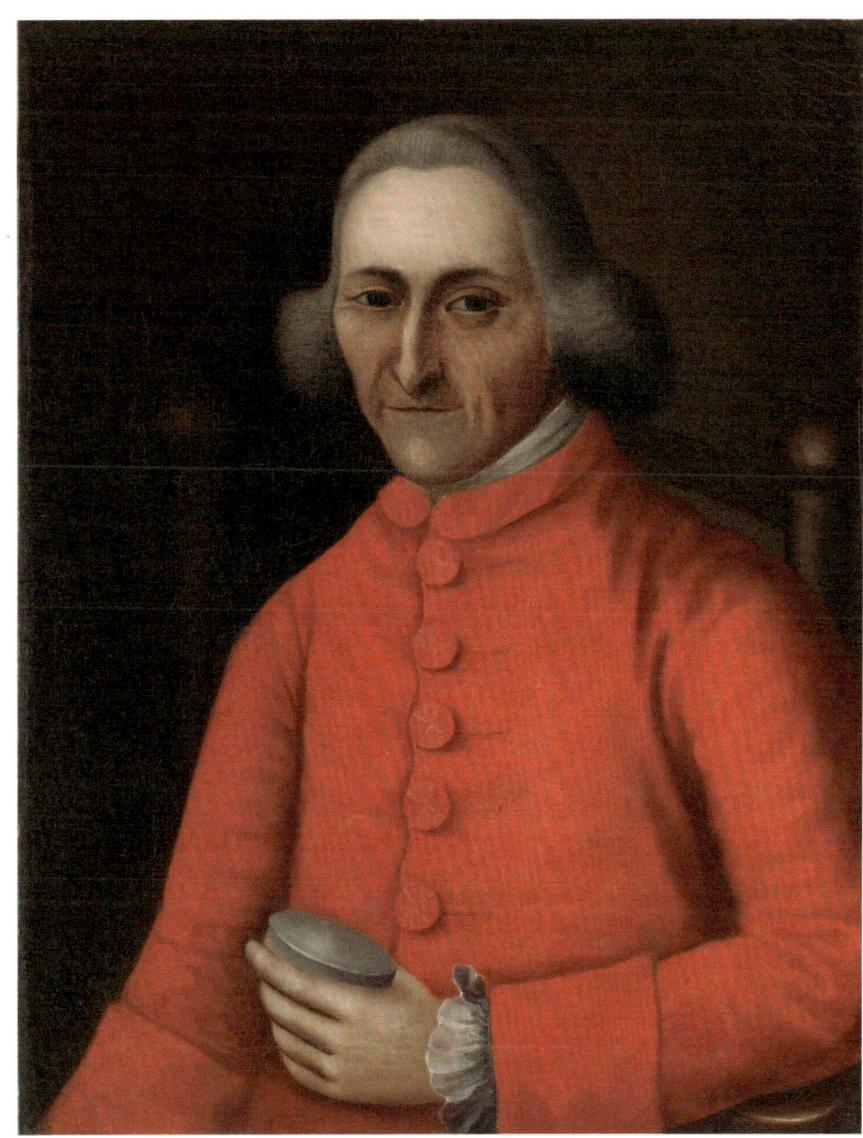

Ezekiel Hersey
Oil painting by Benjamin Blyth, ca. 1770
Courtesy of the Harvard University Portrait Collection H383,
bequest of Dr. Harold C. Ernst to Harvard Medical School, 1927

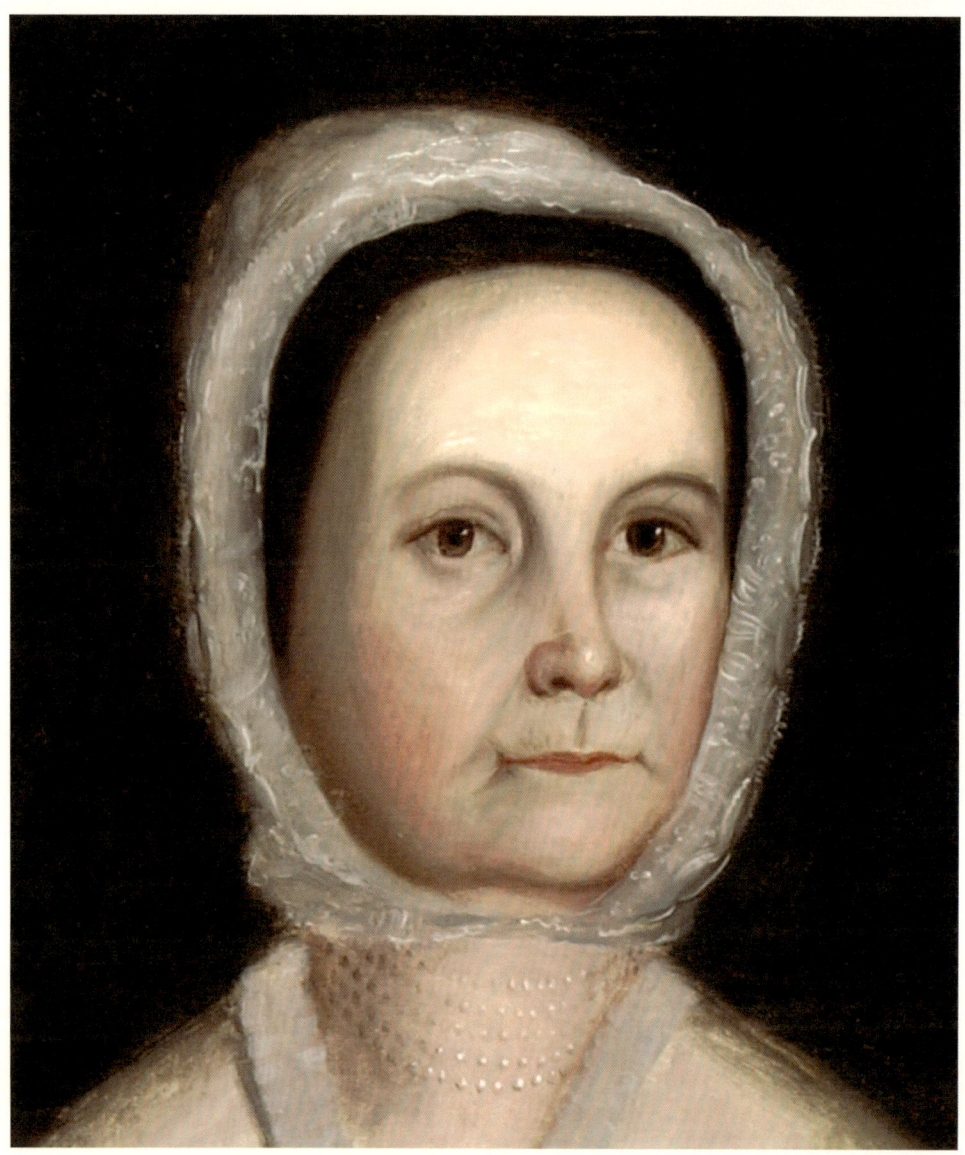

Sarah Hersey
Detail of oil portrait by Samuel Stillman Osgood, mid-19th c., based on a lost pastel by Benjamin
Blyth, probably 1770
Courtesy of Derby Academy, Hingham, MA, bequest of Sarah Hersey Derby, 1790

Sarah Hersey (1714–1790)

Oil painting (detail) by Samuel Stillman Osgood, based on a lost pastel by Benjamin Blyth,
probably 1770, measurements unknown
Location unknown, possibly destroyed; Derby Academy, bequest of Sarah Hersey Derby, 1790

A mid-nineteenth-century oil portrait of Sarah Hersey Derby hangs in the library of Derby Academy in Hingham, Massachusetts, of which she was the founder. The portrait, by Samuel Stillman Osgood (1808–1885), was based on an original, now lost, by an unrecorded artist. However, the face in the portrait is strikingly similar to the pastel portraits of Elizabeth Cabot (Cat. 23), Abigail Love Pickman (Cat. 106), and Margaret Gibbs Appleton (Cat. 5), done by Benjamin Blyth in the late 1760s. Sarah Hersey was at that time another elderly woman, among Blyth's early subjects. He also had painted contemporaneously an oil portrait of Sarah Derby's husband, Dr. Ezekiel Hersey (Cat. 66).

Sarah was born in Hingham on April 18, 1714, to Hannah (Vickery) and John Langlee, a tavern keeper. She married Hersey, also of Hingham, in 1738. A year after his death, she married Richard Derby, Sr. of Salem (Cat. 47). After he died in 1783, she returned to Hingham to live at the large farm she had inherited from Hersey until her death in 1790.

According to *Sibley's Harvard Graduates*, "It is a tradition that she was a woman of great beauty and small education." Bentley wrote disparagingly of her at the report of her death that she was "constantly changing her disposition of affairs. She was short of stature, naturally ingenious, but above instruction. The specimens of her needlework, &c., resemble the efforts of an uninstructed native. . . . Her conversation was about her own affairs, at church she slept, from a mental inaptitude for reflection. . . . Great curiosity is excited respecting the particulars of her last will & Testament." Her will stipulated that both her clock and her portrait be placed in the Derby Academy building. Both now are displayed in the George S. Terry Library of the Academy.

Osgood, the artist of the oil portrait copy, was probably responding to the wishes of Derby Academy for a more impressive, full-body portrayal portrait of its founder. The large bow at Sarah Derby's midriff and treatment of the sleeves with voluminous lace suggest a source such as at least one of six portraits of women by John Singleton Copley.

The later oil portraits of Dr. Hersey and his wife have the distinction of being the only known example of a couple whose pastel portraits by Blyth were the source of images to create, albeit independently, larger full-figure oil portraits by adding fictitious bodies.

Bentley 1:178-79
Derby Academy Archives
Hingham Historical Society, "Out of the Archives," April 18, 2014
Sibley 8:432–36
SIRIS
WPA 616 under Derby, Sarah

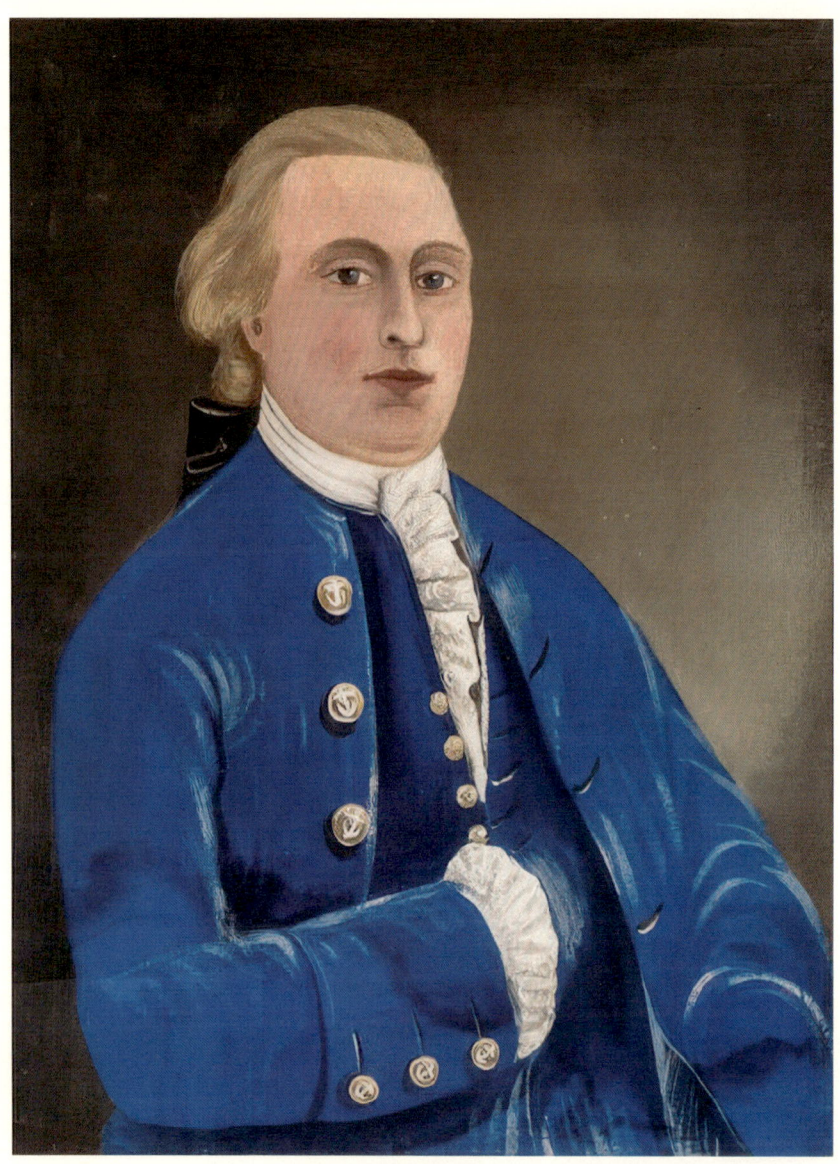

Hugh Hill
Oil painting by an anonymous artist, early 20th century, presumably after a lost pastel attributed to
Benjamin Blyth, early 1770s
Courtesy of Historic Beverly, gift of Mrs. Richard Ober of Beverly in 1937
Photograph by Michael C. King

[68]

Hugh Hill (1741–1829)

Oil painting by an anonymous artist, early 20th century, after a presumed pastel by Benjamin Blyth
(attr.), early 1770s, measurements unknown
Historic Beverly, gift of Mrs. Richard Ober of Beverly in 1937.

Capt. Hugh Hill, born in Ireland, was a seaman by age fifteen. He sailed for Robert Hooper of
Marblehead and eventually moved to Beverly, where he sailed for the Cabots. A strong supporter
of the Revolution, he became a successful privateer, commanding the great *Pilgrim*, owned by
Moses Brown and Andrew Cabot of Beverly. In 1781, he commanded a new ship, *Cicero*, that took
several valuable prizes and returned to port with the artist John Trumbull; Charles Adams, son
of John and Abigail; and Lt. John Barney, who had escaped from Britain's Mill Prison. After the
war, Hill engaged in commercial fishing. In 1812, he moved to a farm in North Beverly, where he
died in 1829.

This oil was probably painted in the second quarter of the twentieth century, approximately
one hundred years after Hill's death, and most likely was based on a Blyth pastel, now lost. This
attribution is based on the format of the composition and the fact that among Hill's associates
were men with whom Blyth interacted, either as an artist or as a privateer. Hill looks to be in his
mid-thirties, suggesting that a pastel could have been drawn in the early 1770s, when Blyth was
very active.

The oil of Hill is illustrated in James Duncan Phillips' book, *Salem in the Eighteenth Century*,
published in 1937—the year in which it was given to Historic Beverly.

Phillips, *Salem 18th c.*, pp. xix, 411–12, 418–19, 427–28, 429; illus. opp. p. 412
WPA 1038

69

Woman of the Hiller(?) Family

Benjamin Blyth, mid-1770s
Pastel on two sheets of paper, 23¼ x 18 in. (59 x 45.5 cm.)
Current location not known; Sotheby's;
Ted Samuels Antiques, San Francisco, California; provenance unknown

This pastel, sold by Sotheby's in 2003, was tentatively identified in an article in *Antiques and Fine Art* magazine in 2012 as of Elizabeth Hiller (1750–1806), sister of Joseph Hiller of Salem, and was attributed to John Singleton Copley. The identity of the subject, or at least the family, is credible. However, the pastel is here attributed to Benjamin Blyth. It has a harder, more linear quality as seen in the repetitive dark lines in the bonnet ruffles, the pearl necklace, and the strokes outlining her eyes and the base of her nose. The unvarying brown line separating the lips is one of Blyth's most consistent characteristics. Also, the sitter's dress does not show the deft handling of fabric associated with Copley. The bow at her neck is too close to the surface plane, and her cap is depicted as parallel to it, examples of Blyth's difficulty with perspective. The subject's hand, limp and knuckle-less, is more typical of Blyth than Copley, as seen in his pastels of Mrs. Gawen Brown (illus., p. 61), Mrs. Henshaw (Museum of Fine Arts, Houston), Joseph Barrell (Worcester Art Museum), Jonathan Jackson (Museum of Fine Arts, Boston), or Mrs. Henry Hill (Chicago Art Institute). The diaphanous frilled cap resembles those in Blyth's pastels of Elizabeth Cabot, Lydia Fisk, and Priscilla Ropes (Cats. 23, 53, 112).

The portrait, described in Sotheby's auction as "American school/18th century/Portrait of a dark-haired young woman in a gray satin dress . . . Glass cracked, stains and split," was listed with two silkworks and a theorem painting, with the estimate of $300–$500. The lot sold for $3,600.

Deborah M. Child, the author of the article attributing the portrait to Copley, includes a superb account of the early use of pastel in this country—the history, composition, and evolution of crayons, and the drawing techniques. Copley's portraits of women illustrated are of Mrs. Joseph Barrell, Mrs. Andrew Tyler, Mrs. Elijah Vose, Mrs. Edward Green, and Mrs. John Singleton Copley, all of which are intended to encourage stylistic resemblance to the Hiller(?). Child convincingly compiled the connection to the Joseph Hiller family through Ted Samuels, an antiques dealer in California, who had bought furniture from the Foster, Hiller, Appleton, and Wentworth families of Boston. Wentworth was not a name associated with either Salem or Blyth, Fosters were few, and the Appleton family were primarily from Ipswich (which would not preclude them), but Joseph Hiller (1749–1814) moved to Salem in 1770. After his marriage to Samuel Blyth's sister-in-law, Hiller and the Blyths became partners in several printmaking ventures, so Hiller's wife Margaret would be a more likely subject of the pastel, begging the question of whether Blyth ever did one of Hiller.

Child, "Deborah M, "A Portrait to be treasured once again: A Copley Pastel of a Boston Maiden," *Antiques and Fine Art Magazine,* 9 (Spring 2012):6.

Jeffares email, Mar. 22, 2016, accepting the Child attribution to Copley

Shelley, Marjorie, ——, "Painting in Crayon: The Pastels of John Singleton Copley," *John Singleton Copley in America*. New York: The Metropolitan Museum of Art (1995), 127–42

Sotheby's 2003 Americana auction 07954, Lot 106

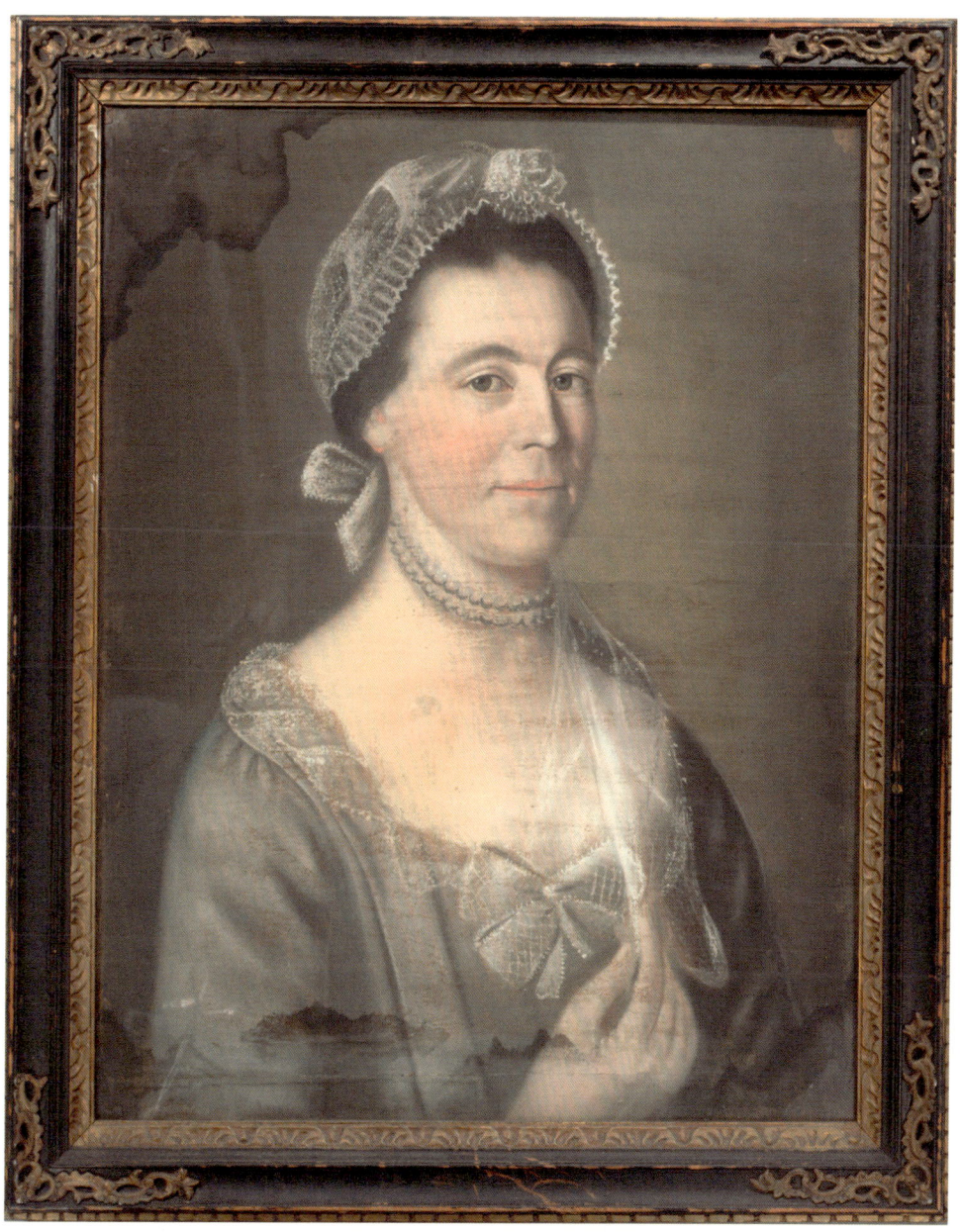

Woman of the Hiller(?) Family
Photograph of pastel attributed to Benjamin Blyth, mid-1770s
Photograph courtesy of Sotheby's, 2003

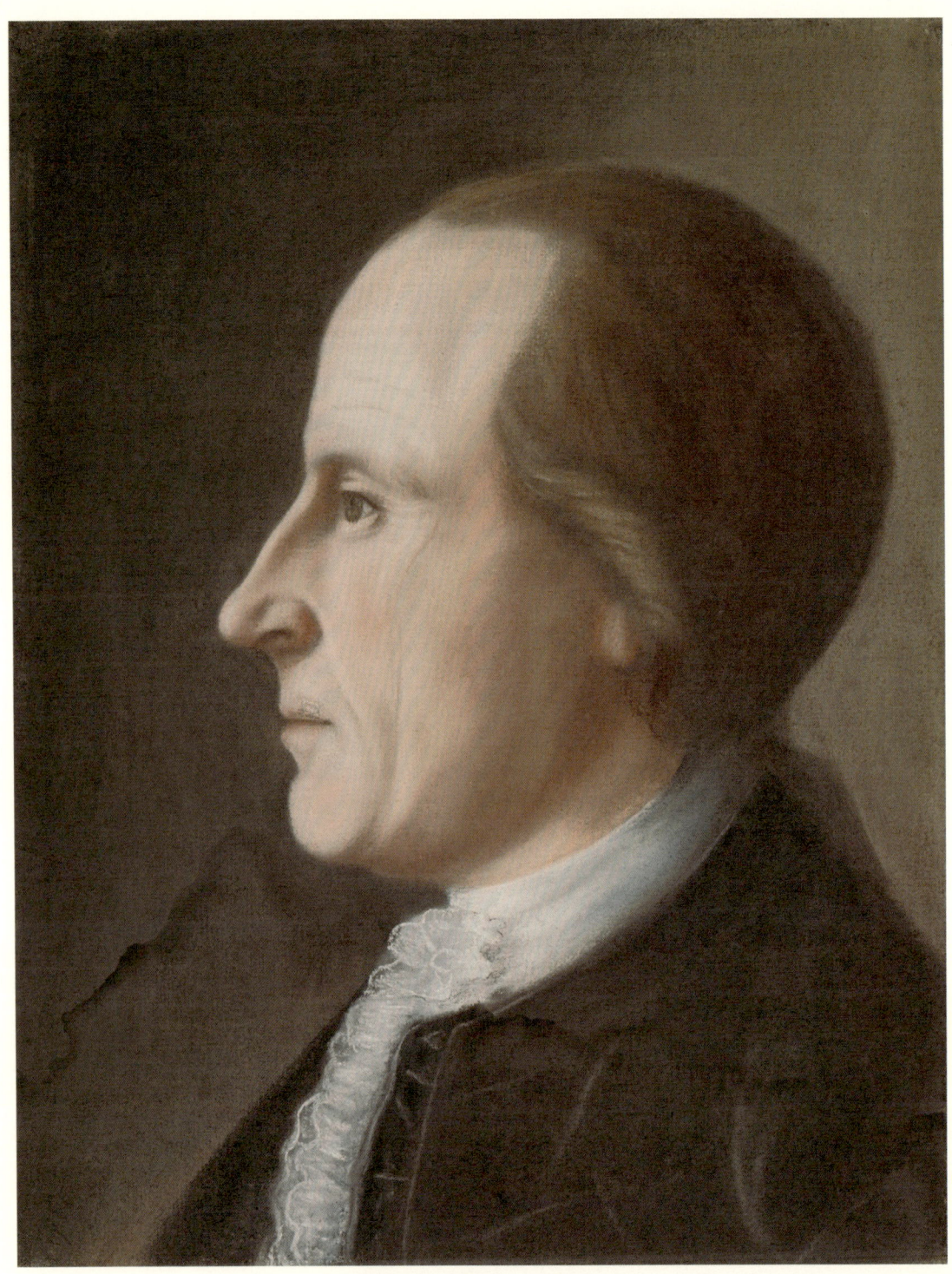

Edward Augustus Holyoke
Pastel by Benjamin Blyth, 1770
Courtesy of the Museum of Fine Arts, Boston, 2020.6, gift of Nancy, David, and Christopher Osgood
in loving memory of William B. Osgood

70

Edward Augustus Holyoke (1728–1829)

Benjamin Blyth, 1770
Pastel on paper mounted on fabric, 14¾ x 11¾ in. (37.5 x 28.6 cm.), Samuel Blyth frame
Museum of Fine Arts, Boston 2020. 6, gift of Nancy, David, and Christopher Osgood
in loving memory of William B. Osgood; William and Nancy Osgood; Northeast Auctions, 2007,
Lot 1636; Osgood family; Susanna Holyoke

Dr. Edward Augustus Holyoke was a revered Salem figure. "On Aug. 21, 1828, many of Salem's most important citizens gathered at the Essex House to pay tribute to one of the town's most beloved citizens on his 100th birthday, noted the *City Guide to Salem* in 1828. "The highlight of the event was a toast offered by the honoree to his beloved Massachusetts Medical Society." Holyoke traveled by horseback, chaise, or on foot throughout the North Shore, until retiring in 1821. The Reverend William Bentley, who had died two years earlier, had called Holyoke "the most interesting character of my own times in Salem, from his professional reputation & unspotted character & the warm affections of all our citizens." The two men dined together and constantly exchanged information on many subjects, especially computations and instruments on the weather.

Son of the Reverend Edward Holyoke and Margaret (Appleton), Holyoke was born on August 1, 1728, in Marblehead, Massachusetts, where his father was minister of its Congregational Church. When he became president of Harvard College in 1737, the family moved to Wadsworth House in Cambridge. Edward Augustus graduated from Harvard with the class of 1746. After teaching school for a few years, he moved to his mother's hometown of Ipswich to study medicine under Dr. Thomas Perry. At the completion of his two-year apprenticeship in 1749, he settled in Salem and opened a practice that he maintained for eighty years. Among his thirty-five students of medicine was William Paine (Cat. 102). Holyoke's first wife, Judith Pickman, daughter of Benjamin Pickman of Salem, died in childbirth at age nineteen. Holyoke then married Mary Vial (Cat. 71) three years later, in 1756.

He made a contribution to Salem's public health during the 1777 smallpox epidemic. After making out his will, Holyoke allowed himself to be inoculated. He survived the controversial treatment and subsequently convinced more than 600 of his own patients to let him inoculate them. Only two died, and the success of this treatment made Holyoke an early adherent of smallpox vaccination. The *Guide* continues, "Tragically, all of Holyoke's expertise and experience often failed him when it came to treating his own family." He had twelve children, but only four survived infancy.

An avowed Loyalist who was friends with Thomas Hutchinson, royal governor of Massachusetts Bay, Holyoke at first lost much of his standing in heavily patriotic Salem when the American Revolution began. Nonetheless, he stayed to care for his patients, although he sent his family to live in Nantucket. In that year, he became the first recipient of an honorary M.D. from Harvard. He also was president of the Salem Athenaeum, the Salem Dispensary, the

Salem Savings Bank, and first president of both the new Massachusetts Medical Society and the Essex Historical Society, precursor of the Essex Institute (now Peabody Essex Museum), founded in 1821.

Mary Vial Holyoke's diary entry for October 12, 1770, provides the only known precise date when Benjamin Blyth drew a pastel. She wrote, "Doctor Sat for his Picture." This is also one of the few portraits Blyth did in silhouette. Its stylistic characteristics indicate Blyth's best work: the emphasis is on the face of a very serious, dedicated man.

Bayley Papers, MHS

Bentley 1:326; 2:293; 3:30, 160, 569; many other references

Bolton, *Portrait Draughtsmen*, 7

[Brazer, John], *Memoir of Edward Holyoke*, frontis. illus., Pendleton lithograph

CAP DLR00940

Cole, "Limned by Blyth," 331–33

Dresser, Louisa, "Attribution and Authenticity in American Painting," Art in America 33 (October 1945), illus. opp. 199

EIHC, 1972:50, 275

FARL, Blyth, Benjamin 157–3b

Foote, "Blyth," 72–73, 92–93

The Holyoke Diaries, 75–76; illus. between 56–57

Jeffares, http://www.pastellists.com/Articles/Blyth.pdf

Little, "The Blyths of Salem" 50, illus. opp. 56

Norton, "Brothers Blyth," 62

Osgood, Nancy, typescript, The Holyoke and Ward Families

Osgood, *Sketch of Salem* 3:224, 242–45

Prown, 1:108, 219 (Copley oil)

Sibley 12:9, full text 30-44, illus opp. 30

Visitor's Guide to Salem (1892), 10

Visitor's Guide to Salem (1895), 12, 74

[71]

Mary Vial Holyoke (1737–1802)

Benjamin Blyth, 1771
Pastel on paper, measurements not known
Current location not known; Mary Eliot Nichols, Hathorne (Danvers), Massachusetts; Nichols family in 1957

Mary Vial was born on December 19, 1737, to Nathaniel, a Boston shopkeeper, and Mary (Simpson) Vial. She was their third child given that name. She and Dr. Edward Augustus Holyoke were married in October 1759. Of their twelve children, three successively named Edward Augustus, only four survived infancy. Mary Vial Holyoke died in 1802, leaving her husband a widower for the second time.

Her diaries are a valuable but little-known resource on the social history of Salem in the latter half of the eighteenth century. Many entries indicate that she tended often to the needs of others, including members of the Blyth family: "Mrs. Blyth Brought to Bed" on March 18, 1768, referred to the wife of Samuel Blyth, who was thereafter an invalid, and noted her burial on August 22, 1787. Mary Holyoke also "watched" Betsy Cabot, daughter of Francis, who soon died on April 6, and was a friend of Lydia Fisk and Priscilla Ropes (Cats. 53, 111). In the entry for May 24, 1781, Holyoke wrote, "At Judge Olivers By invitation to tea and hear the harpsichord." Perhaps it was one of Samuel Blyth's manufacture, as he was making harpsichords at the time and may even have played it.

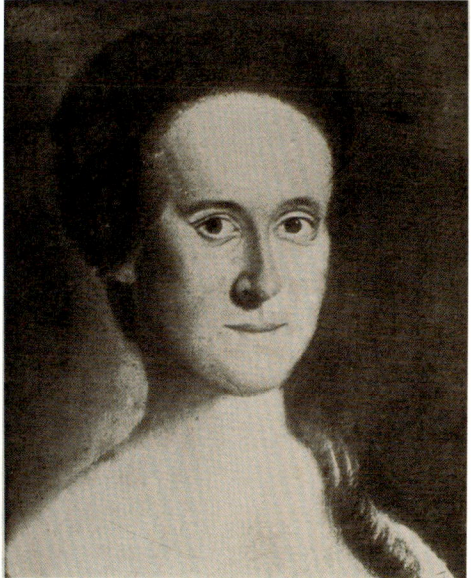

Mary Vial Holyoke
Photograph of unlocated pastel by
Benjamin Blyth, 1771
Illustration from *Holyoke Diaries*, Salem, Mass., 1911
Courtesy of the Boston Athenaeum

In addition to noting the date of her husband's pastel by Blyth (Cat. 70), she entered in her diary on February 27, 1771, "First sat for my picture." Her portrait does demonstrate what Alan Burroughs noted about Blyth pastels in general, "a Badgeresque honesty of purpose." Mary Holyoke's charity, openness, and kindness are indeed recorded in Blyth's representation of her.

Burroughs, Limners and Likenesses, 70
Cole, "Limned by Blyth," 331–333
FARL, Blyth, Benjamin 158-3a
Foote, "Blyth," 72–73, 93 ("Mrs. Edward Augustus Holyoke")
Holyoke Diaries, Mary Vial Holyoke diary, 75, 76, illus. opp. 77
Jeffares, http://www.pastellists.com/Articles/Blyth.pdf
Little, "The Blyths of Salem," 50
Norton, "Brothers Blyth," 62
Osgood, Nancy, typescript, The Holyoke and Ward Families
WPA 1073

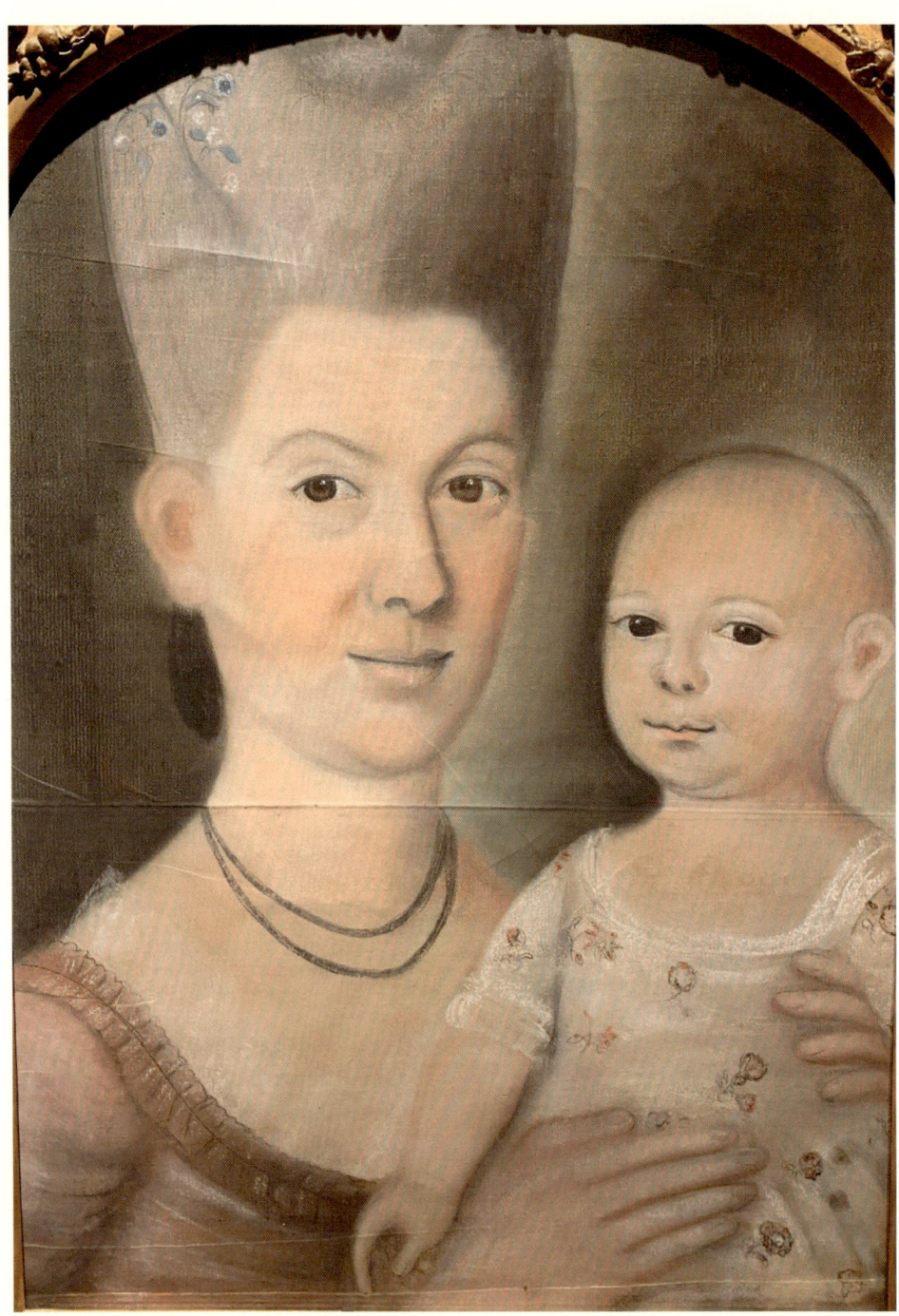

Relief Homans and Phoebe
Pastel by Benjamin Blyth, 1781–82
Historic Beverly 988.193, gift of Mrs. Nancy Bates

Relief Homans (1755–1842) *&*
daughter Phoebe (1779–1815)

Benjamin Blyth, 1781–82
Pastel on paper mounted on linen, 19⁷⁄₁₆ x 13⅜ in. (49.3 x 34 cm.), later frame
Historic Beverly 988.193, gift of Mrs. Nancy Bates, in 1935; Homans descendants

Relief Brown, born in Charlestown to Stephen and Mary (Barrow) in 1755, was named for her grandmother. After the death of her mother and then of her father Stephen, a Charlestown mariner, she, as a minor over age fourteen, petitioned for Nathaniel Brown of Wenham to be guardian for her and her younger sister, Phebe. In May 1777, Relief ("Relephy") married William Homans, a widower with two very young children. They had nine more children. She witnessed the deaths of three of her sons as young men: William, Jr., of consumption, in 1798, at age twenty-four; Charles, of fever, in Martinique in 1808, at age twenty-two; and William Albert, lost at sea "abt. 1832," at age thirty-four. She outlived many of her children and stepchildren, including Phoebe, and died at age eighty-seven on August 14, 1842, of "lethargy." The Reverend William Bentley called Relief a "Good Woman with whom I boarded" when he preached in Beverly. After her funeral, he wrote, "Mrs. Homans is a woman who has suffered the greatest mortifications & changes with exemplary fortitude."

Phoebe, her second child, born on August 20, 1779, married Daniel Rogers of Gloucester on January 21, 1806. She died from typhoid fever in January 1815, leaving six children, ages two to seven. This portrait and its companion of Maj. William Homans belonged to the family until they were given to Historic Beverly by Mrs. Nancy Bates, but they were not delivered to the Society until after the death of her aunt, Mrs. Anna Rogers Dodge, a daughter of Phoebe Homans Rogers. The portraits probably were framed in 1809, the date of the Salem newspaper which lines them. Relief, holding Phoebe, looks proud and happy in this portrait. Baby Phoebe is the epitome of the Blyth baby portraits.

Bentley 3:314, 4:309
Foote, "Blyth," 94 ("Mrs. William A. Homans and child Phoebe")
Norton, "Brothers Blyth," 62
Middlesex County, MA Probate Records, 3206, 1770
WPA 1076
Historic Beverly 988. 193, gift of Mrs. Nancy Bates

[73]

William A. Homans (1749–1839)

Benjamin Blyth, 1781–82

Pastel on paper mounted on linen, 19⁷⁄₁₆ x 13⁷⁄₁₆ in. (49.4 x 34 cm.), later frame

Historic Beverly 988.194, gift of Mrs. Nancy Bates, in 1935; Homans descendants

William Homans first appears in Beverly vital records with the baptism of his son William in 1774, in which he was listed as "William, Jr. of Marblehead." Indeed, Marblehead lists many residents with the name Homan or Homans in the eighteenth century. William was born there in 1749 to Richard and Hannah (Gooding) Homan. The young family next appeared in Ipswich, where William's older brother, Capt. Richard Homans, had settled. No marriage record has been found, but a daughter Elizabeth was born there in March 1776. William's wife, Elizabeth, died six months later, at age twenty-seven, and in May of the following year he married Mrs. "Relephy" (Relief) Brown of Wenham. Their first son, Richard, was born in Ipswich in 1778, but soon, William and family settled in Beverly.

During the Revolution, Homans achieved the rank of major and is the central figure in a local legend (possibly apocryphal) about the war. In the battle between the *Hannah,* the first armed vessel of the new colonial Navy, and the British ship *Nautilus* in Beverly Harbor in October 1775, "a Tory named Wyer climbed to the roof of his home at 112 Cabot Street to encourage the British." Homans was reported to have told him to 'come down and shut up his mouth or he would shake his daylights out.'" Wyer reportedly complied.

The Homans family were members of Beverly's First Parish Church, and their house was on Cabot Street, north of Edwards Street. The Reverend William Bentley recorded in his diary entry for April 3, 1790, "Spent the day in Beverley at Mʳ. Homans's at whose house I tarried while I was a Candidate in Beverly." On another occasion, Bentley wrote, Capt. Homans "entertained us with a most exact imitation of low life, in the most indelicate, honest, but vile language of low life, for which he deserved the shouts in the execution, but a whipping under the gallows when the story was ended." When Major Homans died of old age on August 15, 1839, it was recorded in Gloucester as well as Beverly.

Homans' portrait and its companion, of his wife Relief with daughter Phoebe, were a gift from Mrs. Nancy Bates, but did not become part of Historic Beverly's collections until the death of her cousin, Phoebe's daughter, Anna Rogers Dodge, who is believed to have written the notes on the back of the portrait. The donors provided the identifications, but they might not be correct, as the clothing and hair styles of both spouses bespeak the early 1770s. Homans also powdered his hair, an uncommon practice by the late 1770s. His upper lip looks to have been completely redrawn with brown crayon, along with delicate black strokes that underlined his nose. This was probably done when the companion portraits were given elaborate carved and gilded frames. Homans does look like a man who could be bawdy, as both Bentley and the tale of the Tory Wyer intimated.

Bentley 1:158, 304; 3:314–15; 4:309
FARL, Blyth, Benjamin 157–2a
Foote, "Blyth," 93
Norton, "Brothers Blyth," 62
WPA 1077

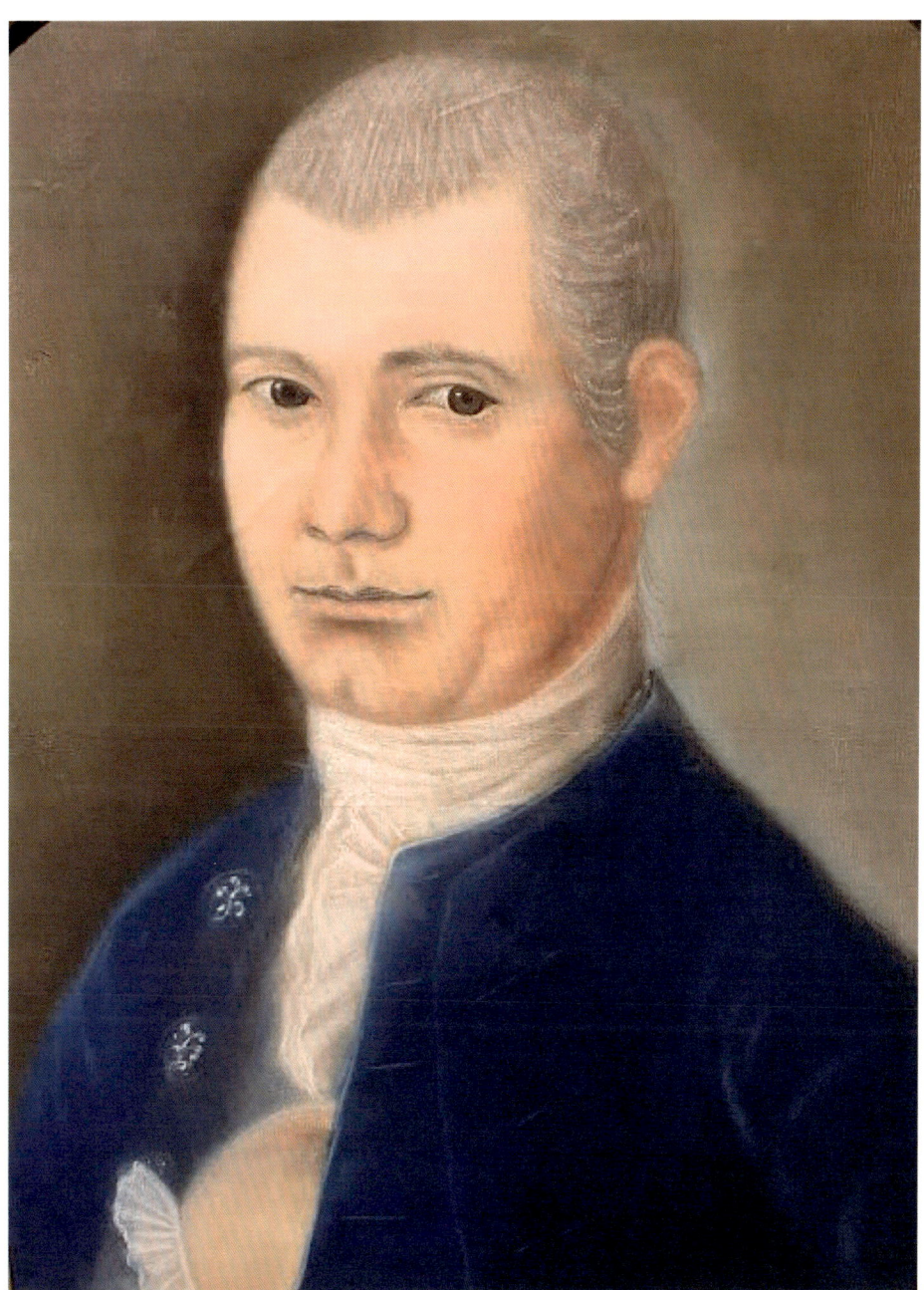

William A. Homans
Pastel by Benjamin Blyth, 1781–82
Historic Beverly 988.194, gift of a granddaughter, Mrs. Nancy Bates, in 1935

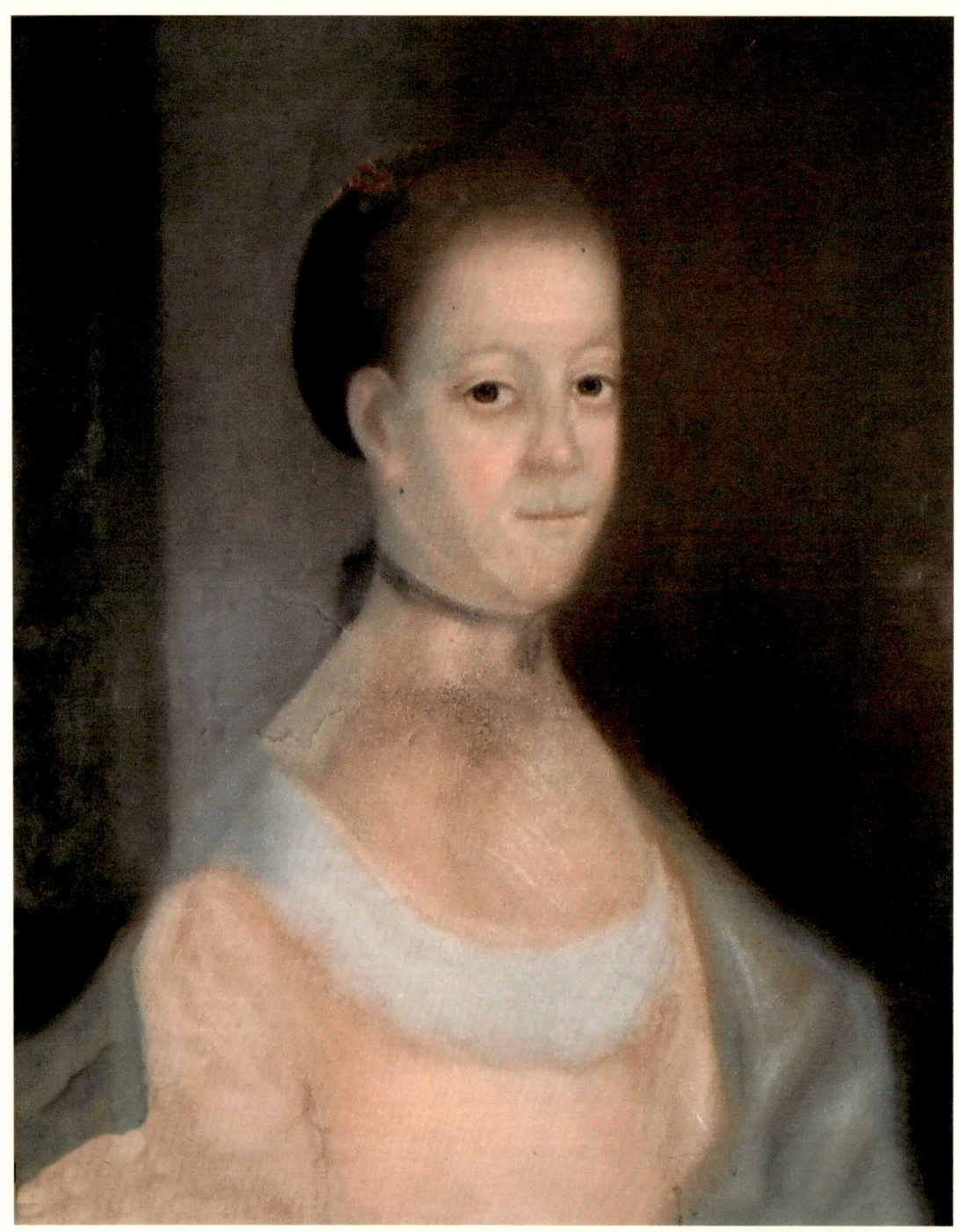

Rebeckah Hooper
Pastel by Benjamin Blyth, ca. 1775
Leffingwell House Museum, Society of the Founders of Norwich, CT, Inc.

[74]

Rebeckah Hooper (1755–1790)

Benjamin Blyth, ca. 1775

Pastel on paper mounted on linen, 22¹¹⁄₁₆ x 17⁹⁄₁₆ in. (sight), (58.2 x 44.6 cm.), Samuel Blyth frame
Leffingwell House Museum, Society of the Founders of Norwich, CT, Inc., gift of Mr. and Mrs. Howard
T. Brown; unknown dealer; Sarah C. Currier, Newburyport, MA; Mrs. F. G. Hale, Newburyport, MA

This pastel was among the Blyth portraits once attributed to Copley that was doubted by Parker and Wheeler, who also noted its poor condition at the time. Assuming she is the Rebeckah born in August,1755 to Robert, Esq., and Ruth Hooper, the attribution to Copley would be understandable, as many members of the Hooper family of Marblehead were painted by him. However, the portrait is obviously by Benjamin Blyth and might have been done after Copley left for England in June 1774.

Rebeckah Hooper, as her name was spelled both in her birth record and by the donor of her miniature (Cat. 75), was born on August 15, 1755. She was the youngest of Hooper's four daughters. Known as "King" Hooper, his mansion at 8 Hooper Street in Marblehead is a National Historic Landmark. In 1780, Rebeckah married Lewis Jenkins at St. Paul's Episcopal Church, Newburyport. They had four children, Rebeckah Hooper, born on August 3, 1782; Joseph Marien, born on September 20, 1783; Robert Dalton, born on November 19, 1785; and Susannah Caroline in January 1789. Rebeckah died the following year, at age thirty-five, and was buried in the Presbyterian Church. Six months later, her husband married Ruth Hooper (probably a relative). He died eight years later and was also buried in the Presbyterian Churchyard.

Cementing its connection to Newburyport, the pastel at one time belonged to Mrs. F. G. Hale of that town. A miniature of Rebecca (Rebeckah) Hooper in the collections of the U. S. Department of State was also attributed to Copley but is credited here to Blyth.

Bayley, *Copley*, 126

Jeffares, http://www.pastellists.com/Articles/Blyth.pdf

Leffingwell Inn Association, letter from Richard Guidebeck, Mar. 20, 2016

Norton, "Brothers Blyth," 62

Parker and Wheeler, 258

Perkins, Supplement, 19

[75]

Rebeckah Hooper (1755–1790)

Benjamin Blyth (attr.), ca. 1778
Miniature on ivory, 1⅛ x 15⁄16 in. (sight), (2.9 x 2.4 cm.)
U. S. Department of State Diplomatic Reception Rooms, Washington D. C., RR–1977.0039,
gift of Mr. and Mrs. James O. Keene

This miniature was once mistakenly believed to have been painted by John Singleton Copley, who painted oil portraits and a miniature of Robert "King" Hooper and one (or possibly two) portraits of his four wives and several of his eleven offspring—(and quite a few others in Marblehead, mostly related to him, even if by marriage). However, Copley had already left for England just after the outbreak of the Revolution, which also brought about a reversal of Robert Hooper's fortunes. And stylistically, it fits into Blyth's oeuvre. Rebeckah is portrayed as gentle, if not somewhat withdrawn. Although the available biographical information creates ambiguities, the pastel (Cat. 74) and the miniature are clearly of the same young woman.

Judith Anderson, historian, Marblehead, MA, correspondence

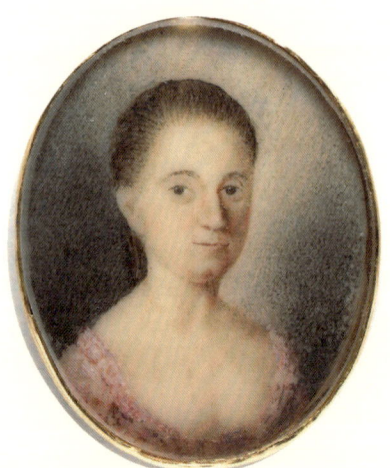

Rebeckah Hooper
Miniature by Benjamin Blyth, ca. 1778
Courtesy of the U. S. Department of State
Diplomatic Reception Rooms, Washington D. C., Gift of Mr. and Mrs. James O.
Keene, RR-1977.0039

Molly Hoyt (1773–1846)

Benjamin Blyth, ca. 1782

Pastel on paper mounted on linen, 16½ x 13 in. (sight), (41.9 x 32.5 cm.), Samuel Blyth frame

Perry Hopf, Kennebunkport, ME; John Hardy Wright; Blackwood/March Antiques, Essex, MA; Pingree family

The partial biography written on the back of the pastel of young, strawberry-blond Molly Hoyt fills in some of her biography. Molly was one of twins born to Moses and Mary (Stickney) Hoyt of Newburyport, "at Hawk, NH", on Feb. 14, 1775. The Reverend William Bentley corresponded with her father and visited with him several times. On October 19, 1797, Molly married Daniel Robertson Pingree (Pingry), a cordwainer in Newburyport. They had six children. The first Daniel died at eight months, in 1801; the second Daniel was born in 1802. Mary, born in 1804, died in 1808, four days before her fourth birthday. Samuel died at birth in 1810. Seven years later, Daniel and Molly had their last child, Elizabeth, from whom the portrait descended. Daniel Pingree died in 1841, age sixty-nine, and Molly (listed as Mary) died on December 20, 1846, at age seventy-three.

This pastel was exhibited in "Vernacular Visions: Folk Art of Old Newbury," at the Cushing House Museum in 1994. Molly is shown as alert, bemused, and enjoying a favorite pastime—reading.

Benes, *Old-Town and the Waterside*, 148

Bentley I:48, 61, 200; 2:55, 56

Blackwood/March Antiques, catalogue, Essex, MA, 30

Cole, "Limned by Blyth," 331

CRN Auctions, Cambridge, MA, catalogue, April 2005

Jeffares, http://www.pastellists.com/Articles/Blyth.pdf

Little, "The Blyths of Salem" 50, 54, 57

Norton, "Brothers Blyth," 62

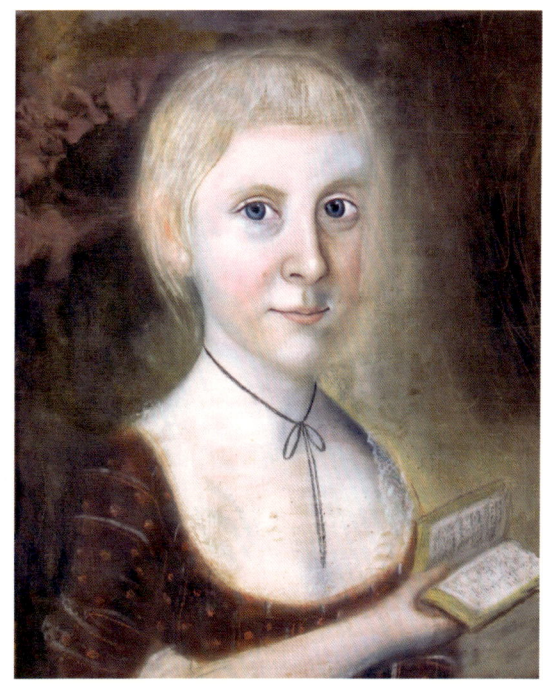

Molly Hoyt
Pastel by Benjamin Blyth, ca. 1782
Courtesy of Perry Hopf, Kennebunkport, ME

[77]

Man of the Hunnewell family(?)

Benjamin Blyth, late 1760s
Pastel on paper mounted on linen, 22½ x 17½ in. (55.9 x 44.4 cm.), elaborate Hogarth-type frame,
probably later
Collection of Jacob E. Mitchell; Jeffrey B. Anderson; Skinner, Inc.; Carl Crossman;
estate of Eleanor Hunnewell

The identity of the couple who sat for these portraits, clearly important commissions for Benjamin Blyth, are unknown. They came from the Hunnewell estate. According to the late art historian and gallery owner Carl Crossman, the family of Eleanor Hunnewell, whom he knew well, were not known to be collectors, lending credibility to the surmise that the portraits were inherited. The Hunnewells were a prominent family in Charlestown in the eighteenth century, but whether the provenance extends back through the Hunnewells or those whom they married cannot be determined. The man looks to be in his late forties or early fifties, which would mean he was born in the 1720s or early 1730s.

Crossman discounted the attribution of this portrait and its companion to Copley. The treatment of the wig, like those of John Adams and Samuel Curwen, and that of the clothing suggest attribution to Benjamin Blyth's work in the late 1760s to early 1770s. However, the face and hair appear to have been redrawn with white and flesh-colored crayon, presumably when it and its companion portrait were reframed.

Carl Crossman correspondence
James Hunnewell correspondence
Skinner, Inc. auction, "A Discerning Eye: The Carl Crossman Collection," Jan. 14, 26, 2021

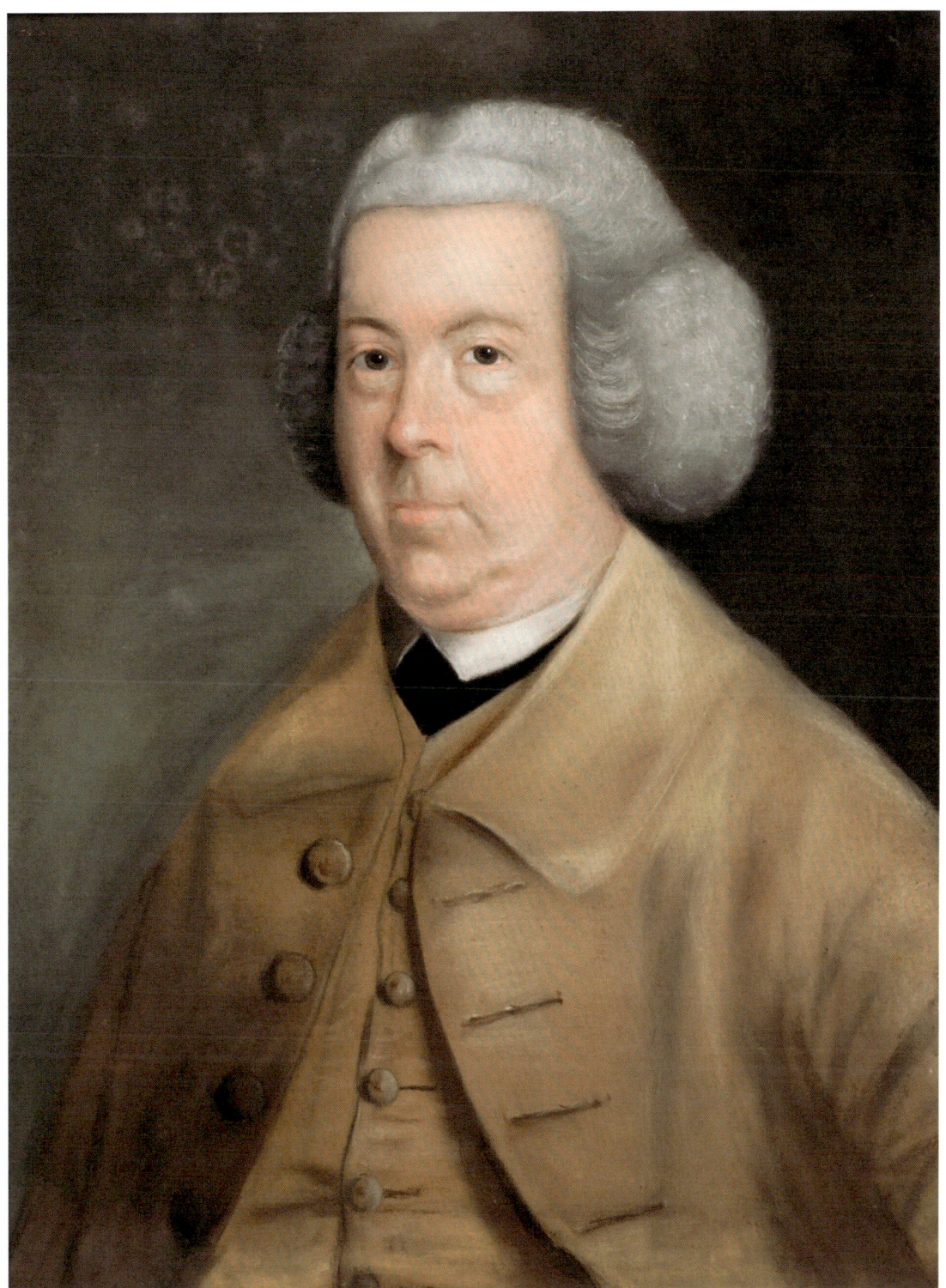

Man of the Hunnewell Family(?)
Pastel by Benjamin Blyth, late 1760s
Collection of Jacob E. Mitchell

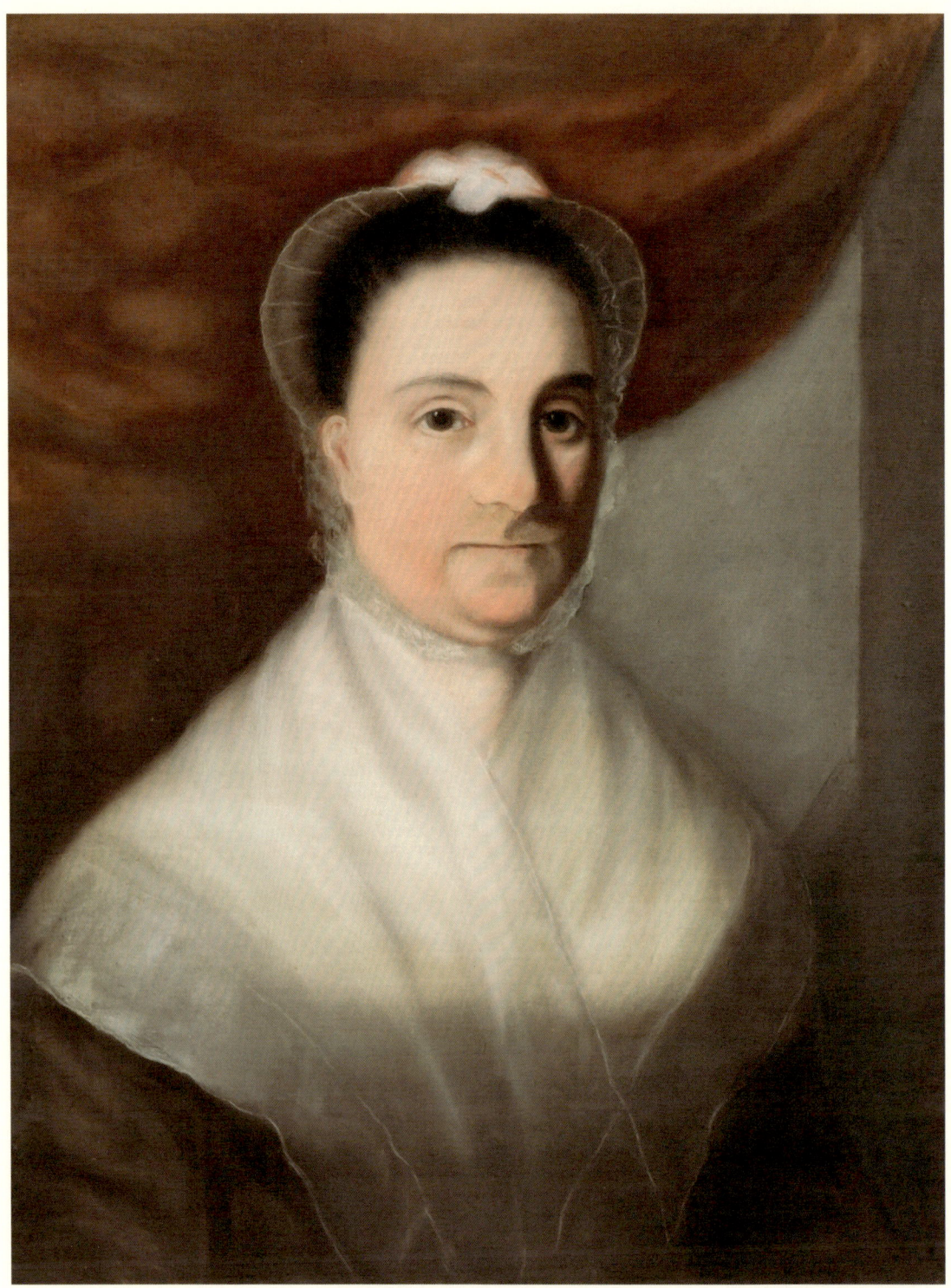

Woman of the Hunnewell Family(?)
Pastel by Benjamin Blyth, late 1760s
Collection of Jacob E. Mitchell

Woman of the Hunnewell family(?)

Benjamin Blyth, late 1760s

Pastel on paper mounted on linen, 22½ x 17½ in. (55.9 x 44.4 cm.), elaborate Hogarth-type frame, probably later

Collection of Jacob E. Mitchell; Skinner, Inc.; Carl Crossman; estate of Eleanor Hunnewell

The woman, like her husband, also looks to be in her forties, making the time of her birth around 1730 and placing the portrait in the late 1760s to early 1770s, as does her outfit. The presence of a drape in the background is atypical of Blyth, but not unknown, especially in his earlier pastels, and the depictions of her ear and mouth make a solid attribution to the Salem artist.

Carl Crossman correspondence

James Hunnewell correspondence

Skinner, Inc. auction, "A Discerning Eye: The Carl Crossman Collection," Jan. 14 and 26, 2021

Henry Jackson (1747–1809)

Benjamin Blyth, 1778–80
Oil on canvas, 36 x 30 in. (91. 44 x 76. 2), possible Samuel Blyth frame
Peabody Essex Museum 102242, gift of the Estate of Mrs. Elizabeth A. Knight, 1909

Catalogued by the former Essex Institute as an unidentified American Army Officer by an unknown artist, this portrait was recently identified as Col. Henry Jackson by art and antiques dealer James Kochan. Indeed, Jackson's facial features resemble those in his portrait as an older man by Gilbert Stuart. (A prior tentative attribution to Edward Savage (1761–1817) as the artist has been discounted.) This portrait is now attributed to Benjamin Blyth, specifically for similarities to his portraits of Stephen Abbot and Benjamin Moses—the treatment of facial features, the tight vests over a stomach paunch, handling of the cloudy sky, and palette. The curve of the fingers on Jackson's right hand also conveys Blyth. He often painted outlines for fingernails, and the one on Jackson's right hand, although anatomically impossible, is painted the same way as those on the right hand of Benjamin Moses. The distant encampment and Jackson pointing to it are similar to those elements in the Putnam mezzotint, for which Blyth contributed the original. Extensive use of small daubs of well-executed overpainting, skillfully amplifying volume and shadow throughout the canvas, especially on Jackson's hair and face, obscured the identity of the artist. Untouched areas, however, strengthen the case for a Blyth attribution.

The youngest son of Joseph and Susannah (Gray) Jackson, Henry was baptized on October 19, 1747. Before the American Revolutionary War, he was an officer of the First Corps of Cadets in Boston. After the evacuation of the British from Boston, he became commander of the Boston Independent Company. In January 1777, the unit was designated Jackson's Additional Continental Regiment, which took part in the Philadelphia Campaign and at Monmouth, New Jersey. His unit then was ordered to join a division under the Marquis de Lafayette to march to Rhode Island in August 1778, where American and French forces were preparing for a joint operation to try to seize British-held Newport. After taking command of the 4th Massachusetts Regiment, Jackson received a brevet promotion to brigadier general on September 30, 1783, and in that year was admitted as an original member of the Society of the Cincinnati in Massachusetts. From 1792 to 1796 he was major general of the Massachusetts Militia and became the agent supervising the building of the frigate USS Constitution at Boston in 1797. Unmarried, he died in Boston on January 4, 1809.

For the Newport campaign, Colonel Jackson commanded about 200 Massachusetts Continentals under Gen. Charles Lee. The intended engagement at Monmouth was a fiasco, and Jackson retreated without orders. Lee was later court-martialed, and Jackson subjected to a Court of Inquiry. Both men survived the interrogations, although the muted conclusion of Jackson's trial held in July 1779, was that there appeared to be nothing against him "sufficiently reprehensible to

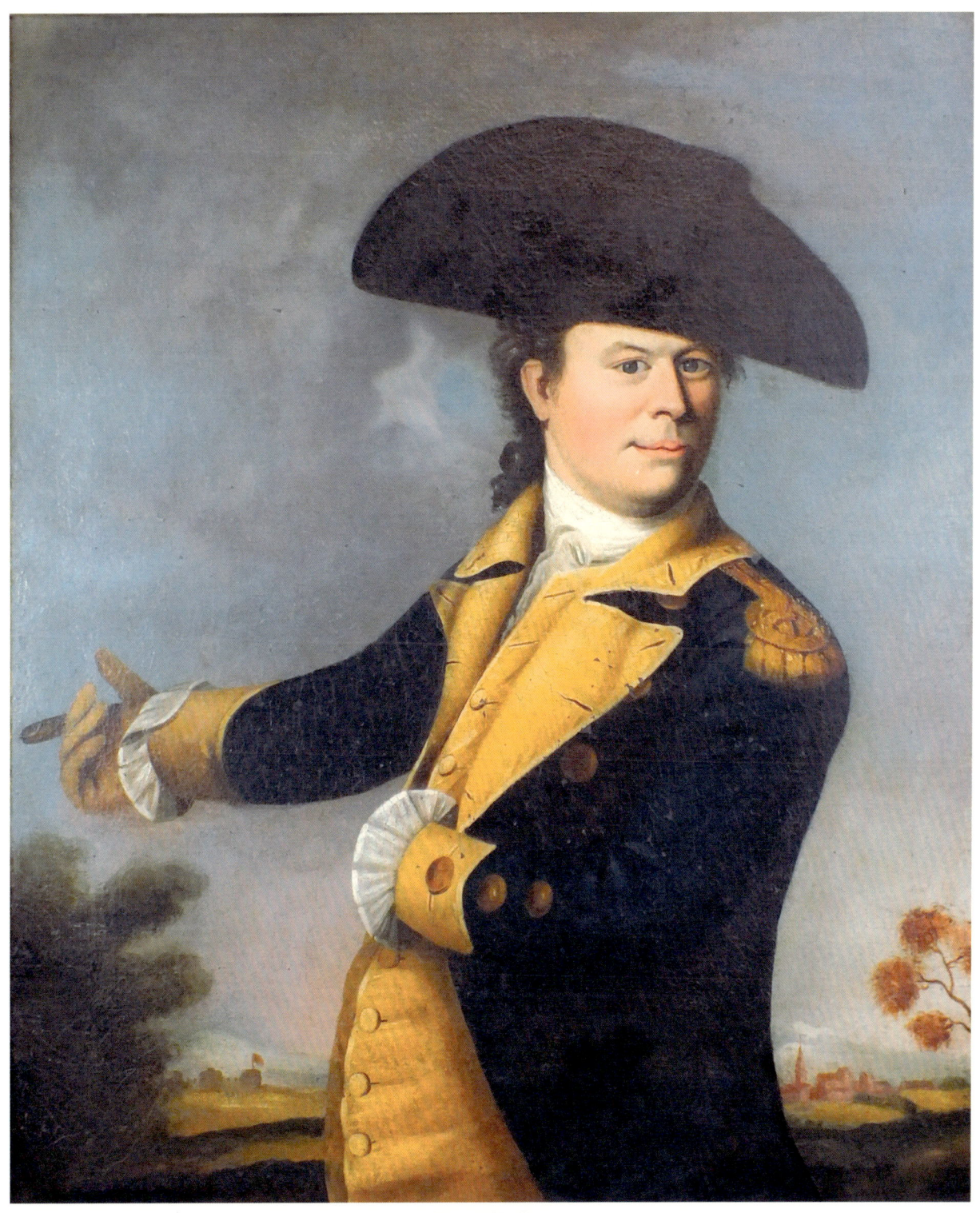

Henry Jackson
Oil painting by Benjamin Blyth, 1778–80
Courtesy of the Peabody Essex Museum 102242, gift of the Estate of Mrs. Elizabeth A. Knight, 1909

call him before a Court Martial." Redeeming testimony had noted that Jackson's detachment performed superbly during the Battle of Rhode Island in Portsmouth on August 29, 1778, an important engagement in Salem's participation in the Revolution, although he got little or no mention in several accounts. (General Lee was also a subject for a mezzotint attributed to Joseph Hiller and reissued by Samuel Blyth, perhaps indicative of some sympathy in Salem for the two men.)

Jackson points with obvious pride to the fort in the left background. Although one source referred to it as Castle William in Boston, the surrounding terrain, showing the fort on a low hill in a large, treeless field lined with stone walls, belies this. In the right background is a church amidst a cluster of houses. Both images, using "artistic license," are meant to suggest symbolically the fort and the nearby small town of Newtown. Such is the terrain at the battle site on northern Aquidneck Island and as it must have been at the time. A similar portrayal is in Blyth's mezzotint of Gen. Israel Putnam, depicting him pointing to the Battle of Bunker Hill, in which he took a prominent part. The portrait of Jackson serves to provide more evidence of Blyth probably having gone on the Rhode Island Expedition.

Jackson's swagger reflects pride in his accomplishment. Here as elsewhere, a strong portrayal of character is a Blyth hallmark.

allthingsliberty. com, website of the *Journal of the American Revolution*
EIHC "Catalogue . . .", 370
McBurney, Christian M., *Rhode Island Campaign,* Yardley, Pa: Westholme Pub., 2011
Schmidt, Gloria, Butts Hill Fort Restoration Committee, correspondence
Siris IAP 22620339
Henry Jackson, Continental Army general, Wikimedia Foundation, last edited 28 August 2021
Wikipedia, Henry R. Jackson

[80]

Benjamin King (1740–1804)

Benjamin Blyth, ca. 1780
Oil on canvas, 36½ x 30½ in. (92.71 x 77.47 cm.)
Peabody Essex Museum 120269, gift of the Estate of Howard Jackson, 1929;
Jackson, Norris, Holman families

Benjamin, son of Daniel and Elizabeth (Coes) King, was baptized at Salem's First Church on November 23, 1740. His father was one of the first persons in New England to deal in mathematical instruments, a career that Benjamin also pursued, with Salem's prominent citizens among his customers. On September 27, 1764, he married Sarah Northey, daughter of David and Miriam (Bassett) Northey, from a family of Quakers in Lynn. Predictably, the Reverend William Bentley had something to say on the subject: On June 21, 1792, "Visited Lynn, saw a woman aged 100, a Quaker, was a Blaney . . . The old matron said she was related to the Kings of Salem. Wondered why there were so many Quakers there." None of the King children's birth records were found, because of this affiliation, it can be assumed, but King's probate record led to marriage records indicating that there were at least three daughters, Mary Mason, Ann Churchill Norris, and Elizabeth Holman. Elizabeth's husband was Samuel Holman, Jr., executor of his father-in-law's estate, and Mary was the second wife of Jonathan Mason, who, Bentley recorded, was "much respected" and schooled with his older brother Thomas (Cat. 91), "an eminent merchant of Salem."

The Kings had much contact with the Northeys, a Quaker family of silver- and goldsmiths; Benjamin rented his shop from Ezra Northey and at his death owed William Northey a substantial sum. Although Benjamin's religious affiliation was probably Quaker, he did have a pew in Dr. Prince's meeting house; in 1776, he also gave money to help Dr. Whitaker, minister of the Third Church, to manufacture nitre for saltpeter. Bentley noted King's death on December 26, 1804, adding that he had "supported a very good character through life & was much esteemed." One item in the will was that his slave John Jayne be given his freedom, clothes, and fifty dollars. King was buried in the family plot in Broad Street Cemetery.

For many years, the artist of Benjamin King's portrait, like the one of his wife with one of their daughters, was classified simply as "American School." Attribution was undoubtedly hindered by the overpainting in dark brown, evident on the hair at the right side of his face, and in red on his mouth, line of nose, and left eye. Crackling occurred after the overpainting. Nonetheless, many of Blyth's characteristics remain: the palette, the pose, the facial modeling, the hands, and the telescope, even the treatment of the fabric buttons. As for the telescope, Blyth could handle metals very well, as seen in the brass end of ghe telescope and the silver snuff box held by Dr. Hersey (Cat. 66), also an oil.

The King portraits were passed down from a succession of family members named Elizabeth (Holman, Norris, and Jackson) to Howard Jackson, whose heirs donated the portraits to the

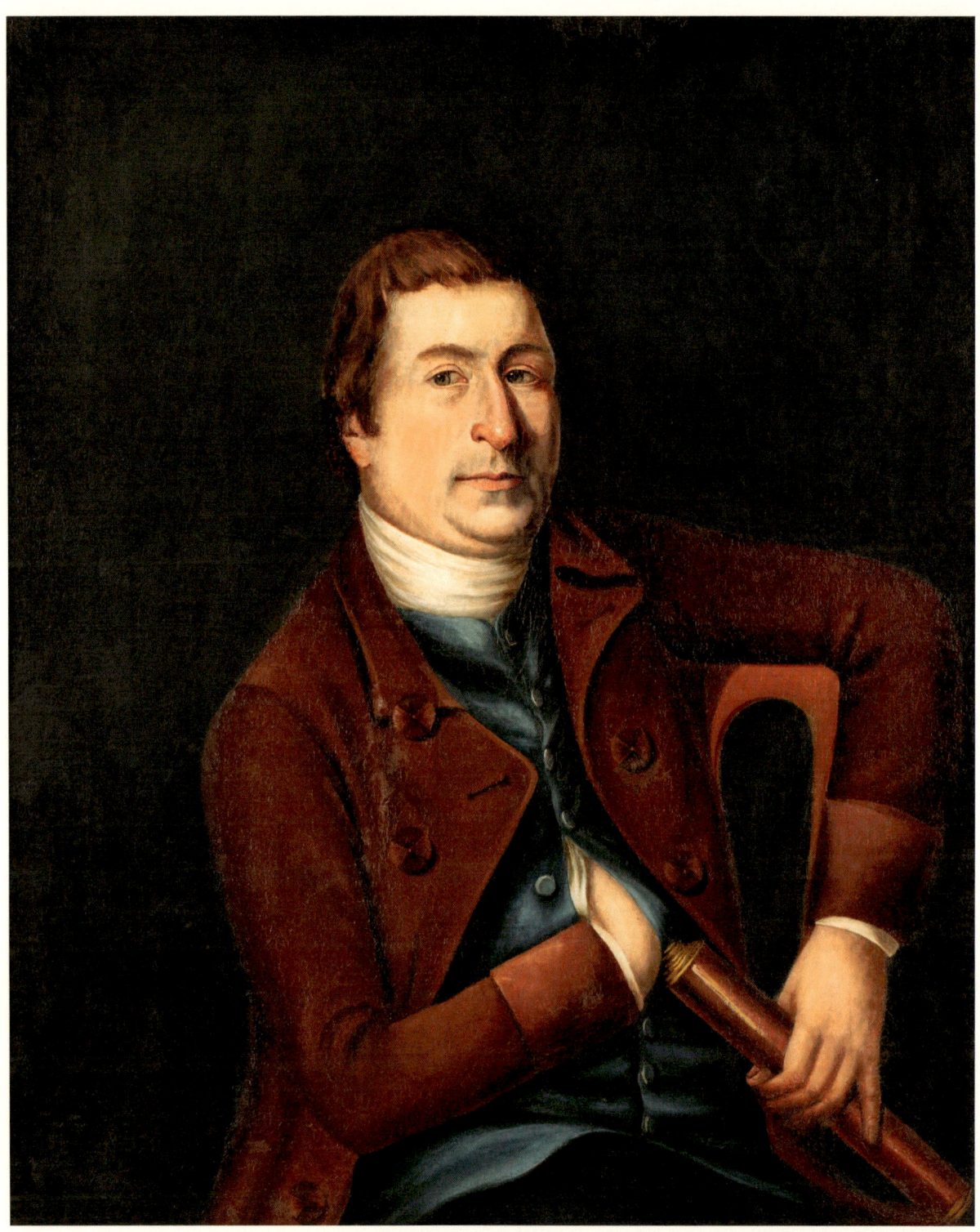

Benjamin King
Oil painting by Benjamin Blyth, ca. 1780
Courtesy of the Peabody Essex Museum 120269, gift of the Estate of Howard Jackson, 1929

former Essex Institute; they also gave an oil portrait of Benjamin King's father, Daniel (PEM 120268); its dimensions, 33 x 26 in., suggest it also is a three-quarter figure portrayal. Other family portraits were given by the heirs of Miss Annie F. King in 1926 with a Bible that provided information on the family. During the 1960s, the portraits of Benjamin King and Sarah with Betsy hung in the parlor of the Crowninshield-Bentley House.

American art historian Alan Burroughs, who wrote that he suspected there were many more portraits by Blyth to be discovered, described this one of Benjamin King as an example of "arbitrary but wholesome and vivid anonymous portraits." A good description. Benjamin appears as a successful man with a sense of his own worth and pride in his profession.

Belknap, 103

Bentley 1:373; 3:130, 373; 4: 439

Burroughs, *Limners and Likenesses*, 59 fn. 51, 89, illus. Plate 66

Essex County Probate Record 15785, 1805

EIHC 71:239, cat. 150, "unknown artist"

Fales, Dean Jr., "The Furnishings of the House," April 1961, *EIHC* 97:109; illus. Fig. 10, betw. 128–29

FARL, American School, Massachusetts (1751–1800) 121-6h

Felt 2:177

SIRI, Daniel King

WPA 1224

[81]

Sarah Northey King (1743–1803) *& Ann* (1778–1812)

Benjamin Blyth, ca. 1780
Oil on canvas, 34 x 28 in. (86.36 x 71.1 cm.), original frame
Peabody Essex Museum 120270, gift of the Estate of Howard Jackson, 1929;
Jackson, Norris, Holman families

Sarah Northey King came from Lynn, a community that prompted the Reverend William Bentley to observe that many Quakers lived there. She was born to David and Miriam (Bassett) Northey in 1743. David became a goldsmith in Salem, although both Sarah's great-grandfather and grandfather John were glaziers. David's estate at his death in 1778 included a mansion house with "dependences" in Ferry Lane, plus six acres of land and three rights to the common pasturage. The three appraisers for his estate were his sons William and Abijah Northey and Capt. Samuel Flagg. Blyth drew pastels of the last two (Cats. 97, 55).

On September 27, 1764, Sarah married Benjamin King, Salem instrument maker. Their known surviving children were three daughters: Mary, born in 1765/6; Ann Churchill, born in 1778/9, and Elizabeth, born in 1790. Ann, the child in the portrait, married Edward Norris in 1804 and died in 1812 "in her 35th year." There are no recorded children, which probably explains how the portrait descended through her younger sister Elizabeth's family. Sarah died on March 3, 1803, and is buried at Broad Street Cemetery.

The subdued color of the draped clothing worn by Mrs. King has a timeless quality, and with the lack of lace or jewelry, is probably indicative of her Quaker sensibilities. Much of the surface of the portrait shows and contrasting shiny surfaces with dull patches, due to many abrasions, and there are signs of later overpainting, viewed during a visit with the late American art historian Lucretia Giese. The overpainting is primarily in brown: strokes, some quite broad, that cover a portion of Sarah's hair and pearls, outline the crease in her chin, create strange shaping of her nose, and her daughter's, and in added shadowing. The entire stretcher was strengthened and backed with a Styrofoam sheet. Nonetheless, it shows many attributes of Blyth's work: the pose of mother and child, almost identical to that of Nancy Lane and her child; the palette; and the treatment of Sarah's hair, her large ear, the delineation of their hands, and the handling of the drapery, which compares to the oil portrait of Mrs. Cary (Cat. 26) and even to the pastel of Anstiss Derby (Cat. 40).

Bentley 3:14
Essex County Probate Record 19597, 1805
EIHC 71:244, cat. 158, "unknown artist"
FARL, American School, Massachusetts (1751–1800) 124-6a
Salem VR, P. R. 290: Bible then in the possession of Miss Annie F. King
WPA 1232

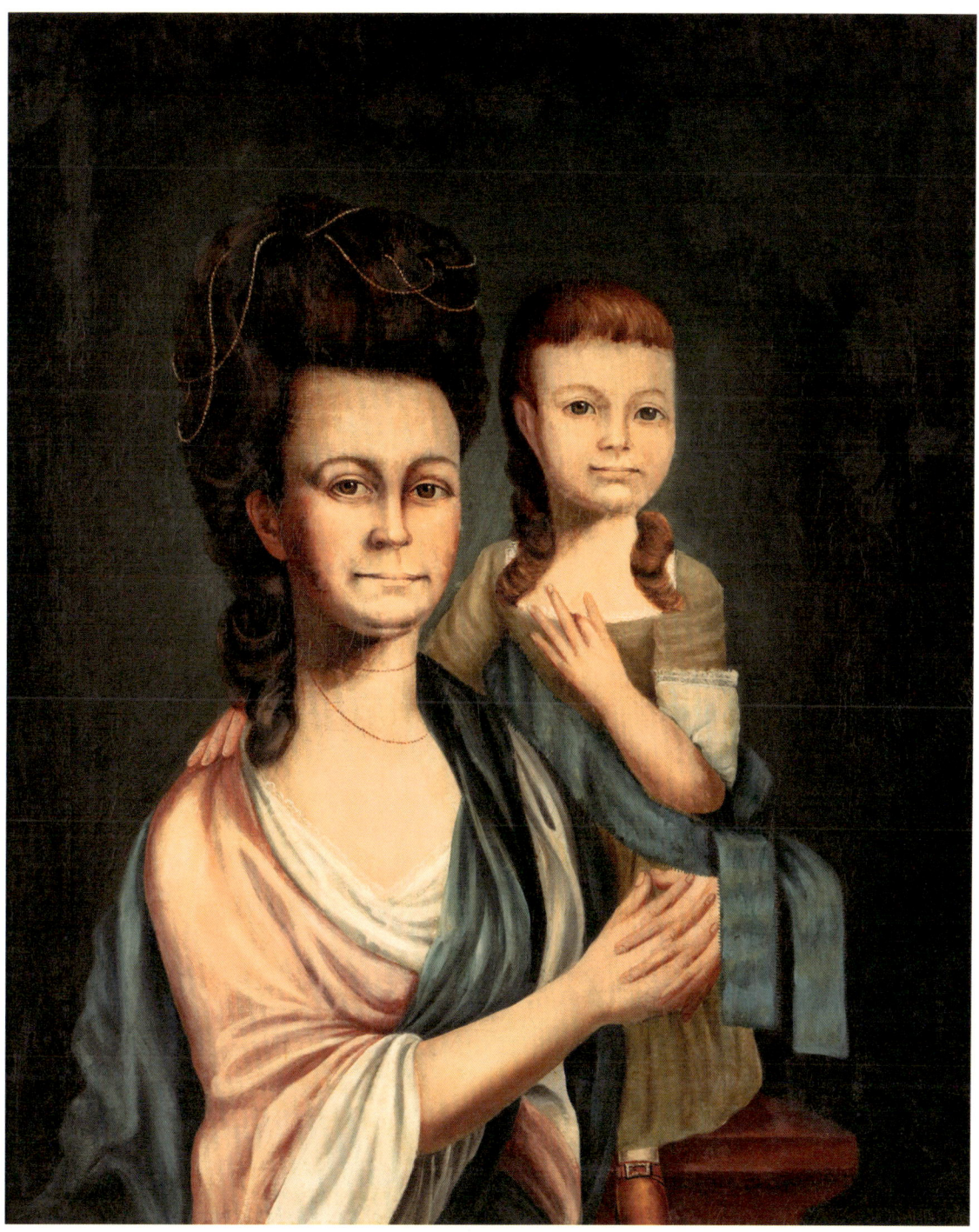

Sarah Northey King and Ann
Oil painting by Benjamin Blyth, ca. 1780
Courtesy of the Peabody Essex Museum 120270, gift of the Estate of Howard Jackson, 1929

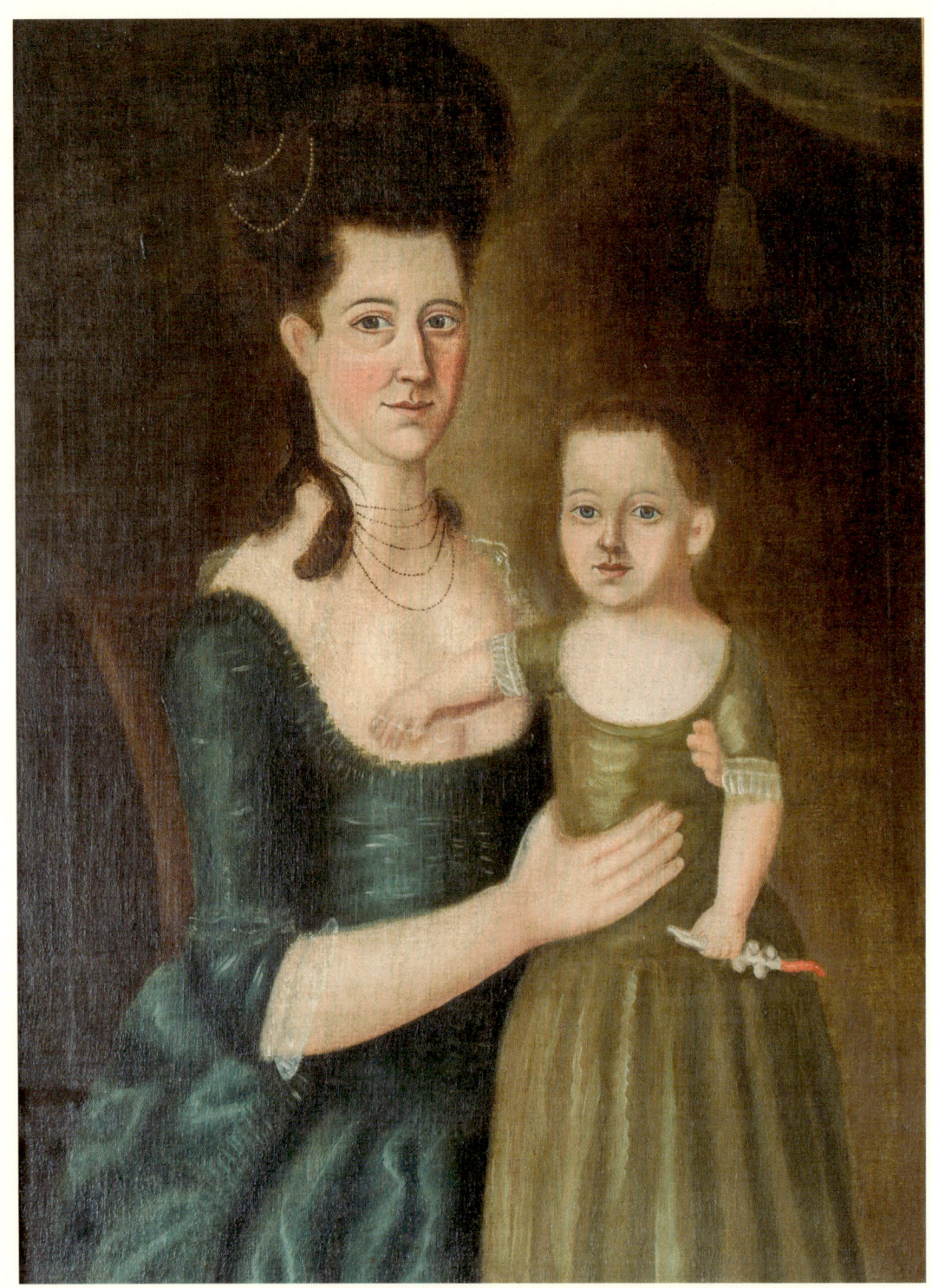

Anna "Nancy" Lane and Betsy
Oil by Benjamin Blyth, 1782–83
Courtesy of the Collection of Randy and Nancy Root
Photograph by Loren J. Root, Photography

Anna "Nancy" Lane (1751–1800) *& Betsy* (1781–1816)

Benjamin Blyth, 1782–3
Oil on canvas, 38½: x 25½ in. (97.79 x 64.8 cm.), Samuel Blyth frame
Collection of Nancy and Randy Root; collection of Marvin Sadik; F. O. Bailey Antiquarians;
family descendants

When a portrait said to be of Anna "Nancy" Bezoil Lane and her daughter came on the market in 2005, offered by F. O. Bailey Antiquarians, the late Marvin Sadik, former director of the Smithsonian's National Portrait Gallery, bid aggressively and won, confident that it was a work by Benjamin Blyth. He paid $32,480, surely the top price ever paid for a Blyth portrait at the time." I've had it cleaned and it looks terrific and the woman has a wonderful coiffure," he told *Maine Antiques Digest*. He noted the similarity to the Blyth portrait of Mrs. Moses and her child (Cat. 95) at the Peabody Essex Museum. Not only is the pose of Nancy and Betsy the same as in both the mother-and-child portraits of Sarah and Betsy Moses and of Sarah Northey King and Ann (Cat. 81), but the rattle held by Betsy appears in other children's portraits by the Blyths.

Anna Bezoil, known as Nancy, was born on April 29, 1751, the daughter of Capt. William and Mercy (Giddings) Bezoil of Gloucester. Described by the Reverend William Bentley as "one of the handsomest women of the Country," Nancy married Nicholas Lane, a sailmaker from Gloucester, on March 10, 1771, just shy of her twentieth birthday. (Bentley said she was seventeen, also noting that "Lane's cove is from his ancestors.") The Lane family moved to Salem by 1780 and lived on Derby Street, between Carlton and Becket. At first members of Salem's First Church, they later joined Bentley's East Church. Nancy Lane died of rheumatic fever at age forty-eight on February 16, 1800, and was interred in the Charter Street Burial Ground. Her husband Nicholas, left with five minor-age children, married Mary Buffum, from Middletown, Connecticut, in 1802.

A paper attached to the back of the portrait said the Lanes had thirteen children, and the child portrayed was Betsy, their fifth. Her life was marked by tragedy. Baptized at Salem's First Church on February 11, 1781, she married Josiah Gatchel, a ship carpenter originally from Brunswick, Maine, in 1800. Two weeks later, her mother died. Betsy and Josiah had two sons, William, and Josiah, who died in 1803 at the age of fourteen months. Josiah the father, by then called a house-wright or carpenter, died two years later, on April 11, 1805, at age twenty-eight, after suffering for a few weeks from rheumatism and cramps. They both were buried at Bentley's East Church. Five months after the death of her husband, Betsy married Alexander Buchanan, a mariner. Their son Alexander, born in February 1807, also died at the age of fourteen months; Bentley recorded the "melancholy occurrence in English street. A Mrs. Buchanan, alias Getchel, alias Lane, . . . was in the afternoon setting before the fire with a child in her arms, in a fit of intoxication. The child fell from her arms into the fire. . . . The woman has always been thought below the ordinary character of her sex & her habits were known from the difficulty of rousing her." At the death of her father Nicholas in 1815, Betsy inherited the south side of his "mansion house" on English Street in Salem. Bentley recorded her death of dropsy at age thirty-seven on November 24, 1816, adding that her husband was an Englishman "supposed to be living. Last seen on board of an English man-of-war."

The portrait shows mother and child at a happier time. When consigned to the Bailey sale by a family said to be Smith/Frothingham from Wayne, Maine, both the canvas and the frame had been repaired, and it was re-backed. The portrait is one of Blyth's best, and the unusual added details, such as the curved-back chair in which Anna sits and the drapes were probably meant to signify the opulence of her house. Given that each of the other portraits of a woman with a baby painted by Blyth at this period—Sarah Moses, Mary Somes, and Sarah King—had a companion portrait of the husband, there may have been or possibly is one of Nicholas Lane.

ancestry. com/genealogy/records/william-bezoil_32866487, illus.

Bentley 3:151, 152, 343; 4:332–33

Bentley, *Deaths*, 498, 52.

Essex Antiquarian 9:92

EIHC 13:77

Maine Antiques Digest Jan. 2006, p. 32-D, courtesy of Lois Avigad

[83]

Edward Symmes Lang (1742–1830)

Benjamin Blyth, 1783

Oil on canvas, 28 x 23 in. (71.1 x 58.4 cm.), Samuel Blyth frame

Owner anonymous; Thomas F. and Tess L. Schutte Collection; Robert Thayer, Inc.; Mrs. L. Henry Montgomery, Charles City, Iowa; Montgomery family; Edward Symms Lang Richardson; Richardson family, Charles City, Iowa

Edward Symes Lang was born in Salem on September 3, 1742 to Jeffrey, a gold- and silversmith, and Hanna Simes ("Symmes"/ "Sims") Lang. His mother died in 1748, just after he turned six, and his father died ten years later. Edward took over his father's business and began renting shop space from J. Crowninshield. In 1768, he married Rachel Ward. He rented his house from Susan Babbage and taught her son Edward at the Evening School. Lang's account book shows that he taught school even while he had an active business as a silver- and goldsmith. Among his pupils was the enslaved man of David Ropes (Cat. 111).

Lang's account books that start in the year 1765 and show an extensive clientele, including Crowninshields and Derbys. By 1777, he had customers for his business from Topsfield, Middleton, and Wenham, and sold Stephen Emery of Boston a gold necklace, a string of beads, and buckles. Lang traveled primarily by horse. In October 1781, he sold Benjamin Blyth four silver "Lokets," suggesting that indeed Blyth was making miniature portraits in Salem.

Lang joined the Salem Masonic Lodge on March 1, 1781, the same day as Benjamin Blyth, and became secretary, treasurer, then master in 1808—the first member to hold all offices. Lang's business suffered from the economic hardships brought on by the Revolution, so in 1785, in "reduced circumstances" and at the urging of the Reverend William Bentley, he took a teaching position for the East School and taught there for over twenty-three years. During that time, he and Bentley spent much time together, visiting farms, even walking to Marblehead together one dark and rainy evening after a town alarm was sounded, to help extinguish a fire. Bentley had called Lang "a most worthy man" in 1793, but by 1810 he asked him to resign, writing, "I urged him to take the office, not because he had a trade but because he was poor & in debt. I did not dismiss him in old age without emotion." Lang deeply resented it, according to both his son and Salem historian Joseph B. Felt. A bitter man, Lang then took a position in the Essex Bank as bookkeeper. He died in 1830 of "old age."

His portrait, depicting a sober, handsome man about forty years old, was done when his fortunes already were suffering because of the Revolution. It is in a Samuel Blyth frame and is in its original condition. A label on the back attributes it to Benjamin Blyth/ Salem 1783. An unspecific entry in Lang's account book in 1783 credits Benjamin Blyth "By 2 Pictures, unfinished, 4-1-4." It is assumed to be a reference to the portraits. Another old label is unintelligible. Thomas and Tess Schutte bought the portrait from Robert Thayer, antiques dealer in Sheffield, Massachusetts, and had it professionally conserved by Tom Yost.

Bentley 1:360; 2:31, 88, 188, 219; 3:360, 533, 535; 4:545, 594

Felt, 1: 454, 462

EIHC 66:329

Historic Deerfield, Inc., letter from Lang grandson Edward L. Richardson, Aurora, Ill, [1897] to Charles L. Mason

PEM Phillips Library, Lang Account Book

Montgomery, Joseph, correspondence

"Portraits in Iowa: Portraits of Americans, made before 1900 and now located in Iowa," [n. p.]: National Society of the Colonial Dames of America in the State of Iowa, 1975.

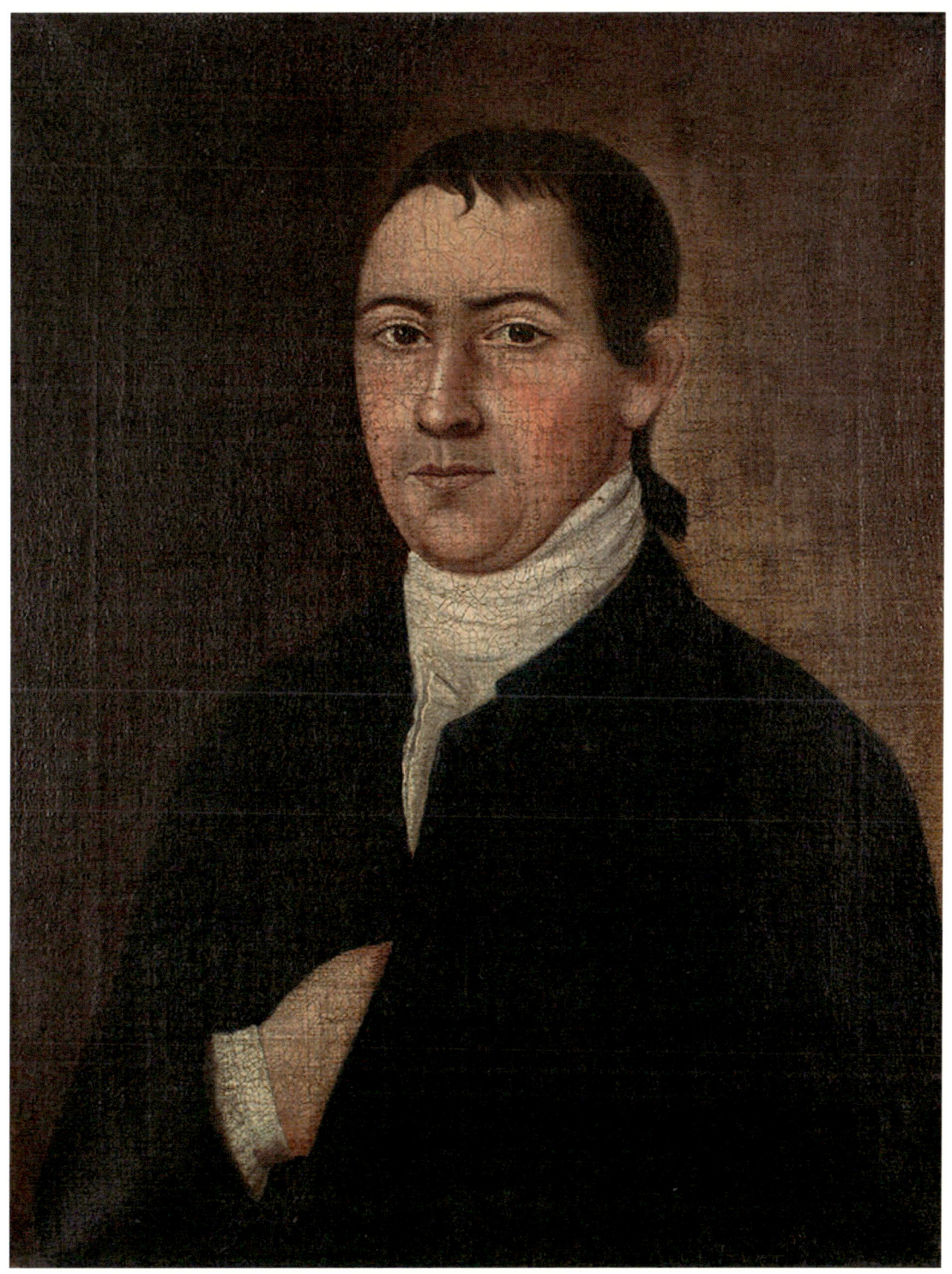

Edward Symes Lang
Oil painting by Benjamin Blyth, 1783
Private collection
Photograph by Matt Kalinowski

[84]

Rachel Ward Lang (1745/6–1819)

Benjamin Blyth, 1783
Oil?, 24½ x 18 in. (62.2 x 45.7 cm.)
Current location not known; Mr. and Mrs. Henry L. Montgomery family, Charles City, Iowa;
Richardson family

Neither Rachel's birth nor those for any other siblings are recorded in the list of Wards in Salem Vital Records. But her birth was ascertained from Benjamin Pickman's bequest of £30 to his sister—Rachel's mother—when he died in 1773. So Rachel was his niece, daughter of Ebenezer and Rachel Ward. (Pickman also left the same sum to his other sister, Sarah Curwen, wife of George Curwen.)

Rachel married silver- and goldsmith Edward Lang (Cat. 83) in 1768. They had nine children. Their eldest son Edward, one of twins born in 1777, married a daughter of Joseph Hiller, but according to the Reverend William Bentley, they lived apart for years. Of the Lang's six daughters, three died in their teens, one—Edward's twin, Elizabeth—in 1793 and two in 1795. Rachel Lang died of "old age" in May 1819, and was the last member of the Ward family, Bentley noted. She was buried in the Gardner Hill Burial Ground at the western edge of Salem. To accommodate development of the area in the 1840s, 150 graves, including hers and those of Bentley, Jacob Crowninshield, and Lt. Benjamin West (Cat. 135), who died at the Battle of Bunker Hill, were moved to Harmony Grove Cemetery.

The portraits of Edward and Rachel Lang were given by Edward Symm[e]s Lang Richardson to Mr. and Mrs. Henry L. Montgomery of Charles City, who owned them in 1975, according to the checklist of an exhibition of Iowa portraits. The State Historical Society of Iowa lists them in the checklist, but there are no illustrations.

Bentley 4:594
Historic Deerfield, Inc., letter from Lang grandson Edward L. Richardson, Aurora, IL, [1897] to Charles L. Lang
PEM, Phillips Library, Lang Account Book
Lang Family Correspondence, letter from Edward Symmes Lang Richardson to Charles R. Montgomery, Aug. 3, 1897
"Portraits in Iowa: Portraits of Americans, made before 1900 and now located in Iowa," [n. p.]: National Society of the Colonial Dames of America in the State of Iowa, 1975

[85]

Joseph Lemmon (1715–1772)

Benjamin Blyth, ca. 1778
Pastel on paper mounted on fabric, 20⅛ x 16 in. (51.1 x 40.7 cm.), Samuel Blyth frame
Smithsonian American Art Museum 1977.131, gift of Mr. and Mrs. Flew Murphy;
descended through the family

Joseph's father, Joseph, "Esq.," was a businessman in Charlestown, whose extensive holdings included a wharf and shops and several other parcels of land. He was both a selectman and treasurer of the town for over eighteen years. His son Joseph, the fourth generation of Josephs, was born on February 5, 1715, and graduated from Harvard College in 1735, the same class as brothers Samuel and George Curwen. Lemmon then moved to Marblehead, where he practiced medicine, but, unlike his father, he avoided public office. In 1742, he married Hannah Swett; she died eight years later, leaving three daughters, Elizabeth, age seven; Mary, age five; Ruth, age three; and Joseph, an infant. Six months later, the widower married Jane Goodwin, about whom there is no record, and in 1765, he married Elizabeth (Gookin) Skinner, a widow. Lemmon, who died in 1772, named his three sons-in-law to be executors and left money for a silver baptismal basin to the Church of Christ in Marblehead, specifying that if that was no longer needed, the money was to be used for the poor widows of the parish.

The portrait of Joseph Lemmon is one of a number attributed by early-twentieth-century art dealer Frank W. Bayley to "Copley's early manner." His gallery may have enhanced Lemmon with its characteristic touches of well-placed thin black lines. For many years, the portrait's location was not known. The Copley historians, Barbara Parker and Anne Wheeler, writing in the 1930s and basing their opinion on a photograph in the Frick Art Reference Library, were the first to suggest it was a "Blythe"; but four decades later, the attribution was still being disputed. In a lively correspondence between the owner at the time and several museums and institutions, the director of a private library deemed it a Copley, as it was "too good" to be by Benjamin Blyth. Now securely identified as by Blyth, it is part of the collection at the Smithsonian American Art Museum. One of Blyth's most successful portraits, this shows an essentially private and beneficent man, whose portliness is shown in the pull of his buttoned vest.

Bayley, "Copley's early manner," 163
FARL, Blyth, Benjamin 157-3h
Foote, "Blyth," 94
Jeffares, http://www.pastellists.com/Articles/Blyth.pdf
Norton, "Brothers Blyth," 62
Historic New England, glass neg: 3612–B; Baldwin Coolidge Photo 16973

Perkins, Augustus Thorndike, *A sketch of the life and a list of some of the works of John Singleton Copley*, [Boston]: Privately printed, 1873, 81, listed as a Copley, "whereabouts unknown"

Parker and Wheeler, *Copley*, 258

Sibley 9: xii, 549, illus. opp. 550 ("lost portrait")

Smithsonian Institution, National Museum of American Art, Lemmon Object File

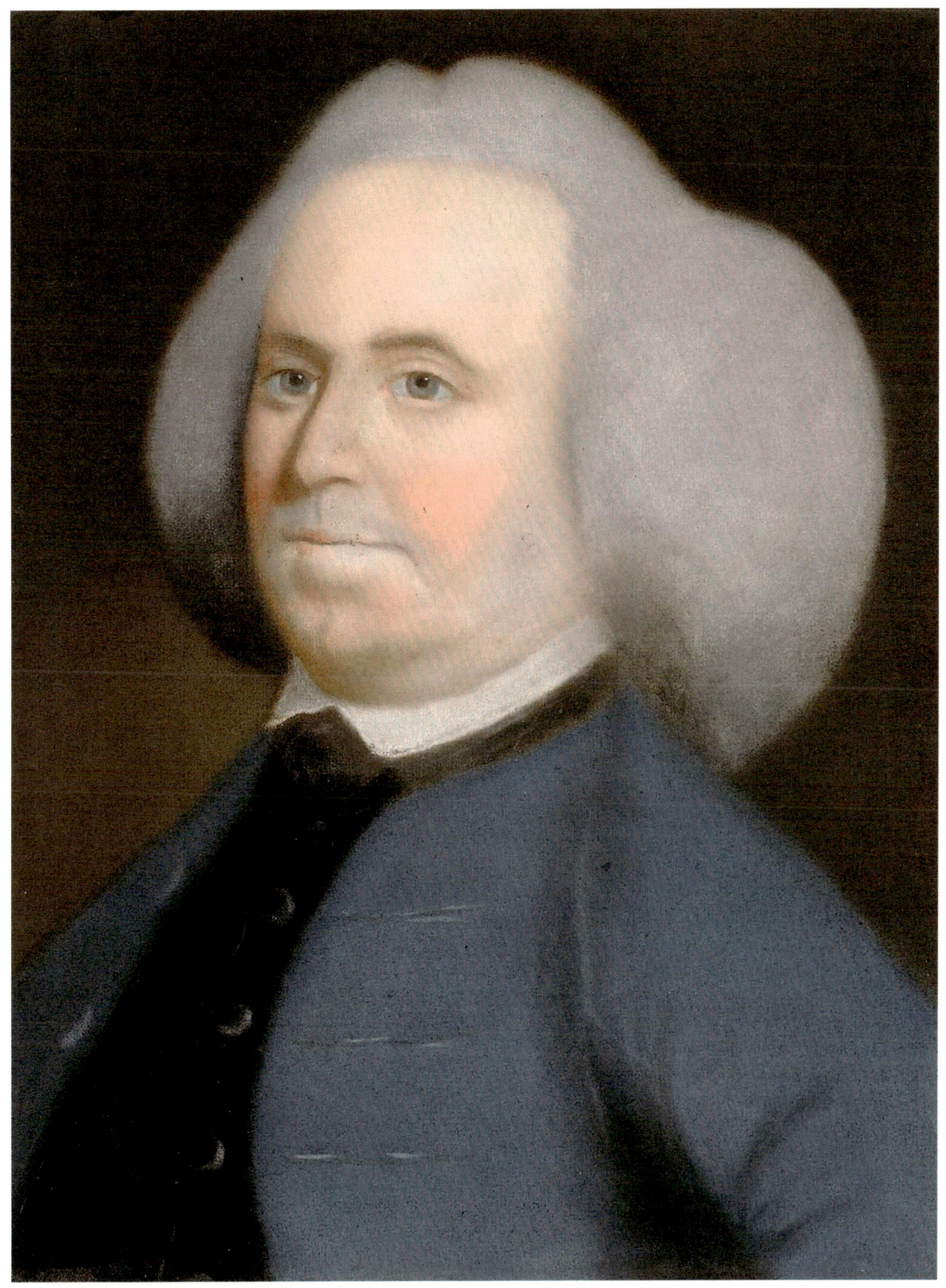

Joseph Lemmon
Pastel by Benjamin Blyth, ca. 1778
Courtesy of the Smithsonian Institution 1977.131, National Museum of American Art

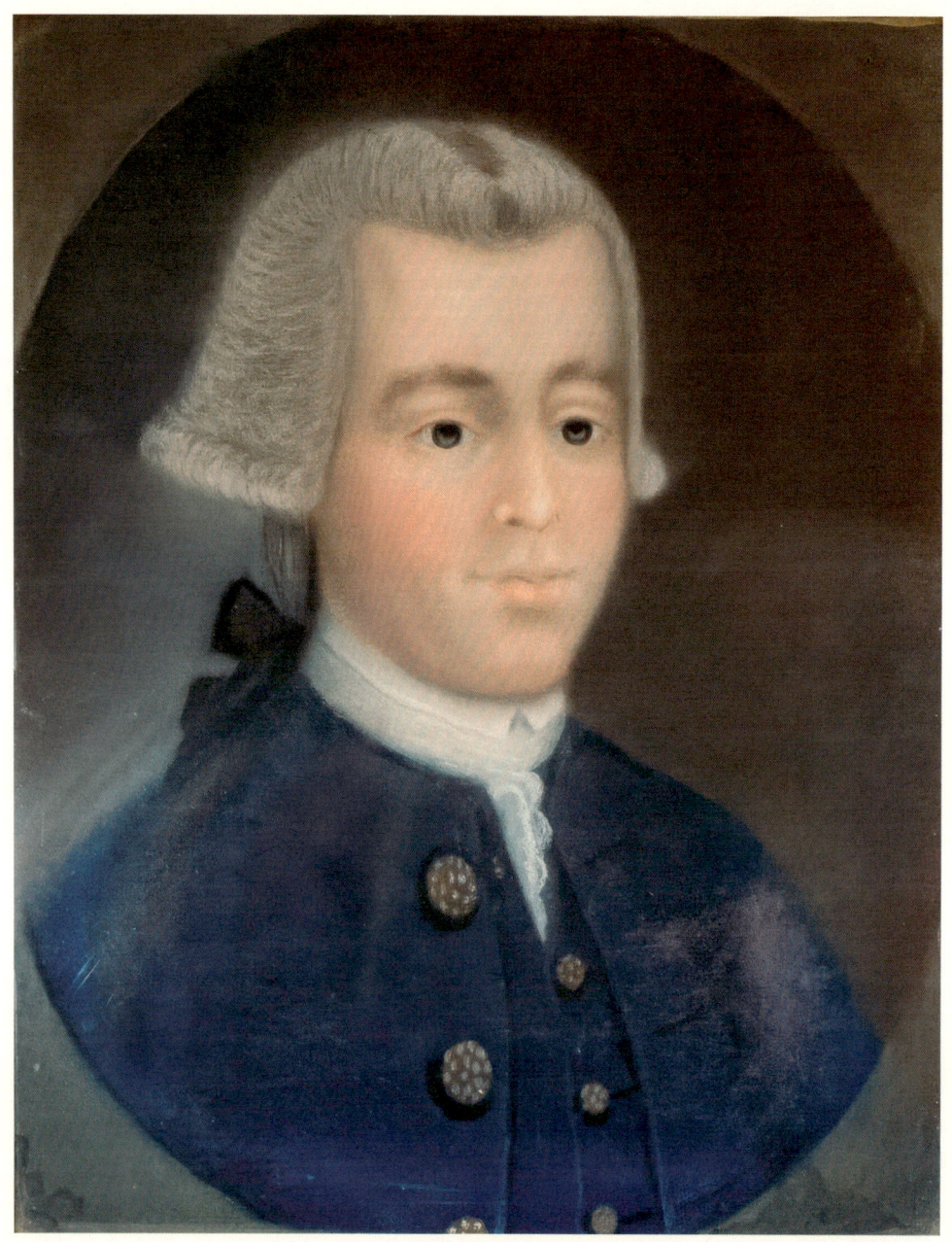

Bela Lincoln
Pastel by Benjamin Blyth (attr.), late 1760s
Courtesy of the Hingham Historical Society
Photograph by Michael C. King

[86]
Bela Lincoln (1734–1773)

Benjamin Blyth (attr.), late 1760s
Pastel, 17⅛ x 14 in. (43.5 x 35.56 cm.), early-19th-c. frame with center hanging hook
Hingham Historical Society, Benjamin Lincoln House

This portrait of Bela Lincoln came to notice when the Benjamin Lincoln House was purchased by the Hingham Historical Society in January 2021. The house contains many of its original furnishings, including manuscripts from Gen. Benjamin Lincoln, its owner during the Revolution and older brother of Bela.

Bela Lincoln was born to the Hon. Benjamin and Elizabeth (Thaxter) Lincoln of Hingham, Massachusetts, on March 11, 1734. He graduated from Harvard College in 1754, in the same class as John Hancock. A contemporary, Nathan Fiske, wrote that little was expected of Lincoln, an opinion that rose from his "natural bashfulness . . . the effects of which were shiness [sic] and silence." But Lincoln maintained an excellent college record, although "sick with the slow Fever." In 1760, chided by his father for avoiding his obligation, he married Hannah Quincy. After studying medicine with Dr. Ezekiel Hersey (Cat. 66), Lincoln practiced for a time and then traveled to Scotland, where he received a Degree in Medicine from Marischal College (now part of the University of Aberdeen) in 1765. Three years later, back at home, he was appointed a Justice of the Peace for Suffolk. Lincoln was sympathetic to the Patriot cause but died before the Revolution began. He practiced medicine in Hingham until he became ill again, retreating with his wife to George's Island in Boston Harbor, where he died at the age of thirty-nine, on July 16, 1773. His widow then married Ebenezer Storer.

Although there are definite signs that the pastel was worked on, it shows several characteristics that suggest it was drawn by Blyth. According to Dierdre Anderson, director of the Hingham Historical Society, the portrait was altered either in the late 1800s by the Samuel T. Crosby family or by Elizabeth Lincoln Scaife Beveridge (1910–1998), who lived in the home from 1940 until her death. Alterations presumably were made in the pastel to the face, especially the mouth, the eyes, and the wig, which obscure the characteristics that would have defined his personality as well as Blyth's stylistic attributes. The background oval may have been added at that time, along with the later, undoubtedly fancier, frame. But the general composition and the jacket with buttons and stock, which show no evidence of overdrawing, clearly point to a Blyth attribution. Whether it was done in Hingham or Salem is unknown at this time, but a pastel of another Hingham resident, Samuel Norton(?) (Cat. 98), also is attributed to Blyth.

Hingham Historical Society, object file
Scottish Notes and Queries. Aberdeen. L Ref Per A A5 SNQ2.I:7
Sibley 13:455–56

[87]

Aaron López (1731–1782)

Benjamin Blyth (attr.), ca. 1778
Pastel, 10½ x 8½ in. (54.9 x 21.6 cm.), oval
Currently unlocated; American Jewish Historical Society, New York; Rose Art Museum;
provenance unknown

Aaron López was a Portuguese Jew who emigrated to Newport, Rhode Island, in 1752 and became its wealthiest resident. He established a lively business, especially in the spermaceti trade, with an attendant candle factory, and with extensive trade in the West Indies. He also underwrote twenty-one slave ships. A leading contributor to building the Touro Synagogue, he laid one of its cornerstones, purchased books for the Redwood Library and Athenaeum, and contributed lumber to help build the college that later relocated to Providence and became Brown University. In 1761, López had applied to the Rhode Island Superior Court to become a naturalized citizen. After being denied three times by the courts, he moved temporarily in April 1762 to nearby Swansea, Massachusetts, to pursue his cause. On October 15, López became what historians believe was the first Jew to become a naturalized citizen of Massachusetts. He died twenty years later. On May 28, 1782, while returning with his family to Newport, he drowned when his horse and carriage fell into a pond. He was buried in the Jewish cemetery in Newport.

An unattributed pastel of López, formerly in the collections of Brandeis University, was reported lost when being moved to the American Jewish Historical Society in New York City. Existing images show an oval with much surface damage and badly wrinkled paper and measurements smaller than those for a typical pastel by Benjamin Blyth. As for the oval, the pastel may have been cut down, especially if the intent was to eliminate areas that had been damaged. The small size might seem another deterrent to attribution, but two rectangular portraits by Benjamin Blyth of the Paines, brother and sister, are nearly the same size, and about ten others by him are only slightly larger. The illustration of López in Seymour Brody's biography of him, based on the missing portrait, is in a rectangular format. The question of when Blyth could have done it hinges on whether López was still in Newport during the Rhode Island Expedition. However, no biography of him makes clear when he moved his family out of Newport to Massachusetts to avoid the conflict.

Of the known Blyth portraits, that of the Reverend Thomas Cary (Cat. 27) presents similar technique and physical attributes. The pastel of López, like that of Cary, also conveys a sober, thoughtful man, one whom Ezra Stiles (1727–1795), Congregational minister in Newport and future president of Yale College, described as "a merchant of the first eminence . . . probably . . . surpassed by no merchant in America."

Aaron Lopez, Wikimedia Foundation, last edited 28 January 2023

American Jewish Historical Society

Brandeis University Archives

Brody, Seymour, "Aaron Lopez—Merchant King who Kept the Revolutionary Army Supplied," *Jewish Heroes and Heroines in America from Colonial Times to 1900.* https://web. archive.org/web/20080517040213/http://www. fau. edu/library/brody7.htm

Gutstein, Morris A., *The Story of the Jews of Newport* (New York: Block Publishing Co., 1936)

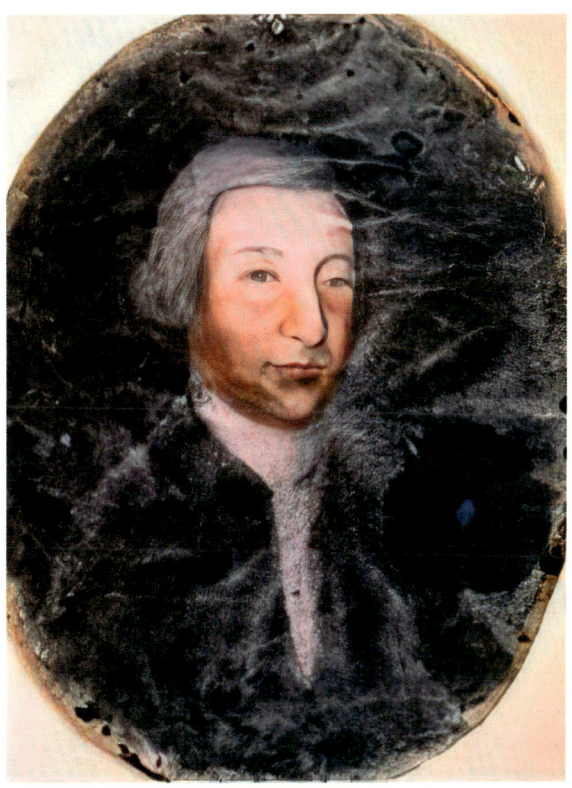

Aaron López
Photoreproduction of a lost pastel attributed to Benjamin
Blyth, ca. 1778
Currently unlocated

[88]

John Lowell (1743–1802)

Artist unknown, early 19th-century, based on a pastel by Benjamin Blyth(?), mid-1770s
Oil, 20⅞ x 16¾ in. (53.02 x 42.5 cm.), period frame
Mr. and Mrs. Edward L. Stone; provenance unknown

John Lowell, Esq. was born in Newburyport on June 17, 1743, to the Reverend John and Sarah Lowell. His father was "a divine of largely scholarly attainments . . . a liberality of mind unusual to the period," according to a history of Newburyport. His son John graduated from Harvard College in 1761 and, as a young lawyer, roomed with Jonathan Jackson, a classmate. The two men vowed never to marry, but both broke their vows on the same day, January 3, 1767. Lowell married Mrs. Sarah Higginson of Salem. At the time, Lowell, the "favorite attorney of exiled loyalists," according to *Sibley's Harvard Graduates*, reasoned that Newburyport's trade with Britain that included the sale of ships precluded joining the embargo. His practice extended into Maine and New Hampshire, and he lived, John Adams noted, "in great splendor" in "the Palace of a Nobleman" on High Street. He was described by the Boston chronicler Annie Haven Thwing as a "Lawyer, Retailer, Gentleman" of Newburyport and Boston.

Despite his early Loyalist leanings, John Lowell was elected to the House of Representatives in May 1776 and soon opened an office in Boston. Later, he took the seat in the Continental Congress that had been held by John Adams. Lowell became Judge of the Court of Appeals for Admiralty Cases in 1782 and a Fellow of the Harvard Corporation in 1784. Very active in charitable and social causes, he was highly lauded at his death.

Lowell's first wife Sarah, daughter of Stephen and Elizabeth (Cabot) Higginson of Salem, died at age twenty-eight on April 17, 1774, leaving him a widower with three young children. Later that year, he married twenty-year-old Susanna Cabot, daughter of Francis and Mary (Fitch) Cabot, but she died in 1777 after a long and painful illness. The following year, Lowell was married for the third time, to Mrs. Rebecca (Russell) Tyng of Dunstable. Notice reached Samuel Curwen in London, who recorded in his diary: "Heard of Rebecca Tyng's marriage to John Lowell of Newburyport."

This oil portrait of Lowell, offered by Christie, Manson & Woods International Inc., in its sale of April 24, 1981, was attributed to "Benjamin Blythe" with a disclaimer on authenticity for good reasons. It is more smoothly modeled than most of Blyth's portraits in oil, and the background details, (the drapery and an obelisk memorializing the death of Lowell's first wife, Sarah) pose a problem. Although the date of Sarah's death on the obelisk is correct, her age was not; she was twenty-eight, not thirty-three. If the painting were done when Lowell was still alive, it presumably would have had the correct death date for his wife. However, the composition and the draftsmanship of the face bespeak Blyth, and the age of the sitter dates the portrayal to the mid-1770s. The likely possibility is that the oil was based on a pastel by Blyth and that the obelisk, along with the background drapery, may have been added when the oil was painted. Provenance would help solve the question, but a valid surmise is that it was done for one of the children by his first marriage. According to a recent owner, the oil was reframed at some point and may have had some restorative repainting.

A later oil portrait by John Johnston in the Harvard Art Museums shows the same benevolent person as depicted by Blyth. A miniature of Lowell by Charles Willson Peale, in the Museum of Fine Arts, Boston, shows the same calm demeanor but Lowell is older, heavier, with white hair.

Bentley 1:1

Butterfield, *Adams Correspondence*, 1:114

Christie's catalogue, *American Paintings, Drawings, and Sculpture of the 18th, 19th, and 20th Centuries*, April 24, 1981, Lot 3

Curwen diary, April 8, 1778, 185

Eldred Auction Gallery sale July 27, 2022, not sold

PEM, Phillips Library, Orne, Timothy, interleaved almanacs

Sibley 14:650-64

Smith, Mrs. E. Vale, *History of Newburyport*, (1854) 2:706

Thwing Collection, *Boston, 1630–1822*, 12542

Steward, Scott and Christopher Child, *The Descendants of Judge John Lowell* (Newbury Street Press, 2010), illus. on dust jacket

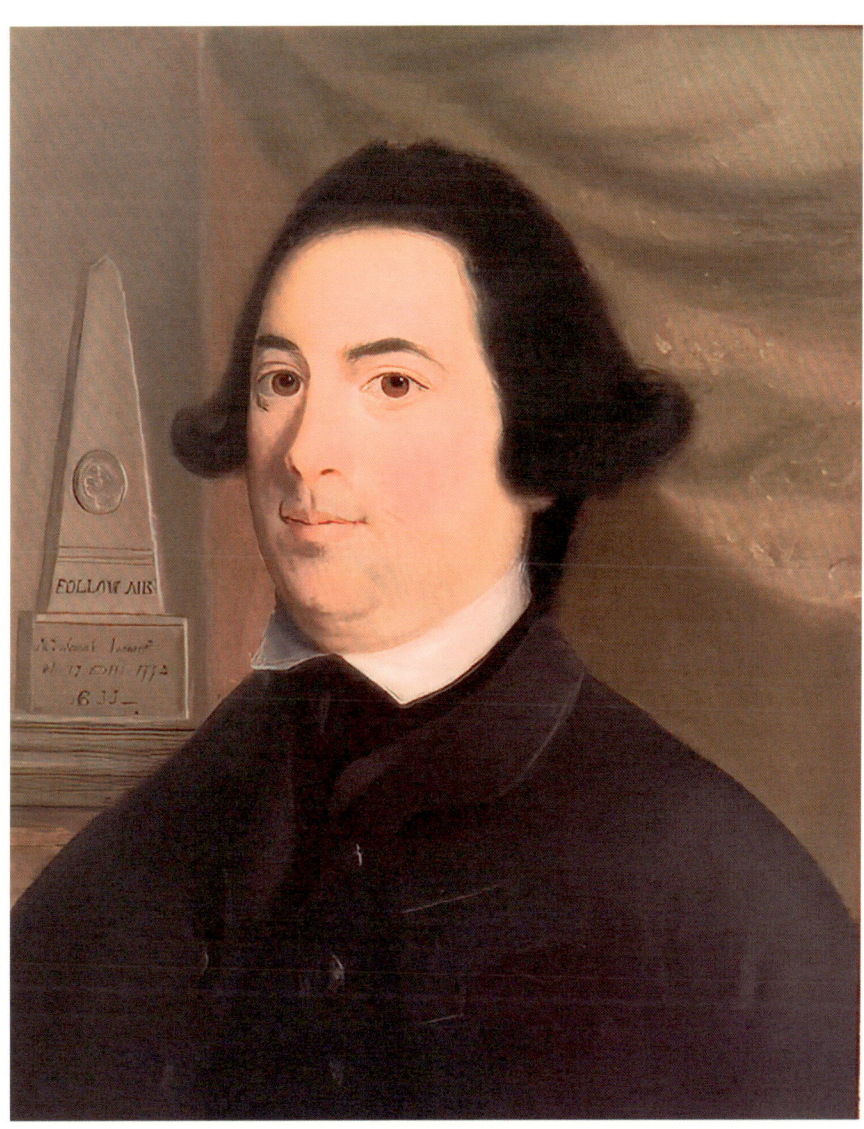

John Lowell
Oil by an anonymous artist, based on a lost pastel by Benjamin Blyth, mid-1770s
Collection of Mr. and Mrs. Edward L. Stone
Photograph by Eldred Auction Gallery

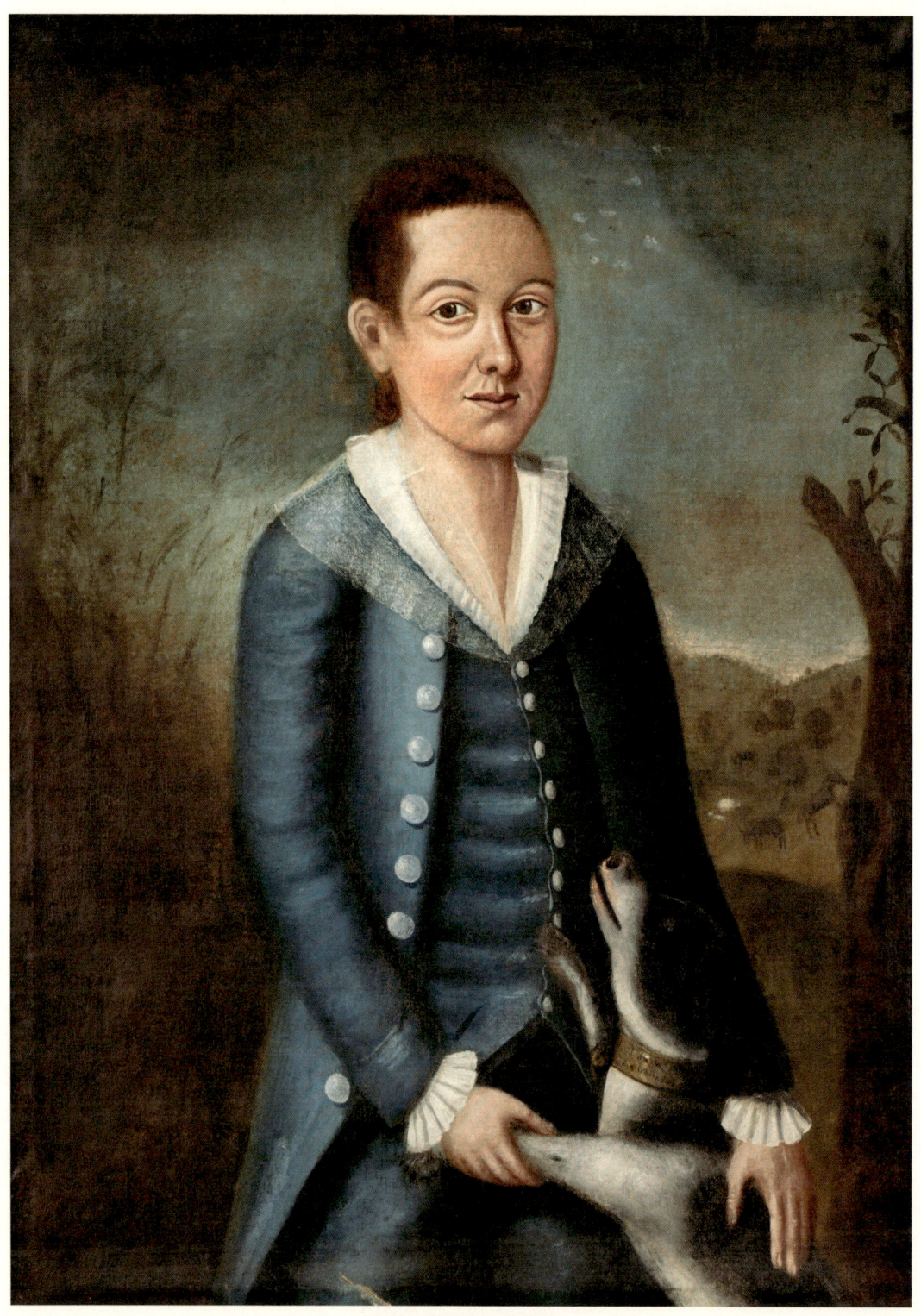

William Luscomb (?)
Oil painting by Benjamin Blyth, with Samuel Blyth? ca. 1782–83
Courtesy of the Peabody Essex Museum 101888, gift of Mrs. Francis H. Lee, 1908

[89]

William Luscomb(?) (1774–1820)

Benjamin Blyth (attr., with Samuel Blyth?), ca. 1782–3
Oil on linen, 37¾ x 27½ in., incl. contemporary frame
Peabody Essex Museum 101888, gift of Mrs. Francis H. Lee, gift of Mrs. Henry R. Luscomb, 1908

The collar inscription on this young boy's attentive dog reads: "I am Wᵐ Lu[worn away]'s dog. Whose dog are you?" It is a play on the Alexander Pope couplet, "I am His Highness's dog at Kew. Pray tell me, Sir, whose dog are *you*?" The William Luscomb most likely portrayed was baptized at The North Church, Salem, on April 17, 1774. He was the son of William and Susannah (Cook) Luscomb, who took out a certificate of marriage on January 20, 1773. The family were active members of the church. According to the Reverend William Bentley's diary, "The alterations under the pulpit undertaken this week by Mʳ Ward, & the Painting by Mʳ Liscombe."

William III became a painter. In 1794, he married Mehitabel Ward, a daughter of Richard and Mehitable [*sic*] (Curwen) Ward (Cat. 127). The first recorded children were triplets, born on January 16, 1800. One was a William, the fifth generation of that name. His death is not recorded, but another William was born the following year. There were three more children, all girls. William, the subject of this portrait, died of consumption at age forty-six, on February 4, 1820.

Although the official record cites the donor as Francis H. Lee, in 1908, the year of his death, the entry in the *EIHC* "Catalogue of Portraits...", published in several volumes in the 1930s, gives the inscription in full, citing the assumed identity of the subject as "[Luscomb's?]," and that the portrait was given to the Essex Institute by Henry R. Luscomb's widow the year after his death in 1907. Although there is now a family name rather than simply "Boy with dog," there are no parents recorded for the birth of his father, Henry, in 1813, so the family connection remains unresolved.

When William's portrait was painted, he was probably about eight or nine. He is dressed very fashionably, with the wide lace-edged gossamer collar worn beginning in the late 1770s by young boys from well-off families, like the one worn by Ezekiel Hersey Derby in his pastel portrait by Blyth (Cat. 45). The Luscomb portrait, however, contains several elements that are more closely associated with Samuel Blyth: the linearity of details of the face, the gnarled tree trunk framing the side of the painting, the cartoon-like drawings of horses scattered randomly in the field in the background, and the witticism written on the dog's collar. Perhaps it was begun by Benjamin and finished by Samuel. Either brother might have known of Joseph Badger's portrait of young Jeremiah Belknap for his depiction of William's dog, in a similar stance and not very furry. William's pet seems even more hairless, as Benjamin Blyth depicted cats and dogs. Nonetheless, the pet clearly adores his owner. The viewer knows whose dog *he* was.

Bentley 1: xlii, 49, 375
EIHC 73:78. cat 369, "Boy with Dog" in "Unknown Portraits"
Norton, "Brothers Blyth" (under "Lemon/Lewis"), 62

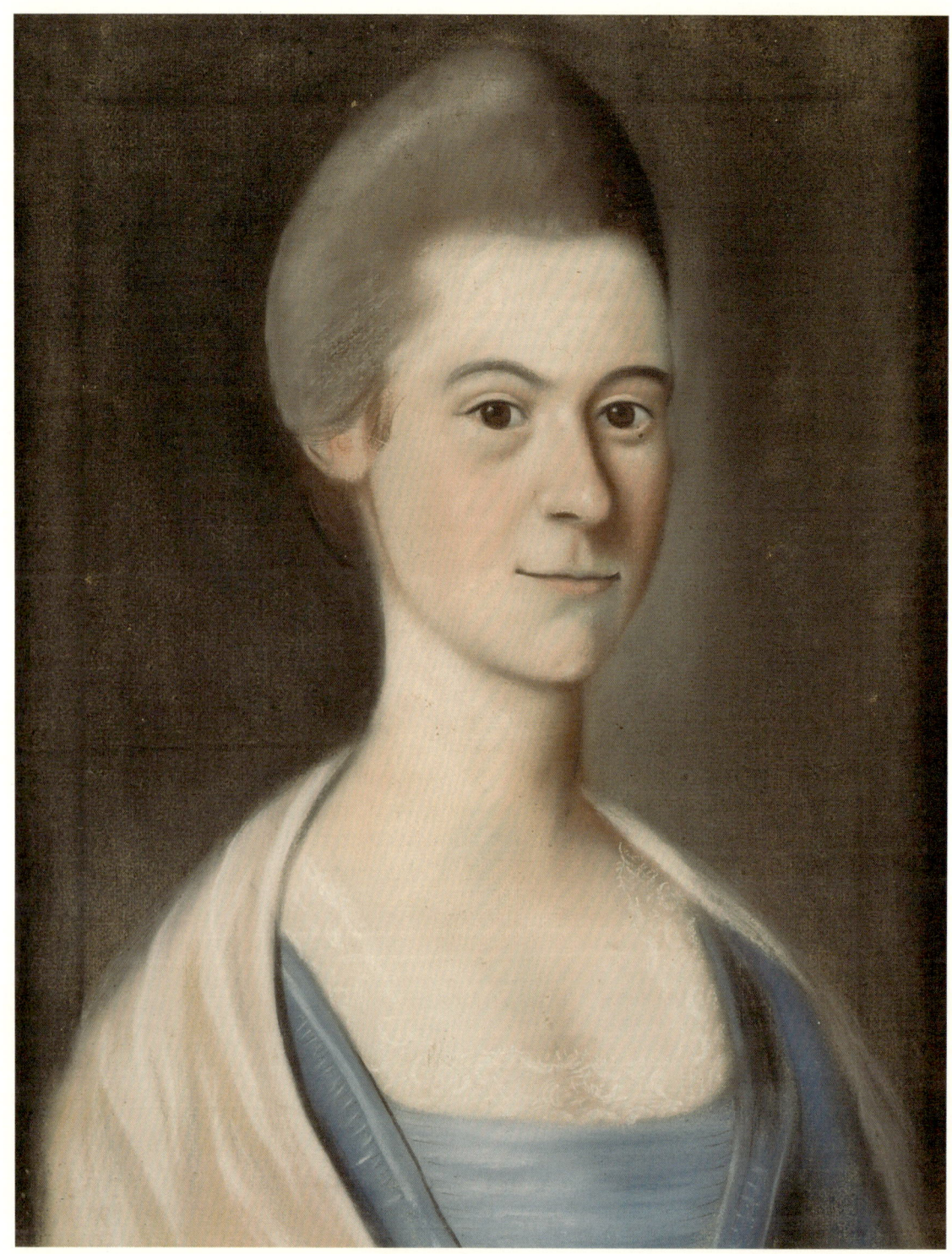

Eunice Diman Mason
Pastel by Benjamin Blyth, probably 1774
Courtesy of the Massachusetts Historical Society Artwork 01. 141, gift of Mrs. Irving W. Bailey
(Helen Diman Harwood), 1972

[90]

Eunice Diman Mason (1752–1796)

Benjamin Blyth, probably 1774
Pastel on paper mounted on linen, 19½ x 15⅜ in. (49.3 x 39 cm.), Samuel Blyth frame
Massachusetts Historical Society Artwork 01.141, gift of Mrs. Irving W. Bailey (Helen Diman Harwood), 1972;
James Diman Green; Harriet Haraden Ropes; Haraden family

Eunice's birth, like the other two daughters and two sons born to the Reverend James Diman, minister of the Second (East) Church in Salem, is not recorded in Salem Vital Records. However, an early label on the back of the portrait states that Eunice was born on January 9, 1752. Her mother was Mary Orne, from a prominent family in Salem and Marblehead. Eunice married Thomas Mason on April 12, 1774, and after his death, she married Jonathan Haraden in 1782. Their house is illustrated in the Bowditch *Pickering Genealogy*. There were no children recorded from either marriage. She died on November 12, 1796, at forty-four, from "hectic," in nineteenth-century medical usage, a fever usually accompanying tuberculosis. Her husband, Capt. Jonathan, "a distinguished naval commander," also died of "hectic" in 1803, at age fifty-nine.

Local vital records were compiled from churches and family Bible records, so the fact that Eunice's father withheld record books in his feud with his church and the Reverend William Bentley, engaged to supplant him, might be the explanation for the absence of Diman births. Diman, a conservative Congregationalist, was a controversial figure in Salem. "Even his daughters now openly consorted socially with his bitterest opponents, with whom he was not on speaking terms," wrote Bentley. When Eunice's sister Lois was married on June 10, 1789, Bentley mentioned the Diman house for sale, adding "the other Daughter [Eunice], was reconciled before the others removed." In turn, in 1796, after the sisters and families left Bentley's congregation, he wrote, "gone among those who happen to ask them to dine, of whatever persuasion."

As no other member of the Diman family evidently was drawn by Blyth, it is presumed that her portrait and the one of her first husband, Thomas Mason, were done around the time of their marriage. Also, they face each other and are to the same scale. So, the former pastel title of Eunice Diman has been changed to reflect this. It depicts a very sympathetic, amiable, pert woman in her early twenties. This portrait, like that of her first husband, can be characterized as one of Blyth's sketchier ones, yet such touches as the delicacy of the lace bordering her "handkerchief" (shawl) and her piercing dark brown eyes are admirably portrayed. The portrait is at the Massachusetts Historical Society, and that of her husband Thomas Mason, Jr., also unfinished, is in the collections of the Peabody Essex Museum.

Bentley 1:26, 106–7; 2:205

Bowditch, *Pickering Genealogy*, xx, betw. 196–97, 198–99

Norton, "Brothers Blyth," 62

Oliver, *Portraits in the Massachusetts Historical Society,* illus. 32–33

Sibley 7/8:699

[91]

Thomas Mason (1750–1781/2)

Benjamin Blyth, probably 1774
Pastel on paper mounted on fabric, 20½ x 16½ (52 x 41.25 cm.), Samuel Blyth frame
Peabody Essex Museum 2750, gift of Mary Jane Scobie, 1890

Thomas Mason, son of Capt. Thomas and Abigail (Emmerton) Mason, was baptized at Salem's Tabernacle Church on April 8, 1750. Nothing is found on Thomas's mother Abigail (Emmerton)—although it was a later Emmerton, James A., who compiled a thorough book on eighteenth-century baptisms in Salem from "hitherto unpublished" sources in 1886. Thomas's father, Capt. Thomas Mason, commanded the brigantine *Salem* that "sailed for many years to the West Indies" for the Cabot brothers and Timothy Orne.

Thomas Mason, Jr. married Eunice Diman (Cat. 90), daughter of the Reverend James Diman of the Second Church, on April 12, 1774. They had no children. Thomas, reportedly lost at sea in late 1781 at age thirty-one, died intestate and insolvent. At the request of his widow, his father became administrator for his son's estate. He outlived his son by twenty years, and at his death, Bentley noted, "he amassed a great estate, which he has chiefly spent in acts of kindness to his dependent relatives, & to the needy in general. His children died young." The Mason house was on Essex Street, presumably where the Gideon Tucker House is now and across from the Peabody Essex Museum's John Tucker Daland House.

The portraits of Eunice and Thomas Mason complement each other and were probably done at the time of their marriage. These portraits are now in separate collections, his at the Peabody Essex Museum, hers at the Massachusetts Historical Society. Given the similarity in handwriting to a letter from Eunice Mason in the probate record of her husband's death, she probably wrote the inscription "Thomas Mason of Salem" on the back of the portrait. It is one of the few known Blyth pastels that seems unfinished; black crayon lines outline areas that would have been covered with pastel, and the differing blues of the jacket have not been resolved. In Blyth's depiction, Mason seems gentle and beneficent and a bit more sober minded than his wife.

Bentley, 2:378, 3:373
EIHC 71:266, Cat. 190, "unknown artist"
Essex County Probate Record 17979
Foote, "Blyth," 94–95
Jeffares, http://www.pastellists.com/Articles/Blyth.pdf
Norton, "Brothers Blyth," 62
Phillips, *Salem . . . 18th C.*, 246
Visitor's Guide to Salem (1895), "Merchant. Pastel," 195

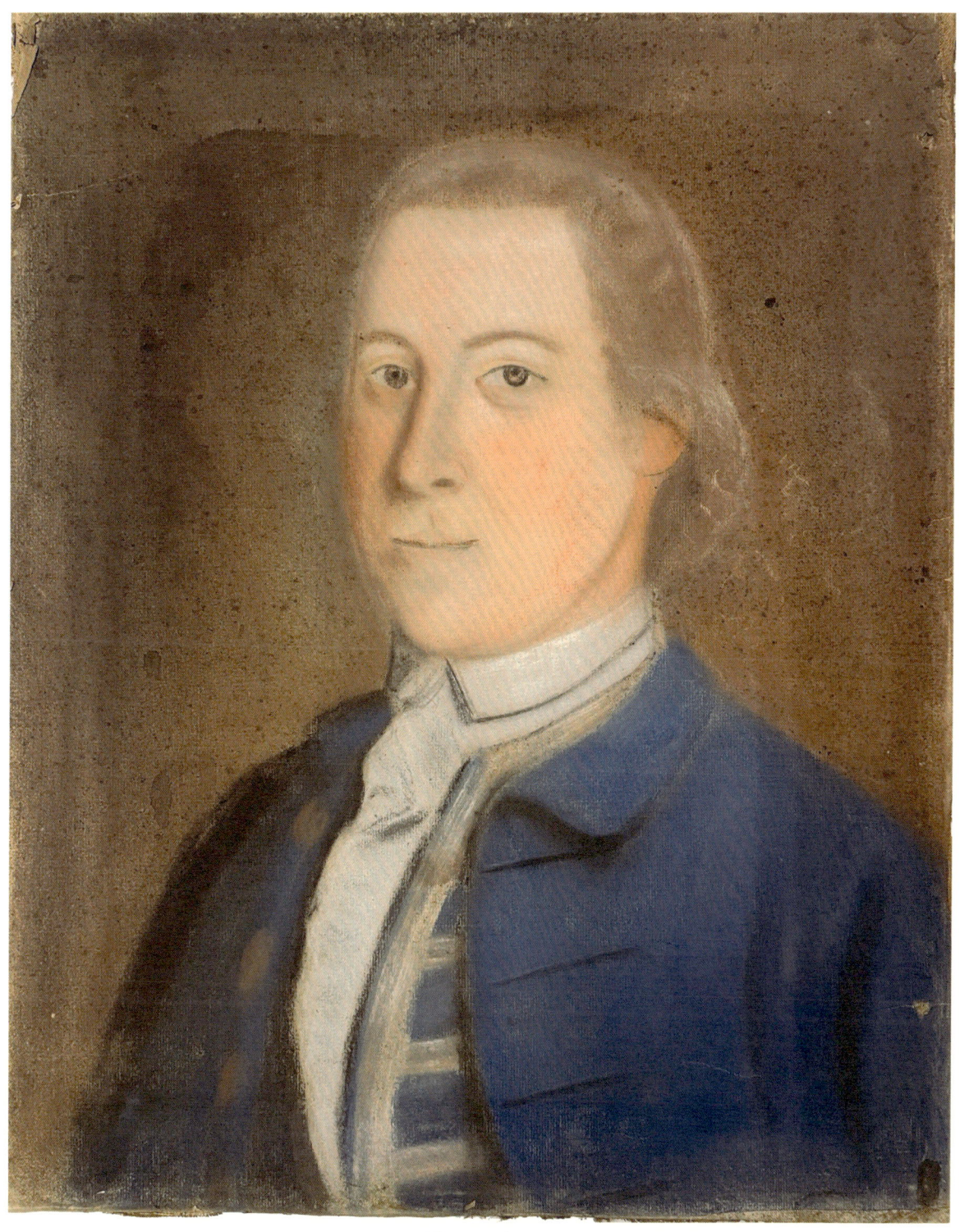

Thomas Mason
Pastel by Benjamin Blyth, probably 1774
Courtesy of the Peabody Essex Museum 2,750, gift of Mary Jane Scobie, 1890

[92]

Thomas Melville (1751–1832)

Benjamin Blyth, ca. 1778
Pastel on paper mounted on canvas, 23½ x 17¾ in. (59.7 x 45 cm.), Hogarth-type frame
Revolutionary Spaces 1914.0002.001A, gift of John S. Damrell, Charles S. Damrell, 1914

Thomas Melville (Melvill) was the only known member of the Boston Tea Party drawn by Blyth. It was assumed that he had participated in the Boston Tea party, *Sibley's Harvard Graduates* noted, "because the family found that commodity in his shoes the next morning." Melville, then "a young radical," was an aide to Gen. Joseph Warren (Cat. 130), one of Boston's most prominent merchants, and at his death at age eighty-one, the firemen's organization, which he headed for twenty-five years, held a thirty-day mourning period.

Melville's father Allan, who emigrated from Fife, Scotland, sold shoes and stockings on Dyer's Wharf in Boston. In 1749, he married Jean/Jane Cargill in the Presbyterian Church, and their only child, Thomas Jr., was born on January 16, 1751. Thomas's mother died in 1759, and his father died two years later, so Thomas was brought up by his grandmother. Intending to follow in the footsteps of his Presbyterian minister grandfather, he graduated in 1769 from the College of New Jersey (later, Princeton).

Melville didn't pursue the ministry after all, but began accumulating property and in 1774 married Priscilla Scollay, of a prominent Boston family. They moved to a brick house on Green Street. He was awarded an honorary degree "*ad eundem*" from Harvard College and made an honorary member of its class of 1769. By then, he was known as "Gentleman." At first a colonial naval officer, Melville became an early patriot, joining the Sons of Liberty, the new Freemasons in 1772, and the Long Room Club. "On May 10, 1776, he was commissioned a captain of artillery and took great pleasure in firing the parting shots from Nantasket at the last British ships to leave." He also served in the Rhode Island Campaign and was part owner of the privateer *Speedwell*, among other vessels. After the American Revolution, Samuel Adams helped him secure the post of Collector of Excise and Impost and later, Surveyor of the Port of Boston. Melville also was a state representative, a founder of Massachusetts General Hospital, and a president of the Massachusetts Charitable Society. By 1798, he was titled "Esquire," confirming the observation in *Sibley's* that "his skill in the art of political survival was remarkable." He died in 1832 and along with his wife, who died the following April, was buried in the Melville Tomb in Copp's Hill Burial Ground.

For many years his portrait was attributed to Copley, although "authorities at the Museum of Fine Arts" in 1936—presumably Barbara Parker and Anne Wheeler—disputed it. Copley had left Boston for England before the sitter attained the presumed age in the portrait, and their politics were diametrically opposed. Third, characteristics of Blyth include the askew perspective of the far eye, the bland treatment of the hair, and the concentration on character. This pastel, as with so many others by Blyth, sustained damage—in this case, water, and insect droppings—and in

1973 was conserved but "not up to modern standards," according to current staff at Revolutionary Spaces (formerly the Bostonian Society).

Melville's red sash connotes his standing as an officer in the American Revolution; the artist John Trumbull noted, "however worn and ragged and dirty his [i. e., an officer's] other clothing might be, when this was thrown over it, he was in elegant uniform." A handsome man known for being well-dressed, Melville also appears comfortably self-assured. Indeed, although damaged, this is one of Blyth's best pastel portraits, done, like that of John Gibaut, at the height of his abilities with the medium. Revolutionary Spaces owns two other oil portraits of Melville, one as a youth, probably by Joseph Badger, and a later one by Francis Alexander.

Melville was a grandfather of American author Herman Melville (1819–1891).

Foote, "Blyth," 95–96

Revolutionary Spaces, object file

Sibley 17:115, 184-6

Thwing Collection (with some errors)

Trumbull, quoted in Staples and Shaw, *Clothing through American History*, 345-46.

Wehle, *American Miniatures*, 25, pl. 9

WPA 1430, attributed to Copley

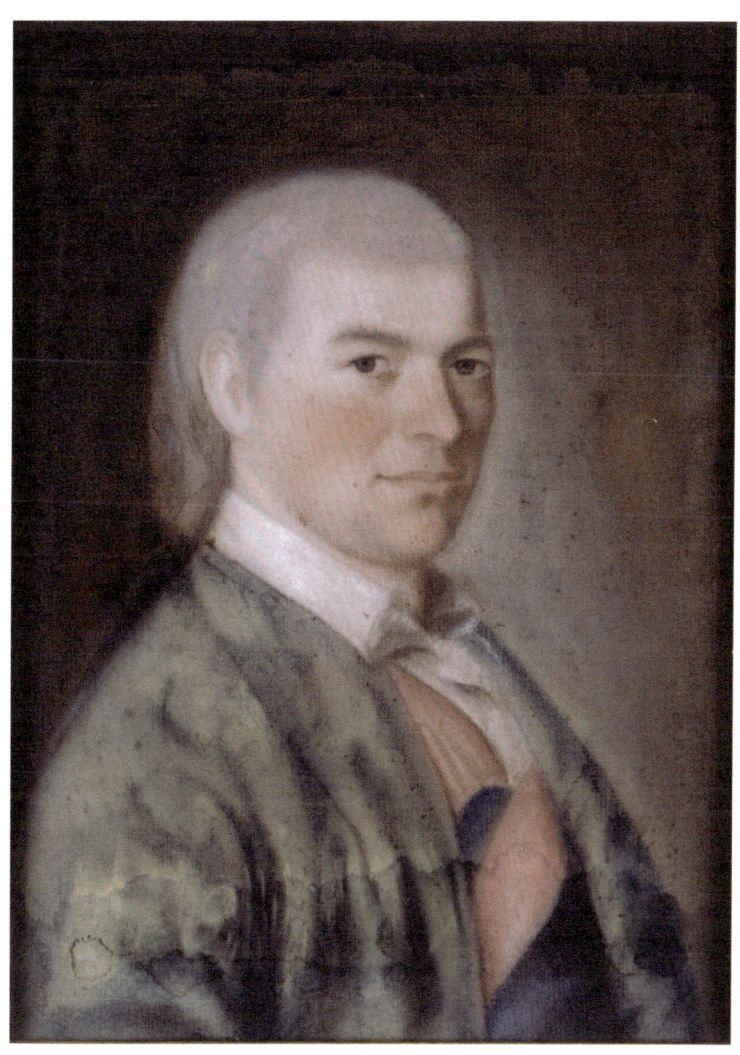

Thomas Melville
Pastel by Benjamin Blyth, ca. 1778
Courtesy of Revolutionary Spaces 1914.0002.001A, gift of John S. Damrell, Charles S. Damrell, 1914

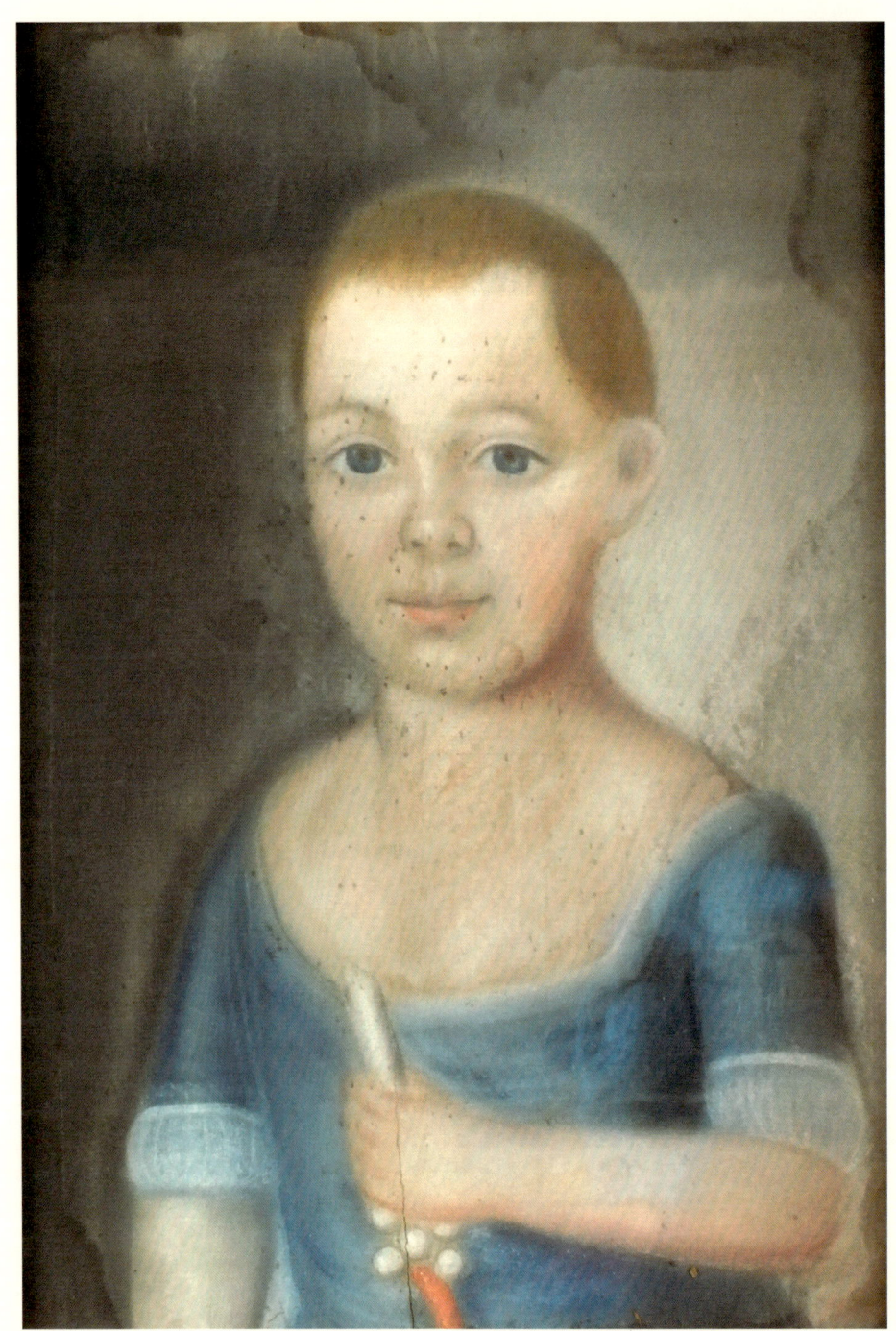

William Messervy
Pastel by Benjamin, probably 1783
Courtesy of the Peabody Essex Museum 100271, gift of George P. Messervy, 1904

[93]

William Messervy (1780–1852)

Benjamin Blyth, probably 1783
Pastel on paper mounted on canvas, 15½ x 11 in. *(37.5 x 25.9 cm.)*, Hogarth-type frame
Peabody Essex Museum 100271, gift of George P. Messervy, 1904

The Peabody Essex Museum owns two portraits of William Messervy. The earlier first portrait, painted when Messervy was two to three years old, is this pastel by Benjamin Blyth. The other is an oil by an unknown artist, painted when Messervy was middle-aged. The entry states that he was born "about 1780" to William and Hannah Messervy. This is the only known information on William's parents. The family belonged to St. Peter's Church, for which there are few records during the Revolution because the church was closed.

In 1810, Messervy married Elizabeth Passarow, daughter of a glass manufacturer of Boston and member of King's Chapel. They lived at 13 South Street in Salem. "From the very first, Capt. Messervy proved himself a skillful and adventurous navigator," reads the *EIHC* entry for the oil portrait. During the War of 1812, his brig *Coromandel* was captured, but he retook it and returned to Salem; and the *Hunter* was chased by privateers on the way to Havana, but he evaded them "by superior sailing." He also commanded the *Restitution* on several foreign voyages between 1815 and 1817. William and Elizabeth (Eliza) gave their names to their son and a daughter; the son became mayor of Salem, but Eliza died in 1834. William died on August 11, 1852, at "age 71, 11 mo. 29 da"; indicating that he was born in August 1780.

Although the portrait was classified by the former Essex Institute as by an unknown artist, it clearly is by Benjamin Blyth; one of the most charming of the Blyth child portraits, it seems too well done to have been drawn by Samuel. The frame also may not have been made by him. William is dressed very fashionably. His wide lace-edged gossamer collar, like the one worn by Ezekiel Hersey Derby in his portrait by Blyth (Cat. 45), was popular for young boys from well-off families worn beginning in the late 1770s.

Bentley 1:12

EIHC 71:319–20, cat. 192, "unknown artist"

Foote, "Blyth," 75, 97

Jeffares, http://www.pastellists.com/Articles/Blyth.pdf

Norton, "Blyth," 62

Tapley, 43

WPA 1435, artist unknown

[94]

Benjamin Moses (1737–1803)

Benjamin Blyth; signed "B. Blyth pinx^t 1781," middle right
Oil on canvas, 37 x 27 in. (93.98 x 68.58 cm.)
Peabody Essex Museum 121030, purchase from Miss Alice R. Meek, 1931

As the only known oil signed and dated by Benjamin Blyth, the portrait of Benjamin Moses and the companion portrait of his wife Sarah and child Betsy have had to serve as the baseline for other attributions. There are some caveats, however, related to earlier mistakes and omissions: in the *Catalogue of the Portraits of Essex Institute* published serially in the mid-1930s, Benjamin and Sarah Moses (Cats. 94, 95) were listed as "anonymous" and given the incorrect date of 1791. Nonetheless, they are two of the only four examples of portraits by Blyth that the Institute purchased; the others are the miniatures of Elias Hasket and Elizabeth Derby.

Benjamin Moses, son of Capt. Eleasar and Mary (Henderson), was baptized on February 6, 1737. His father was a sailmaker who was a "welcome man in all social clubs" and "a well known attender upon the King's Customs and a celebrated Devourer of food of all kinds &c, . . ." wrote the Reverend William Bentley. Benjamin, who originally followed his father into sailmaking, became a major shipowner during the American Revolution, heading an extensive privateering coastal trade between Salem and Boston, with the *Creature* (previously the *Oliver Cromwell*), and later, was Master of the *Indian*. He was admitted as a member of the Essex Lodge on April 9, 1779.

On June 7, 1761, he married Sarah Caryll (Carroll, Cariel), and they had twelve children, including Sarah ("Sally") (Cat. 96). Their eldest son Benjamin died at age thirty-five on his passage from Cadiz to New York in early 1800. Although the Moses family was not members of his parish, Bentley attended the funeral of one of their grandsons, aged fourteen months, in 1787. By 1814, on the death of another, Samuel Moses, age twenty-nine, Bentley noted, "The large family of Moses has now disappeared from Salem & those who remain are scattered."

Nina Fletcher Little was responsible for ascertaining the names of the sitters and the correct date of execution. She described the companion portraits as "large and handsome. . . . While they are obviously lacking in many elements of professional skill, they compensate for this in personality and vigor." The Frick Art Reference Library photograph, made in the 1940s, shows the painting in its original condition, before it was cleaned and overpainted, somewhat crudely (See p. 69).

Benjamin Moses, in the tradition of so many portraits of leading figures of eighteenth-century New England, shows pride in his success. In the background a ship under sail alludes to his livelihood.

Bentley 1:28, 75, 370–71; 4:271
Little, 52–53
EIHC 73:80, cat. 382, "Man" in "Unknown Portraits"; 5:130
Hadley, *Essex Lodge*

FARL, Blyth, Benjamin 121-6a

Foote, "Blyth," 75, 97

Museum of Fine Arts, Boston, exhibition *Paintings by New England Provincial Artists 1775–1800*, 1976

Norton, "Brothers Blyth," 63

Oliver, *Windows on the Past*, illus. 18

Ropes, James Esq., manuscript

Salem Gazette, July 29, 1803

WPA 2563, under Unidentified: Man, 1791

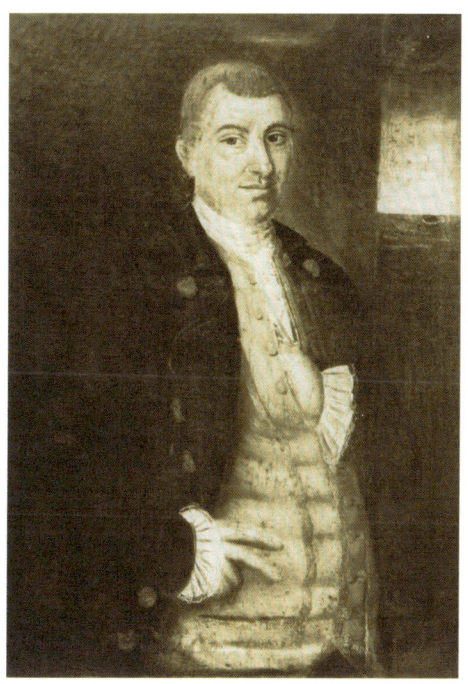

Benjamin Moses
Photograph of oil painting by Benjamin Blyth,
prior to restoration
Courtesy Frick Art Reference Library, Blyth,
Benjamin 121-6a

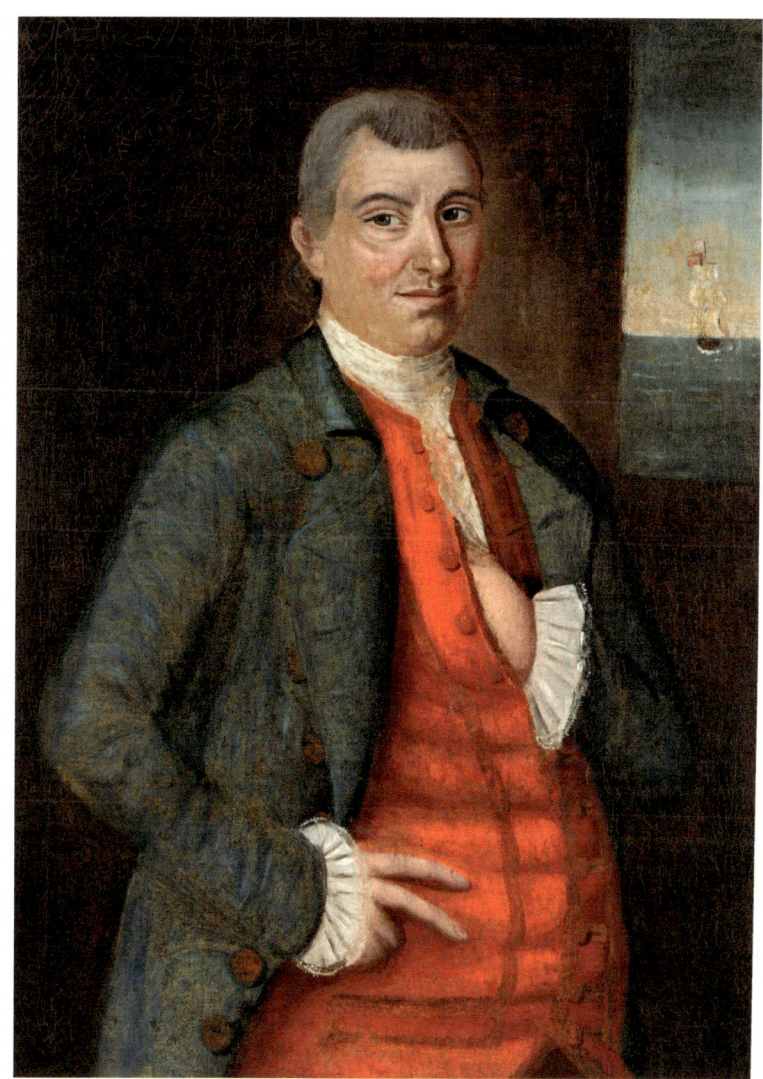

Benjamin Moses
Oil p;ainting by Benjamin Blyth, signed and dated 1781
Courtesy of the Peabody Essex Museum 121030,
purchase from Miss Alice R. Meek, 1931

[95]

Sarah Moses (1734–1835) *& Betsy* (1780–1851)

Benjamin Blyth, 1781
Oil on canvas, 37 x 27 in. (93.98 x 68.58 cm.)
Peabody Essex Museum 121031, purchase from Miss Alice Meek, 1931

The identity of Sarah Moses and her daughter Betsy, like that of her husband, also was not known when the collection was published in the *Catalogue of the Portraits of Essex Institute,* published serially in the mid-1930s. Sarah Caryll's birthdate eludes confirmation, but she probably was born in Middleton to John and Rebeckah Cariel on March 20, 1734. She married Benjamin Moses of Salem in 1761. The birth records for children of Benjamin are not precise enough to determine the number of children that preceded Betsy, who was born on December 1, 1780, but at any event, there is no "Rebecca," the name that Foote used in his description. Three of their children had names that also were those of Sarah's sisters, Mary, Betsy, and Susannah, and two were twins, as were two of her siblings.

Their first child Benjamin, born in 1763, died as an infant. A set of twins born in 1766 were followed by six more children. The record for Betsy's birth on December 1, 1780, confirms that the family transferred their church allegiance from the First Parish in Salem to the Anglican church of St. Peter's.

Betsy married Benjamin Hale, a mariner, on October 9, 1806. She lost both her husband and her first-born son, Benjamin, in foreign ports: her husband, second officer of the ship *Two Brothers,* at Batavia, on August 5, 1823, at age forty-five, and her son, a seaman on board *Sumatra,* at Canton, in August 1828, at age twenty-one. By 1830, the census shows a household headed by Sarah Moses that included two other women, elderly and middle-aged, and a young boy, ten to fifteen years old. She presumably was the great-grandmother, and Betsy the widowed daughter, then aged forty-nine.

According to the *Salem Gazette,* Sarah, widow of Benjamin, having outlived many of her children died, on Nov. 8, 1835, "a. 97 y. 6 mo." Betsy, who never remarried, died of cancer on May 14, 1851.

This portrait and that of Sarah's husband Benjamin were heavily touched up sometime before 1957. They were exhibited in *Paintings by New England Provincial Artists 1775–1800* (1976). The Museum of Fine Arts, Boston restored the paintings again for a second exhibition, *Little by Little,* featuring the collection of Nina Fletcher Little and Bertram K. Little in 1984.

EIHC 5:29; 73:80, cat. 383, "Woman holding child" in "Unknown Portraits"

Essex County Probate record 12082

FARL, Blyth, Benjamin 124-6a

Foote, "Blyth," 75, 97–98 ("Mrs. Benjamin Moses and Child")

Little, Nina Fletcher, *Little by Little*

Norton, "Brothers Blyth," 63

Oliver, *Windows on the Past*, illus. 19

Salem Census, 1830

WPA 2564, as Unidentified: Woman holding child

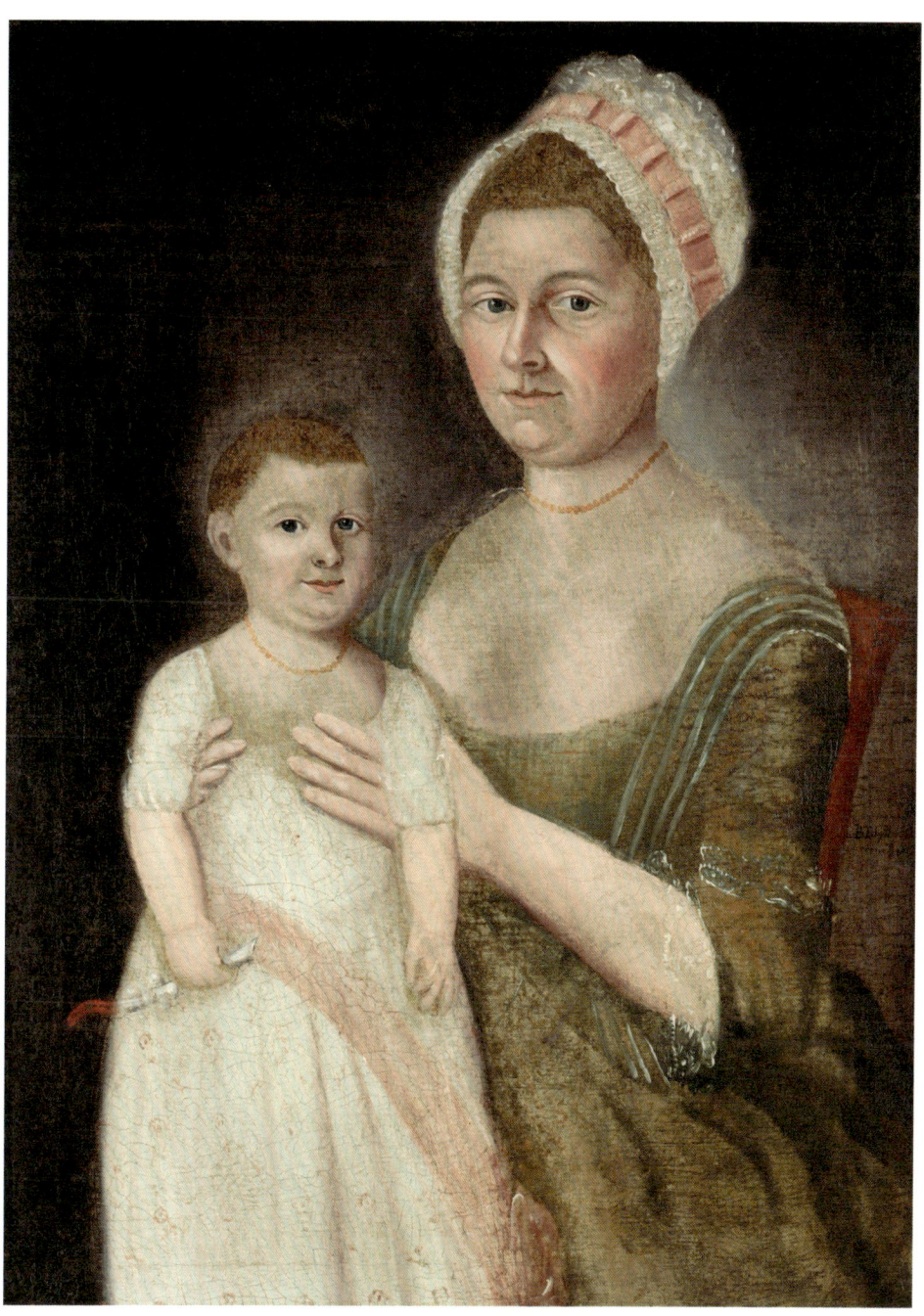

Sarah and Betsy Moses
Oil painting by Benjamin Blyth, 1781
Courtesy of the Peabody Essex Museum 121031, purchase from Miss Alice Meek, 1931

[96]

Sarah "Sally" Moses (1769–1840)

Benjamin Blyth, probably 1781
Pastel on paper mounted on linen, 22½ x 18 in. (57.2 x 45.7 cm.), Samuel Blyth frame
Collection of the Dennis family; Moses/Martin/Dalton families

This of a winsome child portrayed with a pet bird descended through the Dalton and Dennis families of Salem, who believed it to be of Eleazer Dalton. But the pastel has the hallmarks of work by Benjamin Blyth. Eleazer was born in 1797, long after Blyth had left Salem. Moreover, the clothing, a dress trimmed with lace, indicates that the child is a girl, probably between ten and twelve years old.

A better case can be made for the subject being Eleazer's mother, Sarah "Sally" Moses. Although the newspaper account of her death in 1840 indicated that she was born in 1756, there is only one Sarah Moses born between 1750 and 1780 in Salem Vital Records, "d.[aughter] Benjamin, bp. Sept. 3, 1769." She would have been ten to twelve years old, the age of the child in the portrait; this coincides with the portraits of her father Benjamin and of her mother, Sarah Moses with baby Betsy (Cats. 94, 95), painted by Blyth in 1781.

Babies and children drawn by Blyth had distinctive facial details, and Betsy's features are almost identical to her sister's. Mother and the two girls all wear thin gold chain necklaces. Notably, Betsy is the only Blyth pastel of a baby shown with one.

Further confirmation of the family geneaology and their tight relationships is included in an article on the *Essex Lodge of Freemasons in Essex Institute Historical Collections*, published in 1859. It states that member John Kehoo [sic] married Mary Moses, "daughter of Benjamin," and Edward Dalton married her sister, Sarah. Fellow émigrés from Ireland, Kehoe and Dalton were mariners, "fast friends, and boarded at Mulkey's house, ... both remarkably handsome, and promising men, and by their circumspect conduct, and industrious habits, soon gained the respect and confidence of the community."

Edward and Sarah (Sally) Moses Dalton had seven children, six boys and one girl, the last of whom was Eleazer Moses, named after Sally's paternal grandfather and once thought to be the subject of this pastel.

Blyth used the same, somewhat simplified, visionary landscape with pale brown and moss-green-aqua coloring in his oil of William Luscomb (Cat. 88). A small bird is perched on Sarah's hand, as in Blyth's pastel of Patty Webb (Cat. 133). Blyth might have been familiar with this motif from the Joseph Badger portraits of young children, such as that of John Gerry (1741–1786), from a prominent local Marblehead family, now in the Museum of Fine Arts, Houston.

This pastel is one of Blyth's most ambitious child portraits, as were the oils of his parents at the time. Benjamin Moses, a successful sea captain, evidently had money to spend on portraiture! Sally is an appealing child, with a pert smile, as if she is pleased to be the subject of this portrait. One can imagine a ten- or twelve-year-old child with such a personality, watching her parents and baby sister being memorialized in oil, and insisting, "How about me?"

Dennis family documents
EIHC 3:122

"Leavitt, William, "History of the Essex Lodge of Freemasons," *EIHC* 3:121, 123 (1861)

Salem VR , some citing as source PR 401 ("The Misses Martin")

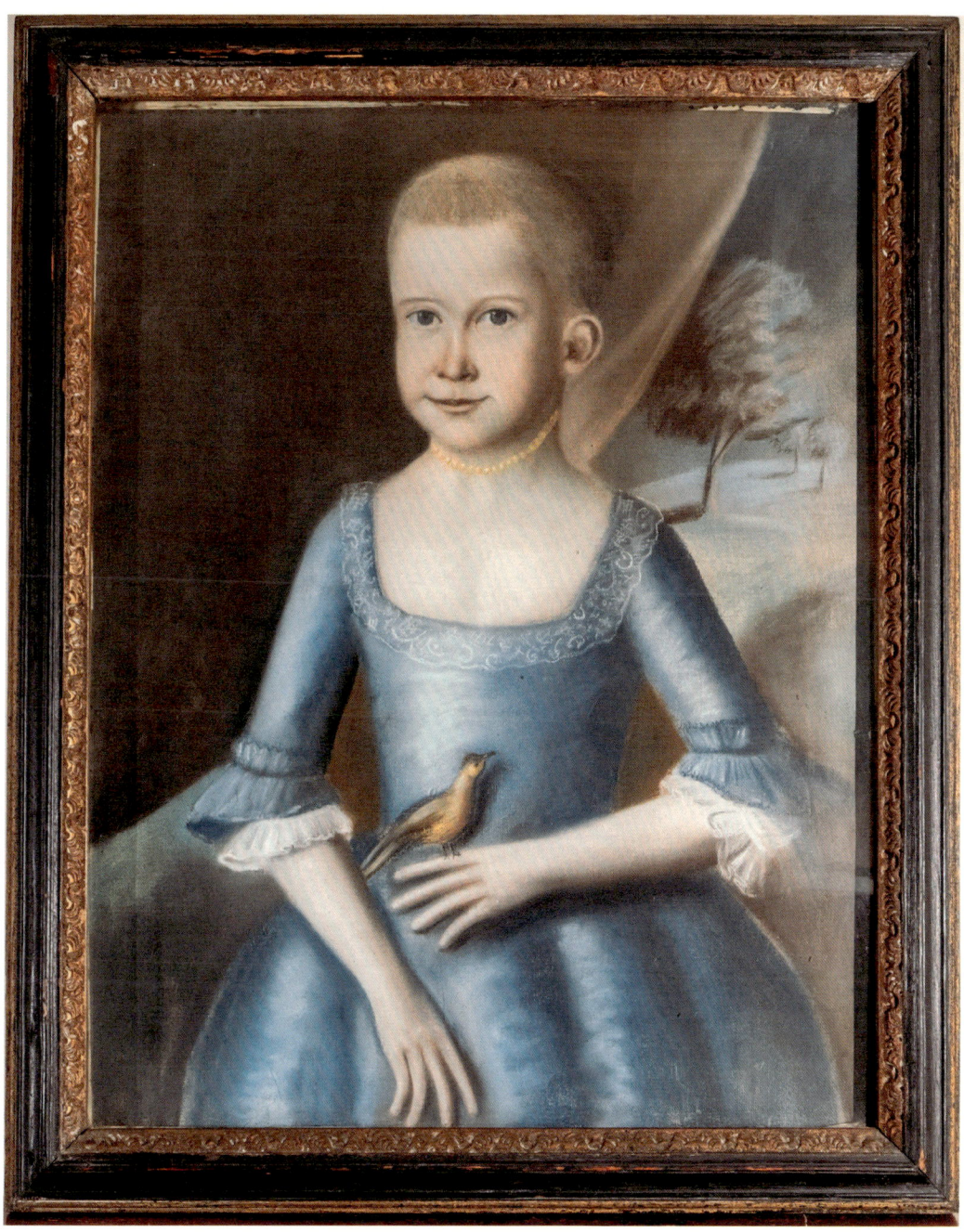

Sarah Moses
Pastel by Benjamin Blyth, probably 1781
Courtesy of the collection of the Dennis family
Photograph by Michael C. King

[97]

Abijah Northey (1741–1816)

Benjamin Blyth (attr.), early 1770s
Pastel on paper mounted on canvas, 29½ x 17½ in. including frame (57.2 x 43.8 cm.), Samuel Blyth frame
James and Patricia Goode; Eldred Auction Gallery, April 2022; location not known; Sotheby's;
Childs Gallery; Bertram and Nina Fletcher Little; Northeast Auctions; Mrs. Atherton Noyes;
W. Eliot Fette; Wm. Makepeace; Betsy Hill.

Nina Fletcher Little believed that "A portrait of a Gentleman" in her collection was of Abijah Northey "of Salem and Newburyport." She undoubtedly based her conclusion on a "brooch" (miniature portrait) of him which was at one time also in her collection. The location of the miniature is currently not known.

Abijah Northey was born in 1741 to David and Miriam Northey, active Quakers. David was a goldsmith, a career which Abijah also followed. In 1765, he married Abigail Wood in Charlestown. The family lived above Northey's shop opposite the Parkman house, in Salem. They had three children, David born in 1770 (who died in 1791); Abigail, born in 1772; and Abijah Jr., born in 1774. Northey's family had many interconnections with the King family. His sister Sarah married Benjamin King (Cat. 80). His wife's sister Mary married Samuel King. After she died in 1782, Northey was appointed guardian for her two daughters, Sally Gerrish, "about eleven" and Polly. Northey's son Abijah Jr. married his cousin Sally in 1795.

Abijah Northey owned a windmill and mill house. Although a Quaker, he was on the committee with other Salem notables to assign pews in the North Meeting House in 1796. He also was one of the many Salem men to join the Rhode Island Expedition in August 1778. The author of an article on church plate in Salem, John H. Buck, noted that Paul Revere was said to have "frequently exchanged works" with Northey. Abijah also sold hardware to the Salem cabinetmakers Elijah and Jacob Sanderson and appears in the account book of Edward Lang (Cat. 83), another Salem gold- and silversmith, for providing a horse and "slay" for Lang to go to the farm in Beverly with "Mrs. Dabney" (Cat. 39).

Northey died in 1816, two years after his wife Abigail. Considered "well respected," Abijah's portrait exudes the epitome of the philosophy of the Society of Friends: gentleness, calm, and tolerance, qualities that did not hinder his success or that of his brother in business or public affairs. Barely visible in the right background is a large, draped curtain. The portrait was the property of Mrs. Atherton Noyes when it was loaned to the Museum of Fine Arts, Boston for exhibition and was later purchased by Nina Fletcher Little. Northey himself may have made the case. Another portrait of Northey by John Brewster, ca. 1820–30, is in the Peabody Essex Museum, as well as more than two dozen gold- and silversmith tools given in 1964 by a descendant, John T. Northey.

Bentley 4:380–81

Buck, John, H., "The Early Church Plate of Salem," *EIHC* 43:98, citing the *Boston Transcript*, Jan. 20, 1900

EIHC 1:113; 4:80; 7:70–71, 158; 43:98; 70:354; 75:13; 100:207; 108:49–57

Essex County Probate Record 15816, Administration

Felt, 2:66

Little, *Paintings by New England Provincial Artist 1775–1800*

PEM Phillips Library, Northey family papers

Phillips, *Salem . . . Indies*, 21–22

SIRIS

Sotheby's auction, Little collection, 1994

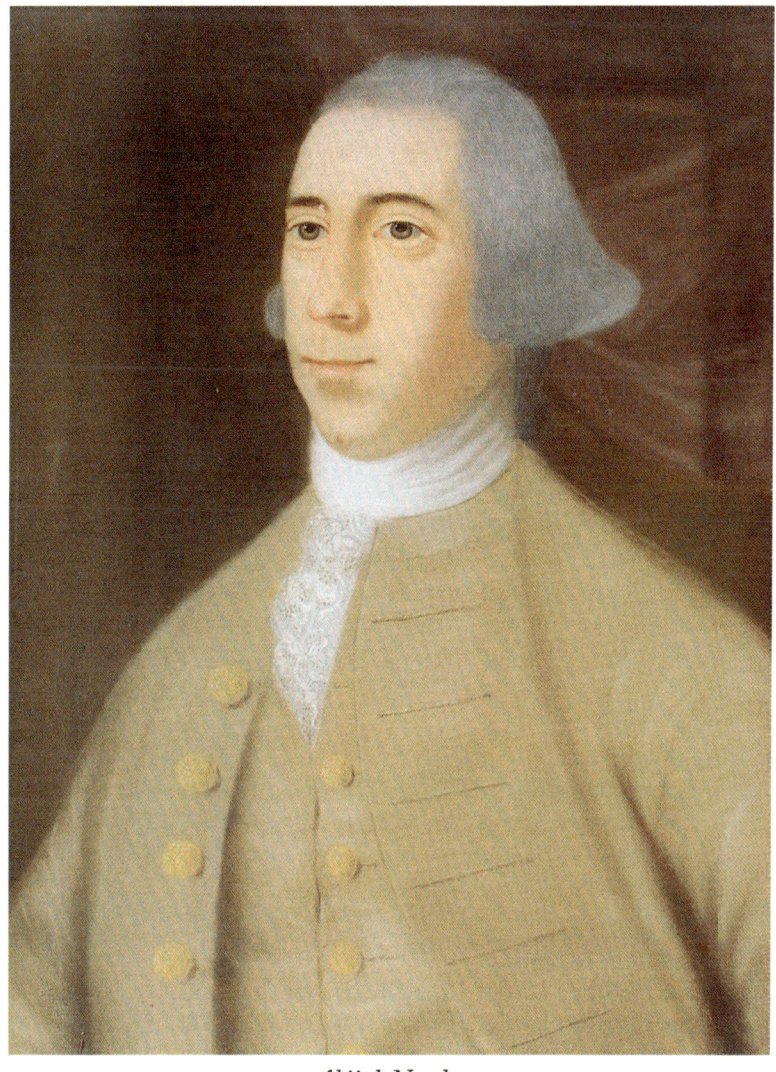

Abijah Northey
Photograph of pastel by Benjamin Blyth, early 1770s
Photograph by F. Lee Eiseman, courtesy of Sotheby's, Little collection, 1994

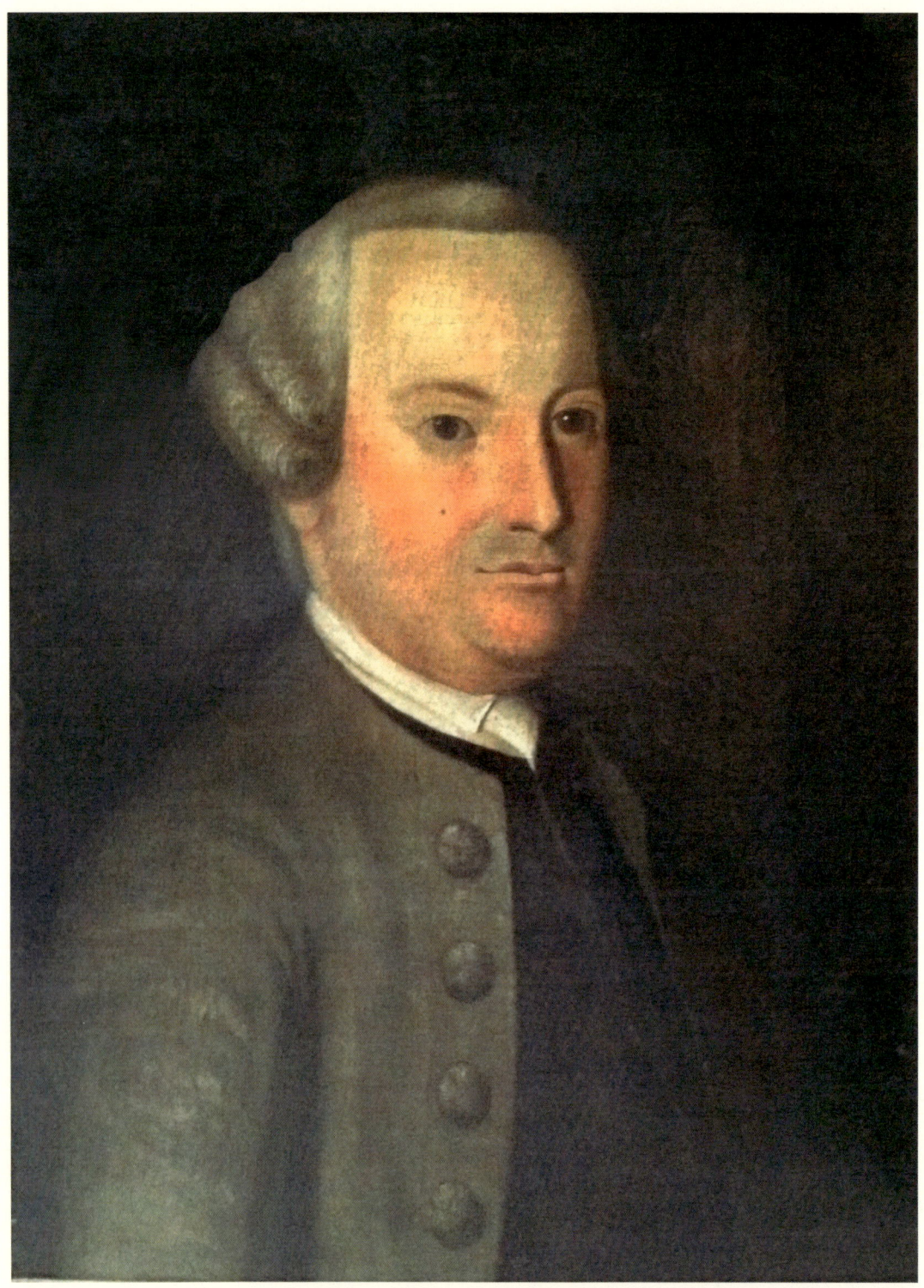

Samuel Norton (1743–1832?)
Oil painting by an anonymous artist, based on a lost pastel by Benjamin Blyth, early 1770s
Courtesy of Historic New England

[98]

Samuel Norton(?) (1743–1832?)

Anonymous artist, 19th c., based on a lost pastel by Benjamin Blyth, early 1770s
Oil on canvas, 23 x 18⅛ in., 26½ x 21¾ in., with frame
Historic New England 1990.101, gift of Susan B. Norton; Norton family; Wigglesworth

This oil portrait in the collections of Historic New England (HNE), catalogued as "Man of the Norton Family," has many features that suggest that it is a copy of a Blyth pastel, including the same dimensions as many of them. The writing on the back indicates that the sitter was thought to be "Samuel Norton's father/or grandfather. This may/ be a copy of a Wigglesworth/-owned portrait," affirming that there may have been an earlier portrait. The format also suggests it was a pastel.

The portrait was a gift to HNE from the Norton family of Hingham. Based on the estimated age of the sitter and the attribution to Benjamin Blyth, it most likely is of Samuel Norton (1743–1832), who had a son named Samuel, and a family member who married a Wigglesworth. A connection between the Norton and Wigglesworth families in the Newburyport/Salisbury area of Essex County bolsters the case for an original by Blyth: on June 21, 1843, in Salisbury, Sarah T. Norton married John H. Wigglesworth. However, Sarah's father is not Samuel, and there is only one Samuel among all the Norton births in Essex County from 1730 to 1890.

HNE correspondence

[99]

Thomas Fitch Oliver (1757–1797)

Benjamin Blyth, ca. 1780
Pastel on paper, measurements unknown
Current location not known; Mrs. George Francis Crane in 1944

The Rev. Thomas Fitch Oliver served St. Peter's Church in Salem, the Blyth family's church, as lay reader, warden, and vestryman, for four years before entering the ministry and becoming rector in 1786 of St. Michael's Church in Marblehead. Grandson of Gov. Andrew Oliver of the Massachusetts Bay Colony, Thomas Fitch was born on May 4, 1757, to Judge Andrew and Mary (Lynde) Oliver. At the age of seven, he inherited 2,078 acres of land in Lunenburg, Massachusetts, from his maternal grandfather, Thomas Fitch. Thomas Fitch Oliver graduated from Harvard College in 1775, when many of the Anglican churches in New England were already shuttered. He studied law at Brown University and was a lay reader at St. John's Church in Providence. In 1778, he married Sarah Pynchon, daughter of William Pynchon, the founder of Springfield, Massachusetts. Oliver probably is the minister mentioned by Bentley, who served the churches of Marblehead and Beverly and finally settled at St. Thomas's Church at Garrison Forest, Maryland, where he died of consumption in 1797, at age forty. Three sons named after him all died. A surviving daughter, Mary Lynde Fitch, married noted nineteenth-century jurist Joseph Story in December 1804.

Oliver revered more formal Anglicanism, noting of his service while at Marblehead from 1789 to 1791, "Will it do you any pleasure to learn that our quire at St. Michael's do constantly chant the Venite – the Te Deum and in the afternoon the Cantate and Nunc Dimittis to great acceptation. This I assure you is the case and I believe mine is almost the only church in the continents in which this [is] done."

The only known illustration of this portrait is in the history of St. Peter's Church by Harriet Sylvester Tapley. In an essay in the *Essex Institute Historical Collections*, Harold D. Hodgkinson wrote that the portrait "shows a fine looking, upstanding, intelligent gentleman of strong personality." He quoted Oliver: "I have been of the opinion that to all his creatures God allots even in this life a small proportion of happiness and as misery has been almost my constant companion,..." The Reverend William Bentley did not share Hodgkinson's opinion of Oliver: "The bigotry of Oliver [was] joined to an honest but uninformed mind [referring to a Rev. Thayer who had adopted Catholicism]." The portrait of Oliver also shows signs of redrawing on parts of the face, but it does convey his stern rectitude, haughty demeanor, and sense of privilege.

Baltimore Chronicle, Feb. 23, 1797
Bentley 1:58. 141, 165, 282, 289, 313
Essex Antiquarian, 170
Hodgkinson, Harold D., "A Clergyman's Comments on the Life of Young America, 1787–1791," *EIHC* 102:74-85
MHS, Oliver (and Lynde and Pynchon) Family Papers
Tapley, *St. Peter's Church*, illus. opp. 60

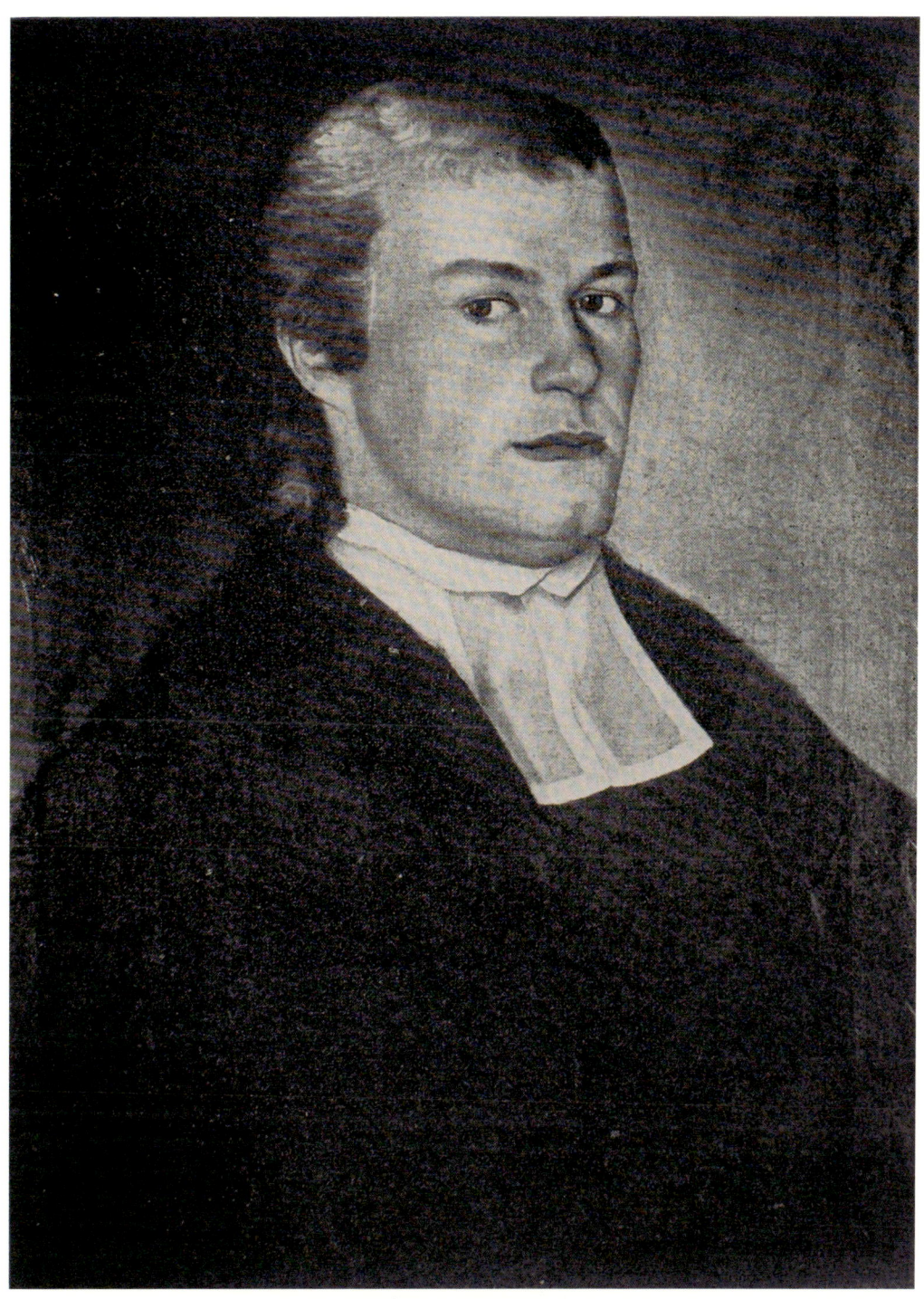

Thomas Fitch Oliver
Photograph of unlocated pastel by Benjamin Blyth, ca. 1780
Illustration from Tapley, *St. Peter's Church* (1944)
Courtesy of the Boston Athenaeum

James Otis (1725–1783)

Benjamin Blyth, late 1760s
Pastel on paper, 19 x 15 in. (est.)
Massachusetts Historical Society, before 1888; destroyed by 1957

James Otis, Jr. was an early critic of British policies that led to the Revolution. In 1761, he delivered his famous speech in Boston against Writs of Assistance, and his phrase, "Taxation without representation is tyranny" became the rallying cry of the patriots. Born in Barnstable, Massachusetts, on February 5, 1702, to James and Mary (Alleyne) Otis, he graduated from Harvard College in 1743 and soon became one of Boston's leading lawyers. In 1760, he was appointed Advocate General of the Admiralty Court but promptly resigned when Gov. Francis Bernard failed to appoint his father to the promised position of chief justice of the Massachusetts Supreme Court and gave the position to Otis's longtime opponent, Thomas Hutchinson.

The next February, Otis argued against the Writs of Assistance, a British ruling allowing its troops to search homes without a warrant and attempting to enforce existing British-enacted trade and navigation laws. Although Otis failed to win his case, John Adams, who heard it, considered it a major propellant to the coming of the Revolution. Later that year, Otis was elected to the provincial legislature of Massachusetts, serving every year until his illness. Otis published his speech on the Writs of Assistance in an expanded version in 1765, and Adams embellished it in two later publications, which led to the adoption of the Fourth Amendment to the U. S. Constitution that prohibits illegal search warrants. Otis also advocated equal rights for African Americans. He then served as Chief Justice of the Court of Common Pleas from 1764 to 1776. But by the late 1760s, he began to exhibit signs of mental instability, believed at the time to have been aggravated by a blow on his head from his opponents in 1769. After the Revolution, he was moved to Andover, where he was killed by lightning in 1783.

The 1888 catalogue of Massachusetts Historical Society paintings notes that Otis's pastel portrait was "nearly obliterated"; by 1939 it was "unlocated," and it had disappeared by 1957, when Foote wrote his article on Blyth. The Smithsonian Institution Research Information System of American paintings and sculpture (SIRIS) lists the Blyth pastel three times: one in the collections of the MHS, and two, unlocated.

The oil portraits of Otis and his wife by Joseph Blackburn were on loan for many years to the Museum of Fine Arts, Boston, but were given to Historic New England in 2017. Because Blyth is known to have copied Blackburn portraits, it is possible that Blyth copied the Blackburn portrait of Otis as well. As his pastel of Otis is now destroyed, the Blackburn oil portrait of Otis is illustrated here. Blyth's debt to Blackburn is clear.

Another oil portrait of James Otis, by John Singleton Copley, ca. 1760, is in the Wichita Art Museum.

American Portraits found in Massachusetts, cat. 1566

Bentley 3:233

Foote, "Blyth," 99

Jeffares, http://www.pastellists.com/Articles/Blyth.pdf

Norton, "Brothers Blyth," 63

Prown 1:111, 225

WPA, 1566

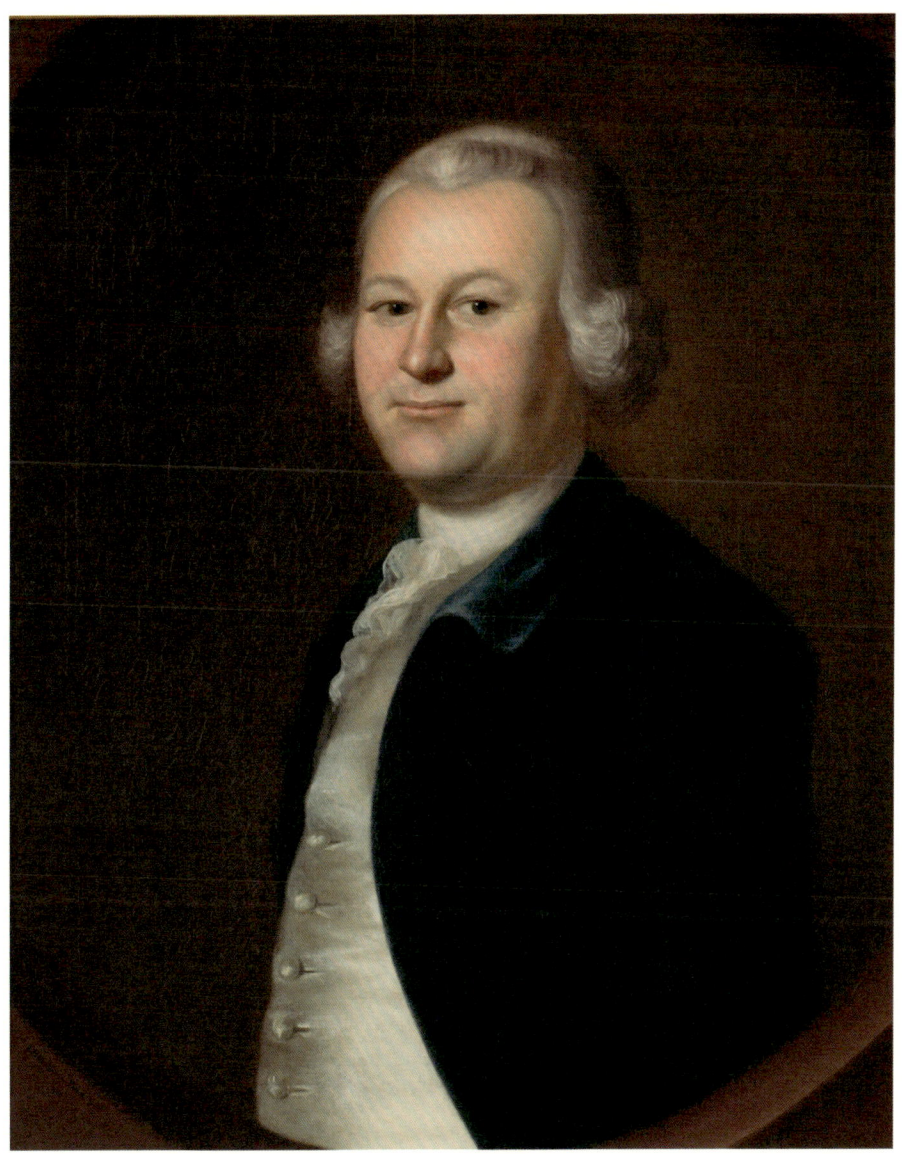

James Otis
Oil painting by Joseph Blackburn (ca. 1703–1787)
28⅝ x 23½ in.
Historic New England 2017.148.1AB, gift in memory of Gertrude and Carlos Hepp

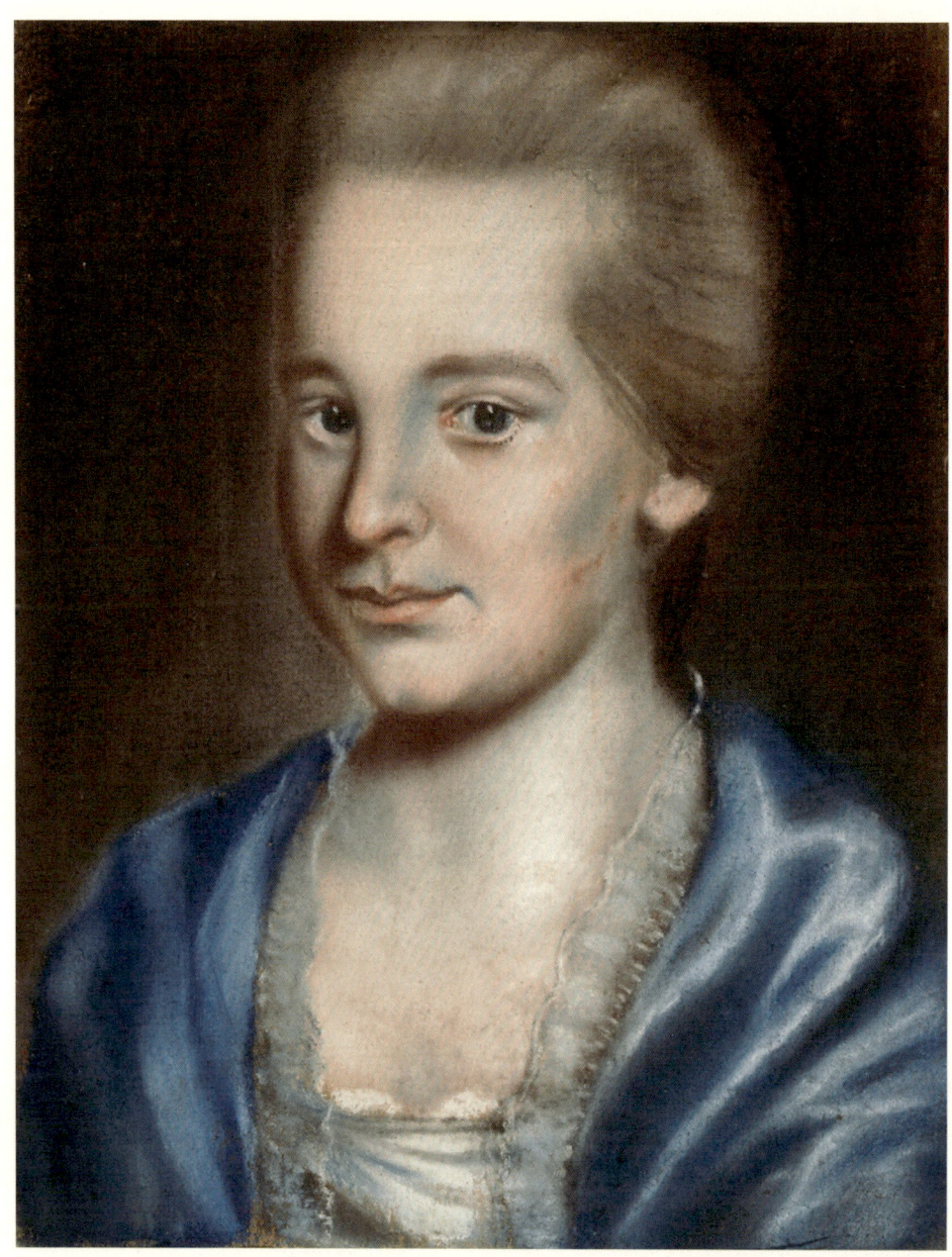

Hannah Paine
Pastel by Benjamin Blyth, 1771
Courtesy of the Worcester Art Museum 1959.42, bequest of Russell Sturgis Paine, 1959

[101]

Hannah Paine (1755–1842)

Benjamin Blyth, 1771
Pastel on medium, smooth blue laid paper mounted on fabric, 9¹⁵⁄₁₆ x 7⅞ in. (25.2 x 20 cm.),
Samuel Blyth frame and glass
Worcester Art Museum 1959.42, bequest of Russell Sturgis Paine, 1959; Trumbull Mansion
under custody of Louisa Trumbull Roberts, Louisa Jane Trumbull Lea, Jane (Lea) Holzhausen, NY

Hannah Paine was drawn by Blyth when she visited her brother, William Paine, who was studying medicine in Salem under Dr. Edward A. Holyoke. The doctor's wife, Mary Vial Holyoke, noted in her diary that "Mr. Paine brought his Sister" for a visit in 1771; just a month earlier, Mary Vial had sat for her own portrait by Blyth. Hannah, born to Timothy and Sarah (Chandler) on July 22, 1755, would have been seventeen at the time. The following October 22, 1772, shortly after her brother married Lois Orne, Hannah married Ebenezer Bradish. Ten years her senior, he was born in Cambridge in 1746 to Ebenezer and Eunice Bradish. They lived in Cambridge, probably at the west end, known as Menotomy, which separated in 1807 to become Arlington. Two sons were born there, Ebenezer Jr. in 1773, and Timothy in 1775. By the time Elizabeth Willard was born in December 1776, the family was living in Lancaster, where Timothy died at age two. Another son, also named Timothy Paine, was born in 1781.

Hannah moved to Worcester after Ebenezer committed suicide at the home of a friend, John Ballard, in Lancaster on April 29, 1818. The record of her death on April 3, 1842, reads "Widow Hannah, a. 87, d.[aughter] of Timothy Paine," with no mention of her deceased husband. Her will indicated that she died a wealthy woman.

Her portrait shows areas of the mouth and eyelashes on the lower lid that appear to have been added later and resemble work now thought to have been done in Frank W. Bayley's Copley Gallery. In Historic New England's Baldwin Coolidge collection is a photograph of this pastel with an inscription on the back that it was made by Baldwin Coolidge, in Boston, on Jan. 24, 1906. The same statement is also on the back of the pastel, with "Restored" instead of "made." Among the numerous pasted labels naming successive owners, one records that it was included in the Portland Society of Art Spring Exhibition, 1911.

The wide-eyed Hannah was an attractive, even coquettish, young woman.

American Portraits found in Massachusetts, Cat.1
HNE, Baldwin Coolidge Photograph Collection
Holyoke Diaries, 75
Jeffares, http://www.pastellists.com/Articles/Blyth.pdf
Norton, "Brothers Blyth," 63
WPA 1580, artist unknown

[102]

William Paine (1750–1833)

Benjamin Blyth, 1771

Pastel on medium, smooth cream, laid paper mounted on fabric, 9¹⁵⁄₁₆ x 7¹⁵⁄₁₆ in. (25.3 x 20.2 cm.),
Samuel Blyth frame and glass

Worcester Art Museum 1959.41, bequest of Russell Sturgis Paine, 1959; Frances (Lea) Moroney, Paris

William Paine's life was one of those torn asunder by the American Revolution. Born in Worcester in 1750 to Timothy and Sarah (Chandler) Paine, he moved to Salem after his graduation from Harvard College in 1768 to study medicine with Dr. Edward A. Holyoke. The Reverend William Bentley noted that the two doctors examined dead female animals together (" . . . exquirebant injuriam aeconomiae animali Puellae defunctae."). There, Paine met Lois Pickering Orne, of a distinguished Salem family, and they were married in September 1772, when she was seventeen. An orphan, she was a ward of Francis Cabot, whose sister-in-law, Elizabeth Higginson Cabot (Cat. 23), and Francis and George Cabot (Cats. 24, 25) were drawn a few years earlier by Blyth. In honor of his marriage, Paine ordered a forty-five-piece set of Paul Revere silver, said to be the largest commission Revere ever received. The couple soon moved back to Worcester, where Paine opened an apothecary shop in 1773.

Paine, a Loyalist, considered the Boston Tea Party "scandalous." Fearing for his life, he left for England in 1774, initially leaving his wife with his father, Judge Timothy Paine, in Worcester. Appointed apothecary to the British forces in America, Paine returned and served in the Carolinas, Rhode Island, and New York, where his wife and family joined him. After trips to England and Portugal, they were next in Halifax, where he was rewarded for his service at the end of the war with a pension and 5,000 acres at La Tête (now Frye's Island) in Passamaquoddy Bay. The family then moved to St. John, New Brunswick. Lois Paine's concerns that the children could not be properly educated there apparently prompted William to petition Gov. Thomas Carleton to establish an academy, which eventually became the University of New Brunswick.

When the ban against Loyalists was rescinded in 1787, the family moved back to Salem, where Paine was helping patients *gratis* and, according to Salem nineteenth-century historian Joseph B. Felt, was inoculating hundreds against smallpox "by the Suttonian method." Dr. Paine continued to do so at Perkins's Derby-Neck farmhouse and Col. Pickman's farm until, after his father's death in 1793, the family moved back to the ancestral home, The Oaks, in Worcester. The connections with Salem continued; two years later, his daughter Esther, like her father "an uncompromising British subject," married Joseph Cabot, and Paine also kept in contact with Bentley.

Paine's portrait was probably drawn, along with the one of his sister in 1770–71. It is one of the few portraits by Blyth of Loyalists, but Paine's, along with those of Robert Traill (Cat. 124) and Peter Frye (Cat. 56) were all done several years before the outbreak of war. Although an accompanying note from a descendant notes that Paine was depicted in "court dress," he actually was wearing a shirt, stock and coat of the period. The Paine portraits, uncharacteristically small for Blyth, along with the Revere silver, are now in the Worcester Art Museum. Paine was a founder of the American Antiquarian Society, which owns a portrait of him by Chester Harding.

Bentley 1:102, 173, 295, 326, 409, 411; 2:272–73

Bowditch, *Pickering Genealogy*, illus. betw. 189–190, "From a pastel portrait by Earle"

Felt 2:432

Jeffares, http://www.pastellists.com/Articles/Blyth.pdf

Norton, "Brothers Blyth," 63

SMS: Plate 2, no. 95

Sturgis, Mrs. E. O. P., "A Sketch of the Children of Dr. William Paine," *Proceedings of Worcester Society of Antiquity.* 20:1480192 (1904) Worcester: Hamilton Press [n. d.]).

WPA 1586

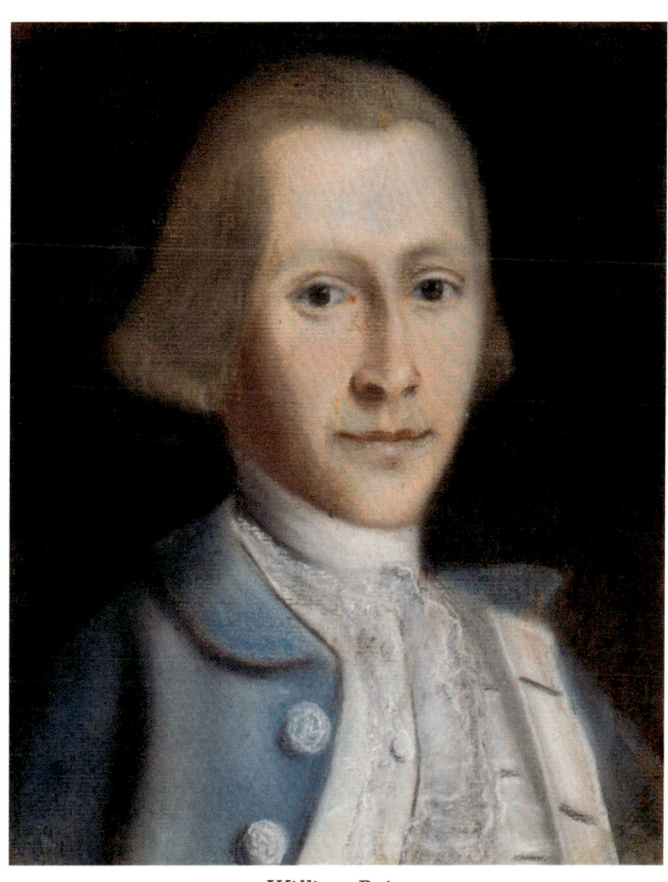

William Paine
Pastel by Benjamin Blyth, 1770–1771
Courtesy of the Worcester Art Museum 1959.41, bequest of Russell Sturgis Paine, 1959

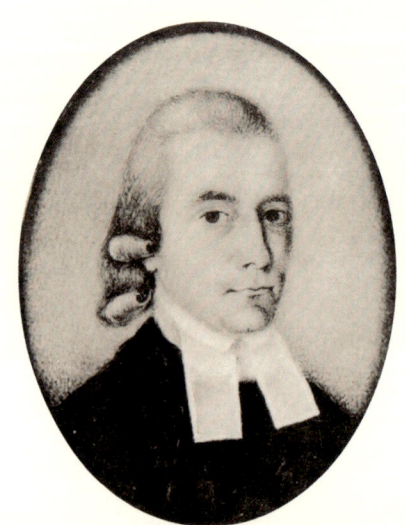

Samuel Parker
Photograph of unlocated, unattributed
miniature by Benjamin Blyth, probably 1780
Illustration from *Sibley's Harvard Graduates,*
vol. 16
Courtesy of The Boston Athenaeum

[103]

Samuel Parker (1744–1804)

Benjamin Blyth, probably 1780
Miniature, measurements unknown
Current location not known; formerly in the collection of S. Parker, Brookline, MA

Samuel Parker was born in Hollis, New Hampshire, to the Hon. William and Mary Parker, on August 17, 1744, and graduated from Harvard College in 1764. He taught for several years before being ordained in England to become assistant minister of Trinity Church, Boston, in 1774. When the British evacuated the city in 1776, the rector of the church left with them, along with those of Boston's two other Anglican churches—King's Chapel and Christ Church. However, Parker was able to continue holding services by omitting the prayer for the king. He and the Reverend William McGilchrist, rector of St. Peter's Church in Salem, reportedly were the only two active Anglican clergy in Massachusetts during the Revolution, although their duties were curtailed. On November 28, 1776, Parker married Anne (Nancy) Cutler of Boston.

After independence, King's Chapel converted to Unitarianism by amending the Book of Common Prayer to its new religious philosophy, Unitarianism, but as the Reverend William Bentley observed, Parker called it "irregular, unconstitutional, diametrically opposite to every principal adopted in any Episcopal church." Parker became a prime mover in establishing The Society for the Propagation of the Gospel and the Episcopal Church in America. In 1803, he was unanimously elected third bishop of Massachusetts. He developed gout, however, and never served in the post. He died in Boston on December 6, 1804. The Widows' Fund of Trinity Church, still functioning, was originally established to help care for his widow and thirteen children.

A tall and powerful man, "with a broad, cheerful, and rubicund face," he was called "astute" and "sagacious" by church historian S. D. McConnell and was praised for "a pulpit presence and clarity which drew Dissenters to his services." Parker was a guest preacher at St. Peter's Church at least twice, and in April 1780, he delivered the funeral sermon for McGilchrist. Blyth, a member of St. Peter's Church, could have made the miniature on one of these occasions. It is the only known image of Parker; according to *Sibley's Harvard Graduates*, he "always refused to sit for his portrait."

Bentley 1:87, 125–26, 196; 2:427; 3:113

EIHC 91:282

FARL, American School, Massachusetts (1751–1800) 175–10w

McConnell, *American Episcopal Church*, 259, 293

Norton, Bettina A., "Trinity Never Closed its Doors," bicentennial exhibition at Trinity Church, 1976

Sibley 16:76-84; illus. betw. 297–98

Tapley, *St. Peter's Church*, 55, 57

Trinity Church in the City of Boston, Boston: D. B. Updike, The Merrymount Press, 1933, illus. 13

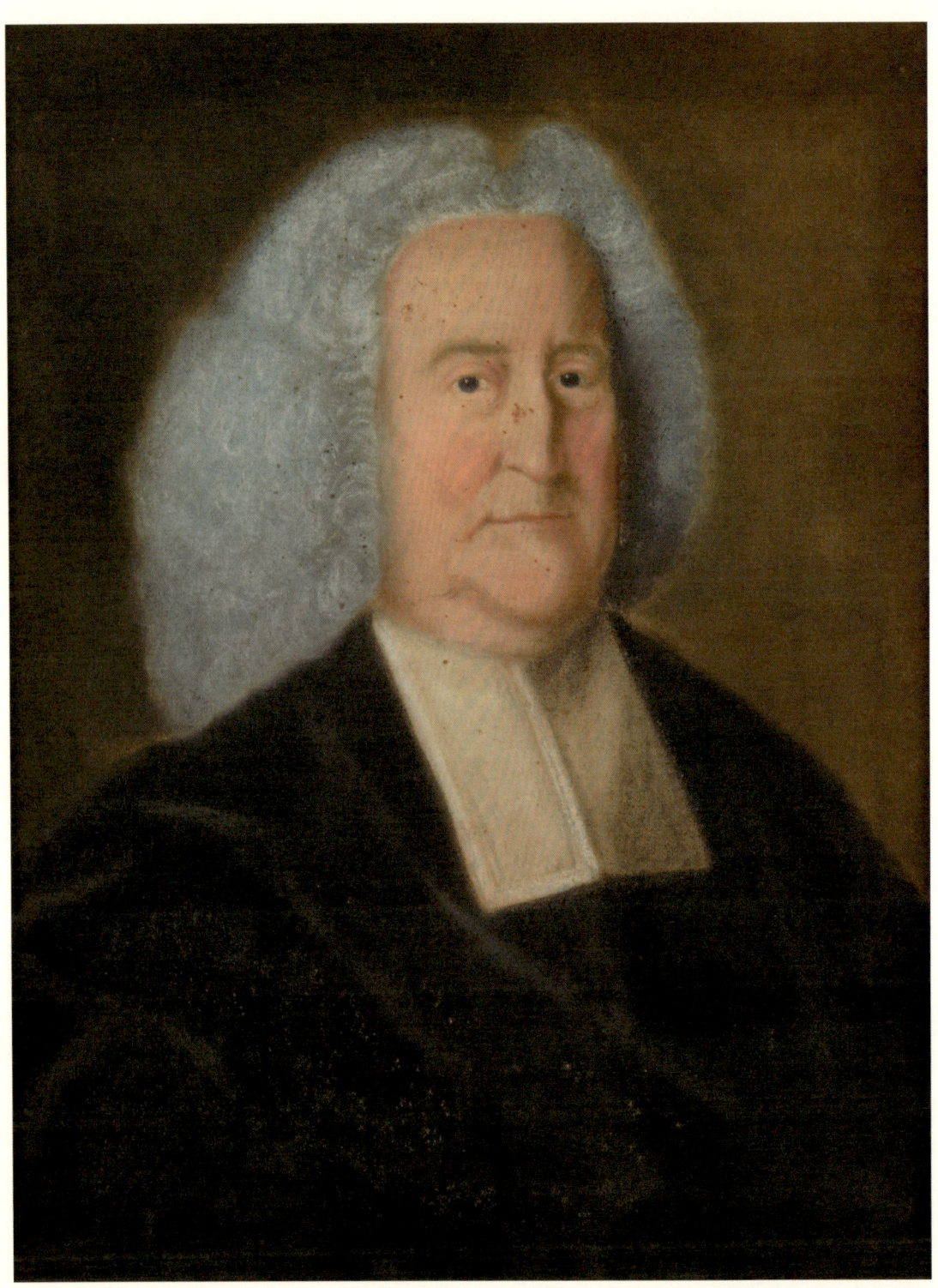

Ebenezer Pemberton
Pastel by Benjamin Blyth, early 1770s
Princeton Portrait Collection, Princeton University, bequest of F. Huntington Babcock, 1973

[104]

Ebenezer Pemberton (1705–1777)

Benjamin Blyth, early 1770s
Pastel on paper mounted on linen, 23½ x 18⅜ in. (59.7 x 46.7 cm.), Hogarth-type frame
Princeton Portrait Collection, Princeton University, bequest of F. Huntington Babcock, 1973

The Reverend Ebenezer Pemberton, a New Lights supporter, was born in Boston in 1705, son of the renowned Reverend Ebenezer Pemberton of Old South Church and Mary (Clark) Pemberton. He became chaplain under Capt. William Dummer at Fort William in 1722, the year after he graduated from Harvard. Four years later, he began a long career as pastor of the First Presbyterian Church in New York City. Thanks to his marriage into a prominent and wealthy family, the congregation was rescued from near destitution and flourished until religious differences led to his departure. He was the only member of the clergy in New York City to welcome the New Lights Evangelist George Whitefield (Cat. 139) into his pulpit.

Pemberton returned to Boston in 1754 to become the minister of the New Brick Church in North Square. In 1770, he received an honorary doctorate from the College of New Jersey (now Princeton University), as one of its founders, along with Gov. Jonathan Belcher (Cat. 14). In 1771, Pemberton was the only minister in Boston who read Gov. Thomas Hutchinson's proclamation from the pulpit for the annual thanksgiving, with the Whigs leaving the service "in great indignation." Moreover, his close friendship with the governor, a member of his congregation, caused him to be accused of loyalty to the crown. In 1774 his church was closed, and he probably did not preach again after the evacuation of Boston in March of 1776. He died the next year at age 72 and is interred at the Granary Burial Ground.

Pemberton was married four times. His first wife, Catherine Harris left him a mansion and 300 acres at Fish-Kills; the others were Catherine Stilwell, Rebecca Smith, and Anne Powell, niece of Lt. Gov. Dummer. There is no record of any children, but he raised his nephew and namesake.

The likely time for Blyth to have done the portrait was in 1771, when Pemberton delivered the sermon for the ordination of the Reverend Isaac Story at the Second Congregational Church in Marblehead. Around that time, Blyth was also copying other portraits in pastels. These included the Blackburn portrait of Jonathan Simpson (Cat. 117) for Mary Vial Holyoke (Cat. 71), Gov. Jonathan Belcher (Cat. 14) for a client unknown, as well as Whitefield in oils (Cat. 139), for the Reverend John Chipman of Beverly (Cat. 28).

The Pemberton portrait, however, is one of two known original pastels by Blyth that were later copied in oils—this one, twice: for Harvard (H354), as an alumnus, and for Princeton, as one of the university's founders, a trustee, and recipient of its first doctoral degree. A letter from the Harvard Archives to Alan Burroughs at the Fogg Museum on May 26, 1941, relates, "The unidentified portrait of Ebenezer Pemberton, given to Harvard by Mrs. H. F. Osborn, turns out to be a copy of the original in the possession of F. Huntington Babcock, 250 West 57th Street,

New York, New York. She borrowed the portrait with the specific purpose of making a copy for Princeton, and appears to have made us one too." She subsequently bequeathed the original by Blyth, reproduced here, to Princeton in 1973.

Pemberton does look like a man beset upon by controversy.

Felt 2:25
oasis.lib.harvard. edu
Sibley 6:537–44; illus. (not attributed) opp. 536
WPA 1644

Man of the Perkins Family

Benjamin Blyth, mid-1770s, reproduction frame by Perry Hopf
Pencil and pastel on paper mounted on board, 21½ x 16½ in. (54.6 x 41.9 cm.)
Collection of James and Janet Laverdiere; Skinner, Inc.; Sotheby's; Nina Fletcher Little;
Roger Bacon Antiques

Most of what is known about the subject of this portrait comes from the Sotheby's catalogue for the sale of the collection of Nina Fletcher Little. She had acquired it from Roger Bacon Antiques, now no longer in business. The twentieth-century jelly label pasted on the back, mentioning "Per-

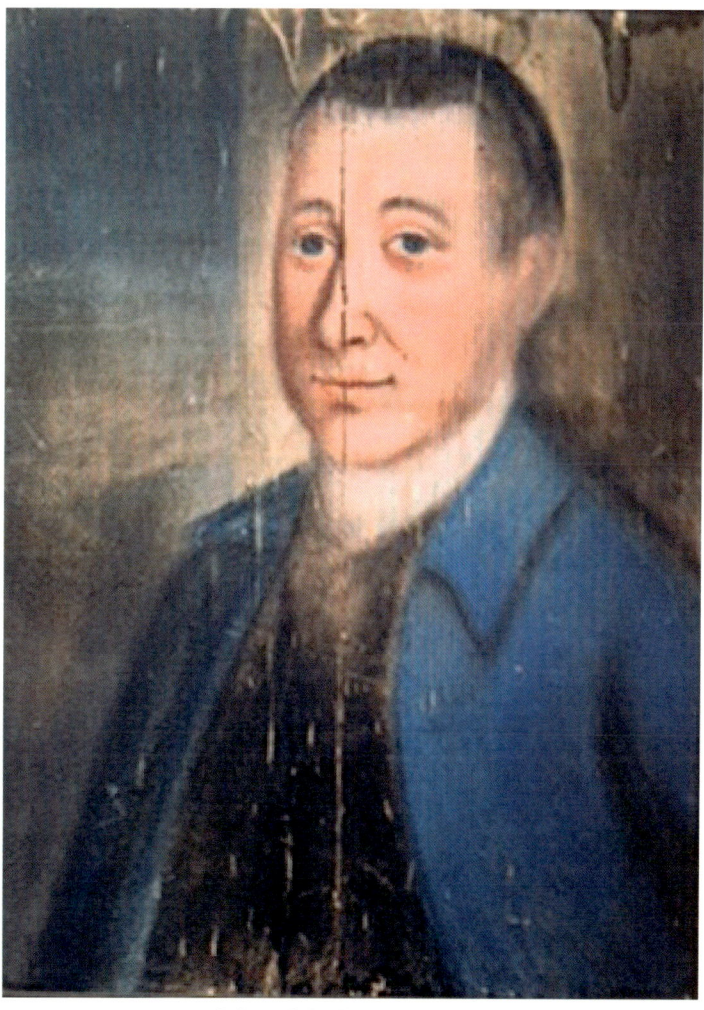

Man of the Perkins Family
Pastel by Benjamin Blyth, mid-1770s
Courtesy of the collection of James and Janet Laverdiere
Photograph by Michael C. King m

kins Family Newburyport," cannot be confirmed, and according to the family of Nina Little, the label is not in her handwriting. Blyth's name is also misspelled. Perkins was a prominent family name in Topsfield, with only a few recorded births in other neighboring towns of northern Essex County between 1740 and 1760, and none in Newburyport—or Salem or Beverly.

Because the portrait was not finished, it provides hints as to Blyth's method of sketching. The face probably was drawn first. He would have filled in the background last, which allows a glimpse of his redrawing of Perkins's right shoulder. However, the pastel is badly damaged, with vertical cracks and tears and much surface abrasion because it lacks a canvas or linen backing and was glued directly onto a pine board.

The man in this portrait, who appears to be in his twenties or early thirties, seems mournful.

`Little family correspondence
Little Sale, Sotheby's, Oct. 1994

[106]

Abigail Love Rawlins Pickman (1709–1786)

Benjamin Blyth
Pastel on paper, mid-1760s, 22½ x 17½ in. (57.2 x 44.4 cm.)
Current location not known; Northeast Auctions, 2000

Abigail Love Rawlins, born in 1707 to Abigail (Lindall) and Capt. Rawlins of Boston, married Benjamin Pickman of Salem in 1731. About twenty years later, John Greenwood painted oil portraits of the couple, now at the Peabody Essex Museum. Abigail Pickman's face shows the same physiognomy as in this pastel, but she was in her early forties for the Greenwood portrait, whereas the pastel was drawn in the late 1760s, when she was approaching her sixties. The handling of the composition is similar to Blyth's portrait of Elizabeth Higginson Cabot (Cat. 23) and

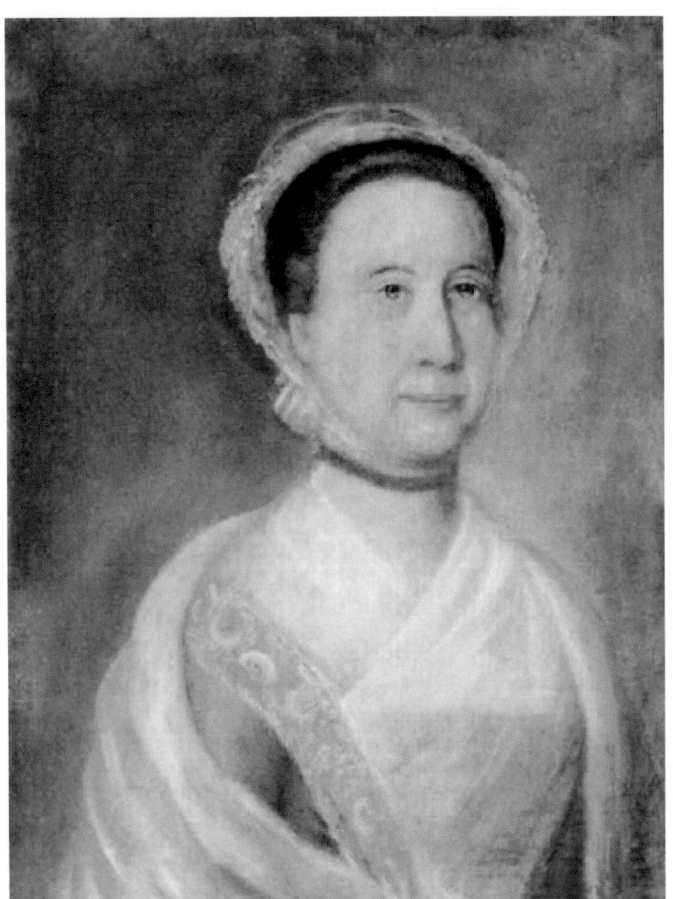

Sarah Hersey (Cat. 67), done at that time. Her cemetery inscription reads, "Madam Love Pickman died June the 9th, 1786." Blyth's portrayal is synchronous with the description given by the Reverend William Bentley, on the day she was buried: "A very respectable Character."

ArtNet, attributed to Blyth (with incorrect dates)
Bentley 1:38
EIHC 6:95 "Some Account of Houses and other Buildings in Salem, . . ."; 39:95, nos. 9, 10.
Felt, 2:64, 220, 511–13, 564–65
The First Centenary of the North Church, 154
Historic American Buildings Survey, Frank O. Banzetti photo, 1940
Jeffares, http://www.pastellists.com/Articles/Blyth.pdf
Northeast Auctions sale, Nov. 2000, Lot 739
Phillips, *Richard Derby of Salem*, 31

Abigail Love Rawlins Pickman
Photograph of unlocated pastel by Benjamin Blyth, mid-1760s
Courtesy of ArtNet

[107]

William Pickman (1748–1815)

Benjamin Blyth (attr.), ca. 1775
Current location not known; once owned by Dudley Leavitt Pickman

William Pickman, son of Col. Benjamin and Love Rawlins Pickman, was born on March 12, 1748. After graduating from Harvard College in 1766, he entered his father's counting house and was part owner of several vessels and a shop on India Wharf. He served as a selectman, a representative, Justice of the Peace, then Naval Officer for the Port of Salem and Beverly. He also became a shareholder in Salem's Social Library. As the country was heading toward Revolution, he, like many persons of his social class, was a friend of both Loyalists and patriots and signed the letter expressing sympathy for Lt. Gov. Hutchinson. However, his Harvard biography noted that he objected to British officers who were "Guilty of the Greatest Indecencies to every Female." Despite retracting his signature to the Hutchinson letter, Pickman's store and shop burned on Oct. 4,

1774. He also lost his position in town government. Amid fear that the British might burn Salem, he left for Haverhill and there married Elizabeth, daughter of the Rev. Dudley and Mary (Pickering) Leavitt, on Oct. 27, 1776. His renowned privateering vessel, *Black Prince*, was burned to prevent its capture at Penobscot. His wife died in 1782, leaving children William, five, Dudley, three, and Elizabeth, six months old. Later, his son William drowned on his passage from Naples, on December 14, 1798. Having "expended his estate" and becoming "much enfeebled," the subject of this pastel spent his last years at the home of his son Dudley and died on Nov. 3, 1815.

Samuel Curwen called him a member of the "new aristocracy," a peculiar designation, as Pickman was descended from one of Salem's old, prestigious families. Bentley wrote of him that he had "a fine person and agreeable manners." His portrait validates the description of his character.

The attribution to Blyth is made with reservations. A very sympathetic portrayal, it is very

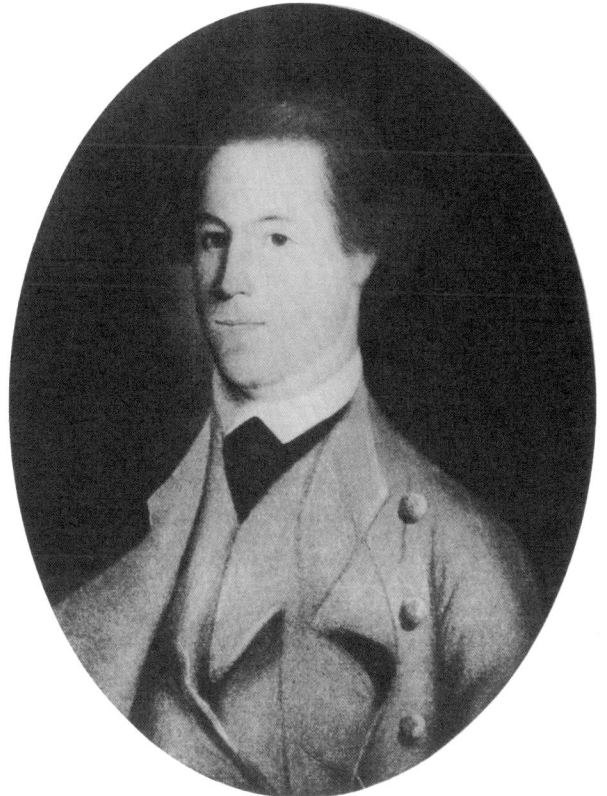

William Pickman
Photograph of unlocated pastel attributed to Benjamin Blyth, ca. 1775
Sibley's Harvard Graduates, photograph courtesy of Boston Athenaeum

well drawn and seemingly more proficient than much of Blyth's work. However, many of his attributes, such as seen in the portraits of James Flagg, Peter Frye, James Russell, and especially Gibbs Atkins are apparent. In addition, Blyth was *the* pastel portraitist in Salem until 1782, and he had drawn a portrait of William Pickman's mother, Abigail (Cat. 106). Also, Blyth's brother Samuel made the Pickman coat of arms (Illus. 43). Lastly, because this portrait is known only in the reproduction, details about its draftsmanship or whether it had been worked on, as is the case with so many Blyth pastels, cannot be ascertained.

Bentley, IV:359
Curwen, *Journal* . . . , 257
Pickman, Benjamin, *Diary and Letters of Benjamin Pickman*, illus. 22
Sibley, 11:403–405, 45:405

Hannah Porter (1757–1838)

Benjamin Blyth, mid-1770s
Pastel on paper mounted on linen, 17½ x 13⅜ in. (44.5 x 34 cm.)
Current location not known; Mrs. Roe R. Adams, Versailles, Kentucky; Breck family

Known simply as "A woman of the Breck family," this unfinished portrait is catalogued in the Frick Art Reference Library as of Hannah, daughter of Elijah Porter and Dorothy Clark(e) Porter of Topsfield. It probably was drawn more than a decade before her marriage to the Reverend Daniel Breck in February 1786. Thirteen years older than his wife, he was minister at the Topsfield Congregational Church. In 1787, the congregation grew so dissatisfied with him that it sought to have him dismissed. The following year a council of six men, including the Reverend William Bentley and the Reverend Thomas Barnard of Salem (Cat. 8) deliberated for two weeks before unanimously upholding his dismissal. Bentley, who had called him "that stupid Breck of Topsfield," recorded that he was "bred in the occupation of a Cooper, went late in his studies, & being destitute either of address or abilities . . ." Bentley concluded, "That tho' the charges against Mʳ Breck did prove nothing against his moral character, & only the frailties incident to the most prudent men, yet as the disaffection was great & inveterate, it was recommended that he should ask a dismission" with settlement. Breck then moved to Hartland, Vermont, as the first minister of a newly formed church.

The first three of the Brecks' five children were born while he was still officiating in Topsfield. The last two were born in Hartland. Hannah died in Vermont on June 15, 1838, age seventy-nine, and is buried in Center Cemetery, Hartland, with her husband, who died in 1845 at age ninety-seven, three of their children, and other descendants.

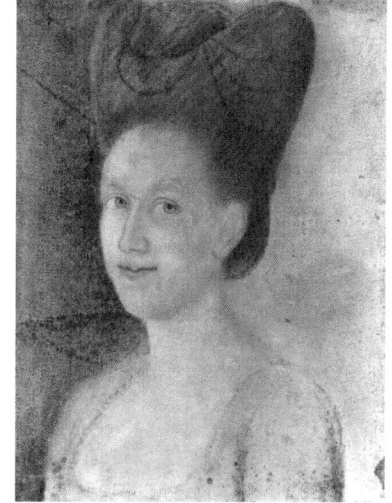

Hannah Porter
Photograph of unlocated pastel by Benjamin Blyth, mid-1770s
Courtesy of the Frick Art Reference Library Photoarchives

Her portrait is known solely in the black-and-white photograph at the Frick Art Reference Library. Its report also provides the only known description: "Light red-brown hair dressed with two pink feathers at the back and black beads draped across the front. Light blue eyes, pale complexion, pale blue background." It shows a coquettish young woman with the fashionable upswept and bejeweled hairdo of the early 1770s.

One of Blyth's inexplicably unfinished portraits, it descended through Robert L. Breck, Versailles, Kentucky, to his granddaughter, Mrs. Roe R. Adams, née Martha Rodes Carter.

Bentley 1:63, 89–91; 2:364; 4:164
FARL, American School, Massachusetts (1751–1800) 158-3c
Hartland (Vt.) Historical Society
Versailles Area Historical Society
Woodford County Public Library

The Honble Israel Putnam Esqr

Major General of the United Forces of America

B Blyth del. /Hiller &, Blyth fec^{nt}

Mezzotint, ca. 1775, image and text 37 x 29 cm., sheet 41 x 32 cm., from an unknown original

Courtesy American Antiquarian Society, 42722

Benjamin Blyth contributed the original artwork for Joseph Hiller's mezzotint of Gen. Israel Putnam. He is pointing to a hill with encampments, an apparent allusion to the Battle of Bunker Hill on June 17, 1775, in which he had a prominent role. The rare print—only one other copy is known—is inscribed at the left background, "B. Blyth del.", and at bottom right, "Hiller & Blyth fece^{nt}." The script beneath the image is beautifully engraved by Hiller.

The portrait is too particular to have been a copy of the English mezzotint by J. Wilkinson, published in London in September 1776. Although it may have alluded to the Hiller & Blyth, it is decidedly fictitious. In Blyth's portrayal, Putnam's nose and jowls are very pronounced, and his piercing, light blue eyes distinctive. Given Blyth's reputation for physiognomic accuracy and that he is not known to have done any portraits, other than copies, that were not from life, this print should be considered more reliable than the scores of other images that exist of Putnam. Far from flattering, this is a factor that might have dampened enthusiasm for the print.

The AAS impression is uncolored, but the only other known one, sold recently to the Society of the Cincinnati, has red-orange on Putnam's sash and the flag, which raises questions. Gen. Washington's order on July 14, 1775, stated that generals "be distinguished in the following manner, the Commander-in-Chief a light-blue ribbon wore across his breast . . . the majors and brigadier generals by a pink ribbon . . . , the aid de camps by a green ribbon." Also, images of flags in American prints of that period were usually painted with red and white stripes. The assumption is that the color was added later.

Whether the original of Putnam by Benjamin Blyth was a drawing, pastel, or oil painting has long been a mystery. A drawing seems likely, as was probably the case with Blyth's original for one, if not both, of the full-length mezzotint portraits of General Washington in the Elkin collection.

Israel Putnam was born in Salem Village (now Danvers) on January 7, 1718, to Joseph and Elizabeth (Porter) Putnam. He and his first wife, Hannah Pope, had thirteen children. After her death in 1767, he married Deborah Lothrop Gardner. Putnam died in Pomfret (now Brooklyn), Connecticut, on May 29, 1790. His home, now called Putnam Farm, the oldest part of which dates to about 1750, is on the National Register of Historic Places.

"Two Portraits of Washington," 12, quoting Charles Allen Munn, *Three Types of Washington Portraits*, 25.

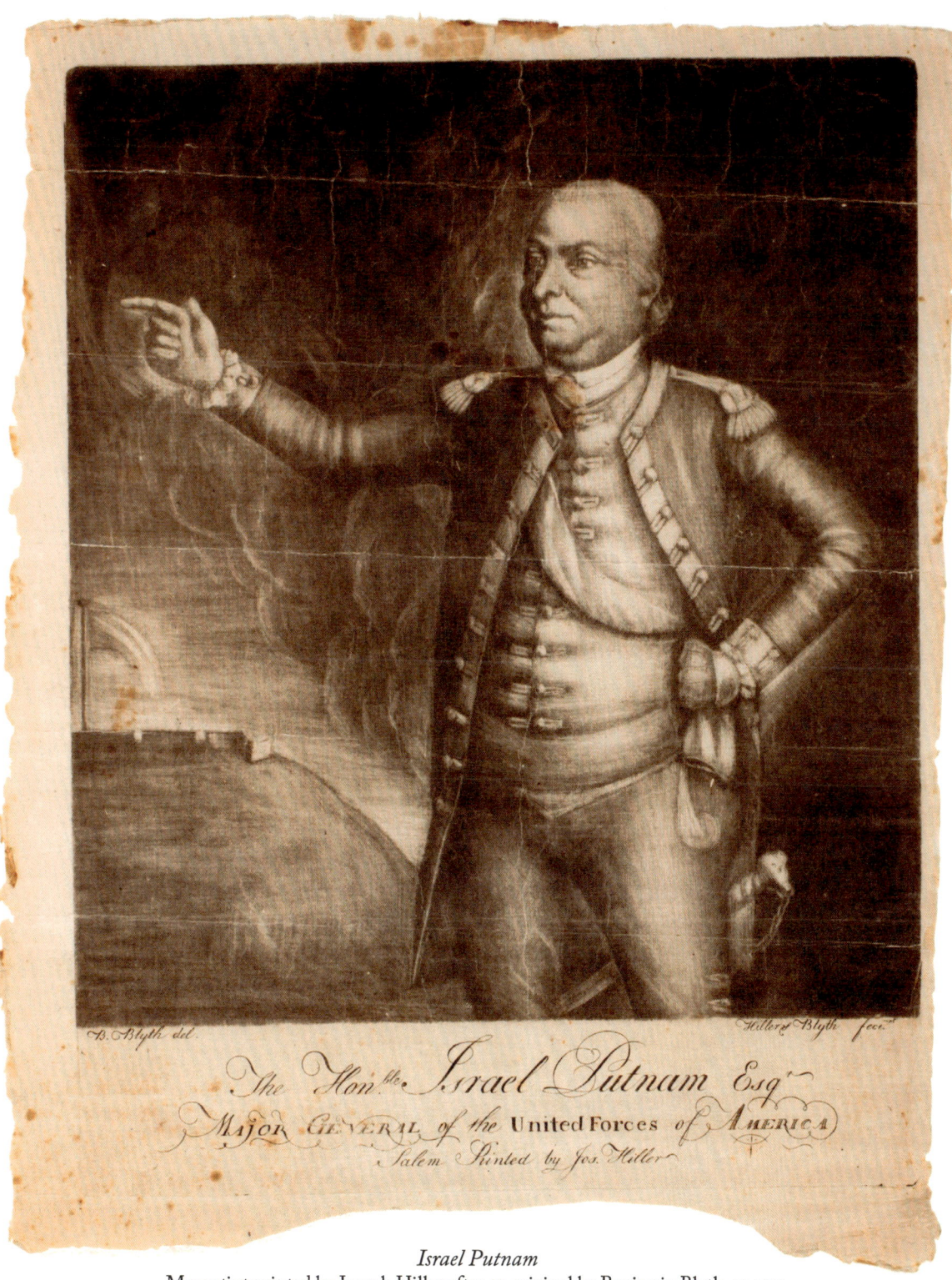

Israel Putnam
Mezzotint printed by Joseph Hiller after an original by Benjamin Blyth, ca. 1775
Courtesy of The American Antiquarian Society, Engrf Blyt HillB Putn

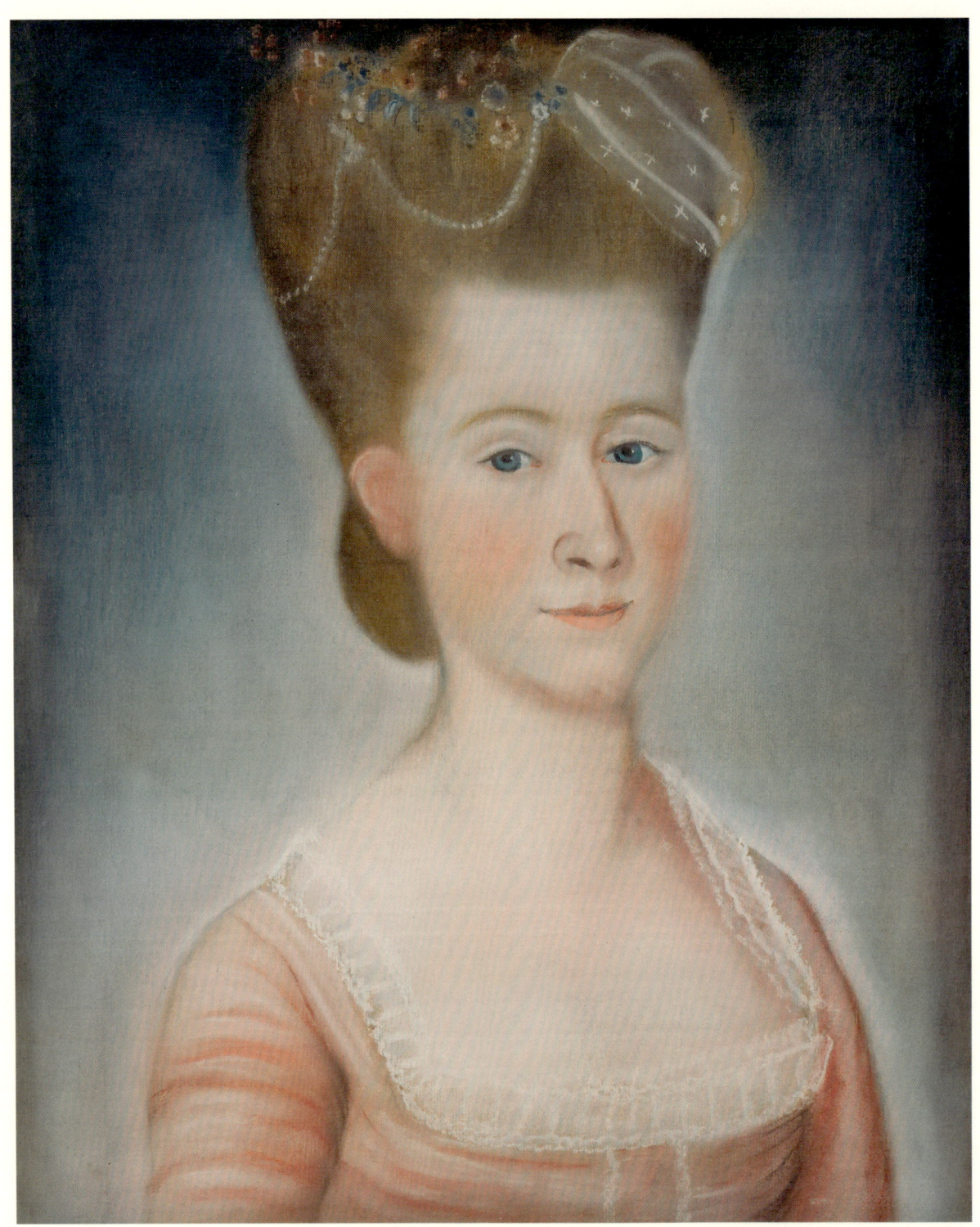

Elizabeth or Rachel Rogers
Pastel by Benjamin Blyth, late 1760s to early 1770s
Courtesy of the Cape Ann Museum 2333.3, gift of the estate of Elizabeth Alling, 1982

Elizabeth (1739–1769) *or Rachel* (1750–1833) *Rogers*

Benjamin Blyth, early 1770s, possibly late 1760s
Pastel on paper mounted on linen, 18½ x 15½ in. (sight), (47 x 39.37 cm.)
Cape Ann Museum 2333.3, gift of the estate of Elizabeth Alling, 1982; Rogers family

The inscription on the back of this pastel identified it as a portrait of Elizabeth Rogers Low (1764–1810), who married Capt. David Low on February 16, 1786, in Gloucester. Also on the back, "prob. work of itinerant artist/pntd. ca. 1785." The chronology, however, does not work on two counts: the dress and hair style of the sitter dates it fifteen or more years earlier, and Benjamin Blyth, who clearly was the artist, was already in Virginia by 1785. So, this portrait is either of Elizabeth Rogers, Elizabeth Low's mother and wife of Gloucester merchant Daniel Rogers, or his second wife, Rachel.

Elizabeth Gorham, born on December 10, 1739, to John and Elizabeth (Allen) Gorham, married Daniel Rogers, "a highly respected shipmaster," on November 6, 1759. She died on March 4, 1769, at age twenty-nine, five days after the birth of an unnamed child, who also probably died. She left four children, ranging in age from two to nine. After his wife's death, Daniel Rogers married Rachel Ellery on March 20, 1770, just after her twentieth birthday. They had fifteen more children, including three named Rachel. Rachel Rogers died at age 84 in 1833. The Reverend William Bentley recorded that he spent a "pleasant visit" with Daniel Rogers, along with Lt. Somes (Cat. 120) and others, in 1791 and stayed at the house, where "Esqr. Rogers . . . collected his family & finished the scene by an act of devotion."

The sitter was a pretty woman, quite *au courant*, with her bejeweled upswept hair, and looks to be in her early twenties, as was Rachel. On the other hand, as the portrait came down through the Low family, the sitter probably was Elizabeth, the mother of the Elizabeth who married David Low. Either way, it begs the question if there was once a portrait of Daniel Low. On the other hand, as the portrait came down through the Low family, the sitter might be Elizabeth, the mother of the Elizabeth who married David Low. Daniel and Elizabeth Rogers' first son, Daniel Jr., married Phoebe Homans, whose portrait as a toddler, held by her mother, Relief, was drawn by Blyth (Cat. 72). It is now at the Beverly Historical Society and Museum in Beverly, Massachusetts.

Bentley 1:266, 267

Col. John Gorham's Waste Book

Gloucester VR deaths, 263

The New-England Historical and Genealogical Register, "Jno. Gorham," 1745

The New-England Historical and Genealogical Register, "Jno. Gorham," 1745 Norton, "Brothers Blyth," (under "Low"), 62

Staples and Shaw, *Clothing*, 278

WPA 1829

[111]

David Ropes (1739–1793)

Benjamin Blyth, ca. 1774
Pastel on canvas, 25 x 19½ in. (63.5 x 49.53 cm.)
Peabody Essex Museum 1721/107943, gift of M. W. Shepard, 1871

Son of Thomas and Sarah (Hodges) Ropes, David was baptized on April 14, 1739, according to a note on the back of his portrait, although both Salem Vital Records and the catalogue entry in *EIHC* give the date of his baptism as October 14, 1739. The entry states that he "was variously styled 'cooper,' 'trader,' 'innkeeper,' and 'Merchant.'" Ropes kept a boarding house on Derby Street and then in 1774 opened the Salem Coffee House, near both St. Peter's Church and the house of Samuel Blyth. During the Revolution, Ropes ran a tavern on Essex Street and engaged in real estate. He also joined the Essex Masonic Lodge in March 1780. However, towards the end of his life, he lost a considerable amount of his fortune. After his death on December 20, 1793, the Rev. Bentley wrote, "Every one loved David Ropes."

This meticulously drawn pastel, with the companion of Ropes's wife Priscilla (Cat. 112), is one of Blyth's most ambitious. Larger than others, it was folded at one time. The horizontal seam can be detected near the center of the image. The pastel was treated for mildew by the Museum of Fine Arts, Boston, in 1969, along with those of Lydia Phippen Fisk (Cat. 53) and John Gibaut (Cat. 59). Some of the drawing may have been strengthened, as in the black piping and a strip of brown, representing part of the vest.

The inscription on the back reads "Presented to J W Shepard by his aunt Betsy, April 12th, 1881." Yet the object sheet from PEM gives the accession date of 1871, and the *EIHC* "Catalogue . . ." says, "before 1919."

Bayley, *Little Known . . . Portrait Painters*, "Blyth," no. 2, illus.

Bentley 1:132; 2:77

EIHC 3:125, 7:162–63; 72:144–45, 151, cat. 262, "unknown artist"

Felt 1:422–23; 2:265, 273

Foote, "Blyth," 99–100

Holyoke, Mary Vial diary, 1763

Jeffares, http://www.pastellists.com/Articles/Blyth.pdf

Norton, "Brothers Blyth," 63

Visitor's Guide to Salem (1895), "Pastel," 195

WPA 1836

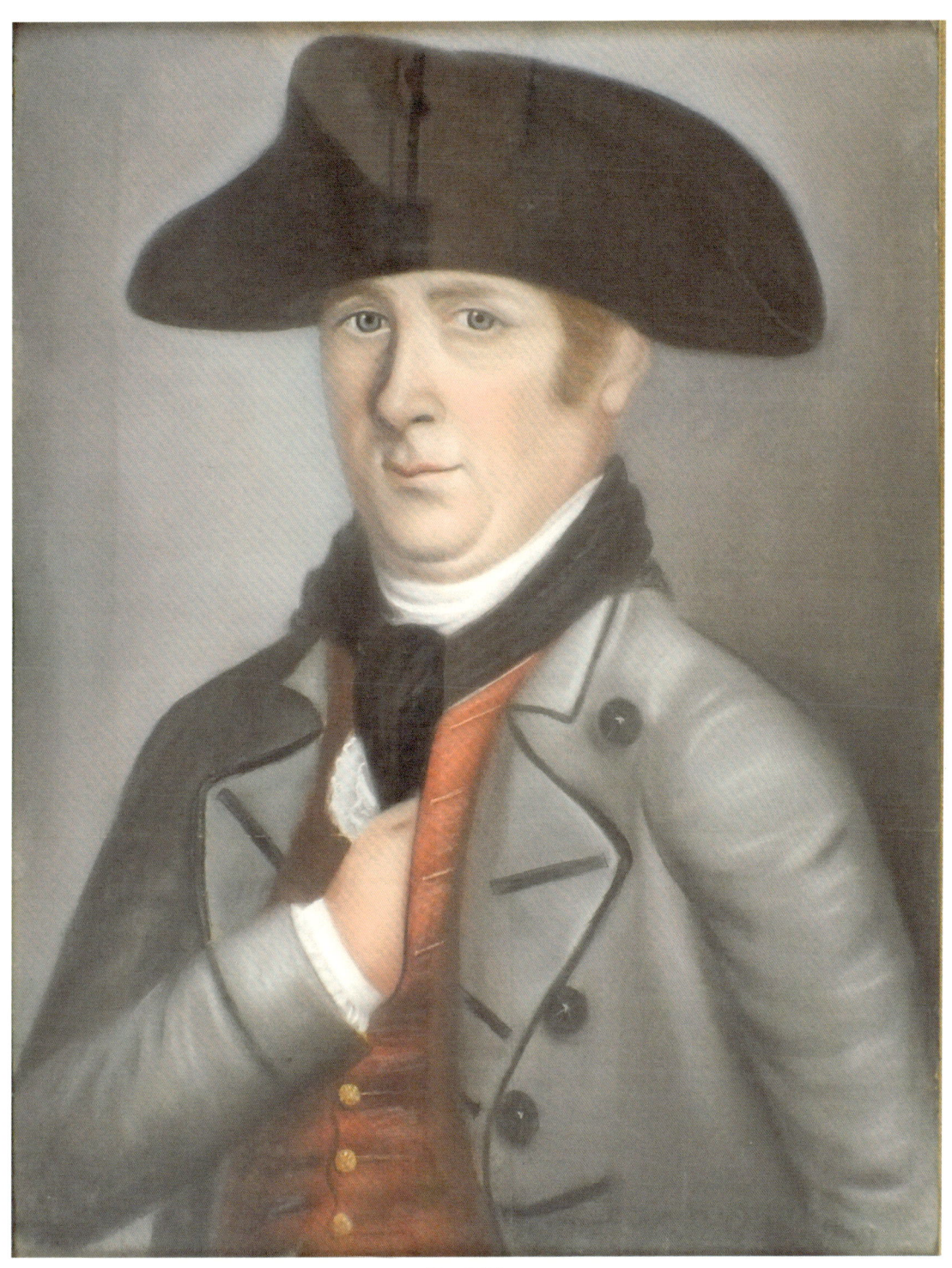

David Ropes
Pastel by Benjamin Blyth, ca. 1774
Courtesy of the Peabody Essex Museum 1721/107943, gift of M. W. Shepard, 1871

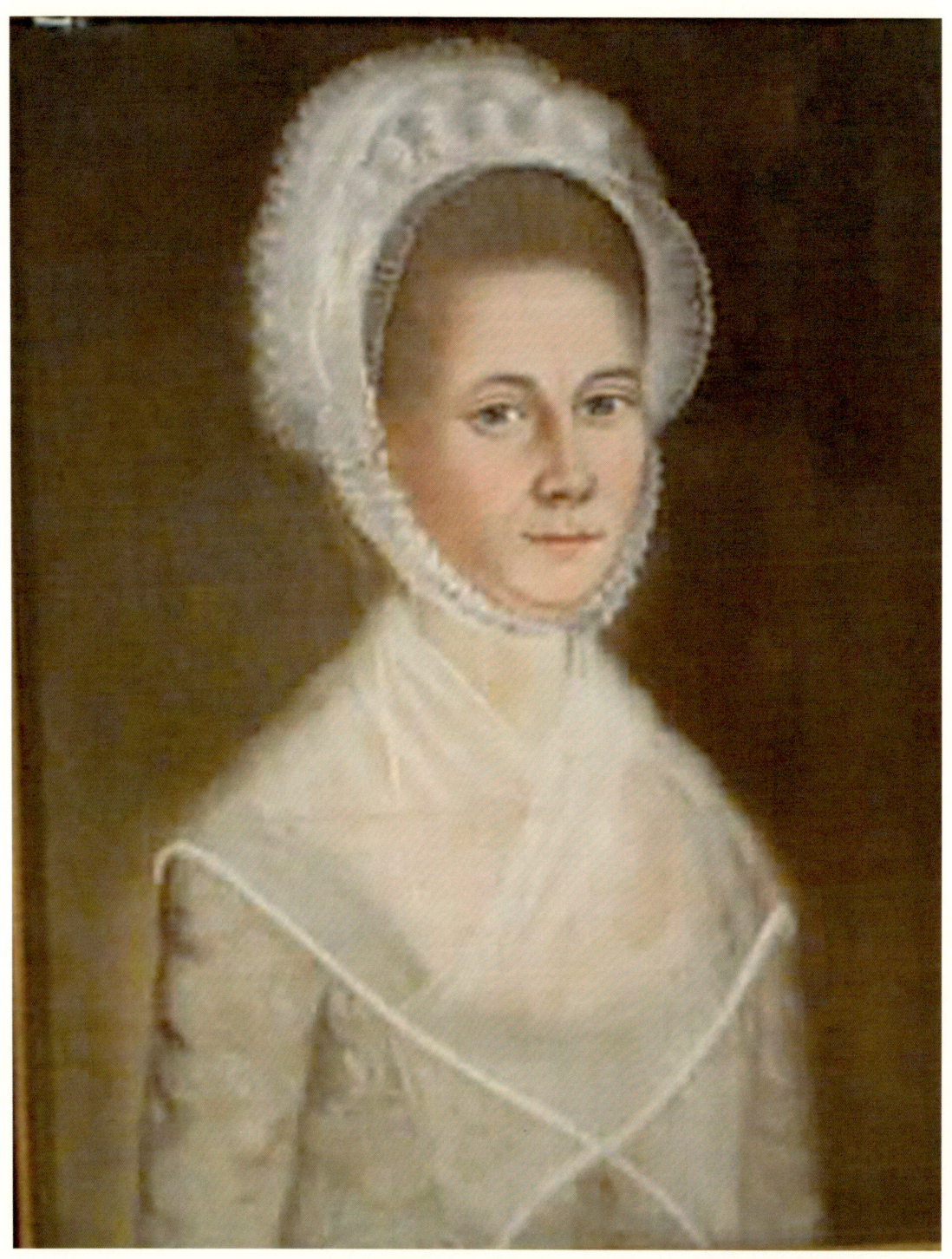

Priscilla Ropes
Pastel by Benjamin Blyth, ca. 1774
Courtesy of the Peabody Essex Museum 1721/107944, gift of M. W. Shepard, 1871

Priscilla Ropes (1741–1831)

Benjamin Blyth, ca. 1774
Pastel on paper mounted on linen, 25 x 19 in. (63.5 x 49.53 cm.)
Peabody Essex Museum 1721/107944, gift of M. W. Shepard, 1871

The three records of Priscilla Ropes' birth date give differing information. Salem Vital Records state that she was born to Jonathan Webb, Jr., and Elizabeth on April 21, 1741, taken from a Bible record of Miss Sally Shepard, of the family that donated the portraits. The Webb family evidently were then members of the Tabernacle Church. The catalogue entry in the Essex Institute Historical Collections reads September 14, 1741, spelling her mother's maiden name as Saunders. However, the inscription written in ink on paper and pasted on the back of her portrait reads "Priscilla, dau. of Jonathan and Elizabeth (Sanders) Webb. bapt. Nov. 8, 1747."

Priscilla's father was a mariner and a tavern keeper, the profession taken up by her husband, David Ropes, whom she married on October 9, 1760. Only two of their children are listed in Salem Vital Records, both named Ruth, from records of the First Church; knowledge of one other comes from entries from the Holyoke diaries, beginning in 1763 that Priscilla was "brought to bed" with the first child—named for her. By the time of the birth of their son, Nathaniel, in 1773, the family had joined St. Peter's Church, the church of the Blyths. A newspaper of October 7, 1831, recorded her death "in her 91st year."

Also written on the back of her portrait is: "Presented to – Shepard by his Aunt Betsy April 19, 1850." This was followed thirty-one years later, with the gift of the portrait of Priscilla's husband David. In her portrait, Priscilla appears to be in her early to mid-thirties, and her costume suggests a date in the early 1770s, although she wears her gossamer shawl in the demure style of the 1760s, as is her bonnet. This portrait, along with her husband's, are two of Blyth's most ambitious. Her face is delicately modeled, with a touch of red at the inner eye and subtle coloring of her hair; as with many Blyths, the lace also is delicately painted.

Bayley, *Little Known . . . Portrait Painters*, "Blyth," no. 2, illus.

Earle, *Two Centuries of Costume*, illus. of bonnet, dated "1761," 2:541

EIHC 16: 219; 72:144–45;151, Cat 271, "unknown artist"

FARL, Blyth, Benjamin 158-3f

Foote, "Blyth," 100 ("Mrs. David Ropes")

Hadley, *Essex Lodge*

Jeffares, http://www.pastellists.com/Articles/Blyth.pdf

Norton, "Brothers Blyth," 63

Visitor's Guide to Salem (1895), "Pastel, 195"

WPA 1838

James Russell, Esq. (1715–1798)

Benjamin Blyth, ca. 1770

Pastel on paper mounted on linen, 26 x 21 in. (sight), (66 x 53.3 cm.), Samuel Blyth frame

Private collection

The portraits of James and Rebecca Russell were among seven rewarding leads that turned up because of an article, "Where have all the portraits gone?" by this author, published in *Maine Antiques Digest* in 2019.

Born in Boston to Daniel Russell, Esq., and Rebeka [*sic*] Russell on August 5, 1715, James Russell, who represented the town of Charlestown for many years in the General Court, was County Treasurer, Judge of the Court, and member of the Honorable Council. He was married on April 13, 1738, to Katherine Graves (Greaves), daughter of Hon. Thomas Graves, also of Boston, by the Reverend Hull Abbot. Their nine children were born between December 27, 1738, and December 8, 1757. His rising career is reflected in the birth record for his eighth child in 1755, by which time he was listed as "Esq." After the war, he proposed a bridge from Charlestown to Boston, which became in 1786 the first one ever built in the United States across a broad river.

A Loyalist, Judge Russell was appointed in 1774 as a Mandamus Councilor, but he did not take the official oath. He was allowed to stay in his home when the Revolution began, although his sons were not. His wife Katherine died very suddenly, after an illness of only three days, on September 17, 1778, at age 61. The Hon. James Russell died April 24, 1798, at age eighty-three.

This portrait shows a sober, thoughtful, admirable man. According to his biography on the Stedman Family History Research Center site, "He was not solicitous to shine, but was anxious to do good, and to be on friendly terms with his neighbors. . . . He was incessant in his endeavors to promote the happiness and advance the prosperity of the community in which he lived." Given that Blyth also drew Russell's daughter Rebecca, perhaps he also did a portrait of his wife.

Loyalists of Massachusetts, 453

Stedman Family History Research Center, http://www.tqsi.com/stedman/earlyresearch.html

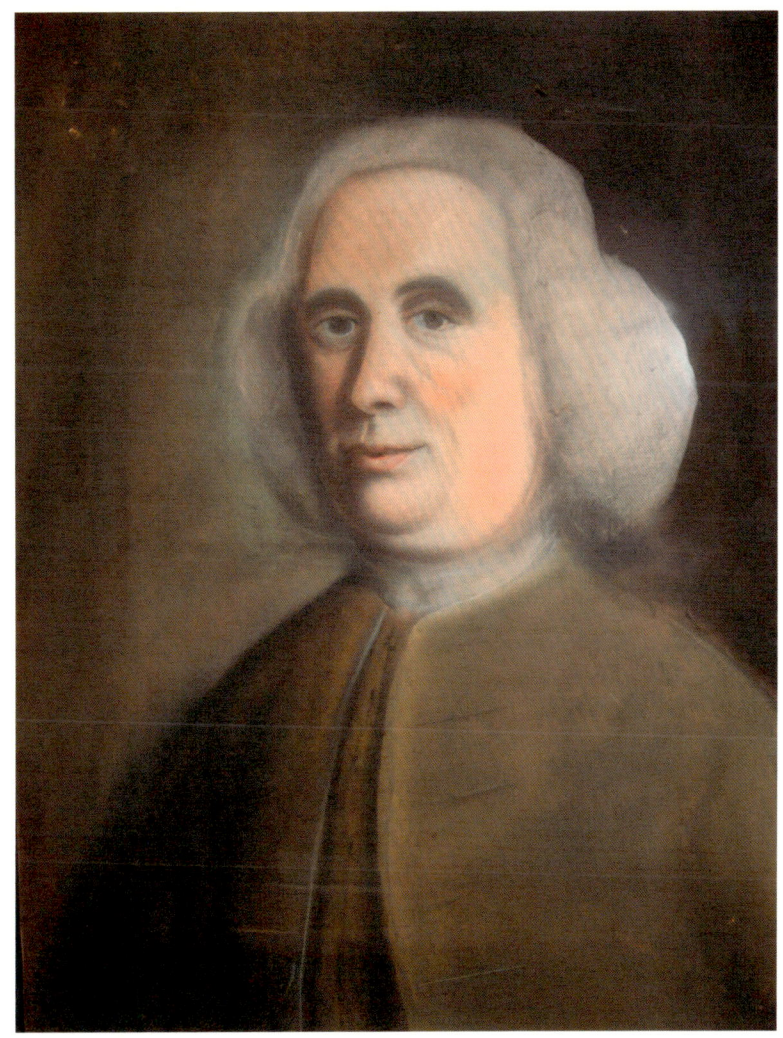

James Russell
Pastel by Benjamin Blyth, ca. 1770
Private collection

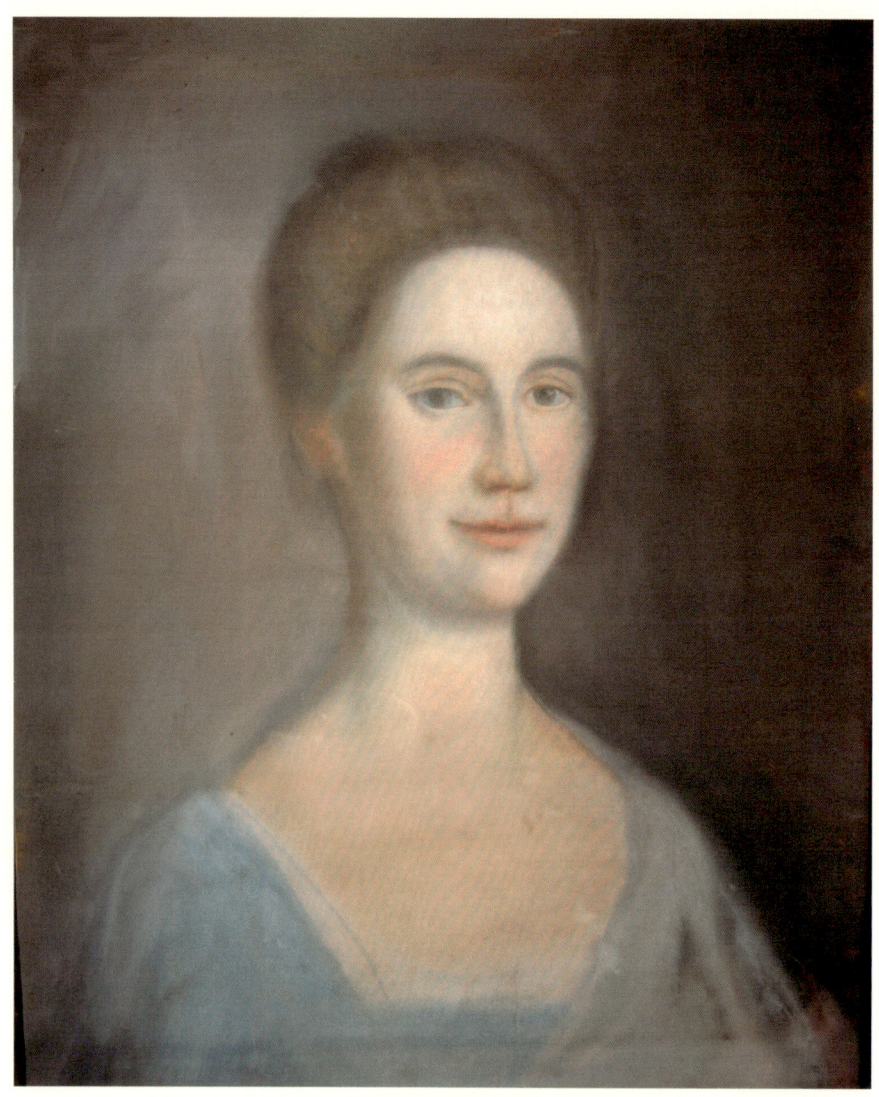

Rebecca Russell
Pastel by Benjamin Blyth, ca. 1770
Private collection

[114]

Rebecca Russell (1747–1816)

Benjamin Blyth, ca. 1770
Pastel on paper mounted on linen, 26 x 21 in. (sight), (66 x 53.3 cm.), Samuel Blyth frame
Private collection

Rebecca, born to James Russell and his wife Katherine Greaves on February 27, 1746, was named after their first child, who died on the day she was born. Both were named after James Russell's mother. Rebecca married twice. Her first husband, James Tyng (1730–1775), whom she married on June 11, 1772, in Charlestown, died three years later. There were no children. Her second husband was John Lowell (Cat. 88), whom she married in Chelmsford on January 27, 1778. They lived in Boston. Their youngest son, Charles Lowell (1782–1861), became the father of the poet, James Russell Lowell (1819–91).

Rebecca died in Boston in 1816. The Lowell Tomb, where she was buried, was among those removed in 1895 from the Central Burying Ground in Boston Common to Forest Hills Cemetery to allow for the construction of the Boylston Street subway.

An example of Blyth's ability to portray character, her compelling portrait, like that of the young John Gibaut, conveys an inner thoughtfulness.

Seth Thayer, correspondence

[115]

Gibbons Sharp (ca. 1715–1805)

Benjamin Blyth, late 1760s
Pastel on paper mounted on linen, 27 x 22½ in. (68.9 x 57.1 cm.), early-19th-c. gilt wood frame
Historic New England, on unresolved loan; E. G. Prescott to Frederick Lincoln in 1833

Records for Gibbons Sharp (Gibbins, Gibbens) are scant. His birth date is not known, but he married Hephzibah Oliver on October 29, 1765 and died on September 15, 1805. He was in the French and Indian Wars, and in 1771, he sued his next-door neighbor, Gibbs Atkins (Cat. 6), for trespass. Sharp was an active member of the New North Church on Hanover Street in the North End of Boston, an area "in which the most aged men have been found," noted the Reverend William Bentley in 1805, adding "Deacon Sharp is now living about 90." He died later that year. The manuscript titled "List of Wards, 1800," notes his real estate valued at $900, with the comment, "Ship Wright. Old. no Businefs."

Sharp's portrait has been dated in various sources to either 1755 or 1767. Given his age and clothing, and that it was drawn by Blyth, the 1767 date is more likely. Also, since there is a companion portrait of his wife, Hepzibah Oliver, the portraits would have been drawn after the couple was married on October 29, 1765. These portraits are among the few in which Blyth depicted hands, which argues for an early date in his oeuvre, as Blyth later abandoned the practice.

The framing history of this portrait and its companion of Hepzibah Sharp are the most thoroughly documented of any by Blyth. The printed label on the back of Gibbons Sharp reads that the portrait was framed by E. Lothrop, Gilder, of Court-Street, Boston, probably in the early 1830s, and another typed label reads "Cleaned & Refitted" by Foster Brothers/Feb. 1, 1940." The portrait must have been given an additional mount, because a strip of paper was added across the bottom, 1½ inches high (sight), and another one inch (sight) vertically at the right side. They both were in-painted to match the pastel. Another label on the back, written in ink, reads "This picture of my beloved Uncle Deacon Sharp I give and bequeath to Frederick Lincoln." It is signed E. G. Prescott and dated Boston, 1833.

Bentley 3:151
Jeffares, http://www.pastellists.com/Articles/Blyth.pdf
New North Church, Boston records
Norton, "Brothers Blyth," 63

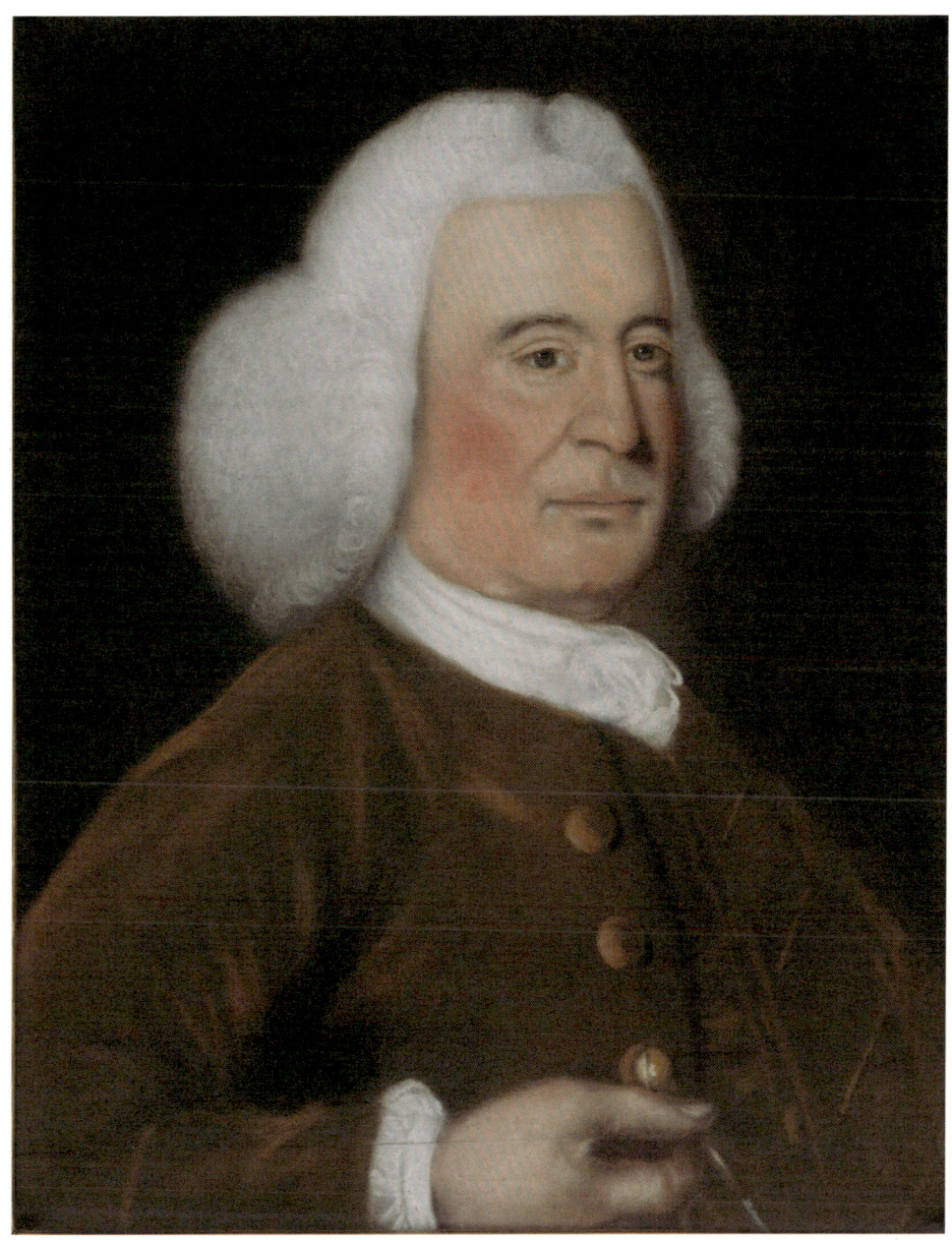

Gibbons Sharp
Pastel by Benjamin Blyth, late 1760s
Courtesy of Historic New England, on unresolved loan

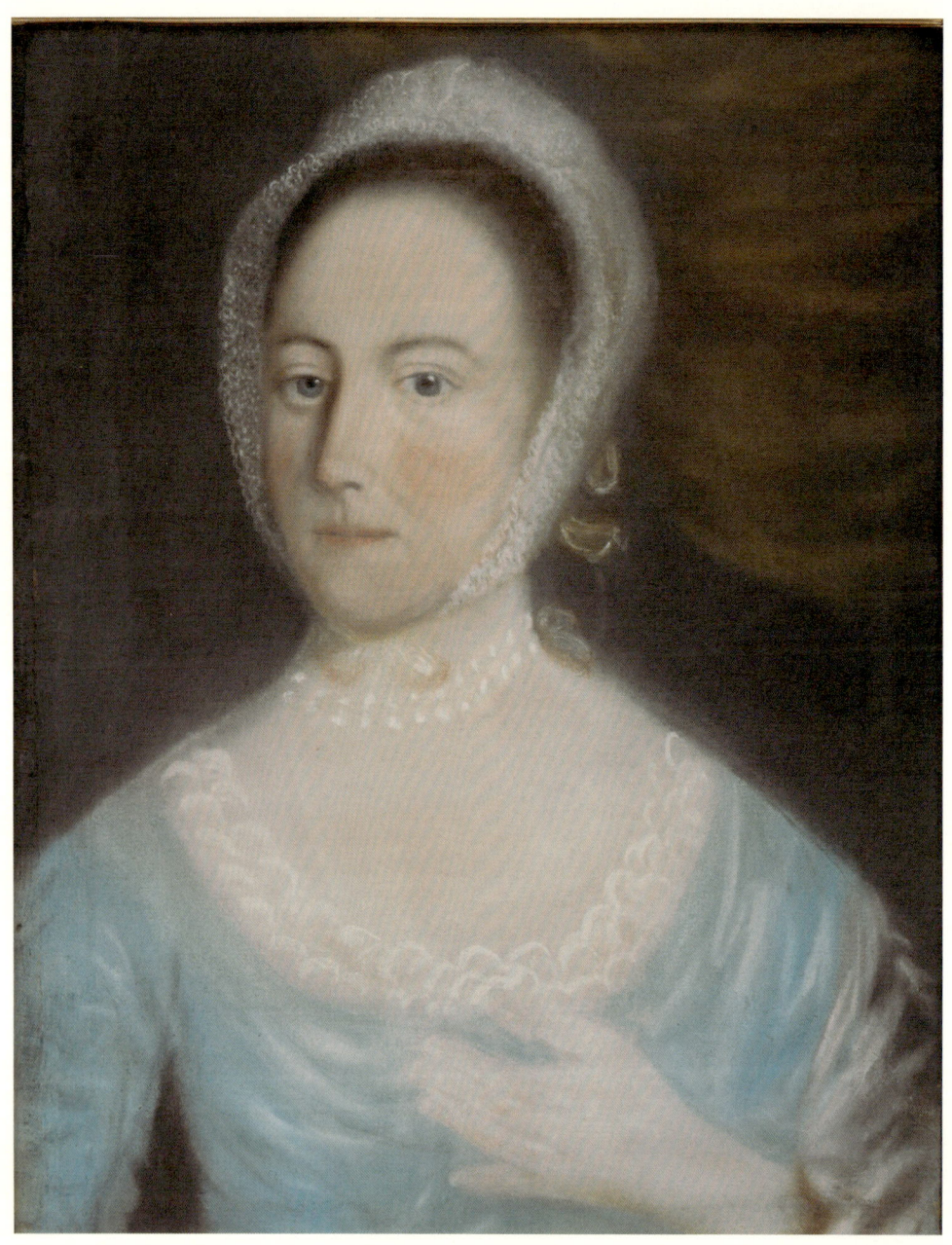

Hepzibah Sharp
Pastel by Benjamin Blyth, late 1760s
Courtesy of Historic New England, on unresolved loan

[116]

Hepzibah Sharp (1726/7–1801)

Benjamin Blyth, late 1760s

Pastel on paper mounted on canvas, 27 x 22½ in. (68. 9 x 57. 1 cm.), early-19th-c. gilt wood frame

Historic New England, on unresolved loan; E. G. Prescott to Frederick Lincoln in 1833

No record of the birth of a Hepzibah Oliver in Massachusetts in the 1720s has been found, but the record of her death on November 26, 1801, at age 74, would indicate that she was born in 1726/7 and was twelve years younger than her husband.

Both her portrait and that of her husband show their hands, an early practice by Blyth which he generally thereafter abandoned. In the background is a drape with baubles, a feature also soon abandoned in favor of unadorned backgrounds. Hepzibah's portrait, like that of her husband, was mounted on a slightly larger canvas, adding about ¾", which was in-painted on the left side. This probably was done when this portrait and that of her husband were framed in the late 1820s or early 1830s by E. Lothrop, Gilder on Court-Street, Boston. Written in ink on the back is a pasted label, similar to that on the portrait of her husband: "This picture of my beloved Aunt Hepzibah Sharp I give and bequeath to Frederick Lincoln." It is signed E. G. Prescott and dated, Boston, 1833.

Jeffares, http://www.pastellists.com/Articles/Blyth. pdf

Norton, "Brothers Blyth," 63

[117]

Jonathan Simpson (1685–1763)

Benjamin Blyth, probably 1771
Pastel on paper on linen, 21½ x 16 in. (54.6 x 40.6 cm.), Samuel Blyth frame
James and Janet Laverdiere; Northeast Auctions; Mary Eliot Nichols, Danvers, MA

Resolution to a problem of identifying portraits often comes about fortuitously, sometimes because an owner values historical accuracy. Such was the case with the Blyth pastel of Jonathan Simpson, painted by Joseph Blackburn in 1757/8. When described for sale by Northeast Auctions, the inscription on the back was read as Jonathan Simpson *Ward*. (Indeed, it is almost the mirror image of the pastel purported to be of Gov. Richard Ward of Rhode Island, attributed to Blyth (Cat. 146). However, when the current owners of the Simpson, James and Janet Laverdiere, were contacted, they clarified that the inscription is "Jonathan Simpson Merch[an]t."

Jonathan Simpson, a prominent shopkeeper of Boston, was born on April 3, 1685. His parents were Jonathan and Wait (Clap) Simpson of Charlestown. In 1707, he married Mary, daughter of Thomas and Mary Baker. Their daughter Mary married Nathaniel Vial, another Boston shopkeeper, in 1736; and their daughter and only child was Mary, who married Dr. Edward Augustus Holyoke. Simpson died in Boston on February 16, 1763.

Blyth drew this pastel copy for Simpson's granddaughter, Mary Vial Holyoke, when Blyth was drawing her portrait (Cat. 71) and that of her husband, Dr. Edward Augustus Holyoke (Cat. 70) in 1770–71. Henry Wilder Foote did not know this about the pastel and so could not explain the supposed anachronism, given Simpson's death date, but nonetheless correctly assigned it stylistically to Blyth. For the portrayal, Blyth eliminated the chair and background seen in the Blackburn oil, but otherwise his pastel is faithful and in many ways equal to the Blackburn original, now in the Museum of Fine Arts, Springfield, Massachusetts. Both images capture a contented, successful merchant. (See p. 24) The pastel also shows just how often, and how well, Benjamin Blyth copied oil portraits of Salem residents done by earlier artists, Joseph Blackburn and two others as yet unidentified. The Blyth copy of Simpson once belonged to Mary Eliot Nichols, who also was a previous owner of the Holyoke portraits.

James and Janet Laverdiere also recently purchased two of Blyth's most ambitious portraits, of the Gardners (Cats. 57, 58) and shortly before this book went to press, the pastel of Patty Webb (Cat. 134).

Foote, "Blyth," 100–1
Jeffares, http://www.pastellists.com/Articles/Blyth.pdf
MHS, Frank William Bayley Papers
Northeast Auctions catalog (information unobtainable)
Osgood, Nancy, typescript biography, The Holyoke and Ward Families

Park, Lawrence, "Joseph Blackburn, a Colonial Portrait Painter"
SIRIS, Control number 80960035

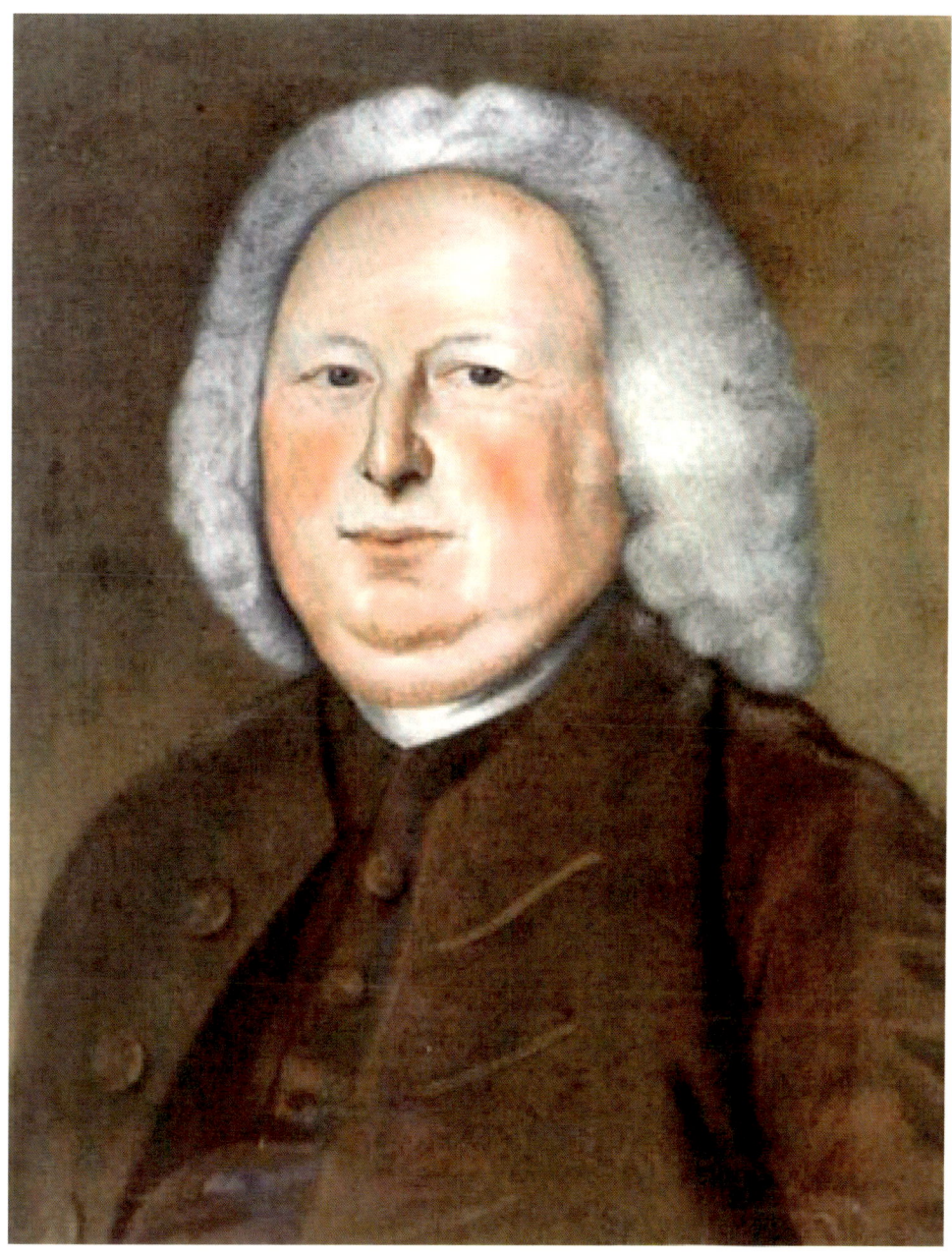

Jonathan Simpson
Pastel by Benjamin Blyth, probably 1771
Courtesy of the collection of James and Janet Laverdiere

John Small (1726–1796)

Benjamin Blyth, probably 1774
Pastel, measurements unknown
Current location not known, Boston Antique Shop, William Inglis Morse, C. Howland White,
Capt. Gideon White

The British Brigade Major John Small, stationed in New England during the American Revolution, found himself fighting at the Battle of Bunker Hill with friends who were on opposing sides: Gen. Israel Putnam, whose life Small later claimed credit for saving, and Gen. Joseph Warren, for whom his self-proclaimed efforts were less successful. All three, who had been drawn by Blyth (besides Small, Cats. 108 and 129), are featured in *The Death of General Warren at the Battle of Bunker's Hill, June 17, 1775*, painted by John Trumbull in London after the war. It incorporated much advice from Small. He is shown prominently (not surprisingly, though possibly not accurately) staving off the attack by bayonet on Warren, whose death was caused by a shot to his head. Small also suggested adding Putnam, shown at the left rear.

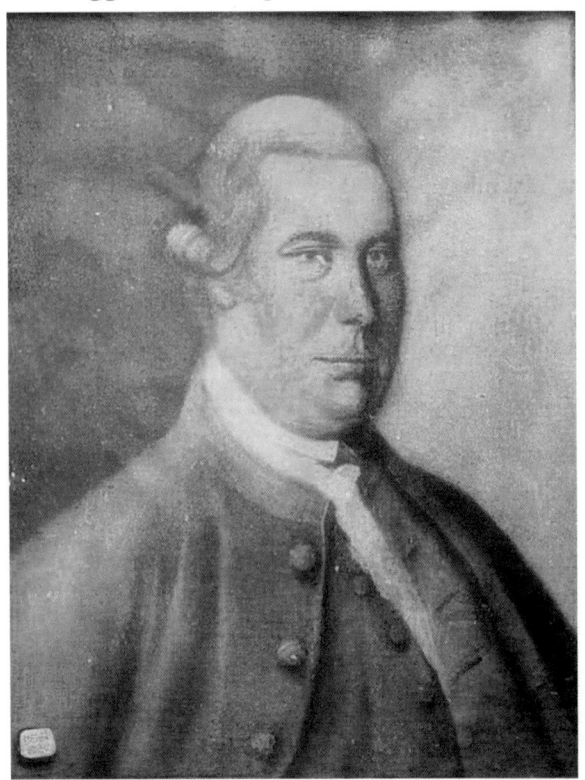

John Small
Photograph of unlocated pastel by Benjamin Blyth, 1774?
Courtesy of the Frick Art Reference Library Photoarchives

Born in Scotland in 1726, Small became a British military officer in 1756 and served with distinction in the Seven Years' War. In 1774, he was in Salem and Danvers with the contingent of General Thomas Gage and then was sent to Nova Scotia to raise what became the 84th Regiment of Foot, Royal Highland Emigrants. After the war, he settled with other British soldiers in Douglas Township, Hants County, Nova Scotia. The British Crown granted land to them to encourage settlement. Small built a manor house "Selma Hall," and Selma then became the name of the town. However, he soon returned to Great Britain, where he was appointed lieutenant governor of Guernsey and promoted to major general, serving from 1793 until his death in March 1796 in Saint Peter Port, Guernsey. According to Elisa Tamarkin, author of *Anglophilia*, Small was "distinguished by acts of humanity and kindness to his enemies, as by bravery and fidelity to the cause he served." He never married.

On September 17, 1769, from New York, Small

wrote to John Singleton Copley, "[T]he Miniature you took from my Crayon Picture has been very much admired. … I want much to have a Copy of my Crayon picture, Mr. Dumaresq will Let you have the use of it for that purpose." In his book on the artist, Bayley wrote, "the crayon was made for Mr. Philip Dumaresq and a copy made for Capt. Small with some alterations, according to the Copley correspondence." Pastel scholar Neil Jeffares discovered that Blyth's pastel of Small was found in 1921 in Shelburne, Nova Scotia, by C. Howland White, who claimed that Small gave it to his great-grandfather, Capt. Gideon White, before leaving for England.

By 1932, it was owned by William Inglis Morse, who reproduced it in his book, *The Land of The New Adventure*. Morse may have thought the pastel was by Copley, but Barbara Parker and Anne Wheeler, who examined it around then, said it was "not characteristic of Copley's work." The pastel does fit stylistically with the work of Blyth. The modeling of the face is quite proficient, but the flatness of the back of the head betrays problems with perspective, which is also true with Blyth's portrait of Elizabeth Dabney (Cat. 39). Small's portrait is further diminished by the small size and awkward placement of the wig. The eyes, however, are very penetrating, his expression, determined.

One question is, why would Small have Blyth do a pastel of him, presumably in 1774, if he already had one or two by Copley? Had he given both away, or did he decide to add another? A possible explanation is that Bayley was mistaken, and there never was a second Copley portrait. As Copley had left for England in June 1774, Small may have turned to Blyth. A later pastel of Small as a British major general in the Chateau Ramezay Museum in Montreal, Canada, ca. 1793, shows a more robust, handsome man, which raises another question, about the identity of the sitter in the pastel. Blyth was known, however, for the accuracy of his portrayals. The pastels or miniature by Copley that Small alluded to in his correspondence would really solve the mystery. They must be in Canada or England, if still extant.

Adams, Charles F., et al, *Letters & Papers of John Singleton Copley and Henry Pelham*, 77–78

Bayley, *Life and Works* . . . (attributing it to Copley), 227

Bolton, *Copley*, no. 46, 21

FARL, Copley, John Singleton 157-3k

Jeffares, Neil, correspondence

Morse, William Inglis, *The Land of The New Adventure* (London, 1932), illus. 50

Parker and Wheeler, 259, 267-278

Prown (attributing it to Copley), 1:229

Tamarkin, *Anglophilia*, 134

Wikimedia Foundation, 18 June 2022, https://en. wikipedia. org/wiki/ John_Small_(British_Army_officer)

[119]

William Smith (1707–1783)

Benjamin Blyth, late 1760s
Pastel on paper, 23½ x 18½ in. (59.7 x 47 cm.)
Current location not known; Mrs. Lewis Greenleaf, Nantucket, 1970s; Greenleaf family

The Reverend William Smith was a liberal Congregationalist emphasizing reason and morality over the Puritan doctrines of predestination and original sin. He had no sympathy for the revivalist New Lights and at a meeting in Weymouth in 1745, publicly disparaged the Reverend George Whitefield. Born to Capt. William Smith, a wealthy mariner and merchant, and Abigail (Fowle) Smith of Charlestown on August 3, 1707, he was regarded as a "pious lad," though with a humorous bent. According to *Sibley's Harvard Graduates*, his diary "recorded as funny, stories which today seem dirty and entirely without humor. However, the people of that age never doubted his devotion to religion." Smith graduated from Harvard College in 1725 and nine years later was called to the First Church of Weymouth, a position he held for forty-nine years. The announcement of his intention to marry Elizabeth Quincy of Braintree was published on his thirty-third birthday. The daughter of John and Elizabeth (Norton) Quincy, she "seems to have been one of that series of unusual women who contributed to the presidential Adams family the strain of greatness," *Sibley's* recorded. They had one son and four daughters, of which Abigail (Cat. 2) was the third. At Abigail's marriage to the young, ambitious lawyer, John Adams (Cat. 3), later to become second president of the United States, Smith, who had an aversion to lawyers, chose as the subject of his sermon, "John came neither eating nor drinking, & they say he hath a devil."

His mother's family owned an eighty-acre farm on the Mystic River; and Smith, who had a lifelong interest in grafting trees and other agricultural pursuits, later bought a farm in Medford. At his death on September 17, 1783, he also owned a farm in Lincoln and land in Concord. His will offered freedom to Phoebe, an enslaved woman in his household, but stated that if she chose to remain with one of his daughters, she "should have an additional £100 from his estate for her trouble."

This portrait of Smith was one of those attributed to Copley by Theodore Bolton, who noted that it was on loan to the Metropolitan Museum by Mr. R. C. Greenleaf from 1913 to 1921. Bolton also provided the measurements. Parker & Wheeler considered the attribution doubtful.

Bolton, *Portraits . . . Draughtsmen*, 21
The Book of Abigail and John: Selected Letters of the Adams Family, 1762–1784, 2002, illus. 20
Jeffares, http://www.pastellists.com/Articles/Blyth.pdf
Parker & Wheeler, 259
Proceedings of the MHS 19:386
Sibley 7:560, 588–91

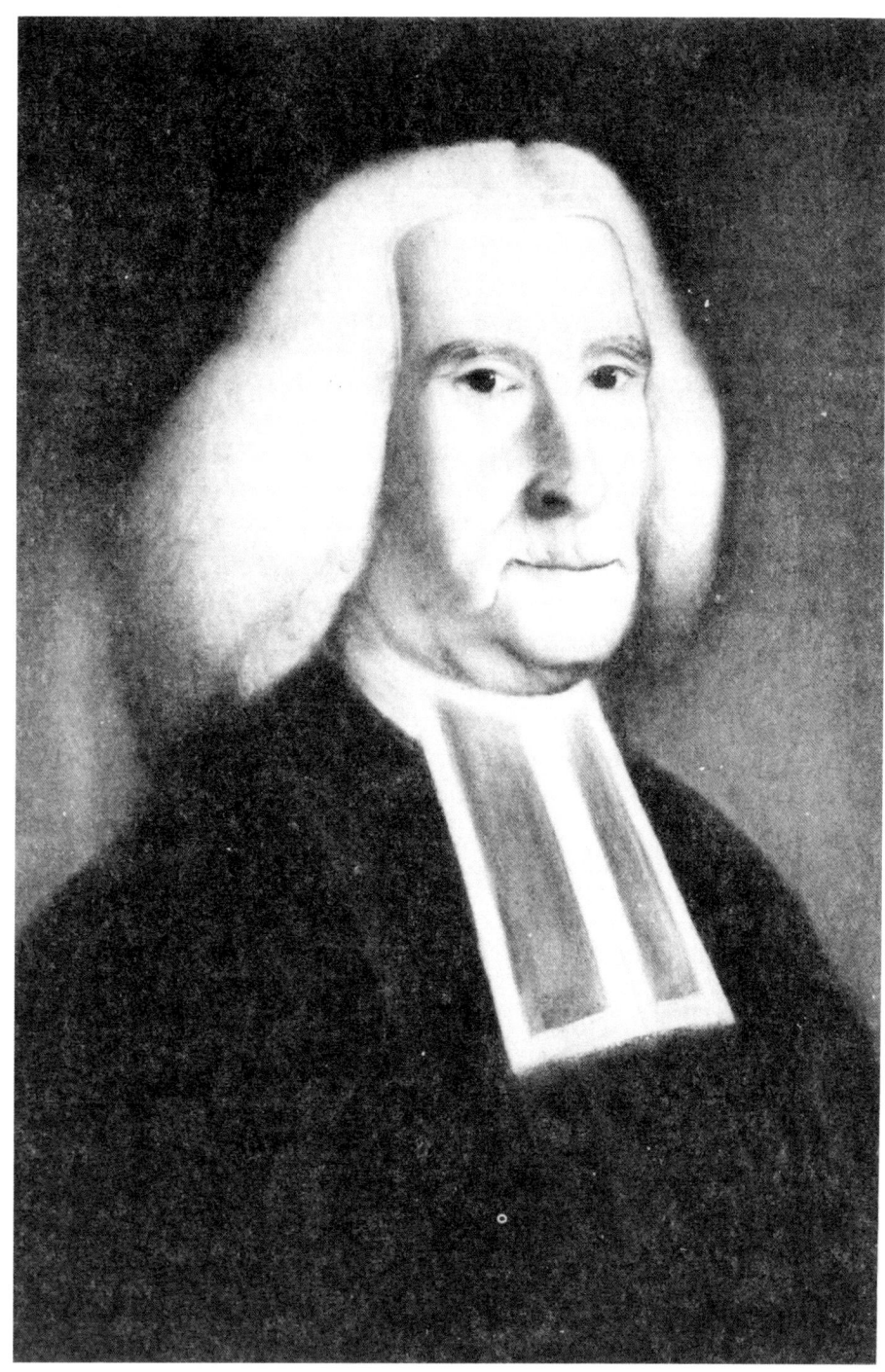

Reverend William Smith
Photograph of unlocated pastel by Benjamin Blyth, late 1760s
The book of Abigail and John: Selected Letters of the Adams Family, 1762–1784, 20
Courtesy of the Boston Athenaeum

[120]

John Somes (1745–1816)

Benjamin Blyth, early 1770s
Pastel on paper mounted on coarse linen, 21. 8 x 19 in. (55.37 x 48.26 cm.), Samuel Blyth frame (?)
with original hanging hooks
Cape Ann Museum 1,596, gift in 1952 of the estate of Josephine Dolliver, a Somes descendant
through her mother

The large Somes family was prominent from the early settlement of Gloucester. In 1692, Abigail Somes was accused of witchcraft and jailed in Boston from May 23 to January 3, 1693, but she, like four other women in Gloucester, escaped execution.

Capt. John Somes was baptized in June 1745, the seventh of nine children of Abraham and Martha (Emerson) Soams, as the surname of this line of the family was spelled in records of the early to mid-eighteenth century. In 1771, his intention of marriage to Mary Smith, who was eighteen at the time, was published. Neither the birth of any children nor her death was recorded. Then on October 1, 1780, Somes married Anna (or Anne) (Dolliver) Coullson (Colson), whose first husband had been lost at sea in 1777. She had a daughter, born in March 1778, but she and Somes had no children.

Somes was a noted privateer captain during the Revolution. His ship *America* out of Newburyport in 1779 and 1780 took three ships of the Quebec fleet in the mouth of the St. Lawrence. He was on the *America* out of Newburyport again in the summer of 1780 which took with the aid of the *Brutus* the ships *William* and *Everetta,* and brigantines *Duke of Burlue, Kitty and Bell, Snow Beaver,* & *Nancy.* However, his armed letter-of-marque brig *Ranger* was captured on the way from Cape Ann to Cap François within sight of Hispaniola on June 18, 1781.

After the war, Somes became a merchant. He also ran a tavern, earning him the nickname, "Old Toby." By 1791, he owned a house, a barn, a wharf and a store, the brig *Three Friends* and its cargo, a coasting sloop, a horse, a pig, and a cow. He was the first president of the Gloucester Bank, a position he held for many years. He also represented Gloucester in the General Court in 1806 and 1807 and was a member of the Universalist Church. Somes died on August 17, 1816, at age seventy-three. His age was given variously as seventy-six, which would have made his birth date earlier; his baptism may have been as a child and not as an infant. The first listings in the inventory of his estate—a part interest in the schooner *Jolly Robin*, "276 gallons of rum, 28 bags of cotton and 40 hog's head of salt"—indicate that he was a trader at his death. His assets, all left to his wife, included shares in several banks as well as a mansion house and several other parcels of land and buildings, a farm on Eastern Point, as well as outstanding loans and rents from real estate. He was buried in a private lot in Universalist Yard.

Three years after his death, an entry in the Reverend William Bentley's diary suggests that Somes did not leave bank affairs in order. "We have in this County two desperate if not unexampled frauds. At Gloucester were left signed by the Cashier & not improbably innocently by President Somes & left after his death, a great amount of bills left in a very exposed place & afterwards put into circulation. Many of these were received and accredited at Salem bank & for these the bank sues. It has been heard it is upon an appeal from judgment given for G. Bank.... We see the general character of Banks throughout the United States."

The buttons and lace in Somes's portrait are especially well done. His hair is fashionably powdered, and he has the demeanor of a successful merchant—a slightly wrinkled brow and calculating air. The portrait probably was done as a companion with the one of his wife (Cat. 121). Now unaccounted for, it was in a private collection in Gloucester in 1963. American art historian John Wilmerding noted that the well-known nineteenth-century American luminist Fitz Henry Lane made an oil copy.

Bentley 1:257, 267; 4:628

Cape Ann Museum records

Essex County Probate Record 25869

EIHC 45:158; 76:52; 99:197 (Wilmerding, "Fitz Hugh Lane 1804–1865")

Hawes, Charles Boardman, *Gloucester by Land and Sea* (Boston: Little, Brown and Company, 1923, 28

Jeffares, http://www.pastel-lists.com/Articles/Blyth.pdf

Norton, "Brothers Blyth," 63

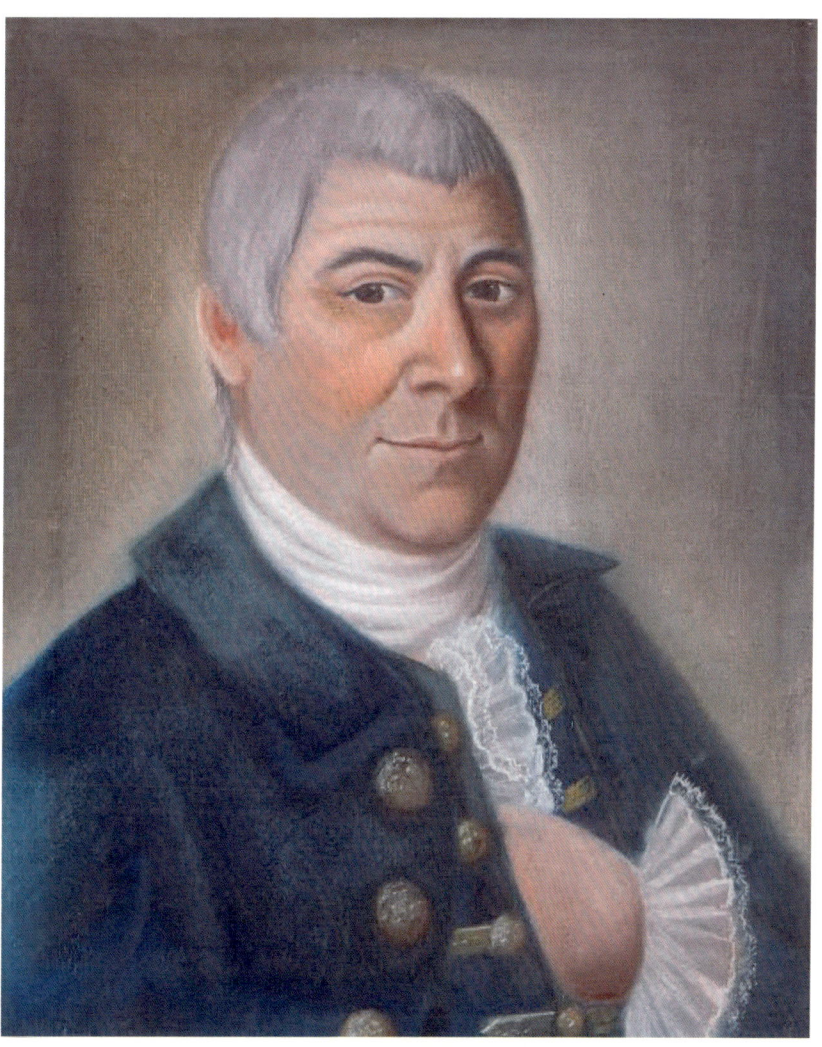

John Somes
Pastel by Benjamin Blyth, early 1770s
Courtesy of the Cape Ann Museum 1,596, gift in 1952 of the estate of
Josephine Dolliver, a Somes descendant through her mother

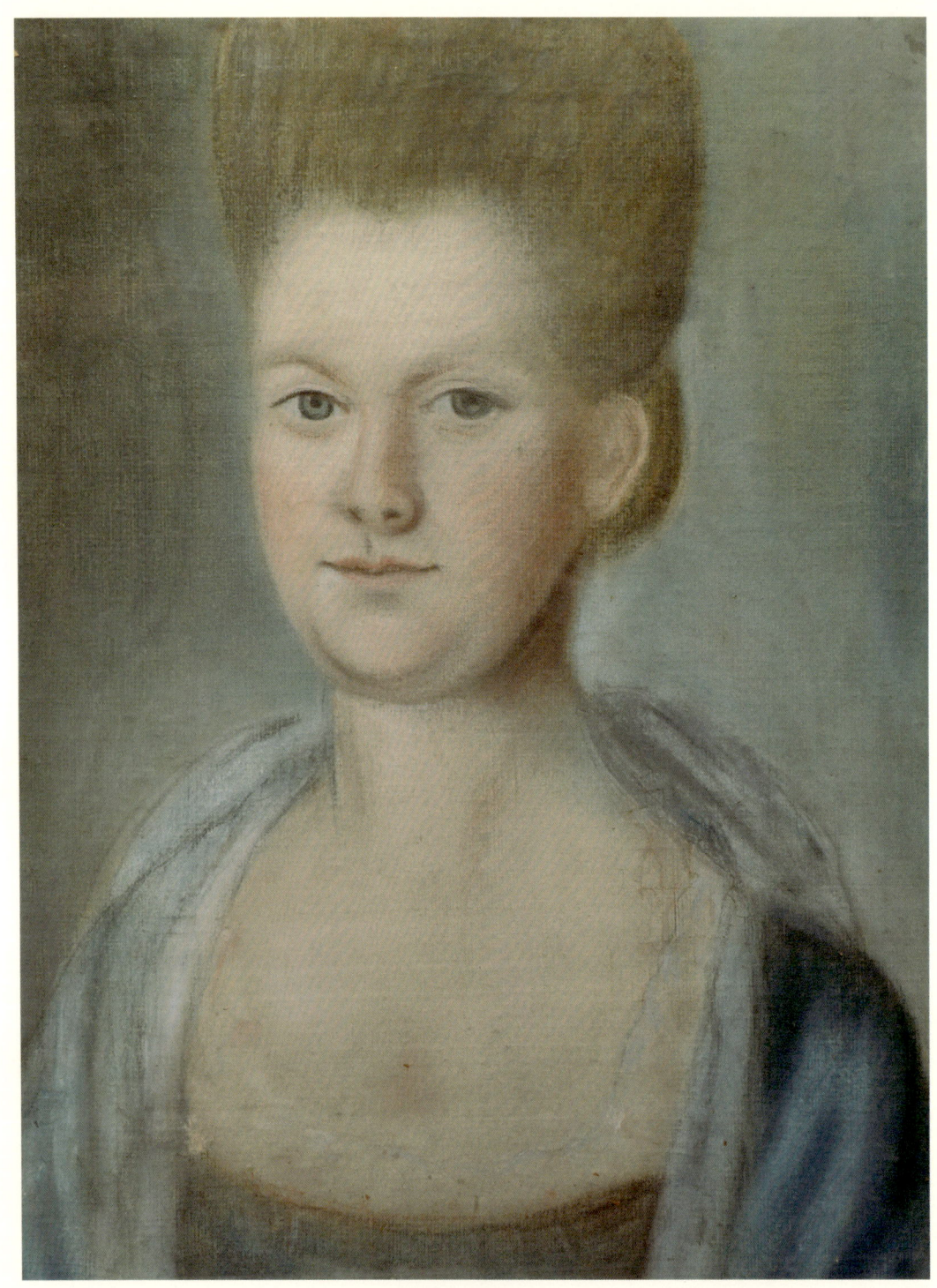

[Mary?] Somes
Pastel by Benjamin Blyth, early 1770s
Courtesy of the Cape Ann Museum 1,596A, gift in 1948 by Miss Annie S. Webber, a Somes descendant through her father

[121]

Mary(?) Somes (1753–177?)

Benjamin Blyth, early 1770s

Pastel on paper mounted on coarse linen, 17.8 x 13.6 in. (45.21 x 34.54 cm.), Samuel Blyth frame

Cape Ann Museum 1,596A, gift in 1948 by Miss Annie S. Webber,

a Somes descendant through her father

The old label on this portrait says "Mrs. John Somes." Somes had two wives. He and Mary Smith were married on August 18, 1771. Most likely, she was the Mary Smith baptized on April 22, 1753, whose father was Alexander Smith of Gloucester. The records of the Smith family are almost non-existent, so there are no births of children listed, and her death is not recorded.

Somes married widow Anna Dolliver on October 1, 1780. She was born on September 18, 1755, to Paul and Rachel (Barber) Dolliver. Her father died in 1761, when she was six years old, and her mother remarried. Anna's first husband, Capt. John Colson (Coulsen), was lost on the Brig *Gloucester* soon after leaving port on July 1, 1777. Their daughter Nancy, baptized eight and a half months later, would have been a toddler when her widowed mother married Somes. When he died in 1816, he did not name his stepdaughter in his will; he left his entire estate to his wife, who outlived him by thirty years. This could be a portrait of her, well before she married Somes, but that seems unlikely.

The hairstyle and clothing of "Mrs. Somes" bespeak a date of the early 1770s for the portrait, like that of John Somes. The frames on the two portraits do not match and the portraits are different sizes, which might suggest they were done at different times, although the one of Mary (or Anna) most likely was cut down and reframed. Hers is sketchier than his, suggesting that she may have become ill or died before Blyth was able to finish it. So, it likely is of Mary.

Hawes, Charles Boardman, *Gloucester by Land and Sea*, (Boston: Little, Brown and Company, 1923), 28

Jeffares, http://www.pastellists.com/Articles/Blyth. pdf

Norton, "Brothers Blyth," 63

☞ Elizabeth Dabney Bridges Stevens; see Elizabeth Dabney (Cat. 39)

[122]

Ebenezer Syms (1767?–?)

Benjamin Blyth, ca. 1780
Pastel on paper mounted on linen, 14⅔ x 11¼ in. (37.2 x 26cm.), later frame
Current location not known; Nina Fletcher Little, Sotheby's,
American Classics Antiques (Woodstock, VT), Mrs. Thomas C. Dunnington, NH

This portrait, said to be of Ebenezer Syms, was probably drawn at about the same time as that of young Ezekiel Hersey Derby. Both are among Blyth's more successful of this genre, and the dog that Ebenezer holds is rendered more successfully than Blyth's other attempts at pets. The oval format that Blyth drew is very unusual for his work.

The advertisement in *Maine Antiques Digest* from the dealer Meryl Weiss gave the specific age of Ebenezer as "13 years and 7 months," suggesting that this, along with his name, was written on the back of the portrait. However, the dealer made no guess at a date of execution. The clothing on the boy, as on Ezekiel Derby, places it around 1780, when the collar for boys' jackets came into fashion. So, the boy may have been born around 1767. No record has been found under various spellings of the surname.

The portrait was exhibited in Nina Fletcher Little's exhibition, "Paintings by New England Provincial Artists 1775–1800" at the Museum of Fine Arts, Boston, in 1976. Referred to later as "Capt. Sims," it was once owned by Mrs. Thomas C. Dunnington of Dover, New Hampshire. From the Little collection, it was sold by Sotheby's for $2,200 to American Classics Antiques.

Lois Avigad, correspondence
Maine Antiques Digest, Nov. 1997
Sotheby's

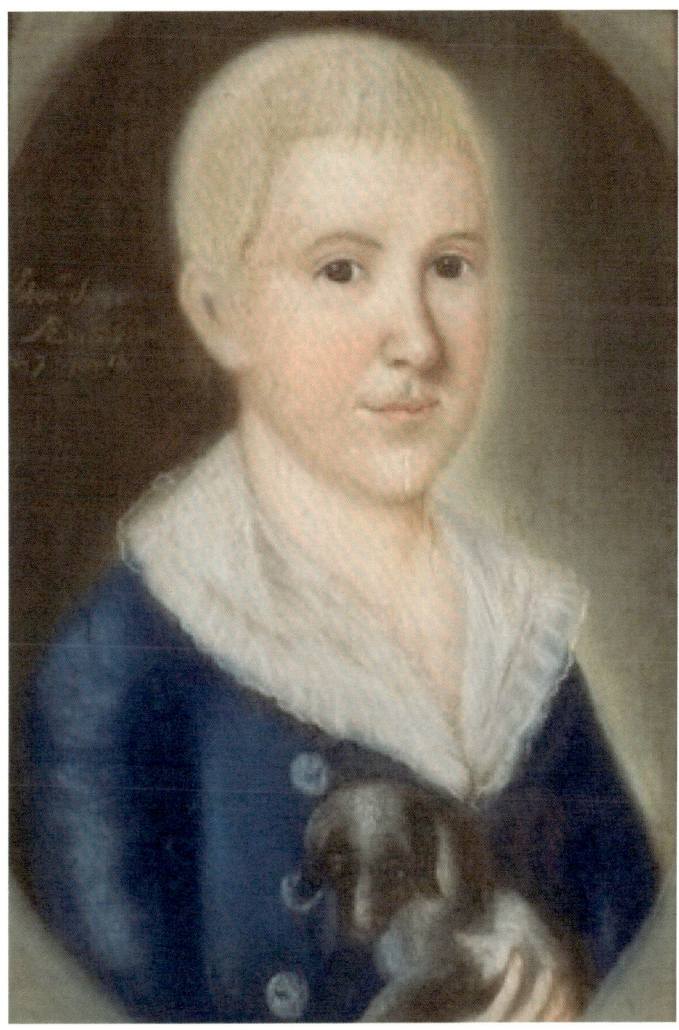

Ebenezer Syms
Photograph of pastel by Benjamin Blyth, ca. 1780
Courtesy of Sotheby's, Little collection, 1994

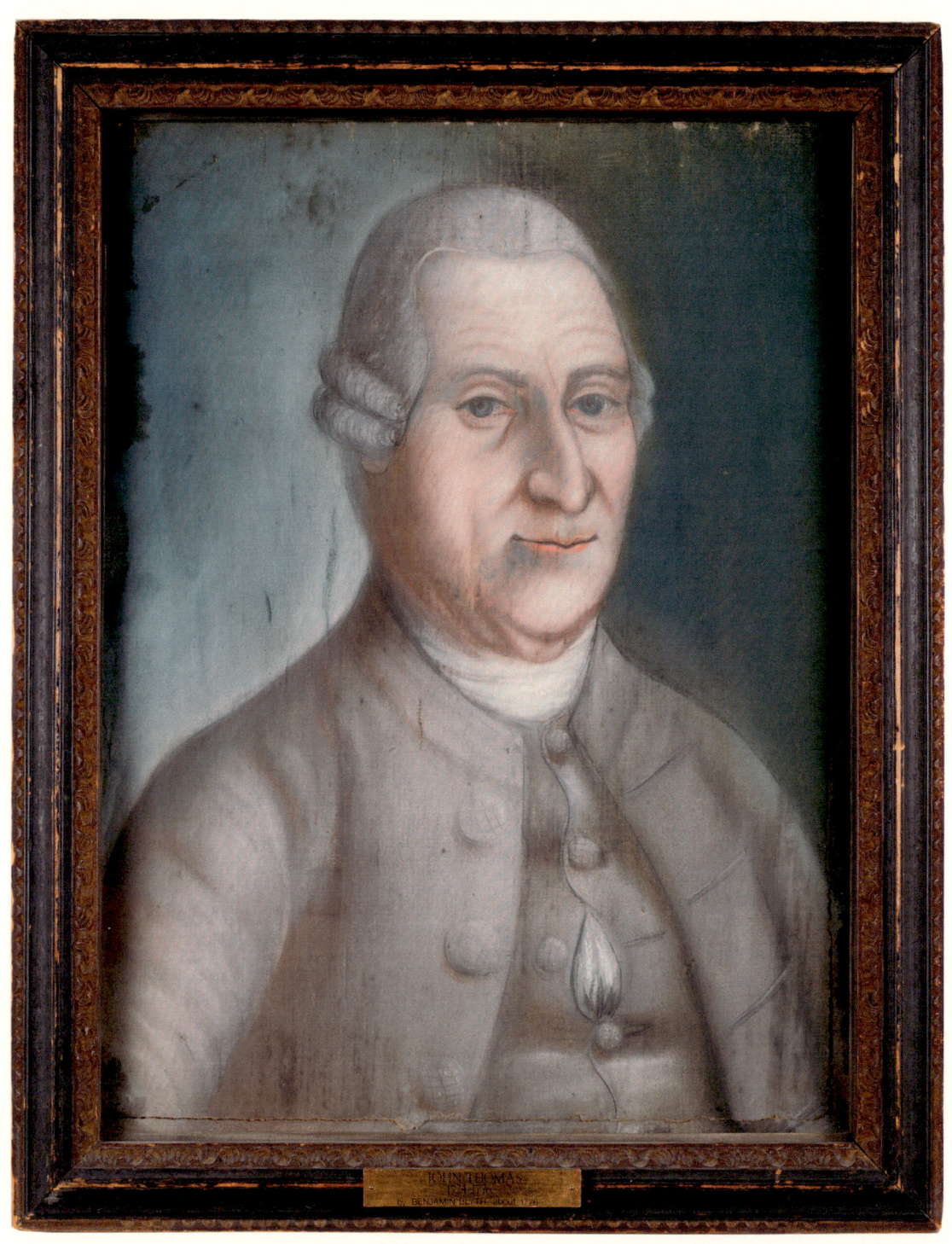

John Thomas
Pastel by Benjamin Blyth, 1776, with documented frame from the Blyths
Courtesy of the Massachusetts Historical Society Artwork 01.142, Rm. 205 (MA3303),
gift of descendants Sarah and Joanna Williams

John Thomas (1724–1776)

Benjamin Blyth, 1776
Pastel on paper mounted on board, 20¹¹⁄₁₆ x 15¹¹⁄₁₆ in. (52.5 x 39.8 cm.), Samuel Blyth frame
Massachusetts Historical Society Artwork 01.142 (MA3303), gift in 1923 by direct descendants,
the Misses Sarah and Joanna Williams

Born in Marshfield in 1724 to John and Ledia (Lydia) Thomas, John Thomas began the practice of medicine in Kingston. In 1761, he married Mrs. Hannah Thomas (no relation) of Taunton. The birth records for their three children give his title as "Col." or "Esq.," noting his importance to the town even before his service in the American Revolution. They were Hannah, born in 1762; John, born in 1766; and Nathaniel, born in 1769. Thomas's early service in the Continental Army was as a lieutenant and surgeon in three military expeditions. Elected a brigadier general by the Continental Congress on June 22, 1775, he was chosen by Washington to be in charge of the troops that marched through Roxbury to occupy Dorchester Heights on the night of March 4–5, 1776. (The British evacuated Boston two weeks later.) Thomas used the parsonage of Roxbury's First Church, the Dillaway House, as his headquarters; one of the few eighteenth-century houses in Boston associated with the Revolution, it is now an historic site. Abigail Adams, writing to her husband on July 16, 1775, noted that Thomas was very highly regarded. Adams himself visited him in Roxbury on the morning of January 24, 1776, and wrote to his wife that when they ate at Col. Mifflin's house "with a group of Indians, . . . the general was going to give them gifts of trinkets and clothes." Thomas, by then a major general and commander in chief of the army in Canada, died on June 2, 1776, of smallpox caught on the retreat from the attack on Quebec in December 1775.

Thomas's face is portrayed as unusually pale, without Blyth's usually rosy complexions, and he looks tired and pensive, old for his age—fifty-one. because Thomas's portrait shows him as an elderly man in civilian dress, Henry Wilder Foote thought that it was drawn shortly before Thomas joined the army. This is probably incorrect, given his age and the date of the bill from Blyth. Perhaps these were signs of Thomas's illness, as he died of smallpox shortly after his portrait was drawn.

The portrait must have looked much better when Frank W. Bayley called it "a fine example" of the work of Blyth in his 1917 pamphlet on little-known artists. He also mentioned the owner at the time. The pastel likely was at Bayley's gallery, where Baldwin Coolidge, an artist who worked for him then, may have enhanced the composition with deft strokes in black crayon, as he is assumed to have done with other portraits by Blyth. However, the brown lip line appears far too prominent, perhaps an amateur attempt at restoration. Through the years, this pastel has suffered much damage; water stains are visible along the left side, and because it was mounted directly on wood, it shows the consequent buckling, tears, and abrasion that detract from a proper assessment of Blyth's work.

Adams, Abigail and John *Letters*, 102, 114

Bayley, *Little Known . . . Portrait Painters*, Blyth No. 2

Bolton, *Portrait Draughtsmen*, 7

Cole, "Limned by Blyth," 333

Dillaway Thomas House, Roxbury Heritage State Park

FARL, Blyth, Benjamin 157-3i

Felt 1:317

Foote, "Blyth," 73–74, 102

Irving, Washington, *Life of Washington*, illus. with bill, then in possession of descendants.

Jeffares, http://www.pastellists.com/Articles/Blyth.pdf

MHS, John Thomas Papers

Norton, "Brothers Blyth," 63

Portraits of The Massachusetts Historical Society, 103

John Thomas (American General) Wikimedia Foundation, last edited August 16, 2022, https://en. wikipedia. org/wiki/John_Thomas_(American_general)

WPA 2130

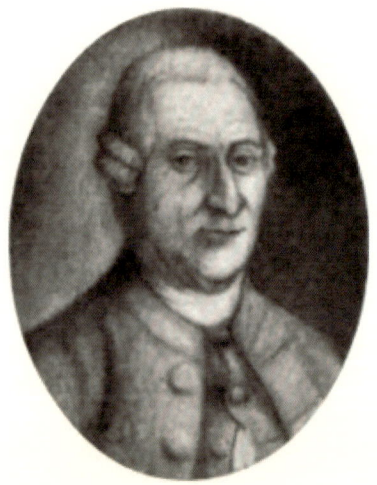

This reproduction from a web source now untraceable shows the pastel of Gen. John Thomas before the crude redrawing.

Robert Traill (CA. 1725–AFTER 1789)

Benjamin Blyth, probably 1769–70
Pastel on paper, 20 x 16 in. (50.8 x 40.6 cm.)
Current location not known; Nancy Heffenger Kennedy, Dover, MA; Heffenger family

Robert Traill was a key witness in the sensational 1769 trial—*Rex vs. Corbet*. John Adams was defense attorney for Seaman Michael Corbet, one of four "Marblehead sailors" being tried for the murder of Mr. Parton, a crew member on an English ship. The verdict hung on whether Corbet so feared he was going to be impressed into the English Navy that the death would be deemed justified manslaughter, based on the statute that forbade impressments of American seamen. The British Navy asserted that its crew had boarded the colonist's ship to look for undeclared goods. The testimony that exonerated Corbet came from questions asked by Traill.

The date of his birth in the Orkney Islands is not known, but he was in Portsmouth, New Hampshire, by 1748, where he married Mary Whipple, the daughter of the comptroller of customs, and succeeded his father-in-law in that office. Traill was the first person in New Hampshire licensed to brew and sell strong beer, doing so in an outbuilding behind his house known as the "Old Brewery." After the outbreak of the Revolution, he returned to London with his twenty-seven-year-old son, Robert Jr., leaving his wife and daughter behind. By 1780, Robert was dispatched to the Bermudas to serve as collector of customs. Two years later, he was also appointed judge of the vice-admiralty. Traill's death date is unknown, but he and his wife never reunited, and she died in Portsmouth in 1791.

Traill's portrait, designated a dubious attribution to Copley by Parker and Wheeler, shows all the characteristics of Benjamin Blyth and was attributed to him by the respected art historian, William Sawitsky (1879–1947). Early-twentieth-century art historian Theodore Bolton (1889–1973), noting that it was owned at the time by Dr.

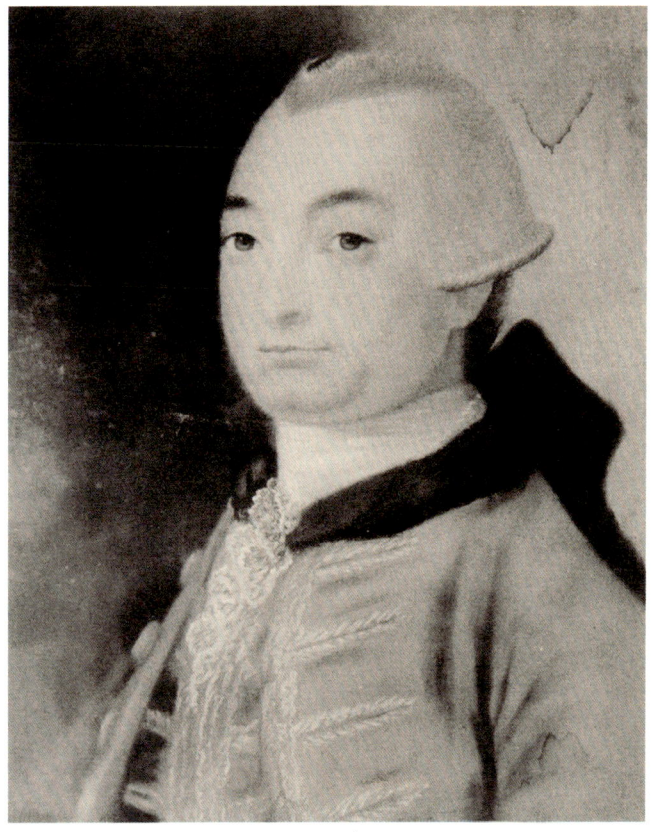

Robert Traill
Photograph of an unlocated pastel by Benjamin Blyth, probably 1769–70
Courtesy of the Frick Art Reference Library Photoarchives

A. C. Heffinger of Portsmouth, New Hampshire, provided its measurements and the guess that it was done around 1762. In the object file for Traill at the Frick Art Reference Library is a 1937 testament, "In spite of documentary evidence that Copley had made portraits of Robert Traill and the acceptance of the portrait as a Copley pastel for many years, Mr. Heffenger is willing to allow his portrait to be listed as attributed to Benjamin Blyth."

Traill is shown as a somewhat haughty Loyalist.

Bayley, *Loyalists of Massachusetts* (erroneously credited to Copley), 257

Bolton, *Portrait Draughtsmen,* 21

FARL, Blyth, Benjamin 157-3g

Felt 2:263

Jarvis, *In the Eye . . .* , 429

MHS, Legal Papers of John Adams LJA 2:292, LPA Case 56, 278

Parker and Wheeler (discounting it as a Copley), 258

Siebert, 5

Elizabeth Cutty Turner (1750/1–1790)

Benjamin Blyth, early 1770s

Pastel on paper mounted on linen, 22 x 13½ in. (55.9 x 34.3 cm.), later frame

United Missouri Bank of St. Louis, St. Louis, Missouri; Mr. and Mrs. Wright Morrow, Houston, TX; Knoedler
Gallery; Mrs. James Wolfe, Cambridge, Massachusetts

Elizabeth Cutty, whose birth date is unknown, married George Turner in the Parish Church of
St. Nicholas, Portsmouth, New Hampshire, on December 14, 1771, "According to the rights and
Ceremonies of the Church of Ireland as by Law Establish'd[,] Cork, December 14th, 1771 by me,
Robert Austin, Rector." She died in Portsmouth in 1790, at age 39.

    Jules Prown credited this portrait to John Singleton Copley, "but the style indicated that it
was painted before she married Capt. Turner in 1771." Copley decorated his own portrait of Mrs.
Turner with clouds in a blue sky, but Blyth's unadorned portrait shows a serious woman against
a darker background. It also shows signs of water damage. Both her portrait and that of her husband (Cat. 126) were reframed.

Jeffares, http://www.pastellists.com/Articles/Blyth. pdf

Prown, *Copley* 1:231

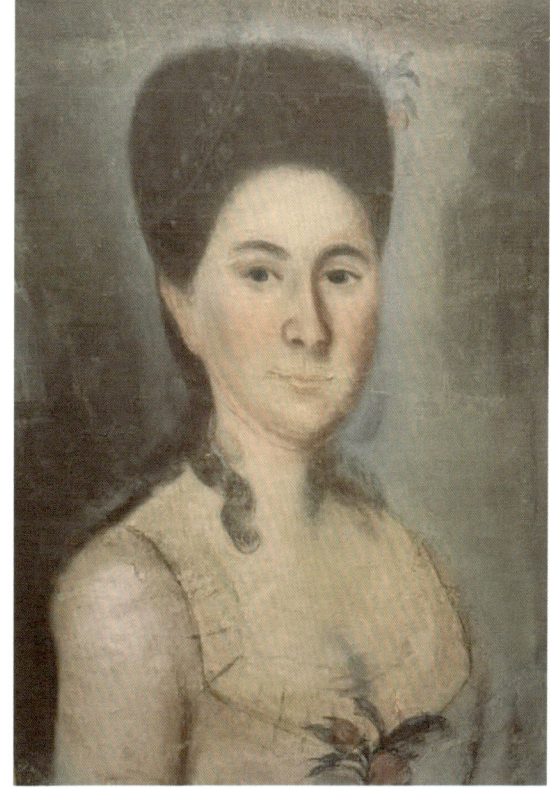

Elizabeth Cutty Turner
Pastel by Benjamin Blyth, early 1770s
Courtesy of the United Missouri Bank of St. Louis,
Denver, Colorado office

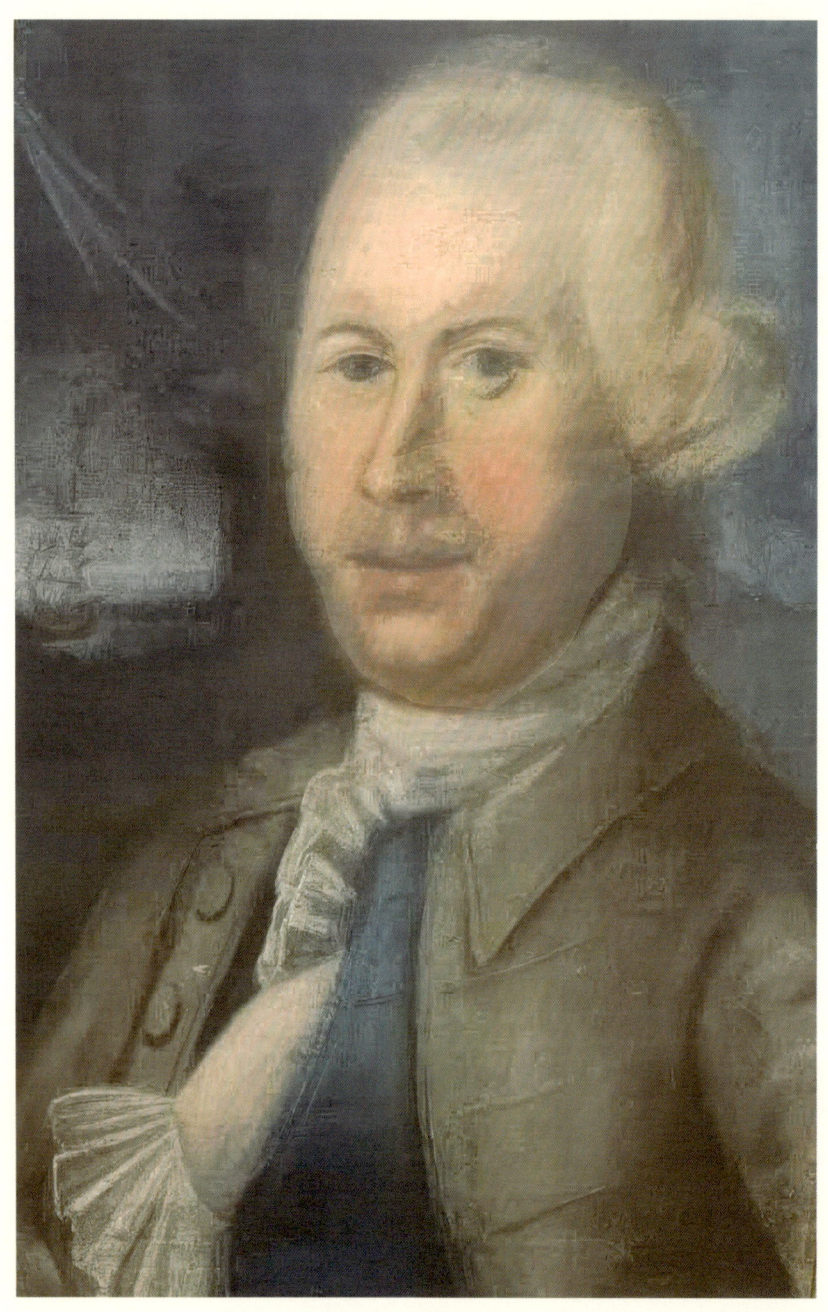

George Turner
Pastel by Benjamin Blyth, early 1770s
Courtesy of the United Missouri Bank of St. Louis, Denver, Colorado office

[126]

George Turner (1731–1821)

Benjamin Blyth, early 1770s
Pastel on paper mounted on linen, 22 x 13½ in. (55.9 x 34.3 cm.), later frame
United Missouri Bank of St. Louis, St. Louis, Missouri; Mr. and Mrs. Wright Morrow, Houston, TX;
Knoedler Gallery; Mrs. James Wolfe, Cambridge, MA

Capt. George Turner was a sea captain and merchant in Portsmouth, New Hampshire. He captained his own ships and then sold the goods he brought into port. Born in Cork, Ireland, in 1731, he was in Portsmouth by the mid-1760s and conducted maritime trade into the nineteenth century. Turner caused an imbroglio when trading with the West Indies in the mid-1760s by advertising that he did not water his rum. In 1770, he returned to Ireland with his first wife, but after her death the following year, he returned to Portsmouth and in December married Elizabeth Cutty, reportedly his first wife's sister. His vessel at the time was *Irish Gimlet*, and he was selling "St. Ubes salt." As the Revolution got underway, he was appointed one of three men to inventory the town's artillery to choose sites for fortification.

His trade continued to be active after the war. *The Oracle of the Day*, a publication issued out of Portsmouth from 1783 until 1799, recorded the voyages of two of Turner's brigs: the *Gustavus*, which arrived from Liverpool in 1797, and the *Betsey*, which sailed from Portsmouth on February 23, 1798, for Laguira (in the Cinque Terre region of Italy). The journal also recorded that Turner offered for rent a house with a garden and well in October 1798, and was an agent for selling a brig, *Blossom*, in 1799.

The portraits of Elizabeth Cutty Turner and George Turner are not mentioned in Parker and Wheeler, but Prown listed Turner under "Attributed Pictures." His portrait is one of the very few by Blyth (other than those of children) that depict more than the face and upper torso of the sitter. In the background, a ship is framed by a swag of a curtain.

Bentley 4:371, 509
Brighton, *They Came to Fish*, 61, 66, 67, 102, 103
Jeffares, http://www.pastellists.com/Articles/Blyth.pdf
Oracle of the Day (Portsmouth, NH), April 27, 1797; October 20, 1798; June 1, 1799
Prown, *Copley in America*, 1:231

[127]
Mehitabel Curwen Ward (1741–1813)
Benjamin Blyth, probably 1772
Pastel on paper mounted on linen, measurements unknown, Samuel Blyth frame
Current location not known; photocopy location also unknown

Mehitabel Curwen was born to George and Sarah (Pickman) Curwen on January 23, 1741, and married Richard Ward in Salem on November 8, 1764. Ward was very successful, eventually earning the title "Esq." Their first child, a son, presumably was named for her father George, the second, for her uncle Samuel, the third, for her maiden sister Sarah, and the fourth, for her. There were four more children. She died in April 1813, at age seventy-two.

After Samuel Curwen fled to England, he and Richard Ward corresponded regularly, with Curwen enclosing letters to his wife, Abigail. Shortly before Curwen's return from England, the remains of his valuable library were sold by Ward, so Curwen's will left Mehitabel only the portrait of her unmarried sister and almost everything else to a grandnephew. The will was hotly contested by Ward, with no success.

Samuel Curwen's grandson George Rea Curwen, one of Salem's most illustrious collectors, gave the family's thirty-nine portraits and numerous artifacts to the Essex Institute in the well-known "Curwen accession," 4134. The pastel of Mehitabel, however, reportedly was not in this collection, and its whereabouts is unknown. Known only in this photocopy, now lost, the original portrait seems unfinished, perhaps damaged. It is also curious that there is at this time no known portrait by Blyth of Mehitabel's husband, Richard Ward.

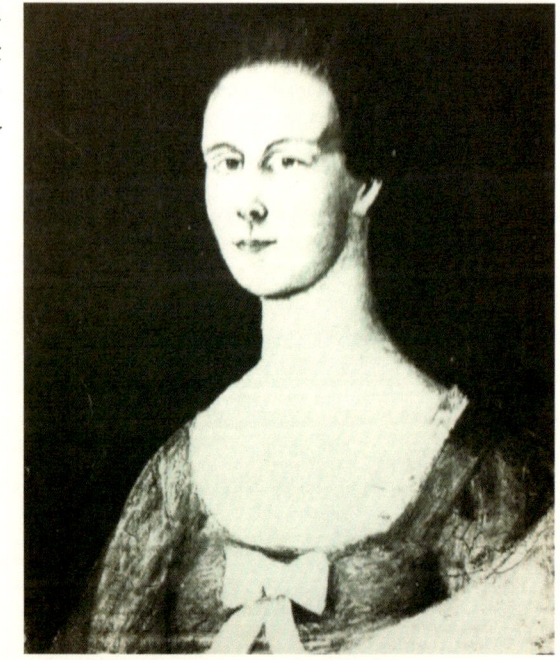

Mehitabel Curwen
Photocopy of a lost pastel by Benjamin Blyth,
probably 1772

EIHC 36:249; 72:300, cat. 336 (oil), later portrait by "unknown artist"
Jeffares, http://www.pastellists.com/Articles/Blyth.pdf
Norton, "Brothers Blyth" (under "Ward"), 63

[128]

Miles Ward (1744–1796)

Benjamin Blyth, early 1770s
Pastel, 15 x 12½ in. (38.1 x 31.75 cm.)
Peabody Essex Museum 115485, gift of the heirs of Miss Ellie P. Ward, 1920

This portrait was catalogued by the former Essex Institute as Unknown Man in Light Brown Coat, 115485, "gift before 1918." The subject appears to have been in his twenties. The artist also was listed as unknown, but it clearly is Benjamin Blyth. The pastel was unframed in 1969 when it suffered water damage, along with Blyth pastels of John Gibaut, Lydia Phippen Fiske, and David Ropes. The latter three were sent to the conservation laboratory of the Museum of Fine Arts, Boston, but not this pastel, presumably because at the time the identity of the sitter was not known. Due to the pastel's fragility, the back could not be examined for any further clarifying information.

However, the description of another portrait in the former EI collections, of Miles Ward, noted that the sitter had "long dark hair worn over [his] ears and was wearing a light brown coat and waistcoat." The background is described as "black." Although it was listed as "currently unlocated" and still is technically unaccounted for, this description suggests that the pastel Unknown Man in Light Brown Coat is the missing pastel of Miles Ward. Presumably because it was unlocated, it had never been given a catalogue number. The slight size discrepancy may be due to similar inconsistencies in the old EI records. So, for this catalogue, with the acquiescence of the Peabody Essex Museum, the two object records are merged. The catalogue number for Unknown Man in Light Brown Coat is now assigned to Ward.

Miles Ward, a son of Ebenezer and Rachel (Pickman) Ward of Salem, was born on July 12, 1744. In 1772, referred to as "Miles 3d," he married Hannah Chipman, daughter of the Reverend John Chipman (Cat. 28), minister of the First Church, Beverly. The Ward family belonged to Salem's North Meeting House. They had two children, Joseph Chipman and Elizabeth. Ward was a glazier and merchant who owned a mansion house and wharf in Salem and a large property with an old house, barn, and sawmill in Gouldsborough, Maine. He died in Salem on October 23, 1796. His carefully worded will awarded his estate equally among his wife and two children, with various scenarios spelled out.

Ward's father-in-law, the Reverend Chipman, was drawn by Blyth in the early 1770s, so it is even more likely that Blyth drew Ward as well, and for that matter, maybe both men's wives. This pastel has special interest, as the subject not only seems ambivalent about the process but is informally attired in a frock coat, the only such example in a known Blyth pastel. Most sitters wore more formal clothing, probably their best outfits at the time. Ward appears a handsome, alert, and somewhat wary young man, staring right at the artist—and now, the viewer.

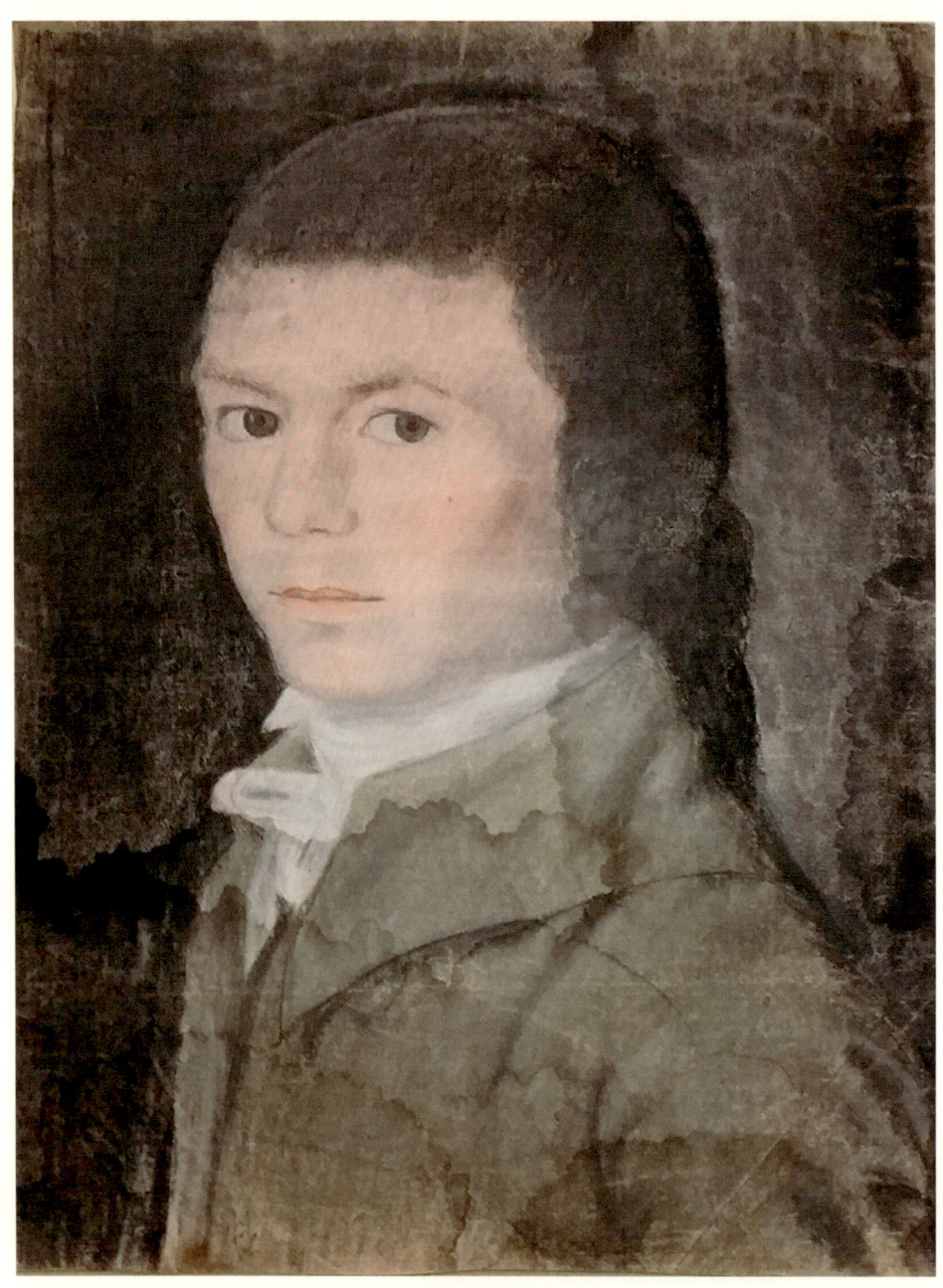

Miles Ward
Pastel by Benjamin Blyth, early to mid-1770s
Courtesy of the Peabody Essex Museum, 115485, gift of the heirs of Miss Ellie P. Ward, 1920

Baumgarten, Linda, *What Clothes Reveal*, 109
Bentley 2:169, 203; 4:77–79, 453
Chipman, *Chipmans of America*, 19
EIHC 5:208–9; ll:292; 72:300–01, Cat. 337; 73:81, Cat. 389
Essex County Probate Records docket 28923
Jeffares, http://www.pastellists.com/Articles/Blyth.pdf
Norton, "Brothers Blyth," 63
Perley, *History of Salem*, 2:104
PEM, Phillips Library, Lang Account Book

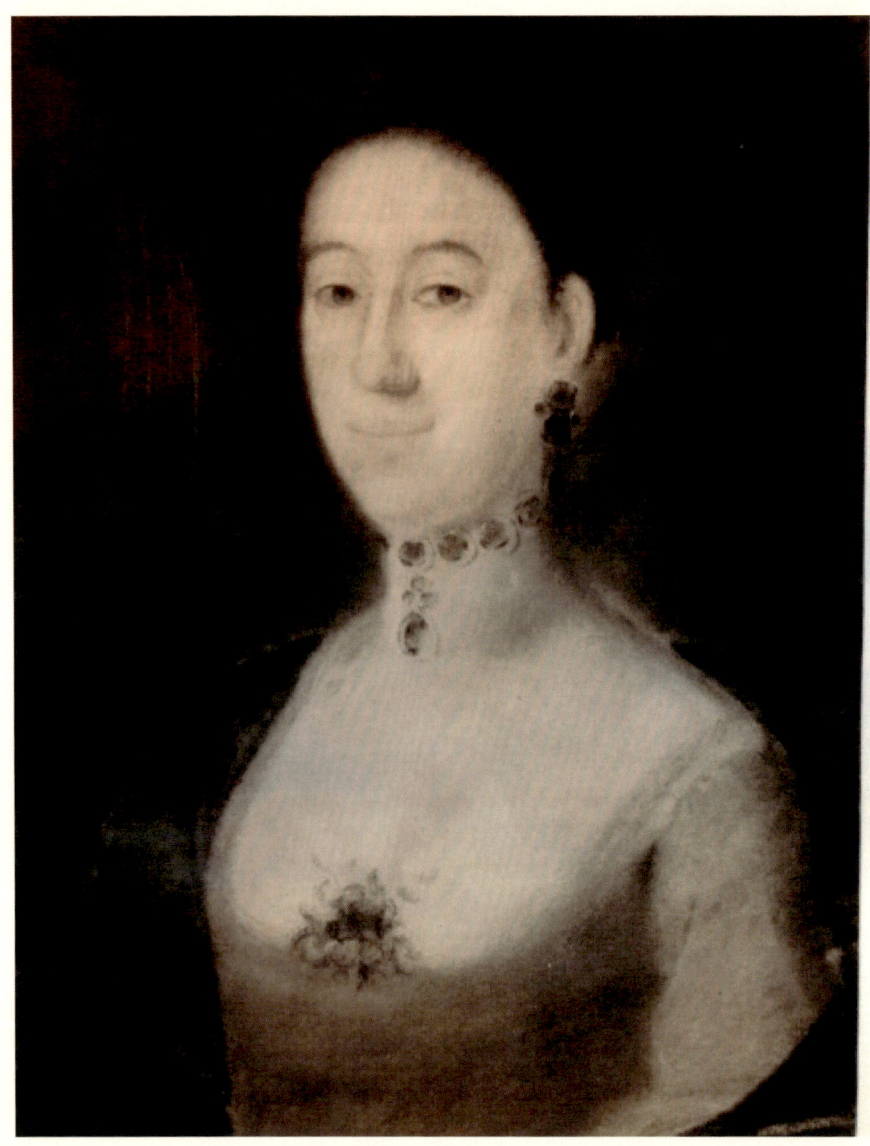

Elizabeth Warren
Photograph of unlocated pastel by Benjamin Blyth, probably mid-1760s
Courtesy of the Frick Art Reference Library Photoarchives

Elizabeth Warren (1746–1773)

Benjamin Blyth, probably mid-1760s
Pastel on paper, 22 x 17 in. (55.9 x 43.18 cm.)
Current location not known; Ferargil Galleries, Rain's Gallery (1935), Charles H. Hart,
Mr. and Mrs. Frederic Fairchild Sherman, Caroline E. Lyman, Lyman family, Mary Warren Lyman

Elizabeth Hooten was born in 1747, the daughter of Dr. Richard Hooten, a Boston physician who died shortly after her birth. Her mother's name is not known. In 1764, at the age of eighteen, Elizabeth married Joseph Warren (Cat. 130). She died nine years after their marriage, leaving her husband a widower with four young children.

The Ferargil Galleries, which offered the pair of portraits at an estimate of $1,000 in October 1943, corrected the earlier Rains catalogue identification of her as Mary, Joseph Warren's mother, to his wife, Elizabeth. The gallery also provided a description: "An aristocratic lady dressed in a low-cut light blue gown over which is draped a dark blue wrap, wearing a blue sapphire necklace and large pendants and earrings to match and a blue brooch." A photograph of the pastel shows that she is placed in a rondel and is seated in a dark chair. The portrait of Mrs. Warren by John Singleton Copley shows her in an Italian Renaissance painting-inspired landscape with an enormous garden urn, to indicate the sitter's wealth. However, this portrait does not show her wearing the necklace that is so elegant and prominent in the Blyth. (The sapphire necklace and earrings worn by Mrs. Warren are very similar to those in the Copley portrait of Elizabeth Cutty, however.)

Previous owners of the portraits, Mr. and Mrs. Frederic Fairchild Sherman, loaned them to an exhibition at the George Walter Smith Art Gallery, Springfield, Massachusetts, in 1914. The inscription on the back, "Mary Warren, Drawn by B. Blight, Salem," is a later addition, but this pastel may have been signed by Blyth, as was the one of her husband.

Copley's portrait is decidedly complimentary, as was his practice, and the focus is on the spectacular satins. Blyth concentrated on her face and portrayed her as she looked. Although Mrs. Warren was not a handsome woman, her expression conveys her as an aristocratic, confident woman with a sense of humor.

Exhibition catalogue, *A Showing of the Private Collection of Mr. and Mrs. Frederic Fairchild Sherman*, . . .
Ferargil Galleries Catalogue, Oct. 1943, lot 63
FARL, Blyth, Benjamin 158-3i
Jeffares, http://www.pastellists.com/Articles/Blyth.pdf
Norton, "Brothers Blyth," 63

Joseph Warren (1741–1775)

Benjamin Blyth, probably mid-1760s
Pastel on paper, 22 x 17 in. (55.9 x 43.18 cm.)
Current location not known; Ferargil Galleries, Rain's Gallery (1935), Charles H. Hart, Mr. and Mrs.
Frederic Fairchild Sherman, Caroline E. Lyman, Lyman family, Mary Warren Lyman

Joseph Warren was a doctor as well as a general officer in the Continental Army, whose death was one of the first of many tragedies of the Revolution. Born in Roxbury in 1741 to Joseph and Mary Stevens Warren, he graduated from Harvard College with high honors in 1759, then taught school while studying medicine. He served as physician to many of the prominent families of Boston, both Patriots and Loyalists, and was inoculating against smallpox in the 1760s. In 1764, he married Elizabeth Hooten (Cat. 129), from a wealthy Boston family. She died in 1773. Of their four children, one son also became a doctor.

In addition to practicing medicine in Boston, Warren, who was a friend of John Adams, became a major force in building resistance to British control over the Commonwealth affairs, giving speeches and writing pamphlets such as the influential Suffolk Resolves and an incendiary newspaper essay under the pseudonym "A True Patriot." In 1775, Warren won election as president of the Massachusetts Provincial Congress. He turned down an appointment as physician general of the Continental Army and deferred his position as major general to participate as a combatant, first at Lexington and Concord. He was killed at the Battle of Bunker Hill on June 17, 1775. His death at age thirty-four robbed the Commonwealth of a top medical practitioner, one who successfully helped thwart smallpox. A leader of the provisional government, he became one of the first heroes of the war.

Before his death, he was planning to marry Mercy Scollay. His four small children were left "in indifferent circumstances," according to a plea sent out by the Boston branch of the Lodge of Masons in 1780, of which he had been Grand Master. His death prompted strong reactions. Many mourned the loss, though some were ambivalent. Henry Pelham, John Singleton Copley's half-brother, wrote to Copley's wife Susanna on July 23, 1775, "I have passed Doctr. Warren's Grave. I felt a disagreeab[le] Sensation, thus to see a Townsman an old Acquaintance led by unbounded Ambition to an untimely death and thus early to realise that Ruin which a lust of Power and Dominion has brought upon himself and partly through his means upon this unhappy Country.... I would wish to forget his principles to Lament his Fate."

Pelham's characterization of Warren is counter to the personality Blyth portrayed—a generous, kind, open-hearted man, perhaps a bit idealistic. Moreover, such was the regard for Warren that streets in many communities were named for him, including the street on which he lived in Roxbury and a main east-west thoroughfare in Charlestown, at the base of the hill where he was killed. John Trumbull memorialized Joseph Warren's death in a monumental historical painting

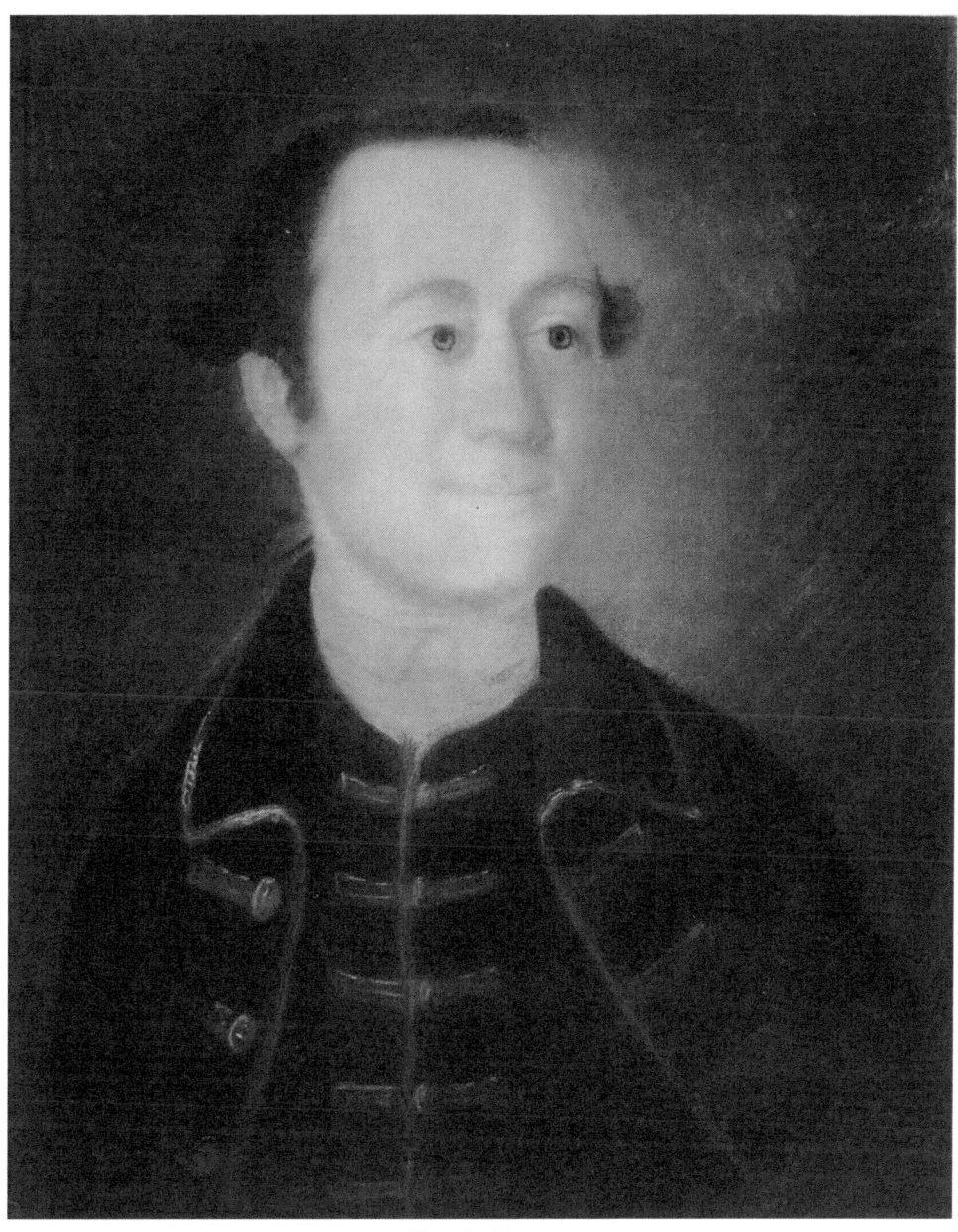

Joseph Warren
Photograph of an unlocated pastel by Benjamin Blyth, probably mid-1760s
Courtesy of the Frick Art Reference Library Photoarchives

by using information from Maj. John Small (Cat. 118). Based on Small's account, Trumbull portrayed him as the British officer repelling a bayonet thrust to Warren's chest.

John Singleton Copley painted an oil portrait of Warren in 1765–67, and John Norman issued a print of Warren for *Boston Magazine* in April 1784. Although Blyth's pastel portrait is known at this time only in a black-and white photograph, the Ferargil Galleries catalogue entry 62 in 1943 noted that Warren was wearing a blue uniform trimmed with gold braid. The back of the pastel is inscribed in pen, "D^r. Joseph Warren/drawn by B Blyth Salem." The entry noted the inscription on the back, "in the artist's handwriting," but misspelled his name as "Blight."

The provenance of the portraits of Joseph and Elizabeth Warren includes two major early-twentieth-century scholars of American art, Charles Henry Hart, then Mr. and Mrs. Frederic Fairchild Sherman, who loaned the pair to an exhibition at the George Walter Smith Art Gallery, Springfield, Massachusetts, in 1914. The author was shown photographs of the Warren pastels in January 2019, but the individual could neither permit reproduction of the photographs nor disclose the location of the original pastels.

The early pastel is one of the most important ones drawn by Blyth. It is also one of only two that he is known to have signed, although in this instance, on the back. George Cabot (Cat. 25) is signed twice within the image.

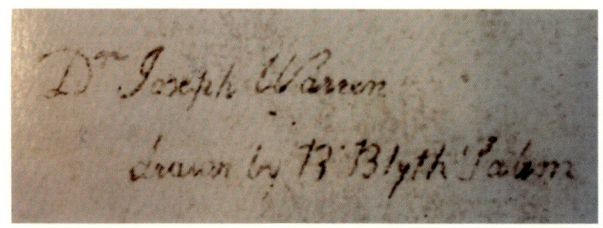

Inscription on the back of the photograph of the pastel of
Joseph Warren
Courtesy of the Frick Art Reverence Library photoarchives

Adams, *Letters & Papers of John Singleton Copley and Henry Pelham*, 346

"A Collection of American Revolutionary Engravings in the William M. Elkins Library located in The Rare Book Department of the Free Library of Philadelphia"; document courtesy of Ellen Shaffer

EIHC 3:44

Ferargil Galleries Catalogue, New York City, Oct. 1943, lot 62

FARL, Blyth, Benjamin 158-3n

Jeffares, http://www.pastellists.com/Articles/Blyth.pdf

Norton, "Brothers Blyth," 63

Prown, 1:115, 233

Sibley 14:510–27

HIS EXCELLENCY GENERAL WASHINGTON

B. Blyth Pinx't

Joseph Hiller (attr.)

Mezzotint, hand-colored, 33 x 25 cm. (sight), ca. 1776

William M. Elkins Collection of Americana, Rare Book Department,
Free Library of Philadelphia, ELK0020001

The print is known in only one impression, at the William M. Elkins Collection of Americana, Rare Book Department, Free Library of Philadelphia. Blyth is cited for the original, but the engraving and printing, although not credited, is attributed here to Joseph Hiller. Like the original by Blyth for the print of *The Hon-ble Israel Putnam Esq'*, neither the extent of what he contributed to the composition, its medium, nor its whereabouts (if even extant) are known. The lush landscape in this version of Washington, with prominent large cannon, three smaller ones firing away, and large billows of smoke is far more ambitious than landscapes seen in Samuel Blyth prints. However, Samuel Blyth probably is responsible for the coloring. The two wavy lines of birds painted in the background are identical to those seen, but in far bigger flocks, in the two Elkins prints of Generals Washington and Lee, also attributed to Hiller with coloring by Samuel Blyth.

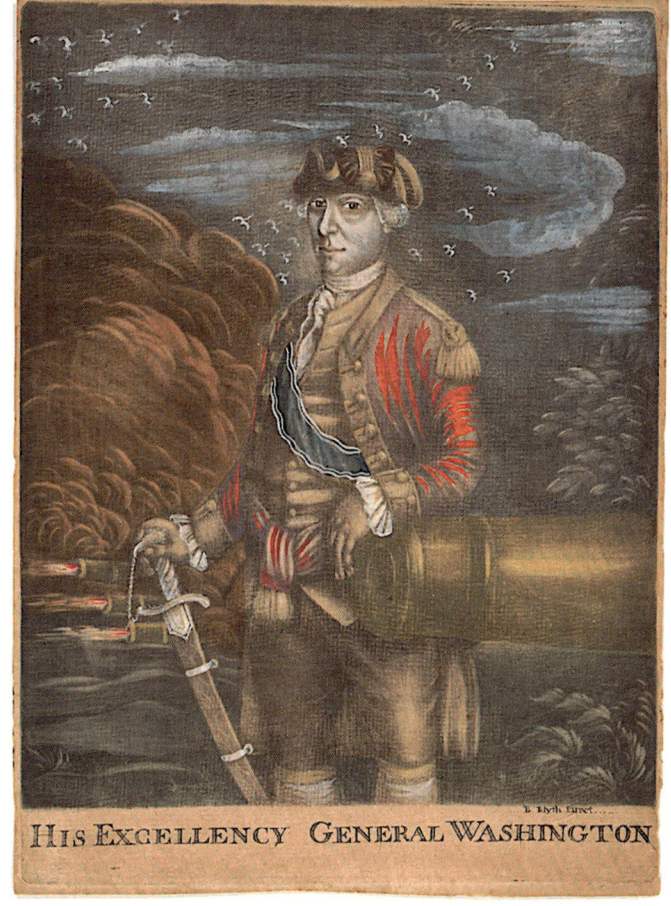

HIS EXCELLENCY GEORGE WASHINGTON
B. Blyth Pinx't, 1775–6
Joseph Hiller (attr.)
Courtesy of William M. Elkins Collection of Americana, Rare Book
Department, Free Library of Philadelphia, ELK0020001

His Excell^{cy} George Washington, Esqr
General and Commander in Chief of the Allied Armies

Supporting the Independence of America
Taken from an Original Picture in possession of his Ex^{cy} Govr Hancock
Engraving with etching and stipple, 33.3 x 24.1 cm.
B. Blyth del., J. Norman sculp,
Published by John Coles, Boston, March 26th, 1782
Courtesy of the Henry Francis du Pont Winterthur Museum 58. 2413

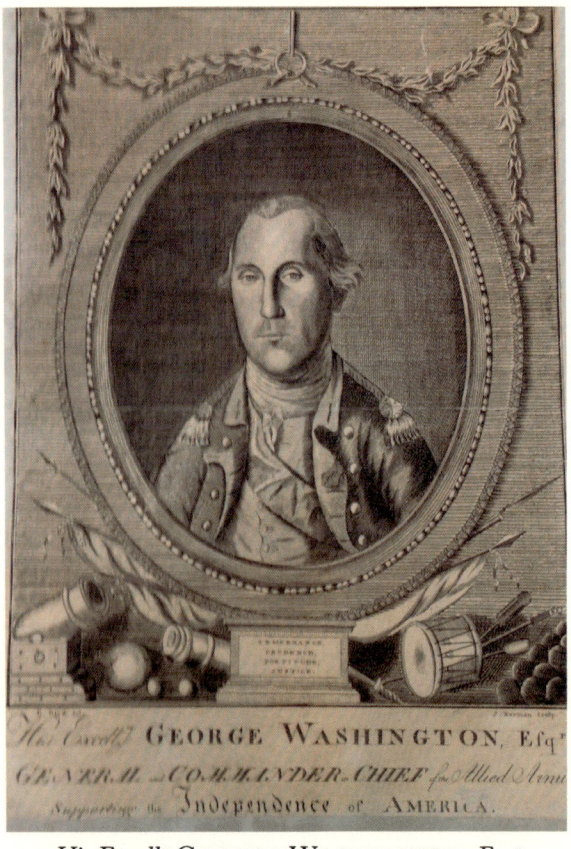

His Excell^{cy} GEORGE WASHINGTON, *Esqr*
Engraving with etching and stipple, 33.3 x 24.1 cm.
B. Blyth del., J. Norman sculp.
Courtesy of the Henry Francis du Pont Winterthur
Museum 58. 2412

This portrait and its companion of Mrs. Washington were based on miniatures by Charles Willson Peale, then in the collection of John Hancock. The assumption for these engravings is that Blyth provided the drawings for the portraits, and the embellishments of borders, including guns, drums, cannon balls, furled flags, and leafy garlands, were provided by the engraver, J. Norman, or the publisher, John Coles. He was affiliated in another printmaking venture with Samuel Blyth, who also may have taught him how to draw coats of arms. And Coles and Benjamin Blyth had been agents for the six-gun privateer brig *Brandywine*.

Henry Wilder Foote, in his article on Blyth in 1957 for the Massachusetts Historical Society, found the engraving "very poorly done." Other impressions of this engraving and the companion of Mrs. Washington are in the John Carter Brown Library; the Metropolitan Museum of Art; the Museum of Fine Arts, Boston; the Smithsonian's National Portrait Gallery; and the Peabody Essex Museum.

Fowble, Cat. 198, 303
Little, *The Magazine Antiques,* Feb. 1969, 240
Stauffer and David McNeely, *American Engravers Upon Copper and Steel,* 401–2.

MRS. WASHINGTON

Engraving with etching and stipple, 29.5 x 23.1 cm.
B. Blyth, del., J. Norman Sculp.
Published by John Coles, Boston, March 26th. 1782
Courtesy of the Henry Francis du Pont Winterthur Museum 58.2413

This engraving of Martha Washington is especially valued, as it shows her as a young woman, whereas most images depict her as older. Once thought by print historian Mantle Fielding to be a "fictitious portrait," the image on which Blyth was believed to have based his print was either the miniature of Martha Washington done in 1776 by C. W. Peale or the mezzotint by Hiller of Lady Washington, made a few years earlier. Blyth must have appropriated her hat and clothing from other sources, using his earlier pastels such as that of Mrs. Nathaniel Appleton, Mrs. Abigail Glover, or Mrs. J. Gardner as a source.

Other impressions of this engraving and the companion of General George Washington are in the John Carter Brown Library; the Metropolitan Museum of Art; the Museum of Fine Arts, Boston; the Smithsonian's National Portrait Gallery; and the Peabody Essex Museum.

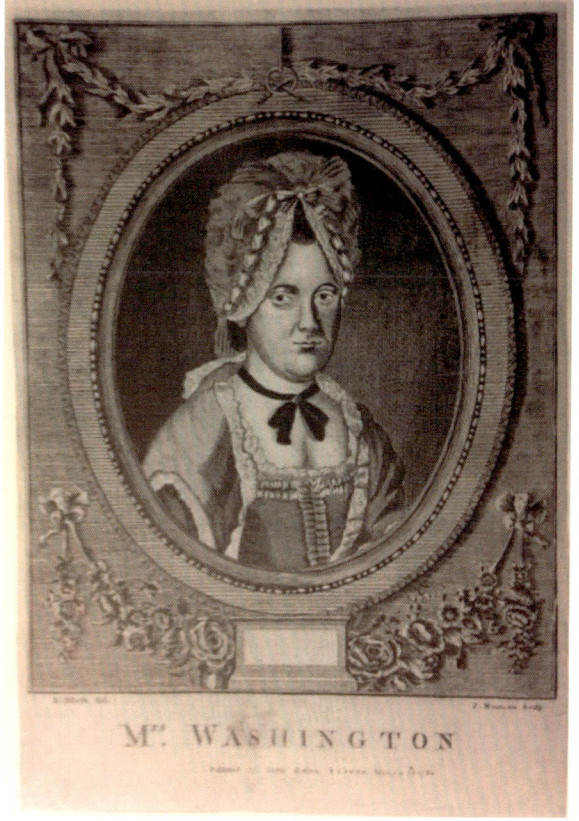

MRS. WASHINGTON
B. Blyth, del., J. Norman Sculp.
Published by John Coles, Boston, March 26th. 1782
Courtesy of the Henry Francis du Pont Winterthur Museum
58.2413

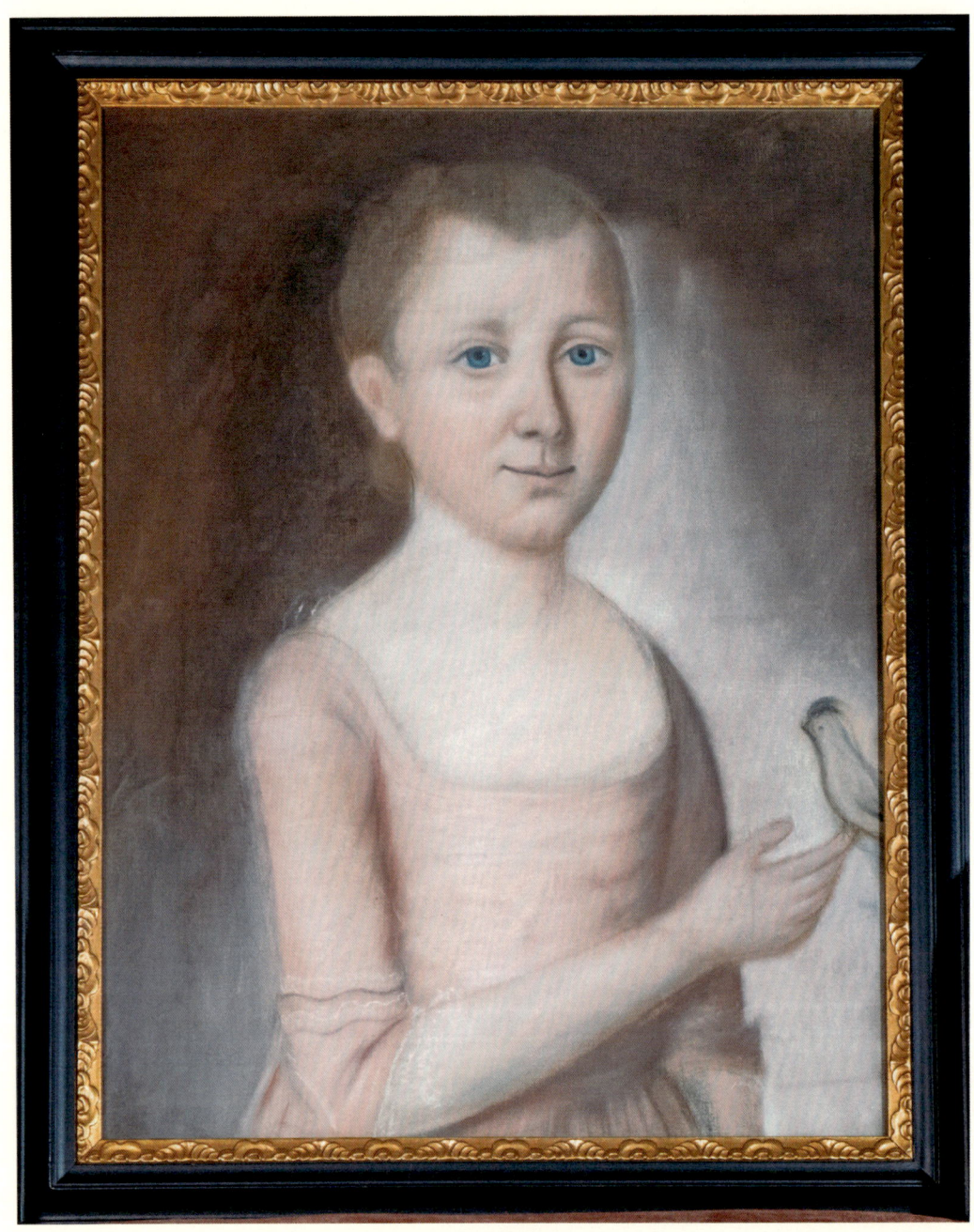

Patty Webb
Pastel by Benjamin Blyth, ca. 1783
Courtesy of James and Janet Laverdiere
Photograph by Michael C. King

[134]

Patty Webb (1777–1817)

Benjamin Blyth, ca. 1783
Pastel on blue laid paper on plain-weave fabric, 18⅝ x 14⁹⁄₁₆ in. (47.3 x 37 cm.),
Reproduction frame by Perry Hopf
Collection of James and Janet Laverdiere; Judy Herdeg and the late John Herdeg; James D. Julia Inc.,
Dorothy Harper Dean, Hooper family, Elizabeth Harding

Patty Webb, also known as Martha, was born on September 7, 1777, to Capt. Nathaniel Goyet (Gaiset/Coit) Webb and Martha Needham Archer Webb. In 1780, she was baptized "Patty" at Salem's North Church. Capt. Webb commanded several privateer sloops during the Revolution, including the *America*, a privateer sloop, and the *Hazzard*. When Patty was eleven years old, her father died at sea: he was thrown overboard by two English hands, who had just been taken on and seized the ship. They were tried for murder and executed in Charleston, South Carolina.

In 1794, Patty married James Brewer of Boston, whose father had participated in the Boston Tea Party and was a confidential messenger between Hancock and Washington. She was the mother of six children, James, Henry, Martha, Thomas, Isaac, and Elizabeth. Patty died after a long illness in Boston, March 17, 1807, at age thirty, and her husband died in Boston on January 13, 1817.

This portrait was found as a result of this author's plea, "Where Have All the Portraits Gone?" in *Maine Antiques Digest* in 2015. It was purchased in 2009 by Judy and John Herdeg, who generously provided their research information. They had the pastel professionally conserved, removing particulates that included flyspecks, cleaning surfaces, and repairing losses. The pastel, in a reproduction Samuel Blyth frame, is charming, showing Polly's obvious pride in her pet crested bird.

The inscription on the back of the portrait says it was drawn when Patty was three years old. "Patty' appears to be older than three, which suggests that it might have been done later, and possibly by Benjamin's brother, Samuel. However, the concentration on her facial expression and lack of background detail keep it in the oeuvre of Benjamin, probably one of his last portraits before he left Salem.

This pastel of Patty Webb, originally owned by her daughter, Elizabeth Harding, was sold on Jan. 17, 2025 by the auction house Pook and Pook, Inc., to James and Janet Laverdiere. They now own seven other pastels by Blyth: Gideon Baty (Cat. 11), J(onathan?) Gardner (Cat. 57), Sarah Putnam(?) Gardner (Cat. 58), Man of the Perkins Family (Cat. 105), Jonathan Simpson (Cat. 117), Unknown Boy in Brown Suit (Cat. 142), and Unknown Woman in Blue Dress with Black Lace (Cat 151).

John Herdeg, correspondence
Maine Antique Digest, May 2015

Benjamin West (1747–1775)

Benjamin Blyth, probably 1775
Pastel on paper mounted on wood, 25 x 16 in. (63.5 x 40.64 cm.)
Peabody Essex Museum 116640, gift of Mrs. Sarah C. Bacheller, 1922

Benjamin West, the son of Mary (Massey) and Samuel West, Jr., was born on Oct. 8, 1747. The term "Capt." in the record of the births of Samuel's children suggests that his profession was at sea. Benjamin and Hannah Phippen's intention to marry was published on August 8, 1762, when they both were fifteen years old. They had three children. The girls, two-year-old Elizabeth and Susanna, an infant, were baptized into the First Church in Salem on September 29, 1765. Their son Benjamin was born three years later.

West enlisted in Capt. Andrew Haskell's Company and was commissioned a Lieutenant on June 12, 1775. He died less than a week later, in the Battle of Bunker Hill. Abigail West never re-married. In 1799, the year after Abigail's death, the *Salem Gazette* noted that a tomb to Capt. West, was put up in Harmony Grove Cemetery, Salem.

The original pastel remained in the family until given to the former Essex Institute in 1922. It had been pasted directly onto a one-inch-thick pine board. The surface of the portrait also suffered from smoke damage and is replete with small vertical tears throughout from the board warping, probably from having been hung over a fireplace. Two copies were made, most likely for Caleb Foote, who gave one to the Essex Institute in 1889.

In 1890, Caleb Foote wrote to the City of Boston asking it to rectify an omission:

> I have learned from newspapers that the name of Lieut. Benjamin West is not included in the list of those killed at Bunker Hill. . . . That he was then killed I have the testimony of my grandmother, who was the widow of Samuel West, a brother [*sic*] of the Lieutenant. . . . This great-uncle of mine had some taste and talent for portrait-painting, and a life-size portrait bust of him, in his lieutenant's uniform, painted by himself, hung in the house. . . . A copy of it is now in possession of the Essex Institute, in Salem, and another is in the family of the late Reverend Henry W. Foote, of Boston.

The Essex Institute copy given by Foote was published in the first *Visitors' Guide to Salem* (1892): "West, Benjamin. Killed at the battle of Bunker Hill. Copy of a portrait by himself."

Foote's grandson, historian Henry Wilder Foote, made a correction in his 1957 article on Blyth, "That it was a self-portrait was a mistaken family tradition, formed by persons who had forgotten Blyth and his relationship to West. There is no evidence that Benjamin West ever drew any pictures, and this portrait can with assurance be attributed to his cousin, Benjamin Blyth." There also are several errors, uncharacteristic for Foote, in the caption for West in his article. Foote does not appear to have known that his grandfather had given one of the copies that he had likely commissioned to the Essex Institute.

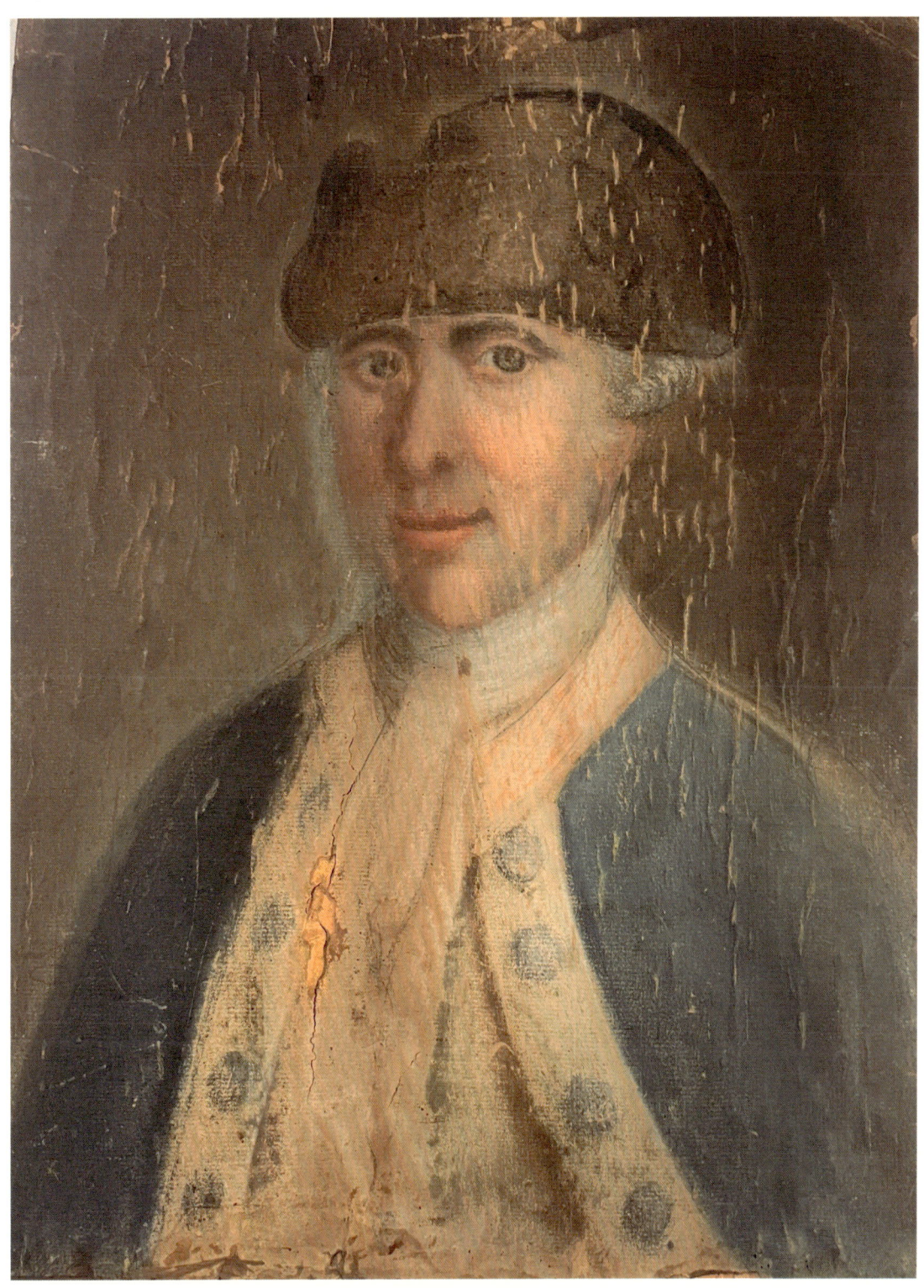

Benjamin West
Pastel by Benjamin Blyth, probably 1775
Courtesy of the Peabody Essex Museum 116640, gift of Mrs. Sarah C. Bacheller, 1922

The full, red lips in the original portrait question the attribution to Blyth, but the eyes are very similarly drawn to those of John Collins (Cat. 29) and George Cabot (Cat. 25), the only pastel signed by Benjamin Blyth. That, and happenstance, seems to corroborate Henry Wilder Foote's surmise, that the original was done by Benjamin West's cousin, Benjamin Blyth. Perhaps the nineteenth-century copyist added a few touches to the original, as on the lips, a too-common practice at the time.

The very poor condition of the pastel is due primarily to its having been mounted on board, causing the paper to buckle and crack as the wood expanded and contracted. The damage is extensive throughout the pastel but fortunately spared the face, which shows a genial, contemplative man, who proved to be selfless as he appears here. At any event, this Benjamin West should not be confused with the contemporary British-American artist, Benjamin West (1738–1820).

Boston, City of, Archives, Document 54, Boston Registry Dept., 1890

EIHC 73:65, Cats. 349, 350

Felt, 2:520

Foote, "Blyth," 102–3

Jeffares, http://www.pastellists.com/Articles/Blyth.pdf

MHS Adams Papers: James Warren to John Adams, Oct. 1, 1775, 1:122

Massachusetts Gazette, —, 1799

Massachusetts Soldiers and Sailors of the Revolution, 16:890

Norton, "Brothers Blyth," 63

Salem Gazette, Jan. 2, 1798

Visitors' Guide to Salem (1892), 165; — (1985), 196

WPA 2407, artist unknown; notes two copies

Elizabeth Stone White (1749–1822)

Benjamin Blyth, early 1770s
Pastel on paper mounted on linen, 21 x 16 in. (53.4 x 40.64 cm.), unframed
Peabody Essex Museum 2988, gift of Benjamin Barstow, 1891

Elizabeth Stone, born in 1749 in Beverly to Mary and Josiah Stone, Jr., married Joseph White on October 18, 1770, and died from "disorder of the heart" on August 13, 1822, at age 74. The Whites were childless but took care of a niece who had been orphaned. They "were fond of her & she dutiful to them," the Reverend William Bentley wrote. Another child, Joseph, son of his brother Henry, also "was patronized by his Uncle Joseph."

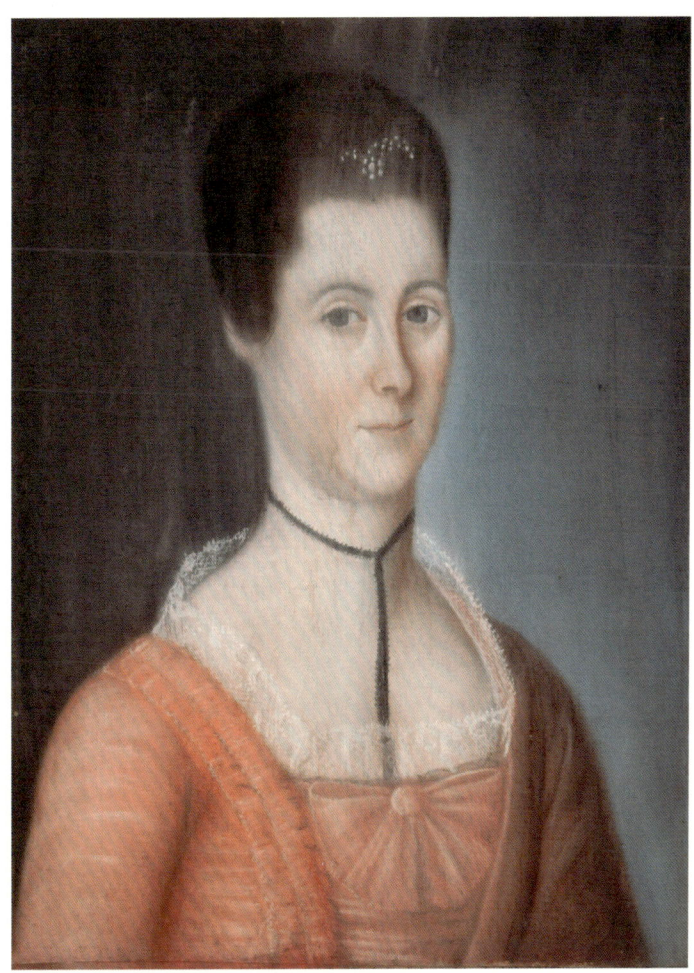

Elizabeth White
Pastel by Benjamin Blyth, early 1770s
Courtesy of the Peabody Essex Museum 2988, gift of Benjamin Barstow, 1891

Elizabeth's upswept, bejeweled hair style of the early 1770s, her dress, and a thin ribbon around her neck that hangs to the top of the bodice, suggest that this portrait was done soon after her marriage to White (Cat. 138). Blyth paid particular attention to the coral-colored, scoop-neck dress and its elegant lace edging, which indicate the wealth of her husband, one of Salem's most successful shipmasters and traders. It also is one of the few portraits for which Blyth used blue in the background, quite effectively in this one of Elizabeth White, as he did with other portraits, such as of Abigail Adams (Cat. 2), Lydia Phippen Fisk (Cat. 53), and Sarah Putnam(?) Gardner (Cat. 58).

The portraits of Elizabeth and Joseph White and that of John Gibaut descended through the Barstow family and were early gifts to the Essex Institute. Elizabeth appears rather stiff and formal, even aloof, for a woman her age. William Verstille also painted and signed a miniature of her, dated ca. 1802, in the collections of the Peabody Essex Museum. It is obviously of the same woman, though about thirty years older and less assured.

Bayley, *Little Known . . . Portrait Painters*, "Blyth," no. 2, illus.

Bentley 4:555.

Bolton, *Portrait Draughtsmen*, (as Stone), 7

Burroughs, *Limners and Likenesses*, Plate 53, 69–70

Cole, "Limned by Blyth," illus. 332 illus. 332

EIHC 73:74, cat. 363

FARL, Blyth, Benjamin 158-3b

Foote, "Blyth," 103-4 ("Mrs. Joseph White")

Jeffares, http://www.pastellists.com/Articles/Blyth.pdf

Johnson, Dale T., *American Portrait Miniatures in the Manney Collection*, 225, cat. 260, reproduced in color, plate 7e

National Historic Records Survey 460

Norton, "Brothers Blyth," 63

Phillips, *Pepper and Pirates*, 50

Visitor's Guide to Salem, 1895, "Unknown Artist," 196

WPA 2439

Henry White, Jr. (1777–1778)

Benjamin Blyth, 1778
Pastel on paper, measurements unknown
Current location not known; Cowan Auctions; Mrs. George C. Beach, NY; Carl Crossman; Dr. Hayes;
Mary (Stone Hodges) Silsbee; Elizabeth Hodges

A hand-written inscription on the back of the portrait reads "This is a Portrait of Henry White Jr. taken when 14 mos. old. Son of Henry and Phoebe (Brown) White, Born 14th July 1777 - Died 16 Sept. 1778. . . ." His parents were married on October 8, 1776. Salem Vital Records give his age at death as fourteen years, not months.

The portrait seems unfinished, suggesting that the young Henry died before it was completed. Yet it gives a rare glimpse into Benjamin Blyth's method of drawing his pastel by showing delicately drawn outlines that would have been covered with further crayon work. Comparing it

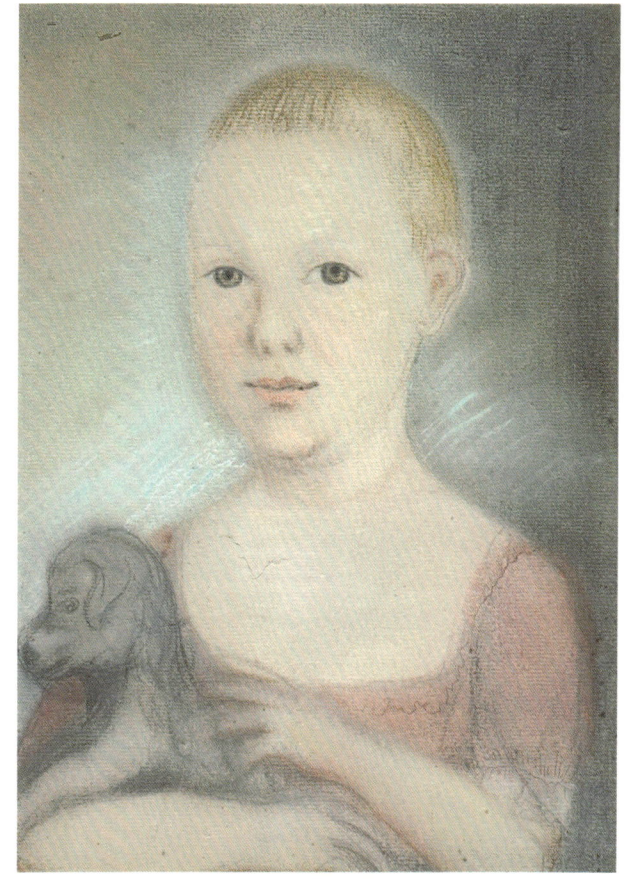

Henry White, Jr.
Pastel by Benjamin Blyth, 1777–78
Private collection; Cowan Antiques

to two pastels of children now tentatively assigned to Samuel Blyth, the Jones child and the Putnam child, Henry appears as more of a portrait, whereas the other two seem composites of facial parts, all of which could have been copied from a pastel such as this of Henry. The pastel is in its original Samuel Blyth frame. It is the more elaborate version with gilt outer edge and inner molding and lined with contemporary newspapers. Elizabeth Hodges, whose name was written three times on the back of the portrait, gave it to her sister, Mary (Stone Hodges) Silsbee. The Silsbee family was related to the Derbys and the Crowninshields.

Jeffares, http://www.pastellists.com/Articles/Blyth.pdf
Norton, "Brothers Blyth," 63

Joseph White (1748–1830)

Benjamin Blyth, early 1770s
Pastel on paper mounted on linen, 21 x 16 in. (53.34 x 40.5 cm.), Samuel Blyth frame
Peabody Essex Museum 2987, gift of Benjamin Barstow, Esq., 1891

Capt. Joseph White was one of Salem's most prosperous merchants in the East India trade in the last quarter of the eighteenth century and into the nineteenth. Born in 1748 in the Isle of Shoals, White married Elizabeth Stone in 1770. They lived in what is now the flagship Federal-style property of the Peabody Essex Museum, the Gardner-White-Pingree House, where he was murdered at age eighty-two. The marriage of one of White's grandnieces to Jenkins Knapp, Jr., for which White disinherited her, precipitated the murder. White was childless and a widower, so potential inheritors included the brothers Joseph Jenkins Knapp, Jr., and John Francis Knapp, who plotted the murder with Richard and George Crowninshield, "disreputable scions of an eminent Salem family." Richard committed suicide in jail, the two Knapps were hanged, and George was acquitted. In the collections of the PEM is the club that was one of the murder weapons.

The Reverend William Bentley, who lived in the adjoining Crowninshield-Bentley House (also now owned by the Peabody Essex Museum), had little regard for his neighbor White's stand on slavery, which had been abolished in Massachusetts in 1783; Bentley expressed his opinion in September 1788, when the *Felicity,* of which White was one of the owners, set sail: "The owner confesses he has no reluctance in selling any part of the human race ... and in consideration of the owner's easy circumstances, is supposed to betray signs of the greatest moral depravity."

White was little involved in town affairs, though he did speak out in 1808 on the Embargo. He was also considered something of a miser; James Duncan Phillips, writing about one of White's ships, *Eliza,* noted that when it arrived in Salem with a record load of pepper, it was "in bitter trouble. She was not an old ship ... but one gets the impression that he made his money out of cheap ships for his ships were often in trouble." Yet he patronized relatives such as his nephew, Col. Joseph White, who died in 1816 at age thirty-five, leaving three young children. Bentley reported that he was "a young man of high relish for social life & has long been paying for his freedom of his pleasures."

The portraits appear to have been drawn soon after the Whites' marriage, given his youth and the costume and hairstyle of Elizabeth White. Known to have been prone to use his wealth as a cudgel, White is depicted as a rather harsh, autocratic man, which is how he was considered by some in Salem at the time.

Bayley, *Little Known. . . Portrait Painters. . .* no. 2, "Blyth"
Bentley 1:104; 3:105, 391; 4:387
Cole, "Limned by Blyth," 331–33
EIHC 73: 74–75, Cat 364

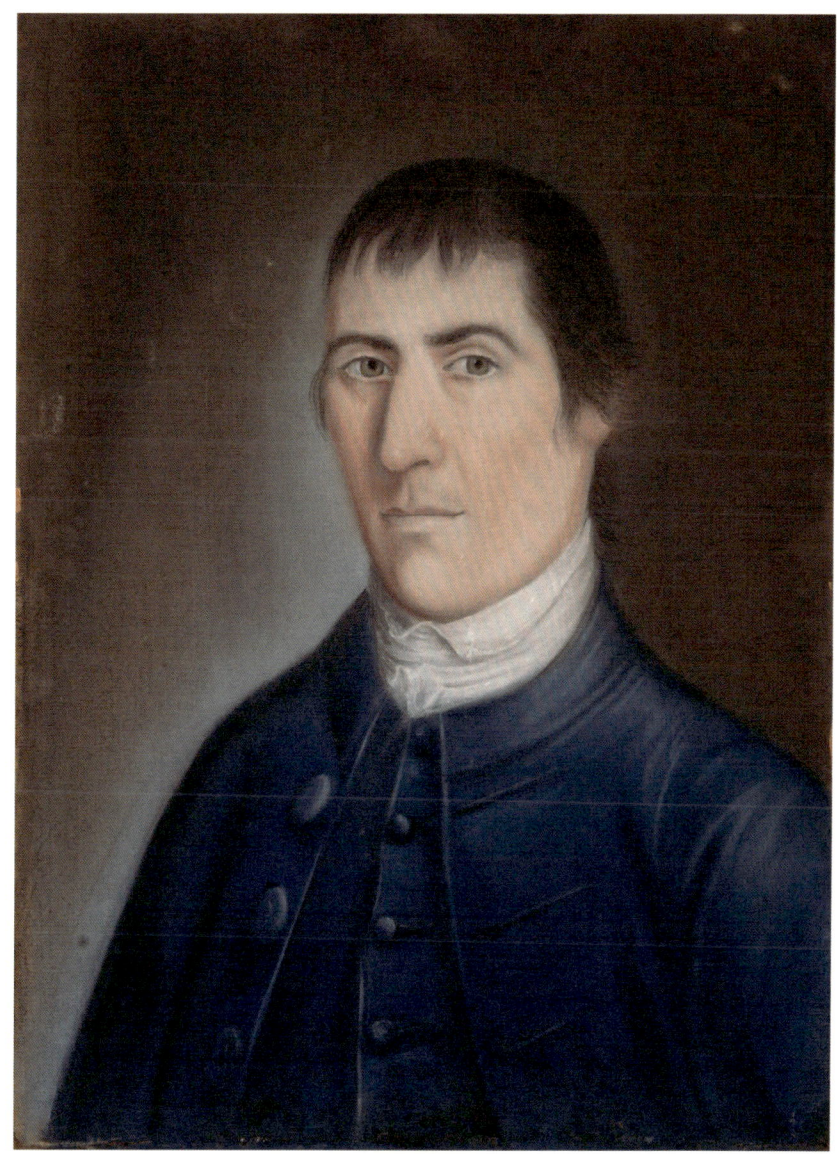

Joseph White
Pastel by Benjamin Blyth, 1780
Courtesy of the Peabody Essex Museum 2987, gift of Benjamin Barstow, Esq., 1891

EIMS, 55

FARL, Blyth, Benjamin 157-3d

Foote, "Blyth," 103

Jeffares, http://www.pastellists.com/Articles/Blyth.pdf

Norton, "Brothers Blyth," 63

Phillips, *Pepper and Pirates*, 50

Visitor's Guide to Salem, 1895, "Pastel," unknown artist, 196

Wagner, E. J., "The Tell-Tale Murder," *Smithsonian*, 41:7 (Nov. 2010), 60–68

WPA 2441

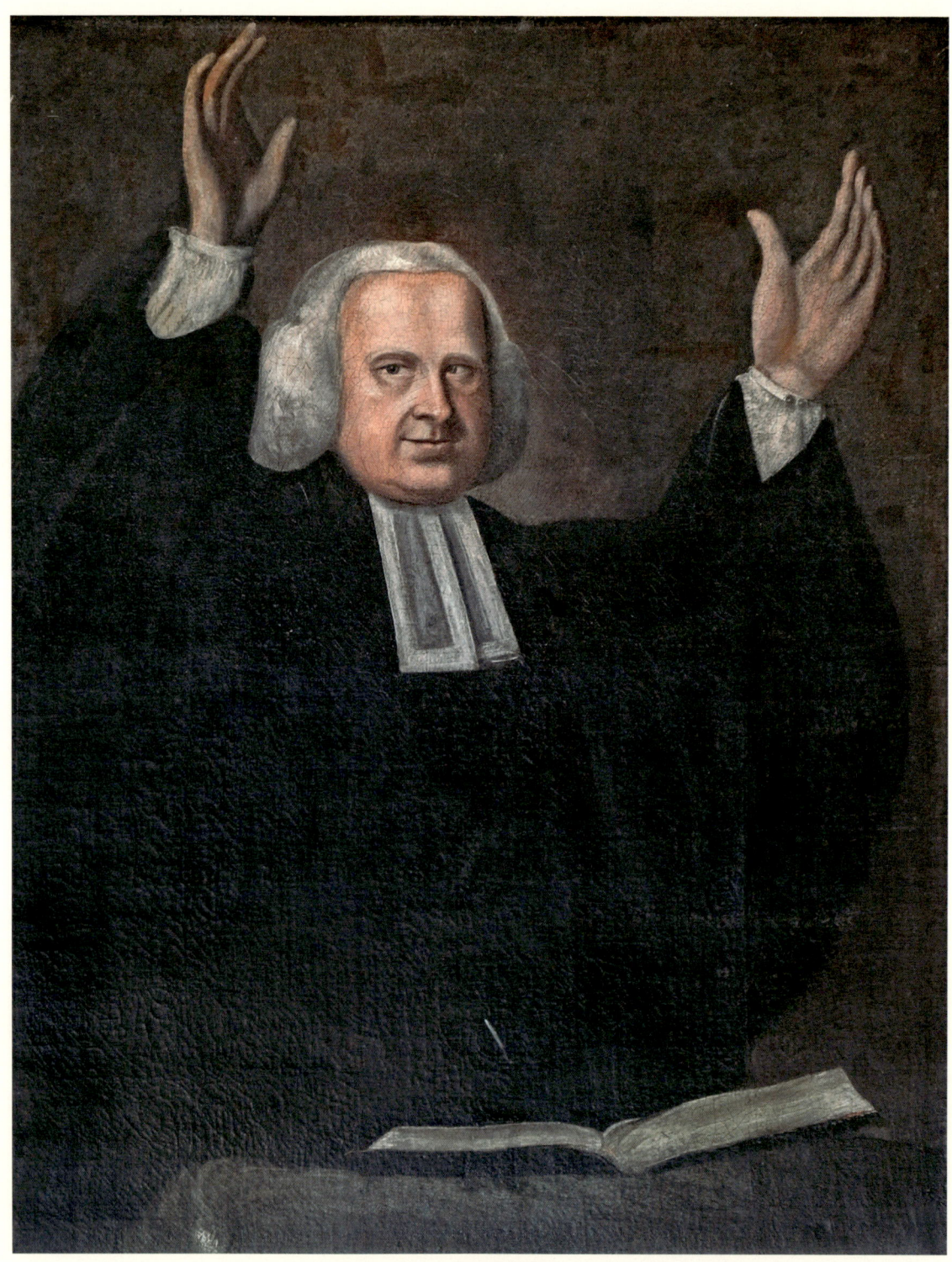

George Whitefield
Oil painting by Benjamin Blyth, 1770–72
Courtesy of the Congregational Library, Boston, Massachusetts
Photograph by by F. Lee Eiseman

George Whitefield (1714–1770)

Benjamin Blyth, 1770–72
After the British mezzotint by John Greenwood, 1764 (first) or 1768 (second) state
Oil on canvas, 46 x 33½ in. (116.8 x 85.1 cm.), 19th-c. gilt frame
Congregational Library & Archives, Boston, bequest of Miss Eliza Chipman, 1891

The Reverend George Whitefield was born on December 27, 1714, in Gloucester, England to a family of innkeepers. He attended Oxford and after receiving his degree was ordained in the Anglican church. Influenced by John and Charles Wesley, founders of Methodism, Whitefield became an itinerant evangelist preaching in Britain and, after 1738, in the North American colonies. He traveled the length of the East Coast, including in Salem and environs, conducting revivals, and promoting his brand of Methodism, the "Great Awakening." He died in Newburyport on September 30, 1770.

When Whitefield first visited Salem in 1740, he was hosted by the Reverend Thomas Barnard Sr., minister of the First Church, but Barnard and other clergy would later stay clear of Whitefield's "disorders and confusions in which so many towns and churches in the country were involved." Whitefield preached in Salem twice in 1754 and twice again on September 5 and 7, 1770, but in the words of nineteenth-century Salem historian Joseph B. Felt, "This was the last time that his eloquent appeals were made to our population in behalf of their spiritual welfare." The Reverend William Bentley thought little of Whitefield, whom he dismissed as one of the "Itinerants," and often brought up his name in his excerpts on the various sects of religion. After Whitefield's death, the *Salem Gazette* published an elegiac poem by Phyllis Wheatley, "with a representation of him as he lay dead." Bentley viewed Whitefield's corpse in the vault under the pulpit of the Presbyterian Church in Newbury, but not until seventeen years after his death.

Blyth copied the mezzotint by John Greenwood, originally published in England in 1764, that was based on an oil portrait by Nathaniel Hone (1718–1784). Greenwood had many connections to Salem and was a strong influence on Blyth before leaving in 1751 and eventually returning to England. Blyth simplified the print, focusing on Whitefield and his Bible and eliminating other background details. Blyth did a creditable job of producing the copy, capturing the evangelical pose, and employing such deft strokes as the white to highlight the left edge of his clerical collar and a book (the Bible?). The fingers of the left hand are the elongated, jointless arcs typical of Blyth, but here with bulges.

The portrait most likely was commissioned by the Reverend John Chipman of Beverly. It hung for many years in the Chipman mansion before it was given to the Congregational Library by his great-granddaughter. Felt probably saw it in the mansion, but his recollection of the medium was inaccurate, noted Henry Wilder Foote. Badly blistered, the portrait was restored by the Congregational Library in the 1950s, when its importance was recognized. Foote found that Whitefield's face in the oil painting copy by Blyth more "animated" than in the print and concluded that he "must have carefully observed the evangelist's countenance" when he was preaching in Essex County.

Bentley 1:61; 2–9, 10, 75, 147; 3:469, 476–77; 4:61, 513, 608

Bolton, *Portrait Draughtsmen*, 8

Felt, 2:597, 600, 602, 614

Foote, "Artist of the George Whitefield Portrait," *Bulletin of the American Congregational Society*, 10, no. 3 (May 1959), 7–8

Foote, "Blyth," 71–2, 83, 104–5

Congregational Library, Boston, correspondence

Fowble, cat. 56, 109 (Greenwood print, with dates 1764-76, state 4)

Jeffares http://www.pastellists.com/Articles/Blyth.pdf

McClennan, *History of Costume*, 224

Norton, "Brothers Blyth," 63

Phillips, *Salem . . . Indies,* 165

Sibley 7:559–60

WPA 2445, artist unknown

[140]
Joanna Whiting (1763–1843)
Benjamin Blyth, probably early 1770s
Pastel, measurements unknown
Current location not known; C. J. & Miss Alice Whiting (in 1967),
Mabel Robbins Whiting, Maria Fuller

The Frick Art Reference Library photoarchives is the only source of current information on this pastel. Alice M. Whiting of Santa Barbara, California, who sent the photograph to the library, wrote that Joanna Whiting was born in Franklin, Massachusetts, in May 1763. She had a brother, Thurston Whiting, and the family moved to the Waterville-Augusta area. In 1786, she married William Richards. Alice Whiting's notes stated that the pastel was probably done in East Winthrop, Maine, in 1779, and was attributed at the time to Blyth.

Joanna Whiting, twin daughter of Jonathan and Elioenai, was born on April 23, 1763, in Wrentham, not Franklin, Massachusetts. Her twin was Susanna, and she had two brothers, Elias and Abijah. But there is no record yet found in Vital Records of a Thurston, nor of her parents. Presumably the family were in Maine by the early 1770s, where Thurston Whiting "preached often prior to 1776 at the Congregational Church of Winthrop. . . ," according to *History of the Congregational Churches in Maine*, by Calvin M. Clark.

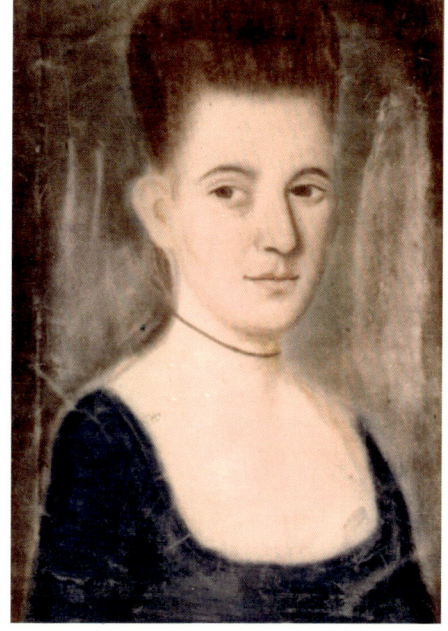

Joanna Whiting
Photograph of unlocated pastel by Benjamin
Blyth, probably early 1770s
Courtesy of the Frick Art Reference Library
Photoarchives

The portrait said to be of Joanna Whiting was not finished. Her dress was probably edged with lace, and the background is incomplete. Both her hairdo and her dress suggest a date of the early 1770s. It is very similar to the pastels of the Bradish sisters (Cats. 18, 19), coincidentally portraits that also came with what is deemed to be inaccurate information on the sitters and suggesting Maine as the place where they were drawn. Nonetheless, the portrait deemed of Joanna Whiting is undoubtedly by Benjamin Blyth, but with so little confirmed information, who she is, and when or where he did it, cannot be determined. This may be another instance when a donor assigns a family portrait to the wrong ancestor.

Clark, Calvin M. *History of the Congregational Churches in Maine*,
Vol. II, (1935)
FARL, Blyth, Benjamin, 1746–

UNIDENTIFIED SITTERS

Unknown Boy "from Salem"

Benjamin Blyth, late 1770s
Pastel on paper, dimensions unknown; Samuel Blyth frame
Current location not known, Roger Bacon Antiques

When offered for sale in 1961 by antiques dealer Roger Bacon of Exeter, New Hampshire, this pastel portrait was attributed to portrait artist William Johnston (1732–1772). Johnston is known to have painted a few portraits in oil of Salem people, but he is not known to have used pastels, and he had died several years before this portrait probably was done. No documentation has been found to determine why the young man in the portrait was thought to be from Salem. It probably was assumed because of its attribution to Benjamin Blyth, and it is in a Samuel Blyth frame. This illustration, as a possible Blyth, was sent to the author by the late New York collector, Lois Avigad.

Foote, Henry Wilder, "Benjamin Blyth of Salem: Eighteenth-Century Artist," *Proceedings of the Massachusetts Historical Society, Third Series* 71 (Oct. 1953–May 1957): 64–107

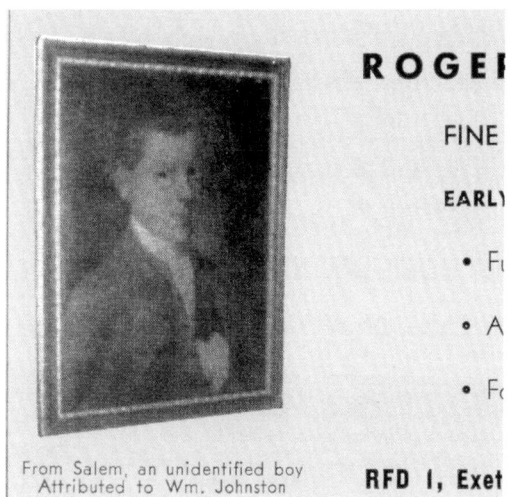

Unknown Boy "from Salem"
Photograph of unlocated pastel by Benjamin Blyth,
late 1770s
Courtesy of *The Magazine Antiques*

[142]
Unknown Boy in a Brown Suit

Benjamin Blyth, ca. 1780
Pencil and pastel on paper. 15¾ x 11½ in. (40 x 29.21 cm.), reproduction frame by Perry Hopf
Collection of James and Janet Laverdiere; Skinner, Inc. sale, Nov. 2018; Sotheby's sale, 1994;
Bertram and Nina Fletcher Little

This unfinished portrait of a young boy reveals how Blyth worked on his pastels, in thin charcoal outlines, still visible on collar and lace. The identity of this self-assured young man, probably around ten years of age, is not known, but the text in the newspaper on the entire back, although badly worn, contains at least six names from Newburyport, Massachusetts. So, the portrait can be said confidently to have originated in Essex County.

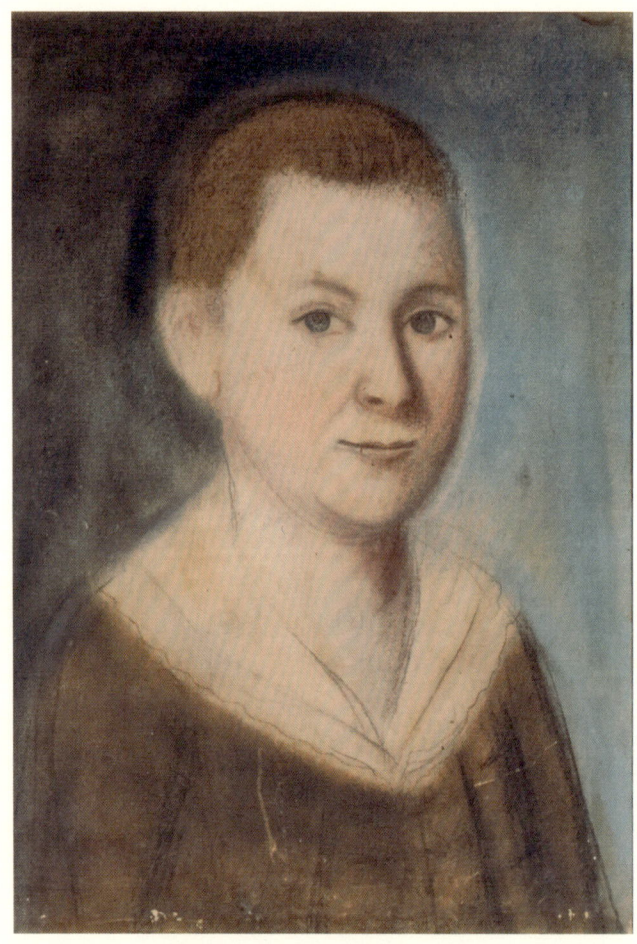

Unknown Boy in a Brown Suit
Pastel by Benjamin Blyth, ca. 1780
Photograph by Michael C. King

[143]

Unknown Man

Benjamin Blyth, ca. 1780
Miniature, measurements unknown
Unknown; owned by an unidentified resident of Worcester, MA in 1994

This miniature was shown to the author at a time when it could not be properly researched. Contact with the owner is now lost.

[144]

Unknown Man,
possibly Lt. Gov. Thomas Hutchinson

Benjamin Blyth (attr.), early 1770s
Pastel, 21½ x 18 in. (54.6 x 45.7 cm.)
Current location not known; H. L. Shattuck, Boston, MA; Copley Gallery, Boston; provenance unknown

A pastel said to be of Lt. Gov. Thomas Hutchinson, signed by Joseph Blackburn, was sold by Boston art dealer Frank Bayley's Copley Gallery to Mr. H. L. Shattuck, Boston, Massachusetts, in 1929. John Hill Morgan and Henry Wilder Foote, in their article on Blackburn seven years later for the *Proceedings of the American Antiquarian Society*, cast doubts not only on the identity of the sitter, but also the artist: "... Mr. Morgan and Mr. Foote do not believe that Blackburn worked in pastel and withhold agreement with the attribution to Blackburn." They subsequently felt that the signature "I. Blackburn Pinxit 1760" was added later, not only to the purported Hutchinson, but also to the ones Bayley had called Lt. Gov. Oliver (now "unknown," Cat. 145) and Mrs. Oliver. (See pp. 21–23.)

SIRIS located the pastel in the collection of the Museum of Fine Arts, Boston, in the 1980s, still attributed to Blackburn, but the museum could find nothing in its files to corroborate this, nor could it be located. So the description by Morgan and Foote is all that is known of the image: "Pastel in which head and bust of subject are drawn against a gray-blue shaded background; half front; the head nearly full front. Youthful in appearance; brown eyes; arched eyebrows and light brown hair brushed off forehead and tied with large, black bow; white stock and lace ruffles; brown coat and orange satin waistcoat."

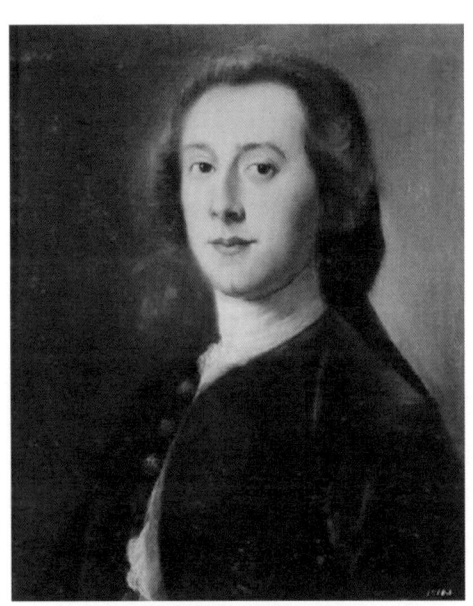

Unknown Man, possibly
Lt. Gov. Thomas Hutchinson
Photograph of unlocated pastel by
Benjamin Blyth, early 1770s
Courtesy of the Bayley Collection,
Historic New England

Given that the face and hair in this portrait have been extensively redrawn, the burden of authentication of the artist turns to handling of costume, pose of the sitter, and background. The rest of the pastel was relatively untouched and closely resembles the work of Benjamin Blyth. The tilted forward angle of the head is not typical, but it is seen in Blyth's pastel of Traill, another Tory. The treatment of the lace on the shirt may be the same as that on Traill, ascertained from the photograph. And at least five of Blyth's portraits had some gradation of grayish blue in the background.

Lack of provenance prior to acquisition by Bayley's Copley Gallery in the 1920s eliminates any identification of the original sitter. It might even be of Lt. Gov. Hutchinson. It shows great similarity to the only known portrait of him painted by Edward Truman, ca. 1740. And Hutchinson was popular in Salem. Blyth could have drawn him on one of his state visits to the town.

FARL, 17183
HNE, Bayley Negative Collection 3548-B
Morgan and Foote, "An Extension of Lawrence Park's Descriptive List . . .", 58–73
SIRIS, IAP 80970135, attr. Blackburn
WPA 1545, attr. Blackburn(?)

Unknown Man, formerly "Lt. Gov. Thomas Oliver"

Benjamin Blyth (attr.), early 1770s
Pastel on paper mounted on canvas, 21½ x 18 in. (54.6 x 45.7 cm.)
Museum of Fine Arts 29.931; purchase from Copley Gallery, Boston
with Archibald Cary Coolidge Fund, 1929

This pastel was purchased as a portrait of Massachusetts Lt. Gov. Thomas Oliver by the Museum of Fine Arts, Boston, for $2,500 in 1929 from Frank W. Bayley's Copley Gallery in Boston. His shop had skillfully enhanced it, probably adding the elaborate carved frame, and added the in-

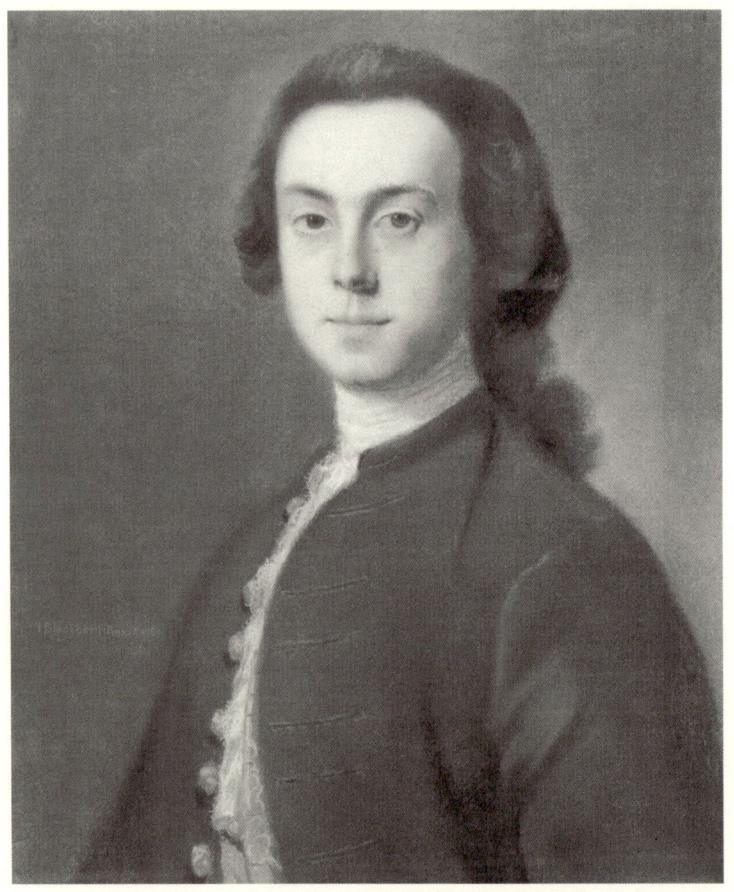

Unknown Man, formerly "Lt. Gov. Thomas Oliver"
Pastel by Benjamin Blyth (attr.), early 1770s
Courtesy of the Museum of Fine Arts 29.931; purchase from Copley Gallery,
Boston with Archibald Cary Coolidge Fund, 1929
Image provided by the Museum of Fine Arts, Boston

scription: "I Blackburn · Pinxit 1760." Additions include flesh-colored strokes on the eyelids and dark brown strokes on the eyebrows and lower eyelashes, as well as short strokes under the left nostril, the corners of the lips, and many areas of hair. (See the discussion, with a color image of a detail of this pastel, on pages 66 through 68). The fraudulent attribution and provenance were exposed by Yale Professor John Hill Morgan shortly after Bayley's death in 1931. Morgan also thought that the crayon color for the inscription had not been used elsewhere in the pastel, but on examination, this appears to be inconclusive.

This now-unidentified sitter was probably originally drawn by Benjamin Blyth. Aside from the face, which was altered, the portrait's draftsmanship resembles that of John Adams (Cat. 3), Gideon Baty (Cat. 11), and even Lydia Phippen Fisk (Cat. 53). The latter two also had some skillful pastel work added later. Further, the handling of lace and buttons is comparable in execution to the pastels of Baty, Joseph Lemmon (Cat. 85), and William Paine (Cat. 102), but especially to those of Samuel Curwen (Cat. 33) and David Ropes (Cat. 111), neither of which was worked on. The somewhat imperious pose is mindful of the pastel of Peter Frye (Cat. 56)—coincidentally, a Loyalist. The unfortunate result of Bayley's subterfuge is that any provenance is lost, and the actual sitter remains unknown.

Bayley Negative Collection

Correspondence from John Henry Morgan in object file, Museum of Fine Arts, Boston

Email correspondence from Neil Jeffares, http://www.pastellists.com/Articles/Blyth. pdf

Morgan and Foote, "An Extension of Lawrence Park's Descriptive List . . .", 64, 70–73

Shattuck Papers, letter from H. W. Foote to Henry Shattuck, Sept. 1935, MHS

Unknown Man, formerly "Gov. Richard Ward"

Benjamin Blyth, probably early 1770s, copy of an unknown sitter by an unknown artist
Pastel, 15¾ x 11¾ in. (sight), (41.9 x 33 cm.)
Rhode Island School of Design, 17.380, Jesse Metcalf Fund. Provenance unknown

The pastel was sold to the Rhode Island School of Design (RISD) in 1917 as the portrait of Richard Ward (1689–1763), early governor of Rhode Island, by John Singleton Copley. His name and the date, 1754, now barely visible, were scratched into the upper left corner. In their book on Copley published in 1937, Barbara Parker and Anne Wheeler doubted the attribution on stylistic grounds and noted that the purported date predated other known pastels by Copley by five years. The attribution was discounted by the museum in 1967, the year after the same conclusion was reached by Jules Prown. Ward would have been in his mid-sixties, a reasonable assumption for the man depicted in this pastel that would infer that the identity of the sitter was correct. However, he does not resemble the oil portrait of Ward at the Redwood Library in Newport, RI, first attributed to John Smibert and now to Nehemiah Partridge (1683–before 1737), ca. 1722.

At around the time of the sale to RISD, Frank W. Bayley, owner of the Copley Gallery in Back Bay, Boston, sold several portraits reputed to be, but subsequently shown *not* to be, of former Massachusetts Bay governors to unsuspecting public collections. The surmise is that he may have been the one who sold this to RISD. Although the Massachusetts Historical Society, Historic New England, Inc., and the Smithsonian Archives of American Art have collections of Bayley Papers, no financial records or logs of the Copley Gallery sales have been found in them or in other likely repositories.

As the pastel is very similar to the pastel copies of portraits Benjamin Blyth drew of Gov. Jonathan Belcher and Jonathan Simpson, it is now surmised that this is another copy by Blyth of an earlier portrait whose identity is unknown. This pastel is the only example seen by the author that shows the nails attaching the back board to the stretcher as, essentially, staples. The unresolved question is where such a frame with its peculiar nailing technique originated, and if it precludes a Blyth attribution. One source states that the technique was seen in the colonies as well as in England. Another source suggests that the pastel might have been framed later in China, shortly after it was drawn. So, the position taken here is that the pastel and its framing were not necessarily done at the same time, although not far apart, and that an attribution to Blyth is tenable.

Bulletin of the Rhode Island School of Design, 6 no. 1, (January 1918), 1–3, cover illus.

Haines, Andrew, email on frames, Oct. 2022

Parker & Wheeler, under "Attributed Pastels," 259

Prown, under "Attributed Pastels," 243

RISD, file correspondence, including a letter to Theodore Bolton, Nov. 1, 1922, in which it was assumed to be a Copley of Gov. Ward

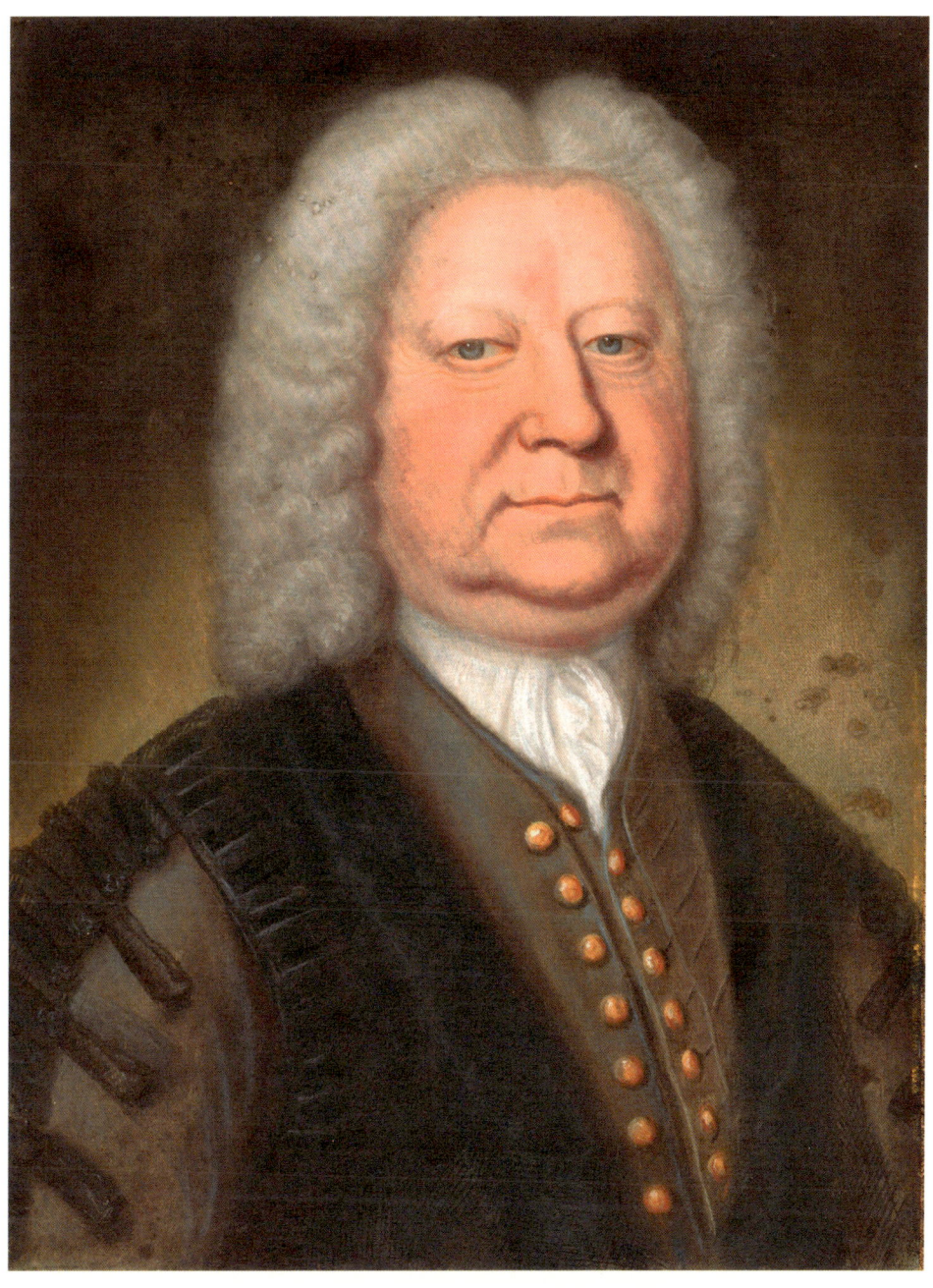

Unknown Man, formerly "Gov. Richard Ward"
Benjamin Blyth, probably early 1770s,
copy of an unknown painting by an unknown artist
Courtesy of the Rhode Island School of Design

☞ Unknown Man in Light Brown Coat, formerly PEM 115485. See Miles Ward (Cat. 128).

Unknown Man with Ledger Books

Benjamin Blyth (attr.), ca. 1775
Pastel on paper, size unknown, contemporary frame
Current location not known; formerly Austin T. Miller American Antiques, Inc.

"Young Man with Ledger Books" was sold by Austin T. Miller American Antiques, Inc., as "In the manner of" Blyth, but it is likely that this pastel was actually done by him, and it seems to have a Samuel Blyth frame. It is very similar to "Unknown Man with Powdered Hair" (Cat. 148). According to the dealer, the portrait originated in New England. It looks as if it was heavily worked on throughout, but especially on the face, with overdrawing in light coral, but the lip line and ear are indicative of Blyth. Although a detail like the bookcase is unusual for Blyth, it seems to be original, as the man's blue coat actually slightly overlaps the frame. A similar bookcase, in the same location, was used in the oil portrait of the Rev. Samuel Haven (1727–1806) attributed to Joseph Steward, in the collections of the Massachusetts Historical Society. Regrettably, the location of the original pastel, and therefore the size, are unknown.

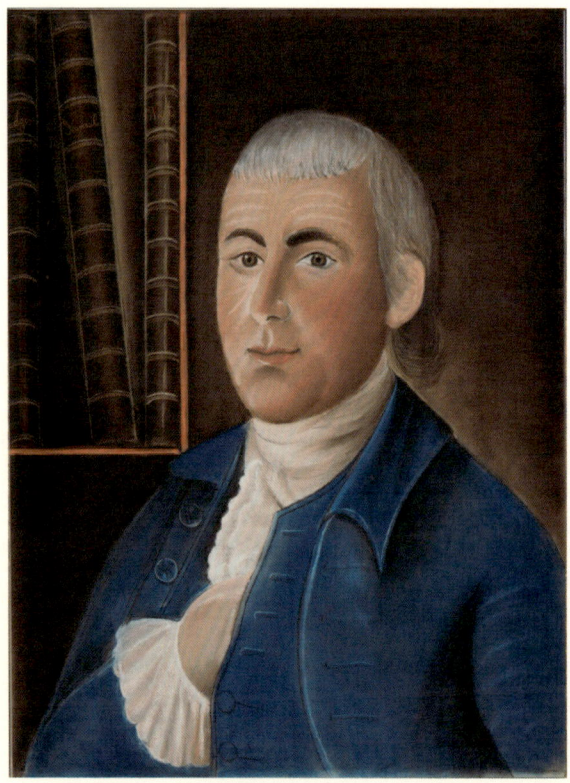

Unknown Man with Ledger Books
Photograph of unlocated pastel by Benjamin Blyth, ca. 1775
Courtesy of Austin T. Miller American Antiques, Inc.

Unknown Man with Powdered Hair

Benjamin Blyth, early 1770s
Pastel on paper mounted on linen, 13¾ x 9⅝ in. (sight), (34.92 x 25 cm.); 19th-c. frame
Private collection; Michael Baumann American Antiques, Newburyport

This portrait was purchased about twenty-five years ago at an onsite estate auction by dealer Michael Baumann from the contents of the Coolidge/Toppan house at the intersection of Winter and High Streets in Newburyport, Massachusetts. The long-time occupants had not been known to be collectors, so it could be assumed that the portrait might be a member of either family. If so, and given that Blyth sought to draw people important to the town, one possible candidate is Edward Toppan, born in 1754 to Edward and Sarah Toppan. His father was a partner in the mercantile house of Hoyt, Coolidge, Toppan. However, the probate record for his estate in 1850 notes that he lived at High and Park Streets, five blocks to the east.

This pastel is very similar to "Man with Ledger Books" (Cat. 147). Regardless of his identity, it is one of Blyth's deftly drawn and compelling portraits, of a somewhat sad, contemplative young man in his early twenties, similar in emotional impact to the young Patty Webb (Cat. 133).

Essex County Probate Record 55411
Newburyport Historical Society

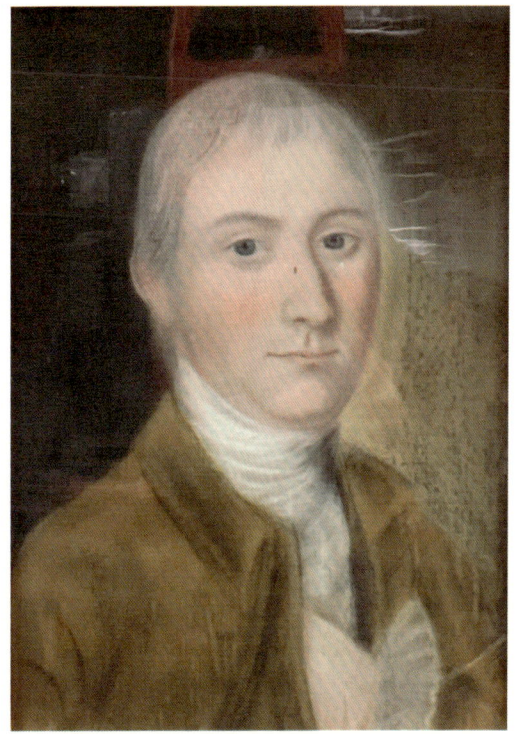

Unknown Man with Powdered Hair
Pastel by Benjamin Blyth, early 1770s
Photograph by F. Lee Eiseman
Private collection

[149]
Unknown Man in Thick Ebony Frame

Benjamin Blyth, early 1770s
Pastel on paper, 11½ x 9½ in. (29.21 x 24.13 cm.), all black Hogarth-type frame
Current location not known; D. Roger Howlett, Childs Gallery, Boston

This pastel, in poor condition, is known only in this equally poor photograph. It looks unfinished; however, there is much evidence of surface abrasion. The contemporary frame also is badly worn, and inner gilding looks to be almost completely eroded. Once thought to be by either Benjamin or Samuel Blyth, both it and its companion, "Unknown Woman in Thick Ebony Frame" (Cat. 150), are attributed to Benjamin. He drew an intriguing portrait of a sober, introspective young man.

Maine Antiques Digest, Feb. 1980, 38-A

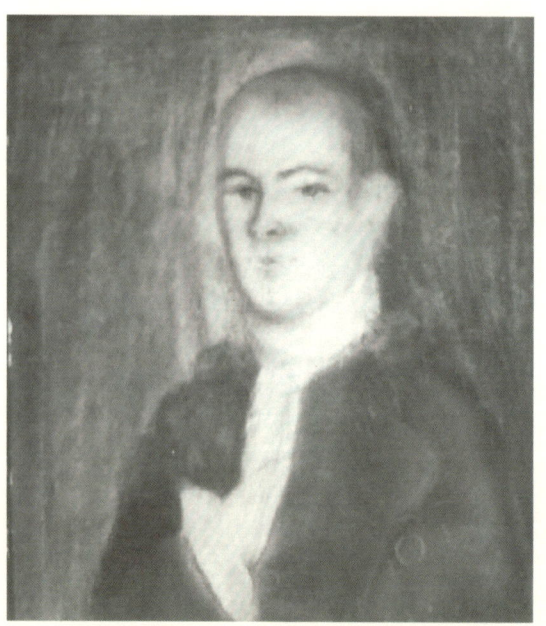

Unknown Man in Thick Ebony Frame
Photograph of unlocated pastel by Benjamin Blyth,
early 1770s
Courtesy of Roger Howlett, Childs Gallery, Boston

Unknown Woman in Thick Ebony Frame

Benjamin Blyth, early 1770s
Pastel on paper, 11½ x 9½ in. (29.21 x 24.13 cm.), all black Hogarth-type frame
Current location not known; formerly D. Roger Howlett, Childs Gallery, Boston

This pastel, in poor condition, is known only in this equally poor photograph. There is evidence of surface abrasion and water stains. The frame is badly worn, and inner gilding looks to be almost completely eroded, like the companion "Unknown Man in Thick Ebony Frame" (Cat. 149). Although once thought to be by either Benjamin or Samuel Blyth, Benjamin's characteristic portrayal of character comes through. It is very similar to the two pastels of the Bradish sisters (Cats. 18, 19).

Maine Antiques Digest, Feb. 1980, 38-A

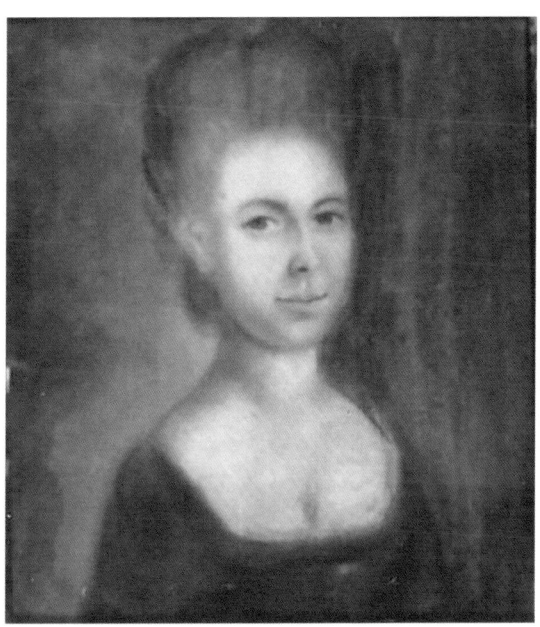

Unknown Woman in Thick Ebony Frame
Photograph of unlocated pastel by Benjamin Blyth,
early 1770s
Courtesy of Roger Howlett, Childs Gallery, Boston

[151]

Unknown Woman in Blue Dress with Black Lace

Benjamin Blyth, early 1770s
Pastel on paper mounted on linen, 14½ x 10¼ in. (36.8 x 26 cm.), early-19th-c. frame
Collection of James and Janet Laverdiere; private collection, Pook & Pook, Inc., auction house,
Downingtown, PA; provenance unknown

This portrait is one of the most elaborate of Blyth's pastels—like those of Sarah(?) Gardner (Cat. 58) and Unknown Woman of the Hiller(?) Family (Cat. 69)—and is testimony to the unfortunate lack of provenance of three important pastels in the Blyth oeuvre. Great care was taken with drawing the white lace on her pink shawl and the unusual black lace lining the neckline of her light blue dress, as well as the pearls and flowers in her hair. The colors of pale pink and blue, with the unusual delicacy of the black lace, have created a lovely composition, one of the few for which

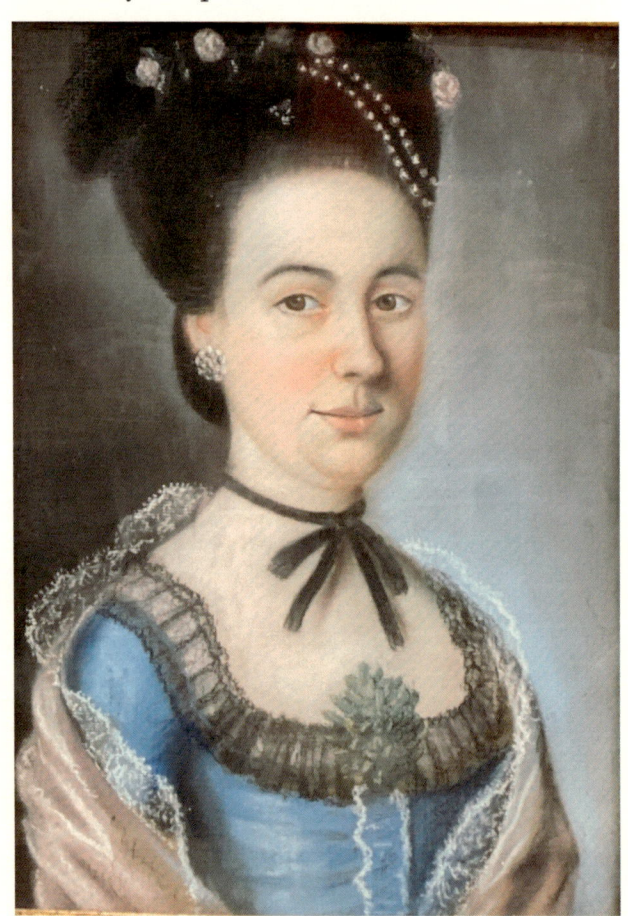

these details trump the emphasis on her personality. Its ambitious handling lends credence to the theory that Blyth may have been better paid for emphasizing sumptuous, expensive fabrics, an important element in the work of Copley. As with the portrait of Hannah Paine, there are strokes for lashes on the underside of the woman's eyes as well as enhancing strokes of black along the lace that suggest that this portrait may have been worked on by a dealer and conservator, most likely Frank W. Bayley's Copley Gallery in Boston. Visible in the text of the newspaper lining the portrait is "Derby, Esqr.," buttressing a Salem source.

The subject, looking dignified and obviously wealthy, appears to be from one of the most substantial families of Essex County.

Unknown Woman in Blue Dress with Black Lace
Pastel by Benjamin Blyth, ca. 1772
Courtesy of the Collection of James and Janet Laverdiere

Unknown Woman in Blue Dress, Wrap, & Black Neckband

Benjamin Blyth, ca. 1772

Pastel on paper mounted on wood, 10½ x 8½, (26.67 x 21.6 cm.); 13½ x 10½ in. with Samuel Blyth frame

Peabody Essex Museum 106735, gift of Henry FitzGilbert Waters, 1876

The unknown woman in a light blue dress with a dark wrap "lined with pink" over her left shoulder and a black velvet neckband wears her powdered hair high, with a spray of blue beads or flowers. The donor, Henry FitzGilbert Waters, gave several other portraits of family members to the museum, so it can be assumed that this woman also was an ancestor. Henry Wilder Foote noted that she appeared to be about twenty years old. He believed the attribution on the back, " . . . Painted by Samuel Blyth, Southward Coll." to be a mistake, as he also found the earlier attribution of Elizabeth Dabney (Cat. 39). He thought, correctly, that the woman's portrait resembled "Benjamin Blyth's larger and finer portrait of Sarah Curwen, but it is now in poor condition and badly spotted." In her erect bearing and some facial details, it shows affinity with the pastels once said to be of Lt. Gov. Hutchinson (Cat. 144) and Lt. Gov Oliver (Cat. 145). It was probably unfinished.

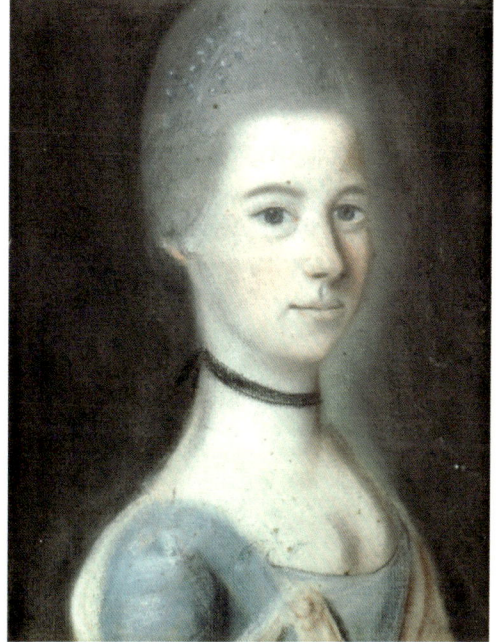

In addition to being smaller than most Blyth pastels, it was pasted directly on wood. At one time, it was given a proper mat and put on display in the Crowninshield-Bentley House, Room 7.

She was one of Blyth's more contemplative, serious subjects, like the youthful John Gibaut (Cat. 59).

EIHC 73:81, Cat. 388

FARL, Blyth, Benjamin 158-3h

Foote, "Blyth," 79, 105

Norton, "Brothers Blyth," 63

WPA, 2565

Unknown Woman in Blue Dress, Dark Wrap, and Black Neckband
Benjamin Blyth, ca. 1772
Peabody Essex Museum 106735, gift of Henry FitzGilbert Waters, 1876

Unknown Woman with Handkerchief Cap & Pink-Bowed Yellow Dress

Benjamin Blyth, early 1770s
Pastel on paper mounted on linen, 22¼ x 15⅜ in. (56.4 x 39.1 cm.), replacement plain Hogarth-type frame
Private collection; Avigad collection; Sotheby's 1994

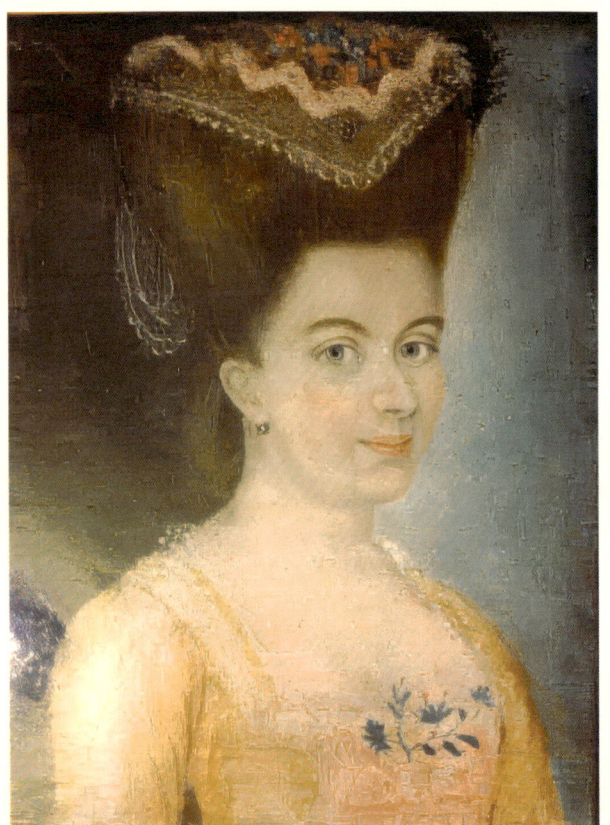

At the request of the late owner, Lois Avigad of New York City, the title she gave it is retained. Mrs. Avigad, who bought the portrait at a Sotheby's sale in 1994, was a knowledgeable collector and amassed much documentation on Blyth that she and her husband shared for this publication. This portrait is certainly one of the most florid of Blyth's depictions, with the sitter's elaborate upsweep hairdo and embellishments. It is a shame that the woman's identity is unknown. From the expression on her face, she seems quite pleased with her hair decoration, in high fashion in the early 1770s.

Lois Avigad, Dr. Gad Avigad, correspondence

Unknown Woman in Handkerchief Cap and Pink-Bowed Yellow Dress
Pastel by Benjamin Blyth, early 1770s

POSSIBLE ATTRIBUTIONS

The following are likely subjects, although there are either no known images or insufficient information to validate them.

Abigail Cooper, miniature or pastel?

Abigail "Nabby" Cooper is listed by Parker and Wheeler in their book on Copley under "Questionable Copley miniatures," page 260: "Mr. and Mrs. Joseph Sayer Hixon . . . Mrs. Hixon was Abigail Cooper . . . mentioned as a miniature . . . may be the pastel portrait owned by Richard H. Taylor, Los Angeles, Cal." An Abigail Cooper married Joseph Hixon in Boston in 1777. However, a connection with Essex County is tenuous.

Northey, Abijah, miniature

In 1957, a "brooch" of Abijah Northey from the collection of Bertram K. and Nina Fletcher Little was exhibited at the Museum of Fine Arts, Boston. Northey was a Salem silversmith whose pastel portrait was drawn by Blyth (Cat. 97). Northey himself may have made the case. The location of the miniature is currently unknown.

Unknown Subject, pastel

A pastel, no further information, on loan by Ann Colman Moody to the Essex Institute, was withdrawn and returned to the "Newbury Society," in October 1955. In 1927, Moody had founded The Sons and Daughters of The First Settlers of Newbury, Massachusetts. The society has no record of a donation.

Anonymous Man and Woman, pastels

In 1937, Mrs. William C. Endicott donated pastels of an unidentified man and woman, listed as copies by Martha Endicott Peabody Rogers (1826–1866), to the Essex Institute ("Addition to the Catalogue of Portraits" *Essex Institute Historical Collections*, 86:173–74). The man is described as "Half length facing right. Pink coat, white waistcoat, ruffled shirt and sleeve ruffles, holding cane, white wig." Rogers may have added the cane, a typical practice of copyists in the nineteenth century, viz. Benjamin Crowninshield (Cat. 31). The woman is described as "Half length facing left, seated in chair. Pink dress, low neck, lace trimming, black neck band." They have not been located for many years. Since both copyist and donor were from Essex County, it is surmised that the artist of the original pastels was Benjamin Blyth.

Historic New England's pastel of an unknown woman from an unknown donor was tentatively attributed to Benjamin Blyth because of its presumed date, the composition, and the dark background. Also, the sitter presumably was from the area. However, the drawing, especially of the bosom, is awkward, and the lace does not have Blyth's characteristic delicacy. Typically, his hair ornaments are delicately sketched portrayals of flowers and pearls, in blue, pink, and white. The one in this portrait not only is out of scale (cf. Elizabeth or Rachel Rogers (Cat. 110), Elizabeth Dabney (Cat. 39), and Unknown Woman in Blue Dress with Black Lace (Cat. 151), but some leaves are green, a color not used by Blyth. Too many problems preclude the pastel being a possible Blyth, although it may have been a copy of one.

POSSIBLE SITTERS

Benjamin Blyth also depicted several people for whom there are no known images of their spouses. Those who might once have been drawn as companion portraits include Nathaniel Appleton (d. 1784); Lois (Mrs. Thomas) Barnard (d. 1819); Sarah (Mrs. Edward) Bass (d. 1789); Nathaniel Dabney (d. 1784); Lydia (Mrs. Richard Jr.) Derby (d. 1777); Abigail (Mrs. Abijah) Northey (d. 1814); and Daniel Rogers (d. 1824). Blyth drew a number of clergymen. Among Salem clergy whom he might have drawn are James Diman, pastor of the East Church, Thomas Barnard Sr., minister of the First Church, or the popular rector of Blyth's own church, William McGilchrist.

DUBIOUS ATTRIBUTIONS

Several pastels formerly attributed to Benjamin Blyth have been found to be stylistically incompatible with his work. Azor Orne and his wife Mary were thought at one time to have been done by Blyth (see Foote, "Benjamin Blyth of Salem: Eighteenth-Century Artist," 98–99), but after Barbara Parker finally saw them, she stated in a letter to the Frick Art Reference Library on May 27, 1954, that Orne probably was by Copley and his wife was probably a nineteenth-century copy of an image, medium unspecified.

Benjamin Blyth's pastels show less of the patterned linearity associated with more primitive artists, such as the painter of the Morehouse and the Emerson portraits, here removed from prior attribution to him. The composition and draftsmanship of them and the pastel of the Reverend John Murray are stylistically dissimilar to the work of either Benjamin or Samuel Blyth, and the biographies of the Mo[o]rehouse and Murray families make an attribution to Blyth more problematic.

The variety among contemporary pastel portraits by anonymous artists that have been discounted as by Benjamin Blyth points out that not only were there others trying the medium at the time, but that Blyth clearly was a superior artist to all of them.

APPENDIX
SPONSORS OF PUBLICATION

I am very grateful for the financial assistance and moral support from the following:

Akash Agarwal
Laura Norton Agarwal
Georgia and James Barnhill
Laurence D. Berman
Joan Toland Bok
Gary Borisy and Sally Casper
Diane* and John Paul Britton
Christopher Bryant
Margaret R. Burke and Dennis A. Fiori
Nym Cooke
Heather Damelio
Jane Deland
Bonneau H. Dickson, Jr.
F. Lee Eiseman and Mary Runkel
Jean Fuller Farrington
Cynthia* and T. Corwin Fleming
Lora Elderkin Fleming
Ronald Lee Fleming
Hilary Bacon Gabrieli
Lucretia Hoover Giese*
Diana and Joseph Govern
Shirley Hale
Dan Hennessee
Sarah Ropes Hinkle
Henry B. Hoover, Jr.
Maisie Houghton

Madeleine G. and Marvin Kalb
Katherine Kimball and Charles Warren*
Claire and Michael C. King
Patricia Krol
James and Janet Laverdiere
Lynne and Sidney Levitsky
Barbara and John Marden
Mary Markis
Gary M. Milan
Patrice and Stephen Minton
Virginia Newes*
The family of Benjamin R. Norton
The family of Prof. Dee Norton
Giulia di Stefano Norton
Catherine Parmelee
Karen and Michael Rotenberg
Ann and Malcolm Russell
Duncan and Grace Smith
Joseph Peter Spang III*
Roger E. Stacey
Mary Fran and Thomas Townsend
John* and Marie Vander Sande
Helena E. Wright
Katharine Young
Anonymous (4)

*Deceased

ACKNOWLEDGMENTS

This project has been almost ten years in the making. The research was extensive, but it was hampered by the epidemic of Covid and by my late husband's gradual, heart-breaking and time-consuming descent into dementia. The book is dedicated to him and our late son.

Six fellow historians and long-time friends have given enormous help, encouragement, and support throughout this enterprise, which took more time than originally was anticipated: Marjorie B. Cohn, retired Carl A. Weyerhaeuser curator of prints, former conservator of "Works of Art on Paper,"and acting director (twice) at the former Fogg Art Museum of Harvard University; Dennis A. Fiori, president (now retired) of the Massachusetts Historical Society; the late Lucretia Hoover Giese, former professor of art history from Rhode Island School of Design; the late J. Peter Spang, former long-time curator of Historic Deerfield, Inc.; Helena Wright, former curator of the Division of Culture and the Arts of the Smithsonian Museum of American History; and John Hardy Wright, former assistant curator at the Essex Institute. Major credit for the development of this manuscript goes to Caroline F. Sloat, who provided editorial suggestions that have vastly improved the text. For directing me to her, I am indebted to Richard Candee, professor emeritus of American and New England Studies, Boston University, who also offered cogent observations and suggestions. Valuable suggestions were also contributed by my daughter, Giulia di Stefano Norton, and Claire R. King. I could not have completed the manuscript without the steady, long-time help with other tasks from my late husband John and our former house resident, Dr. Lawson Ung, and current tenant, Chase du Maurier. Friends F. Lee Eiseman and Michael C. King contributed professional-quality photography.

It was my good fortune to work throughout the production with one of the most knowledgeable, affable, aesthetically satisfying designers in the trade, Jerry Kelly. And thanks to the suggestion of Beacon Hill author John Spooner, this book is published by TidePool Press, overseen by two highly capable and, again, affable, editors, Jock Herron and Ingrid Mach. Their insights and corrections were invaluable. Nor could I have worked "off grid" through the summers without the hospitality from two restaurants in Acton, MA, the former Ginger Court, which willingly provided wi-fi access, even when I was not dining or imbibing wine, and Dunkin' Donuts on Great Road.

The following acknowledgements credit those individuals who were at the respective institutions at the time. The major source for works by the Blyths is of course the Peabody Essex Museum, created by a merger of the Essex Institute and Peabody Museum in 1993. Executive Director and CEO Lynda Roscoe Hartigan generously encouraged her staff to assist me, and this cooperation was invaluable. John Childs and Suzanne Inge searched the old records of the PEM for important clarifying information. Christine Bertoni, Claire Blechman, Adam Brooks, Kathryn Carey, Marta Fodor, Ani Geragosian,Dean Lahikainen, Alyssa Langlais, Donald A. McPhee, Kathryn White, Eric Wolin, and Tiffany Yee also provided assistance, as did Kathy M. Flynn, Amanda Fowler, Jennifer Hornsby, Dan Lipcan, Catherine Robertson, and Meaghan Wright of the museum's Phillips Library. The assistance of former directors/CEOs Dan L. Monroe and Brian Kennedy, was also helpful. The Massachusetts Historical Society's Anne E. Bentley, Peter Drummey,

Hannah Elder, Elaine Heavey, Dan Hinchen, Sara Martin, Christopher Minty, Rakashi Chand, and Conrad Wright provided superb help with research. The Boston Athenaeum's extensive holdings going back to nineteenth-century tomes were in continual use; I am grateful especially to Will Evans, James P. Feeney, Jr., Elizabeth O'Meara, Robert Sanford, Arnold Serapilio, and Mary Warnement for innumerable services; also, Carolle R. Morini, and former staff members Patricia Boulos, Emily Cure, David B. Dearinger, Samantha Dodgen, Thomas Gearty, James Kraus, and Robert West. The very comprehensive index was provided by Shannon Li.

The response to three chapters of the text sent early on to Theodore E. Stebbins, Jr., former John Moors Cabot Curator of American Art at the Museum of Fine Arts, Boston and more recently Consultative Curator of American Art at Harvard University, was a big boost in the effort to continue with the project. "I like it!!" he wrote in the summer of 2016. He also offered several valuable suggestions, as did the late Carl Crossman, Chinese Export scholar and former co-owner of Childs Gallery, Boston. It was my good fortune to have encouraging correspondence from the late Bernard Bailyn, professor of American history at Harvard. In the early stages, British art historian Neil Jeffares, author of the *Dictionary of Pastel Artists before 1800* (www.pastellists. com), offered valuable information and suggestions. I also am extremely grateful for the careful reading and suggestions on order given by Dr. Ellen Miles on my chapter on Blyth's pastels. For critical help on miniatures, I am indebted to Donald Shelton, Edward Sheppard, and Ron Tauss. I am also grateful to Sarah Pierce, former curator of prints at the Boston Athenaeum and editor emerita of *Imprint*, in which an earlier version of the chapter on Blyth prints appeared in Spring 2019, and to S. Clayton Pennington and *Maine Antiques Digest* which ran my article "Where Have All the Portraits Gone?" and led to seven productive leads. Other individuals who contributed their expertise include Dr. Donna A. Seger, professor of medieval and early modern history at Salem State University and producer of the website streetsofsalem.com; editors Anne Swanson and Christine Chamberlain; independent scholars Judith Anderson, Marblehead, MA, Seth Thayer, Belfast, ME, Christopher Bryant, Manchester-by-the-Sea; Dr. Françoise Little, for providing catalogues from sales of the Bertram and Nina Fletcher Little collection from which illustrations were not provided by the dealers; and many other current and former owners of Blyth portraits.

During the course of research and writing, a number of the listed individuals have left the institutions where they worked and offered help. Other persons, some dear friends, have died. I remain grateful to all.

Institutions and staff that provided timely and valuable assistance during the project:

Abby Aldrich Rockefeller Folk Art Museum, Colonial Williamsburg Foundation, Lea C. Lane, Marianne Martin; Acadia University, Meg Townsend; Addison Gallery of American Art, Phillips Andover Academy, Susan C. Faxon, Julia McDonough; Allen. E. Roberts Grand Lodge Museum, Richmond, VA, Marie Barnett, Bernard L. Brock; American Antiquarian Society, Brianne Barrett, Vincent Golden, Lauren B. Hewes, Thomas G. Knoles, Ashley Lauren Szumita; American Arts Consulting, LLC, Seth A. Thayer, Jr. ; American Congregational Society Library Cary Hewitt, Claudette Newhall, Steven Picazio; American Jewish Historical Society, Tanya Elder, Elizabeth Hyman; American Textile History Museum, Jane A. Ward; *Antiques and Fine Arts Magazine*,

Peter Hannan; Arlington Street Church, Boston, Jeffrey Bouchard; ArtNet Worldwide Corporation, Kate Hyman, New York office; Berkeley Art Museum, University of California, Stephanie Cannizzo, Genevieve Cottraux; Boston Public Library, Henry Scannell, Calder Sell, Karen Schaft; Bowdoin College Museum of Art, Joachim Homann, Laura Layton, Sarah Montros; Brandeis University, Carrie Van Horn; British Museum, Hugo Chapman; Brooklyn Museum, Susan Fisher, Margarita Karasoulas, Nancy Rosoff, Joseph Shaikewitz, Shea Spiller; Brown University, John Hay Library, Ann Dodge; Butts Hill Fort Restoration Committee (Portsmouth, RI), Gloria Schmidt; Campus Martius Museum and Ohio History Connection, Jason Crabill, Cliff Eckle, Glenna Hoff, Bill Reynolds; Cape Ann Historical Association and Museum, Stephanie Buck, Leon Doucette, Martha Oaks; Christie's Auction House, Inc., Grace Baljon; Casco Bay Auctions, Andrew Davis; Cleveland Museum of Art, June De Phillips; Colby College Museum of Art, Lauren Lessing, Ramey Mize, Diana Tuite; Colonial Williamsburg Foundation, Lea C. Lane; Columbus Memorial Library, Local History and Genealogy, Michelle Caldwell; Concord Free Public Library, Special Collections, Jessie Hopper, Constance Manoli-Skocay, Jessica Steytler, Leslie Perrin Wilson Anke Voss; Concord Museum, Jessica Desany Ganong, Erica Lome, David Wood; Congregational Library, Margaret Bendroth; Connecticut Historical Society, Melica Bloom, Tasha Caswell, Diane Lee; Copley Society; Cornell University Library, Cheryl Beredo, Kheel Center, Aliqae Geraci; Crosby Company, Tara Cederholm; Cowan Auctions (now Hindman Auctions), Leah Vogelpohl; Custom House Maritime Museum, Sean Palmatier, Jason D. Roberts; Joan Whitlow; Dalhousie University, Canada Karen Smith; Dartmouth College, Hood Museum, Barbara MacAdam; Derby Academy, Deborah "Squeakie" Thompson; Dedham Unitarian Universalist Church, the Rev. Rali Weaver; Deerfield Academy Lydia Hemphill; Derby Academy, John Houghton; Detroit Institute of the Arts, Nancy Barr, Kenneth Myers, Carol Rogan; Episcopal Diocese of Massachusetts, Lynn Smith; Essex County South District, Kosta Psiakis; First Church in Salem, the Rev. Elizabeth Ide; Diane Smith: First Parish in Concord, Douglas R. Baker; First Religious Society of Newburyport, Robert Heenehan, Edward Mair; Florida Atlantic University Libraries; Florence Griswold Museum Amy Kurtz Lansing; Franklin D. Roosevelt Library and Museum, Herman Eberhardt, Mary Jikhars; Free Library of Philadelphia, Caitlin A. Goodman, Karen Kirsheman, J. Eytan Shemtov; Frick Art Reference Library, Ralph Baylor, Sally Brazil, Eugenie Fortier, Suz Massen; Gibbes Museum, Joyce Baker; Gold Leaf Studios, William Bruce Adair; Golden Ball Tavern, Joan Bines; Grand Lodge of Ohio, Darlene Shirk; Greenwich (CT) Public Library, Mary Cuff, Carl White; Harvard University: —Harvard Art Museums: Portrait Collection, Theodore E. Stebbins, Tara Cerretani, Sam Dollenmayer, Emily Driscoll, Ethan Lasser, Nicole Lindermann, Mary Lister, Kathryn Press; Print Collection, Erica Lawton; Straus Center for Conservation; — Baker Library, Harvard Business School, Katherine Fox, Melissa Murphy; —Harvard Divinity School, Fran O'Donnell; —Houghton Library, James Capobianco, Susan Halpert, Hope Mayo; —Harvard Medical School, Dolores Toston; Huntington Library, Morex Arai, James Glisson; Haverhill Historical Society, Jay Williams; Haverhill Public Library, Amanda Levy, the late Greg Laing; Hingham Historical Society, Michael Achille, Dierdre Anderson; Historic Deerfield, Inc., David Bosse, Tara Cederholm, Philip Zea; Historic New England (formerly SPNEA) Nancy Carlisle, Nora Carleson, Nicole Chalfant, Lorna Condon, Jeanne Gamble, Donna Russo, Madison Vlass; Historical Society of Princeton, Stephanie Schwartz; Mariannne Litty; Kennedy Galleries, Inc., Martha Fleischman; King's College, Pat Chalmers; Lancaster [MA] Historical Commission, Heather Lennon; Leffingwell House Museum, Gregory and Camilla Farlow; Leslie Antiques Ltd., Ronald Tauss; Library of Congress, Katherine Blood; Lincoln County Historical Society, Maine, Edward Kavnagh, Jonathan Lee; Lyman Allyn Art Museum, Tanya Porht, Erin Walker; *The Magazine Antiques*, Kathryn Kiick, Donald Sparacin; Maine Maritime Museum, Nathan Lipfert; Marblehead Museum, Emilia Boehm Emig, Lauren McCormack; Marblehead Public Library; Mead Art Museum, Stephen Fisher, Vanya Malloy; Massachusetts State Art Commission, Susan Greendyke; Metropolitan Museum and Thomas M Watson Library, Melissa Bowling, Sean Farrell, Elizabeth Mankin Kornhauser, Catherine Mackay, Constance McPhee, Lauren Ritz, Marjorie Shelley, Adrianna Slaughter, Elizabeth Zanis; Milwaukee Art Museum, Lydelle Abbott, Liz Flaig; Mount Desert Island Historical Society, Mount Desert, ME., Patrick Callaway; Musée McCord Stewart, Heather McNabb; Museum and Historical Society of Beverly, Abby Battis, Darren Brown, Daniel F Fish, Susan Goganian, Terri McFadden; Museum of Fine Arts, Boston, Janet L. Comey, Mauri Fagan, Lee-Anne Famolare, Andrew Haines, Erica Hirshler, Fred Hee Jung Lee, Paul McAlpine, Meghan Melvin, Maureen Merton, Pamela A. Parmal, Taylor Poulin, Deborah Barlow Smedstad, Stephanie Loeb Stepanek, Christine Storti, Jennifer Swope; Museum of Fine Arts, Houston, Remi S. Dyll, Cyrus Kohanloo; Museum of Old Newbury, Susan C. S. Edwards; Museums of Old York, Cynthia A. Young-Gomes; Muskingum County, Ohio: Court Clerk's office, Eugenia Starr; Probate Court, Abby Garber; Muskingum County Library System, Heather Phillips; Nantucket Historical Association, Betsy Tyler; National Gallery of Art, Peter Huestis, Dr. Ellen Miles, Zoe Samels; National Park Service:— Adams National Historic Site; — Independence National Historical Park, Karie Diethorn;—Longfellow House-Washington's Headquarters National Historic Site, Kelly Cobble, Kate Hanson; —Salem Maritime National Historic Site, Emily Murphy; National Society of Colonial Dames (NSCDXVIIC), Nan Ackerman, Scott Scholz; National Society of Daughters of the American Revolution, Carrie Blough; New Bedford Free Public Library, Mrs. Goodman; New Bedford Whaling Museum, D. Jordan Berson, Christina Cannette, Melanie Correia; New Britain Museum of American Art, Elizabeth Sirrine; New England Historic and Genealogy Society, Curt di Camillo, Alice Kane, Ann Lawthers, Judy Lucey, Ken Salls; New Hampshire Historical Society, Jonathan Olly; New Haven Museum, Donna Wardle; New-York Historical Society, Scott Wixon; New York Public Library, The Irma and Paul Milstein Division of United States History, Local History and Genealogy, David G. Christie, Margaret Glover, Rebecca Szanty; Newburyport Maritime Museum, Michael Mroz; Newport Historical Society, Bridget Sullivan; Nichols House Museum, Flavia Cigliano, Linda Marchall, Claire Senatore, Emma Welty; Northeast Auctions, Ronald Bourgeault; Ohio History Connection and Campus Martius, Jason Crabill, Glenna Hoff, Bill Reynolds, Lisa Wood; Old Colony Historical Society, Katie MacDonald; Philadelphia History Museum, Kristen Froelich; Philadelphia Museum of Art, Emily Leischner; Pollard Memorial Library, Lowell, MA, Pam Colt; Pook & Pook Inc., James Pook; Portland Art Museum, Charles Campbell; Preservation Society of Newport County, Paul Miller; Princeton University:— Art Museum, Lisa M. Arcomano, Emile Askey, Jennifer E. Garey, Karl E. Kusserow; —Harvey S. Firestone Library, April C. Armstrong; Ralph Waldo Emerson Memorial Association, Margaret

Emerson Bancroft, Ellen Emerson, Marie Gordinier; Redwood Library, Whitney Pape; Revolutionary Spaces (formerly Bostonian Society), Patricia Gilrein, Brian LeMay, Elizabeth Roscio; Rhode Island Historical Society, Kirsten Hammerstrom, JD Kay, Dana Munrow; Rhode Island School of Design, Shannon Gunther, Sarah Mirseyedi, Maureen O'Brien, Britany Salsbury; Saint Louis Art Museum, Pat Boulware; Saint Paul's Church, Newburyport, Bronson de Stadler, Deborah Hay; San Francisco de Young Museum of Art, Jane Glover, Natasha Morovic, Leni Velasquez; Second Congregational Church in Beverly, Mary Jane Clark; Shelburne Museum, Allison Gillette, Jacquelyn Oak, Barbara Rathburn; Skinner, Inc. Elizabeth Haff, Brianna Lovensheimer; Smithsonian Institution:—Research Information System (SIRIS); —National Gallery of American Art, Elizabeth Anderson, Randy Arnold; Jennifer Bauman, Anne Evenhaugen, Richard Sorensen, Denise Wammaling;— National Museum of American History, Joan Boudreau; — National Portrait Gallery, Brandon Fortune, Sue Garton, Linda Thrift; Society of the Cincinnati: Ellen McCallister Clark, Rachel Nellis, Paul Newman; Society for the Preservation of Long Island Antiquities, Tara LaWare; Somerville Historical Society, Ann Benson; Sotheby's, Amanda Bass, Sarah Goslin, Julia Hernandez, Madeline Hurst, Kristin Nottebaum, Timothy O'Connor, Yasmeen Sabet, Aimee Scillieri, Sophie Shapiro; Somesville Museum, Patrick Callaway; Springfield Museum of Art, Joanna Hanna; Stanford University, Cecil H. Green Library, Christopher Matthews; Thayer Memorial Library, Lancaster, MA, Victoria Hatchell, special collections and archives librarian; Toledo Museum of Art, Mark Yappueying; United Missouri Bank of St. Louis, Kathryn Mueth, Eric Nesbitt, Tracy Shatto, Carol Sturm; U. S. Dept. of State, curatorial offices; University of Aberdeen (Scotland), Sarah Miller, Jan M. Smith; Virginia Historical Society, Frances Pollard; Wadsworth Athenaeum, Zenon Gansziniec, Erin Monroe; Wenham Historical Society, Jane Bowers; Henry Francis Dupont Winterthur Museum, Jason Brudereck; E. McSherry Fowble, Amanda Hinckle, Brock Jobe, Susan Nelson; Woodford County Public Library (Versailles, Kentucky), Heather Plumkett; Worcester Art Museum, Director Emeritus James A. Welu, Elizabeth Athens, Nancy Burns, Kate Dalton, Sarah Gillis, Delaney Keenan; Yale University:—Art Gallery, Suzanne Greenawalt, Janet M. Miller, Kathleen Mylen-Coulombe, Casey Thomas;—Beinecke Library, Elizabeth Frengel, Michael Frost, Amy Jacaruso.

BIBLIOGRAPHY

The major sources were *The Diary of William Bentley, D. D., Essex Institute Historical Collections,*
Sibley's Harvard Graduates, the Smithsonian Institution Research Information System (SIRIS), and vital records
from individual cities and towns in both the United States and England, found on Ancestry. com.

Adair, William Bruce. *The Frame in America, 1700–1900/A Survey of Fabrication Techniques and Styles.* The American Institute of Architects Foundation, 1983.

Adams, Abigail. *Book of Abigail and John: Selected Letters of the Adams Family, 1762–1784.* Ed. L. H. Butterfield, Marc Friedlaender, and Mary-Jo Kline. Cambridge, Massachusetts: Harvard University Press, 1975.

Adams, Charles Francis et al., eds. *Works of John Adams*, vol. 2. Boston: Charles C. Little and James Brown, 1850.

Adams Family Papers, Massachusetts Historical Society.

Alden, John Richard. *General Charles Lee, Traitor or Patriot?* Baton Rouge: Louisiana State University Press, [1951], 307–8.

Allen, Charles Dexter. *American Book-Plates: A Guide to Their Study with Examples.* New York: The Macmillan Company, 1905.

American Art News 13, no. 19 (Feb. 13, 1915): 7. Art Book Reviews/ Bayley's Copley Catalog.

An Impartial History of the War in America: Between Great Britain and Her Colonies, from Its Commencement to the End of the Year 1779; . . . Illustrated with a variety of beautiful copperplates, representing real and animated likenesses of those celebrated Generals who have distinguished themselves in the important contest. London, 1780.

Avery, Kevin J. *American Drawings and Watercolors in the Metropolitan Museum of Art/with an Essay by Marjorie Shelley.* New York: Metropolitan Museum of Art; New Haven: Yale University Press, 2002.

Bailyn, Bernard. *The Ordeal of Thomas Hutchinson.* Cambridge, Mass.: Belknap Press of Harvard University Press, 1974.

Baitjer, Katharine, and Marjorie Shelley. *Pastel Portraits: Images of 18th-Century Europe.* New York: Metropolitan Museum of Art; New Haven: distributed by Yale University Press, 2011.

Baker, C. H. Collins, "Notes on Joseph Blackburn and Nathaniel Dance," *The Huntington Library Quarterly* 9, no 1 (Nov. 1945):33–48.

Baker, W. S. *The Engraved Portraits of Washington*, with Notices of the Originals and Brief Biographical Sketches of the Painters. Philadelphia: Lindsay & Baker, 1880.

Barratt, Carrie Rebora and Lori Zabar. *American Portrait Miniatures in the Metropolitan Museum of Art.* New York: Metropolitan Museum of Art, New Haven: Yale University Press, 2010.

Baumgarten, Linda. *What Clothes Reveal.* Williamsburg, VA: The Colonial Williamsburg Foundation, in Association with Yale University Press, 2002.

Bayley, Frank W. *The Life and Works of John Singleton Copley, founded on the work of Augustus Thorndike Perkins.* Boston: The Taylor Press, 1915.

——. *Five Colonial Artists of New England: Joseph Badger, Joseph Blackburn, John Singleton Copley, Robert Feke, John Smibert.* Boston: Privately printed, 1929.

——. *Little Known Early American Portrait Painters.* Boston: Copley Gallery, 1917; five pamphlets.

Belknap, Henry Wyckoff. *Artists and Craftsmen of Essex County, Massachusetts.* Salem: The Essex Institute, 1927.

Bell, Carol Willsey. C. G. Ohio Wills and Estates to 1850: An Index. Columbus Ohio: C. W. Bell [1981].

Benes, Peter. *Old-Town and the Waterside: Two Hundred Years of Tradition and Change in Newburyport, and West Newbury, 1635–1835.* Newburyport: Historical Society of Old Newbury, 1986.

Bentley, William, D. D. *The Diary of William Bentley, D. D., Pastor of the East Church, Salem, Massachusetts.* 4 vols. Salem: The Essex Institute, 1905–14.

——. *Record of the Parish List of Deaths 1785–1819.* Salem: Printed for the Essex Institute, 1882.

——. *A Sermon delivered in the East Meeting-House, Salem: occasioned by the death of Jonathan Gardner, Esq . . . .* Salem [Marine Society]: printed by Thomas C. Cushing, 1791.

Bolton, Charles K. *Circulating Libraries in Boston*. Boston, 1907.

Bolton, Theodore. *Early American Portrait Draughtsmen in Crayons*. New York: F. F. Sherman, Inc., 1923.

——. *Early American Portrait Painters in Miniature*. New York: Frederick Fairchild Sherman, 1921.

——, Theodore and Harry Lorin Binsse, "An American Artist of Formula: Joseph Blackburn." *Antiquarian* 15 (Nov. 1930): 50-53, 88-92.

——, Theodore and Harry Lorin Binsse, "John Singleton Copley," *Antiquarian* 15 (Dec. 1930): 76-83.

Bosse, David, "'To Promote Useful Knowledge': An Accurate Map of the Four New England States by John Norman and John Coles," *Imago Mundi* 52 (2000): 143-57.

Bowditch, Charles Pickering. *The Pickering Genealogy*. Cambridge: University Press, J. Wilson and Son, 1897.

Bowditch, Dr. Harold, "Early Water-Color Paintings of New England Coats of Arms," [*Publications of the Colonial Society of Massachusetts 35* (1944), 172-209.

Boyle, John. *A Journal of Occurrences in Boston*. Houghton Library MS Am. Cambridge: Harvard University, 1926.

Brazer, John. *A Discourse Delivered in the North Church, in Salem, on Saturday, 4th of April, 1829: at the Internment of Edward Augustus Holyoke, M. D., LL. D., A. A. S., &c., &c*. Salem: Foote & Brown, 1829.

——. *Memoir of Edward Holyoke, M. D, LL. D*. Boston: Prepared in compliance with a vote of the Essex South Medical Society and published at their request. Boston: Published by Perkins & Marvin, 1829.

Briggs, L. Vernon. *History and Genealogy of the Cabot Family, 1475–1927*. Vol. 1. Boston: Charles E. Goodspeed& Co., 1927.

Brighton, Raymond A. *They Came to Fish*, Vol. 2. Portsmouth, NH: Portsmouth 350, Inc., [1973].

B[rown]. J. *A Catalogue of the Members of the North Church in Salem, with an Historical Sketch of the Church in Salem*. Salem, Massachusetts: Printed by W. & S. B. Ives, 1827.

Burroughs, Alan. *John Greenwood in America, 1745–1752*. Andover, Massachusetts: Addison Gallery of American Art, Phillips Academy, 1943.

——. *Limners and Likenesses, Three Centuries of American Painting*. Cambridge, Mass: Harvard University Press, 1936.

——, "Young Copley," *Art in America* 31 (October 1943): 160-71.

Carr, Carolyn Kinder and Ellen G. Miles. *A Brush with History: Paintings from the National Portrait Gallery*. Washington, D. C. : National Portrait Gallery, Smithsonian Institution, 2001.

"Catalogue of the Portraits at the Essex Institute." *Essex Institute Historical Collections,* vols. 70-73 (1934-37).

Child, Deborah M. "A Portrait to be treasured once again: A Copley Pastel of a Boston Maiden," *Antiques and Fine Art Magazine* 9 (Spring 2012):6.

Cleveland, Edmund Janes. *The Genealogy of the Cleveland and Cleaveland Families* (1899).

Coburn, Frederick W., "The Johnstons of Boston/Thomas Johnston (1708–1767), Painter, Engraver, Japanner, Organ Builder," *Art in America* 21 (Dec. 1932): 132-39.

Cole, Ruth Townsend. "Limned by Blyth," *The Magazine Antiques* 69 (March 1956): 331-33.

Cresswell, Donald H. *American Revolution in Drawings and Prints; A Checklist of 1765–1790 Graphics in the Library of Congress*. Compiled by Donald H. Cresswell, with a foreword by Sinclair H. Hitchings. Washington: U. S. Government Printing Office, 1975.

Curley, Juanita Bradish. *A Genealogy & History of Robert Bradish in America*. Northville, Michigan: Unicorn Press, 2000.

Curwen, Samuel. *Journal and Letters of the Late Samuel Curwen, Judge of Admiralty, etc., An American Refugee in England, From 1775 to 1784*. Edited by George Atkinson Ward. New York: C. S. Francis, 1842.

Cutler, William Parker. *Life, Journals and Correspondence of Rev. Manasseh Cutler, L. L. D*. Cincinnati: R. Clarke & Co., 1888.

Darrach, Mrs. William, and Mrs. Ernest G. Vietor. "Reverend Manasseh Cutler, LL. D. 1742, 1825, His Career as a Botanist," *Essex Institute Historical Collections* 90 (1954), 111-22.

Detwiler, Frederic C., "Thomas Dawes's Church in Brattle Square," *Old-Time New England* 69 (1979): 1–17.

Dow, George Francis. *Arts & Crafts in New England, 1704–1775; Gleanings from Boston Newspapers . . . 1927.* Topsfield, Mass. : The Wayside Press, 1927.

——. *The Holyoke Diaries, 1709–1856.* Salem: The Essex Institute, 1911.

——. *The Diary and Letters of Benjamin Pickman (1740–1819) of Salem, Massachusetts . . . .* Topsfield, Mass. : The Wayside Press, 1927.

Dresser, Louisa. "Attribution and Authenticity in American Painting," Art in America 33 (October 1945): 193-209.

Dunlap, William. *A History of the Rise and Progress of the Arts of Design in the United States.* New edition by Frank W. Bayley and Charles E. Goodspeed. Boston: C. E. Goodspeed & Co., 1918.

Earle, Alice Morse. *Child Life in Colonial Days.* New York: Charles Scribner's Sons, 1894.

——. *Costume of Colonial Times.* New York: C. Scribner's Sons, 1894.

——. *Two Centuries of Costume in America, MDCXX — MDCCCXX.* Vol 2. New York: The Macmillan Company, 1903.

Eleazer Brooks Papers, 1776–1793, William Munroe Special Collections, Concord Public Library, Concord, MA.

Elliott, Clark A., and Margaret W. Rossiter, eds. *Science at Harvard University/ Historical Perspectives.* Bethlehem: Lehigh University Press, 1992.

Endicott, Charles M. *Account of Leslie's Retreat at the North Bridge in Salem on Sunday Feb'y 26, 1775.* Salem: Wm. Ives & Geo. W. Pease, Printers, 1856.

Endicott, William Crowninshield. *John Endecott and John Winthrop.* Boston, 1930.

Emmerton, James A. *Eighteenth Century baptism in Salem, Massachusetts' Hitherto Unpublished.* [Salem]: Salem Press, 1886.

Felt, Joseph B. *Annals of Salem,* 2d ed. 2 vols. Salem, Massachusetts: W. & S. B. Ives; Boston: J. Munroe, 1845, 1849.

Ferguson, David L. *Cleopatra's Barge.* Boston: Little Brown and Company, 1976.

The First Centenary of the North Church and Society, in Salem, Massachusetts. Salem: Printed for the Society, 1873.

First Church, Salem, Mass. *Exercises in Commemoration of the Three Hundredth Anniversary of the Gathering of the First Church in Salem.* [Salem, Mass.]: Privately printed, 1930.

Flexner, James Thomas. *First Flowers of Our Wilderness.* Boston: Houghton Mifflin, 1947.

——. *John Singleton Copley.* Boston: Houghton Mifflin Company, 1948.

Foote, Henry Wilder. "When was John Singleton Copley Born?" *New England Quarterly* 10, no. 1 (1937): 111-20

——. "Benjamin Blyth of Salem: Eighteenth-Century Artist," *Proceedings of the Massachusetts Historical Society, Third Series* 71 (Oct. 1953–May 1957): 64-107.

——. Introduction, *Catalogue of Portraits in the Essex Institute.* Salem, Mass: The Essex Institute, 1936.

Fowble, E. McSherry. *Two Centuries of Prints in America/ 1680–1880 /A Selective Catalogue of the Winterthur Museum Collection.* Charlottesville: Published for the Henry Francis du Pont Winterthur Museum by the University Press of Virginia, 1987.

Frank, Robin Jaffe. *Love and Loss/ American Portrait and Mourning Miniatures.* New Haven, Conn.: Yale University Press, 2000.

Frick Art Reference Library, New York, New York.

Gardner, Frank Augustine. *Gardner Memorial/ A Biographical and Genealogical Record. . .* Salem, Mass.: Newcomb & Gauss, printers], 1933. 76-77

Gerdts, William H. *American Still-Life Painting.* New York and London: Praeger Publishers, [1971], 48-49. -

——. *Art Across America: Two Centuries of Regional Painting in America, 1720–1920.* Vol. 1. New York: Abbeville Press, 1990.

——. *Painters of the Humble Truth: Masterpieces of American Still Life, 1801–1939* Columbia, MO: Philbrook Art Center, University of Missouri Press, 1981, 66, 68.

Goodspeed, Charles E. *Yankee Bookseller: Being the Reminiscences of Charles E. Goodspeed.* Boston: Houghton Mifflin Company, 1937.

Grant, James. *John Adams, Party of One.* New York: Farrar, Straus and Giroux, 2005.

Greenwood, Isaac J. *The Greenwood Family of Norwich, England, in America.* Concord, N. H.,1934.

Groce, George, and David H. Wallace. *The New-York Historical Society's Dictionary of Artists in America, 1564–1860*. New Haven: Yale University Press, 1957.

Gutstein, Morris A. *Aaron Lopez and Judah Touro: A Refugee and a Son of a Refugee*. New York: Behrman's Jewish Book House, 1939.

Hadley, Harold P. *Two Hundred Years of Masonry in Essex Lodge*. Massachusetts: Essex Lodge, 1979.

Hansen, David. "Gawen Brown, Soldier and Clockmaker." *Old-Time New England* 30 no. 1 (July 1939), 1-9.

Hart, Charles Henry. "An Etched Profile Portrait of Washington by Joseph Hiller, Jr., 1794," *Essex Institute Historical Collections* 43 (1907): 4-5.

———. *Catalogue of the Engraved Portraits of Washington*. New York: The Grolier Club, 1904. (Author's annotated copy at the Boston Athenaeum.)

———. Original portraits of Washington. Detached from: *Century Illustrated Monthly Magazine* 37 no. 6 (April 1889). New York: Century Company, 1890.

———. "Peale's original whole-length portrait of Washington: A plea for exactness in historical writings." *American Historical Association: Annual report . . . 1896*. Washington, [D. C.]: 1897, 189-200.

———. "Original Portraits of Washington," *The Century Illustrated Monthly Magazine*, New York: The Century Company, 43 (Feb. 1892).

———. *Some notes Concerning John Norman, Engraver (died June 8, 1817, Æt. 69)*. Cambridge: John Wilson and Son, 1904. Reprinted from the *Proceedings of the Massachusetts Historical Society*, (Oct. 1904).

Harvard University. *Quinquennial Catalogue of the Officers and Graduates, 1636–1930*. Cambridge, Massachusetts, Published by the University, 1930.

Hawes, Charles Boardman. *Gloucester by Land and Sea*. Boston: Little, Brown and Company, 1923.

Hecksher, Morrison M. "Copley's Picture Frames," *John Singleton Copley in America*. New York: The Metropolitan Museum of Art, 1995, 143-69.

Hendy, Sir Philip, preface. *Loan Exhibition of One Hundred Colonial Portraits: Massachusetts Bay Colony Tercentenary*, Museum of Fine Arts, Boston, 19 June–21 Sept. 1930. [Boston, 1930].

Henkels, Stan. V. *Important Collection of Rare Engraved Portraits of General George Washington and other Notable Americans . . .* Catalogue compiled, and sale conducted by Stan. V. Henkels at the book auction rooms of David & Harvey, 1112 Walnut Street, Phila, Pa. Friday, May 4th, 1906.

Heydenryk, Henry. *The Art and History of Frames/ An Inquiry into the Enhancement of Paintings*. New York: James H. Heineman, Inc., 1963.

Historical Records Survey (Mass.). *American Portraits, 1620–1825, Found in Massachusetts*, 3 vols. Prepared by the Historical Records Survey, Division of Professional and Service Projects, Works Progress Administration, 1939. Boston: Historical Records Survey, 1939–1942.

Hitchings, Sinclair. "Thomas Johnston," *Boston Prints and Printmakers, 1670–1775, Publications of the Colonial Society of Massachusetts* 46 (1973), 83–132.

Hodgkinson, Harold D. "A Clergyman's Comments on the Life of Young America, 1787–1791," *Essex Institute Historical Collections* 102:74-85.

Holman, Richard B. "William Burgis," *Boston Prints and Printmakers, 1670–1775. Publications of the Colonial Society of Massachusetts* 46 (1973), 57-81.

Holyoke Diaries, 1709–1856; with an introduction and annotations by George Francis Dow. Salem: The Essex Institute, 1911.

Hijiya, James A. "Four Ways of Looking at a Philanthropist: A Study of Robert Weeks de Forest," *Proceedings of the American Philosophical Society* 124, no. 6 (Dec. 17, 1980), 404–18.

Important Americana: The Bertram K. and Nina Fletcher Little Collection, Part II, Sotheby's Sale 6612, Friday, October 21 - Saturday, October 22, 1994. (Annotated copy with prices, courtesy of the Little family).

Jackson, Russell Leigh, comp. *Additions to the Catalogue of Portraits in the Essex Institute, Received since 1936*, Salem, Mass.: Newcomb and Gauss, 1950; repr. from *Essex Institute Historical Collections*, 85-86.

Jarvis, Michael J. *In the Eye of All Trade: Bermuda, Bermudians, and the Maritime Atlantic World,* Chapel Hill: University of North Carolina Press, 2010.

Johnson, Dale T. *American Portrait Miniatures in the Manney Collection.* New York: Metropolitan Museum of Art, distributed by Harry N. Abrams, Inc., New York, 1990.

Jones, E. Alfred. *The Loyalists of Massachusetts, Their Memorials, Petitions, and Claims.* London: St. Catherine's Press, 1930.

Jones, Guernsey, ed. *Letters & Papers of John Singleton Copley and Henry Pelham.* Boston: Massachusetts Historical Society, 1914.

Kayser, Stephen J. *Early American Jewish Portraiture: Exhibited February to July 1952.* New York, N. Y. : American Jewish Historical Society, ca. 1952.

James Kimball, comp. "Orderly Book of the Regiment of Artillery Raised for the Defence of the Town of Boston in 1776," *Essex Institute Historical Collections* 13:110-28.

Lahikainen. Dean T. *Samuel McIntire: Carving an American Style.* Salem, Mass.: Peabody Essex Museum, distributed by University Press of New England, 2007.

Leach, Robert J. *Quaker Nantucket: The Religious Community Behind the Whaling Empire.* Nantucket, Mass. : Mill Hill Press, 1999.

Lee, Cuthbert. *Early American Portrait Painters.* New Haven: Yale University Press, 1929.

——. Portrait Register. [Asheville, N. C.]: Biltmore Press, 1968.

Little, Nina Fletcher. "The Blyths of Salem: Benjamin, Limner in Crayons and Oil, and Samuel, Painter and Cabinetmaker," *Essex Institute Historical Collections* 108 (1972): 49-57.

——. *Little by Little: Six Decades of Collecting American Decorative Arts.* New York: E. P. Dutton, 1984.

Lord, Priscilla Sawyer, and Virginia Clegg Gamage. *Marblehead/ The Spirit of '76 Lives Here.* Philadelphia: Chilton Book Company, [1971, 1972].

Magra, Christopher P. *The Fisherman's Cause: Atlantic Commerce and Maritime Dimensions of the American Revolution.* Cambridge: Cambridge University Press, 2009.

Maguire, J. Robert, "His Excellency and Lady Washington: A Pair of Mezzotint Portraits by Joseph Hiller, Sr., or Samuel Blyth?" *Imprint* 30, no. 2 (Autumn 2005): 22-33.

Massachusetts Historical Society. *Portraits in the Massachusetts Historical Society: An Illustrated Catalog with Descriptive Matter by Andrew Oliver, Ann Millspaugh Huff, Edward W. Hanson.* Boston: Published by the Society, 1988.

McClellan, Elisabeth. History of American Costume, 1607–1870. New York, Tudor Publishing Company, 1937.

McConnell, Reverend S. D. *History of the American Episcopal Church: From the Planting of the Colonies to the End of the Civil War.* 3d ed. New York: Thomas Whittaker, 1891.

McCullough, David. *John Adams.* New York: Simon & Schuster, 2001.

McLaughlin, Jane A, "Baldwin Coolidge, Photographer," *Spritsail, A Journal of Falmouth History* 1, no. 1 (Summer 1987).

Middlebrook, Louis F., "A Few of the New England Engravers," *Essex Institute Historical Collections* 62 (1926): 359-63.

Miles, Ellen G. *American Paintings of the Eighteenth Century, The Collections of the National Gallery of Arts Systematic Catalogue.* Washington, D. C. : National Gallery of Art, c. 1995.

——, ed. *The Portrait in Eighteenth-Century America.* Newark: University of Delaware Press, 1993.

Mitchell, Paul & Lynn Roberts. *Frameworks: Form, Function & Ornament in European Portrait Frames.* London: Paul Mitchell Ltd. in association with Merrell Holberton, 1996.

Morgan, John Hill and Henry Wilder Foote. "An Extension of Lawrence Park's Descriptive List of the Work of Joseph Blackburn." *Proceedings of the American Antiquarian Society* 46, pt. 1 (April 1936): 15-81.

—— and Mantle Fielding. *The Life Portraits of Washington.* Philadelphia: printed for the subscribers [Lancaster, Pa. : Lancaster Press, Inc.], ca. 1931.

Morison, Samuel Eliot. *The Maritime History of Massachusetts, 1783–1860.* Boston: Houghton Mifflin, 1961.

Morse, William Inglis. *The Land of the New Adventure/ (The Georgian Era in Nova Scotia).* London: Bernard Quaritch Ltd., 1932.

Morris, Richard J. "Redefining the Economic Elite in Salem, Massachusetts, 1759–1799," The New England Quarterly 73, no. 4 (Dec. 2000): 603-24.

Munn, Charles Allen. Three Types of Washington Portraits. New York: Privately printed,1908.

Museum of Fine Arts, Boston. American Paintings in the Museum of Fine Arts, Boston: An Illustrated Summary Catalog by Carol Troyen, Charlotte Emans Moore and Priscilla Kate Diamond, introduction by Theodore E. Stebbins, Jr. Boston: Museum of Fine Arts, 1997.

——. A Descriptive Catalogue of an Exhibition of Early Engraving in America, December 12, 1904 - February 5, 1905. Cambridge: The University Press, 1904.

——. Loan Exhibition of One Hundred Colonial Portraits, Museum of Fine Arts, Boston, 19 June-21 September 1930.

North Church, Salem, Mass. The First Centenary of the North Church and Society, in Salem, Massachusetts. Salem: Printed for the Society, 1873.

Norton, Bettina A. "Anglican embellishments: The Contributions of John Gibbs, Junior, and William Price to the Church of England in Eighteenth-century Boston," The Dublin Seminar for New England Folklife, 1979, Boston, Mass. : Boston University, [1980], 46-63.

——. "Benjamin and Samuel Blyth's Roles in Printmaking," Imprint 44, no. 1 (Spring 2019), 2-23.

——. "The Brothers Blyth: Salem in its Heyday," Painting and Portrait Making in the American Northeast, Dublin Seminar for New England Folklife, Peter Benes, ed., Jane Montague Benes, associate ed. Boston, Mass: Boston University, 1995.

——. Prints at the Essex Institute, Essex Institute Museum Booklet Series 2. Salem, Mass: Essex Institute, 1978.

——. editor and contributor. Trinity Church: The Story of an Episcopal Parish in the City of Boston. Boston: Published by the Wardens and Vestry, 1978.

Oliver, Andrew, comp. Faces of a Family. Boston: Privately printed [Portland, Me.]: Anthoensen Press, 1960.

——, ed. The Journal of Samuel Curwen, Loyalist. Cambridge: Harvard University Press, for the Essex Institute, Salem, Massachusetts, 1972.

——. Portraits of John and Abigail Adams. Cambridge: The Belknap Press of Harvard University Press, 1967.

——. Windows on the Past: Portraits at the Essex Institute, Essex Institute Museum Booklet Series 5. Salem, Mass: Essex Institute, 1981.

Osgood, Charles S., and H. M. Batchelder. Historical Sketch of Salem/1626–1879. Salem: Essex Institute, 1879.

O'Toole, Dennis A., and Lisa W. Strick. "In the Minds and Hearts of the People": Five American Patriots and the Road to Revolution. Washington: National Portrait Gallery, 1974.

Park, Lawrence. "Joseph Blackburn, A Colonial Portrait Painter; with a Descriptive List of His Works," Proceedings of the American Antiquarian Society 32 (Oct. 1922): 270-329.

Parker, Barbara Neville, and Anne Wheeler. John Singleton Copley: American Portraits in Oil, Pastel, and Miniature. Boston: Museum of Fine Arts, 1938.

——. New England Miniatures, 1750–1850, Sponsored by the National Society of the Colonial Dames of America in the Commonwealth of Massachusetts. Boston: Museum of Fine Arts, 1957.

Perkins, Augustus Thorndike. A Sketch of the Life and a List of Some of the Works of John Singleton Copley. [Boston], 1873.

Perley, Sidney. The History of Salem, Massachusetts, 3 vols. Salem: S. Perley, 1924-28.

Phillips, James Duncan. The Life and Times of Richard Derby, Merchant of Salem, 1712–1783. Cambridge: Riverside Press, 1929.

——. Pepper and Pirates, Adventures in the Sumatra Pepper Trade of Salem. Boston: Houghton Mifflin Company, 1949.

——. "Political Fights and Local Squabbles in Salem, 1800–1806," Essex Institute Historical Collections 82, no. 1 (1946): 1–11.

——. Salem and the Indies, The Story of the Great Commercial Era of the City. Boston: Houghton Mifflin Company, 1947.

——. Salem in the Eighteenth Century. Boston and New York: Houghton Mifflin Company, 1937.

Prown, Jules David. American Painting: From its Beginnings to the Armory Show. [Geneva]: Skira [distributed in the U. S. by Rizzoli International Pubs.], 1987.

——. John Singleton Copley. Cambridge: Published for the National Gallery of Art [by] Harvard University Press, 1966.

Quincy, Josiah. *The History of Harvard University*. Cambridge: J. Owen, 1840.

Rebora, Carrie, Paul Staiti, Erica Hirshler, Theodore E. Stebbins Jr, Carol Troyen. *John Singleton Copley in America*. New York: The Metropolitan Museum of Art, Distributed by Harry N. Abrams, 1995.

Reeves, Wendy Wick. See Wick, Wendy C.

Reichlin, Ellie, "Double Exposure and William Sumner Appleton," Old-Time New England 69, no. 255 (Winter/Spring) 1979. 34-41.

Ribeiro, Aileen. "'The Whole Art of Dress': Costume in the Work of John Singleton Copley," *American Drawings and Watercolors in the Metropolitan Museum of Art*. New Haven: Yale University Press, 2002.

Richardson, Robert D. Jr. *Emerson: The Mind on Fire*. Berkeley: University of California Press, 1995.

Ring, Betty. *Girlhood Embroidery: American Samplers & Pictorial Needlework, 1650–1850*. New York: A. A. Knopf, 1993. 100–101.

Saunders, Richard H. *John Smibert/ Colonial America's First Portrait Painter*. New Haven and London: Yale University Press, 1995.

——— and Ellen G. Miles. *American Colonial Portraits 1700–1776*. Washington, DC: Published by the Smithsonian Institution Press for the National Portrait Gallery, 1987.

Schimmelman, Janice C. "Books on Drawing and Painting Techniques Available in Eighteenth-Century American Libraries and Bookstores," *Winterthur Portfolio* 19 (Summer–Autumn, 1984).

Sellers, Charles Coleman. *Charles Willson Peale*, 2 vols. New York: Scribner [1969].

———. "Charles Willson Peale and His World," *Memoirs of American Philosophical Society* 23, pts. 1-2. Philadelphia: American Philosophical Society, 1947.

———. *Portraits and Miniatures by Charles Willson Peale*. Philadelphia: Transactions of the American Philosophical Society, 42 (1952).

Shadwell, Wendy J. "An Attribution for His Excellency and Lady Washington," *The Magazine Antiques* (Feb. 1969): 240-41.

Shaffer, Ellen. *Portrait of a Philadelphia Collector: William McIntire Elkins (1882–1947)*. Philadelphia: Free Library, 1956, 3, 11–12, 13.

Shelley, Marjorie. "American Watercolors and Drawings in the Metropolitan Museum of Art," *A Catalogue of Works by Artists Born before 1835*, vol. 1. New York: Metropolitan Museum of Art, 2002.

———, "The Craft of American Drawing: Early Eighteenth to Late Nineteenth Century," *American Drawings and Watercolors in the Metropolitan Museum of Art*. New York: Metropolitan Museum of Art, 2002, 86.

———, "Painting in Crayon: The Pastels of John Singleton Copley," *John Singleton Copley in America*. New York: The Metropolitan Museum of Art, 1995, 127-42.

Sherman, Frederic Fairchild. *Early American Portraiture*. New York: Privately printed, 1930.

———. "John Singleton Copley as a Portrait Miniaturist," *Art in America*, 18 (June 1930): 207-214.

Sibley, John Langdon. *Biographical Sketches of Graduates of Harvard University in Cambridge, Massachusetts*. Cambridge: C. W. Sever, 1873–1973, vols. 5–14, 16–17.

Smith, Huldah M. "Some Aspects of William Bentley as Art Collector and Connoisseur," *Essex Institute Historical Collections* 97 (1961): 152-64.

Sizer, Theodore, ed. *The Autobiography of Colonel John Trumbull: Patriot-Artist, 1756–1843*. New Haven: Yale University Press, 1953.

Smith, Philip Chadwick Foster, ed. *Portraits of the Marine Society at Salem in New-England*. Salem: The Marine Society at Salem, 1972.

Smith, Ralph Clifton. *A Biographical Index of American Artists*. Baltimore: The Williams & Wilkins Company, 1930.

Smithsonian Institution Research Information System (SIRIS).

Staples, Kathleen A., and Madelyn Shaw. *Clothing through American History*. Santa Barbara, CA: Greenwood, 2013.

Stauffer, David McNeely, Mantle Fielding, and Thomas Hovey Gage. *American Engravers upon Copper and Steel*. New York, The Grolier Club of the City of New York, 1907, 2 vols.

Stebbins Jr., Theodore E, et al. *American Paintings at Harvard: Paintings, Watercolors, and Pastels by Artists Born before 1826,* Cambridge, Massachusetts, Harvard Art Museum, vol. 1. Yale University Press, 2014.

——, "An American Despite Himself," *John Singleton Copley in America.* New York: The Metropolitan Museum of Art, 1995, 79–101.

Streeter, Gilbert. "Salem Before the Revolution," *Essex Institute Historical Collections* 32 (1896): 83.

Tamarkin, Elisa. *Anglophilia: Deference, Devotion, and Antebellum America.* University of Chicago Press, 2008.

Tapley, Harriet Silvester. "Francis Cabot and the Beginnings of Washington, D. C." *Essex Institute Historical Collections* 73 (1937): 348-62.

——. *St. Peter's Church in Salem, Massachusetts before the Revolution.* Salem: The Essex Institute, 1944.

——. Salem Imprints, 1768–1825: A History of the First Fifty Years of Printing in Salem, Massachusetts, with Some Account of the Bookshops, Booksellers, Bookbinders, and the Private Libraries. Salem: The Essex Institute, 1927.

Tolles, Bryant F., and Carolyn K. Tolles. *Architecture in Salem: An Illustrated Guide.* Salem: The Essex Institute,1983.

Tomkins, Calvin. *Merchants and Masterpieces: The Story of the Metropolitan Museum of Art.* New York: E. P. Dutton & Co., Inc., 1970.

Tuckerman, Henry T. *Book of the Artists: American Artist Life.* New York: G. P. Putnam & Sons, 1867.

United States Department of the Navy Bureau of Naval Personnel, "History of U. S. Navy Uniforms."

Appendix 2. United States Navy Uniform Regulations. NavPers 15665D. Washington, D. C.: U. S. Government Printing Office, 1981.

Vaughn, Malcolm, "American Pastels: Late Eighteenth Century," *International Studio* 89 (Apr. 1928).

Visitor's Guide to Salem. Salem, Mass.: Eben Putnam, 1892.

Visitor's Guide to Salem/ Thirty-Fifth Thousand. Salem, Mass: The Essex Institute, 1895.

Warren, David B., et al. *American Decorative Arts in the Bayou Bend Collection.* Houston: Museum of Fine Arts, Houston, in association with Princeton University Press, 1998.

Watkins, Walter K., "Crown Coffee House; A Story of Old Boston," Boston: Fidelity Trust Company.

——. "John Coles, Heraldry Painter," *Old-Time New England* 21, no. 3 (1931):129-43.

——. "The New England Museum and the Home of Art in Boston," *Bostonian Society Publications* 2, no. 2 (1917): 112–14.

Wehle, Harry B. *American Miniatures, 1730–1850: One Hundred and Seventy-three Portraits Selected with a Descriptive Account.* Garden City, NY: published for the Metropolitan Museum of Art by Doubleday, Page & Company, 1927.

Whitehill, Walter Muir, intro. *Portraits of Shipmasters and Merchants in the Peabody Museum of Salem.* Salem: Peabody Museum, 1939.

Whitney, Janet. *Abigail Adams.* Boston: Little, Brown & Co., 1947.

Wick, Wendy C. *George Washington, an American Icon: The Eighteenth-Century Graphic Portraits.*

Washington, D. C: Smithsonian Institution Traveling Exhibition Service: National Portrait Gallery, Smithsonian Institution; Charlottesville, Va.: Distributed by the University Press of Virginia, 1982.

Wilner, Eli. *The Gilded Edge/ Art of the Frame.* San Francisco: Chronicle Books, 2000.

Winer, Laurence B. *The Loyalists of Lynn, Salem, and Marblehead.* Ph. D. diss., Wayne State University, 2008.

WEBSITES

allthingsliberty. com, Journal of the American Revolution

loebjewishportraits. com, Jewish portrait database

The Dictionary of Pastellists before 1800

INDEX

NOTE: Page numbers in *italics* denote illustrations. Catalogue numbers are indicated as (Cat. #).
Works are by Benjamin Blyth unless otherwise indicated.

Feke, Robert, 16, 19

Felt, Joseph B., 27, 41, 55, 140, 162, 167, 247, 286, 327, 357

Ferguson, David L., 145

Fielding, Mantle, 20, 34, 345, 390, 392

Fisk, John, 85, 93, 95, 186
Blyth portrait of (Cat. 52), 184–85

Fisk, Lydia Phippen, 93, 95, 184, 223
Blyth portrait of (Cat. 53), 24, 43n61, *63* (detail), 108, 186, *187*, 202, 218, 302, 369

Fisk, Martha Hibbert, 184

Fisk, Samuel, 184

Fisk, Sarah Gerry, 184

Fiske, Nathan, 255

Fitch, Eunice Brown
Blackburn portrait of, 19, 24n23

Fitch, Timothy
Blackburn portrait of, 19, 24n23

Flagg, Dorothy Drowne, 190

Flagg, James
Blyth portrait of (Cat. 54), *188*, 189, 190, 296

Flagg, Samuel, 242
Blyth portrait of (Cat. 55), 38, 60–61, 190–91, *191*

Flexner, James, 26

Foote, Caleb, 348

Foote, Henry Wilder, 27n30, 44, 45, 47, 84, 87, 112, 134, 136, 139, 158, 167, 175, 178, 181, 190, 272, 314, 327, 344, 348, 357–58, 366, 377

Foote, Mary Wilder, 189

Forest, Robert M. de, 66n90

Fowble, E. McSherry, 52

frames, styles and techniques, 40–43, *42* (details)

Freeman, Watson, 106, 111

Freemasons. *See* Masons

French and Indian War, 98, 147, 156, 170, 195, 310

Frye, John, 193

Frye, Love Rawlins Pickman, 193
needlework by, 15–16, *16*

Frye, Peter, 37, 148, 177, 190
Blyth portrait of (Cat. 56), 39, 40, 65, *65* (detail), 65–66, *66* (detail), 67, *192*, 193–94, 286, 296, 369

Frye, Peter, Jr., 193

Gage, Thomas, 28, 29, 316

Gale, William, 77

Gardiner, Samuel
Johnston portrait of, *25*, 43n59

Gardiner, Mrs. Samuel
Johnston portrait of, *25*, 43n59, 62

Gardner, Elizabeth Pickering, 195

Gardner, Jonathan, 37, 169
Blyth portrait of (Cat. 57), 158, 195–96, *197*, 314

Gardner, Lois Gardner, 101, 158

Gardner, Samuel, 101

Gardner, Mrs. Samuel
Blackburn portrait of, 24n23
Greenwood portrait of, 26

Gardner, Sarah Derby, 195

Gardner, Sarah Putnam, 195
Blyth portrait of (Cat. 58), 24, 61, *63* (detail), 142, 158, *198*, 199, 314, 345, 376

Gatchel, Betsy. *See* Lane, Betsy

Gatchel, Josiah, 245

Gee, Joshua
Greenwood portrait of, 22n20

Gerdts, William H., 16, 159

Gerrish, Abigail
Greenwood portrait of, 19n11

Gerrish, Benjamin, 18–19
Greenwood portrait of, 19n11, 26

Gerrish, Margaret Cabot
Greenwood portrait of, 19n11

Gerry, Ann, 77–78

Gerry, Elbridge, 77–78, 205

Gerry, John
Badger portrait of, 19, 44n46, 274

Gibaut, Abigail, 200

Gibaut, Edward, 184

Gibaut, John, 85
Blyth portrait of (Cat. 59), 43n61, 56, 62, *63* (detail), 64, 67, 68, *68* (detail), 68, 186, 200–202, *201*, 267, 302, 335, 352, 377

Gibaut, Sarah Crowninshield, 200

Gibbs, Henry, 96

Gibbs, John, 18

Gibbs, John, Jr., 18

Giese, Lucretia, 242

Glover, Abigail Burnham, 205
Blyth portrait of (Cat. 60), 203, *203*, 204, 345

Glover, John (1732–1797), 204

Glover, John, Jr. (1755–1811?)
Blyth portrait of (Cat. 61), 80, 204, *204*

Glover, John (brother of Jonathan), 205

Glover, Jonathan (1731–1797), 51–52, 103, 125, 203, 204
Blyth portrait of, copy (Cat. 62), 205–7, *206*

Glover, Mary Greely, 203

Glover, Tabitha, 205

Set in the types of
William Caslon and John Bell.
Printed at Puritan Press in Hollis, New Hampshire.
Design & typography by
Jerry Kelly.